GW00371141

16 MAPS OF HELL*

(*with a Rough Draft of the Exit)

For Mike

16 MAPS
of HELL*

· ·

The Unraveling of
Hollywood Superculture

· ·

(*with a Rough Draft of the Exit)

from JASUN H.
DEC 20 20

JASUN HORSLEY

Images by Michelle Horsley

First published in 2020 by Auticulture

http://auticulture.com

Copyright © 2020 by Jasun Horsley

Cover design and images © 2020 by Michelle Horsley

ISBN: 978-1-7751590-2-5

"We are double in ourselves, so that we believe what we disbelieve and cannot rid ourselves of what we condemn."

—MONTAIGNE

For Emerald, and those who come after
As the City of Wizards falls

CONTENTS

PART TWO:
THE FORGETTING CHAMBER

ACKNOWLEDGMENTS

This work is nothing if not a conglomeration of influences, many of which are cited, examined, honored, and exposed in the pages to come. I will confine this segment to those *not* named herein, starting with my wife, an invaluable inspiration, guide, and instigator in shaping this work, as with my last two books, sometimes in open defiance of my cries of "No more links, leads, or citations!" Also for her beautiful work with the images and cover art.

After that, a word of thanks is due to Dave Oshana, and to those who have congregated around his "signal," for providing me with a welcome and I think necessary contrast to the darkness mapped herein, as well as a growing, felt sense of the possibility of exiting/integrating Hell.

A special word of thanks is due to "TN," the *official* instigator of this work, who passed through my hometown and dared me *not* to self-publish, by volunteering to build an index for the book and suggesting the crowd-funding method. TN went on to proofread the MS, not once but twice, thereby witnessing its last-minute transformation, and offered valuable editorial suggestions that were incorporated into the work, included by the end as footnotes (chapter 15) when I was too tired, lazy, or content with the book to try rework the text itself. Thanks also to Jeff Williams for assisting with the formatting and interior design of the book.

Last, but evidently not least, the 209 contributors to the *16 Maps of Hell* crowdfunding campaign that made the book's publication possible: Aaron C, Adam B, Adam J, Adam O, Alex T, Alexander H, Alistair S, Andrew C, Andy W, Ann B, Ann D, Ann GM, Anna M, Ashley H, Ben F, Benett F, Benjamin A, Benjamin C, Benjamin G, Benjamin R, Benjamin S, Birdie S, Björn S, Brandon A, Brendan O, Brian M, Brian S, Cara D, Carlos L,

Catherine AF, Cedomir M, Chester, Chris F, Chris M, Chris S, Christoph K, Christopher D, CMR, Daniel A, Daniel E, Daniel L, Daniel M, Daniel T, Darick C, Darren W, Dave E, David C, David G, David M, David M(2), David O, David R, Denise G, Devyn E, Dianne B, Dominic U, Don H, Donald F, Donna H, Dora B, Douglas McL, Duncan M, Eileen M, Eleanor G-S, Ellen B, Ellen W, Emerald G, Eric C, Evgeny A, Fergus L, Francisco JCA, Gabor D, Gavin W., Glenn R, Gordon Y, Grant A, Grant J, Greg D, Greg H, Greg M, Gudjon G, Heather T, Holly GS, Hugo D, Isaac R, Isaac W, Jake L, James McD, Jared R, Jared W, Jason B, Jason T, Jeff G, Jill D H, Jim S, Joan L, Joe A, Joel K, Joel S, John C, John H, John R, John S, Jonathan B, Jonathan L, Jose A, Joseph B, Joseph F, Joseph V, Josiah F, Juan E, Julia T, Julie T, Julius T, Justin A, Kali M, Kate L, Kay L, Keith A D, Kelly R, Kelsey J, Kevin H, Kevin P, Kristjan S, Kurt J, Kurt L, Kyle P, Louis P, Louise C, Louise W, Luke D, Maria L, Marianne F, Marina G, Marsha M, Martin F, Martin J, Martin M, Mathias D, Matthew D, Matthew S, Michael Mi, Michael Mu, Michael T, Michael W, Michaelangelo, Mike B, Mike P, Mollie B, Nat B, Nathaniel R, Neely T, Neil D, Nina P, Norton F, Oli D, Paul H, Paul H(2), Paul P, Paul S, Paul W, Rea M, Reed G, Richard H, Richard B, Richard S, Richard T, Rick S, Rishabh A, Rob D, Robert D E, Roger H, Ronald V, Russell D, Ruth R, Ryan V, Samuel C, Sarah W NP, Scott McG, Sean A, Shawn K, Simon A, Simon K, Simon M, Steffany L, Stephen A, Stephen W, Steve M, Steven R, Steven S, Suzie M, Tamar W, Taylor RV, Ted M, Terence H, The Skrauss, Thomas A, Thomas M, Timothy F, Timothy K, Tony M, Travis M, Valerie O, Vincent C, William B, William B, William K, William R, Xavier McC.

I hope this work fully recompenses and justifies your interest and support, and that you enjoy it especially for your (democratically) participatory role in its genesis.

JASUN HORSLEY
August 8, 2020

Author's Foreword

FAREWELL TO HELL
(FOR THE READERS)

"Feel my fingers as they
Touch your arms
I'm spinning around but I feel alright
The book I read was in your eyes"

—TALKING HEADS *"The Book I Read"*

I f you can't step in the same river twice, what about a book? This is not the same book as when I started it—or even when I first finished it. Far from it. Not only is the river always in flux, we are too, and a lot has changed since I last read through *16 Maps of Hell* back in late 2019, even if the book hadn't (yet) changed (though now it has).

Continuity is a necessary fiction. Every book emerges partially out of a theory the writer has about the mind of the reader. If I didn't have any sort of theory about the future reader of this foreword, I would hardly be motived to write it. This foreword is for you, *personally*—because via the *16 Maps of Hell* campaign that funded this book's publication, you probably helped it to happen. Now not only do I know your name, I know where you live.*

The original foreword that comes immediately after this was written in 2019, while I was hunting for a publisher for a 600-page denunciation of pop culture and mass media as one giant mafia of soul control, heavily regulated by "old seers" hungry to fill their inner emptiness with endless slices of world domination. The old foreword was an attempt to sugar coat the red

---

* That is, if you got the book directly from me.

pill and Trojan Horse it through the gates of Empire, making it seem topical, responsible, conscientious, and relevant (I hope it is all these things) in a way compatible with the predominant sensibility/ideology of (mafia) publishers, agents, editors, reviewers, and their homogenous value set (I fear it is not).

Since *16 Maps of Hell* is apparently the sort of book that you want to read, you are probably sick to death with the "superculture," with the mainstream media's endlessly manipulative and exploitative fake narratives, even, perhaps, with the rapidly mutating forms of "conspiracy theory" being churned out by a controlled opposition of alternate perceptions websites and YouTube channels. Perhaps you are losing both your desire and capacity for suspending disbelief, and being drawn ever closer to a Void Of Increasing Disbelief? If so, I can't promise this book will disabuse you of your illusions, or that it will cure you of the need for an ongoing cultural fix of sociological propaganda to assuage a lifetime's alienation. Unless you are already on the brink of that, it probably won't push you over.*

The culmination of the advanced alienation agenda known as "Hollywood" that *16 Maps* aims to lay bare *is*, I think, visible today in a world of soul-snatched bodies hooked into their smart screens, oblivious to the flesh and blood existence around them. It is observable as a matrix currently being realized in and through our colonized minds and bodies, via a "parasocial" reality (see 3.3) in which we have all become figments of each other's impoverished, unnaturally inflated imaginations. This book is an optimistic, maybe *hubristic*, and certainly risky "adios" to that coming smart new world, as well as a hopeful initiation into a forgotten but (*because* forgotten) unsullied world of *true* wonders, outside the cave of digital shadows. That latter is a world that, just maybe, you have signed up for by participating in this "dear Hell" letter.

If I find myself a different person than when I first wrote this book, I like to think *some* of those changes are due to having written this book (which is not the same book you are now reading, since it changed as I did).

---

* It *may* help to transmute your relationship with the media to one of exponentially increasing ambivalence, on the one hand (even cognitive dissonance), while, more importantly, offering a "transitional matrix," a halfway house for movie and TV (or world news or video game) addicts, where together we can slowly wean ourselves off our chosen poisons, via the gradual mapping, sensing, and experiencing of a new-old form of *communal sense-making*.

I choose to believe this—I keep open the possibility—because it means that writing this book has helped draw out some of the Hollywood toxins from my own system, with one ironic result that it has reduced my interest for the subject matter of this book —hence the last minute restructuring and the many "outtakes."* *C'est la vie, c'est la guerre.* To succeed is to fail. Every map is disposable once it gets you where you are going. The other factor that has brought about this last-minute transformation, as you will discover if you make it all the way in and through to the "exit," is you, the reader—or at least *my* theory of *your* mind. *16 Maps of Hell*, then, is the first truly reciprocal book I have ever written. I think it shows.

JASUN HORSLEY
July 1, 2020

---

* As regards the Outtakes section, the reader is advised of two ways to proceed while reading: sequentially, saving the outtakes to the end or ignoring them altogether; and comprehensively, jumping to the outtakes as they are cited in the main body of the book, and then back again.

Author's Foreword

(FOR THE GATEKEEPERS)

I n his seminal 1962 work *Propaganda: The Formation of Men's Attitudes*, Jacques Ellul juxtaposes "the need on the part of regimes to make propaganda," with "the need of the propagandee," describing them as twin conditions that "correspond to and complement each other in the development of propaganda" (p. 121). Ellul's book is a philosophical treatise that makes a compelling case for modern propaganda as being nothing less than "the expression of modern society as a whole" (p. 118). This present work is less of a treatise than a body of evidence with accompanying analysis, to indicate what I think the evidence points to. What it points to, I hope, is the current shape of a cultural symbiosis between rulers and the ruled described by Ellul sixty years ago, which is now in what appears to be an almost unimaginably advanced stage of development.

Loosely said, *16 Maps of Hell* is an attempt to understand the nature of the system that we loosely call, these days, "the world," this latter being a more unified, interconnected, and homogenized system than at any other previous time in history. My approach to this, possibly Promethean, task is to look at one, seemingly discreet aspect of the world-system, the one loosely known as "Hollywood." It seemed expedient, as well as appealing, to isolate one corner of the world-system (or tentacle, if what we are talking about is a living system) in an attempt to understand it. Without doing so, the map would end up as large as the territory being mapped (there is no way to understand the world in its entirety, not even with reference to all the books in the world).

The paradoxical, and problematic, nature of this procedure may be apparent. Insofar as Hollywood represents the system of the world, it is also

unmappable, being too vast and complex to submit to any remotely comprehensive representation. Nonetheless, the territory to be mapped has at least
been significantly reduced. All of this is to say, in a roundabout way, two
things: firstly, that the *means* of my thesis is the gradual revelation of a terrain
previously concealed. This entails a degree of unfamiliarity, or "lostness,"
not only for the reader but for the author, since the terrain can't be mapped
before entering it, only after. With any luck, I am not making excuses for
my incompetence here, but underscoring, again, how what is being mapped,
since it is under our feet and all around us, can't be isolated for study without
reducing it in resolution so drastically as to risk making it meaningless.

Secondly (a declaration of the book's thesis): the all-pervasive nature of
Hollywood is central to what this work will attempt to argue, namely, that
myths, narratives, storytelling, ideology, propaganda, and the technological
media which creates and distributes these things, including also their effects
on social policies, fashions, movements, communities, and the micro-details
of our individually lived lives, are all threads of *a single tapestry of social reality
construction and narrative transportation.* Ellul calls this "sociological propaganda," but this hardly captures the pervasiveness of it, and for me the
mythopoetic word "spell" comes closer to the actual truth. The key to my
thesis is that of a collective *occupation, or possession,* by sociocultural "propaganda," extending over centuries, by which we have become, not only the
captives, but also the carriers and disseminators of a false narrative.

This makes the thesis of this book both childishly simple and crush-
ingly complex. In some ways, it is closer to science fiction than social science.
Simply put, both as individuals and as a collective, we have been lured—and
lured ourselves—into *a counterfeit reality,* a dream world. Hollywood, as a
place and a state of mind, is both a primary causal agency of this condition
(over the past century), and a crucial (because visible) symptom *of* it. It is the
equivalent of a metastasized tumor on the world psyche.

This model (which is only a map, not the territory) presents me, and if
I am right, all of us, with a living conundrum: the source of our oppression
is at the same time our chosen means of pseudo-escape from oppression.
In Ellul's own terms, we are addicted to and dependent on the propaganda
that enslaves us. This living conundrum is currently exemplified, I think, by
the increasingly fervent public debate about the moral responsibility of art
and of artists to uphold positive, humanitarian values. Many people in the

Western world are currently feeling, and expressing, a visceral need to call our cultural media and the artists and communicators who create it to moral accountability. There is a growing imperative to confront, expose, and reject all forms of "patriarchy"—power abuse, lies, exploitation—wherever we find it, including, or especially, when it comes to our political leaders and designated culture makers.

But how are we to judge either our culture *or* its makers when our capacity for judgment—our set of values—has already been formed for us by the very agents we hope to bring to account? It might be easier to remove a tumor from our own brains, alone and unaided, than to undertake such a cultural extraction process. Fortunately, as serious, even critical, as our condition appears to be, *we are not alone*.

That was a simple summation of this book's thesis. What follows, over the next few hundred pages, is the more comprehensive version.

JASUN HORSLEY
May, 2020

ONCE UPON A TIME IN HOLLYWOOD

CHRONIC FANTASY SYNDROME / A TOWN OF CONFABULATORS

"Film was no less than a secular religion."

—PETER BISKIND, *Easy Riders, Raging Bulls*

I was twenty when I made my first trip to Hollywood. I had moved to New York in 1987, on my twentieth birthday. I was rich at the time, having received a large inheritance when I turned eighteen. Renting a tiny room on Third Ave, I settled in and began reading *Crime and Punishment* and writing a script about a philosophical serial killer called Ed. I was drinking every other night in the East Village, and discovered cocaine via some shady bar buddies. After seven months, I bought an old Plymouth Fury and drove across country to the Promised Land. I arrived on Christmas Eve. After a night on the town—in which I was hoping to get laid but nearly got busted with a vial of cocaine in my pocket (I got away with a ticket for jaywalking)—I fell severely ill the next morning. Happy Christmas. Welcome to Hollywood.

I was staying at the Holiday Inn, on N. Highland Ave, just off the Walk of Fame, and I ended up stuck in that hotel room, wasting away with a high fever, unable to leave my bed or eat, for going on two weeks. During the first several days, I was lost in a fevered trance in which I could barely sense my body or remember who I was, a ghost-like consciousness, spread out across the hotel room, held together by the four walls. As I gradually grew stronger, I was able to sit up and turn on the TV, and I whiled away the sickly nights by watching a steadily deteriorating stream of pay-per-view movies, while drifting in and out of awareness. I dimly remember watching *Someone to Watch Over Me* and, God help me, *Slam Dance*, with Tom Hulce and Virginia Madsen. I was still unable to eat anything, drinking an endless stream of soda from the dispensing machine in the hallway, to combat the hideous dry taste in my mouth (the sugar probably kept me alive). The stronger I grew, the more desperate I was to eat; but when I ordered room service, I couldn't face more than a mouthful or two. I spent sleepless nights fantasizing about the different kinds of food I would eat when I got out. I spent hours methodically trying to recall every meal my mother ever cooked for me.

Eventually, I was strong enough to visit a doctor, who told me I had the worst case of tonsillitis he'd ever seen. This turned out to be a misdiagnosis: when I got back to England, in early 1988, I was told I had glandular fever, a chronic condition. Twenty years later, it was diagnosed as chronic fatigue syndrome (CFS), from which I suffered into my forties. Looking back now, with the hindsight of these thirty years, my first Hollywood pilgrimage, in which the dream turned instantly to nightmare, looks a lot like a blueprint, my first Map of Hell. If I'd known how to read it, I could have saved myself a lot of grief.

✦

My dream of an epic Hollywood-sponsored life first began to take conscious, proactive form (morphing from embryonic fantasy to full-blown ambition) roughly around the age of twelve, when Clint Eastwood became the center of my "parasocial universe" (see 3.3). Since then, I had doggedly pursued the culturally incepted dream of becoming a "star." The dream mutated and morphed over the years, as aspirations of artistic success cross-bonded with occultist-spiritual dreams of empowerment. But there was no reduction in intensity or fervor—on the contrary, I kept trying to fly higher, faster, wilder.

In the forty years since I wrote my first film reviews and movie scripts, at age thirteen, I have published five books on film and worked on maybe two dozen screenplays. One of the later ones, written in 2006, was inspired by my growing frustration at being *constantly ignored by Hollywood*. It was called *S.P.A.M.* and it was about a failed screenwriter living in Los Angeles: on the point of suicide, he meets a beautiful movie star trying to *escape* from Hollywood. Believing it will be his big break, he sets out to save her and slowly discovers that the film industry is controlled by a sinister cabal of movie agents. It was a comedy, based on a combination of direct experience and paranoid intuition. With hindsight, this too was something of an early "map."

✦

"I hope you're not keeping notes. I learned long ago that keeping notes can be dangerous to your health."

—SIDNEY KORSHAK, *"the real Godfather of Hollywood,"*
to Paramount executive Peter Bart[1]

In the formative years of my film obsession, I was most captured by the 1970s movies. One of the most popular and enjoyable books on Hollywood—specifically the "artistic renaissance" of the late 1960s and early 1970s—is Peter Biskind's *Easy Riders, Raging Bulls*. That the book only scratches the surface of that time, and has served more to mythologize it than *de*mythologize it, is something Biskind seems to acknowledge in the opening words of his book:

Hollywood is a town of confabulators. The people who dwell there create fictions for a living, fictions that refuse tidily to confine themselves to the screen, but spill over into the daily lives of the men and women who regard themselves as stars in the movies of their own lives. Although this book tells readers altogether more than they may wish to know about the Hollywood of the 70s, I do not flatter myself that I have arrived at "the truth." At the end of this long, twisted road I am once again struck with the force of the old maxim, the more you know, the more you know what you don't know. This is particularly true in the case of Hollywood [where] very little of what matters is committed to paper. . . . In a town where credit grabbing is an art form, to say that memory is self-serving is to say that the sun rises in the east and sets in the west (p. 7).

In a television interview about Biskind's book, Jack Nicholson quipped, with his trademark eyebrow curl, "I don't read fiction." At the time I heard this line (around 2002, living in Hampstead; on second thought, it may have been Dennis Hopper quoting Nicholson[2]), I presumed Nicholson was insinuating that Biskind's accounts were salacious and exaggerated. Now I wonder if his remark could just as easily be read the opposite way: inferring that the book *romanticized* the period, obscuring a much darker, uglier reality? Biskind's book is both salacious *and* romantic; in the documentary based on the book, Richard Dreyfuss made a comment about Julia Phillips' disclosures in *You'll Never Eat Lunch in this Town Again*: after his initial anger, Dreyfuss realized that "what really happened was *so* much worse."[3] At the very least, what Nicholson (or Hopper) was saying, I think indisputably, was "You had to be there." There's no arguing with that: hard as I may aspire to present a *counter-narrative* to the official Hollywood story, I wasn't there, I am not there still, and I will almost certainly never *be* there.

In Bret Easton Ellis' *White*, published in 2019, Ellis expresses his frustration with how, when interviewing Hollywood actors for his podcast, he can never get them to say anything negative or controversial about *anyone*. There is *an unwritten clause* in Hollywood not to tell tales out of school. It's not *seen* as snitching, because, at the most ordinary level, it simply means don't criticize your co-workers. You can't say, "That was a crappy performance," or, "They were difficult on set," or, "That shoot was a fucking nightmare," because it upsets people who you might need to work with, or get work from, in future. To some degree, this is the case within any industry or work place; but it's especially so in Hollywood, because so much there depends on *image*.

As Tim Adler writes in his introduction to *Hollywood and the Mob*, "the key resemblance between Hollywood and the Mafia is that both are to an extent secret societies, whose members never speak to outsiders" (p. 8). And as with the Mafia, it's not that hard to imagine what might be going on that Hollywood insiders don't even want to *think* about, never mind go on record about. Imagine the power abuses, sexual exploitation, illegal activities, and whatever else is happening behind the scenes of every movie deal and film shoot: why *wouldn't* we imagine that Hollywood—the state of mind that's also a business that's also a close-knit community, almost an extended family— might operate, like the Mafia, under an *omertà*—a vow of silence, on pain of death—or at least career suicide?

HOLLYWOOD SECRET SOCIETY

"Our impulses are being redirected. We are living in an
artificially induced state of consciousness that resembles
sleep. . . . The poor and the underclass are growing. Racial
justice and human rights are nonexistent. They have created a
repressive society, and we are their unwitting accomplices. Their
intention to rule rests with the annihilation of consciousness. We
have been lulled into a trance. They have made us indifferent to
ourselves, to others. We are focused only on our own gain. Please
understand. They are safe as long as they are not discovered.
That is their primary method of survival. Keep us asleep, keep
us selfish, keep us sedated."

—*They Live*

So if Hollywood is a secret society, what *kind* of secret society is it? And,
since we all know of its existence, what exactly makes it secret? While working on this book, I discovered a treasure chest of clues to this mystery. In *The
Power of Ritual in Prehistory: Secret Societies and Origins of Social Complexity*,
Brian Hayden makes a very clear and essential point about secret societies: it
is not their *existence* that is concealed from the public, but rather the rituals,
powers, privileges, and knowledge that become available to those who join.

Hayden is a professor emeritus of archaeology at Simon Fraser University
who has performed years of extensive archeological research, worldwide. His
interest in cultural and political ecology has led to the development of a
compelling thesis regarding the use of resources and energy to achieve political goals. Setting out to "rescue secret societies" from a "state of oblivion in
archaeology," Hayden has demonstrated how they "played pivotal roles in
sociopolitical and religious developments in the past": amounting to a form
of covert social organization by what he calls "aggrandizers." At one end
of the secret society spectrum, Hayden posits "open associations"—such as
religious charity organizations—that are accessible to all and "have no secret
doctrines." At the other end, he describes the "secret associations . . . which
exhibit exclusive access to knowledge that is generally used for purposes of
controlling spirits as well as controlling people" (all quotes, p. 7–8). Many,
though not all, of their activities *are concealed from the public*. Of these

practices (with special focus on the North American West Coast), Hayden writes:

> In order to persuade community members of the power of the super-natural forces that secret societies claimed to control, they periodically put on dances, displays, and processions of some of those powers for everyone to see. Society members impersonated spirits by the use of masks, costumes, and unusual noise-making devices. They also developed highly sophisticated stage magic techniques, all of which provided fascination and entertainment for non-initiated spectators, as well as instilling terror. . . . Creating altered states of consciousness (ASCs) or sacred ecstatic experiences (SEEs) in initiates was very frequent, if not universal, in secret societies, [as inferred by] rock art associated with vision quests and the use of dark, claustrophobic locations (e.g., caves), hallucinogens, masks, and mind-altering sound effects (p. 38, 292).

In case the parallels with the Hollywood of a few millennia later aren't immediately apparent, Hayden puts it in even more simple terms in his conclusion: "Since power was the primary goal and interest of these societies, they advertised their control over power on appropriate occasions, especially at initiations . . . Their displays and performances were competitively lavish in order to attract more members with wealth and power" (p. 346–7). Is this a case of the more things change . . . ?*

As *16 Maps of Hell* will attempt to make palpable, regarding the function and methodology of psychological operations, *people lie*. And they lie not only for the purposes of glamorizing the truth but also—less easily understood—with the end of making it sordid, grisly, and terrifying. This work is largely dependent on people's testimonies, as well as on provable facts; yet the very *last* thing I want to do is create a delivery device for the tall

---

* I came upon Hayden's work relatively late in the process of writing this book, though it turned out that Hayden is my neighbor, in Western British Columbia. What I will attempt, at key points in the book, is to weave in references to the remarkable discoveries Hayden has made (as well as the earlier researchers whose work he builds on), in the hope they will provide a deeper, more ancient and mysterious context for the cultural history, anecdotes, and arguments I will be presenting.

tales of intelligence operatives, criminals, and chronic attention merchants. Unfortunately, this is a risk I have to take, because the alternative is simply to let the myth—i.e., a *known* set of lies—stand.

I have been locked for a lifetime inside another CFS, a chronic fantasy syndrome. But if I hadn't fallen under that spell—like millions before and after me—I would never have been compelled to try and *unspell* my way out of it and this book would not exist. If the business of the Hollywood dream factory is creating illusions and making us suspend our disbelief, I believe there are two levels to this process: the first is the product itself; the other (which is also a product) is the myth of Hollywood, of movies and movie stars, directors, writers and producers. That's the deeper layer of fiction—the hidden terrain—which this book maps. *16 Maps of Hell* is an attempt to finish what an earlier book, *Seen and Not Seen*, started, to make peace with my culture by, paradoxically, formally declaring war on it. More accurately and less paradoxically, by recognizing the cold war that's been raging inside me, ever since those first "implants" were installed. And I'm not talking about my hairline.

I have been immersing myself in Hollywood and movie lore since I was twelve. That's four decades watching movies, documentaries, hearing interviews with industry people, reading about the business, studying the craft, writing scripts, forging connections, even making movies of my own. You could say I know Hollywood inside out, except that I am not, nor have I ever been, a Hollywood player. This is not for lack of trying; nor, I believe, lack of talent—or even connections. It is something else that has prevented me.

I think the main reason I never broke through was *attitude*: the wrong one. While I desperately wanted to join the creative class and hobnob with the hotshots of Hollywood, I also deeply distrusted that desire within myself, and always suspected it was foreign to me in some way, even antithetical to my nature. The house that's divided cannot stand, and the horse that's pulling in two directions at once is unlikely to carry its rider very far. In 2010, when my brother Sebastian Horsley died in the midst of growing fame and artistic success, it confirmed a powerful intuition I'd had for many years: if anything would prove fatal to him, it would be success within the entertainment industry. As I had feared, becoming a celebrity turned out to be the death of my brother, and the penny finally started to drop for me. I began to see, not just believe but *see*, that Hollywood represented something fundamentally ugly and destructive. And that knowing this *still* wasn't enough for me to turn away.

What I realized was this: All my study and research, my deep immersion in the Hollywood industry and mindset—the location, the culture, the state of mind—was geared to the end, not of joining the "family" but *of extricating myself from it*. For decades, I thought I was on the outside, struggling to get in. It turned out I was on the inside, trying to get out.

And I was making maps on my way out.

Part One

TORTURE THE WOMEN

"The trouble today is that we don't torture the women enough."

—ALFRED HITCHCOCK

"As Marion is to Norman, the audience of *Psycho* is to
Hitchcock; as the audiences of horror film in general are to
the directors of those films, female is to male. Hitchcock's
'torture the women' then means, simply, torture the
audience. . . . Cinefantastic horror, in short, succeeds in
incorporating its spectators as 'feminine' and then violating that
body—which recoils, shudders, cries out collectively in ways
otherwise imaginable, for males, only in nightmare."

—CAROL J. CLOVER, *Men, Women, and Chain Saws*

1

THE MEN WHO
WOULD BE KINGS

1.1   THE ART OF THE IMPOSER

"If the extreme self-interest personality types are given free rein,
they usually ruin the lives of others, erode society and culture,
and degrade the environment. They have always been a force to
be dealt with by community action, and they are so today."

—BRIAN HAYDEN

There is a 1971 *Esquire* article by the theater critic Kenneth Tynan about the Polish film director Roman Polanski, entitled "The Polish Imposition." The piece is accompanied by a black and white photograph of Polanski, wielding a sacrificial dagger menacingly. A *Psycho*-like shadow looms on the wall behind him, of an arm raised holding a knife (it doesn't correspond with Polanski's pose). On Polanski's right, behind him and adjacent to the knife, is Tynan himself, a grinning munchkin with only his head visible. This eerie photo was taken sometime around August 1971, two years after the murder of Polanski's wife, Sharon Tate. It is clearly designed to give the director the imposing appearance of a murderer.

On the third page of the article, Tynan describes Polanski as possessing "the assurance of all great imposers":

a quality of temperament or personality [that] denotes the ability not only
to impose one's will on others (although that is part of it) but to dictate the
conditions—social, moral, sexual, political—within which one can operate
with maximum freedom. . . . Success or failure, fulfillment or frustration
in almost every sphere of human activity is dependent on whether or not
one has the trick of imposing.[1]

Tynan was close friends with Polanski and wrote the screenplay for
Polanski's *Macbeth*, which the article serves to promote. Presumably he was
speaking from experience when he claimed that Polanski possessed the trick
of imposing "in spades—sometimes to an extreme degree," and that, "Like
many imposers, he divides the world into Lenin's categories of 'Who' and
'Whom'—those who do, and those to whom it is done." For good measure, somewhat superfluously, he adds: "With people like this, there is
always a sense of danger." Just how dangerous Roman Polanski's circle of
influence may have been is the focus of the opening chapters in *16 Maps of
Hell*, and without my conscious intention, in the last stages of preparing this
work for publication, Polanski has become something of the hub around
which this work revolves. With hindsight, the first indication of this was
the obscure *Esquire* article which I hunted down because of having heard
about the photograph. The quality Tynan calls "imposition" is, I suspect,
absolutely essential for understanding the sphere of human activity known
as Hollywood. In some ways, I realized, this book's entire thesis may be
summed up by those few disarmingly frank—perhaps unwittingly sinister—
words from Polanski's friend and collaborator. It is the will to operate with
maximum freedom, no matter the cost in collateral damage to others.

In *The Power of Ritual in Prehistory*, Hayden describes a "transegalitarian" society made up of "aggrandizers," a term that seems to correspond
closely with Tynan's "imposer": human beings who, throughout history, have
sought to increase their personal power via the imposition of their will onto
others, and via (an added wrinkle Tynan omits) *covert cooperation and networking*. Hayden posits a small percentage of all populations that possess
strongly developed aggrandizer traits and who, "by and large, become the
elites and gravitate toward positions of power, including memberships and
high positions in secret societies." He describes them as "relentlessly aggressive in getting what they want and in trying to change attitudes, norms, and

rules to favor their strategies" (p. 18). In other words, advanced imposers. Hayden attributes the imposer-aggrandizers with a combination of (two very obvious human behaviors) a hunger for power and *the practice of lying*.

If there is one, overarching theme to this work, it might be summed up thus, as the systemic (and all-too-human) pathology of *self-aggrandizement through deception*. When it comes to understanding Hollywood, one must proceed from the assumption that *everything we have heard so far is a lie*. In any event, that is how I mean to proceed.

1.2   AN UNDERGROUND HISTORY OF "THE NEW HOLLYWOOD" (ROGER CORMAN & AIP)

"We Americans have always considered Hollywood, at best, a sinkhole of depraved venality. And, of course, it is. It is not a protective monastery of aesthetic truth."

—DAVID MAMET

The period in Hollywood history documented in Peter Biskind's *Easy Riders, Raging Bulls*, the "New Hollywood" of the late 1960s and early 1970s, has always been especially exciting to me. I have read Biskind's book four or five times now, and I never seem to tire of the vicarious thrill it gives me. At the same time, this was the period of probably the most infamous crime to ever occur in Hollywood, the murder of Sharon Tate, Jay Sebring, and others at Tate and Polanski's home on Cielo Drive in Los Angeles, on the night of August 8, 1969. These crimes not only impacted a Hollywood nexus of power but seem to have emerged *out of* that nexus. It is a nexus that includes many of the major New Hollywood players—Jack Nicholson, Mia Farrow, Dennis Hopper, Warren Beatty, Robert Evans, Robert Towne, and many others less well-known. As a result, I have, after many drafts of this work, decided that this is the logical—the *necessary*—point of departure for my dark and convoluted journey into the Hollywood heart of darkness.

In my opinion, the logical place to begin a potted *alternate* history of the New Hollywood is, not *Bonnie and Clyde*, as Biskind does, but Roger

Corman. As improbable as it seems, and as unexpected to the author, I will hence begin with a brief look at Corman's career. As I wrote back in 2005, in *Dogville vs Hollywood*, "Corman was a unique player in the history of Hollywood . . . he seemed to emerge less of his own accord and more like an avatar bringing a new religion—in response to a need, a void within the medium itself" (p. 64). This raises a question that I think is central to this work: how to tell the difference between an upsurge of the *zeitgeist* and an irresistible psy-opportunity?

Corman's career spanned nearly 40 years and included well over 500 pictures as producer and/or director, and occasionally actor (such as in *The Silence of the Lambs* and *The Godfather Part II*). As a director, Corman is best remembered for his 1960s Edgar Allan Poe adaptations; as a producer, Corman dedicated himself to "exploitation" films that catered to the lowest common denominator of audience interest—sex, violence, drugs, monsters, spaceships, prisons, and bikers. It was out of this cauldron that "the New Hollywood," rife with toil and trouble, bubbled forth. From *Dogville vs Hollywood*:

> During his time at [American Independent Pictures], Corman pretty much established his own film school/studio and recruited and nurtured a legion of up-and-coming players . . . among them Peter Fonda, Dennis Hopper, Bruce Dern, Francis Ford Coppola, Jack Nicholson, [Robert Towne, Willian Shatner, Sylvester Stallone] Monte Hellman, Woody Allen, Peter Bogdanovich, Charles Bronson, Robert De Niro, Brian De Palma, Martin Scorsese, Paul Bartel, John Sayles, Jonathan Demme, John Milius, Joe Dante, Jonathan Kaplan, Ron Howard, and James Cameron. Corman created a unique arena for writers, directors, and actors to develop their gifts in and discover their strengths. Everybody was happy, and everybody won. Ironic that this methodology was reviled (by both Hollywood and critics) as "exploitation," since it was a far less exploitative environment than that of Hollywood. At AIP, the artists got to make movies, Corman [and AIP] got to make money, and audiences got the movies they wanted (and no doubt deserved). It was a trash movie utopia (p. 66).

As the primary intelligence behind this unofficial recruiting and training ground for Hollywood operatives, it becomes expedient to inquire—what sort of witch's cauldron did Corman himself issue from? He was born in Detroit, Michigan, on April 5, 1926, his father an engineer. He and his brother (who also became a film producer) were raised Catholic, and Roger went to Beverly Hills High School, after which he studied Industrial Engineering at Stanford University. With only six months to complete, Corman (legend has it) decided he didn't want to be an engineer and enlisted in the V-12 Navy College Training Program, serving from 1944 to 1946. The V-12 program's goal was similar to the Army Specialized Training Program (ASTP): to produce officers, as well as technically trained personnel in fields like engineering, foreign languages, and medicine. Running from 1942 to 1944, the ASTP recruits were expected, though not required, to become officers at the end of their training. It seems fair to ask—without expecting an answer—if this included the undercover kind.

After his two-plus years in the Navy, Corman returned to Stanford to finish his degree, receiving a Bachelor of Science in Industrial Engineering in 1947. While he was there, he was initiated into the fraternity Sigma Alpha Epsilon.[2] The Sigma Alpha Epsilon is "one of the largest and best-known fraternities in the US—and the deadliest" (there were over sixty hazing-related deaths at SAE between 2005 and 2013).[3] Greek letter fraternities are an entire culture in US college and university life, less sub- than super-, and one that dates back further than US independence. (The first college fraternity in North America was Phi Beta Kappa, founded at the College of William and Mary in 1775.[4]) Today, in 2020, there are well over a hundred men's fraternities, all presumably with nationwide networks, and perhaps half as many women's ones. As for what sorts of "characters" are being built via these fraternity initiation methods—since this is after all their spoken directive—several articles in recent years, citing a number of studies, have claimed that fraternity men are three times more likely to commit rape than other men on college campuses![5] Evidently, either the training-via hazing rituals isn't "taking," or it's designed for a purpose *diametrically opposed* to the one publicly declared.

Whatever the implications of Corman's background in "Greek life," having been duly hazed, he did a brief stint at US Electrical Motors in Los Angeles in 1948, where his career in engineering sputtered out after only four days. Since his brother, Gene Corman, was already working in the film industry as an agent, Roger decided to follow that route instead. At age 23, he became a story analyst at 20th Century Fox, but apparently lost interest again and, under the G.I. Bill—a law that provided a range of benefits for returning World War II veterans (though he never saw combat)—he went back to college, this time to Oxford, to study literature.

Corman then returned to Hollywood, where he worked briefly as a television stage hand at KLAC, became a messenger at Fox, and then an assistant to literary agent, Dick Hyland. At 27, he sold his first screenplay (*Highway Dragnet*) to Allied Artists and was given the job of associate producer on the film. One of his first films as producer was the racing car thriller, *The Fast and the Furious*, in 1955—now a popular franchise—which he sold to a new independent company, the American Releasing Company. The company was run by James H. Nicholson and Samuel Z. Arkoff. Soon after Corman arrived, ARP changed its name to AIP, American International Pictures, and the rest is history.

Or, perhaps I should say, myth?

1.3   THE BOY FROM NEPTUNE:
CASE STUDY # 1, JACK NICHOLSON

> "When you meet the producers of movies, you very often think
> you're not connected with a businessman at all. You feel more as
> if you're dealing with a gangster. I think the shocking thing . . . is
> talking to a studio head or to a bigshot producer, because you
> have a very strange feeling that you're dealing with a mafia man.
> They think strictly in terms of very harsh reality. Flesh and
> money are the primary considerations. Flesh, money, and power."
>
> —PAULINE KAEL, *in conversation with Studs Terkel, 1966*

When it comes to exactly how the world of the entertainment industry cum organized crime cum intelligence and military psyop is configured or directed, it is tempting to let the data speak for itself—or not. The problem with this is it can leave things vague and unsatisfactory. Linking Corman to the inception of the New Hollywood and at the same time to Naval training and hardcore fraternity initiation does not count as hard evidence that he was part of a deliberate intelligence program to recruit agents of cultural engineering. Yet within the deeper context of my thesis, and that created by all the other documented history, it does become at least *highly suggestive*.

As a point of comparison, I offer *Who Paid the Piper? The CIA and the Cultural Cold War* by Frances Stonor Saunders. Saunders' book painstakingly demonstrates how the Central Intelligence Agency played an active role in the infiltration, co-opting, and in some cases whole-cloth creation, of artistic movements in the mid-20th century, ostensibly to counteract Communism and expand American political influence. Much of the CIA's funding went through the Congress for Cultural Freedom, and as Saunders writes: "Whether they liked it or not, whether they knew it or not, there were few writers, poets, artists, historians, scientists, or critics in postwar Europe whose names were not in some way linked to this covert enterprise" (p. 2).

So, while it would be presumptuous to deduce from this slice of hidden history that the same applies to the US film industry, or to any particular period of it (e.g., Corman's AIP stint and the ensuing flood of new talent that became the New Hollywood), it would be just as rash to deny that the possibility exists. When we have the means, the motive, and the opportunity *clearly* in view, as well as a dead body, it becomes not unreasonable to suspect a crime. Once this is recognized, then any and every significant player on the field becomes, not guilty by association, but under suspicion of aiding and abetting.

All that said, let's move on to possibly the most celebrated of all Corman's discoveries, Jack Nicholson. Nicholson first came to Hollywood in 1954, when he was seventeen; according to Patrick McGilligan's biography *Jack*, this was to visit his sister, though as we shall see, telling Nicholson's sister from his mother is something even Nicholson himself was unable to do for going on the first forty years of life. Jack took a job as an office worker for Hanna-Barbera at the MGM cartoon studio, and trained to be an actor with a group called the Players Ring Theater. After that, he found small parts performing on the stage and in TV soap operas, then made his film debut in the Roger Corman-produced teen drama, *The Cry Baby Killer* (1958), in the title role. Corman went on to direct Nicholson in *The Little Shop of Horrors, The Raven, The Terror*, and *The St. Valentine's Day Massacre*. Nicholson branched out as a writer and then director, writing the screenplay for the 1967 counterculture film *The Trip*, directed by Corman and starring Peter Fonda and

Dennis Hopper, as well as *Head*, the movie that took The Monkees from small to big screen—and for which Charles Manson may or may not have auditioned.*

Head also precipitated Nicholson's move from Corman's stable to a new kind of "family," Raybert Productions, founded by Bob Rafelson and Bert Schneider. Besides *Head*, Raybert's principal works were the situation comedy *The Monkees* (and the group of the same name), and *Easy Rider* (co-produced with Peter Fonda's Pando Company). *Easy Rider*, as we all know, was Nicholson's breakout role in 1969 (he got the part when Rip Torn came to blows with Hopper—Hopper was by most accounts narcotically-demented during this period). On the strength of *Easy Rider*, Nicholson was cast by Stanley Kubrick in the part of Napoleon, for a film Kubrick never managed to make. Instead, Nicholson took the part of Bobby Dupea, written for him by Carol Eastman, in *Five Easy Pieces*, which was produced by Raybert, now known as BBS Productions, standing for Bob, Bert, and Stephen Blauner, the new partner. *Five Easy Pieces* became a career-defining role for Nicholson and may still be his best performance.

BBS released the Oscar-winning *The Last Picture Show* in 1971, as well as three more films with Nicholson: *A Safe Place* (1971), *The King of Marvin Gardens* (1972), and *Drive, He Said* (1971), Nicholson's directorial debut. Peter Biskind devotes quite a few pages to BBS in *Easy Riders, Raging Bulls*, including some observations that are relevant for my present thesis. An anonymous source tells Biskind, for example, that working at BBS "was all like *The Godfather*, very dynastic, very Mafioso-like. . . It was almost like you mingled your blood with Bert when you were his friend or business associate. He'd do anything for you if you were in trouble, but if you made any mistakes, that was it" (p. 55). Biskind comments:

> Rafelson and Schneider considered themselves, and indeed behaved like, sexual outlaws, for whom nothing was taboo, nothing too flagrant.

---

* There is a bit of urban legend that Charles Manson auditioned for the TV show *The Monkees*; since he was in jail when that show was starting up, this would seem unlikely. The Monkees movie *Head*, however, *was* cast during the period when Manson was schmoozing the Hollywood scene and hanging out with the Beach Boys, so it's conceivable that this is the factual basis of the legend.

[Schneider's good looks and intelligence were] gilded by wealth and an innate sense of privilege, unclouded by self-doubt, a dynastic assurance that everything he did was right. [As] Bert's brother Harold put it more succinctly, Bert would fuck a snake. [S]ex was a publicly traded commodity among the [BBS] guys, sexual exploits a variation of who could piss further. [Schneider] helped himself freely to the decade's smorgasbord of liberation theologies, spiritual and corporeal, developing a highly evolved ideology of promiscuity to justify his behavior (p. 58–59).

According to Richard Dreyfuss on that time, "everybody wanted to be Bert Schneider."[6] In case we might want to cut Jack some slack here, Biskind quotes James Nelson, a post-production worker at BBS, describing Jack Nicholson and Schneider as being "close like brothers"; Nicholson's longtime friend Harry Gittes describes the BBS guys as

the meanest people I'd ever met in my life, brutal, inhumane inflictors. Respect and loyalty, that was the way BBS operated. They had a gangster mentality. This was the Jewish, Bugsy Siegel type of hipness—"We are not the soft Jews." And believe me, these were *not* the soft Jews. These were the toughest coldest Jews I had ever met in my life . . . I have never forgiven Jack for getting involved with these guys. BBS brought out his mean side (p. 117).

Maybe so, but you can't bring out what the boy doesn't have in him, and it might not be too much of a stretch to say that Nicholson was born into "the life." He was literally born in Neptune City (astrologically, Neptune is the planet of illusion, magic, dreams, drugs, deception, and movies), in New Jersey in 1937, the son of a showgirl called June Frances Nicholson (stage name June Nilson). Add to an already illusion-soaked childhood this fact: the year before Jack was born, June married Italian-American showman Donald Furcillo (stage name Donald Rose) only to find out he was already married, making their marriage null and void. McGilligan believes June's manager, Latvian-born Eddie King, and not Furcillo, may have been Nicholson's actual father. And the final layer of deception-intrigue: since June was only seventeen years old and unmarried when Jack's ETA was announced, her parents agreed to raise Nicholson as their own child, without revealing his true parentage to anyone (not even little Jack). June the showgirl was then cast in the part of Jack's sister—making Nicholson's entire childhood effectively "staged"—a make-believe. As Dave McGowan points out in *Weird Scenes Inside the Canyon*, there is no record of Nicholson's birth "either at the hospital or in the city's archives. . . . It appears then that there is no way to determine who Jack Nicholson really is" (p. 94).

Nicholson himself officially only found out that his sister was his mother in 1974, after *Time* magazine did some digging. He claimed it was no big deal, since he was by then already "psychologically formed." Bizarrely, this revelation was coincident with the release of Roman Polanski's *Chinatown*, in 1974, a film in which Nicholson's character, Jake Gittes (named after Harry), repeatedly slaps Evelyn Mulwray (Faye Dunaway) until she gets her story straight regarding whether the girl in her care is her sister or her daughter. This is the dark secret at the core of *Chinatown*: the girl is the result of Evelyn's being either raped or seduced by her father, Noah Cross. "She's my sister *and* my daughter!"—just as Jack was June's brother *and* her son.

1.4   HOLLYWOOD INCEST:
CASE STUDY # 2, GEORGE HODEL

> "If art has any goal . . . it is to banish the enthrallment of the
> human agent with morality and to allow a person to experience
> the ecstasy of both saintliness and wickedness. 'Salvation' comes
> when one can say . . . 'I obey my law' and 'I seek and commit acts
> of evil through intention and principle.'"
>
> —CARL RASCHKE, *Painted Black*

Noah Cross was played by John Huston, father of Nicholson's longtime partner Anjelica Huston, and one of the most powerful and esteemed movie directors in Hollywood history. Esteemed especially by Jack Nicholson, who said of him: "I consciously knew for a certain period with John that the greatest guy alive was a friend of mine. . . He's one of those people in life whose approval I seek. . . When John Huston dies . . . I'll cry for the rest of my life" (Wasson, p. 195).

This is the same Huston who was best friends with George Hodel, who married Huston's first wife Dorothy, after they divorced in 1933. Hodel was "an admirer of the Marquis de Sade and a friend of movie, literary and art libertines like . . . Huston, [Surrealist artist] Man Ray, [film director and Mia's father] John Farrow and Henry Miller."[7] He was also a physician whose clinic was dedicated primarily to treating the rich and famous for venereal disease—"Top people from the movie industry," according to Steve Hodel's *Black Dahlia Avenger: A Genius for Murder* (p. 358). Hodel also performed illegal abortions there. Steve Hodel quotes Joe Barrett, a friend of Dorothy, remembering how his father's clinic provided ample opportunity for blackmailing:

> Directors, producers, actors, and also police officials . . . it was a very active place, especially in the late thirties and early to mid-forties, before penicillin had been discovered. . . . The socially elite came to be treated, along with their girlfriends and prostitutes. Dorothy [Huston Hodel] said that George kept detailed files on all his patients and that in her words "The files made for some interesting income" (p. 358).

As Steve Hodel's various books discuss, Hodel was accused, though never formally charged, with the 1947 murder and mutilation of Elizabeth Short, a.k.a. the Black Dahlia. Under suspicion, his house was bugged for several days and the wire-recordings capture secret conversations in which Hodel confessed to police payoffs, performing illegal abortions, and having committed the 1945 murder of his personal secretary, Ruth Spaulding, as well as the 1947 torture-murder of Elizabeth "Black Dahlia" Short. The transcripts[8] also contain the probable real-time murder of a woman as recorded by detectives during a 1950 stakeout. Though only minutes away from the residence, the police officers take no action. According to Hodel, this is the "smoking gun" that law enforcement cannot allow to be made public—possibly one of several around Hodel's illicit activities.

By April 1950, there was enough evidence to charge Hodel for Short's murder and he was about to be arrested when he fled the US to counsel prisoners in the Territorial Prison in Hawaii for three years. After that, he moved on to the Philippines, started a new family, and appears to have remained there until 1990. He died in 1999 in San Francisco, without charges ever being filed. Many years later, he was accused by his son, Los Angeles homicide detective Steve, of several other murders. Most relevant of all for this current unveiling, Hodel was also accused in 1949, by his daughter Tamar, of raping her and getting her pregnant at the age of fourteen (unlike Evelyn Mulwray's in *Chinatown*, the child was aborted, against George's wishes). Despite two eye witnesses, Hodel was acquitted.

Most bizarrely of all, perhaps, Hodel has been implicated (also by Steve Hodel, though others have supported the claim) of being involved in the infamous Zodiac Killings of the late 1960s and early 1970s in Northern California (more on that tangle later). Clearly we are deep into the twilight zone where movie plots, true crimes, and elaborately confabulated cover-ups have become inextricably entangled. Nor is this the exclusive province of disturbed sons or conspiracy researchers: respected film critic David Thomson has been hinting at just such a deep, dark Hollywood conspiracy around the Black Dahlia case for going on twenty years:

> George got away with [raping his daughter] because a shameless lawyer created the idea of "Tamar the liar," and because the L.A.P.D. wasn't as judiciously hostile to Dr. George as it might have been. He was part of an abortionists' circle in Los Angeles, and he knew which cops you could lean on. So he never made it past the level of "prime suspect" in the Elizabeth Short case. [The fact he] mixed freely with Man Ray and John Huston . . . doesn't mean that Man Ray or Huston was an accomplice, but neither does it exclude them from knowing damning stuff about the suave doctor and his hobby. . . . Huston had his own strains of cruelty and cynicism. He could do nearly anything he turned his hand to—it was inevitable that he became a hit in Hollywood. (He once said that the secret to direction was the sadism it required.) . . . And George Hodel was their friend, their fellow partygoer, and someone eager to impress more famous men. As it turned out, murder was his art, especially the cut-up jobs on attractive young women, just the sort who hoped that Man Ray might photograph them, or John Huston give them a test.[9]

This last implies that culture—whether Hollywood screen tests or Surrealist photoshoots—served as a perfect honey trap for hapless murder victims.

✦

"Scumbags and superstars
Tell me your names
I'll make a bet, you're
Both the same."

—TALKING HEADS, *"Lifetime Piling Up"*

As film critic Jeff Simon wrote in 2019:

Even before his son convincingly accused his father of the Black Dahlia murder, Hodel has lurked in the background of Hollywood movies. A particularly sinister overtone of Polanski's sardonic masterpiece *Chinatown* is that Hodel's friend Huston played Noah Cross, whose incestuous rape of his daughter is the nightmare around which the whole film is built.[10]

Back in 2006, David Thomson again, who seems to have an atypical awareness of—or willingness to discuss—the criminal underbelly of Hollywood culture, more-than-hinted at Huston's complicity, making the highly unfashionable suggestion that Huston's *movies* were evidence of it.

Was Huston a part of the circle? Can an artistic hero have been that close to murder? I don't know. But Huston was a strange man, with a cold, sadistic streak. He killed a man in a driving accident when he was young and it was covered up. He was also one of the first directors who made films where the rats—the criminals—were the appealing characters: I'm thinking of *High Sierra* (which he wrote), *The Maltese Falcon, The Asphalt Jungle*.[11]

Unless Huston killed more than one person in a driving accident, Thomson has his facts wrong here: Huston killed a *woman*, dancer Tosca Roulien, when he hit her with his car in 1933. When her husband, the Latin actor Raul Roulien, attempted to seek compensation for her death, his career was systematically destroyed by John's father, Walter Huston.[12] There were rumors at the time that the actual culprit was Clark Gable, and that Huston was selected to take the fall.[13] He moved to Europe after the event and drifted around before returning to Hollywood in 1937 (the year of Nicholson's birth, and that *Chinatown* was set). When Huston met Hodel is hard to determine with accuracy—some accounts call them childhood friends—though the first obvious connection is when Hodel married Huston's first wife, in 1940.

Tamar Hodel's experience has been receiving more attention lately, not just via her brother's writing on the Black Dahlia but because it forms the loose basis for the recent TV show, *I Am the Night*. I had not even heard of Tamar when I began this chapter, but she ties together so many different threads within it that it's potentially mind-boggling. For starters: Tamar "had an interesting role in the forming of the Mamas & the Papas [a band that will soon become central to this "detour"]. While living in California, Tamar became the mentor of her 11-year-old neighbor, Michelle Gilliam, who would become Michelle Phillips of the Mamas & the Papas. Tamar introduced Michelle to John Phillips, her future husband and band-mate."[14] Phillips became a highly successful singer and actress in the 1960s and 70s and enjoyed(?) extra-marital flings with Warren Beatty and Roman Polanski, as well as being Jack Nicholson's girlfriend for a couple of years after her break-up with John. Michelle Phillips "apparently told [Nicholson] Tamar's story [and it] allegedly made its way into the script for *Chinatown*."[15] What's more, for a brief period, Polanski would even suspect John Phillips of killing Sharon Tate out of jealous rage over Polanski's fling with Michelle (more on this later).

Flashback: Before John Phillips married Michelle, he had a daughter with his first wife, Susan Stuart Adams. The daughter was named Mackenzie and Mackenzie became a minor celebrity at the age of twelve when she got a featured role in George Lucas's breakout film, *American Graffiti*. Flash-forward 36 years to 2009: Mackenzie Phillips published a memoir, *High on Arrival*, and while promoting it on *The Oprah Winfrey Show*. She spoke of how her father had injected her with cocaine when she was eleven, leading to a lifetime's addiction.* But the real bombshell she lobbed during her Oprah

---

* Mackenzie went on to suffer a lifetime of drug addiction, culminating in 2008 when she was arrested by the Los Angeles Airport Police for trying to get through airport security carrying cocaine and heroin. In October 2008, she pleaded guilty to a felony count of

interview was this: At the age of 19, on the night before her first wedding in 1979, Mackenzie "woke up that night from a blackout to find myself having sex with my own father." Months later, she confronted him and demanded why he had raped her; Phillips insisted it hadn't been rape but a consensual act of love.[16] Mackenzie entered into a sexual relationship with her father, later describing it as "sort of Stockholm Syndrome, where you begin to love your captor."[17] The affair ended—after ten years—when Mackenzie got pregnant and Papa John arranged for her to abort it.[18]

Tamar Hodel spoke out in support of Mackenzie, also in 2009. She recalled seeing her in Hawaii performing *The Vagina Monologues*: "She was onstage, talking about incest, and there was no doubt she was talking about herself. . . There is much more incest out there than people are aware of. It's hidden and it destroys lives. I look at Mackenzie and realize I was fortunate: I was raped only one time by my father."[19] A less-well-publicized fact brings all of these sordid scenarios into a single tapestry: before her death, in 2015, as was included in her brother Steve Hodel's *Black Dahlia Avenger III*, Tamar claimed that John Huston attempted to rape her, also at age eleven. In her account, quoted in Hodel's book, Tamar describes Huston as "a tall, very powerful man . . . Almost overshadowing my own father," adding that "they were in competition with each other." The assault occurred "when I was eleven, we were sunbathing nude before we were told not to, and John was drunk. And, he tried to rape me. . . . No, it was not a party. And I never did experience a party as has been described so often. I'm talking about normal, everyday life at the house" (p. 113).

Tamar's denial that she attended her father's sex parties is significant, as we'll see, but then so is the reference to "normal, everyday life," because all the evidence would suggest that there was no such condition in George Hodel's universe. The house Tamar grew up in, the Franklin House in Los Angeles, was described by art photographer Edmund Teske as "an evil place.

---

cocaine possession and was sentenced to a drug rehabilitation program. See: "Mackenzie Phillips arrested at LAX on suspicion of narcotics possession," *The Seattle Times*, August 28, 2008: https://www.seattletimes.com/entertainment/mackenzie-phillips-arrested-at-lax-on -suspicion-of-narcotics-possession/ and: "Mackenzie Phillips Pleads Guilty to Cocaine Possession," by Ken Lee, People, October 31, 2008: https://people.com/crime/mackenzie -phillips-pleads-guilty-to-cocaine-possession/

. . Women were tortured for sport there. Murders happened there."[20] Hodel
was known to have thrown "drug-infused, hedonistic parties and orgies in
his gold bedroom," and these parties—which Tamar later claimed not to
have attended—she had previously described as her reason for running away
in 1949:

> When questioned by the police, she said she had left because "her home
> life was too depressing," on account of "all the sex parties at the Franklin
> House." Tamar then accused her father and other adults of raping
> her during a party at the house. When questioned by police, George
> responded bizarrely, stating that he had recently been "delving into the
> mystery of love and the universe," and that the acts of which he was
> accused were "unclear, like a dream. I can't figure out whether some-
> one is hypnotizing me," he insisted, "or I am hypnotizing someone."
> When police raided the home, they seized pornography and questionable
> objects.[21]

Hodel's bizarrely dreamy statement, and Tamar's changing versions of
history, both suggest that we are dealing with (possibly) deliberate manipulation of memory, and that the disseminators of twilight language are
themselves forever lost in that zone. (And in case we might think his sons
were somehow exempt, Hodel was also said to "frequently beat his sons in
the basement" of the house—perhaps as part of their Spartan training, see
4.2.) In a further case of art overlapping with nightmare and with brutal
reality, Tamar was named after the heroine of a poem—written by Hodel's
friend, the Big Sur poet Robinson Jeffers—about "a tormented woman
who had sex with her brother." "My father took avant-garde to the hilt, and
the women went along with this," Tamar told Sheila Weller in 2015. "But
it was hidden." Tamar also describes how Man Ray took nude pictures of
her and, somewhat conflicting her claim above, how she "was pressured to
sunbathe nude." She also describes being forced to fellate her father at the
age of eleven. "The pharaohs had sex with their daughters," he would rave
to her. Her father, she said, was determined "to make me a sex goddess."

One final detail seems especially chilling: "L.A. artist William Copley
did a painting in 1961, showing a doctor with torture-inflicting tools and a
dead nude woman on the floor. A hard-to-escape conclusion: the Surrealists

were winking at the murder of the Black Dahlia."[22] If so, it may have been reciprocal: Steve Hodel's stated belief is that his father was trying to emulate Man Ray's surrealist artwork via the mutilation of Short's body. "This is dad's surrealistic masterpiece . . . his scalpel being his paintbrush and her body was the canvas. It's that twisted." Hodel suspects that Short posed for Man Ray in 1943 for a painting in which the female subject has her face scratched out—similar to Short's body when found. Man Ray's "Minotaur" (1934) may have served as a similar inspiration for the Black Dahlia mutilation:

> Made from the torso of a woman's body, the photograph references the mythological beast imprisoned in a labyrinth on the Greek island of Crete, where youths were sacrificed to appease the gods; as a surrealist work, it also references the suppression of libidinal impulses *a la* Freud. . . . "One of the early clues was my recognizing through Man Ray's artworks," explained Hodel during his segment on Dr. Phil. "This exact picture of a woman bisected at the waist, carefully posed . . . it's of course identical to the crime scene photography."[23]

1.5 ALL MOBBED UP: CASE STUDY # 3, ROBERT EVANS & THE KINGMAKERS

> "There are some crimes for which you get punished, and there are some crimes that our society isn't equipped to punish, and so we reward the criminals. . . . So there's really nothing to do but put their names on plaques and make them pillars of the community."
>
> —ROBERT TOWNE

It's hard to imagine anything more baroque—elaborately grotesque—than committing grisly torture-murders as a form of artistic one-upmanship. And yet, in the years since the Black Dahlia murder, this has become the trope of a seemingly endless stream of serial killer movies, comic books, pulp novels, and TV shows. It may actually date back—if not to reality itself, to comic book supervillains like the Joker, whose madness involves a kind of deranged desire to establish themselves in the public eye by performing flamboyant, elaborately staged acts of destruction. And if there's a thesis emerging via the unexpected leads that I have found myself pursuing in this current chapter, it may be this: insofar as Hollywood is a place where mobsters, psy-operatives, and murderous madmen have chosen to ply their trade—or maybe even built it from the ground up—then the products it creates, the dreams it manufactures, may not only be a cover for their activities, but a kind of covert celebration of them.

John Huston played the title role in the 1969 *De Sade* (co-directed by Roger Corman, uncredited), a film Wikipedia describes as "characterized by its psychedelic imagery and go-go sensibilities." In Andy Warhol's *Interview* magazine, Huston was complemented on his performance:

> *Interview*: You scared the hell out of me in the DE SADE thing.
> **Huston**: I've never seen it.
> *Interview*: You were terrifically perverse.
> **Huston**: Why thank you![24]

What greater show of power is there than to flaunt one's abuses openly and suffer no consequences? Perhaps the Hollywood criminal elite take it one step further and not only flaunt their murderous, sexually aberrant proclivities openly, but bestow *awards* upon each other for doing so, thereby getting to bask in the adoration of the public being victimized? It's been remarked how movie stars seem to enjoy playing gangsters and criminals to a bizarre degree. The assumption has generally been that it's a way for them—soft and pampered as they are—to live wild vicariously. Perhaps it's closer to the reverse, and is a way for them to be *who they actually are* without suffering the consequences—and more, be celebrated for it?

One of the very first movie gangsters was George Raft in Howard Hawks' *Scarface*, and Raft was a boyhood friend of Bugsy Siegel (also a suspect in the Black Dahlia murder case). Before he became a movie star, Raft was a "wheel man" (getaway driver) for the mob,[25] and claimed to have narrowly avoided a life of crime. Or was he assigned to the glamorous end of the vice business? Bugsy Siegel himself hobnobbed in Hollywood and, though he never got to see it, he was played by Warren Beatty in 1992's

Bugsy. Meyer Lansky was played by Ben Kingsley in the movie; in real-life he was known as the "Mob's Accountant" and was instrumental, along with his associate Charles "Lucky" Luciano, in the development of the National Crime Syndicate in the US. Strange characters to be immortalized by Oscar-winning movie stars. That is, until we look a little closer at the Oscar winners and the Oscar-givers.

✦

"[W]hen you're building something you're spinning a web and tend to become a prisoner of the web."

—CHARLES BLUHDORN

Hollywood super-lawyer Greg Bautzer worked for Siegel and Lansky, and Bautzer has been credited with getting Robert Evans his job running Paramount pictures in 1966—a position that led to *Rosemary's Baby*, *The Godfather*, and *Chinatown*. Is a picture starting to emerge? Perhaps a few more hard, cold facts are required first. In *The Man Who Seduced Hollywood*, B. James Gladstone writes how Robert Evans met Sidney Korshak at the Racquet Club in Palm Springs sometime in the 1950s. Korshak's power, writes Gladstone, "derived from his ability to act as a go-between for respectable businessmen, such as Universal topper Lew Wasserman, and underworld figures who controlled the unions. Korshak's other business was investing mob revenue in legitimate businesses" (p. 237). Evans, Gladstone reports, would "sit at Korshak's knee soaking up gangland tales"; emphasizing the paternal imagery, he adds that Korshak "virtually adopted him as a son" (p. 241). Eventually, Korshak introduced Evans to Bautzer,[26] who took Evans under his wing and "helped him start a fledgling career as a producer, optioning books to adapt for the screen"—i.e., securing a "legitimate business" for investing "mob revenue."[27]

One of those books was a 1966 novel titled *The Detective*, which Evans purchased before it was released and which became his "in" at Paramount (it was made into a movie in 1968, starring a mobbed-up Frank Sinatra). The official version for how Evans became the youngest studio head in movie history since Irving Thalberg is as follows: in August 1966, Peter Bart (later editor of *Variety*) wrote an article for *The New York Times'* Sunday Arts & Leisure section on Evans, describing him as "the most aggressive young producer in

Hollywood." The article, legend has it, proved "prescient" when Bart pointed out that Evans was the only actor to ever portray Irving Thalberg in film (*Man of a Thousand Faces*), and now was well be on his way to becoming him in life. (More likely, Evans was cast in the role as a way of grooming—and auditioning—him for his future position.) The article caught the attention of the head of the Gulf+Western conglomerate, Charles Bluhdorn, who hired Evans as part of a shakeup at Paramount Pictures (which included bringing in Bart, recruited by Evans as a Paramount executive). So much for the legend. Albert S. Ruddy (who went on to produce *The Godfather* for Evans) tells a different story; "privy to the machinations that put Evans on top [Ruddy] confirms that they were not accomplished by a mere newspaper article":

> "Greg Bautzer's the guy that set Bobby Evans up with Charlie Bluhdorn," said Ruddy in 2011. [Bautzer] gave Bluhdorn a line of bullshit about how this kid knew everyone in Hollywood." It was Bautzer who knew everyone. Bluhdorn, on the other hand, was new to Hollywood. . . . [Says Bautzer's ex-wife Dana Wynter:] "And [Bluhdorn] wanted a studio. He wanted 'the business.' You know, show business. And Greg got it for him. And he also got Bob Evans his spot." . . . "Greg was known as 'The Kingmaker' [said Ruddy]. He was handling Howard Hughes, Kirk Kerkorian, everybody. [Bluhdorn] was smart. If you're going into the movie business, you go to Greg Bautzer" (p. 242).

Author Gladstone emphasizes how Evans neglected to mention Bautzer's involvement in his ascent, "giving credit instead to Korshak and implying that the mob got him his job as head of Paramount. The razzle-dazzle story has the cloak-and-dagger allure of one of Evans' movies, but it is pure fiction." Al Ruddy "laughs at the notion: 'Bob is still trying to hang on to that whole thing that Sidney Korshak and the mob ran everything and got him his job. That's such bullshit'" (p. 242). Neither Ruddy nor Gladstone explain why leaving out Bautzer's part in his ascension makes Evans' claim that the mob got him his job "bullshit," exactly. Korshak *was* the mob, after all, and since he worked for Korshak, Bugsy Siegel, and Meyer Lansky, so was Bautzer! Not to mention Charlie Bluhdorn, the man who picked out Evans for the job while steering Gulf+Western. Are we to suppose Gulf+Western is an example of what Gladstone calls "legitimate businesses"? Here's Peter Biskind's summary of Bluhdorn:

> Bluhdorn had vast holdings in sugar and cattle in the Dominican Republic, where he reigned like a medieval lord. He had his own landing strip, where the company Gulfstream would sit in readiness, and where his own armed guards patrolled. . . . Evans swore by him but to Peter Bart, 'He was a thug, a terrible person, an absolutely unmitigated awful human being.' [Don] Simpson says, 'He was a mean, despicable, unethical, evil man . . . . He had no problem breaking the law. He was a criminal." [These testimonials were presumably made after Bluhdorn was already dead, hence unable to exact reprisals.] Indeed there was a rank smell about Paramount in those days; it was better not to know too much. Bluhdorn seemed to have few qualms about turning to gray money. He was under investigation by the [Securities and Exchange Commission] throughout the '70s, and he was close to Korshak, the real Godfather of Hollywood (p. 144).*

It seems likely that Bluhdorn himself was only a puppet for mob interests, especially considering his buyout of Paramount was vouchsafed by Sidney Korshak.† According to one source, Bludhorn's "backing to buy Paramount parent company Gulf and Western came from . . . Meyer Lansky."[28] Certainly, the two moved in *very* tight circles, as extensively documented by Dan E. Moldea's *Dark Victory: Ronald Reagan, MCA and the Mob*. The book maps out the many-headed hydra of organized crime, power politics, big business, and entertainment media, and states that Lansky knew

---

* In *Infamous Players: A Tale of Movies, the Mob (and Sex)*, Peter Bart casually mentions that "one of the girls provided for Bluhdorn [by Evans] was hospitalized after a prolonged evening of sexual activities with the chairman" (p. 43).

† "Bludhorn was unable to complete the purchase of Paramount on his own—he needed to gain the approval for the buyout from Paramount's executives and board members. Enter Sidney Korshak" (Russo, p. 320).

perhaps better than anyone else that the successful annihilation of organized crime's subculture in America would rock the "legitimate" world's entire foundation, which would ultimately force fundamental social changes and redistribution of wealth and power in this country. Lansky's dream was to bond the two worlds together so that one could not survive without the other. Those of us that recognize the vast power of the underworld in our nation today also understand how close that dream—and our nightmare—is to coming true.

And into this "family," Robert Evans was initiated—though at what precise moment in his career remains open to speculation.

1.6 JINXED: ROBERT EVANS COMES BOTTOM UP WITH *THE COTTON CLUB*

"I have seen almost every movie star, top models, heads of studios and heads of states walk into his home. Bob Evans is the Godfather of Hollywood."

—MEREDITH RHULE *(Evans' live-in "movie projectionist")*

Before we get to the flaming intersection of Roman Polanski and Charles Manson, a brief account of Robert Evans' post-Paramount career arc is probably due, considering how much it brought his criminal connections out from deep background to lurid foreground. The first strike against Evans was in 1980 when, along with his brother Charles Evans and his brother-in-law Michael Shure, he was convicted of buying $19,000 worth (five ounces) of cocaine from a federal narcotics agent posing as a drug dealer.[29] He was sentenced to a year's probation and obliged to channel his creative gifts into making an anti-drug television spot called *Get High on Yourself* (this was around the time Nancy Reagan's "Just Say No" campaign was warming up). The film was done with a bunch of singing celebrities, such as Bob Hope, Carol Burnett, Muhammad Ali, Paul Newman, Scott Baio, Mark Hamill, and Bruce Jenner (now Caitlin). *Dangerous Minds* called it "one of the biggest TV mega-turds of all time."[30] In Evans' popular memoir (the closest he came to a real comeback), *The Kid Stays in the Picture*, he claims this was the highpoint of his career (yes). He also describes showing a clip to Bob Hope, who was so impressed he immediately called Ronald Reagan at the Whitehouse (p. 324).

So where were Evans' mobster ties—or his "close friend" Henry Kissinger—when it came time to dodge this rap? It seems more likely that, for whatever reason, Evans was being brought down a notch or two (as had happened to his pal Polanski three years earlier); but if so, it apparently didn't suffice, seeing as he was further hobbled four years later. *The Cotton Club* started out as Evans' "comeback" project by which he hoped to redeem himself, read: muscle his way back into the big leagues. This was in early 1983, and by an odd stroke of timing, Evans' former boss, Charlie Bluhdorn, died in February of 1983, under conditions "regarded by many as mysterious."[31] (A *Vanity Fair* piece indicated that both the cause and location of his death was never fully confirmed.*) Evans planned to make his debut as a director with *The Cotton Club*, and having paid $350,000 for the rights to the book (by James Haskins), he set about securing a budget. This was before he even had a script, and he went to Cannes selling it to anyone who would listen as "*The Godfather* with music."

Evans' first investor was the Arab arms trader (and associate of Jeffrey Epstein), Adnan Khashoggi, who would soon become infamous for his involvement with the Iran-Contra affair. Khashoggi invested $2 million into the project, half of which went into hiring Mario Puzo to write the script. When Khashoggi read Puzo's script, however, he backed out of the production. Evans then managed to secure a full-budget, estimated at $18 to $20 million, from the Doumani brothers, owners of the Tropicana Hotel and El Morocco Casino in Las Vegas (i.e., mobsters). He also got Richard Gere—fresh from *An*

---

* "Hurricane Charlie," by Robert Sam Anson, *Vanity Fair*, April 2001: "One [report] had it that cancer, not heart failure, had killed Charlie. Another, that he'd died not aboard his Gulfstream II but in the plush confines of his Dominican estate, then been loaded aboard his plane as if alive, in the manner of El Cid. No, said still another, Charlie had died on the plane, and of a heart attack—experienced while communing intimately with a comely business reporter. There was even a report, which *Variety* checked out, that Charlie had been murdered—the means poison, the poisoner acting on instructions of the Mafia." https://www.vanityfair.com/magazine/2015/02/archive-march-2015-charlie-bluhdorn#~0

Officer and a Gentleman—to commit, and with Gere on board, Orion Pictures offered $10 million to distribute the film.

After weeks of work from Puzo, the script was in such terrible shape that the Doumanis threatened to pull out, whereupon Gere started to have doubts too. In desperation, Evans called his old nemesis, Prince Machiavelli (Evans' pet name for Francis Coppola), and gave him a quarter of a million dollars to rework the script (based on suggestions Coppola had offered for free). Coppola came back with a script that (according to a dismayed Evans) had nothing to do with Coppola's original pitch, leaving Evans with no choice but to pay Coppola another quarter million to do it *again*. The Doumanis had refused to authorize the Coppola rewrites, so all of this money was coming out of Evans' own pocket (or so he claimed). Coppola was under pressure of his own, as his beloved studio, Zoetrope, was in the process of going down the tubes, forever.[32]

As the final straw to sink the ship, the Doumanis hated Coppola's script so much they pulled out of the movie; this was the point that Evans, his back squarely against the wall, made a deal with variety show promoter Roy Radin. Together they formed a holding company in Puerto Rico worth $35 million (the money supposedly coming from the Puerto Rican government) with *The Cotton Club* as the company's first project. Soon after they signed their agreement, however, Radin was shot multiple times in the head, his face partially destroyed by dynamite, and his body found rotting in a canyon just outside LA.

Evans was introduced to Roy Radin by Karen Greenberger, a.k.a., Lanie Jacobs. Jacobs was deep into the LA cocaine trade and her connections—via both her husband Larry Greenberger and Milan Bellechesses (compared by his lawyer to Al Pacino in *Scarface*)—went all the way to the Medellin cocaine cartel in Columbia. Evans entered into a business-*and*-pleasure relationship with Jacobs (they were lovers) that led to Evans bringing in Radin as a financer. Roy Radin had his own sordid history: in 1980, 23-year-old television actress Melanie Haller (*Welcome Back Kotter*), after attending one of Radin's notoriously "wild" parties, "was found bruised, bleeding and barely conscious, draped over a seat on the Long Island Railroad car as it cruised toward New York City. [Haller] said she had been raped and beaten at the party, then deposited on the train." A New Jersey businessman eventually pleaded guilty to the assault; Radin was charged with menacing Haller and possession of a gun.[33]

In the Radin murder trial, Greenberg/Jacobs was convicted of second-degree murder and kidnapping. William Mentzer, a known Los Angeles hit-man apparently hired by Jacobs, was convicted of first-degree murder, along with three others. Mentzer may or may not have known Charles Manson and Abigail Folger (a victim of what became known as "the Manson murders"). Mentzer has also been connected—tenuously—to the Son of Sam killings, as well as claiming to have met the Zodiac killer.* Truth, lies, or disinformation with a purpose, Evans' *Cotton Club* enterprise cut suspiciously close to the same criminal underworld that had already spilled out into his Hollywood circle, with catastrophic results, back in August of 1969.

In the Roy Radin trial, during a 1989 preliminary hearing, under advice from his attorney Robert Shapiro (who later represented Robert Downey Jr. and O.J. Simpson), Evans invoked the Fifth Amendment to avoid incriminating himself, and refused to testify. Although police reports indicate that at least two witnesses testified that Evans *was* involved in the murder of Radin, Evans was never charged.[34] Apparently, he still had a few friends left in high places.

---

* The main source is Maurice Terry's *Ultimate Evil*—viewed by some as dark gospel truth and others as a mess of lurid sensationalism.

2

THE MEN WHO
KNEW TOO MUCH

2.1. HOLLYWOOD'S HALL OF MIRRORS

"It helped me so much that I wonder how politicians
who have not received this training can do without it."

—RONALD REAGAN, *on being a movie star*

At the time of the murder of Sharon Tate, the governor of California
was Ronald Reagan. Leaving aside Reagan's less-publicized mob
ties (c.f. *Dark Victory*, a book which borrows its title from a 1939
movie with Bette Davis and Humphrey Bogart), what just about everyone
knows is that Reagan got his start in the movie business, playing "white-hat"
Western heroes. What's less-known is that his final role was as a black-hat
corporate killer in *The Killers*, in 1964, starring Lee Marvin and directed by
Don Siegel (who went on to make several films with Clint Eastwood, including *Dirty Harry*). Siegel's career took off more or less in tandem with the
appearance of Allied Artists, the company that gave Roger Corman his first
movie deal; Siegel's breakout work was *Invasion of the Body Snatchers*, in 1957.

The Killers was made for TV but was released theatrically when NBC
deemed it too violent to broadcast. It was released in the UK as *Ernest
Hemingway's "The Killers"*—presumably to highlight its literary credentials

(Hemingway has some strange meta-ties to both Huston and Evans'). The film is about a boxer hunted by paid assassins, who makes no attempt to flee when he has the chance. The murdered boxer with no will to live was played by John Cassavetes, four years before, as Guy Woodhouse, he made a pact with Satanists, trading his wife's baby for a Hollywood career. *The Killers* was not only Reagan's last role but the only time he ever played a vil-lain. According to Kirk Douglas' autobiography, *The Ragman's Son*, Reagan regretted doing the movie, particularly the scene in which he slaps Angie Dickinson. This is what I wrote about it in *The Blood Poets*:

> Siegel, or someone, had a flash of pure genius, and cast the soon-to-be governor of California Ronald Reagan in the role. Reagan gives a restrained, modulated, and suitably rank performance as the wealthy, corrupt Jack Browning, the man behind all the events of the film, who seems motivated less by financial gain than by sheer nastiness. It's as if he just can't help himself . . . Reagan's presence in the film [serves a func-tion] the filmmakers could hardly have been aware of at the time [Or could they?]—it gives the film . . . historic, even mythic, significance. For Jack Browning represents corporate corruption, big banking, the Establishment, and what better actor could there possibly be to portray the corruption of modern American society than Ronald Reagan? (p. 20)

Ronald Reagan is arguably the most famous, or infamous, case of how compatible a Hollywood career is with the highest and deepest forces of social control and world politics. More specific to this current analysis, whether or not Reagan regretted doing the role of Jack Browning—just one year before running for governor of California and setting out for the American

---

* Robert Evans' second major role was as the bullfighter in an adaptation of Hemingway's *The Sun Also Rises*, and the picture that Daryl Zanuck decreed "the kid" got to stay in (hence the title of Evans' memoir). A recent book by Jeffrey Meyers called *John Huston: Courage and Art* begins with a prologue called "John Huston and Hemingway," under-scoring the many parallels between the two men. The first line quotes Andrew Sarris calling Huston "a Hemingway character lost in a Dostoyevsky novel"; this is followed by Normal Mailer's estimation of Huston as "the only film artist who bears comparison to Hemingway." Meyers then quotes Huston himself, professing to have been influenced by both Hemingway's writing and his values (2011, p. 1).

presidency—his choice is consistent with the idea that organized criminals, either disguised-as or in-cahoots-with movie stars, can't resist tipping their hand in ways that don't compromise the security of their work. Simply put, like John Huston playing Noah Cross in *Chinatown*, Jack Browning was probably the closest Reagan ever got to playing *himself*. And, much like some of the other stories recounted in *16 Maps of Hell*, no amount of political skullduggery or gangster affiliations—before, during, and after his ascent to high office—seems to have tarnished his stellar reputation. While Reagan may not be remembered as a great Hollywood actor along the lines of Jimmy Stewart or Henry Fonda—or even Lee Marvin—he *is* widely seen today as one of the US's greatest presidents (seriously).*

✦

> "The unblinking acceptance of perversity—in the most general social sense—within the art world is presented as a prerequisite for entry into the cultural elite, distinguishing its members from the common people. Morality is detached from the consumption of cultural artefacts. This is almost a textbook definition of decadence."
>
> —ALEXANDER ADAMS,
> *"The exhilarating nihilism of Michel Houellebecq," 2019*

So what of Robert Evans? As we have seen, he was within a phone call of Ronald Reagan's ear even at his lowest point, and he made a big tallyho of his friendship with Henry Kissinger, a man sometimes seen as the *éminence grise* behind several presidencies. In *The Kid Stays in the Picture*, Evans describes his struggle to get Kissinger to attend the world premiere of *The Godfather*, and his glow of pride at getting to enter the event with Kissinger. He also describes running into Sidney Korshak at the event, who grabs Evans and warns him: "Don't ever bring me and Kissinger together in public. Ever!"[1] It seems curious that it's Korshak the mobster balking, not Kissinger, the man

---

* He comes in at number 9 in a *Business Insider* list of "the greatest US presidents, according to political scientists." JFK comes in at 16; Trump comes in last. Brennan Weiss, Feb 18, 2019: https://www.businessinsider.com/greatest-us-presidents-ranked-by-political-scientists-2018-2

of high renown. Certainly, known associations with mobsters is something Evans has bragged about as much as denied. And whatever has become of his Hollywood career—which may have more to do with tasteless choices than blacklisting—Evans' reputation has, if anything, improved with age (rather like Ronald Reagan's).

When Evans came to Paramount, the now-secure legend has it, the studio was floundering and the golden boy "revolutionized the movie industry."[2] Evans helped to birth the New Hollywood by bringing to term some of the embryonic talents seeded by Corman at AIP (and occasionally watered by the hard-Jew hipsters at BBS), talents such as Peter Bogdanovich, Woody Allen, Robert De Niro, and most notably, Francis Ford Coppola, the man who "single-handedly" turned the Mafia into a *cause célèbre*. In fact, Paramount and Evans shaped Puzo's book, never mind Coppola's film, from its earliest stages. Perhaps this was part of the terms by which Bautzer, Korshak, Bluhdorn, and co. got Evans his job?

During Evans' tenure, between 1966 and 1974, Paramount released *Barefoot in the Park, No Way to Treat a Lady* (a ribald comedy about murdering women), *The Odd Couple, Barbarella, The Italian Job, If . . . , The Brotherhood* (mobsters again), *True Grit, Once Upon a Time in the West, The Conformist, Love Story, Harold and Maude, The Godfather, Play It Again, Sam, Paper Moon, Bang the Drum Slowly* (De Niro's first major role), *Serpico, Don't Look Now, On a Clear Day You Can See Forever, Save the Tiger, The Conversation, The Godfather Part II,* and *The Great Gatsby.* The cherry on Evans' cake was *Chinatown,* his first film as an independent producer, after which he stepped down as production head. And in some ways, it is *Chinatown* which brings together the threads revealed in this present chapter most visibly.*

---

* In *The Big Goodbye,* though author Sam Wasson mostly prints the legend around the making of *Chinatown,* he provides one telling bit of evidence, regarding the uncredited co-author of all of Robert Towne's scripts, including *Chinatown,* Edward Taylor. Quoting Mike Koepf: "'Robert was the strong one and Edward was the weak one, but Edward was the brilliant one. I mean the guy was smart, character psychology and motivation were his forte. The guy deserves credit indeed.'" . . . "It was a given that Edward wrote the movie with Robert," said Taylor's stepdaughter, Katherine Andrusco. "Whatever Robert was working on, Edward was working on. Every day." "Robert never wrote on his own," Payne said, "he never paid Eddie enough, and Eddie never asked for more." Many in Taylor's family were at a loss to understand the terms of his arrangement with

Some forty years later, in 2017, *The Kid Stays in the Picture* was turned into a stage production at the Royal Court in London by actor and writer Simon McBurney (whose most recent role, in 2019, was as Rupert Murdoch in *The Loudest Voice*). McBurney's play was an unabashed celebration of Evans' legacy, but also, or so he claimed, an exploration of the blurry liminal zone between history and mythic representation. In a *Guardian* piece called "How Robert Evans changed movies for ever—and for the better" (note the spin), he cited the preface to *The Kid Stays in the Picture*: "There are three sides to every story: yours . . . mine . . . and the truth. No one is lying." (Which brings to mind Joe Eszterhas' quip: "all lies ever told anywhere about Robert Evans are true," Eszterhas, p. 29.)

In allegiance with McBurney, *The Guardian* piece seemed more than happy to print the Evans legend, despite the mountain of facts pointing to incest, drugs, and murder. "The distinction between fact and fiction," the article waxes philosophically—sopho-moronically—"is particularly irrelevant in the case of Evans because of the bizarre hall-of-mirrors effect created by his films."[3] How exactly does the Hollywood hall of mirrors make the truth irrelevant? Is it because *The Guardian* (at least its arts section) has given up all attempts to ever get to the truth, and expects its readers to do the same? Wouldn't that be *a highly convenient situation for organized criminals running a business of make-believe?*

Is it a minor detail that the part of Evans in McBurney's stage adaptation was played by Danny Huston, John Huston's youngest son (legitimately at least)? More mirrors within mirrors?

Towne, how Taylor could so comfortably consent to anonymity and what the precise nature of his contributions were. When pressed for details, Taylor himself was vague to the point of contradiction. . . . Taylor's genuine equanimity led his friends and family to wonder who, or what, he may have been protecting, and why. Taylor's widow, Virginia Kennerely, wrote that she "did brood for some time on *what shameful secret there could be that accounted for Robert's remarkable and apparently unconditional, almost Svengali-like, hold on Ed*." [Emphasis added. Taylor, said a former girlfriend,] "was not ambitious in the sense that he did not devote himself to self-advancement." To Taylor, loyalty took clear precedence over work. . . . Towne, Taylor knew better than anyone, suffered from the reverse tendency. "His father was very successful," their friend Nicholas Coster said, "and I saw Robert competing with that image. He was fiercely competitive'" (p. 103, 104, 106, 107). There may be a microcosm in how Hollywood secret society functions here: the aggrandizers aggrandize, "the slaves shall serve."

2.2.   THE DIVIDED CONSCIOUSNESS OF
ROMAN POLANSKI (CASE STUDY # 4)

"You projected fear. You made me a monster and I have to live
with that the rest of my life because I cannot fight this case. If
I could fight this case and I could present this case, I would take
that monster back and I would take that fear back. Then you
could find something else to put your fear on, because it's all
your fear."

—CHARLES MANSON, *November 19, 1970 (Trial Testimony)*

One of the first projects Robert Evans greenlit at Paramount was
Rosemary's Baby, and it was Evans—and by extension the Hollywood mob—
who first lured Roman Polanski to Hollywood. This is how Peter Bart
"recalled" it in 2019: "as production vice president at Paramount in 1967,
I admired [Polanski's] early films and conspired with Robert Evans to persuade him to come to Hollywood. . . . our purpose was to interest him in
Rosemary's Baby, which we felt would connect with his opaque sensibility."[4]

It would be hard to say how many times I've covered this material since,
as an adolescent, I first became aware of the details (probably via reading
Barbara Leaming's *Polanski: His Life and Films*). As I wrote in *Secret Life of
Movies*, Polanski was my first movie director obsession, due to his "European
'respectability'—his modernist/surrealist/existentialist credibility with the
art house—combined with his obvious affinity for the grand guignol of
Hollywood—his glee for violence and sensationalism." This, I wrote, "made
him the perfect choice for a still-forming, cheerfully perverse, adolescent film
buff." I emulated Polanski's "delight in appalling and disturbing audiences
with his perversity, and in mocking and deriding us for our susceptibility to
his devices. He was a postmodern master of suspense, torturer as entertainer,
Hitchcock by way of the Marquis de Sade" (p. 130).

Curiously enough, during the same period I was discovering, and identifying so strongly with, Polanski, I was reading Colin Wilson's *A Criminal
History of Mankind* and becoming mildly obsessed with the popular idea of
"serial killers" who seek to leave their mark on society the only way they can,
choosing notoriety over anonymity. The first time I wrote about Polanski,

in "The Perversities of Roman Polanski" in *The Blood Poets*, I expressed my inner-outer conflict between celebrating an artist's affinity for evil and cautioning against the pitfalls of such a predilection:

> When evil triumphs in a Polanski film . . . we are permitted to get a weird kick out of it, as if acknowledging that it's what we secretly hoped for all along . . . (Even "evil" has its good points, he seems to be saying, and certainly his films do a fair job of persuading us.) . . . . For the artist there is no subject more fascinating, more enticing (because more challenging) than the subject of evil. And evil can only really be communicated with appropriate power and horror if the artist forms a (temporary) allegiance with it—so that this very affinity serves to suck us into the abyss, and alert us as to its allure. . . . Morality has no place whatsoever in art. Perversity, on the other hand, is most at home there, for only there does it come into its own (p. 67–8, 70–71).

Polanski, I wrote, "was an intelligent man flirting with disaster," and the "flirting slipped tragically into foreplay and led inexorably on to a consummation." This was when "Polanski himself paid the highest price that any artist can," and "the demons of genius that he unleashed came after him, demanding payment for their services" (p. 71). It's curious for me to read this material now, because I know I had no inkling, nor ever intended to suggest, that Polanski was complicit in the murder of his wife. Yet this is how it reads to me now.

Perhaps the Polanski story—the juxtaposition of a film artist achieving ultimate success and then experiencing ultimate tragedy—encapsulates my lifelong struggle to reconcile two opposing interpretations of reality? My first "imprint" of this slice of psychohistory would have been the official one: Polanski's wife, and the mother of his unborn child, was murdered in a senseless act of brutality, after which Polanski was doubly victimized when the press confabulated a correlation, even causation, between his films, his lifestyle, and the murders. I would have read Polanski's expressions of anger and disgust at these insinuations in the Leaming bio, and I would have also read, in the same period, Pauline Kael's introductory paragraph to her review of *Macbeth*, the first film Polanski made after the murders, an extravagantly bloody film, complete with scenes of murdered children:

In the Manson case, there was an eerie element that the public responded to. Even though we knew that Roman Polanski had nothing to do with causing the murder of his wife and unborn child and friends, the massacre seemed a vision realized from his nightmare movies. And there was an element of guilt and embarrassment in this connection we made, particularly when Polanski said that the crime was being "reviewed in terms of my films." He didn't quite seem to understand why the connection was inevitable. Now it suggests either a strange form of naiveté or a divided consciousness for Polanski to complain that his *Macbeth* is being reviewed in terms of the Manson case (1975, p. 399).

Soon after, in early 1984, at the age of sixteen, I would have seen the ITV program "Roman Polanski Meets Clive James," a filmed dinner interview between the two men. I would have been impressed by Polanski's eloquence and apparent sincerity (as I was the last time I rewatched it). I would have felt sympathy for his suffering and admiration for his stoicism and survival abilities. Even in my twenties and thirties, when I began to allow for the possibility of correlation between Manson and Polanski and wrote about it, it was a mystical sort of correlation, the power of *zeitgeist* combined with Polanski's creative unconscious, combined with a psyop in which little Roman was still the victim, albeit of much larger and more organized forces than a deranged hippie enclave. In *The Blood Poets*, I contemplated that

> The Manson killings themselves were, at some level, an "act" inspired by the movies. There is as much relationship between the murders at Cielo Drive and the movies that came before them, as there is with those that came after. *Bonnie and Clyde* and *Repulsion* and *Rosemary's Baby* and *If . . .* led to the Manson killings just as much as the killings themselves led to *Straw Dogs*, *Macbeth*, and *Chinatown*. [B]oth the killings and the movies were expressions of the one "spirit."

By such sleight of consciousness, I managed to dodge probably the most haunting question around these murders, that of Hollywood's, and by association Polanski's, complicity with them. And like so many others, like Polanski himself, if to a far lesser degree, I had a significant *investment* in doing so. Polanski was my identification figure; central to that sympathetic bond was viewing him as a tragic victim, as well as a creative spirit, surviving against the odds. Polanski is a charismatic and seductive personality; in the Clive James interview, as elsewhere, he comes across as charming, soft-voiced, self-effacing, thoughtful, humble and unaffected. Even now, it is difficult for me to believe that he could have been complicit with the horrors of what occurred at Cielo Drive, at least except for one fact. As I was aware even when I wrote *Blood Poets*, as even Kael acknowledges, Polanski's movies make *some* sort of correlation unavoidable.

16 Maps of Hell attempts to demonstrate that the movies we go to, seeking escape, are only the thinnest end of a sociopolitical wedge being driven into the collective psyche; that they are part of a veritable *manufactured zeitgeist*, a cultural psyop. The only way to avoid Polanski's complicity, then, is to suggest that any artist, or any human being, has no accountability, or responsibility, for his fantasies or for the creations of his mind. Yet clearly this is not the case; in fact the truth is probably closer to something I wrote about Polanski (in the chapter on *The Tenant*) in *The Secret Life of Movies*: "Artists adhere to the highest morality of all, that of assuming responsibility for their dreams" (p. 136). This may have been wishful thinking on my part, but if so it is also a fair and reasonable standard to demand of our cultural overlords. What I wasn't able to consider, in 1999 or in 2009, was the degree to which Polanski's fantasies were backed, funded, and promoted by a mass-media, mob-backed conglomeration, making both him and his movies part of a massive deep-state criminal conspiracy that dwarfs anything that could ever be leveled at the so-called "Manson family."

2.3. HIGH-LEVEL CONFABULATIONS

"And the only man of energy, yes the revolution's pride/He trained a hundred women just to kill an unborn child."

—LEONARD COHEN, *"Diamonds in the Mine," 1971*

In his autobiography, *Roman*, published in 1984, Polanski devotes eighteen pages (chapter twenty-two) to Tate's murder, the immediate aftermath, and the trial and conviction of Manson and the others accused. Where Polanski's speaking style and personality are charismatically persuasive, his writing style is considerably less so: the book is a grade or two above William Friedkin's autobiography (see chapter 6), in terms of style and content (it's over 400 pages and Polanski is occasionally candid); but it is still oddly weightless, lacking conviction or intensity, especially when one considers the intensity of the life being recounted. The book feels as if it were done under orders, like a homework assignment (or perhaps for the money).

Polanski describes his reaction to the news of Tate's death in some detail, including micro-movements he made, as if to establish the reality of his grief. He mentions the funeral and Steve McQueen's absence, for which he never forgave him. After that, he launches into an angry diatribe against the press, accusing them of "taking their cue from Hollywood gossip and . . . churning out allusions to orgies, drug parties, and black magic. Not only the bitchiest but also the most insecure community in the world, Hollywood was striving to find an explanation that would put the blame fairly and squarely on the victims and thus reduce the threat to Hollywood as a whole" (p. 310). Polanski dedicates another page to the "false" media stories, and then writes:

A year had to pass before the truth emerged at the trial and five years before a full and reasonably accurate account of what happened was presented in *Helter Skelter*, a book by Vincent Bugliosi, the L.A. district attorney. Even so, the harm done during the days immediately after the murders has never been put right. To this day there must be large numbers of people who remember only what they were fed by the media. . . . Sex, drugs, arcane rites—that, the media obviously felt, was what the public wanted, so that's what they gave them. The truth, as one of the girl killers testified before a grand jury, was less colorful (p. 313).

Robert Evans, in *his* autobiography, *The Kid Stays in the Picture*, offers more or less the exact same line:

The horrific murders of Sharon and her friends by the insane followers of Charles Manson sent a shock wave through Hollywood that is still felt today. What made them even uglier was the media orgy of lies, all of which came down to one outrageous innuendo: because of their "decadence," the victims had somehow brought it on themselves. . . . The press even implicated Roman. It didn't matter that he was six thousand miles away when the tragedy occurred. Somehow the "master of the macabre" had to have been involved (p. 148).

For the purposes of denial, Polanski focuses specifically on the element of drugs as being spuriously placed at the center of the murders. "I told the police we all smoked pot" he writes, "but by local standards we were almost abstainers." He mentions that Wojtek Frykowski and Abigail Folger "experimented with mescaline," and that Jay Sebring "was a secret coke user," then insists that "The press painted an astonishingly inaccurate picture of Wojtek Frykowski, describing him as a 'major drug purveyor.' In many ways, Wojtek was one of the squarest people I've ever known." "The myth of Wojtek the big-time drug-dealer," Polanski claims, "stemmed largely from a report that he'd had dealings with known pushers" (p. 313–14).

Rather than specify what sort of report he is referring to, Polanski offers an anecdote about Frykowski throwing out some dope dealers who gatecrashed a party at Cielo Drive and swore revenge. There may be more than a kernel of truth in this account, as we'll see. But Polanski's denial of Frykowski's involvement in drug deals is insubstantial fluff compared to the numerous testimonials that confirm it, and it is mostly dependent on our sympathy for him *as a victim of both tragedy and press slander.* His assertion that the truth came out via the trial, and the book *Helter Skelter*, has not stood up well to the test of time. In 2020, as we will see, Bugliosi's version of the killings is more or less in tatters.

Polanski also mentions in passing a "videotape of Sharon and me making love, found by a detective," adding that "One writer later claimed that the police had unearthed a whole collection of pornographic movies and stills involving famous Hollywood stars. Although I was never questioned about the tape, I should no doubt be accused of concealing a significant aspect of our life-style if I failed to mention its existence" (p. 314–15). It is curious how Polanski repeats the claim about Hollywood porn without ever actually refuting it—the implication being that it is too absurd to require denial. But why absurd? The rest of the chapter covers Polanski's attempts working with private detectives to hunt down the guilty parties—something that would seem consistent with the idea that he knew the perpetrators, or at least had reason to think so. Polanski then offers up his *pièce de résistance*, his pop-psychology assessment of Manson's motives:

> Manson's rage was that of a spurned performer—one who seeks revenge on others for his own lack of talent and recognition. Bitterness and frustration were his probable motives for sending a raiding party to what he still thought of as Terry Melcher's house: to get his own back on someone who had declined to cut a record for his mediocre compositions (p. 323).

Not insignificantly, this quickly became the dominant theory regarding Manson's motive, and by the time of *Roman*, few were likely to refute it. But even here Polanski is caught in an error, if not an actual lie: the owner of Cielo Drive, Rudolph Altobelli, testified in court that Manson went to the house looking for Melcher on March 23, 1969, and was told Melcher moved out in January.[5] If Polanski still believed his version, it can only be because he badly *needed* to. Polanski winds up the chapter with his lamentation that Tate lost her life "because of this obscene perversion of hippie values," then closes with this line: "In these ways I shall remain faithful to her until the day I die" (p. 324). He is not referring to his sexual activities here (he admits he began having sex again within a month of Tate's death), but to how he still thinks of her whenever he sees a sunset.

The only person Polanski ever admitted to suspecting, as far as I know, was John Phillips of the Mamas and the Papas, even going so far as to search his car for blood-stains, compare his handwriting to the words written in blood at the scene of the crime, and putting a kitchen knife to Phillips' throat, demanding to know if he killed Sharon. As we'll see, the Mamas and the Papas, most especially Mama Cass, are—or would have been if there had ever been an honest investigation—key witnesses to the Cielo Drive murders. In his autobiography *Papa John*, John Phillips (the afore-mentioned father and lover of Mackenzie Phillips) mentions the knife incident (p. 232), describing Polanski as on the verge of cracking up at the time. Before that, Phillips also offers what became The Official Narrative *vis a vis* Tate's murder:

The dream of Peace and Love had turned into a living nightmare with real demon killers stalking the hills. We didn't know then, but they had been senselessly sacrificed by the slaves of Charlie Manson. The maniac Manson ordered his worshipers to kill anyone living at the Cielo address. He assumed that Melcher—the man he believed in his paranoid derangement, had kept him out of the music business—still lived there. . . There were bizarre theories that attempted to link the murders to LSD and Satanic rites, kinky and deadly sexual perversions, and, somehow, to Polanski's own penchant for violence in movies like *Knife in the Water, Repulsion*, and *Rosemary's Baby* (p. 228).

Were all of these key witnesses—like the wives in the second season of HBO's *Big Little Lies*—meeting regularly to make sure they kept their stories straight? On the other hand, Phillips does let slip some information about Frykowski that *would* have proven absolutely vital to the case, if it hadn't been promptly swept under the rug by Polanski, Evans, Bugliosi, and the Hollywood clean-up team: shortly before he was killed, Phillips writes, Frykowski "had come to my door unexpectedly and demanded to be let in. He seemed slightly incoherent and had a bizarre presence about him. . . He was rumored to have had weird drug connections and was part of a crowd that had been feeding off Cass. I apologized and closed the door in his face" (p. 229).

---

* One possible intersection point between Manson and Tate (and intelligence operations) in the days leading up to the murders, one that receives almost no airplay, is the human potential center in Big Sur, Esalen. "Esalen was an important gathering spot/spa/think tank for the rock stars and also the political elite (read: CIA) of California. Musicians and government officials rubbed elbows and other appendages, and traded ideas. Sharon Tate and Abigail Folger were frequent visitors to the institute. Little spoken of is that they were reported to have called there on August 1, 1969. . . Manson left for Big Sur on August 3, 1969. There is a good chance Folger and Tate were there at the institute when Manson arrived, and with the way the institute operated, crossed paths with him. . . . Esalen quietly issued death threats to several reporters investigating the Manson angle, including author of the definitive book on the Family, Ed Sanders (the usually detail oriented Sanders get uncharacteristically vague in his timeline regarding Manson's visit, likely due to the aforementioned snuff threat). . . . Nobody has ever come up with any clue as to what transpired there." "Charles Manson: Music Myth Murder

2.4.   HOLLYWOOD SEX CULT BRINGS DISASTER ON ITSELF! (MANSON: THE COUNTER-NARRATIVE)

"There's been fifty-million people that died since Sharon Tate died and I got everybody in Santa Claus land chasing me, trying to make me feel remorse for one psychotic episode of [Tex] Watson."

—CHARLES MANSON, *1994* *

There can be little doubt by this point that much of the story around the Manson murders—the whole *Helter Skelter* narrative put forward by Vincent Bugliosi—is a manufactured narrative. What's not so easy to determine is how much this narrative was created *after* the event as an improvisatory cover-up, and how much was pre-scripted, ahead of time, as both a prepared cover-up and a psyop: a deliberate means to generate a story that would not only conceal the truth, but also terrorize a nation in a very specific way—just as Polanski designed his movies to do, albeit at a whole other level. In my

---

Mysticism Magick Magus Mayhem," *Carwreckdebangs*, November 30, 2017: https:// carwreckdebangs.wordpress.com/2017/11/30/charles-manson-music-myth-murder -mysticism-magick-magus-mayhem-a-look-back-at-the-untold-story-of-the-manson- family-or-more-manson-than-youd-ever-want-to-know/

* Charles Manson was quoted in 1985 (*Vacaville Reporter*): "I did not teach Tex. I told Tex to do what you think is right and ride your own beef. All that confusion at the Ranch was from Tex. I didn't show Tex how to burn people, someone else taught him that. Tex was trying to be Manson in his mother's body and Tex took a knife and a gun that someone else showed him how to use. So, why was Manson at the top when Tex was the man at the top with the knife and with the gun and with the will?" And in a 1986 interview with Charlie Rose: "So, Tex's got a little problem and he gives me his gun; he can't deal with it, so I gotta go deal with his problem. I had to go shoot somebody for him, because he's too much of a coward. He's laying up underneath the bed with it. I had to shoot Lotsapoppa; some guy in the drug world. I had to go down and take care of some business that was not my business. So Tex owed me one. I said, 'Every time I stand up for you, brother, I got to face your life and your death. I'm tired of carrying you on my back.' I threw him the gun and I said, 'Now you owe me one. And if you don't pay me when you owe me, I will pay you what you owe me.' So, I had to go into another face and playact. So when my brother gets busted and my brother is in jail, I tell Tex, 'Go pay him what you owe me. However you do it, you do it.'"

opinion, after four decades mulling, the Manson case is at least on a par with the JFK assassination, if not the UFO, in terms of being beyond the ken of mortal men. It is "a riddle wrapped in a mystery, inside an enigma." *Millions* of words have been written about it, and I doubt if any two researchers can agree even on the overall nature, motive, or purpose of the crimes, never mind the countless details (even, in some cases, if they ever happened[6]).

For my present purposes, I will be placing a number of testimonials side by side to see what, if anything, can be deduced, or intuited. Specifically, the landmarks my rapid flight over the charred earth of "Heaven Drive" will be using for cartography are these: Ed Sanders's *The Family*, possibly the most well-known and widely-read book (besides *Helter Skelter*) on what I have chosen to call the Manson-Hollywood war. Several interviews by Nikolas Schreck, an ex-Satanist who made a documentary called *Charlie Manson: Superstar* in 1998; Schreck knew Manson personally and wrote a 900-page book on the subject, *The Manson File: Myth and Reality of an Outlaw Shaman*, that attempts to exonerate Manson from direct involvement in the killings and rename them "the Tex Watson murders."[*]

Lastly, I will refer to a 2019 release, *Chaos: Charles Manson, the CIA, and the Secret History of the Sixties*, by Tom O'Neill, which as far as I know is the first book to focus on Manson's links to the CIA and the MKULTRA mind control program—though this latter is not my primary interest. What interest me here are not these writers' conclusions, or even necessarily their arguments, but where the facts and testimonies they cite overlap and agree, thereby supporting one another, while at the same time suggesting a hidden counter-narrative to the official Bugliosi-Polanski-Evans one.[†]

The first things I want to look at are the testimonials relating to Polanski and Tate's relationship and the Hollywood set that the murders both happened within and spewed out of. Many, though not all, of these come from Hollywood insiders, the first being Terry Melcher, Doris Day's son. A quote from A. E. Hotchner's *Doris Day: Her Own Story*, for example,

---

[*] The curious fact that the names are almost identical—flip the W in Watson and you have Charles Matson—would seem to reinforce this *doppelgänger* effect.

[†] The other source I will be citing is Manson himself, who, though this may seem borderline perverse to suggest, may actually be the person with the least to gain by lying, and with the least to lose by telling the truth.

is cited by Sanders: "Michelle [Phillips] told me she and John [Phillips] had dinner one night, to discuss maybe getting back together and afterward he had taken her up to visit the Polanskis in my old house. Michelle said that when they arrived there, everyone in the house was busy filming an orgy and that Sharon Tate was part of it. That was just one of the stories I had heard about what went on in my former house" (Sanders, p. 118).

Doris Day: Her Own Story was published in 1975. In 2019, O'Neill's *Chaos* quotes journalist Dominick Dunne (whose daughter Dominque, the actress best known for her part in the film *Poltergeist*, was murdered in 1984): "I never went to the orgies, but I know they existed" (p. 62). He then cites James Toback's claim to have known about them. (Toback—who cast Robert Downey Jr. in his first lead role as *The Pickup Artist*—faced his own multiple charges of sexual harassment, in October 2017.[7]) For a third inside-source, in *Papa John*, published 1986, John Phillips mentions leaving a party at Cielo Drive with his wife, Michelle Phillips, Roger Vadim and *his* wife, Jane Fonda, and Warren Beatty, and going to Vadim's Old Malibu house for group sex. Phillips is coy about the details and writes merely: "it seems hard to believe it could actually have happened the way it did. So hard, in fact that some of the people in that room now prefer not to remember. . . But that was a different, more innocent and permissive era—California Dreamin', vintage 1969. The possibilities seemed limitless" (p. 221). Indeed. The correlation between permissiveness and innocence is particularly telling.

Melcher reiterates his experience on another occasion, also quoted in *The Family*: "I hadn't been in the house since I moved out, but I had pre-sumed that the murders had something to do with the weird film Polanski had made, and the equally weird people who were hanging around that house. I knew they had been making a lot of homemade sadomasochistic porno movies there with quite a few recognizable Hollywood faces in them" (p. 252). We know from Polanski himself (in *Roman*) that a video of him hav-ing sex with Tate was found, and returned to him by police. Polanski explains this tape as a spontaneous and playful act between two people in love. Yet everything else around that tape indicates it was very far from an isolated thing, and paints a significantly less rosy picture. In *Chaos*, Tom O'Neill cites a tape found by police, "clearly filmed by Polanski, [that] depicted Sharon Tate being forced to have sex with two men" (p. 54). According to Sanders, as well as home porno, there were rumors—considered serious enough for police to investigate—that "residents at 10050 Cielo Drive were into collecting humans from Sunset Strip and from various clubs in that area for casual partying at the estate" (Sanders, p. 252).

2.5.   CELEBRITY PORN BLACKMAIL RING EXPOSED!

> "You are upset because one of your actors got on the wrong lane doing something with the wrong people. And you want to blame somebody else for it. And you got to dig up some poor-ass idiot that don't have the brain of a retarded spastican and make him a cult leader!"
>
> —CHARLES MANSON, *2004, Crime Magazine*

Further testimony supporting Polanski's penchant for celebrity porn comes from Nicholas Schreck, citing a friend of "Playmate" Connie Kreski. In 1969, Kreski was the girlfriend of Polanski's buddy Victor Lownes, the *Playboy* ambassador to the UK, who set up the first *Playboy* office in London and hosted (in)famous parties both at his house and at the London Playboy club, where Polanski and Tate had their wedding reception. Lownes' parties were attended by the A-List set, including the Beatles, Warren Beatty, Michael Caine, Steve McQueen, Judy Garland, Peter Sellers, and Woody Allen.[8] According to Schreck, Kreski told him that

> Polanski and Victor Lownes spent a fortune collecting what she called "fame porn" . . . like a picture of Joan Crawford dancing naked, Marilyn Monroe giving a blowjob, whatever they could find, they would spend top dollar for . . . And in 1969, Robert Evans . . . gave Roman Polanski a new video camera and video playing system as a thank you for the success of *Rosemary's Baby*. [Polanski] began to record orgies and sexual activities.[9]

With all of these insider-testimonials, it seems beyond reasonable doubt that Polanski was regularly filming home sex movies with Tate and others during the period leading up to her death. Sanders' various sources, within the media at least (though also possibly the police and FBI), believed it was for more than home-use. "In the matter of movies, police found a bunch of videotapes during the follow-up investigations. Some were found in the Polanski residence in the main bedroom closet. . . . Part of the films involved an elite underground film group in Hollywood that swapped torrid films of each other" (p. 249). Sanders' friend at *Life* magazine, Barry Farrel, claimed "police had obtained an erotic videotape featuring, among torrid others, Peter Sellers, Yul Brynner, and Mama Cass Elliot, of the Mamas and the Papas. The video was supposedly somehow connected with the case, and the $25,000 reward"—the one offered by Brynner, Sellers, and others for information leading to solving the case (p. 330–31). John Swinney, who worked for attorney Harry Wiese, believed "Hollywood people were willing to put up the money for the reward because they thought they were going to be next" (p. 411).

According to Paul Fitzgerald, defense attorney on the Manson case, a TV personality was trying to help a starlet locate footage shot at Cielo Drive; Fitzgerald claimed "there was erotic footage found in Polanski's house that showed the ex-wife of a California governor balling one of Howard Hughes' powerful attorneys" (Sanders p. 383). A private investigator confirmed the rumors: "there's tapes with all kinds of people," he told Sanders, worth half a million dollars (which would be perhaps four times that today). The PI also mentions "a [porno] film from the set of *Valley of the Dolls*," "a climate of fear regarding the films," and "an erotic ski film with Peter Sellers." He also tells Sanders there are "films of the [Manson] Family with some Hollywood people" (p. 386). He believes "Manson had them killed because 'they knew too much about what was going on'" (p. 387).

Manson, or someone with more to protect? In *Repulsion: The Life and Times of Roman Polanski*, Thomas Kiernan writes of the period following the success of *Knife in the Water*, after Polanski moved to Paris: "One of his favorite activities became participating in the shooting of the private pornographic films that were made almost nightly at various parties around the city" (p. 168). Polanski began as an observer, graduated to a light-holder or camera-operator, and finally joined in as a performer. Soon after this, Polanski met Gene Gutowski, who became his first producer-partner.

Gutowski had a history of intelligence work, having joined the US Army Counterintelligence Corps in 1945 after the end of the war and worked as a special agent until March 1947. At that time he married the US State Department employee, Zillah Rhoades, and moved with her to New York (Zillah was close to Polanski also). As Kiernan has it, Gutowski's initial idea was to serve as "a liaison between Polanski and the Anglo-American film industry" (p. 199). He actually became significantly more involved in bringing Polanski to Hollywood, when he produced Polanski's first English-language films, *Repulsion, Cul-de-Sac,* and *Dance of the Vampires.*

Polanski's intelligence connections are further evidenced by the fact that, following the murders, he was assigned a "bodyguard" in the form of Danny Bowser, "a retired lieutenant from their LAPD homicide squad." As O'Neill notes in *Chaos*, Bowser had recently (in 1965) been "appointed the first commander of the LAPD's new Special Investigations Section (SIS), an elite, high-tech unit that served as 'professional witnesses' by running covert surveillance on known criminals" (p. 267). The *Times* called SIS "a fearsome and mysterious bunch" rumored—in a variation on the plot of *Magnum Force*—to have been "conspiring to shoot suspects and celebrating gunfights with 'kill parties'" (p. 268). O'Neill also points out "the Tate house by then had become a high-profile gathering place for liberal Hollywood—among others, for [Jane] Fonda, Cass Elliot, and Warren Beatty, all three of whom were under FBI surveillance" (p. 219).

In light of George Hodel's dark Hollywood parties on Franklin Avenue, is it possible Cielo Drive was likewise a high-level Hollywood "honey trap," and Polanski a high-level procurer? One of Fitzgerald's sources called this the "case [that] might finish Hollywood" (Sanders p. 383). No such luck: needless to say, "no motion pictures ever surfaced" (ibid.); and since tabloid press (or intel psyop) abhors a vacuum, the possible overlap between an elite underground Hollywood sex ring and a "murderous cult" proved impossible to resist.*

---

* In *Daily News*, August 13, 1969, an article claimed the existence of a "cult—whose members include top Hollywood personalities and show business executives—was revealed as detectives investigated the tangled, bizarre events of the group's last evening" (Sanders, p. 250-51). August 17: "a source close to the investigation declared that there had been a 'wild party' attended by some of 'the biggest freaks and weirdos' in Hollywood. . . . Sharon and the other four might have been victims of an assassin hired by a member of the cult that met regularly in the Polanski home for sex-drug rituals" (p. 251). The yellow press, in other words, may have arrived closer to the truth than Bugliosi did, but in such a way as to help conceal it.

2.6.   HOLLYWOOD HOUSE OF CARDS:
CASE STUDY # 5, JEFFREY EPSTEIN

"Epstein's First Law: Know when you are winning. Epstein's
Second Law: The key question is not what can I gain but what do
I have to lose."

—JEFFREY EPSTEIN

Before continuing with this re-examination of the Cielo Drive murders,
I want to import some possibly crucial data points from a number of different spacetime coordinates, so to speak, with the hope of providing a deeper,
darker background on which to study the Polanski case. First up, there is
another, possibly more striking case of high-level celebrity sex blackmail to
that of George Hodel, and that is Jeffrey Epstein.

In the UK in 2012, following the death of Jimmy Savile, a tidal wave of
accusations from dozens of victims spilled out into public awareness and the
line between "crackpot conspiracy theory" and daily, non-fake news seemed
in danger of vanishing forever. (See for example the 2006 Channel 5 documentary, "David Icke: Was He Right?") A few years later, when the Jeffrey
Epstein case fully broke in July 2019, a similar flurry occurred in US culture,
and once again, cognitions became dissonant. The generally cautious *The
Atlantic*, for example, ran a brief Op-Ed as a brave attempt to stem this rising
tide of justified paranoia:

The more we learn about the allegations against the reclusive billionaire Jeffrey Epstein, the more he seems like a figment of the online
fever swamps. The wealthy financier arrested last week for underage sex
trafficking is accused of operating an international sex ring that could
implicate high-powered men across business, politics, and Hollywood.
Every nightmarish detail of his story—from the creepily decorated
mansion to the flights on "the Lolita Express" to the stays on "Orgy
Island"—sounds like it was conjured by conspiracy theorists. . . . As
Matthew Walther recently wrote at *The Week*, the Epstein story doesn't
fit neatly into any of the dominant partisan-media narratives. The bad
guys belong to both parties. Trump is linked to Epstein, but so is former

President Bill Clinton. The case has less to do with any political tribe and more to do with class and status. The story, as it's been alleged, is one of rich, powerful men careening through the world with complete impunity, treating the young and the vulnerable as props, and protecting one another from accountability. You don't have to believe in lizard people or baby-eating politicians to understand why so many are looking at our leaders and letting their imagination run wild.[10]

For those who aren't familiar with the lore, the lizard people are © David Icke, while baby-eating politicians belong to the domain of Alex Jones and InfoWars™ (Jones made the claim about Hillary Clinton). These are low hanging fruit: both wildly improbable and hugely popular versions of reality, hence easy, and politically safe, for the self-appointed East coast intelligentsia to deride. But what about first-hand testimonials that aren't at all theoretical but are every bit as challenging to the mainstream-media-dependent mindset exemplified by *The Atlantic* as any c-theory? When does a #MeToo cry for justice become too disturbing and distasteful to receive the support, or the respect, of being taken seriously?*

The police investigation against Jeffrey Epstein began in 2006, when a woman contacted Florida's Palm Beach Police Department claiming that her 14-year-old stepdaughter had been taken to Epstein's mansion by an older girl, for sexual purposes. Police found hidden cameras throughout the property and a number of sources reported that Epstein used them to photograph and video tape orgy sessions for VIPs and other dignitaries for the purpose

---

* At the same time, the sociopolitical context for these sorts of claims is becoming increasingly sympathetic *with* them. In October of 2018, the Australian Prime Minister Scott Morrison made a national apology to "Australian survivors and victims of child sexual abuse" that referred to "17,000 survivors coming forward." The speech described "crimes of ritual sexual abuse" occurring in "schools, churches, youth groups, scout troops, orphanages, foster homes, sporting clubs, group homes, charities, and in family homes." It pointed to how "systems within these organizations allowed it to happen and turned a blind eye . . . day after day, week after week, month after month, and decade after decade. Unrelenting torment. . . . Trust broken. Innocence betrayed. Power and position exploited for evil dark crimes." "Scott Morrison's national apology to Australian survivors and victims of child sexual," *The Guardian*, 22 Oct, 2018: https://www.theguardian.com /australia-news/2018/oct/22/scott-morrisons-national-apology-to-australian-survivors -and-victims-of-child-sexual-abuse-full-speech

of blackmail. The orgies included underage girls.[11] One woman, Virginia Roberts, "accused Epstein of keeping her as a sex slave for four years when she was just 15 [to be] pimped out to many important people including Prince Andrew." Roberts claimed to have had paid sex with Prince Andrew in London, New York, and on Epstein's private US island, as part of an orgy that included other underage girls. "I was a pedophile's top girl, being trained up for a British prince," Roberts alleged in her lawsuit.[12]

The FBI eventually compiled reports on "34 confirmed minors" making allegations of sexual exploitation by Epstein, including corroborating details.[13] A 2018 exposé in the *Miami Herald* identified about 80 victims and located about 60 of them.[14] Alexander Acosta, the US Attorney for the Southern District of Florida, took a plea deal that granted immunity from all federal criminal charges to Epstein, as well as to four *named* co-conspirators (including Ghislaine Maxwell), and all unnamed "potential co-conspirators."[15] The *Miami Herald* reported that the non-prosecution agreement "essentially shut down an ongoing FBI probe into whether there were more victims and other powerful people who took part in Epstein's sex crimes."[16]

In 2008, Epstein pleaded guilty to a state charge of procuring for prostitution a girl under 18, and was sentenced to 18 months in prison. Instead of being sent to state prison, however, as is customary for convicted sex offenders in Florida, Epstein was given a private wing of the Palm Beach County Stockade. According to the sheriff's office, he was allowed to leave jail on "work release" after 3½ months. Then in 2019, Epstein was arrested again on similar charges, at which point Acosta disclosed the reason he backed off from prosecuting Epstein in 2007, despite the ample evidence of his guilt: Epstein, he said, "belonged to intelligence."

This wasn't the first time such a claim had been made. As far back as the 1980s, while Epstein worked his way up the banking system and started his own company (1981), he boasted about being an agent for the CIA (he later denied it). Adding credence to his claim was the fact that one of Epstein's clients at the time was Saudi Arabian businessman Adnan Khashoggi, the middleman between Israel and Iran for trading in American weapons as part of the Iran-Contra Affair. High-level stuff, and Khashoggi was only one of several defense contractors known to Epstein. (He was also Robert Evans' first investor on *The Cotton Club*.) In the mid-1980s, Epstein traveled repeatedly between the US, Europe, and the Middle East. To give an idea of his deep state connections, Epstein also served on the Trilateral Commission and the Council on Foreign Relations, two (infamous) elitist international relations organizations.

✦

"I've noticed that as my reputation grows worse my success with women increases. . . . People are intrigued by the devil and attracted when they discover that on top of having horns and a tail, he's also charming."

—ROMAN POLANSKI, *1971* Playboy *interview*

Regarding Epstein's intelligence-connections, the UK paper *The Observer* had this to comment: "It appears that Jeffrey Epstein was involved in intelligence work, of some kind, for someone—and it probably wasn't American intelligence either. The U.S. Intelligence Community is lenient about the private habits of high-value agents or informants, but they won't countenance running sex trafficking rings for minors on American soil, for years." The tenuous nature of this statement was perhaps evident even to *The Observer*, who contradicted it a few paragraphs later: "What's not in doubt is that a sex trafficking ring centered on minors, which involved numerous global VIPs in compromising situations, would be of *high interest to quite a few intelligence services*."[17] In other words, US intelligence—no slouch in the espionage department, by any standards—would be *interested* in intel of this sort, but be careful not to become accountable to (their own) mainstream media sources (such as *The Observer*) for actively pursuing it. Glad that's cleared up then.

Epstein himself made overt efforts to control the narrative around his activities when, in 2004, he bought *Radar* magazine with Mort Zuckerman, "gaining a foothold in the realm of publications that dished on the salacious doings of the rich and famous."[18] In 2003, he had also tried to buy *New York* magazine, along with Harvey Weinstein, Zuckerman, billionaire investor Nelson Peltz, then-Cablevision chief Jim Dolan, and Donny Deutsch.[19] But even without such total spin control, Epstein's 2007 "deal of the century" extended beyond the legal world and gave him *carte blanche* in high society, including Hollywood, where a sex offense conviction on Mickey Mouse charges that everyone knows concealed the real truth carried no consequences. Whether Epstein's Hollywood associates were complicit, or simply didn't care, Epstein continued to attend high-profile events such as the *Batman Vs Superman* premiere and Oscar season parties. Unlike Weinstein, Epstein dodged the ire of the #MeToo movement almost entirely, for a few years at least.

After Epstein's second arrest in July 2019 on charges of sex trafficking of minors in New York and Florida, however, news outlets began to focus on his ties to high-level government officials (including Bill Clinton and Donald Trump) and on "Epstein's long-cultivated relationships within Hollywood and New York media circles, where he moved with ease well after his high-profile 2008 conviction."[20] The dark legend of Epstein's little black book became part of public record after his 2007 arrest, and it has long promised to implicate "a who's who of entertainment figures." Names disclosed in 2019 included Ralph Fiennes, Alec Baldwin, Dustin Hoffman, Michael Jackson, Andrew Jarecki, Christopher Lambert, David Blaine, Jimmy Buffett, Chris Tucker, Courtney Love, Rupert Murdoch, Jon Peters, David Puttnam, Simon Le Bon, Charlie Rose, Mike Wallace, Barbara Walters, Tony Blair, David Koch, Bob Weinstein, and Prince Andrew.*

---

* A full list of the many entertainment industry names found in Jeffrey Epstein's black book would take up too much space to include here. A *partial* list of Hollywood names listed in Epstein's little black book: Ron Burkle, producer of *Out of the Furnace* with Christian Bale; Richard Branson (not the entrepreneur), producer and actor, known for *Superman Returns* (2006); Peter Barnes, producer, director, writer, and Oscar nominee; Naomi Campbell, producer, actress and model, *Zoolander 2*, etc.; Barbara Carrera, actress, Bond Girl; Jeff Davies, producer, part owner of Dreamland Entertainment Group, Mambo City Music, Entourage Music, Mirror Image Media and Duplication, Evolution Graphics, Davis Partners, Davis Productions, Corner Store Entertainment, Vertical Computer Systems; Griffin Dunne, producer, actor, writer, oldest child of Dominick Dunne; Frédéric Fekkai, celebrity hairstylist and "beauty entrepreneur," with clients that include Kim Basinger, Jessica Lange, Sigourney Weaver, Claudia Schiffer, Renée Zellweger, and Hillary Clinton; Isabel Goldsmith-Patiño, hotelier with longstanding relationships in the entertainment, social, cultural, and business communities of London, Paris, Hollywood, and Mexico; Deborah Green, actress, *The Post* (2017); Barbara Guggenheim, married to Bob and Harvey Weinstein's attorney Bert Fields, who represented Michael Jackson during the 1993 child molestation allegations; Sabrina Guinness, producer and wife of Tom Stoppard; Bobby Kotick, CEO of Activision Blizzard, home to some of the most popular video game franchises in history; had a cameo role in film *Moneyball* (2011); Caryn Krooth, producer-director; Christopher Lawford, actor and member of the Kennedy family; Blake Lindsley, actress, known for *Starship Troopers* and *Mulholland Drive*; married to producer Stephen Nemeth. (*Dogtown, Z-Boys, The Sessions,*

Nor is such high-level hobnobbing restricted to Epstein's Lolita Island: in late 2010, Epstein hosted a dinner party in New York in honor of Prince Andrew; the list of 15 to 20 exclusive guests included Charlie Rose, Woody Allen, and George Stephanopoulos. Epstein's alleged co-conspirator, Ghislaine Maxwell (who was not charged in 2007, thanks to the afore-mentioned non-prosecution agreement), "has been spotted at top-tier awards-season parties in New York and Los Angeles . . . with a pre-scandal Weinstein, Elon Musk and Jeff Bezos. She even attended the 2014 *Vanity Fair* Oscar bash, posing with the magazine's editor, Graydon Carter."[21]

> One top Hollywood veteran notes Epstein was very interested in show business and would reach out for information about the industry. "He would call and ask 'What does this person do? What do you think of Paramount?' Questions like that," this person recalls. "He was an investor. He seemed incredibly smart. I didn't know what his social life was. I wish I had read [about him] more carefully. But based on what I've read, he had a lot of friends in every industry."[22]

Fear and Loathing in Las Vegas, Climate Refugees); Guy J. Louthan, producer; Isabel Maxwell, producer-director; Peter Morton, producer known for *Snatch* and *Lock, Stock and Two Smoking Barrels*, godfather to Matthew Vaughn, director of *Layer Cake* (2004), *Stardust* (2007), *Kick-Ass* (2010), *X-Men: First Class* (2011), and *Kingsman* and its sequels; Robert Morton, writer-producer, known for *The Late Show with David Letterman*; Alan Mruvka, creater and founder of Movietime Channel Inc., now known as E! Entertainment Television with partner Larry Namer; Pliny Porter, producer, President of Production and Development for Julia Roberts' production company; Muffy Potter, producer and actress; Meryl Poster, the president and founder of Superb Entertainment, president of television at The Weinstein Company until October 2014, previously the Co-President of Production for Miramax Films; Joan and Melissa Rivers; Gerald Ronson, uncle of music producer Mark Ronson; Bobby Shriver, producer, known for *True Lies* and brother of Maria Shriver, Arnold's Schwarzenegger's wife; Maria Shriver; Peggy Siegel, publicist and Oscar campaigner; Christy Turlington, actress, director, producer and supermodel; married to actor/writer/producer/director Edward Burns; Rupert Wainwright, director of award-winning features, TV shows, and commercials, known for *Stigmata* with Patricia Arquette; Casey Wasserman, entertainment executive and sports agent executive, grandson of Lew Wasserman; Jason Weinberg, manager, producer, known for *Ray Donovan* and *The Gong Show*; Felicity Waterman, actress, known for *Die Hard 2* (1990) and *Titanic* (1996); Jim Wiatt, senior executive in the global media and entertainment industry, former Chairman and Chief Executive Officer of the William Morris Agency from 1999 to 2009; Lionel Wigram, producer of *Harry Potter* films; Jim Wyatt, producer.

Epstein was a member of and a major financial contributor[23] to John Brockman's Edge Foundation: Third Culture, "an eclectic platform for conversations that involve scientists, artists, and technologists."[24] This ties Epstein closely to Edge founder John Brockman, the self-described "shadowy figure at the top of the cyberfashion food chain." Brockman "emerged from the New York art scene of the 1960s, promoting underground cinema and rubbing shoulders with heavyweights like Andy Warhol" (he put together distribution deals for Warhol's films). Significantly closer to the New Hollywood nexus, in 1968, Brockman "devised a notorious advertising campaign for the Monkees' cult flop *Head* that saw images of his face and the word 'Head' plastered all over New York City." (The poster is now in the Museum of Modern Art.) During these early days of his ascent, Brockman buddied with Dennis Hopper, Hunter S. Thompson, John Cage, Sam Sheppard, Charlie Mingus, Jr., Abby Hoffman, Paul Krassner, Jerry Rubin, Nicholas Humphrey, Jack Nicholson, Bert Schneider of BBS, and Huey P. Newton (founder of the Black Panthers). He was friends with Gerd Stern, the founder of USCO, which meant he was fraternizing with Timothy Leary, Richard Alpert, Ralph Metzner, and Jonas Mekas, among many others. His first client as a literary agent was John C. Lilly, a neuro-scientist with loose ties to MKULTRA, who gave workshops at Esalen and on whom the movie *Altered States* was based.

The kind of friends Epstein had are the kind that—as Roman Polanski found out forty years earlier—quickly turn into enemies the moment you fall from grace. There was a brief period when the media was promising—or threatening—to disclose "almost 2,000 pages of documents that could reveal sexual abuse by 'numerous prominent politicians, business executives, foreign presidents, a well-known prime minister, and other world leaders.'"[25] That came to an end when, on August 10, 2019, as I was finishing up the first draft of this book, Epstein was found dead in his cell at the Metropolitan Correctional Center in New York City under highly suspicious circumstances. The death was widely reported as a suicide, though the evidence suggests otherwise.[26] President Donald Trump retweeted one theory suggesting that Bill Clinton was involved in Epstein's death. Perhaps Clinton retweeted a theory that blamed Trump?

On the other hand, on August 5, five days before his death was announced, someone emailed me this: "I feel defeated today. As if the globalist elites have already won. Next thing we know Epstein will be conveniently suicided, i.e., given another free pass and a new identity in Israel." Sometime later, in early September, a drone picture was circulated of what looked distinctly like Jeffrey Epstein, alive and well on his island.[27]

If we take all of this deep background, the interconnecting world of intelligence agencies, organized crime, sex trafficking, filmed blackmail material, and the lifestyles of the cultural elite; and if we allow, as the evidence clearly indicates, that these networks were fully functional in 1960s London and Hollywood during Polanski's rise to prominence within the industry; it becomes increasingly difficult to view him, or even Tate and the others, as innocent victims of a random act of carnage. What starts to seem vastly more likely is that the official version of "the Manson murders" ("Helter Skelter") was closer to a (yes, Polanski-esque) real-world horror fantasy narrative along the lines of a high-prestige Hollywood production, albeit at considerably deeper levels of make-believe and with a "crew" afforded training, funds, and objectives that far transcend the ordinary aspirations of movie artists.

Or at least what we have assumed these to be.*

---

* In July 2020, William Steel testified about Epstein and Ghislaine Maxwell: "I saw videos of very powerful people—celebrities, world figures—in those videos having sex, threesomes, even orgies with minors. . . . They showed me black-and-white footage of a woman they told me was internationally known, a well-known rock star and another man having sex. It looked like it was taken in the 1960s and without their knowledge." "'Nymphomaniac' Jeffrey Epstein and Ghislaine Maxwell 'filmed powerful people having sex with underage girls'" by Emma Parry, *The Sun*, July 10, 2020: https://www.the-sun.com/news/1120265/epstein-maxwell-people-sex-under-age-girls/

3

DARK CITY

3.1   HOLLYWOOD HARVEST

"The cult of the hero is the absolutely necessary complement of
the classification of society. . . . This exaltation of the hero proves
that one lives in a mass society. The individual who is prevented
by circumstances from becoming a real person, who can no
longer express himself through personal thought or action,
who finds his aspirations frustrated, projects onto the hero all
he would wish to be. He lives vicariously and experiences the
athletic or amorous or military exploits of the god with whom he
lives in spiritual symbiosis."

—JACQUES ELLUL, *Propaganda*

With these opening chapters, I have opened up a massive can of
worms that looks more like a rotting corpse sticking out of the
family rose garden than a simple fishing accessory. The worms
indicate that things are not as they seem. Since freighted hypotheses require
solid tracks to reach their destination, it's not yet time to return to Cielo
Drive. The context for the sort of enormous reality distortion I suggested in
the last chapter is more than merely political or criminal; it is social, cultural,
and even philosophical in its scope. It is the tip of an iceberg that *is* our
culture, and would indicate that *nothing* in our world is as it seems (which

is how we have been trained to see it), and may even be closer to the exact inverse. The deep context for such modern myth creation that both movies and "psyop" aspire to is, naturally, ancient myths. The more the old gods change, the more the new gods remain the same.

In *The Attention Merchants*, Tim Wu describes "the creation of a new pantheon," one that has been indefinitely expanded to "carry the attention merchants into the twenty-first century" (p. 216). This is something that has become fully observable, *experiential*, in the last ten years or so of internet culture and social media, and with the *literal* pantheons of the Marvel and DC universes. Yet it's also, tellingly, in line with ancient religious and sorcerous beliefs. Attention is the currency of existence.

> If the attention merchants were once primitive, one-man operations, the game of harvesting human attention and reselling it to advertisers has become a major part of our economy. [T]he new industries of the twentieth century turned [attention] into a form of currency they could mint. [T]he winning strategy from the beginning has been to seek out time and spaces previously walled off from the commercial exploitation, gathering up chunks and then slivers of our un-harvested awareness (Wu, p. 6).

In Western society, besides corporate CEOs and high-ranking politicians, the largest earners are entertainment figures: sports, movie, and music stars. Compare the $80 million yearly salary of a Downey Jr. or Brad Pitt (or the billion-dollar assets of a Lucas or a Spielberg) with the yearly salary of a school teacher. Low-paid, low-status figures, teachers are not especially respected by young people—but then the education system hardly seems designed to inspire children's respect. Bertrand Russell wrote in 1951, in *The Impact of Science on Society*: "education should aim at destroying free will, so that, after pupils have left school, they shall be incapable, throughout the rest of their lives, of thinking or acting otherwise than as their schoolmasters would have wished" (p. 50). I went to two private schools in the UK, and my experience supports Russell's statement: the purpose of my schooling was not to inspire me, or even to nurture my intelligence, but to *socialize* and prepare me for a certain role within society. Fortunately, I saw through the ruse and rejected the program (at that level at least).

As already implied, the subtler and more insidious tool of mass psychological influence—the good cop to education's bad cop—is entertainment media. To help the reader understand the subtlety and complexity of this scientific social (and mythic) management program, I want to introduce a term coined by Donald Horton and Richard Wohl in 1956, "parasocial interaction" (PSI). PSI refers to a kind of psychological relationship experienced by an audience in their *mediated encounters with performers in the mass media*. PSI is what happens when viewers or listeners start to feel like media personalities are their friends, despite having little or no interaction with them. "Parasocial relationships are cultivated by the media to resemble face-to-face relationships"; over time, we have so many experiences of illusory relationships with celebrities that we start to "feel that they know and understand us," though in truth they have never even heard of us. Studies have indicated that some "viewers perceive the personas as helping to significantly shape their own identity."[1]

What begins as a lifeline, eventually becomes a noose around our necks (cf. *Seen and Not Seen*). Part of the nature of this noose is the instilled drive to break *through* the fourth wall of parasocial reality and storm heaven, to attain the level of a star oneself. In his breakdown of transegalitarian secret societies, Hayden describes how their organization in ancient times combined ecstatic shamanism, a belief in spirits demanding human sacrifice, and "devious conversation" (conspiring in secret). This latter included, when necessary, coming to one another's aid in dealing with "intransigents" who challenged the authority of the elite. Referring to "evolved regional secret society organizations," Hayden describes how "major ritual centers" (e.g. Stonehenge) developed over time and in some cases evolved into more official cultural centers that became involved in the organization of a larger economy. There are sites that even today function on at least two levels, both as economic centers and as "sacred" sites. One way such ritual centers are identifiable—despite having a covert historical function and meaning known only to the aggrandizers—is that they attract ordinary people to make pilgrimages there. Viz a viz Hollywood, formerly Holy Wood.*

---

* Later in his book, Hayden quotes a separate source on how "initiation into religious secret societies was a sine qua non for elite or leadership status." Both access and status "usually correlated with the wealth and the social background of an individual as well as his

Hayden's work implies a hidden infrastructure to society (a super-culture) shaping and informing it, creating both political and cultural "currents," invisible on the surface but quite palpably real in their effects. Such societal undercurrents, in fact, determine the direction of society at large, and they do so by *dint* of their invisibility, which itself depends on a form of *camouflage*. Countless Hollywood movies, for example, are backed, conceived, and created by the US military-industrial complex, and yet they appear to glorify a rebel hero, a lone outlaw figure fighting against a corrupt and abusive government system and prevailing against impossible odds. This distorted, inverted solar hero supposedly stands in for the common man, for the collective, but in fact, like Tony Stark (*Iron Man*), he represents—in covert, symbolic form, though sometimes literally too—the "transegalitarian aggrandizers" of a military-backed elite. While we cheer Robert Downey Jr.—both the actor and the character he portrays—and experience a vicarious thrill of empowerment as the tenacious "little guy" overcomes—or shows up—a monolithic corporate power, we never suspect that we are aggrandizing our oppressors and all of our energy is actually going to the same power system ostensibly being challenged. What we imagine we are defying, we are in fact *deifying*. Jacques Ellul again:

> The well-known mechanism of identifying with movie stars is almost impossible to avoid for the member of modern society who comes to admire himself in the person of the hero. There he reveals the powers of which he unconsciously dreams, projects his desires, identifies himself with this success and that adventure. . . . The propagandee is alienated and transposed into the person promoted by propaganda (publicity campaigns for movie stars and propaganda campaigns are almost identical) (p. 172–3).

---

or her social, intellectual, and technological skills." Such religious-political leaders "served as administrators and statesmen of early California" (p. 91–2). Hayden's book covers a large spectrum of archeological data (from the Americas to Oceania and Africa), beginning with the American northwest and including a chapter on California. His findings show a remarkable degree of consistency in the workings of secret societies on different continents. I have given special attention to the West Coast material, for obvious reasons.

Being in the business of mythic management, the entertainment industry appeals to a layer of consciousness beneath the rational mind. Its function is to perpetuate a permanent transference of our power and autonomy—our life force—onto idealized symbols created by a shadowy elite. We literally *buy* into parasocial interactions with self-aggrandizing movie stars and Hollywood wish-fulfillment fantasies of epic power and success, believing we are too wised up to be sold on real-world political narratives. The mythic narratives being created are not restricted to movies and pop songs, however, because they include the lives (and deaths) of *the celebrities themselves,* all of which are directed and "scripted"—in looser, subtler ways—by backstage spin doctors with the exact same end: shaping and directing the collective dreaming mind by harvesting the energy of our rapt attentions. We are being farmed.

3.2   THEATER OF CRUELTY

> "Theatre develops out of sacrifice and the Greek genius was to
> turn sacrifice into tragedy—because what is sacrifice? It's the
> re-living of the primordial murder—the myth—therefore tragedy
> is telling the story instead of having the victim. That is why when
> you tell the story you must not have a sacrifice. The big taboo is
> you must not even show the violence. You can only use language."
>
> —RENE GIRARD, *CBC Radio, "Ideas"*

Hayden notes that many of the public rituals performed by secret societies included "performers representing Immortals," and that some members were said to "become stars after death" (p. 91, 93). Such high-sorcery didn't come without risks, however: "some of the spirits being impersonated were represented as *so dangerous and powerful that mistakes in the performances could kill the performers*" (p. 94, emphasis added).

It could be argued that any artist—and none more than a performance artist—is looking for attention. This is literally true, but it may also be true in the colloquial sense, implying a childish need to be seen and validated. Children who fail to receive the attention they need from their caregivers "act up" and "act out," via tantrums and transgressions, sometimes even leading to accidents or self-destruction. In the arts, from Shakespeare to *grand guignol* to Hollywood, a guaranteed way to get the undivided attention of audiences (as in Hayden's secret society rituals) is tragedy and horror, specifically *acts that go straight to the most primal, survival-oriented parts of the brain and body*. Significantly, the Greeks—who originated theater as we know it today— *prohibited acts of violence* on stage, partly because of the dangers of mimesis (audience imitation; they also used masks to clearly distinguish the actor from the role).*

When Heath Ledger took on the role of the Joker for *The Dark Knight*, shortly before his drug-related death in 2008, it may have been in an attempt, not only to test his range as an actor, but also to be taken more seriously as one: by shirking the role of pretty boy actor and playing a psychopath (ironically, a comic book psychopath), he might thereby harvest *a particular quality of audience attention*, namely their fear and revulsion, or *horror*.

What exactly was Ledger letting take over his consciousness? The Joker is not merely a psychopath, he's an *archetypal* psychopath; in the ranks of 20th century *tulpas*, he's practically a god. (Research for the first *Batman* movie claimed that the bat insignia was the *second* most recognizable symbol to kids, after the smiley face.) There was some speculation at the time that Ledger's immersion in the role of archetypal maniac precipitated a meltdown that brought about his premature death. Fifty years earlier, the idea that a movie (or stage) actor could become so submerged in a role that it would haunt his interior spaces would have been, if not unthinkable, quite hard for the average moviegoer to grok. By 2008, however, the whole "Method actor" thing was so widely accepted that few people questioned the connection being made.†

Method acting entails the deliberate manipulation of consciousness to summon memories and feelings from the past, bring them into the present, and temporarily transform the personality. Via the Method, actors effectively send their consciousness back in time, to a relevant experience

---

* Another reason given is that having to *imagine* acts of violence increased the audience's awareness of their own complicity.

† For a longer-form exploration of the forces, inner and outer, behind Ledger's death, see Outtake # 1, on page 445.

(remote-viewing it), and relive it. From a recondite corner of the past, they act out the scene, projecting it into the present, while their consciousness remains, so to say, in the past. Like children who play make-believe and get lost in fantasy, actors conspire—with their fellow actors, directors, and writers, and above all with their audience, co-conspirators all—to assemble *a new perception of reality* to temporarily replace the old one. A good Method actor has a propensity for entering into altered states of perception and experiencing parallel worlds—in other words, *a somewhat tenuous grip on reality.* Accomplished Method actors like Robert De Niro are sometimes described as ciphers, empty vessels who only come to life when they hear "Action"—at which point they allow their "character" to animate them—or possess them.*

The adoption of roles by a performer, via the indirect mining of his or her unconscious, might be seen as a healthier and more volitional form of dissociative identity disorder (DID). In previous époques—and even today in more shamanic cultures—what we term DID would have been understood as a kind of entity-possession. So what really happens in cases of DID? It is notoriously hard to describe or define. Perhaps the same can be said for when an actor submerges himself in a role? This is from *The Stars*, by Edgar Morin:

> Like her admirers, the star is subjugated by this image superimposed upon her real self: like them, too, she wonders if she is really identical with her double on the screen. Devalued by her double, a phantom of her phantom, the star can escape her own emptiness only by amusing herself, and can amuse herself only by imitating her double, by miming her movie life. An inner necessity impels her to assume her role completely, to live a life of love and festivals. She must keep abreast of her double.

---

* De Niro even played a character called Louis Cipher (Lucifer) in Alan Parker's *Angel Heart*. This method or modus operandi is echoed by "programmed killers"—or more mundanely, by victims of extreme psychological and/or physical abuse—who remain passive and zombie-like until they receive a "trigger" command and suddenly "snap into character." This is very different from how acting *used* to be, pre-Stanislavski, in the early days of Greek theater, for example. In those days, plays were written and performed for the specific end of healing and catharsis, and the actors usually wore masks (*personae*). This is the exact inverse of the internalized method of modern screen acting, and it brings to mind Jack Nicholson's quip about how all he needed to get in character was his costume.

Thus the screen mythology extends itself behind the screen and beyond it (Morin, p. 66–67).

In *The Dark Knight*, Ledger's Joker sees himself as "an agent of chaos" who is "ahead of the curve."* Curiously enough, the Joker's rationale—even his methodology—is firmly in keeping, not just with modern, self-mythologizing serial killers (and Ed Gein supposedly read a lot of comic books), but also with an artistic tradition with occult underpinnings, one that goes back at least as far as the *avant-garde* of the 19th century. This movement is comprehensively (though controversially) mapped in a 1990 book, *Painted Black*, by Carl Raschke,† in a chapter entitled "The Aesthetics of Terror." Raschke locates aesthetic terrorism's emergence as "a surrogate for political radicalism" in French circles close to Baudelaire, at "approximately the same time the political momentum of revolution throughout Europe was waning."

> The concept of art as a revolutionary battering ram that flattens the old values of society and drives their opposite into the shafts of experience developed during the Romantic age. It became a favorite theory among the artistic radicals of the nineteenth century, whose fellowship frequently overlapped with the occult underworld. *[T]he Illuminist yearning for world transformation through occult conspiracy played easily into the hands of aesthetic terrorists. The prestige enjoyed by the occult among artists in twentieth-century civilization, and by extension the interests of occultists in the use of artistic media, turned on the common bond of 'magic'. . . aesthetics and magic have always been intertwined'* (p. 103, emphasis added).

If Raschke's thesis seems surprising, it may only be because, as with the hidden infrastructure of aggrandizers, the nature of the beast is

---

* "Introduce a little anarchy," he tells Harvey Dent (while dressed as a female nurse), "Upset the established order, and everything becomes chaos. I'm an agent of chaos. Oh, and you know the thing about chaos? It's fair!"

† Raschke, a Professor of the Religious Studies Department at the University of Denver, specializes in continental philosophy, art theory, political theory, and the philosophy and theory of religion, and *Painted Black* has certainly provoked some strong rebuttals (considering his thesis, hardly surprising).

self-concealment. My brother, artist and dandy Sebastian Horsley, was *manifestly* the heir of the romantic tradition Raschke describes (he told me he loved Dadaism, and he once had an exhibition of paintings called "The Flowers of Evil," inspired by Baudelaire's poetry collection). At the same time, he openly scorned all things occult (to me at least). In retrospect, now he is gone, I suspect he protested so much as means to obscure the obvious: that he was *steeped* in occultism, not so much the ideology of it (though that too) as the *aesthetics*.

Polanski—who saw himself as an heir of this same artistic tradition—once compared his encounter with Dada and Surrealism in college to "the discovery of sex in the Victorian era" (Cronin, p. 138). As I wrote in *The Blood Poets*: Polanski's director credit in *Repulsion* "comes slicing across the middle of the eye like a razor blade, [in] a direct (none-too-subtle) reference to Buñuel and Dali's *Un Chien Andalou*, with its famous eye-slicing scene. Polanski here acknowledges his influences and proceeds to uphold a specific tradition" (p. 59). * Another influence that will become relevant to *16 Maps of Hell* is that of Samuel Beckett.

> Polanski loved *Waiting for Godot* and in the sixties in France had met Samuel Beckett, who had always wanted to be a filmmaker and was interested in Polanski's mounting an adaptation of *Godot*. The plans never went anywhere, but Polanski's ideas about terror, like those of many of his peers in film, were shaped by the theater. He lived in London in the sixties when Harold Pinter, Edward Albee, and Beckett were all the rage. In 1966, Kenneth Tynan, the legendary critic then working at the National Theater, wrote the then artistic director Laurence Olivier, advising that he give Polanski a short-term contract: "He has exactly the right combination of fantasy and violence for us," he wrote (Zinoman, p. 22).

In my correspondence with researcher and writer Camille Blinstrub about *16 Maps of Hell*, she told me that her "take on Hollywood as of late is how much 'highbrow' influence was going on behind the scenes. Dali, Anais

---

* Buñuel called *Un Chien Andalou* "a passionate call to murder." See "With a passion that still has the power to shock," by Manohla Dargis, *LA Times*, June 22, 2003: https://www.latimes.com/archives/la-xpm-2003-jun-22-ca-dargis22-story.html

Nin, Henry Miller, Hemingway, Huxley, Crowley. [This included] hiding the amount of influence they had, because in those days Americans did not care for highbrow all that much." Nor do they today, and Ledger's the Joker (and Nolan's *Dark Knight*) may be an example of how the most avant-garde artistic influences are concealed within the "friendly" (laughing and dancing) guise of a pop cultural archetype.

Attention at any cost. Raschke describes aesthetic terrorism as "the notion derived from avant-garde artistic work, and applied to the occult, that power over things ultimately requires social revolution, which in turn demands a subversion of symbols . . . a blunt instrument in the war of values. It slices to the heart of what we mean by satanism" (p. 103). Ledger's the Joker—with his call to chaos—would seem to closely approximate this same dark "revolutionary" spirit.

Raschke writes that the limits of aesthetic terrorism were (possibly) reached in 1960s Vienna, via Austrian playwright Hermann Nitsch's "orgy mysteries." These were stage productions that included drunken and drug-induced revelry by the performers, culminating in a bloody animal sacrifice on stage. The aim: "the liberated joy of strong existence without barriers" (p. 104). Rumors were rife that imitators of these theatrical rituals incorporated human sacrifice into their enactments. Since the goal being advocated was that of transcending all barriers, this would seem to have been an almost inevitable trajectory of Nitsch's methodology, which itself would seem to be a deliberate inversion of the cathartic, community-based principles of Greek theater.

3.3   PARASOCIAL INTERACTIONS

"The Dadaists, unlike the artistic decadents before them, fancied themselves political magicians . . . Dadaism pulled its proposals for an art that would speak a 'secret language' of all humankind from musings of the earlier figures of the occult underworld"

—CARL RASCHKE, *Painted Black*

At the time of Ledger's death, I was well aware of my brother's struggle with a lifetime's drug addiction, and I was convinced fame would be the worst possible thing for him. Consciously or not, Ledger's death confirmed, and enflamed, my fears. My brother's death came a week after the West-End premiere of the play *Dandy in the Underworld*, based on his memoir.* Having seen himself portrayed on stage and found it repugnant—like Dorian Gray gazing at *his* portrait, perhaps—he joked: "I'd rather be crucified again than sit through that. I knew I was obnoxious but I never knew how much."[2] Struggling to put a brave face on it, he then quipped: "They say seeing your doppelganger is an omen of death, so I got quite excited about that and thought, best get my coat on."[3]

For Heath Ledger, the process seems to have occurred in reverse: since he died while filming *The Imaginarium of Doctor Parnassus*, in order not to abandon the film, director Terry Gilliam hired not one but three Hollywood stars as *doppelgängers* for Ledger (Jude Law, Colin Farrell, and Johnny Depp). The film revolves around the leader of a travelling theatre troupe, Doctor Parnassus (Christopher Plummer), who has made a pact with the Devil, trading immortality for his daughter (i.e., soul). The Imaginarium is the feature attraction of his roadshow. Like Hollywood in miniature, it invites audience members to pass through a magical mirror and explore their imaginations, giving them the choice between enlightenment and delusion. Ledger's Tony joins the troupe when he is rescued from hanging. In one scene, with Depp-as-Ledger-as-Tony, we see three floating coffins, identified as the remains of Princess Diana, James Dean, and Rudolph Valentino. Though dead—Depp's Tony eulogizes, all-but inaudibly—these fallen stars are "immortal nevertheless. They won't get old or fat. They won't get sick or feeble. They are beyond fear because they are forever young. They're gods and you can join them. . . . Actually, there's one more thing. Look at me. This is very, very important. *Your sacrifice must be absolutely pure.*"

In a documentary about the anomalies surrounding the death of Ledger ("How It Really Happened"), Ron Koslow, one of the creators of *Roar*, Ledger's first US TV break, described Ledger's acting career as "a Faustian

---

* Though I didn't become fully conscious of it until working on this chapter, there were some eerie parallels between Ledger's death and my brother's, starting with the cause: a "drug cocktail overdose" (for my brother, it included cocaine, heroin, and pain killers).

bargain . . . you have to sacrifice a lot of yourself to do something like that. It doesn't come without a cost."* The indication is that the potential rewards of becoming a Hollywood celebrity are scaled to match the risks. If you are willing to offer up your entire being, not just your body as a sex object but your soul as a vessel for the collective unconscious to consume, you can, like Valentino or Dean, have a shot at becoming a living legend. You may wind up worshiped as one of the "immortals"—human gods living indefinitely on in a parasocial realm.†

In a strange twist on religious tradition, however, the modern deities of our screen idols don't only receive sacrifice from their worshipers (in terms of time, energy, money, and *attention*), they also run the risk of being sacrificed *to* them. The imposers and the imposed upon: "those who do, and those to whom it is done." Is it possible this fact relates—in an obscure if not occult way—to why the casualty rate in the entertainment industry seems so disproportionately high? Before the orgy mysteries—and possible human sacrifices—of Nitsch's stagecraft in 1960s France, Raschke cites Antonin Artaud, the French dramatist working in the 1940s, for whom "The theater of cruelty stood for a spectacle that served to activate the 'magnetism' in the human organism. . . . *The horrors perpetrated [on stage] are not concocted primarily to be watched; they must be 'acted out' in some way by the viewer, who because of their compelling strength is unable to remain a strict voyeur*" (p. 106–7, emphasis added).

The screen mythology that extends itself behind the screen, also reaches beyond it.

◆

---

* In the same show, Heath Ledger said, "Acting [is] all about harnessing the power of belief. Once you do that, you can take yourself anywhere."

† Two of the most celebrated comic book writers, Neil Gaiman and Alan Moore, in *Sandman* and *Promethea* respectively, have played with the idea that fictional creations can become semi-autonomous entities via the psychic energy we give them—also the theory behind the eastern concept of *tulpas*, though it may overlap with parasocial interactions as well (parasocial may also be paranormal).

"To create what it does, Hollywood has to draw young people, often of unstable temperament, from all over the world. It plunges them into exacting work—surrounds them with a sensuous life—and cuts them off from the normal sources of living."

—MAX LERNER, *America as a Civilization*

So what exactly is the correlation being insinuated by this work between systematized exploitation and abuse and the Hollywood culture that both enables it and spreads it around like plutonium, via parasocial loyalties, identifications, and emulations (a.k.a. "possession")? Alyssa Termini writes:

Parasocial relationships are a type of interaction that can be described as an interpersonal relationship where one person, the spectator, knows a significant amount about the other, the persona or celebrity, but that knowledge is not reciprocated. However, . . . the persona has much control over what the spectator knows about them, thus unknowingly controlling the parasocial interaction.[4]

Movies create narratives, using characters embodied by stars, to capture our attention. If done consistently and effectively enough, these characters, so to speak, *colonize our unconscious.* It is as if the actors' Method of using emotional memory to "charge" a performance and give it veracity transfers to us, the audience members. Persuaded by the actor's emotional presence, we summon our own corresponding associations and enter willingly into Dr. Parnassus' Imaginarium. The promise is immortality; the cost, our psychological integrity.

When we see an especially good movie, one that affects us personally and profoundly, we continue to run the images, dialogue, characters and situations in our minds, sometimes for hours or days afterwards. It's as if we continue to narrate—to live—the story, *in and through our own consciousness.* This is also what happens for sufferers of post-traumatic stress disorder.*

---

* Someone like James Holmes, the Aurora *"Dark Knight Rises* shooter"—with his confused Batman-Joker identification—would seem to be a case of both at once: a movie-imprinted PTSD victim. (See Outtake # 2, on page 457.)

When we dream—literally or not—of meeting a movie star, to some degree we are also fantasizing about meeting the characters the star has played on the screen. In my thirties, I dreamed of hanging out with Keanu Reeves and Helena Bonham Carter. It was both Keanu and Helena the movie stars, and Neo and Marla the characters, I was fantasizing about (or connecting to).

Since we have little to no experience of an actor's actual personality, besides through TV publicity, magazine interviews, and suchlike (for which he or she is also acting), we are primarily connecting to the *characters* an actor plays, rather than to the actors who embody them. These characters exist in some twilight zone between imaginal and actual. First of all, they exist in the minds of the writer who created them. Secondly, they exist through the *Method*—the emotional, psychological and physical identification—of the actors. Finally, they come into a full flowering of existence *in and through the consciousness of the audience itself.* At which time, as Antonin Artaud envisioned and Heath Ledger or my brother (possibly) enacted, they spill out the screen or tumble from the stage. The image lives on, but the vessel through which it incarnated is sloughed off.

Since these characters have no *actual* existence—save that embodied by an actor, who barring any sequels sheds the character soon after, like a snake shedding a skin—whatever reality they possess pertains to the *parasocial realms*. And these movie characters become every bit as real, in our thoughts, memories, and fantasies, as they ever could be on the screen (and potentially even more so, since they now have a body to act through—us). The realm from which they emerged is also the realm to which they belong: the imagination. The true nature of this realm is something we can only imagine.

The allure of parasocial interactions—which are not actually *inter*active, more narcissistic, unless we suppose them to be metaphysical—is, ironically enough, that they also offer the illusion of control to the person engaged in the projection-fantasy. "The lack of actual contact with a media figure means that parasocial interactions can offer positive social interactions *with no risk of rejection and consequent feelings of unworthiness.*"[5] Since "a parasocial partner does not interact with you," he or she "does not let you down."[6]

Parasocial interaction is modern jargon for something that existed long before mass media did. It happened whenever a person established—or at least *felt*—a bond with political leaders, priests, gods, or spirits. "Like the Egyptians worshiped their gods and pharaohs, modern-day fans fixate on and try to attach themselves to celebrities' lives. Just as Egyptians worshiped in their temples, contemporary fans gather in arenas to worship their favorite comedian, musician, or upstanding figure."[7] As Hayden observes (p. 83), "In southern California, secret society members claimed that celestial bodies governed everything on earth and that members could travel to the stars and influence the celestial spheres." Since these sorts of rituals "were claimed to be critical to the continuation of life," *they were kept secret.*

The association between secret knowledge, occult power, and public performance art might seem surprising, but if so, that may only confirm the efficacy—and the importance—of the secrecy. Singing and dancing along with our favorite stars echoes ritualistic dances performed for the gods in ancient times. Gods and pharaohs were revered because they were prominent, wealthy, and in a position that appealed to the commoners. In the same way, celebrities are placed "on a media-created pedestal and are portrayed as rich, superhuman, and youthful. [And now they] are more accessible than ever before . . . audiences have been presented with ample opportunities to connect with stars."[8] In Hayden's mapping of prehistorical secret societies, this was how imposer-aggrandizers manipulated the community, via the appliance of mass psychology, and got them "on-side."

> First, inducing SEEs [sacred ecstatic experiences] served to validate claims that the society held the secrets for contacting supernatural powers and entities. They created feelings of transcendence and unity with higher forces (however conceived), if not vivid visions of spirits. Second, these experiences as well as the psychophysiological effects of extreme experiences served to bind individuals to the organizations as well as to the ideologies of the organizations. This helped to guarantee candidates' keeping of secrets and their fidelity to the society—a bond surpassing loyalty to kin or community (p. 339).

TL,DR: The worshipper who persists in his worship may eventually become divine. Both celebrities and their fans are involved in a parasocial relationship, and just not with each other. Their relationship is also, maybe *primarily*, with the characters or *personae* that they create *together*, just as Ledger animated and gave life to the Joker—though *only in return for letting the Joker possess him.* In my brother's case, the fictional creation that slew and replaced him—as in Edgar Allan Poe's "William Wilson"—was himself. "Who is playing me?" he said shortly before his death. "Well it won't be me. I would be completely miscast for the role darling. Nobody can be exactly like me. Even I have trouble doing it."[9]

3.4   IMAGINAL ARCHITECTS

"This spotlight and the actions of a celebrity add to the reasons why people develop infatuations. It is human nature to want to know more about someone who is enviable or desirable. Celebrities seem to have it all: the fame, the fortune, and the ability to maintain the status, a concept many people yearn to experience. Because of this natural desire . . . the infatuation begins; every piece of information the media put into the world contributes to an obsession, and eventually a parasocial relationship is created."

—ALYSSA TERMINI, *"Crazy in Love with a Smooth Criminal"*

As the creation of an unknown number of artists' imaginations, the Joker can never be said to exist entirely independently of his sources, any more than a human child can be fully separated from *its* genealogy, no matter how "independent" it may grow up to be as an adult. Like atoms forever "entangled," there exists a constant, instantaneous line of "sympathy" between them: whatever is done to one, affects the other. How much more so of two atoms that were once single, as in the case of a mother and her child—or a creator and his thought-form?

What then of movie stars who "bring to life" the characters they play? Kirk Douglas as Spartacus (in the 1960 Stanley Kubrick movie) now lives on in the collective imagination in a way that transcends both the actor and the historical Spartacus (some people have only ever *heard* of Spartacus because of the movie). And while Douglas animates the *idea* of Spartacus, the historical fact of the gladiator-slave in revolt, combined with the Hollywood myth, symbiotically gave Douglas the actor a more mythical dimension and status.

Moviegoers now associate him, not only with fictionalized heroes, but with historical ones.

Douglas was one of a tiny handful of stars in the 1950s who came to embody the masculine ideal (John Wayne, Charlton Heston, and Burt Lancaster were prominent others): he inspired women to want to be with him and men to want to be *like* him. It is a kind of parody of how Spartacus inspired other slaves to (literally) stand up and identify themselves *as* him—to fill his sandals in order to both empower themselves and protect Spartacus, their leader. So we may ask, was the Kirk Douglas who raped and brutalized Natalie Wood (see 8.5) a monster, or was he simply ahead of the curve? If so, we may be asking the wrong question. In an age of monsters, he was both.

The superhero-supervillain embodiments of post-millennial cinema would seem to entail a steepening of this curve. As explored in a 2014 paper, "The Birth and Death of the Superhero Film," superheroes inspire similar feelings in us today as saints once did. The paper cites the actor Christopher Reeve's experience with fans of Superman, including "children dying of brain tumors who wanted as their last request to talk to [him]." Reeves claimed these children went "to their graves with a peace brought on by knowing that their belief in this kind of character is intact." Such "near-religious reverence makes psychological sense in that Reeve was seen as *the embodiment of Superman*"[10] (emphasis added).

As we might reasonably suppose, even without Jungian training, there is a dark side to this deification process: an alleged "Superman curse" dates at least as far back as George Reeves, star of the TV show *Adventures of Superman* from 1952 to 1958. Reeves died of a gunshot wound at age 45 under mysterious circumstances (his death was officially ruled a suicide; it was the subject of a 2006 Ben Affleck movie, *Hollywoodland*). Lee Quigley played Superman as a baby in the 1978 film and died in 1991 at age 14 of solvent abuse. Most famously of all, Christopher Reeve suffered a horseback riding accident in 1995, at age 43, was paralyzed from the neck down, and died nine years later.* I once met Reeve, around my seventeenth birthday in 1984. I went backstage after his performance in *The Aspern Papers* at the Theatre

---

* There are quite a few other deaths making up the evidence for this alleged "curse," but these are the most outstanding examples.

Royal in Haymarket, London. He put his arm around me for a photo, and I
remember thinking at the time how sweet he was. He even had a saintly glow
about him, or so I perceived him. Whatever that glow was, it didn't protect
him from the curse.

In Bob Kane's origin story, Bruce Wayne chose to become the Batman
because "criminals are a cowardly, superstitious lot." The same may be true of
actors, who are known to take the curse of Shakespeare's "Scottish play" seriously enough to never name it. Other people regard the Superman curse as
mere superstition and dismiss the deaths as coincidental. There is a third possibility, however, as there is in the case of Heath Ledger's fatal embodiment of
the Joker. As profound as the effect of Reeve "embodying Superman" was for
some of his fans, might it not have been equally profound for Reeve himself?
Is it possible to handle such powerful psychological, emotional and spiritual
energies without risking a meltdown? There may be more to the idea of
hubris than mere religious superstition. Taking on the guise and the motions
of the übermensch—and embodying this ideal for mass audiences—may
require a degree of knowledge and preparation that, when ignored, leads to
catastrophic consequences.

The Joker began his existence as an *idea* belonging to whoever first came
up with it, now lost to history. Yet the Joker is really being constantly *re*-cre-
ated—brought to life—every time a writer, artist, director, actor, or singer
interprets "him." He now "belongs" to—or has possession of—billions of
people's consciousness. All of these imaginations are now working with, on,
through, and *for* the idea of the Joker, through their own personal relationship with "him"—their investment in him and whatever he represents to
them. Clearly, the influence of the Joker on the minds and hearts of children
and teenagers (and the adults who grew up on him) far transcends the reach
of a single writer/creator. At this point, it's not any particular creator, or even
the comics or movies, that are influencing us; it's our own imaginative interaction with the narratives and characters that continue in *a parasocial world*
created by the comics, TV shows, movies, and music—and by us.*

---

* 2019's *The Joker* "reinvented" the character as a vehicle for current social concerns
and turned him into a combination of the alienated anti-hero from 1970s Hollywood
movies with an "incel" (involuntary celibate), an anarcho-surrealist with extreme identity dysphoria. This Joker laughs at all the wrong things—he is not just politically but

Immersion in or possession by fantasy realities (DID meets PSI) is often described as fanaticism, obsession, geekdom, cult phenomena, and suchlike. The degree to which fans have immersed themselves in the "culture"—the mythology—of *Lord of the Rings* or *Game of Thrones*, for example, suggests they are treating these stories not merely *as if* real, but *as* real—*just as in an occult ritual.* This kind of devotion to *a set of narratives* is a game of make-believe (LARPing) that becomes as real as ordinary reality for many people (with or without a belief in magic). At which point, it ceases to be merely a game. When Walt Disney coined the term "Imagineering" in 1952, he was tipping the hidden hand of mythic engineers. The word is only now coming into its own; or rather, we may only now be beginning to understand the necessity of such a word to account for the way in which our parasocial reality has been created, or at least shaped—not merely by the human imagination, but the human imagination as directed, and coopted, by mass media and other invisible forces—by the hidden architects of the Imaginal.

The question then becomes necessary: what are the effects of allowing these imagineered characters and narratives into our psyches? What is the result of our willing collaboration with the process by which popular quasi-archetypes become active forces in our lives and assume mythical dimensions? What happens when popular characters of fiction become icons to be observed, admired, emulated, and finally worshipped as gods? Are these thought-forms made up of audiences' "psychic energy"—the emotional memory, associations, fears, wishes, etc., being invoked by the combination of the fictional characters and the performers through whom they are embodied?

Although the thought-form is essentially our own—having emerged from our shared unconscious to dialogue with our conscious minds—it has drawn, in part, its appearance, its flavor—even perhaps its intent—from a semi-fictional construct made actual through particular cultural artifacts of

---

ontologically incorrect. Like Donald Trump, he is a Joker in the pack, a monster in society's mirror (movie and TV screen). The film consciously plays on this ambiguity—the twilight reality of the *tulpa*-celebrity—by juxtaposing 1970s movie realism with a 2019 DC comic book movie. This contrast, or conflict, is embodied in the Joker himself, who dissociates from reality into self-mythologizing fantasy and back again, to the extent that, by the end of the movie, we are unsure what we have seen.

interpretation. The movie star-*tulpa* then potentially both informs our unconscious (providing symbolic content for it to play with) and *draws energy off it*. This last idea brings us back into the marketplace of attention: movies—and the imposer-aggrandizers lurking behind them—both feed our consciousness and feed *off* it.

Within such a complex and heavily-mediated tapestry of human energies, is it so far-fetched to imagine that Heath Ledger (or James Holmes) was "possessed" by the spirit of the Joker, and so entered into a liminal realm where he could no longer find himself? Or that, for my brother, in a kind of reverse possession, seeing a fictional representation of himself on stage precipitated a crisis in which he no longer knew how to *be* himself?

Or no longer wanted to?

3.5   STALIN'S PET CHICKEN

"On one occasion, so it was narrated, Stalin called for a live
chicken and proceeded to use it to make an unforgettable point
before some of his henchmen. Forcefully clutching the chicken in
one hand, with the other he began to systematically pluck out its
feathers. As the chicken struggled in vain to escape, he continued
with the painful denuding until the bird was completely stripped.
'Now you watch,' Stalin said as he placed the chicken on the floor
and walked away with some breadcrumbs in his hand. Incredibly,
the fear-crazed chicken hobbled toward him and clung to the
legs of his trousers. Stalin threw a handful of grain to the bird,
and it began to follow him around the room, he turned to his
dumbfounded colleagues and said quietly, 'This is the way to rule
the people.'"

—RAVI ZACHARIAS, *Can Man Live Without God*

For an example of the possessive power of movies, let's return to the 1960 Stanley Kubrick-Kirk Douglas hit movie, *Spartacus*. Well before the movie was made, the legend of Spartacus had stood for resistance to tyranny. In January 1919, for example, a German socialist faction called the Spartacists led a general strike (including armed battles) in Berlin while Germany was in the middle of a post-war revolution. In 1951, the communist writer Howard Fast self-published his novel *Spartacus*, depicting the slave revolt in Marxist terms. When (the very-far-from-Marxist) Kirk Douglas set about creating a film version of Fast's novel, as a vehicle for himself, he rescued Dalton Trumbo, a Hollywood communist, from McCarthy's blacklist to write the screenplay. As already mentioned, the climactic scene has the many slaves standing up and claiming, "I am Spartacus!" to show their defiance to the Roman state and protect their leader from Crassus. As a result, Crassus has them all sentenced to death by crucifixion.

Throughout the prison riots at Attica in 1971, the rioters compared themselves to Spartacus, part of a modern "slave revolt."[11] So were they emulating Spartacus, or the man who played him? Soon after the film was released, "Kirk Douglas' press agent told *Newsweek* that the star's Spartacus hairstyle, a crewcut with a short ponytail in the back, designed by Jay Sebring, would start a whole new trend: 'We'll give out prizes for the best Spartacut!'" (Hoberman, p. 16). (Jay Sebring, hairdresser to the stars, became considerably more famous as one of the victims of the Cielo Drive murders.) Inevitably, but also fittingly, "I am Spartacus" has become a "meme" on the internet. (I know someone who claims he ran into Kirk Douglas on the street once, and shouted those three words at him.) The irony of rebellious individualists (even when Communists) collectively identifying with a corporate movie icon needs no unpacking, but maybe it does need emphasizing just how effectively the Spartacus "meme" turns the communist ideal of collectivism on its head. By asserting the centrality of the individual who leads the slaves to freedom, the revolution gets coopted. It is a chilling example of the Hollywood mastery of *sleight of hand*.

✦

"At this point, projection and repression are realized through identification. Research has shown that when watching a well-made film, the spectators repeat in a reduced form the movements of the hero."

—PROF. YU. A. SHERKOVIN & T. K. BELASCHENKO *(Eds.)*,
Social Psychology and Propaganda

In "The Matric E-Motion: Simulation, Mimesis, Hypermimesis," the philosopher and psychiatrist Nidesh Lawtoo[12] writes:

> Socrates inaugurates the discussion of mimesis via the medium of the theatre, and the actor's psychosomatic transformations [during which] the actor (*mimos*) speaking in direct speech (mimetic *lexis*) "assimilates" a fictional character by "likening oneself to another in speech or bodily bearing," thereby "deliver[ing] a speech as if he were someone else" (mimetic impersonation). ["I am Spartacus!"] And this bodily motion, in turn, generates emotions such as "anger" or "pity" that spread contagiously across the body politic. [Mimesis is also memetic.] From the origins of mimetic theory, then, we witness the postulation of *a contagion of emotions and a multiplying series of bodily replications*—a process that moves actors from within and that spectators see, initially at least, from without."[13]

TL;DR: when actors effectively transform themselves into fictional characters, they first *internalize* and then *pass on* the required emotions and impulses to the collective audience. Audience members then replicate both the emotions and the actions *in their own lives*.

Lawtoo describes this process as "the making of shady representations that Socrates called 'phantoms of reality,'" phantoms that understandably cause confusion "between the true and the false world." The "emotional impersonations" that audience members unconsciously perform in response to stage or film dramatization generate what Nietzsche called a "phantom of the ego," and this phantom in turn generates "psychic conjunctions between self and others."[14] This model would seem to correspond with PSI, or parasocial interactions, as previously discussed.

For an example of manufactured mimesis in action, let's take a look at the Joker copycat crimes, as compiled by researcher Loren Coleman. According to Coleman, the trend of Joker copycat crimes is a recent phenomenon that began roughly in 2008.[15] One of the more notorious examples is Kim de Gelder, "the Dendermonde Joker": on January 23, 2009, wearing a bulletproof vest, backpack, and made up to look like the Joker, de Gelder struck at a "Fairytale-land" or "*Fabeltjesland*" daycare in Belgium, killing two babies and a teacher and injuring twelve others in a rampage of knifing. It was the same day Warner Brothers re-released *The Dark Knight* in traditional theaters and IMAX theaters in the US and other countries. De Gelder was described by former workmates as a "film freak" and "movie addict."

Before positing psychological operations as a causal factor for events of this sort (we will get to that in part two), I want to briefly introduce a much wider, little known, psychosocial context, namely *latah*, a condition observed in Southeast Asia. In 1994, the Diagnostic and Statistical Manual of Mental Disorders, or D.S.M.-IV, recognized *latah* for the first time as a member of a new category of psychiatric illnesses known as *culture-bound syndromes—that is, mental disorders induced primarily by culture and not by any bodily pathology.*[16] Beat author William S. Burroughs mentions *latah* several times in *Naked Lunch*, describing it as being *forcibly induced* rather than spontaneously occurring. (He also mentions it in *The Yage Letters*.) Whether artificially induced or spontaneously occurring (or both), *latah* describes abnormal behaviors that result from *a combination of cultural influences and severe shock.*

Just like Socrates' description of theater-induced mimesis, *latahs* (people afflicted, or inflicted, with *latah*) are said to often mimic the actions of people around them or to *obey commands* automatically and without question. (A specifically cited example is obeying requests to take off their clothes, not surprisingly.) Similar to subjects of deep hypnotic trance, after returning to their senses, *latahs* often claim to have no memory of what they said or did during their fugue state. And although *latahs* are said to

> experience profuse sweating and an increased heart rate while they are in a trance, there is no clear physiognomic source for the condition. What *is* clear, however, is that in Malaysia [where the condition is relatively common], interaction with *latahs* has become a complex form of social play. Instead of being shunned, *latahs* are accepted, even celebrated, for their oddity.[17]

Apparently Malaysia is ahead of the curve, having established a consensual recognition of a phenomenon that, in our own society, is perhaps only just beginning to be recognized, dimly, via such phenomena as "Trump-Derangement-Syndrome." Cultural possession. And the strange condition called *latah* may well be key to the (very slowly, perhaps painfully, emerging) thesis of *16 Maps of Hell*, and to a fuller understanding of the power and appeal of Hollywood.

3.6   MINORITY INFLUENCE & SPECTATOR SPORT

"When [journalist and whistleblower Danny] Ellsberg told me
he was a celebrity, he was saying that he underwent a symbolic
transformation the moment he leaked the Pentagon Papers, and
landed in a social realm that alienated him from non-celebrities
like me."

—DOUGLAS VALENTINE, *CIA as Organized Crime*

Minority influence is the name given to how a small group (or even
an individual) becomes an agent of social change. It's based on the reasoning that there are two types of social influence: majority influence, resulting
in conformity and public compliance, and minority influence, resulting in
conversion. Minority influence is generally viewed as a more "innovative"
or "progressive" form of social change, and tends to be associated with bottom-up or "grass-roots" movements, such as the Suffragettes (early feminists
campaigning for the right to vote) or the Civil Rights Movement. Yet the
term might also be applied to the way a cultural elite influences the attitudes of a collective population, from the top down, in service of their own
interests (for example, Edward Bernays' "Torches of Freedom" campaign
to market cigarettes to women by branding smoking as an act of feminist
liberation). The so-called one-percent, after all, is a minority with a disproportionate degree of influence.

One intriguing element of the sociopolitical theory of minority influence is that of "social cryptomnesia." Cryptomnesia refers to when we have
what we mistakenly believe to be an original idea that is in fact a memory of
something we have previously heard, seen, or read. This has the curious effect
of causing us to misattribute something implanted in us as *a self-generated
inspiration or insight*. It's easy to see how useful such a phenomenon could
be for the purposes of indoctrination, were it possible to induce it. As a population adapts its values, perceptions, or beliefs (and behaviors) to conform
to those belonging to a minority group, there is a "changeover"—or tipping
point—at which the minority effectively *becomes* the majority (at least on
the surface, and only by transforming it into a replica of itself). William

Burroughs described his own version of social cryptomnesia, in characteristically paranoid form, in *Nova Express*, as a kind of viral alien invasion:

> We first took our image and put it into code. A technical code developed by the information theorists . . . written at the molecular level to save space, when it was found that the image material was not dead matter, but exhibited the same life cycle as the virus. This virus released upon the world would infect the entire population and turn them into replicas, it was not safe to release the virus until we could be sure that the last groups to go replica would not notice (p. 49).

Once a minority influence has taken hold in society, the newly-adopted value-set becomes an integral part of the culture, and its original source is forgotten, with the corresponding assumption, either that we have always had these values, or that we generated them from within ourselves (or a bit of both). Simply stated, social cryptomnesia is the result of thoughts and ideas that challenge or shock us being stored in *latent memory*, without our remembering the actual source. Ideas that are seemingly forgotten reappear in our minds, as *our own beliefs or thoughts*, at which point, we have effectively been colonized—or replicated.

Part of the effective cover of intelligence agents may be a kind of self-inflicted cryptomnesia: to become efficient conveyors of the ideological virus, the propaganda and the disinformation, they are tasked to deliver, they first need to believe it originates within themselves. "The first duty of an underground worker" wrote infamous double agent Kim Philby, "is to perfect not only his cover story but his cover personality" (p. 201). As high-level psychological operatives (ad-men) in Hollywood, Corman, Evans, Nicholson, Huston or Polanski may be what researcher Joe Atwill called "lifetime actors." It's also possible—perhaps more likely—that they are only partially aware of what they are involved in, and only some of the time. Nor can the possibility be ruled out (though here we begin to enter *Manchurian Candidate*-territory) that some Hollywood players are psychologically fragmented to the degree they really don't know what they are involved with, at least some of the time.

An important thing to consider when it comes to such speculations is that, like actors, intelligence operatives are, among other things, trained liars. (Deception is the central tool of aggrandizers, remember.) This suggests they wouldn't lie the way you or I do, with shifty "tells," moral ambivalence, guilt, or discomfort. They would lie *as if they were telling the truth*, exactly as Method actors do: *because they believe the lies they are telling* (that is, in the necessity of them). This would make trying to gauge whether a given Hollywood player is an operative (is lying) by observing their personal mannerisms, tone of voice, and so on, essentially futile; because if they *were*, they would be trained to fool us via just such qualities. Hollywood's sleight of hand is that, the more we look, the more we are deceived. And like magic, movies are all about *directing our attention to suspend our disbelief.* From Guy Debord's *Society of the Spectacle:*

> In societies dominated by modern conditions of production, life is presented as an immense accumulation of *spectacles.* Everything that was directly lived has receded into a representation. . . . . *Fragmented* views of reality regroup themselves into a new unity as a *separate pseudo-world* that can only be looked at. The specialization of images of the world evolves into a world of autonomized images where even the deceivers are deceived. The spectacle is a concrete inversion of life, an autonomous movement of the nonliving. The spectacle presents itself simultaneously as society itself, as a part of society, and as *a means of unification.* As a part of society, it is the focal point of all vision and all consciousness. But due to the very fact that this sector is *separate,* it is in reality the domain of delusion and false consciousness: the unification it achieves is nothing but an official language of universal separation (p. 7).

"The spectacle is not a collection of images," Debord argues, but "a social relation between people that is mediated by images." This spectacle is not "a mere visual excess produced by mass-media technologies," but a *materialized worldview*, "a view of a world that has become objective." Rather than being "mere decoration"—or entertainment—for the real world, it is "the very heart of this real society's unreality" (p. 7–8). The Matrix, to you and me.

From the movie-spectacles we've seen, we know (or think we do) that undercover agents—to be effective—have to first become their cover. In a similar way, Method actors may immerse themselves in their characters to the point they don't know where their performance begins or ends; they "mind-control" themselves and become "autonomized images"—human-tulpa hybrids. The nature of military "psychological operations" (see chapter 11) is to persuade the Target Audience that the spectacle *is* reality, and the most effective way to communicate authenticity is to persuade oneself of it, to *become* the role—the deceivers deceived.

What counts perhaps most of all in this project is *which values* a given player or performance is transmitting via its work. Are the values ideologically compatible with overarching narratives and agendas—the separate pseudo-world—that the governing body wants to implement? To this degree, determining how much the governing body—Hollywood, CIA, Mafia, the US military, the State—supports and advances the careers of a given player—i.e., *autonomizes their image*—may be the surest gauge for said player's complicity with the pseudo-world being pushed.

At first pass, this may seem like the circular reasoning of much "conspiracy theory." But if we define State power as what always acts in its own interests, it stands to reason that any given power-structure would only be interested in advancing those players who are effective as *carriers for the values that support and extend its hegemony.*

4

WONDER BOYS

4.1   ISLAND OF LOST TOYS:
CASE STUDY # 5, STAGEDOOR MANOR

"Worshipped as heroes, divinized, the stars are more than objects
of admiration. They are also subjects of a cult. A religion in
embryo has formed around them."

—EDGAR MORIN, *The Stars*

In the early drafts of this book, I alternated my arguments with a number of case studies, in the hope of illustrating certain trends, patterns, methods, and forces, running beneath the Hollywood industry like fault lines, out of which the molten lava of an unquenchable *will to power* spills. Before I found myself unexpectedly restructuring this work, for example, and condemning a number of these case studies to the "Outtakes" section, I began with a look at Robert Downey Jr. The reason for that choice was two-fold: first, Downey Jr's career arc is as extreme as any Hollywood actor, alive *or* dead, and arguably even trumps Polanski's in its heights and depths; secondly, he is a true child of the movies.*

---

* Robert Downey Sr. was a cult filmmaker most famous for *Putney Swope* (1969), a successful underground film that Paul Thomas Anderson, Louis C.K., and Jim Jarmusch have all cited as an influence. The title character of *Putney Swope* is the only black man

In Downey Jr's first film role, at age five, he is locked inside a cage surrounded by adults. One of them kneels in front of him and tells him a story about being scared by a hurricane so badly he lost all the hair on his head. Little Downey responds: "Have any hair on your balls?"' This clip was played on *Jimmy Kimmel Live* in 2008 and got a big laugh.[1] Apparently the creepy, pedophile humor went unnoticed, though much can be read into Downey's rueful expression and momentary speechlessness, before he seems to give up and says only, "God bless my dad." The question of whether an adult has hair on his balls is one that would presumably be meaningless to a five-year-old, unless he had already been exposed to an adult's balls.[†]

After a few more early frolics with his father, already initiated into soft drug use, at age ten Downey was sent to the prestigious kids music training school Stagedoor Manor: "a recognized breeding ground for future Disney and musical theater stars" (Falk, p. 17). While there, as fellow camper Dina McLelland recalls it, young Robert "used to rub it in everybody's faces his dad was a producer and director. . . . He wasn't a nice kid. He had an attitude of being better than everybody else because of who his dad was. [H]e kind of isolated himself in some ways." (p. 19, 20).

---

on the executive board of an advertising firm; after the sudden death of the chairman, because board members aren't allowed to vote for themselves, the majority vote for the person they are sure will not win, and Swope is accidentally put in charge. He renames the business "Truth and Soul, Inc.," replaces all but one of the white employees with blacks, rejects business from any companies that produce alcohol, tobacco or toy guns, and eventually draws attention from the US government, who deem the company a threat to the national security.

* *Pound*, made in 1970, is based on an Off-Off-Broadway play written by Downey Sr. in 1961, about several dogs, a Siamese cat and a penguin, at a pound, waiting to be euthanized. The animals are played in the film by human actors.

† In either case (since Downey Sr. was putting lewd lines in his son's mouth), it's a case of very early sexualization. While this has (as far as I know) gone unremarked upon, what did receive an enormous amount of attention was how, a couple of years later, at age seven, Downey was given his first marijuana cigarette by his father. Growing up—he told *People* in 1996—"there was always a lot of pot and coke around. . . . When my dad and I would do drugs together. . . it was like him trying to express his love for me in the only way he knew how." "Hitting Bottom," by Tom Gliatto, *People*, Aug 19, 1996: https://people.com/archive/hitting-bottom-vol-46-no-8/

I had never heard of Stagedoor Manor before reading a Robert Downey Jr. bio, but it turns out it has a semi-legendary status within the industry, even while being almost unknown outside it. From a 2007 *New York Post* article:

> After 33 years in operation, Stagedoor Manor. . . has reached a critical mass in high-powered alumni: A-list actors, producers, directors, casting agents, managers—even showbiz lawyers and entertainment publicists. The result: a sprawling network *so tight and influential that alumni jokingly refer to it as a kind of mob.* "If someone plays that Stagedoor card, it's like whispering the location of a party with a secret location," says Shawn Levy, director of *Night at the Museum.* "I could sing you that song from the camp's yearly cabaret, and that's the equivalent of the secret handshake." . . . Alumni "quietly look out for each other and help each other," Rudin Pearson says. "It's a network that, for me, goes back 25 years—the type of network that, socially and professionally, you can't find anywhere else."[2]

Sort of like the Masons, then? In *The Power of Ritual in Prehistory*, Hayden explains the initial emergence of aggrandizer elites as occurring "preferentially under conditions of resource abundance [involving] a variety of strategies used to manipulate community opinions, values, surplus production, and surplus use."[3] Echoing Kenneth Tynan's theory of imposers, Hayden believes that aggrandizers have been successful in almost every sphere of human activity and, as a result, have shaped the early development of societies. Most intriguingly of all, Hayden (citing anthropologist David Hutton Webster) adds that some secret societies "*degenerated into social clubs, theatrical dance troupes* providing amusement, or fraternities with limited powers" (Hayden, p. 362, emphasis added). Ah, so. The more things degenerate, the more they stay the same.

There can be few cultural in-groups more dedicated—both overtly and covertly—to aggrandizement than Hollywood, and few more tacit acknowledgments of this than celebrity training camps. Author Mickey Rapkin describes Stagedoor Manor as "a summer camp but also an elite training ground for some of our nation's most talented young artists" (p. 7). Famous alumni besides Downey include Jennifer Jason Leigh, Natalie Portman, Helen Slater, Mary Stuart Masterson, Zach Braff, Jon Cryer, Bryce Dallas

Howard, Amy Ryan, and Adrienne Shelly. Bruce Willis and Richard Dreyfuss sent their kids there, as did Courtney Love.* Rapkin quotes singer-actress Mandy Moore: "I don't want to call it the Mafia. . . . It's more like a secret society." Hmm, OK; nothing to worry about then. Secret society, like, with rituals and initiations?

Playwright Jonathan Marc Sherman ("Things We Want") was expelled from the camp in 1986 at age seventeen, ostensibly for drinking hard liquor. While he was there, so he told the *New Yorker* in 2010, "The woman who was choreographing me in 'The Pajama Game' thankfully liberated me from my virginity."[4] The article also quotes playwright and female imperson-ator Charles Busch, who attended Stagedoor Manor's earlier incarnation, Beginners Showcase, in 1969 and 1970: "We were there when all the hot sex and drinking was going on. . . . I think they cleaned it up after we left. In 1970, of course, a lot of the counsellors were on dope. . . . It really was a microcosm of show business, with stars and wannabes and hangers-on . . . "

Another famous child prodigy who wound up at Stagedoor Manor (for all of nine weeks) was Bijou Phillips, the daughter of John Phillips of The Mamas & the Papas, the seducer of his nineteen-year-old daughter, Mackenzie (Bijou's half-sister). Bijou, the youngest of Phillips' children, grew up partly in foster care with a family in New York, making extended visits to her parents. Her father won custody of her when she was in third grade, and she moved with him to Long Island. It would have been around this time that she wound up at SM, age roughly ten. She was on the cover of *Interview* magazine at thirteen, was the youngest model to ever appear on the cover of *Vogue*'s Italian edition, and became a model for Calvin Klein in several advertising campaigns showing adolescents in white underwear. The campaign "was widely condemned as eerily pedophilic."[5] Her first major film role was in James Toback's *Black and White*, opposite other young-starters Robert Downey Jr., Jared Leto, Brooke Shields, and Elijah Wood. All part of the same network?[†]

---

* After sending her daughter there, Love crowed, "I wish I had a fucking Stagedoor when I was a child." Love grew up on a commune, spent time in reform school and became a stripper at age 16.

† Bijou overdosed on heroine at seventeen, ending up in rehab.

A worker at Stagedoor Manor described it, creepily, as "the island of lost toys. . . . Kids who were ignored. Kids who had no community in their high schools. They came to Stagedoor" (Rapkin, p. 130). Other, more powerful agents also came to this lost-and-found to assess and handle the toys: "So serious is the enterprise that New York casting directors and agents turn up on a regular basis [preferably] 'for dress rehearsals and workshops.'"[6] In other words, for more private "auditions."

It would be rash to come right out and suggest that Stagedoor Manor was a modern-day child brothel in the style of Louis Malle's *Pretty Baby*. But perhaps it's fair to wonder, if there *were* such places within the entertainment industry, mightn't they look and sound a lot like Stagedoor Manor? Omertà, indeed.*

4.2   SPARTAN TRAINING, ANCIENT AND MODERN

"We're all after love, aren't we? Love is what people are hungry for. That's absolutely why I became an actor."

—LEONARDO DICAPRIO[7]

Except for kid stars looking up to adult ones, movie stars presumably don't worship one another (though B-listers may look up to A-listers); so it's fair to ask, do celebrities even *believe* in the cult of celebrity once they have joined it? Does the CIA believe its own propaganda? Clearly, they believe in the necessity of these things. It's even possible, to some degree, as Douglas Valentine suggested in *The CIA as Organized Crime*, that the CIA *do* believe in their own propaganda because it's how they justify their actions *in their own eyes*:

---

* Canadian-American actress and author Alison Arngrim said it plainly: "Isn't it horrifying to say there's a casting couch for children and there is."
https://www.insideedition.com/investigative/5086-inside-edition-investigates-hollywood-pedophiles

The mindset of CIA officers and their media co-conspirators is the uni-
fying factor in this conspiracy. [They] truly believe the heroic myth that
they have created about themselves. Indeed, the "Myth of the Hero" has
informed Western literature and philosophy since the Greek elite paid
Homer to pen the Iliad and Odyssey, forever endowing the warrior class
with the highest social virtues, while justifying the tragic consequences of
their imperial marauding as "fate." Since then the theme of the warrior
hero has determined Western social development (p. 241).

Like movie stars giving a consummate performance of *being* movie
stars, there may be a method to the madness. Central to the myth of the war-
rior-hero, the man of violence as the savior of civilization, is the belief that
brutality is not only necessary for warriors to succeed, but also for warriors
to be made. Spartan warrior training in ancient Greece, for example, began,
like Jesuit training, at the age of seven. As Plutarch describes the procedure
(in *On Sparta*), male children were put under the charge of a slave tutor with
the authority to "punish them severely whenever they misbehaved," with "a
squad of young adults equipped with whips to administer punishment when
necessary." Spartan children were taught to steal but also punished with the
whip when they were caught, for the crime of incompetence. (Transgression
was encouraged, but so was discipline.) "[A] short period of pain," writes
Plutarch, "may be compensated by the enjoyment of long-lasting prestige"
(p. 196–7). Trainees

> learned to read and write no more than was necessary. Otherwise their
> whole education was aimed at developing smart obedience, perseverance
> under stress, and victory in battle. So as they grew older they intensi-
> fied their physical training, and got into the habit of cropping their hair,
> going barefoot, and exercising naked. From the age of twelve they never
> wore a tunic, and were given only one cloak a year. Their bodies were
> rough, and knew nothing of baths or oiling (p. 21).

Plutarch is somewhat coy about the question of sexual initiation at the
hands of older men: "men's love for boys," he writes, also "has some connection with their education" (p. 197). He chooses to be deliberately unclear
about what age this form of "education" began. Hayden notes of prehistoric

secret societies: "It was very common for children as young as four to six years old, and sometimes younger, to become members . . . especially if their parents were rich and high-ranking" (p. 292). The parallels between ancient Greek warrior cults and modern CIA-trained soldiers is easy enough to spot; but what of that between secret societies, Spartans, intelligence agencies, and movie stars and other celebrities? At first it may seem a reach, but we may find some surprising overlaps, both in the social and political utility of "ground agents," and in the manner in which future celebrities and culture makers are being "trained."

Research has shown that sexual trauma "sets body and mind into a tailspin of disorganization," and that victims of sexual abuse experience "the traumatic onslaught as a transgression of the self":

> Sexually traumatized children and adults feel stripped of their dignity and sense of control, and often reenact in feeling, thinking, and behavior the dissociated imprints of horrific, and loathsome memories. [This impacts] their bodies, minds, emotions, faith-based values, relationships, and cultural values. [It] deforms the personality [and imbeds] within the survivor a legacy of chronic, unrelenting, inescapable traumatic anxiety.[8]

A 2017 *Wall Street Journal* article cites a 1962 study[9] of celebrities revealing that less than 15% of them were raised in supportive, untroubled homes, while a full 75%—300 individuals—grew up in an environment that included "poverty, abuse, absent parents, alcoholism, serious illness or some other misfortune." "The 'normal man,' is not a likely candidate for the Hall of Fame," went the thesis. "If the Goertzels were to repeat their study today," the article affirms, "they would find many more examples of women and men who rose to great heights after difficult childhoods." The article refers to these types as "resilient people"—"women and men, in every walk of life, who meet the definition of resilience set forth by American Psychological Association: 'adapting well in the face of adversity, trauma, tragedy, threats or significant sources of stress.'"

> Coping with stress is a lot like exercise: We become stronger with practice. University of Nebraska psychologist Richard Dienstbier explains how this works with his "toughness model," first published in 1989 in

the journal *Psychological Review*. Dr. Dienstbier gathered evidence from a wide range of human and animal studies demonstrating that exposure to intermittent stressors, such as cold temperatures and aerobic exercise, made individuals physiologically "tougher." They became less overwhelmed by subsequent difficulties, and by their own fight-or-flight arousal. This makes a difference because when a stressor seems manageable, we perceive it as a challenge, and adrenaline—which boosts energy, focus and coping—is released. . . . What's more, Dr. Dienstbier wrote, toughened individuals increasingly seek out experiences that stimulate them and provide opportunities for more mastery and success. It is a virtuous circle.[10]

Less virtuous is the intentional application of trauma for negative reinforcement, as in the case of the "operant conditioning" developed by B.F. Skinner and ruthlessly applied by Ewen Cameron and innumerable other MKULTRA "doctors." What I wish to underscore here is that what psychically destroys ninety-nine children may bestow *unique benefits* on the one for whom the programming "takes." In these special cases, the crippling effects of trauma—the transgression-destruction of a core sense of self—may be inseparable, even indistinguishable, from the engendering of *special charismatic abilities*.

To cite a well-known historical example, castrati, eunuch singers, date back to ancient Sumer and existed in the West from the early Byzantine Empire (which followed the fall of Rome, in the 5th century AD). Castrati were castrated, either before puberty or in its earliest stages, to prevent the changes in the larynx caused by puberty. The vocal range of prepubescence was thereby retained, and the voice developed into adulthood in a unique way. The lack of testosterone meant the bone-joints of castrati did not harden and the bones of their ribs often grew unusually long, giving the castrati unusual lung-power. Castrati were rarely referred to as such, however, and in the 18th century, *musici* was the preferred euphemism.

In the case of the sort of "hands-on" traumatic conditioning which someone like Michael Jackson was subjected to, there is the added "benefit" (for the abuser-trainer) of forging a special bond between the traumatized "operant" and his or her "trainer," whether child celebrities and their parents, or the Spartans with their slave tutors:

Necessary conditions for traumatic bonding are that "one person must dominate the other and that the level of abuse chronically spikes and then subsides . . . periods of permissive, compassionate, and even affectionate behavior from the dominant person [are] punctuated by intermittent episodes of intense abuse." The balance of dominance and submission is maintained by "an escalating cycle of punishment ranging from seething intimidation to intensely violent outbursts." The victim is isolated from other sources of support, which "strengthens the sense of unilateral dependency."[11]

4.3   WHAT DOESN'T KILL YOU: CASE STUDY # 6, MICHAEL JACKSON

"America invented the movies so it would never need to grow up."

—J.G. BALLARD, *Millennium People*

When the four-hour HBO documentary *Leaving Neverland* was released in 2019, it presented compelling testimonials from two adults, Wade Robson and James Safechuck, who claimed to have been sexually groomed and abused by Michael Jackson from the ages of seven and ten, respectively. Their testimonials were persuasive and supported by a body of circumstantial evidence regarding Jackson's painfully neurotic personality traits and lifelong interest in, and affinity for, prepubescent boys. Jackson's own abuse at the hands of his father, growing up as part of the Jackson Five, only added to the likelihood of his having developed sexual pathologies as an adult. Jackson often spoke of how his abuse at the hands of his father was so vicious that even thinking about him made him feel sick. His father's "explanation" for the abuse was as an extreme form of "tough love"—necessary to ensure Jackson's success as a musician.[12]

What makes this especially disturbing is that there's no way to avoid, exactly, the fact that, at some level, Joe Jackson's violent methodology was effective. Or that Michael Jackson's resulting fame and wealth empowered him to commit his own abuses, in a desperate attempt to reclaim the childhood he never had. It was also what allowed him to avoid the consequences of those actions while he was alive, even when they did come to light. This first happened in 1993–94, when charges were made by 13-year-old Jordan Chalder, and settled out of court; then in 2005, when Jackson was charged with molesting 13-year-old cancer patient Gavin Arvizo and found not guilty.

Despite all of this, and despite how damning many people found the documentary to be (myself included, though I was never a Jackson fan), legions of his followers rose up to defend Jackson's memory. They claimed the documentary was blatantly one-sided, that it deliberately distorted certain facts, and that the two main witnesses (who had sworn under oath regarding Jackson's innocence while he was alive) were lying opportunistically. Some of the more proactive Jackson fans demanded the Sundance Film Festival cancel the premiere of the film, and Robson and Safechuck claimed they received death threats when they attended. There were protests outside the UK Channel 4's office, an internet campaign was mounted against the film, and a crowdfunded advertising campaign insisted on Jackson's innocence with the slogan "Facts don't lie. People do" on buses and bus stops.[13]

In a 2019 article on Kieran Culkin (Macaulay's brother, and star of HBO's *Succession*), *The Guardian* drew attention to how brazen Jackson was about his proclivities ten years after the first legal action against him, and specifically mentioned Kieran: "I have slept in a bed with many children," Jackson told Martin Bashir in 2003. "I slept in a bed with all of them when Macaulay Culkin was little. Kieran Culkin would sleep on this side, Macaulay Culkin was on this side. We all would just jam in the bed."

> Culkin shifts uncomfortably, but he has seen the question coming—he tells me that he realized I would ask him about Jackson before the interview. He points out that he doesn't have media training, signaling that what follows hasn't been publicist-approved. "The only thing I can say is that I can't really say anything and the reason for that is I can't be helpful to anyone," he says earnestly. "To me, it seems like there's two sides to this thing and because I can't be helpful on one side or the other, anything I say and anything that gets put out in print could only hurt somebody and there's already a lot of really hurt feelings. There are already a lot of people who are in a difficult position and if I contribute in any way, it's just going to hurt someone because I can't actually help."

Not bad for someone with no media-training. Listen between the lines and what you may hear is: "Nothing I say on this will be helpful to my career." True enough. The article also points out some parallels between the Culkins' and Jackson's own background: Kieran's "childhood wasn't without its setbacks. His father, Kit, was an unsuccessful actor who brought up his eight children to be performers whether they liked it or not, all of them living in a boxy railway apartment in New York."[14]

In 2005, Macaulay Culkin denied any "inappropriate behavior" at the time.[15] Corey Feldman, a friend of Jackson since a child, also claimed that Jackson never approached him sexually and called the *Leaving Neverland* documentary "one-sided." Backpedaling, he subsequently added that he hadn't meant "in any way to question the validity of the victims."[16] Barbra Streisand's defense of Jackson was perhaps the most emphatic: "his sexual needs were his sexual needs," she said, "coming from whatever childhood he has or whatever DNA he has. . . . You can say 'molested,' but those children . . . were thrilled to be there. They both married and they both have children, so it didn't kill them."[17] Insider subtext: ergo, it made them stronger.*

Living legends flocked together to defend a fallen warrior. Diana Ross tweeted, "This is what's on my heart this morning. I believe and trust that Michael Jackson was and is a magnificent incredible force to me and to many others. STOP IN THE NAME OF LOVE."[18] Madonna criticized the "lynch-mob mentality," and warned that "people are innocent until proven guilty."[19] She questioned *Leaving Neverland*'s intentions, saying, "What's the agenda? What do people want out of this? Are there people asking for money, is there some kind of extortion thing happening?"[20] Ironically, whatever monetary compensation Robson and Safechuck received, and despite a general backlash against Jackson in the media, the documentary also caused a significant increase in his music sales.[21]

---

* For the inside scoop on Streisand as MKULTRA subject, seek out the edited material from *16 Maps of Hell*, as provided to contributors to the fundraiser campaign, or contact the author directly.

4.4   LET'S TALK ABOUT LOVE

"The mission statement is about the individual. It's about power, and powering over."

—MIKE MYERS, 2017, in *The King*

Countless people claim to love Michael Jackson, but what does it *mean*? Through immersion in an artist's work, we come to feel as if we have an intimate relationship with them *through* their work. The fact the celebrity has never laid eyes on us or heard our names, has no feelings about us whatsoever, while it may cause frustration and longing, does nothing to diminish that love for many people. If we have our own distant-parent issues, it may only increase it. But is it really possible to love someone we have never met? The love we experience *may* be real, in some sense; but the object we are directing it towards is not a real flesh and blood person, but an image manufactured by mass media.

Following the release of *Leaving Neverland, The Guardian* noted, "one of the most popular questions . . . sparked is whether people can still listen to Jackson's music." While the writer of the piece dismisses this concern as "a profoundly unhelpful and narcissistic approach to the issue," I think it's actually *the* central question, because the only reason people are talking about Jackson's crimes—and the only reason he was able to commit them in the way that he did—is because of the effect his music had on millions of people. The article is not wrong, however, when it points out how "despite the detailed allegations, so many fans and even some fellow musicians still defend him and refuse to believe his accusers [because] they're resentful at the prospect of losing his music."[22] Since the fans and fellow musicians are not in danger of *actually* losing the music (no one has proposed destroying Jackson's albums or archives), the loss in question is one of *association*.

Jackson fans do not want to be forced, when they listen to his music, to ponder the possibility that their idol was masturbating behind naked prepubescent boys or having them jam their fingers up his anus. For many, this kind of association might stretch the limits of their devotion past the breaking point. When a long-term, one-sided love affair ends in guilt, shame, and disgust, even rage and hatred, it can precipitate a crisis of meaning. As an indication of the lengths fans will go to avoid such a crisis, several groups of them have filed lawsuits against Safechuck and Robson, for a symbolic amount of one euro. The suit was filed in France, where it's illegal to make criminal accusations against the deceased. "I know that it is not possible," one of them said, "It was rotten. It was to make a buzz. It was to make money." "He had a great heart," said another. "It is not right to make these claims against someone who isn't even alive to defend themselves."[23]

How much easier must it be for these devoted fans to double down on their devotion than to seriously examine the evidence? "If it was genuine," said another, "their parents would have said something. The two accusers defended him when he was alive and they are known to have lied in the past." Having learned the Jackson alibi, line for line, they can repeat it like a mantra whenever needed, and keep on believing. "I just don't think Michael was capable of doing something like that . . . He was just very childlike and he spent his time playing with children because he was the boy who never grew up, that's why he was nicknamed Peter Pan."[24]

How is this not complicity? Peter Pan presided over *the lost boys*, and somewhere on the slippery sliding scale between the boy-who-never-grew-up and the Child Catcher—the predator of *Chitty Chitty Bang Bang*—there's an unconscious adoption of the kind of moral relativity espoused by Streisand and Madonna. It begins with "He didn't do it (I know because I love him)" and moves swiftly on to, "Innocent until proven guilty," and "We can't *prove* he did it." From there, it is a small step to blaming the victims as liars and opportunists. The final step is to imply—or outright state, as Streisand did— that they asked for it and that it didn't kill them, so what's the fuss? Since it didn't kill them, it only made them richer and more famous. As it happens, this was Joe Jackson's rationalization for abusing *his* children (with special abuse for Michael): "Joe justified the abuse of his children by saying he was helping them to achieve fame and wealth, just as so many parents would later justify pushing their children into Jackson's clearly unhealthy orbit by telling themselves they were helping their children on to the path of celebrity."[25]

It's easy to imagine a perpetual tape loop, just below the threshold of the Jackson fan's consciousness (ditto with the parents of the children he abused): "Michael would never do this and the people accusing him are only in it for the money. They weren't actually harmed by it and probably asked for it in the first place. It doesn't matter if he did it, all that matters is that I love him." Without going too much into my own personal history (especially since I have already done so elsewhere), I know firsthand how this sort of divided loyalty and cognitive-emotional dissonance is characteristic of abuse victims. I was never able to separate my love for my brother from admiration for him and the desire to emulate him, or from my fear and resentment of him. It was all one tangled up knot inside me. To some degree it still is. Integral to this knot is my incapacity to fully "own" (or remember) whatever occurred between us, when I was an infant and a small child.

Perhaps the most toxic part in all of this is what is smuggled in, via the elaborate machinations and rationalizations of the superculture (in this case the Jackson Estate and the legions of fans): the belief that, to sexually abuse children doesn't actually *harm* them in any lasting way, and that, in fact, it potentially makes them stronger—as well as more charismatic, driven, and gifted. A short period of pain is compensated for by the enjoyment of long-lasting prestige. Any moral questions are cancelled out by Jackson's (or whoever's) enduring musical legend and legacy—just as victory for the Spartans justified the torments of their training.

The main issue then becomes: whatever comes to light, whatever the truth might be about the King of Pop, we who have staked our claims in Neverland never, ever have to leave.

4.5   A SECRET COVENANT

> "It would appear that a lot of people out there are hiding their own dark, socially unacceptable sexual fantasies behind a facade of fake indignant outrage when someone else gets caught with their pants down."
>
> —OLIVER MARKUS MALLOY, *Why Creeps Don't Know They're Creeps*

With the Scumbag-Superstar dyad under examination in cases like Roman Polanski, John Huston, Robert Evans, Michael Jackson, or (still to come) Leonard Cohen, two ideological narratives are pitted against each other. Cultural indoctrination tells us that certain behaviors are unacceptable and must be punished. Yet the same culture that has indoctrinated us has raised up certain individuals and granted them with a power and a freedom consistent with their influence, thereby placing them beyond our reproach. From Hayden's *Power of Ritual in Prehistory*:

> In order to protect themselves against popular resistance, reprisals, or push backs, and to act with impunity, I think that those claiming political or supernatural powers typically maintained resolute claims that they only acted for the good of the community. In addition, they banded together and ensured that their confrères were among the most powerful people in the community (e.g., heads or successful members of kin groups), thereby creating a triple defense: a validating ideological rhetoric, safety in numbers, and safety from powerful individual members backed by their kinship groups (p. 343).

To maintain the illusion of a benign culture, it's easy to see why those who are seen to be breaking taboos need to be removed *post-haste*, not only from positions of power and influence (for "our" protection), but from our already existing artifacts, since to be reminded of them only sours our experience of culture and makes it unpalatable. But of course, they are removed by people in similar positions of power and influence whose *peccadilloes* have not (yet) been exposed and who thereby affirm their own virtue. The interesting thing with Michael Jackson is that his fame, his centrality to the culture, combined with being dead and so beyond castigation, have combined to make his musical oeuvre more or less untouchable, keeping his artistic reputation *somewhat* intact. This is because, while the individual may not be above reproach, the institution he represents (and that bestowed his wealth and power upon him) is, and must always remain so. (No one really tried to hold the BBC or the NHS accountable for Jimmy Savile.)

Soon after the Harvey Weinstein scandal broke (see Outtake # 3, page 463), the UK *Daily Mail* claimed that Weinstein saw himself as "a savior who was born to be accused of sex assault in order to 'change the world.' . . . Sources close to the shamed producer said he has resigned himself to being punished over the allegations 'as a martyr for social change.'"[26] Weinstein's "defense" potentially opened the floodgates for a whole old/new paradigm: praise the sinners, for only through sin does grace come into the world. Totem and taboo. As political activist and novelist Gilad Atzmon wrote[27]:

> Weinstein could be seen as a follower of Rabbi Sabbatai Zevi, who declared himself the Messiah in 1666. Zevi proclaimed that redemption was available through acts of sin and he amassed a following of over one million passionate believers, about half the world's Jewish population during the 17th century. The shift from total sinner into the new messiah figure was certainly rapid for serial predator Weinstein. But this shouldn't take us by surprise. Weinstein's regard for himself as a "martyr for social change" is consistent with Tikun Olam—the misguided Jewish belief that it is down to the Jews to repair the world. I guess we are witnessing a radical shift in the world of criminal defense. Jeffrey Epstein could just claim that in retrospective, he helped to raise awareness of child prostitution. Israel can say in its defense that its history of crimes against humanity made it into a martyr for social justice proving how lethal choseness and chosenism are. But, could Jimmy Saville do the same? What about Stalin? Let us push it even further, could Hitler apply the same strategy in his defense? Is he eligible to become an anti racism martyr? I'll let you ponder that one.*

It might seem odd to suggest that Harvey Weinstein (or Kevin Spacey, who was outed and blacklisted in the same period, see Outtake # 4, on page 467) could be a "scapegoat," since the word implies innocence and there's no reason to presume innocence on his part (on the contrary). Normally,

---

* Weinstein's (unconfirmed) philosophical defense was accompanied by an equally covert, and considerably more proactive, strategic defense. According to Ronan Farrow in the *New Yorker*, Weinstein hired the British-Israeli private intelligence firm Black Cube to suppress the publication of abuse allegations. Using false identities, private investigators from Black Cube tracked and met journalists and actresses, in particular Rose McGowan, who accused Weinstein of rape. Weinstein had Black Cube and other agencies "'target,' or collect information on, dozens of individuals, and compile psychological profiles that sometimes focused on their personal or sexual histories." Farrow, Ronan, "Harvey Weinstein's Army of Spies," *New Yorker*, November 6, 2017: https://www.newyorker.com/news/news-desk/harvey-weinsteins-army-of-spies

a scapegoat is selected (usually unconsciously) as a means to unify a group, and central to that is the agreement about the person's guilt. The consensus of condemnation brings with it a declaration, not only of solidarity but of innocence. This depends on the scapegoat already being an apparent outsider, however (as in the recent case of the ritual hunt and assassination of Osama Bin Laden); so what happens when the guilty party is an *insider*, within a social set in which the majority are *complicit* with his or her crimes?

Whether it's the complicity of looking the other way or the complicity of committing similar or worse acts, in cases such as Weinstein or Spacey, the moral condemnation from Hollywood insiders may be merely *a strategy* that has nothing do to with genuine distaste or outrage. It may be necessary precisely *because* these behaviors are practiced, or at least known about, by the majority within the Hollywood community. Condemnation signals to those on the outside that the community is self-policing and that such behaviors are not the norm. In the case of Jackson, the brightness of his star, above all (more than the paucity of evidence against him), may have emboldened musical luminaries such as Streisand, Diana Ross, and Madonna to risk signaling their complicity with the crimes, thereby acknowledging that the entertainment industry *does*, in fact, condone such behaviors.

If people hiss at Streisand and Madonna for their moral emptiness, or, on the other side of the moral divide, if they believe Matt Damon or George Clooney when they express shock and outrage at the Weinsteins or the Spaceys, it is not only because they want to but because they *need* to. For if the process of accounting continues for too long, who will be left to uphold the Pantheon? What would remain of our nightly rituals after the factory closes, and what becomes of the worshipers when all the idols have fallen?

If the role models that have been created for us as the basis for identification and imitation are acting in ways our moral conditioning tells us are wrong, either we lose our idols—and in the end, the entire value system that raised them up—or we must radically rethink what constitutes morally acceptable behavior. It's a classic double bind, and at base is the fact that our social values about what constitutes success—what count as desirable and meaningful life goals—are inherently at odds with our sense of what constitutes decent or sane human behavior. This is the conundrum it has taken me some forty years to start to see. Precisely because my values were partially incepted in me by Hollywood, I found myself pursuing goals that, at a conscious level, I knew to be vacuous. But because those values were operating at a preconscious level, I have been helpless to act upon that knowledge, powerless to turn away.

4.6   FALSE PROPHETS

> "In the houses of the inheritors the preservation of the
> community is paramount, and it is . . . in this tropism toward
> survival that Hollywood sometimes presents the appearance of
> the last extant stable society."
>
> —JOAN DIDION, *"In Hollywood"*

If mimesis or imitation is one of the foundations of society, ancient and modern, then Hollywood makes not just an art form but an industry, even an entire culture, out of imitation. It manufactures and replicates ways of being and thereby provides relief—even if the relief of fantasy—during increasingly instable social conditions. Liminal times—times of rapid social change in which the future is increasingly unknown—lead to increased mimesis, and the demand for idealized image-leaders to guide us—stars to navigate by—increases . This is from *Liminality and the Modern: Living Through the In-Between*, by Bjørn Thomassen:

> If rites of passage contain a chaotic, void-like liminal stage, then there must be something or somebody standing outside this void to guide people out of it. In anthropology, this figure is called the master of ceremonies. But what happens in liminal situations when there is no designated master of ceremonies? The short answer is that someone will invent himself as such, and present himself as possessing the key to law and order (p. 103–4).

Outside of rituals, when we are existing and seeking direction within the much larger social scale of "the global village," the future becomes increasingly unknown the greater the number of variables we are made aware of. Since there is no clear ritual to history with beginning or end, there can be no ceremony masters, because no one has gone through any given historical or cultural phase before, and there is no one to lead us out of it. This leads to the emergence of *false* ceremony masters to fill the void created by our need to be guided. As Thomassen (after anthropologist Victor Turner) writes, these "self-proclaimed ceremony masters" claim to "have seen the future," and they "establish their own position by perpetuating liminality and by emptying the liminal moment from real creativity, turning it into a sense of mimetic rivalry" (p 210).* They are false prophets who see the future and call it murder.

In Western movies, when villains take over the town, the people call on a violent man who doesn't belong there to save the community. There seems a similar sort of paradox built into how we look to celebrity artists and performers as "ceremony masters" to rescue us from the mundane anxiety of our liminal existence, to lead us through the confusion and chaos and lift us up to a "loftier" or more elevated station in life. When a movie star plays the villain, as Kevin Spacey did in *House of Cards*, he is still our hero. We are conditioned by the manufactured myths, from Homer on down, to believe that what we need to save our community is not a good man but a strong man. By this means—those of perpetuating liminality—we are deceived by the falseness of the prophet. It may be a small step from here to believing Harvey Weinstein's one-size-fits-all defense: That the monsters who rule us are saints, martyrs to our own ignorance. They are the insiders and we are on the outside, clambering to get in. We are in no positon to judge.

Even when our icons commit what we regard as atrocities, we look to them for inspiration, support, and leadership. Why else would we want to hear what movie stars have to say about endemic sexual abuse in Hollywood? Why would we still believe a word they say? Entertainment celebrities—stars—may represent our last bastion of belief in our culture as something solid, lasting, and benign. Artists, musicians, filmmakers, movie stars: surely *they* can be trusted to lead us from despair? They are *escape*

---

* Mimetic rivalry is closely tied to the psychosocial mechanism of "the double-bind," as incorporated by Gregory Bateson into the application of the schismogenesis principle for social control (see 5.4).

artists, after all, and it was *our* love that lifted them up in the first place (or so we choose to believe).

Though love is not really the word for it, celebrities *are* both animated and raised up by the collective energy of *focused awareness or attention*. Elevating a single individual to a high social plateau over the collective—via a fanbase, electorate, or audience cult—is central to the way Western civilization is structured. Democracy tells us we *are* individuals—and obliges us to act that way—but by its very nature the collective mass can't exist as individuals. Its existence depends on our allegiance to the idea of it, and that allegiance, paradoxically, prevents us from *becoming* individuals.

Democracy tells us we are all equal and that we must *conform* to the notion of individuality. This paradox—or internal contradiction—gives rise of necessity to the idea of meritocracy, the belief that exceptional individuals rise to the surface and *rule*. This is an undemocratic notion, but the magician's circle is squared by the belief that the ruling/celebrity class is installed by, of, and for the people. But since the ruling class, not the people, determines who gets raised up, what happens in lieu of meritocracy is that certain individuals are selected by the cryptocracy to maintain order over the masses. In order for this to happen, they require the energy and attention (the support) of the collective to "animate" them.

So what if the stars above us are diamond-hard sociopaths whose success depends on *an artful simulation of goodness*? Not only are we the products of this same sociopathic superculture, our "gods" have only been able to shape it and ascend within it via our consent and support—our "love." Our loyalty and dependency ensures we can't *help* but aspire to the same wealth, power, fame, influence, and social status, even *against* our conscious will, no matter how much we may want to condemn those who have attained it and abused it. Since there is nothing else on offer, when the Hollywood bell rings, we salivate.

When Kevin Spacey made a video in 2018 in which he pretended to be pretending to be Frank Underwood, the character he played in *House of Cards* before he was erased from the show for alleged crimes of sexual harassment and abuse,[28] no one seemed to know the exact purpose or meaning of the act. Spacey seemed to be addressing the real-life charges *as if they were part of a fictional scenario*—which for all we could know for sure, they *might* have been. By making the video, Spacey was willingly entering into a parasocial interaction with his audience, presumably in the hope of restoring his image and increasing his social capital. The strange artifact divided audiences down the middle, between condemnation and support. Mirrors within mirrors.

The same people who wonder at the naiveté of a small-town teenage girl traveling to Hollywood to make it big and ending up as a crack whore on Hollywood Blvd (more or less the storyline of David Lynch's *Mulholland Drive*), also go to mainstream movies and listen to movie stars talking about how they are going to save the environment. They aspire to have their scripts bought (as I did, and still do) or their novels adapted into movies, and so on. All the evidence in the world doesn't count for much if no one takes the time to *look* at it. It is so much more compelling to gaze at images on the screen, at the beautiful people, than to focus on the minutiae of decay creeping through their flesh and bones. A little old man behind a curtain will never capture our attention the way a hundred-foot fire-breathing wizard does.

The most useful metaphor here is perhaps Oscar Wilde's famous story, *The Picture of Dorian Gray*, in which a dissolute young man of great wealth has a portrait done of him, a portrait that supernaturally absorbs all his decadent behaviors. While the portrait becomes ever more uglified and putrid, he remains as young, beautiful, and glamourous as ever. And it is beauty—the skin-deep kind—that persuades us of goodness, truth, or innocence. This is why the plastic surgery industry soars in Hollywood. Hollywood is like the reverse of Dorian Gray's portrait: the movies, the mass media representation, give us a glittering image of eternal youth. But if we look closely at the stars, the filmmakers, at the producers, executives, and studio heads, we may glimpse a horrendous, dead-eyed visage staring back.

5

CONSPIRACY THEORY

5.1.   A FALSE DICHOTOMY
(WHAT SOME CALL CONSPIRACY)

> "In the great chess-board of human society, every single piece
> has a principle of motion of its own, altogether different from
> that which the legislature might choose to impress upon it. If
> those two principles coincide and act in the same direction, the
> game of human society will go on easily and harmoniously, and
> is very likely to be happy and successful. If they are opposite or
> different, the game will go on miserably, and the society must be
> at all times in the highest degree of disorder."
>
> —ADAM SMITH, *The Theory Of Moral Sentiments*

In presenting the evidence of what looks a lot like a worldwide, eons-long conspiracy to enslave the human race, I am acutely aware of walking an ideological and cognitive tightrope. If *16 Maps of Hell is* a conspiracy theory of history, it is also an *anti*-conspiracy theory. The aim of mapping Hell is every bit as much to expose the fundamental errors of popular (or populist) conspiracy theory (whether "RussiaGate" of the liberal mainstream, or QAnon and *Info Wars* of the so-called "Alt-Right") as the lie of conventional history. This book is a map of an ongoing excavation project whose aim is to explore the intersection between the entertainment industry and "deep state" politics, while at the same time bridging the gulf between rigorous sociological, historical, and anthropological research and what's been both sold to us and rubbished for us as "conspiracy theory."

The Oxford dictionary defines the word conspiracy as: "A secret plan by a group to do something unlawful or harmful." Widely speaking, the three main ingredients of conspiracy are collectivity, criminality, and secrecy. Of these three, only the first can be considered absolute because both criminality and secrecy are relative terms that depend on your point of view. This is especially so when the crimes in question cross national borders and hence definitions of what constitutes crime versus what constitutes justified acts of war or espionage. Many acts that are crimes for the rest of us are legally sanctioned under the National Security Act, an idea popularized by (British intelligence agent) Ian Fleming's 007, with his "license to kill." (Bond is a killer, but not a criminal.)

It's been a long time since the word "conspiracy" was simply a neutral descriptor, however. Since the 1960s (courtesy of the CIA, as we'll see), it has been associated with the word "theory" and thereby, for several decades, with crackpots and paranoids. In the last decade or more, the words have become increasingly linked to *dangerous* crackpots and paranoids (Pizzagate shooters and Unabombers), as well as to antisocial extremists (Sandy Hook deniers), right-wing hate criminals, anti-Semites, holocaust deniers, and neo-Nazis. As Floyd Rudmin writes, in "Conspiracy Theory as Naive Deconstructive History":

> The power of this pejorative is that it discounts a theory by attacking the motivations and mental competence of those who advocate the theory. By labeling an explanation of events "conspiracy theory," evidence and argument are dismissed because they come from a mentally or morally deficient personality, not because they have been shown to be incorrect.[1]

The most recent guilty association of conspiracy theory is perhaps the most unexpected of all: in the days of the Donald Trump administration, "conspiracy theories" have become linked to *state power* of the most deplorable kind: dangerously right-wing, extremist, antisocial, wing-nut neo-fascists running—and ruining—Western society. The word conspiracy, then, is an example of how words are increasingly losing their meaning while at the same time accruing a disproportionate amount of power. It even seems as though they may be gaining power *as* they lose all meaning—quite an Orwellian development in and of itself.

◆

> "It might, however, be the case that coming up with a label for the phenomenon actually invents the phenomenon itself, in the sense that a new conceptual category turns what otherwise would have been a set of possibly quite diverse ideas into a coherent style of thought. . . . One thing that makes the historical study of conspiracy theories particularly challenging, then, is that determining what constitutes the phenomenon has become part of the phenomenon itself."
>
> —PETER KNIGHT, *Conspiracy Theories in American History*

There is a mindset shared by both conspiracy theorists and conspiracy debunkers or skeptics. This doesn't apply to *all* conspiracy theorists or debunkers, but those who do share this mindset seem to be in the majority. Ironically, they may have more in common with each other than differences. As a writer-researcher into long-term, deep-state social engineering (including occult or secret society aspects), I have often been met with blanket arguments from serious-minded, intelligent, and informed individuals claiming that they do not "believe" in a "grand conspiracy" or in "puppet masters" working behind the scenes. This opinion (you cannot call it an argument) is (or seems to be) genuinely offered as a response, not to any claim I have made that there *is* a grand, unified conspiracy or group of puppet masters, but only to the suggestion that *some* historical events or social trends might have come into being via conscious, partially concealed manipulations.

Peter Knight (editor of *Conspiracy Theories in American History*) sums this up in the introduction to his thousand-page encyclopedia, citing the well-known author of *The Paranoid Style in American Politics*, Richard Hofstadter, who, he writes,

> recognized that there have indeed been actual conspiracies here or there in U.S. history, but that a conspiracy theorist believes that there is "a 'vast' or 'gigantic' conspiracy as the motive force in historical events"

(Hofstadter, 29). According to this kind of view, conspiracy theory is more than just the odd speculation about clandestine causes; it is *a way of looking at the world and historical events that sees conspiracies as the motor of history.* [Emphasis added.]

Knight goes on to identify—I think correctly—"one of the important functions of conspiracy theory today, namely questioning how much we are in control of our own minds and our own actions through the debate over exactly what is to count as a conspiracy or not" (p. 17). This suggests that an *anti*-conspiracy position is really a *philosophical* (or even ideological) position rather than a historical or factual one. This is supported by my own experience with people who take such a position: they tend to reject *the idea* of long-term, organized conspiracies, *ipso facto*, not on a case-by-case basis but on *principle*. In the same way, a rational reductionist rejects the idea of the supernatural, possibly for the same or similar reasons, and on similarly shaky grounds. In "Agency Panic" (*Conspiracy Nation*, p. 69–70), Timothy Melley writes this:

> If the sense that there are no accidents—that everything is connected, intended, and meaningful—is a hallmark of paranoia, then the difference between a paranoid theory and a brilliant theory may only be a matter of how much explanatory power the theory has for a given interpretive community. And if this is so, then the work of sorting out paranoid claims from justifiable claims—the work of diagnosing, pathologizing, and normalizing—will require a vision at least as penetrating as the one to be judged.

Curiously enough, many people who *do* advocate for a "grand conspiracy" fall into exactly the same trap as those who dismiss the idea: they extrapolate prematurely from certain sets of evidence the existence of a single, cohesive group and agenda behind long-term social engineering strategies (the Illuminati, the Masons, the Jews, etc.). In both cases—whether the philosophical position is to believe or to deny—a perceived order, direction, and design is *literalized*, in much the same way that religious people literalize the evidence of a divine order into hierarchies of angels, gods, and demons.

Nor is this comparison arbitrary, because the religious (especially Christian) belief in demonic forces manipulating human behavior is an almost precise match for the more contemporary, secular belief in malevolent human agencies doing the same. While this is often used to dismiss conspiracy theorists and their various forms of historical revisionism, it might just as well (and perhaps more accurately) be used as a means of *validation.*

The reason I say this is that human beings may have always been aware of *a hidden factor* that makes agency, individuality, and human history radically different than it appears to our conscious minds. What vary may only be the terms in which we attempt to *re-cognize* this fact.

5.2.   CONSPIRACY-THEORY-AS-SCAPEGOATING

> "The British . . . struck me as so disoriented by the sophisticated, eloquent spin of the New Labor government led by Tony Blair that they could no longer see the ground on which to plant their feet. More serious than systematically misinforming them, their government had steadily eroded the conditions for political judgment. In doing so, it not only denied them the evidence with which to assess this or that claim: it undermined what is necessary for the sound application of the concept of evidence."
>
> —RAIMOND GAITA, *"Even Socrates drew the line at spin"*

The problem that the serious, honest, and sincere conspiracy investigator faces is that all of this premature and poorly executed dot-joining, speculation, wild theorizing, and deliberate disinformation has now severely tainted the data. Due to an almost instant association with "crazy" narratives being spun around it, even referring to a salient fact may lead to accusations of belief in said narratives, quickly followed by smug dismissal—not only of the data being raised but of the person raising it. Bingo, subject dismissed. All of this may or may not be the result of deliberate design. Floyd Rudmin again:

> Conspiracy theory is "deconstructive history" because it is in rebellion against official explanations and against orthodox journalism and orthodox history. Conspiracy theory is radically empirical: tangible facts are the focus, especially facts that the standard stories try to overlook. There

is a ruthless reduction down to what is without doubt real, namely, persons. Conspiracy theory presumes that human events are caused by people acting as people do, including cooperating, planning, cheating, deceiving, and pursuing power.[2]

Rudmin points out how "Conspiracy theories arise when dramatic events happen, and the orthodox explanations try to diminish the events and gloss them over," and "when someone notices that the explanations do not fit the facts." Significant political or economic events change power relationships in society; contradictions in the official explanations of these events are noticed by ordinary citizens, leading to the deduction of power abuse and deception. Further information is sought to make the narratives being spun more coherent and expose the deceptions and power abuses. "Most of the evidence discovered is circumstantial, as it must be when investigating conspiracies."

> Conspiracy theory has a special focus on contradictions, discrepancies, and missing facts. The natural sciences similarly seek to find faulty explanations by focusing on facts that don't fit the orthodox explanations. If we want more truthful explanations of events, whether of scientific events or of political and historical events, then we must compare competing explanations. One explanation usually fits the available observations better than the other. By the principle of fit, the explanation that encompasses more of the observations should be preferred. This principle can favor conspiracy theories. . . . It is true that conspiracy theory authors doubt the orthodox explanations and suspect that there are other explanations for events. Such doubt and suspicion, which is the same kind of doubt and suspicion as motivates many scientific discoveries, gets labeled paranoia.

Rudmin prefers the term naïve to paranoid, which is fair enough. (It's often been said that "you can't be too paranoid," but it's hard to imagine the same being said about an excess of naivety.) Literalizing an observable pattern into an actual group and a unified conspiracy is naïve, but it's also understandable. As Sigmund Freud once pointed out, the human mind has a low tolerance threshold for ambiguity.[3] It clutches at straws in order to avoid drowning in uncertainty. Yet the very nature of crimes covertly committed by groups, and of fake narratives being spun to conceal them, involves the proliferation of ambiguity and uncertainty.

The problem with naïve or premature pattern-recognition is that it prevents us from allowing a pattern to remain *a sequence of effects* that can be traced to an array of individuals, groups, and agendas who may or may not be working in cahoots (and may or may not be conscious of what they are doing). This inevitably concretizes an "other" that: a) can be distinguished from oneself; and b) can be blamed for all of the effects (generally seen as negative and undesirable). This sets up a scapegoat, a "diabolic figure" upon whom all the world's ills can be blamed.

In my experience, it's quite common to find people arguing against a "conspiratorial" view of history for the second reason only, i.e., on ideological grounds. They will argue that scapegoating is a problem and that any interpretation of the evidence that isolates a single group or agenda as being responsible for the world's problems must be wrong because it amounts to scapegoating. This comes close to the sort of ideological "reasoning" that's increasingly prevalent today, such as for example the argument that, since claiming obesity is bad for one's health might strengthen a social prejudice against fat people, it is not a credible argument. Or that suggesting a person's homosexuality could be traced back to childhood trauma is *ipso facto* homophobic.* And so on. By this reasoning, conclusions should not be evaluated according to how well they match the evidence, but how socially, morally, or ideologically "correct" they are.

Since there *is* a natural tendency in human beings to seek out scapegoats, it *is* wise to apply a degree of caution when approaching evidence for "grand conspiracies." As Melley writes:

---

* Incidentally, even the word "homophobic" is misleading, firstly because it generally refers to people with a hatred of homosexuals and not a fear of them; secondly because the word *homophobic* actually means, or should, a fear of sameness, just as heterophobia means a fear of difference. This is another—even more socially explosive—example of a word that has a confused (and ambiguous) meaning but a correspondingly enormous amount of social power. Proofreader's comment: "And don't get me started on what Anti-Semitism should mean etymologically."

The most significant cultural function of these texts has been to sustain an increasingly embattled notion of individualism. Conspiracy theory, paranoia, and anxiety about human agency, in other words, are all part of the paradox in which a supposedly individualist culture conserves its individualism by continually imagining it to be in imminent peril (p. 78).

People *are* inclined to want to believe such easy interpretations, because doing so automatically absolves them of all complicity with the social and spiritual circumstances they may feel trapped inside, and of all responsibility for them. To this extent, I would agree that any conspiratorial view of history that adheres to an "us and them" model—i.e., that presents a clear dividing line between supposed conspirators and the rest of humanity—is inherently flawed. Let's face it, there isn't much evidence for clear or absolute dividing lines in *any* kinds of human interactions. This is probably why most extreme "grand conspiracy" theories eventually wind up with either a superhuman or a non-human (or off-planet) element in the driving seat, be it David Icke's Reptilians, Christianity's Satan, Islam's Djinn, or some distant secret space colony run by the Illuminati.

In my own view, the conspiracy debunker is (mostly) correct in dismissing the idea of a hidden clique of puppet masters directing history from behind the scenes, but *not* because there is no evidence that such cliques exist (there is), rather because they exist not so much as *causal agents* but as more deeply concealed *effects*. They are carriers, if you like, of a "conspiracy"—a spiritual, psychological, cultural, social, and political hegemony—that goes back millennia. At any given time, such cliques may be the possessors of unknown power and influence; but if so, it is only because they are also possessed *by* it. As Melley writes, talking of Vance Packard's˙ (and J. Edgar Hoover's) "structural paranoia":

> the very idea of manipulation, in the sense of a *willful* attempt to control others, becomes obsolete, since attempts at manipulation are themselves only products of previous manipulation. In Packard's world, the system of depth manipulation is self-regulating. Control has been transferred

---

* Vance Packard was an American journalist and social critic and the author of *The Hidden Persuaders. The Sexual Wilderness, The Pyramid Climbers,* and *The Naked Society.*

from human agents to larger agencies, institutions, or corporate structures. . . . Packard and Hoover both attempt to describe a *structural* form
of causality while simultaneously retaining the idea of a malevolent, cen-
tralized, and *intentional* program of mass control. This odd conjunction
of the intentional and the structural is the essence of agency panic, the
motive force of postwar conspiracy culture (*Conspiracy Nation*, p. 77).

By this understanding, any hypothetically controlling individuals,
groups, and agendas are only really effective to the extent that a) they are
themselves possessed; and b) they are able to possess the rest of us. By passing
on (transmitting) their "demons" (ideologies and methodologies) *mimeti-
cally*, they ensure we will embody, implement, and extend them into the
world, via our own thoughts, beliefs, words and actions. *Latahs*.

5.3.   GRAND UNIFIED CONSPIRACY THEORY

"Consequently a necessary step for most of us in the work of
renouncing This World is to become aware of it as an engineered
control system. Thus the act of investigating the structure
and exposing the agendas of the New World Order, for those
dedicated to the spiritual path and also called to this work, can
be of direct service to the contemplative life. If we can witness
the darkness of This World with *apatheia*, with detachment and
equanimity, then we will have accomplished the greater part of
the work of 'shadow-integration'; we will be led, God willing,
to the point of supreme nausea where we can vomit the World,
along with the Ego, its master and slave, out of our souls forever."

—CHARLES UPTON, *System of the Antichrist*

Accurate interpretations of reality that are illegitimately arrived at are
worse than worthless. The reason they are worse than worthless is that, by
giving us a premature sense of understanding, they prevent the requisite
investigatory and deductive work for legitimate understanding to occur.
This is a much subtler and more insidious (i.e., far-reaching) method of

disinformation. To provide true descriptions of our social reality—in the form of "conspiracy theories"—without the corresponding deep background and context (the sociopolitical, cultural, anthropological, psychological, and even the spiritual, nuances) means that we, as the target audience of this kind of "true disinformation," are given knowledge that we have not earned, and so cannot possibly apply.

A child can be told that fire burns, but until it has a direct experience of fire, it is none the wiser, because intellectual knowledge that isn't rooted in experience is useless. It becomes worse than useless, or actively harmful, when we mistake intellectual or second-hand knowledge for something practical and real, and begin to act *as if* we had true knowledge. We then put ourselves in harm's way—we put our hand in the fire, so to speak, or, alternatively, we venture into the wilderness in sub-zero temperatures believing we have sufficient knowledge when we do not. So it is with knowledge about secret societies, "deep state" social manipulations, or "conspiracies." "Learning" about them from sources such as David Icke or Alex Jones is essentially no more helpful than basing our understanding of society on movies and TV shows.

We may have seen *North by Northwest, The Manchurian Candidate, Seven Days in May, Rosemary's Baby, A Clockwork Orange, Klute, Three Days of the Condor, The Odessa File, Executive Action, Chinatown, The Parallax View, The Stepford Wives, All the President's Men, Marathon Man, Network, The Boys from Brazil, Capricorn One, Winter Kills, Blow Out, Blue Thunder, The Osterman Weekend, Repo Man, They Live, Jacob's Ladder, Bob Roberts, JFK, Wag the Dog, Conspiracy Theory, The Game, The X-Files, Enemy of the State, The Matrix, Dark City, The Mothman Prophecies, The Bourne Identity, Syriana, Michael Clayton, Inception, Iron Man 3, Captain America: The Winter Soldier, American Ultra,* and *Under the Silver Lake.* We may have allowed these fictions to inform our worldview and make us feel "in the know." But if we expect reality to conform to these fictions, in anything but the loosest and most impractical of ways, we're in for a rude awakening. With the conspiracy-merchants, there is the added pitfall that we aren't protected by the awareness that what we are seeing is a fictionalized (because heavily simplified and symbolic) narrative, a mix of truth with fantasy. It is rather being packaged and presented as a genuinely revisionist history of the world, when in most cases the person presenting the narrative (even giving them the benefit of sincerity) has not arrived at any sort of true understanding, because they have based their own "theorizing" on intellectual and/or second-hand data, rather than experience. This deficiency multiplies as the counter-narratives "go viral," and are passed from hand to hand and eye to eye, diverging further and further from direct personal experience as they do so.

As the author of this work, I freely admit that I do not *know* if there is a unified conspiracy being implemented by a constant and persistent group over long periods of time. But can the "skeptic" admit they don't know there *isn't*? Nor do I feel much need to try and find this out, since the very terms of such a proposition make it impossible to do so. A conspiracy revealed is no longer effective *as a conspiracy* (unless the conspiracy is to make us believe in it).

What I do find myself wondering is this: if the people who promote the idea of a grand, unified conspiracy had a better understanding of the subtlety, intimacy, and intricacy of psychological, social, cultural, and even *spiritual* engineering involved, and of the essentiality of their own complicity, would they be able to maintain their belief? By the same token, on the other side of the Styx, what of those who reject the idea as absurd? If they were to spend sufficient time sifting through the evidence—which generally they haven't—would they feel so secure in their position?

As any Marxist will tell you, there's plenty of evidence of how a "purely" economic-based society acts as *a program of dehumanization*, with all the earmarks of organized malevolence or "grand conspiracy." A medical institution that "unconsciously" (covertly) prolongs people's stays and undermines their healing process to maximize profits comes up with policies *designed* to fragment, destabilize, and unhinge the patients (such as waking up patients every half hour to make sure they haven't died). This can be put down to cynical corporate profit motives, while at the same time, it's quite in accord with how a "CIA MKULTRA front" *would* operate. So which is it? What we have is a case of the *effects* of a conscious conspiracy, without the necessity of positing a fully conscious causal agency. The ball was set in motion long ago, now it is simply rolling along grooves laid down by decades—or centuries— of "business as usual."

In the same way, the cheapest sort of architecture tends to be the ugliest, and it's hardly paranoid to say that ugly architecture undermines people's morale, their sense of meaning, purpose, and community, making them less and less at home in their families, their lives, and their bodies. Nor is it fanciful to suggest this might make them more and more susceptible to *being controlled externally*, whether merely to consume the products being sold to them (such as movies or video games) or, more proactively, to "act out" in ways that benefit the power structures lurking behind corporate-based architectural decisions. Conspiracy, or blind economic forces? Or both/and?

I suspect there are as many examples of this sort of thing as there are destructive (or at least counter-productive) social trends and policies. All of them can be *superficially* accounted for with financial opportunism, greed, corruption and a lack of ethics (even stupidity). Yet all (I suspect) might also be seen as congruent with known psychological principles for demoralization, fragmentation, and dehumanization.

It's generally understood, for example, that, "In Hollywood . . . money is more highly valued than anything else" (Edwards, p. 321). Questioning such a claim would surely be seen by most people as naïve. Yet few of these same people extrapolate—what seems a natural extrapolation—that a culture or community that values money more highly than anything else is fundamentally an *inhuman* one that no good can possibly come out of. To suppose otherwise would *truly* be naïve.

The common thread here is this last effect: running a society on the basis of a (fake) economy is inherently anti-human, because a system that doesn't represent any natural, human reality renders human beings as *currency* within a system of numbers (René Guénon called it the reign of quantity). Could all of this *conceivably* have been researched and formulated in advance? I don't see how this can be ruled out, any more than it can be assumed merely from observing the consistency of the results.

In its loosest definition, conspiracy indicates malevolence, or at least criminality. There is a tendency for both conspiracy researchers and debunkers not to be able to separate the exposure (or simply the seeing) of organized malevolence with the need to *oppose* it. This unnecessary conflation feeds into both the conspiratorial and the anti-conspiratorial mindset. Wikipedia, for example, describes a "conspiracy theory" as "a belief that a conspiracy has actually been decisive in producing a political event which the theorists *strongly disapprove of*" (emphasis added). Making the element of disapproval—moral judgment—central to this definition suggests that the only reason to want to understand something is to condemn it. Yet exposing the hidden machinations of organized malevolence can also be part of a healthy desire to understand ourselves better in relation to the world. It can be a way of seeing more clearly our complicity with, and consent to, the malevolence in the world, but also our distinctness *from* it: how we are not *of* the world we find ourselves in.

This is very different from scapegoating—even the opposite of it—and potentially it can be the means to heal a split within ourselves, a split that was both caused *by* the world, and that is the cause of the state the world is currently in.

5.4.   THE WORLD-PSYCHE AS SPLIT IN THE SOUL

"Socrates believed that oratory was not a morally neutral
skill that can be directed at good, bad or indifferent ends, but
intrinsically rotten because it betrays the trust necessary for
genuine conversation and, in so doing, erodes the conditions
of political (and other forms of) judgment. We should think the
same about spin. For many years, we in the democratic West have
praised conversation in politics as though it expressed an ideal
of democratic accountability. That may be a sentimental illusion
about the nature of politics, encouraged by politicians who
spin counterfeits of conversational intimacy to make us more
vulnerable to manipulation."

—RAIMOND GAITA, *"Even Socrates drew the line at spin"*

Schismogenesis is a term derived from the Greek words skhisma "cleft" (borrowed into English as schism, "division into opposing factions"), and genesis, "generation, creation." The creation of a divide. Anthropologist and intelligence operative Gregory Bateson developed the concept while working for the OSS (Office of Strategic Services, forerunner to the CIA), and coined the term to describe "progressive differentiation between social groups or individuals."

[I]f two groups exhibit symmetrical behavior patterns towards each other
that are different from the patterns they exhibit within their respec-
tive groups, they can set up a feedback, or "vicious cycle" relation. For

example, if boasting is the way they deal with the other group, and if the other group replies to boasting with more boasting, then each group will drive the other into excessive emphasis on the pattern, leading to more extreme rivalry, and ultimately to hostility and the breakdown of the system. . . . Schismogenic behaviors, when put into equations (!) and graphed as curves, are "bounded by phenomena comparable to orgasm." They reflect conscious or unconscious hopes for release of tension through total involvement.[*]

Complementary schismogenesis is the term Bateson coined for what happens when people with different cultural norms come into contact: they each react to one another's differing patterns of behavior with the opposing behavior. This is colloquially known as "doubling down." Given two groups or types of people, the interaction between them is such that one kind of behavior from one side elicits another kind from the other side, as exemplified in the dominant-submissive behaviors of a class struggle or a sexual relationship. Furthermore, the behaviors may exaggerate one another, leading to a severe rift and possibly conflict. One of the factors said to exacerbate conflict is "information asymmetries" between the two groups, that is, when one party has more or better information than the other, creating an imbalance of power.

The imbalance of information asymmetry might be seen to exist within each of us. When denied access to the more instinctive, atavistic wisdom of the unconscious (or the body), our rational minds are rendered helpless in the face of seemingly irrational acts (which the world is full of). At the same time, when our more primitive, instinctive awareness is denied the leavening influence of reason and logic, it sees patterns and meanings—devilish or divine—in *everything*. It has no way of deducing that, while we *are* being

---

[*] Christian Hubert, citing Bateson's *Steps towards an Ecology of Mind*, p. 68, III. http://christianhubert.com/writings/schismogenesis.html Schismogenesis "was built on Bateson's experience as an OSS intelligence officer in South Asia. Bateson spent much of his wartime duty designing and carrying out 'black propaganda' radio broadcasts from remote, secret locations in Burma and Thailand (Lipset 1980:174), and also worked in China, India, and Ceylon (Yans-McLaughlin 1986a:202)." "Bateson's Schismogenesis as a propaganda tool," *Off-Guardian*, February 18, 2015. https://off-guardian.org/2015/02/18/batesons-schismogenesis-as-a-propaganda-tool/

manipulated by shadowy forces, part of the manipulation is designed to engender our belief in something that *isn't* real, to render us even more susceptible to manipulation. Hence we have the maddening paradox of a conspiracy to engender belief in conspiracies, sometimes referred to as "the revelation of the method."*

Another form of schismogenesis is known as "systems of holding back," "mutually aggregating spirals" which lead people to hold back positive contributions they might otherwise make, because they perceive others to be likewise holding back. Again, this is easily observed in a marital, family, or long-term relationship, when we choose *not* to be vulnerable, loving, or considerate because we want to receive reassurance first that the other person will do the same.

Hollywood Screenwriter Arthur Laurents describes this phenomenon in reference to Barbra Streisand: "You can't expect decent behavior from a movie star or anyone else in the industry who stays and who lives in Hollywood. They stop being human beings. They're too insecure. They're afraid. You have to make the first move. You're not saying 'Hello,' I'm not saying 'Hello.'"[4]

Systems of holding back have been called "the single most important key to life-decreasing, reciprocity-trivializing and vitality-downgrading mechanisms in human life,"[5] and unless we make a conscious effort to counter this tendency, our interactions seem to naturally fall into these patterns. But when we are in a society that is structured around power, status, and wealth, such as Hollywood, it becomes almost impossible to counteract the pull of the system that has installed its "logic" within our psyches. To do

---

* "Although [Revelation of the Method] gets referred to as an actual Masonic concept, it's actually a very recent fabrication from a Catholic 'Revisionist Historian' named Michael Hoffman. . . . when the Cryptocracy commits major crimes, they will broadcast their intentions in advance, through popular movies and television. . . . 'Look at the movie *The Matrix* in the wake of Columbine. Look at *The Wicker Man* movie in the same time frame as Son of Sam. The themes of the killings are in the movies.' Whatever its actual merits, the end result of this theory is pattern recognition in the service of a pre-established conclusion. The Revelation of the Method is how the Illuminati, or the Vatican, or the CIA rub it in our faces." "The Revelation of the Method," *Brainsturbator*, November 28, 2010: http://www.brainsturbator.com/posts/212/the-revelation-of-the-method

so is to invite critical attention, failure, and possibly scapegoating, ostraciza-tion, condemnation.

And we have systems within systems. We do it to ourselves, but we also get help. Perhaps the most critical feature of conspiracy theorizing in general is the failure to refer to personal, everyday experience and accountability within the agendas of social control being described. The cartographer fails to include his or her own faulty instrumentalities—which are as compro-mised as everything else—on the map being assembled. There is an outward gaze that projects wounded agency onto the systemic malevolence that has caused the wounding. But there is no *inward* gaze that recognizes how the wounding also causes the systemic malevolence, or malfunctioning. There is the acknowledgment of conspiracy, but no recognition of complicity.

This split of *schismogenesis*—both self- and other-engineered—may be central to maintaining and extending power and control over human psyches, both individually and collectively. Divide and conquer: as within, so without. Our intuitive, subrational mind believes in demons and in the divine aspect of existence because it has direct experience of archetypal—or at least "psychic"—reality. Our conscious, rational mind "knows better": its job is to manage the everyday, mundane realm of hard, cold facts. Yet both are effectively useless without a dialogue with the other. *Schismogenesis* is the key to maintaining territorial jurisdiction over both sides of this divide. As C.S. Lewis's *Screwtape Letters* has it:

> There are two equal and opposite errors into which our race can fall about the devils. One is to disbelieve in their existence. The other is to believe, and to feel an excessive and un-healthy interest in them. They themselves are equally pleased by both errors and hail a materialist or a magician with the same delight (p. xi).

The Conspiracy Demon depends both on our disbelief and our belief, and he uses *whichever modus operandi* suits his ends. Yet his only power over us is by installing his "program" inside us, and ditto with the State. If the conspiracy believers and the conspiracy debunkers were to get together and compare notes, both sides might come away with a more coherent and wholesome picture of the world. For the maintenance of the sociocultural hegemony of "the world," however, it's paramount that such dialogues, both inner and outer, do not happen.

5.5.   HOLLYWOOD CONSPIRACY: JUST THE FACTS

"They who control the cinema can control the thought of the world."

—AMADEO GIANNINI, *founder of the Bank of America*

- A noted pioneer of American radio and television, David Sarnoff, later became a Reserve Brigadier General and was known as "the General." Sarnoff was one of the first to see the potential of radio for not just point-to-point but point-to-mass transmission (i.e., one person speaking to many). He was put in charge of radio broadcasting at RCA. He was also one of the first credited with recognizing the potential for combining motion pictures with electronic transmission, and he pioneered the television medium in 1928. "Sarnoff's law" states that the value of a broadcast network is proportional to the number of viewers.

- Another pioneer in the field was William Paley, who started the first American TV channel Columbia Broadcasting System (CBS), which had its origins in a collection of 16 radio stations purchased by Paley, also in 1928. During World War Two, Paley served as director of radio operations of the Psychological Warfare branch in London, where he held the rank of colonel. It was there that Paley befriended Edward R. Murrow, CBS's head of European news (and subject of the 2005 George Clooney film, *Good Night and Good Luck*).

- During World War Two, "over 90 percent of Disney employees were devoted to the production of training and propaganda films. In all, the Disney Studios produced . . . 68 hours of continuous film."

Der Fuehrer's Face, featuring Donald Duck, won the Oscar as the best animated film for 1943. "Perhaps the importance of the Disney Studios to the war effort is best demonstrated by the fact that the U.S. Army deployed troops to protect the facilities, the only Hollywood studio accorded such treatment."[6] In the 1950s, Walt Disney worked with "two of the most notorious spies in American history": "Wild Bill" Donovan, the founder of the OSS (which eventually morphed into the CIA), whose law firm was hired by Disney in the late 1950s; and Paul Helliwell, "an incredibly shady figure who ran CIA front operations in Southeast Asia and the Caribbean." Both men helped Disney build Florida's Disney World,[7] which established "a private government for constructing and managing an amusement park," the Reedy Creek Improvement District:

> Florida's starstruck lawmakers . . . gave Disney's puppet government the authority to build its own international airport and even a nuclear power plant . . . cemeteries, schools, a police department, and a criminal justice system—services that Disney has so far chosen not to assume. Reedy Creek does, however, "contract" with Disney for an eight-hundred member security force. . .[8]

• The CIA, MI5, US military, and other intelligence agencies have historically been deeply involved in the entertainment industry (BBC, RCA, CBS, Hollywood) throughout the 20th and 21st centuries. Here's an example from a *non-classified* 1994 Field Manual 33-1-1 released by the US military, "Psychological Operations Techniques and Procedures":

> Movies as PSYOP tools are most effective during consolidation, FID [foreign internal defense], and UW [unconventional warfare] operations. Movies combine many aspects of television and face-to-face communication by creating a visual and aural impact on the target audience. Most children and a high percentage of adults accept, without question, the presumably factual

information presented in films. . . . Motion pictures have the advantage of bypassing audience illiteracy. Movies also have an inherent quality of drama and the ability to elicit a high degree of recall. They may include cartoons or special effects. They may gain added credibility by including news events and local settings familiar to the target audience. A producer may rehearse scenes before filming and make the final performance seem highly realistic. *In many cultures, the actor in a movie is considered to be like the part he has played. An actor can be useful because of the credibility he has gained* [emphasis added]. Movies may present a larger-than-life situation, which has great popular appeal. Background music can add to the emotional impact. [Movies] are ordinarily shown to groups and, therefore, have the power to arouse crowd reactions and to stimulate discussion. They lend themselves *almost exclusively* to friendly PSYOP.[9]

- Popular entertainment industry figures with confirmed intelligence-affiliations include actors (Frank Sinatra, Cary Grant, Greta Garbo, Sterling Hayden, Christopher Lee); writers (Noel Coward, Ian Fleming, Roald Dahl); directors (John Ford); and producers (Walt Disney, Arnon Milchan). These lists are far from complete. According to John Rizzo, the former acting CIA general counsel and author of the (CIA-authorized) book *Company Man: Thirty Years of Crisis and Controversy in the CIA*, the CIA has long had a "special relationship" with the entertainment industry.[10] Rizzo's book does not name any Hollywood players because the names are classified.

- Celebrities have made claims of dark conspiracies operating in Hollywood (Randy Quaid, Crispin Glover, Corey Feldman, Roseanne Barr), and/or had affiliations with cult organizations (River and Joaquin Phoenix and Rose McGowan, the Children of God; Tom Cruise and John Travolta, the Church of Scientology). Quaid has gone on record about how early sexual abuse led to his becoming an actor, and how, for many actors, "acting is more than just a career, it's a way of coping, a welcomed survival."* In 2013, comedienne Roseanne Barr told *Esquire* magazine: "A lot of people who are actors and artists who work in Hollywood come from a background of abuse, and you can make abused people very fearful and they'll do what they're told. Hollywood definitely has a point of view that it sells."[11]

• Many celebrities—previously and currently—have shown serious interest in and involvement with occultism; *credibly* alleged members of the O.T.O. (Ordo Templi Orientis), for example, past and present, include David Bowie, Jimmy Page, Jay-Z, Russell Brand, Madonna, Mick Jagger, Jim Morrison, Timothy Leary, and James Franco. Confirmed (or self-professed) celebrity members are few, however, and may be restricted to Marilyn Manson, Kanye West, and the late Peaches Geldof.[12]

• Hollywood has had intimate connections to organized crime from its inception onwards:

> From the days when Lucky Luciano and Al Capone battled over Hollywood turf, to Chicago mob associate, lawyer and legendary fixer Sidney Korshak pulling strings so that MGM would let Al Pacino play Michael Corleone in *The Godfather*, show business and the mob have fit together like a brass-knuckled hand in a silk opera glove. The relationship goes back at least to the 1920s, when the Chicago "outfit"—which controlled the labor unions—arrived in Los Angeles to help studio executives ride herd on their crews. As Gus Russo, who wrote about Korshak in his book *Supermob*, [claimed,] Hollywood "was a mob town" for decades, possibly into the 1980s.[13]

---

* "I was left feeling vulnerable, and the vulnerability in turn manifests itself in personality and behavior, which does not go unnoticed by vicious Hollywood predators where I continue to be taken advantage of by these monsters." "Randy Quaid Reveals He's a Victim of Sexual Abuse," by Kevin Burwick, *Movie Web*, November 2nd, 2017: https://movieweb.com/randy-quaid-sexual-abuse-victim/

That last may be no more than a diplomatic evasion. If Hollywood has been mobbed up since the 1920s, and unless there was a major clean-up operation we never heard about, there's no reason to suppose it isn't today.

- Organized, high-level pedophilia has existed for decades within the UK entertainment industry. TV DJ and children's entertainer Jimmy Savile was sexually abusing people of all ages for five decades, sometimes openly, with the full protection, not only of the BBC where he worked, but at least partial knowledge of UK's MI5, the police force, high-level government officials, and possibly even the Royal family. In a 2015 report from the UK National Police Chiefs' Council (NPCC) regarding Operation Hydrant, 1,433 suspects of child sexual abuse were identified, though not publicly named; 261 were classified as people of public prominence, with 135 coming from TV, film or radio, 76 politicians, 43 from the music industry, and seven from the world of sport.[14]

- On a 2011 episode of *Nightline*, child actor Corey Feldman stated, "The No. 1 problem in Hollywood was and is and always will be pedophilia. . . . That's the biggest problem for children in this industry. . . It's the big secret." In 2016, Elijah Wood revealed that "many of his young peers had been 'preyed upon' by child molesters. Feldman corroborated Wood's accusation, saying, 'Ask anybody in our group of kids at that time: They were passing us back and forth to each other.'"[15] The 2015 documentary, *An Open Secret*, from director Amy Berg, included testimonies of several ex-child actors who claimed that sexual abusers regularly get away with it. "This film could be the start to show people there's a problem in Hollywood," said an ex-child actor interviewed for the film who claimed to have been abused by his ex-manager, Marty Weiss, for six years. The film was unable to find a distributor but has been viewed in large numbers online.

5.6.   THE SCIENCE OF CULTURAL PROPAGANDA, SECRET SOCIETIES, & POLITICAL ORGANIZATION

"In their propaganda today's dictators rely for the most part
on repetition, suppression and rationalization—the repetition
of catchwords which they wish to be accepted as true, the
suppression of facts which they wish to be ignored, the arousal
and rationalization of passions which may be used in the interests
of the Party or the State. As the art and science of manipulation
come to be better understood, the dictators of the future will
doubtless learn to combine these techniques with . . . non-stop
distractions . . ."

—ALDOUS HUXLEY, *"Propaganda in a Democratic Society,"*
Brave New World Revisited

Since the whole subject of conspiracy theory has been so systematically debased, I want to briefly present a couple of alternate contexts for
understanding it: firstly, that of social and cultural engineering, and secondly, closely related, that of secret societies. The term social engineering,
or the scientific management of society, was quite comprehensively explored
(and advanced) in the previous century by highly prestigious English writers
such as H.G. Wells, Aldous Huxley, and Bertrand Russell. All of them were,
to varying degrees, affiliated with the Fabian Society, probably the primary
force behind the social, cultural, and political reconfiguration of Britain in
the 20th century (as documented in *Vice of Kings*). The consensus view of
these men's writings on the subject of a scientific dictatorship seems strangely
split down the middle. There are those who regard them as novelist-philoso-
phers with a humanitarian bent, warning us about the direction society was
taking. And then there are those, in growing number, who regard them as
Machiavellian agents of secret agendas to implement the same policies they
were supposedly warning about. Once again, we have a perceptual divide.

In my opinion, a closer reading reveals that neither perspective is quite
accurate. For one thing, these men weren't so much warning about the
inexorable social advancements towards totalitarianism as, in more subtle
and discreet ways, *championing it*. Most essentially of all, I think their work

offered a loose (but also comprehensive) blueprint by which to achieve certain ends. The "warning" was only surface-deep, since (beyond much doubt) these men *were* deeply involved in scientific and philosophical research about shaping society, and sharing their findings in a *prescriptive* (as well as proscriptive) manner, often by publishing them (Wells named it "the Open Conspiracy," in his work of the same name). On the other hand, since this is largely speculative, I should add that, establishing these writers' particular moral orientations need not be a factor in how seriously we take their words.

In *The Impact of Science on Society*, published in 1951, Bertrand Russell proposes that mass psychology is the subject "of most importance politically." It is, he writes, "scientifically speaking, not a very advanced study, and so far its professors have not been in universities: they have been advertisers, politicians, and, above all, dictators." Of the rapidly growing modern methods of propaganda, "the most influential is what is called 'education.'" Religion, Russell argues, plays a diminishing part, while "the press, the cinema, and the radio play an increasing part" (p. 29).

> The social psychologists of the future will have a number of classes of school children on whom they will try different methods of producing an unshakable conviction that snow is black. Various results will soon be arrived at. First, that the influence of home is obstructive. Second that not much can be done unless indoctrination begins before the age of ten. *Third, that verses set to music and repeatedly intoned are very effective.* Fourth, that the opinion that snow is white must be held to show a morbid taste for eccentricity (p. 30, emphasis added).

If any reader thinks Russell was exaggerating, they have not followed the viral takeover of gender politics in classrooms, from play school up, which quite literally has children believing that male is female, and vice versa.[16] While the science of brainwashing "will be diligently studied," Russell assures that such knowledge "will be rigidly confined to the governing class. The populace will not be allowed to know how its convictions were generated. When the technique has been perfected, every government that has been in charge of education for a generation will be able to control its subjects securely without the need of armies or policemen" (p 30). Beyond state education, Russell points out that, just as printing is impossible without paper and all paper belongs to the State, even leisure reading can be closely regulated. This is even more easily controlled with radio, television, and the cinema. "All this is not imaginary," he assures us: "it is daily and hourly reality. Nor, given oligarchy, is there the slightest reason to expect anything else" (p. 45–6).

In a similar vein, there is the little-recognized question of *sociological* propaganda, as formulated by Jacques Ellul in *Propaganda*. Sociological propaganda is invisible, all-pervasive, and, as posited by Ellul, more or less indistinguishable from culture at large:

> the group of manifestations by which any society seeks to integrate the maximum number of individuals into itself, to unify its members' behavior according to a pattern, to spread its style of life abroad, and thus impose itself on other groups [sociological propaganda implies that] the entire group, consciously or not, expresses itself in this fashion; and . . . that its influence aims much more at an entire style of life than at options or even one particular course of behavior (p. 62).

Fittingly enough for our purposes, Ellul uses the example of an American film producer, with "certain definite ideas that he wants to express, that are not intended to be propaganda. Rather the propaganda element is in *the American way of life with which he is permeated and which he expresses in his film without realizing it*" (p 64, emphasis added). A vigorous society is "totalitarian in the sense of integrating the individual" and instilling him or her with "involuntary behavior." Whether it's advertising, movies, the arts, education, or technology,

> All these influences are in basic accord with each other and lead spontaneously in the same direction. . . . And yet with deeper and more objective analysis [one finds these] influences are expressed through the same media as propaganda. They are *really directed* by those who make propaganda. [T]hose who have this conception of society are right, and those who have another conception are in error. Consequently, as with ordinary propaganda, it is a matter of propagating behavior and myths both good and bad. Furthermore, such propaganda becomes increasingly effective when those subjected to it accept its doctrines on what is *good or*

bad (for example, the American way of life). There, *a whole society actually expresses itself through this propaganda by advertising its way of life* (p. 64–5, emphasis added).

✦

"The architects of power in the United States must create a force that can be felt but not seen. Power remains strong when it remains in the dark; exposed to the sunlight it begins to evaporate."

—SAMUEL HUNTINGTON, *director of Harvard Center for International Affairs, 1981*

Brian Hayden believes that secret societies "constitute a sort of 'missing link' in the cultural evolution of more complex societies" (p. 3). He argues, convincingly, that "secret societies were the first institutionalized manifestation of ritual organizations linked to political power, and that this was, in fact, [their] explicit goal." The "political dimension of secret societies," he believes, may be "critical to understanding the evolution of political systems" in general (p. 6).

Since Hayden's disciplinary field is archeology, his point of ingress to this largely ignored (or secreted) body of evidence pertains to *geographical locations as centers of power.* Secret societies, he writes, "have a strong tendency to form far-reaching regional networks or interaction spheres" (p. 5). Hayden is very clear on this point: "neither the rhetoric of secret societies nor their publicly expressed purposes (special abilities or functions) are critical for understanding their underlying nature or their reasons for existing" (p. 12). In other words, what a given society, institution, or organization *publicly states* about its purpose or its nature is largely irrelevant when it comes to understanding it. We must look beneath. And not despite but *because of* this duplicity, the influence of secret societies is both formative and enduring (and far-reaching). Such a hidden template to culture strongly suggests that *society itself holds a secret from the majority of its members.*

Hayden argues that "the most powerful members of communities generally dominate the highest ranks of secret societies . . . they control significant resources and means to advance their own hegemonic control in the

community." Via these levers of influence, "secret societies constitute powerful driving forces for cultural changes including major changes in ideologies,
cultural values, and beliefs, as well as new sociopolitical relationships including an increased centralization of power" (p. 5). Indirectly, Hayden's thesis
implies that *culture itself might be a tool in the hands of such forces.*

To call another witness: Clotaire Rapaille, a French marketing consultant and the CEO and Founder of Archetype Discoveries Worldwide,
might agree on a number of these points. For example, that what individuals, groups, or societies profess to be *about* is useless for deciphering
their real purpose or intent. In *The Culture Code*, Rapaille writes: "The
first principle of the Culture Code is that the only effective way to understand what people truly mean is to ignore what they say. . . . It is in the
reptilian brain that the real answers lie" (p. 14, 15). In his work as an advertising advisor for IBM, Boeing, Chrysler, General Electric, Ford, DuPont,
GM, American Express, J.P. Morgan, Citibank, NASA, AT&T, Johnson
& Johnson, Kellogg's, Kraft, Pepsi, Shell, Seiko, Renault, Exxon, Evian,
Colgate, and Citroen, among many others, Rapaille juxtaposes Freud's idea
of the individual unconscious with Jung's collective unconscious to posit
a "third unconscious," which he terms "the cultural unconscious" (p. 20,
27). To demonstrate how he applies his model, he describes a commission
he accepted to sell Nestlé coffee to the (tea-drinking) Japanese. After initial research, he advised a *generational campaign*: marketing coffee-flavored
candy to Japanese children, he proposes, is necessary *to introduce an early
imprint into the cultural unconscious of the Japanese.* Only then will future
generations be susceptible to the advertising. His proposal is accepted and
proves successful. His inception-style advertising campaign entails *shaping
the collective psyche in order to prime it for future influence.*

The existence of a cultural unconscious raises essential questions
about what we mean by social control or conspiracy. It places such ideas
into a much wider, less well-defined frame. What Rapaille's coffee-campaign
demonstrates (if true) is that those who are *consciously* engaged in creating
popular culture (or in directing its creation) potentially hold the keys to
unlocking the cultural unconscious—whether to ransack or to colonize it,
or both. Edward Bernays—whose legacy of public relations Rapaille is the
shame-free inheritor of—made no bones about (his belief in) the hidden
power of gatekeepers and culture-makers, in his book *Propaganda*:

The conscious and intelligent manipulation of the organized habits and opinions of the masses is an important element in democratic society. Those who manipulate this unseen mechanism of society constitute an invisible government which is the true ruling power of our country. . . . We are governed, our minds are molded, our tastes formed, our ideas suggested, largely by men we have never heard of. This is a logical result of the way in which our democratic society is organized. . . . In almost every act of our daily lives, whether in the sphere of politics or business, in our social conduct or our ethical thinking, we are dominated by the relatively small number of persons . . . who understand the mental processes and social patterns of the masses. It is they who pull the wires which control the public mind (Bernays, p. 37–38).

Known as "the father of public relations," Bernays was Freud's nephew and a pioneer in the field of sociological propaganda. In 1990, he was named one of the 100 most influential Americans of the 20th century by Luce's *Life* magazine, and his behind-the-scenes work became more widely known via Adam Curtis' *The Century of the Self* (2002). The documentary recounts Bernays' afore-cited "Torches of Freedom" campaign from 1929, not to mention his work for the notorious United Fruit Company to implement the CIA-orchestrated overthrow of the democratically elected Guatemalan government, in 1954. Yet despite such conspicuous examples of behind-the-scenes social and political manipulations, culture and, by extension, the cultural unconscious, are largely seen as natural, inevitable, and spontaneous results of human community, and hence as entirely uncontrolled and undirected. In 1992, Camille Paglia defined pop culture "as an eruption of the never-defeated paganism of the West" (p. vii). This is the liberal-progressive equivalent of the Christian wishful thinking, "If God had meant us to fly, he would have given us wings." God did give us wings, he just used us to build them. And the modern world is filled to the brim with man-made imitations of things that occur naturally (at this point, including life itself). There is no earthly reason not to extend this to culture in its entirety.

Yet Paglia's still-popular perspective, however blinkered, is not entirely wrong. Even culture, as a human creation, may be possessed of a (non-cultural) unconscious. On the one hand, if we are partially controlled by our cultural unconscious—and if this can be coopted via the intentional shaping of culture—we need to dig a *lot* deeper, and reach a much higher plateau, to gauge the terrain currently quarantined (or QAnonomized) as "conspiracy theory." On the other hand, if a third layer of the human unconscious is vulnerable to this kind of exploitation, and inseparable from the process of manufacturing culture, and if it informs our choices and gives rise to our identities, both as individuals and groups, then the levers of control which Bernays is staking his claims on (as a member of his secret society) may be almost incalculably subtler, deeper, and more sophisticated than either Bernays or the average "conspiracy theorist" imagines.

Simply stated, such sophistication must go far beyond any conscious intent or design—even if this truth is itself factored into the design being intended. Like landscape gardening, culture-hacking requires not only a knowledge of the terrain being reshaped and a specific idea about the desired new landscape, but also a familiarity with the indigenous plant and rock life that is the raw material of the new (as well as old) landscape. Jesuits train their children from the earliest possible age to become effective adult agents of the ideology informing their training. But if the trainers are also the trained, at what precise point does conspiracy become complicity? And what of the unconscious desire of the trainers to be free of those internal levers of control?

How literal, tangible, or direct such a legacy of cultural landscaping might be, as compared to a subtler, less conscious or intentional influence, is difficult, if not impossible, to say. Perhaps the now-quaint notion of spirits of the land possessing the consciousness of colonizers, as in *The Shining* (among other horror movies), has a more tangible and less mystical reality? As hinted at in the introduction, it *could* be that secret societies and their "occult" practices were "imported" cross-culturally and so entered a high-culture phase, assuming a modern, westernized guise via movies, musical performances, awards ceremonies, and such like. But even without such speculations, it is becoming apparent that the centrality of Hollywood to the intentional shaping of the cultural collective unconscious can hardly be overestimated.

6

SORCERER

6.1.   CONSPIRACY BY ANY OTHER NAME

"We might wonder, for example, whether the activities of intelligence agencies involved in spying and carrying out covert missions count as conspiracies. . . . They are by their very nature plotted in secret, and they are indeed intended to alter the shape of history, but we might wonder if the everyday machinations of, say, CIA agents constitute a conspiracy because they are merely doing their job. Only in some cases is it immediately obvious that their actions are illegal or improper, and hence a conspiracy rather than merely being a covert operation. The problem with making illegality or impropriety part of the definition of a conspiracy is that it depends who is defining what's illegal or not."

—PETER KNIGHT, *Conspiracy Theories in American History*

The above quote underscores something I think is central to understanding the resistance to the notion of far-reaching, long-term, and multi-level global conspiracies. *It is all about context.* As Lance deHaven Smith's *Conspiracy Theory in America* persuasively demonstrates, the term "conspiracy theory" was subtly promoted by the CIA following

the John F. Kennedy assassination.* This was done as a means to discredit researchers by creating a "soft" categorization for them, a conceptual climate that would gradually suck all the oxygen out of their efforts and reduce it to a shriveled facsimile of itself. Denial and ridicule are invaluable tools for dealing with anything that potentially threatens to undermine the official narrative about how the world (or the entertainment industry) operates.

That the CIA covertly introduced the term "conspiracy theory" into the common vernacular (back in the days when going viral took a decade or so) is not, as the uninformed reader might suppose, itself a "conspiracy theory." Or at least if it is, it's backed by academically collated data, source documents, and rigorous analyses generally considered sufficient to constitute historical fact and not mere theory. My point isn't to offer up more theories—or even evidence—about CIA skullduggery, but to indicate how what's often derided as "conspiracy theory" is just business-as-usual for intelligence agencies like the CIA. Also, how reframing evidence relating to covert operations (to manipulate individuals, society, and even history itself) as "conspiracy theory" has been central to creating a false and unnatural—yet ever widening—gulf in the field of historical research, a gulf between Establishment figures like Noam Chomsky and fringe voices such as Douglas Valentine, Howard Blum, and Michael Parenti, even as conspiratainers like David Icke and Alex Jones enter the mainstream without rocking the ship of state.

If merely naming a thing is, to a large extent, enough to discredit it, this is only possible after a long and concerted effort to create a sociocultural quarantine for data to be confined to. There is an artificial context into which certain kinds of facts (or, yes, theories) are pulled, as if by a psychic gravitational field, and there inducted into narratives that have clearly been marked as "conspiracy theories," and not as history, political science, or the study of espionage.

---

* "The pejorative dimensions of the term 'conspiracy theory' were introduced into the Western lexicon by CIA 'media assets,' as evidenced in the design laid out by 'Document 1035-960 Concerning Criticism of the Warren Report,' an Agency communiqué issued in early 1967 to Agency bureaus throughout the world at a time when attorney Mark Lane's *Rush to Judgment* was atop bestseller lists and New Orleans DA Garrison's investigation of the Kennedy assassination began to gain traction." http://www.informationclearing house.info/article42768.htm

And yet: espionage as a practice, methodology, and central component of statecraft throughout history is so wholly dependent on *conspiracy* as to be very nearly synonymous with it. *Men in rooms* (and women), plotting to bring about specific ends via the manipulation of mass media, military and police action, government policies, legal sanctions, assassinations, technology, commerce, and so forth, all done with flagrant disregard for common laws, in secret, on a "need-to-know" basis, ensuring there is only the communication between levels of hierarchy that's strictly necessary, that almost no one has more than one or two pieces of the puzzle, and that *everyone* has plausible denial—often even to themselves.

How far-reaching is such an ongoing enterprise? The US Intelligence Community is a federation of at least 17 separate government agencies that work separately and together to conduct intelligence activities to support the foreign policy and national security of the US. Member organizations of the IC include intelligence agencies, military intelligence, and civilian intelligence and analysis offices within federal executive departments. The IC is overseen by the Office of the Director of National Intelligence (ODNI) making up the 17-member Intelligence Community, which itself is headed by the Director of National Intelligence (DNI), who reports to the President of the United States. *The Washington Post* reported in 2010 that there were 1,271 government organizations and 1,931 private companies in 10,000 locations in the US working on counterterrorism, homeland security, and intelligence, and that the intelligence community as a whole includes 854,000 people holding top-secret clearances. According to a 2008 study by the Office of the Director of National Intelligence, private contractors make up 29% of the workforce in the US intelligence community and account for 49% of their personnel budgets.

These names and figures are of course not even remotely complete, because they cannot take into account the existence of "black-ops" (and because police forces have their own intelligence branches, as do many corporations and banks nowadays). In 2017, a *Foreign Policy* article brought public attention to a spy agency even Barack Obama, five months into his presidency, didn't know about: the National Geospatial-Intelligence Agency (NGA), whose "headquarters is the third-largest building in the Washington metropolitan area, bigger than the CIA headquarters and the US Capitol."[1]

This is to say nothing of all the deep-undercover agents and informers who, for security reasons, would not be included in *any* publically released statistics.

I think it's safe to say that the scope and reach of "the intelligence community"—of spooks both on the ground and behind desks, at home and abroad—is something few people can even conceive of, much less guess at. And let's not forget Google, Apple, and Facebook—and all of them (or us) working day and night to secure and advance the interests of State power.

Reassuring, isn't it?

6.2.   THE COMFORT OF DARKNESS: CASE STUDY # 7, *THE EXORCIST*

> "A critic can't fight [*The Exorcist*], because it functions below the conscious level. How does one exorcise the effects of a movie like this? There is no way. The movie industry is such that men of no taste and no imagination can have an incalculable influence."
>
> —PAULINE KAEL, *"Back to the Ouija Board"*

One of the reasons I still read Hollywood biographies, despite the sometimes maddening tension of not knowing what to believe, is that, if the view of Hollywood which *16 Maps of Hell* is presenting is at all accurate, we should expect even the most superficial of biographies to offer up the occasional clue—even if only in the way in which it conceals or distorts the truth.

Before I began *The Friedkin Connection*, the rather lazy and insubstantial autobiography of William Friedkin (the director of *The French Connection*, *The Exorcist, Sorcerer, Cruising*, and *Killer Joe*), I had made a comment to a friend about how I half-enjoyed, half-hated, the cognitive dissonance that reading Hollywood biographies caused in me, with their obviously distorted versions of reality. And as I began the book, I thought to myself, "I wonder if there will be any clues that Friedkin was an MKULTRA subject?"

The book begins with a short prologue, after which Friedkin begins his story, on page 9, with his birth. On page 11, he describes his first experience of seeing a film: "An enormous black rectangle came alive with a blinding white light and a loud blast of music. The comforting darkness was shattered by words I couldn't read. My instinctive reaction was to scream at the top of my lungs. I clutched my mother's arms; I couldn't breathe."

The passage struck me at once because, only a couple of days earlier, by one of those peculiar coincidences, I had just re-watched Wim Wenders' *The End of Violence*, in which the movie producer played by Bill Pullman explains that he became a filmmaker because of how movies terrified him as a child. Like Friedkin, he wanted to turn the tables and do the same to others. On page 14, Friedkin writes:

> I discovered that people, especially young people, liked to be scared. Many years later, Dr. Louis Jolyon West, then head of Neuropsychiatric Clinic at UCLA, explained to me why he thought people enjoy suspense and horror films. "You're in a dark room with dangerous, life-threatening events happening before your eyes, but as a viewer you're in a safe place, removed from what's happening on screen." "A safe darkness," he called it.

Dr. Louis Jolyon West was an American psychiatrist who did his psychiatry residency at Cornell University, an MKULTRA institution and site of the Human Ecology Fund. His work focused particularly on cases where subjects were "taken to the limits of human experience." He later became a subcontractor for MKULTRA Subproject 43, and received a $20,800 grant from the CIA while he was chairman of the department of Psychiatry at the University of Oklahoma. The proposal submitted by West was titled "Psychophysiological Studies of Hypnosis and Suggestibility" with an accompanying document titled "Studies of Dissociative States."[2] A few years later, West performed a psychiatric evaluation of Jack Ruby, the man who shot and killed Lee Harvey Oswald. In 1969, he became director of the UCLA's Neuropsychiatric Institute. According to author and psychiatrist Colin Ross, "ESP research was conducted [there] while Dr. West was director. The CIA funded paranormal research through STARGATE and MKULTRA. Dr. West himself obtained funds through MKULTRA."[3]

In a 1958 report on how to train Air Force flight crews to resist brainwashing as prisoners of war, West wrote that "A realistic, undistorted, truthful account of what a man can expect constitutes a major protection for him."[4] Knowing what protects us from enemy brainwashing is, of course, equally useful when it comes to perfecting our own methods of brainwashing. Another, less common word for brainwashing is "menticide," which is to say, mind-murder: the systematic effort to undermine or destroy a target audience's values and beliefs, whether via prolonged interrogation, drugs, torture, or the slow drip of indoctrination, while at the same time (since nature abhors a vacuum) inducing radically different ideas.

I had a hunch and checked the contents page of Friedkin's bio: sure enough, he uses West's phrase "A Safe Darkness" for the title of the 13th chapter of the book, a clear homage to his "teacher" of the dissociative arts. If we ignore the foreword (which is generally written after a book is finished), West is the first public figure Friedkin namedrops in his narrative. In the edition I read, he is listed in the index *incorrectly*, on page 13 (correct reference is p. 14). Is "Jolly" West the Friedkin connection?

Friedkin's career arc was steep. He went from working in the mail room at WGN-TV immediately after high school to embarking on a directorial career at the age of 18, doing live television shows and documentaries. This included *The People vs. Paul Crump*, about Robert Crump, who was sentenced to die in the electric chair for killing a security guard in a Chicago armed robbery in 1953. When Friedkin made his documentary, Crump had been on death row for nine years. The program was deemed by the TV station too incendiary to air, but they sent it to then-governor Otto Kerner, who watched it and wrote Friedkin a letter. Friedkin kept the letter, and quoted it decades later. Kerner was "extremely moved by your film" and said he had decided to change Crump's sentence "to a life in prison without the possibility of parole."[5] (Folk singer Phil Ochs—also speculated to be an MKULTRA subject who claimed he was working for the CIA[6]—wrote a song entitled "Paul Crump" that chronicled Crump's life.) The film's success helped Friedkin get a job with producer David L. Wolper, and he moved to Hollywood soon after.

His breakthrough film was *The French Connection*, which came out in 1971, a few months before *Dirty Harry*, and won Friedkin the Academy Award for Best Director. In her review of the film, "Urban Gothic," Pauline Kael wrote:

The movie presents [its hero] as the most ruthlessly lawless of characters and yet—here is where the basic amorality comes through—shows that this is the kind of man it takes to get the job done. It's the vicious bastard who gets the results. . . . The only thing this movie believes in is giving the audience jolts, and you can feel the raw, primitive response in the theater. This picture says Popeye is a brutal son of a bitch who gets the dirty job done. So is the picture (1975, p. 318, 319).

6.3.   CATHOLIC PSYOP

"[*The Exorcist*] may be in the worst imaginable taste—that is, an utterly unfeeling movie about miracles—but it's also the biggest recruiting poster the Catholic Church has had since the sunnier days of *Going My Way* and *The Bells of St. Mary's*."

—PAULINE KAEL, *"Back to the Ouija Board"*

Friedkin's most successful and famous/infamous movie is undoubtedly *The Exorcist*, which is also his one full-blown foray into the "paranormal." The book was by William Peter Blatty, who studied at a Jesuit school as a boy, went to George Washington University, and completed his master's degree in 1954. After that, he applied for both the FBI and the CIA but was refused. According to Blatty, this was because the number of address changes he'd had before college made a background check impossible.[7] Blatty joined the US Air Force instead and became head of the Policy Branch of the *Psychological Warfare Division*.[8] He also worked for the US Information Agency in Beirut for several years.

In the late 1950s, he became the public relations director at Loyola University of Los Angeles, and publicity director at the University of Southern California. He published his first novel in 1960 and wrote a series of successful comic novels. That led him to Hollywood, where he collaborated with director Blake Edwards. *The Exorcist* was Blatty's attempt to become a more serious writer and contribute to "the welfare of the world"—or so he said.* It was not initially a success (far from it), but by a quirk of fate, sorcery, or social engineering, Blatty landed a last-minute spot on the Dick Cavett show soon after it came out, where he gave a 42-minute monologue about the book. A week later, it hit the number one spot on *Time*'s best seller list.[9]

In her excoriation of *The Exorcist*, Pauline Kael shared her vitriol equally between Blatty and Friedkin:

> And what Blatty didn't manage to have his characters do [in the book] he had them talk about, so there were fresh atrocities every few hundred words. Like the pulp authors who provide flip-page sex, he provided flip-page torture, infanticide, cannibalism, sexual hysteria, werewolves. The book is a manual of lurid crimes, written in an easy-to-read tough-guy style yet with a grating heightening word here and there, supposedly to tone it up. . . . The book turns up on high-school reading lists now, and the Bantam edition carries such quotes as "Deeply religious . . . a parable for our times" (1976, p. 248).

Blatty's experience heading the psychological warfare division may not be unrelated to the success of *The Exorcist*, any more than are Friedkin's childhood experiences or apprenticeship under Dr. West. One of the reasons *The Exorcist* became so infamous is the extreme reactions audiences initially had to the film. This is from "Cinematic neurosis following *The Exorcist*," an academic paper by J.C. Bozzuto, quoted by Chris Knowles in "Uncle Sam's Secret Sorcerers V":

> Following the distribution and release of the movie, *The Exorcist*, much publicity concerning the psychiatric hazards of the film was reported. Numerous cases of traumatic neurosis and even psychosis were supposedly noted. This report confirms the hypothesis that traumatic "cinema neurosis" can be precipitated by viewing the movie in previously unidentified psychiatric patients. This movie seems to be directly related to

---

* "You can't kid around with a man who says that he wrote *The Exorcist* because "as I went along writing my funny books and screenplays, I felt I wasn't making a contribution to the welfare of the world" (Kael, 1976, p. 247).

traumatic neurosis in susceptible people. Classical symptoms and disability were observed following viewing the movie. There are elements in the movie, such as possession with resultant loss of impulse control, that are likely to threaten people with similar problems, and to exceed their "stimulus barrier."[10]

Knowles recounts how, at one showing of the film, a woman lost consciousness and fell down and broke her jaw. Claiming that subliminal effects in the film had caused her to lose consciousness, she sued the film company, successfully: Warner Brothers settled out of court for an undisclosed amount. One reason they may have done so is that there *were* subliminal images in *The Exorcist*:

> Several of them. And it wasn't just imagery, it was also sound. The terrified squealing of pigs being slaughtered was mixed subtly into the sound track. The buzzing sound of angry, agitated bees wove in and out of scenes throughout the film. That's what we've been told about, or has been discovered by fans. What don't we know about? Was *The Exorcist* in fact a movie or an experiment?[11]

Or was it little Billy's revenge for what the movies (and his mother) had done to him? As Kael points out in her review, since *The Exorcist* was rated R, it was "open to children (to those whose parents are insane enough to take them, or are merely uninformed)." The film had been budgeted at four million dollars, but, "what with swiveling heads, and levitations, and vomit being spewed on target, the cost kept rising, and the picture came in somewhere around ten million." Had the film cost under a million or been made abroad, she suggests, "it would almost certainly be an X film, but when a movie is as expensive as this one, the M.P.A.A. rating board doesn't dare to give it an X" (1976, p. 249).

> Apart from the demonic special effects, which are done in staccato quick cuts, the picture is in a slugging, coercive style. It piles up points, like a demonstration. [Friedkin] has himself said that Blatty's book took hold of him and made him physically ill. That's the problem with moviemakers

who aren't thinkers: they're mentally unprotected. A book like Blatty's makes them sick, and they think this means they should make everybody sick. Probably Friedkin really believes he is communicating an important idea to us. And the only way he knows how to do it is by surface punch; he's a true commercial director—he confuses blatancy with power. . . . Aren't those who accept this picture getting their heads screwed on backward? (Kael, 1976, p. 250, 251)

In the period leading up to writing the book, Blatty had formed a friendship with the actress and spiritualist Shirley MacLaine (Warren Beatty's sister). According to Blatty, he based the character of Regan's mother, Chris McNeil, on MacLaine. He even wanted her to play the role, but MacLaine declined and the role went to Ellen Burstyn, who won the Academy Award. MacLaine's daughter, Sachi Parker, mentions in her autobiography *Lucky Me* that Blatty and her mother were "kindred spirits" who would regularly get out the Ouija board to try and contact spirits and "once or twice they even conducted a séance in the house" (Parker, p. 51). Considering Blatty's many claims of being a dedicated Catholic, this is not exactly a devout pastime.

Sachi also claims that "the photo of the little girl on the first edition of the Harper and Row hardcover book looked an awful lot like me." Her mother was sure it *was* her, but Blatty denied it. "Shirley, how could I have gotten Sachiko's picture on the cover of the book?" he said, to which MacLaine accused him of breaking into the house and stealing it—an unnecessary recourse if Blatty was a regular guest at the house. Parker writes, "He insisted he had nothing to do with choosing the photo on the cover, which makes its unsettling resemblance to me even creepier" (p. 52).

6.4.   TOTEM & TABOO

"Terrorism can be advanced through art only if art threatens *action*."

—ADAM PARFREY, *Apocalypse Culture*

Returning to *The Friedkin Connection*, immediately after naming Dr. Louis Jolyon West, Friedkin describes a bully he knew at school, Joel Fenster. In his account, young Billy finally turns on Fenster and overpowers him. "I had the distinct impulse to end his life," he writes, "and I felt it would make me happy if I did" (p. 16). This is a strange thing to confess in the first few pages of an otherwise extremely lightweight, insubstantial, and non-introspective autobiography. A pattern seemed to be emerging in Friedkin's choices of which incidents and encounters to include.

There are a number of obvious mob connections to Friedkin's rise, some of which Friedkin has talked freely about. Some of these mobster allies are also named in the first few chapters of the book, Sidney Korshak being the most obvious and well-known, a man who "had gotten his start as a driver for Al Capone."[12] In his obit, the *New York Times* called Korshak "one of Hollywood's most fabled and influential fixers"; it also quoted producer Robert Evans: "Let's just say that a nod from Korshak . . . and the teamsters change management. A nod from Korshak, and Santa Anita closes. A nod from Korshak, and Vegas shuts down. A nod from Korshak, and the Dodgers can suddenly play night baseball."[13] Korshak's many "friends" included MCA/Universal chiefs Jules C. Stein and Lew Wasserman, MGM chief Kirk Kerkorian, Gulf+Western founder Charles Bluhdorn, Frank Sinatra, Ronald Reagan, Robert Evans, Warren Beatty, and Hugh Hefner. He died at 88, without ever having a criminal conviction, or even an indictment.[14] In 2002, a biopic on Korshak, from a script by crime novelist James Ellroy for producers Robert Evans and Brian Grazer, was announced from Paramount Pictures, called *The Man Who Kept Secrets*. Friedkin was named as the director.[15] (It never happened.)

In a *WTF* interview with Marc Maron, Friedkin mentioned, at the two-hour mark, that he "happened to know the guy who was the head of the west side mob." He was referring to Maddy Ianniello—who controlled the adult entertainment business centered in the Times Square section of Manhattan during the 1960s and 1970s. When he was researching and shooting *Cruising*, Friedkin worked with several members of the Mafia, including Ianniello, since many of the New York City gay bars were run by mobsters (giving a whole new twist to the term, "gay mafia"—see chapter 10). Ianniello is portrayed by actor Garry Pastore in the 2017 HBO series (starring James Franco), *The Deuce*.

As well as pioneering gay clubs, the New York mafia backed the porno industry in the 1970s (as celebrated in *The Deuce*), and the breakout movie was *Deep Throat*, produced by Gerald Damiano Film Productions (according to Tim Adler's *Hollywood and the Mob*, Damiano later became known as "the Scorsese of porn," p. 175). Released one year before *The Exorcist* in 1972, the movie was produced by mobster Louis Peraino and starred Linda Lovelace, whose boyfriend and manager, Chuck Traynor, "forced Lovelace to perform oral sex on [Peraino] every day in order to secure the part" (Adler, p. 176). Nor was the shoot any different.

> Lovelace later said that her performance had been coerced at gunpoint. She said that a gun was held to her head during filming. Cast and crew did nothing when her manager beat her up in an adjoining hotel room, she said. Indeed, bruises are visible on Lovelace's legs in the film. "When you see *Deep Throat*, you are watching me being raped," Lovelace told the Congressional Meese Commission investigation into pornography in January 1986. "It's a crime that movie is still showing. There was a gun to my head the entire time" (p. 177).

The movie has often been called the most successful movie of all time, presumably in terms of cost-to-profit ratio.* It was so successful that for a time, major Hollywood studios considered bringing pornography onto their roster and into the mainstream. In a review of *Inside Deep Throat*, a 2005 documentary, Roger Ebert commented that many theaters that screened the film were mob-connected enterprises, which probably "inflated box office receipts as a way of laundering income from drugs and prostitution" and other illegal activities.[16]

✦

> "The pornographic 'drama,' though as fraudulent as professional wrestling, makes a claim for being about something absolutely serious, if not humanly profound: it is not so much about itself

---

* Estimates of the film's total revenues have varied widely: numbers as high as $600 million (equivalent to $3.6 billion today) have been cited, which would make *Deep Throat* one of the highest-grossing films of all time.

as about the violation of a taboo. That the taboo is spiritual
rather than physical, or sexual—that our most valuable human
experience, love, is being desecrated, parodied, mocked—is surely
at the core of our culture's fascination with pornography."

—JOYCE CAROL OATES, *"On Boxing"*

Another thing *The Exorcist* and *Deep Throat* have in common (besides
mob approval) is that both films rapidly—and somewhat improbably—
pushed the envelope regarding what was permissible to show on cinema
screens at the time. *Deep Throat* brought hardcore pornography to mainstream audiences. *The Exorcist*—with its "Your mother sucks cocks in Hell!"
and its graphic depiction of a 12-year-old girl masturbating with a cruci-
fix then shoving her mother's face into her bloody crotch—left audiences
dazed and numb. Bear in mind that the first time American audiences had
heard the word "fuck" at the movies was only three years earlier, in Robert
Altman's M*A*S*H; people weren't lining up around the block hours before
show time merely to be terrorized. They were there to be shocked and titillated, having received word of mouth from friends and family members
who had already been shocked and titillated. I remember hearing about
the movie as an eleven year-old boy (five years *after* its release): there was
something darkly *forbidden* about the film, an aura of *danger* that made it
all-but-irresistible.

As already discussed, taboo-breaking has long been associated with the
arts (as well as the occult arts), and especially progressive or *avant-garde* art
in which the two fields are more or less indistinguishable. And taboo has
always been closely related to terror (as well as to sexual arousal). In *The
Power of Ritual in Prehistory*, Hayden emphasizes the centrality of terror to
ancient secret society operations, both in their dealings with the public (via
performance art) and in their own secret rituals. "In order to justify the use
of terror and violence," he writes,

> secret societies promulgated a number of key ideological premises. . . .
> Ethnographers on the Northwest Coast rarely discuss motives behind
> forming or belonging to secret societies. However, when they do raise
> such issues they strongly emphasize the practical benefits, particularly

obtaining power over other people and dominating society via the use of terror, violence, and black magic tactics (p. 35, 36).

For New Mexican secret societies, initiations conferred privileged access to ancestors and were performed "especially in caves"—an ancient precursor to the movie theater. "As individuals who dealt with supernatural forces, some society members (in particular the 'clowns') claimed privileges outside normal morality, including the use of black magic, the use of feces, killing at whim, mocking everything, acting contrarily, and generally doing whatever they wanted" (p. 129). Hayden describes the "blatant disregard by members of social conventions, moralities, norms, values, debt agreements, and taboos. They sometimes simply did what they wanted with impunity" (p. 344). It's important to realize that taboo-breaking was not only a matter of wanton self-gratification—as commoners aspiring to such licentious freedom might suppose—but, as we saw with ancient Sparta, *central to the tribulations and sacrifices of participation*:

> In addition to the emotional bonds to the secret society and its members created by undergoing severe physical and emotional trials, many secret societies demanded other costly demonstrations of loyalty and devotion to their organization, much like gang initiations in contemporary industrial societies or the price to be paid for joining the dark side in *Star Wars*. This could simply involve the surrender of large amounts of wealth; however, it could also include giving one's wife away, *or even the sacrifice and eating of one's eldest son.* After such acts, there would be little doubt that an individual was completely devoted to the secret society and would do anything necessary to retain their position (p. 339–40, emphasis added).

If the ruling classes employ taboos to control, oppress, and exploit the masses, it is regardless of color, race, sex, age, or ideological affiliation, and the evidence suggests they do so by creating taboos out of the very things they are secretly doing behind closed doors. (Or perhaps they create laws and then ritualistically break them?) Whichever comes first, the taboo or the totem, psychologically and socio-politically the mechanism being wielded may be as basic as corralling cows with electric fences and cattle prods. First create the structures you want people to enter into, and then provide the "shocks" to make sure they do. When fear drives, the devil rides.

6.5.   THE PAUL BATESON BAG MURDERS

> "I'm not constrained pretty well by anything. The tough thing
> in life is ultimate freedom, that's when the battle starts. Ultimate
> freedom is what it's all about, because you've got to be very
> strong to stand for ultimate freedom. Ultimate freedom is the big
> challenge, now I've got it."
>
> —JIMMY SAVILE[17]

In the interview with Marc Maron, there's another key section in which Friedkin talks about the New York murderer he cast in *The Exorcist,* Paul Bateson. While preparing to make the film, Friedkin had visited the New York University Medical Center to view some medical procedures relevant to the film's action. He was also looking for staff for extras in the film, planning to shoot interiors in New York (the film is set in Washington, D.C.). Friedkin was invited to watch a cerebral angiography, which is performed by puncturing the front of the neck. In the moments between the arterial puncture and the insertion of the catheter, blood gushes from the tube in time with the patient's heartbeat. Friedkin decided to depict this procedure in his film, and wanted the doctor there to perform it on camera, along with the nurse and the technician, Paul Bateson.

The scene, one of the first to be shot, shows Regan (Linda Blair) being examined medically. Bateson speaks most of the dialogue, demonstrating a bedside manner that his coworkers have commented on as something he used with child patients. He is also seen in the background as Regan is wheeled into the room, and helps put her on the table and attach wires to her shoulders. His voice is heard off-camera as Regan's blood spurts into the air and stains her surgical gown. Despite the lack of any supernatural elements, this scene became notorious as the one audiences found *the most disturbing.* Medical professionals praised it as one of the most realistic depictions of any medical procedure in a popular film.

None of this accounts for Bateson's eventual notoriety, however. Three to four years later, in 1977, the dismembered and mutilated remains of six male victims were found wrapped in black plastic bags, dumped in the Hudson River in New York. Some of the body parts washed up on the New Jersey shore, others landed near the World Trade Center; police traced recovered clothing to a shop in Greenwich Village that catered to homosexuals, and were able to identify one of the victims, via distinctive tattoos, as a known homosexual. Lacking identities and confirmed cause of death in several cases, the crimes were not officially classified as homicides, but were listed as CUPPI's—"circumstances undetermined pending police investigation."

A solution came via evidence collected in an apparently unrelated case: on September 14, 1977, film critic Addison Verrill was beaten and stabbed to death in his New York apartment. The man charged with the slaying was Paul Bateson, then 38. Bateson confessed to meeting Verrill in a Greenwich Village gay bar. After having sex at Verrill's flat, Bateson crushed his victim's skull with a metal skillet, then stabbed Verrill in the heart. Since the afore-mentioned bags in which the body parts of murdered homosexuals were found reportedly had wording on them connecting them to NYUMC's neuropsychiatric unit, where Bateson worked, and since the dismemberment of the bodies appeared to have been done by someone skilled in using a knife, investigators publicly named Bateson as a suspect after he was charged with Verrill's murder.

Bateson was convicted of the Verrill homicide on March 5, 1979, drawing a term of 20 years to life. While awaiting trial, he bragged of killing other men "for fun," dismembering their bodies, and dropping the bagged remains in the Hudson River. Although detectives were satisfied of Bateson's guilt, he was never charged for the "bag murders" and they remain officially unsolved. In a strange way, they also inspired Friedkin's 1979 movie, *Cruising*. Here's how it happened, in Friedkin's own words:

> About two or three years after *The Exorcist* came out, I'm reading *The New York Daily News* and I see Paul Bateson's picture in the paper and there's a long story of how he's suspected of having murdered eight or nine people in the S&M clubs in downtown New York. His lawyer's name was in the article and I called his lawyer—Bateson was at Riker's Island . . . I went to Riker's and saw Paul Bateson. I asked him if he

had murdered these people. . . . Bateson told me his story and about
[gay bar] The Mineshaft and it turned out that a friend of mine, Matty
Ianniello—a big mafia figure who's still alive and nicknamed "Matty the
Horse"—owned all the S&M clubs in New York. In fact, he owned the
Stonewall where gay liberation really started. I asked Matty if he would
give me permission to visit The Mineshaft and I did. At the same time,
I knew a police detective named Randy Jurgenson who did what Pacino
does in *Cruising*. Jurgenson was sent into the S&M world to see if he
could find the killer because he resembled most of the victims. That gave
me the story of *Cruising*.[18]

In fact, *Cruising* is also based on a 1970 novel of the same name, about
a serial killer targeting New York City's gay community, and Friedkin had
been approached about making a film of it *as far back as 1972*, shortly after he
made *The French Connection*, and just a few months before he met Bateson.
He wasn't interested in the novel at the time, but considered it more seriously
a few years later.[19] It's hardly accurate, therefore, to say that Friedkin's interest
in Bateson kickstarted the project, only that this was when the final element
fell into place and the project became a "go." In fact, it had been fermenting
for almost a decade, and, in a strange twist of fate that is also characteristic of
psychological operations, on its way from novel to movie, it became reality.

In various interviews that Friedkin has given in recent years, he has
claimed that Bateson (who is well named: the son of Norman Bates) told
him he pled guilty to the other killings as a way to reduce his sentence;
that *he did not remember killing anyone besides Verrill*; and that he must have
committed these murders and dismemberments while in an intoxicated
state. Friedkin never questions this narrative. But committing eight murders
while "under the influence" and having no memory of it sounds more like
a Hollywood melodrama than real life; it suggests that, either Bateson was
used as a convenient patsy to protect the real culprit(s), or, that he was acting
under some kind of "hypnotic suggestibility," while in a "dissociated state."

There's another curious detail, tying all these strands up in a grisly knot:
as already mentioned, Bateson was the assistant to a neuroscientist at the
Neuropsychiatric division of the New York Medical Center. The afore-mentioned Dr. Louis Jolyon West was in charge of the Neuropsychiatric Institute
on the *opposite* coast, in Los Angeles, during his MKULTRA stint, from 1969

to 1989, when, presumably, he advised Friedkin about the safety of darkness, and covering the same period as the bag murders.

One more weave in this tangled web: Paul Bateson makes an appearance in the sixth episode of season two of David Fincher's *Mindhunter*, somewhat randomly, being interviewed by the back-up team of FBI profilers, Wendy Carr (Anna Torv), the closeted lesbian psychology professor, and agent Gregg Smith (Joe Tuttle). In the lead-up to the interview scene, agent Tench (Holt McCallany) is given a line that seems meant to preempt any questions as to Bateson's inclusion in the show. Tench refers to the fact that Bateson was never convicted, or even charged, with any of the bag murders, but only of an unrelated murder (of a movie critic, no less, though the dialogue avoids mentioning this). Nor, as already discussed, was there ever much evidence to link him to these bag murders—outside of Friedkin's own anecdotes, as given in interviews about his film directing career, with special focus on *The Exorcist*. Smith's response to Tench's skepticism in *Mindhunter* is that Bateson "told a friend he was the bag murderer and liked to kill." Not exactly a case-closer, then.

Esquire magazine ran a short piece challenging *Mindhunter* on this point—apparently the claim that Bateson admitted his guilt *was* made in a sentencing hearing, but since "The New York County Clerk was unable to locate the full transcript of the trial . . . it's unclear if this friend was ever brought forth as a witness."[20] The interview scene in *Mindhunter* is about seven minutes long, and mostly focuses on the relationship between sex and violence—specifically, between *homosexual* sex and violence. During the scene, Bateson claims the police tried to strike a deal with him in order to close the six bag murders, promising him less time; yet *the only known source for this claim is the interviews Friedkin did over the years*, most especially in the couple of years leading up to *Mindhunter* season two. Apparently, the writers of *Mindhunter* considered Friedkin a reliable source.*

Curiouser still, when I was looking into this case for this chapter, I found it to be surprisingly under-documented. I couldn't even find anything specifying the exact time in 1977 that the dismembered body parts were first found. If it weren't for "the Friedkin connection," there would be very little

---

* For more on *Mindhunter* and the artful propaganda of David Fincher, see 11.1.

about it online at all. As of 2020, it's not even known if Bateson is alive or not, and if he is, where he's living. In a 2018 interview, Friedkin said he had heard Bateson was living somewhere in upstate New York.[*]

6.6.   PROMETHEAN MIMESIS

"The secret society lies in an area to which the norms of society do not extend."

—GEORG SIMMEL, *"The Sociology of Secrecy and of Secret Societies" (1906)*

One especially unpleasant but I think unavoidable theme that is emerging as our Map of Hell expands in scale and dimension is that of sexual sadism. The use of terror and violence, after all, as I suggested regarding the appeal of *The Exorcist*, is not only to paralyze, desensitize, and numb us—to render us powerless—but also the reverse, to excite, titillate, and arouse in us an illegitimate (deeply unhealthy) *sense of power*. Nor are the two responses mutually exclusive, but rather complementary, compensatory, and codependent. When we are traumatized we dissociate, and as we dissociate we enter into fantasy—not only escape but *revenge* fantasy. As psycho-historian Lloyd deMause writes in "Why Cults Terrorize and Kill Children,"

Sadists live their daily lives full of terrible anxieties about being independent and active. Any success in their lives is terribly fearful, producing regression to infancy and a desire to merge with mommy. But merging means losing one's self, being annihilated. To avoid this, it is necessary to inflict on someone else all the traumas one has had plus all the fantasies of revenge against the persecuting parents.[21]

---

[*] When I first blogged about all this in March 2016, I sent a link to my website to Friedkin, via his official Twitter account, saying: "clues that @williamfriedkin was an MKULTRA subject." To my surprise, Friedkin "liked" the tweet. Sometime later, however (I only found this out in July 2019, while writing this chapter), he blocked me.

De Mause argues that cultic rituals are a means for such regressed individuals to escape the paralyzing terror of their past victimization and "reassure themselves of their potency and separateness." Groups, he suggests, "are particularly effective in achieving this traumatic reenactment." DeMause—whose researches may prove to dovetail in disturbing ways with Hayden's—locates this regressive survival strategy of "group identification with the aggressor" as early as the Paleolithic age, noting that "not only do children's footprints appear in early caves (actually tunnels. . .), but pictures of shamans and other Paleolithic men with erections appear frequently on the walls, showing that the rituals performed there were sexually exciting."

Such ancient coping rituals may be the dark prehistorical basis for the contemporary ritual of collective movie-watching, whether the sexually provocative imagery of *Deep Throat*, or the more overtly violent stimulation of horror or action movies, with or without an explicit revenge motif. Hayden describes how the secret society initiates who construct and employ their member rituals also refashion them into public spectacles to advertise their power, creating both a threat to terrorize the community and an attraction to draw recruits from it. It's easy to imagine how risky and sensitive such an exercise might be, or how such power displays might backfire, either by stirring community members into an overly aggressive fear response, and/ or by stimulating their desire for power and their potential for violence, which might then erupt in mimetic rivalry as they try and take that power for themselves.*

How does all this pertain to movies as psychological operations and means of crowd control? In her 1971 review of *The French Connection*, Pauline Kael included her personal observations, as a New York moviegoer, about the

---

* When Marina Abramović and Debbie Harry theatrically enact taboo-breaking rituals for an elite audience (edited material, to be shared at the author's site, *Auticulture*) , or when Jimmy Savile is bragging about being "untouchable," or talking wistfully about the challenges of ultimate freedom, is this the cultural elite having their bacchanal cake and eating it? Is it a way for them to be both in and out of the closet at the same time, a case of "psychopath pride"—how to be truly "edgy" without being ostracized, imprisoned, or mobbed? Perhaps it's also a way to do one's work as a psychological operative/cultural leader—and get one's due—without drawing unwanted heat, not only to oneself but to one's secret clique. Because, as Jeffrey Epstein may or may not have discovered, if you become a liability to the elite, you risk becoming a casualty of the elite.

disappearing line between violence as depicted, with increased realism, on movie screens, and *latent* violence in movie audiences:

> Horror stories and brutal melodramas concocted for profit are apparently felt on a deeper level than might have been supposed. People don't laugh or applaud when there's a scream; they try to ignore the sound. . . . It is not uncommon now for fights and semi-psychotic episodes to take place in the theaters, especially when the movies being played are shockers. [Y]ou feel that the violence on the screen may at any moment touch off violence in the theater. The audience is explosively *live* (1975, p. 314–15).

This spillover of movie violence into theater violence became fully dynamic with 1979's *The Warriors*, in which audience members were said to find the movie so rousing that fights broke out in the theaters (similar claims were made in 2019 about *Blue Story*). As a result, Paramount Pictures "scrapped its lurid advertising campaign . . . and offered to pay for extra security at any of the 670 theaters where [the film] opened."[22] Apparently it's a thin line between a movie-psyop doing its job and rousing audiences, and doing its job a little *too* well, and having to rethink its "advertising strategies."*

To control a society via the manipulation of taboos requires slicing a razor through the collective eye and then walking that edge. It means flaunting the Promethean fire (that of violent uprising and rebellion) and taunting those for whom it is forbidden in such a way as to constantly reassert superiority *over* them. A good psyop is designed to remind us of our powerlessness and provoke a correspondingly violent response within us, but without unintentionally setting off the powder keg on which such subtle control depends.

---

* In Outtake # 2, I explore the shootings that occurred at the release of *The Dark Knight Rises* in Colorado—an event that itself seems more like a staged psyop than an organic reaction to the movie, and yet the line is clearly blurred. (Perhaps some of the rowdy kids at *The Warriors* were agent provocateurs working for the studio.) As an interesting variable, one we will return to, *The Dark Knight Rises* was part of the first wave of the superhero movie craze, and superhero violence—because of its overtly fantastic and computer-generated qualities—is a far cry from the sort of realism that was popular in the 1970s, which Friedkin was a pioneer of. That would make it that much harder to imitate, that much less likely to spark mimetic violence. Perhaps this was also somewhat calculated?

The trick, presumably, is to trigger audiences, to generate or perpetuate a profound emotional tension within them, without causing them to burn the theater down; or to take their eyes off the screen.

In *Propaganda*, Jacques Ellul writes how propaganda has far less to do with promulgation of doctrine than "psychological manipulation designed to produce action," and so two seemingly contradictory propagandas, "far from canceling each other out . . . have a cumulative effect":

> A boxer, groggy from a left hook, does not return to normal when he is hit with a right hook; he becomes groggier. Now, the modem propagandist likes to speak of his "shock effect." And it is indeed a psychological shock that the individual subjected to propaganda suffers. But a second shock from another angle certainly does not revive him. On the contrary, a second phenomenon is then produced by these contradictory propagandas: the man whose psychological mechanisms have been set in motion to make him take one action is stopped by the second shock, which acts on the same mechanisms to produce another action. . . . The effect of this double shock is so well known that it is utilized as a technique in a single propaganda by the use of either contradictory news or a tranquilizing propaganda designed to appease the public before launching a great shock that will be felt all the more violently: for example, making propaganda for peace before releasing a violent psychological offensive (p. 180–81).

There is a strange split in us by which we seem both drawn to lurid and exaggerated (or over-simplified) stories of Hollywood depravity and its connections to organized crime, etc., while at the same time, hypnotized by the glitzy glamor of industry "spin." It's as if we are equally spellbound by Dorian Gray's shallow beauty as by glimpses of the soul-deep corruption revealed by the hidden portrait. And somehow, these two fascinations, rather than allowing us to reach a coherent conclusion about the truth, are pitted against one another in our psyches. Like a dazed suspect, caught between dread and hope, a good and bad cop on each side of us, we bounce endlessly between two extremes.

A movie like *The Exorcist* has a (somewhat) similarly twin-horned (pun intended) or double-punch function: it sacrifices realism in order to seduce audiences into believing in the reality of the devil (i.e., is openly satanic). Yet at the same time, it poses as a socially conscientious work (claims to be pious). It is possibly the most famous and successful horror movie of all time, and yet its makers deny it's a horror movie: "Blatty and I never spoke about a horror film. We made a film about the mystery of faith, which was his concept, his idea, his believe [sic] system," said Friedkin in 2018.[23]

As Pauline Kael (in sympathy with Ellul) noted, there's no way to counteract the effects of a work like this because, like all effective propaganda, it functions *below* the conscious level. Once it's in our psyches—Hollywood, the Devil, the unholy aspirations of the elite—there seems no way to get it out again. *The Exorcist* is designed to appeal to the atavistic, superstitious parts of us, yet it's considerably more realistically made than *The Sting* or *The Way We Were* (both released the same year), and it's more persuasive too. The very nature of the subject matter—the supernatural—demands an unusual degree of craftsmanship and realism to make sure we suspend our disbelief in the face of something that stretches our credulity this badly. Kael notes:

> The scaring here is a matter of special effects and sound and editing—the roaring-animal noises from the attic coming at the right instant, Regan's bed shaking just enough, the objects in her room flying about without looking silly, and so on. If the audience ever started giggling at the sounds and tricks, the picture might collapse, because it's entirely mechanical and impersonal (1976, p. 249).

The most effective psyop is one that can persuade us it is art, because we associate what moves us with art, and the art of propaganda is *to move us illegitimately.* By appealing to the irrational, unformed part of our minds, it also feeds that part. It's the part that still fears the darkness and imagines monsters lurking under our beds—in our institutions, governments, or the enemies of government—and demons waiting to possess our children. It feeds that part but also feeds *on* it, just as organized religion and occultism do, keeping it alive and hungry within us.* Popcorn and circuses: we line up to be terrorized, to watch heads roll, and then we come out with our nervous systems jangling and our ears buzzing, convinced we have been entertained. Like little Billy, terrorized by subjugation to fright movies by his mother, the only relief we get is by passing *on* the charge and getting others to line up for the same treatment.

What would C.S. Lewis have thought of *The Exorcist*? It's an utterly unfeeling movie about miracles that inspires belief in demons in the worst way possible: a queasy, prurient fascination that, if it drives people to Catholicism, does so with the lowest possible motivation, the fear of sucking cocks in Hell. By combining unusual levels of craftsmanship with profoundly disorienting shock effects and deeply resonant, primal subject matter (fear of Hell), *The Exorcist* is crowd-friendly psyop. It's audience-participation shock treatment, designed to get audiences to *pay* to be terrorized and lobotomized: manufactured masochism.

Was Friedkin, with his weirdly lightweight but creepily revealing biography, signaling to those in the know what his true connections were?

---

* *Hereditary* (2018) is a more recent example of this kind of profoundly disturbing movie "psyop," and (a far better movie than *The Exorcist*) it shows just how effective these manufactured narratives can be. It's perhaps significant that the trailer for the movie was "accidentally" shown before *Peter Rabbit*, a children's movie, across the US. ("Movie Theater Plays Horror Film 'Hereditary' Trailer Before 'Peter Rabbit," *Variety*, April 26, 2018: https://variety.com/2018/film/news/movie-theater-hereditary-trailer-peter-rabbit-1202788535/)

7

THE INSIDER

7.1. KINDLY PATRIARCHS AND TRADITIONAL TERRORISTS: CASE STUDY # 8, LEONARD COHEN

> "Give me back my broken night
> My mirrored room, my secret life
> It's lonely here,
> There's no one left to torture!
> Give me absolute control
> Over every living soul
> And lie beside me, baby,
> That's an order!"
>
> —LEONARD COHEN, *"The Future"*

In September of 2015, I recorded a four-hour-plus conversation with the Canadian author Ann Diamond, the former lover and friend of international monument (even before he passed, in 2016), Leonard Cohen. Diamond revealed some deeply disturbing information about Cohen, ranging from hard facts, to personal anecdotes, to even more personal ruminations and intuitions. Summed up in a sentence, Diamond believed, and believes, that Cohen may have been part of, or at least closely associated with, a Jewish crime family heritage, that he participated in MKULTRA experiments in the 1950s, became an undercover agent for US, Canadian, and/or Israeli intelligence, and that his musical and literary career was facilitated and shaped as a cover for undercover activities, which included international espionage and acts of war.

Long story short: despite being a lifelong fan of Cohen's music, I found Diamond's testimony compelling. I did my own research into Cohen's background to see how much hard evidence there might be for her claims. The bulk of that research makes up this present chapter.

◆

> "[T]he normal, common-sense assumptions, verbal cues, body language, and so on that we use to size up other people and make instant judgments about them often don't apply to sociopaths."
>
> —JOHN E. DOUGLAS, *Mindhunter*

When we identify with cultural (or counter-cultural) figures to the extent that we let them shape our personalities, allowing that they might be *other* than they seem can become the thin end of an identity crisis wedge. There are almost no tools in the current culture to describe or understand this, because our thinking has been shaped by the very forces we are trying to think about. I literally wrote a book about it (*Seen and Not Seen*—I found it almost impossible to market!).

Over the past decade or so, I've had to wrestle to hold onto the belief that, somehow, my personal impression of whether someone was a decent or authentic human being or not was reliable. When it comes to public figures I have never actually met or interacted with in a personal and private setting, I have pretty much lost the battle, and the belief along with it. If actors can persuade us they are someone else in their film roles, why not off-screen? (This was certainly my experience with one of the few celebrities I knew up-close, Billie Whitelaw; see 15.1.) And if so, why wouldn't this be true of intelligence agents, politicians, intellectuals, and an unknown number of "lifetime actors"? This would seem to go double for human predators such as Jimmy Savile, who depend on instilling others with trust and on maintaining a front of likability, honesty, and decency (or at least harmlessness) to secure their prey. The recurring line of reasoning, by which we present our "gut feelings" or personal affinity for this or that public figure as evidence of their innocence (or guilt), may not be evidence of much besides our own naiveté.

In *The Power of Ritual in Prehistory* (p. 345), Brian Hayden describes the officials of the secret societies as both "kindly patriarchs" and "traditional terrorists." Their public persona and rhetoric was "retiring, gracious, and beneficent, whereas they exhibited shocking arrogance in private." Where some secret societies appeared "open, free, and democratic," in practice, "they were aristocratic 'but definitely secretively so.'" Hayden finds it unlikely "the individuals described were schizophrenics, especially since they were the ones making the policies." He believes "these officials displayed a kindly communitarian public persona *as a strategy* to manipulate supporters and the public, but that for the most part, their real motivation was to ruthlessly increase their own power and self-benefits, just as most aggrandizers and sociopaths do even today" (emphasis added).

> This is not to say that there may not have been some genuinely kind venerable patriarchs who wanted to do what was best for their kin and community. However, it is not possible to explain the use of terror, human sacrifices, and the acquisition of personal wealth and power in terms of kindly venerable patriarchs. If such leaders existed, when they entered secret societies they seem to have been outnumbered and powerless to go against the more highly motivated officials promoting their own interests (p. 345).

There's an even darker veil of obscurity to gauging a person's private capacities by their public persona, however: at a certain level of involvement within the secret society of a predatory criminal underworld, a person's entire moral compass may have become reversed. Like Harvey Weinstein, Leonard Cohen may or may not have been affiliated with the followers of Sabbatai Zevi (past or present*), as Ann Diamond believes, but the Sabbateans apparently *do*—or did—believe in committing evil acts as

---

* I have not yet seen any evidence to suggest that the Sabbatean cult exists in any current form, though part of the Sabbateans lived on into the 20th century as "*Dönmeh*" (Turkish for "convert").

a way to hasten the arrival of the messiah, i.e., that greater good can come out of doing apparent evil. Anyone who believes this is already through the looking glass and into a very different paradigm than most of us are relying on to try and get a "read," either on them or their behaviors. Ronan Farrow observed in *Catch and Kill*: "there was a sense that Weinstein was still living in a parallel reality" (p. 284).

The growing body of evidence of counter-cultural icons being part of a hidden subculture that includes extreme forms of child abuse invites us to look a lot more closely at our own values and our criteria for discerning good from evil—which to a large extent is pretty much our aesthetic sense of the distinction between "good" and "mediocre" (it was for me anyway). It's easy enough for me to believe that Jimmy Savile was a human predator capable of unfathomable acts of depravity, because Savile isn't someone I ever took for a serious artist, a role model, or a soulful human being. When it comes to Leonard Cohen, whose body of work has had a massive influence on my life that I have always considered positive, the cognitive dissonance (as for those Jackson fans) becomes extreme.

Shocking as the truth about Jimmy Savile was, or more recently (though far less extreme) about Harvey Weinstein, it didn't really pull the rug out from under our complacency about our culture. It didn't throw into question our ability to identify a predator among us. Though he was quite beloved by British working classes for a period, Savile really *did* act like a creep for much of the time; and Weinstein was loved by hardly anyone and already considered monstrous before the news about his sexual behaviors broke. This makes it easy for people to say, "I always knew he was up to no good!" Even in the case of Michael Jackson—who has legions of fierce defenders to this day —the revelations were not really all that surprising, because Jackson's public persona *was* creepy. Ditto, if to a lesser degree, with Kevin Spacey, who has made a career out of playing psychopaths and scumbags (see Outtake # 4).

Can we imagine anyone saying the same about Leonard Cohen? The man is practically a saint. He is, in almost every regard, as far from what we would think of as a political assassin, spy, or sexual monster as is possible to imagine. He is the archetypal kindly patriarch.

7.2.   FIELD COMMANDER COHEN: JUST THE FACTS

"I said, 'This can't be me, must be my double.'"

—LEONARD COHEN, *"I Can't Forget*
(That I Don't Remember What)"

As Hayden emphasizes, it's not only fair but necessary to examine where our assumptions come from about what undercover agents—or sexual monsters—might look, seem, or act like. How many intelligence operatives wear tuxedos, drive Aston Martins, drink martinis, and say their names in reverse order? Enough that there's no need to wonder about any-one who doesn't fit that bill? Isn't it more likely that intelligence operatives would be highly skilled at covering their tracks and assuming the appear-ance of something *other* than—even diametrically opposite to—spooks? A poet-novelist turned folk singer turned pop star, say? If so, tracking Cohen's activities, uncovering the people he associated with, where his money came from, which groups backed him, where he traveled to and when, what sort of things happened around him or what kind of coded messages might be concealed in his public output, would be the most logical way to proceed.

With that in mind:

Leonard Cohen was born in 1934 of predominantly Jewish lineage. Officially "middle class," his mother was the daughter of a Talmudic writer, Rabbi Solomon Klonitsky-Kline, of Lithuanian Jewish ancestry, and his paternal grandfather was Lyon Cohen, "the head of the largest clothing man-ufacturers in the British Empire, as well as being a pillar of the Canadian Jewish community" (*Leonard Cohen: The Music and the Man*, by Maurice Ratcliff). He was president of the Canadian Export Clothiers Ltd and later became president of the Clothing Manufacturers Association of Montreal, as well as a director of the Montreal Life Insurance Company and founding president of the Canadian Jewish Congress. Lyon "spearheaded the local war effort and encouraged both of his sons to enlist, which they did, becom-ing the first commissioned Jewish officers in the Canadian army" (*Leonard Cohen: A Life in Art*, p. 17). Lyon was supposed to meet the Pope during a

European trip in 1924, but had a heart attack the day before. He died on August 15, 1937, when Leonard Cohen was three years old. (One of the pall bearers at the funeral was liquor magnate for the mob, Samuel Bronfman.*) Cohen: "I had a very Messianic childhood. . . I was told I was a descendant of Aaron, the high priest."

Cohen's father, a clothing manufacturer, died when Cohen was nine. In 1944, Cohen started attending summer camp as a 10-year-old at Camp Hiawatha in the Laurentians region north of Montreal.[1] Cohen excelled at school and college, and was a student council member. As a teenager, Cohen started a band called Buckskin Boys. He hung out on St. Laurent Boulevard to watch "gangsters, pimps, and wrestlers."

Ann Diamond Testimony (ADT): Diamond told me the St. Laurent Boulevard was a largely Jewish-run crime district, but also manufacturing, business, retail, a hub for prostitution and gambling, and a landing point for immigrants. It's also where she went to high school in 196–5. She believes Cohen may have had family who were involved in local business there.

In 1950, Cohen became a counselor at Camp Sunshine, a Jewish community camp. In 1951 (at age 17) Cohen enrolled at McGill University, became president of the McGill Debating Union, and won the Chester MacNaghten Literary Competition for his poetry.

---

* The Bronfman family's success during American Prohibition was due to ties it had cultivated with organized crime during Canada's Prohibition. "Bronfman liquor was purchased in massive quantities by many crime lords who still live on in American legend, including Charles 'Lucky' Luciano . . . and Meyer Lansky." Bronfman's mob associates were members of what later became known as the National Crime Syndicate, "a confederation dominated by Italian-American and Jewish-American mobs." "During that investigation, some of the biggest names in the American mafia named Bronfman as a central figure in their bootlegging operations. The widow of notorious American mob boss Meyer Lansky even recounted how Bronfman had thrown lavish dinner parties for her husband. Years later, Samuel Bronfman's children and grandchildren, their family's ties to the criminal underworld intact, would later go on to associate closely with Leslie Wexner, allegedly the source of much of [Jeffrey] Epstein's mysterious wealth, and other mob-linked 'philanthropists,' and some would even manage their own sexual blackmail operations, including the recently busted blackmail-based 'sex cult' NXIVM." "The Shocking Origins of the Jeffrey Epstein Case," *Geopolitics*, July 21, 2019: https://geopolitics.co/2019/07/21/the-shocking-origins-of-the-jeffrey-epstein-case/

ADT: In 1951, Cohen took part in Dr. Donald Hebb's notorious sensory isolation experiments, for which student volunteers were paid.

Donald Hebb was involved with CIA-backed mind control experiments at McGill University during this time.[2] He did use student volunteers,[3] and paid them $20 a day.[4] The below photograph is of one of these volunteers, or at least precisely matches the conditions they were subjected to. Ann Diamond claims the picture is of Leonard Cohen.

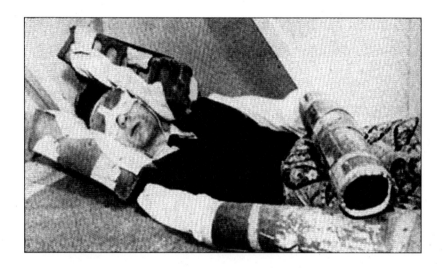

Cohen published his first poems in March 1954 in the magazine *CIV/n*, including "An Halloween Poem to Delight My Younger Friends," describing the ritual burning of birds and frogs on his street in Westmount. It ends with lines about binding a deer and removing its heart. The issue also included poetry by Cohen's poet-professor (who was on the editorial board), Irving Layton. Cohen graduated from McGill the following year with a B.A. degree. In 1956, Cohen's poetry was published as the first book in the McGill Poetry Series, called *Let Us Compare Mythologies*. This was the year after Cohen's graduation and the poems were mostly written when Cohen was between the ages of 15 and 20. Canadian literary critic Northrop Frye praised the book and continued to endorse Cohen's work thereafter. Frye is considered one of the most influential critics of the 20th century.

Cohen supported himself during this period and into his twenties without having regular work, supposedly thanks to a modest trust income from his father's will. In 1958, he participated in looking after children at a McGill-affiliated camp. His main interest appears to have been sex, however.

[Cohen] spent the summer of 1958 as a counselor at Pripstein's Camp Mishmar . . . The camp's philosophy was to take children of varying abilities, background, and behavior and integrate them. . . . The majority of the campers were the children of the middle class and most of the counsellors were McGill students. . . . Many of the counsellors and campers went on to become psychiatrists, social workers and child analysts. . . A camper who ran the darkroom at Pripstein's recalls printing a roll of film for Cohen. They turned out to be a series of photos of nude females. . . . Part of that year was also devoted to visiting his mother, who was being treated for depression in the Allan Memorial Institute (*Various Positions* by Ira B. Nadel, p. 64–5).

The Allan Memorial is where the now-infamous Ewen Cameron conducted his MKULTRA-affiliated experiments during this same period.

ADT: Diamond believes Cohen was also a patient at the AMI in 1958 and claims that this is where she met him, at the age of seven. She admits it would be hard to find corroborating witnesses, as most have died.

7.3.   OPERANT CONDITIONING, EWEN CAMERON & MKULTRA

"I always tell my agents, 'If you want to understand the artist, you have to look at the painting.'"

—JOHN E. DOUGLAS, *Mindhunter*

"Operant conditioning" refers to a scientifically developed method of behavior modification via reward and punishment. It was developed by B.F. Skinner, whose methodology included an "operant conditioning chamber," or "Skinner Box," in which subjects were isolated from their natural environment and exposed to carefully controlled stimuli. Such methods were central to Cameron's mind control program, but may be far more widespread than we think, possibly even culturally ubiquitous. ("Spare the rod, spoil the child.")˙

Cameron's experiments have received widespread coverage in recent years, albeit usually within a context that emphasizes their aberrational nature while divorcing them from their deeper context. A 2018 Guardian piece, for example, "The toxic legacy of Canada's CIA brainwashing experiments: 'They strip you of your soul,'" goes into quite some detail regarding the specific barbarities of Cameron's methods. It cites "a North America-wide project known as MK Ultra," designed "to deepen its understanding of brainwashing, after a handful of Americans captured during the Korean war had publicly praised communism and denounced the US." It claims that, in 1957, "this interest brought the agency north of the border, where a Scottish-born psychiatrist, Ewen Cameron, was trying to discover whether doctors could erase a person's mind and instill new patterns of behavior."

The piece quotes the granddaughter of one of Cameron's victims, Sarah Anne Johnson: "Some of the things he did to his patients are so horrible and unbelievable that it sounds like the stuff of nightmares."

> Patients were subjected to high-voltage electroshock therapy several times a day, forced into drug-induced sleeps that could last months and injected with megadoses of LSD. After reducing them to a childlike state—at times stripping them of basic skills such as how to dress themselves or tie their shoes—Cameron would attempt to reprogram them by bombarding them with recorded messages for up to 16 hours at a time. First came negative messages about their inadequacies, followed by positive ones, in some cases repeated up to half a million times. "He couldn't get his patients to listen to them enough so he put speakers in football helmets

---

* Mistakenly attributed to the Bible, which actually says: "He that spareth his rod, hateth his son: but he that loveth him, chasteneth him betimes" (*Proverbs* 13:24). One interpretation has it that the Biblical reference is to the rod shepherds used to guide their sheep, not to hit them. The phrase, "spare the rod and spoil the child" actually comes from a narrative poem written in the 1600s, titled "Hudibras," by Samuel Butler.

and locked them on their heads," said Johnson. "They were going crazy banging their heads into walls, so he then figured he could put them in a drug induced coma and play the tapes as long as he needed." Along with intensive bouts of electroshock therapy, Johnson's grandmother was given injections of LSD on 14 occasions. . . . "And the doctors and nurses would say to her: 'You're a bad wife, you're a bad mother.'"[5]

A book-length, comprehensive, and well-referenced article on Cameron that appears at The McClaughrys Blog[6] gives a far wider and truer context to these seemingly insane methods. It maps Cameron's involvement in a multi-national, decades-long program of behavior modification so far-reaching and ambitious, and so utterly devoid of ethical considerations, as to more closely approximate dystopian science-fiction than what we think of as history. What follows are some of the pertinent facts about Cameron, as collated and organized at the blog.

Cameron first worked for the OSS (for whom Gregory Bateson also did his pioneer work on schismogenesis), for the Research Division at Albany during World War II. He was "singled out as deserving of more funding for his particularly barbaric methods of interrogation and behavior modification and this relationship with both the OSS and the British intelligence services continued throughout the rest of WWII." Some of the first experiments under MKULTRA used "deep brain stimulation," which entailed opening up the brain and attaching electrodes directly onto it, working with conscious subjects to treat so-called "psychiatric disorders." This was at McGill University under Wilder Penfield; in the US, meanwhile, Jose Delgado and Robert Heath were developing similar or identical methods, using animals and humans.

Also at McGill, under Penfield, a Dr. Scoville surgically removed a structure called the hippocampus from both hemispheres of a man's brain, in an effort to alleviate his epileptic symptoms (September 1st, 1953). The procedure had severe consequences. The "cover" for all this, was that they were researching epilepsy and aging. Penfield operated on about 400 patients altogether in this way, using his electrodes to probe many brain regions systematically. No one really knows just how many people this was done to, because of the atrocious record-keeping that was going on—deliberately—at that time. What we do know, now, is that some of them were children.[7]

Cameron received $69,000 from 1957 to 1964 to carry out his MKULTRA experiments for the CIA at the Allan Memorial Institute. His subproject was number 68. This money "was in addition to the initial 150,000 dollars plus the 30,000 dollars a year for twenty years that had already been guaranteed him by the Rockefeller Foundation fund, set up specifically for his work in July of 1943." Cameron's later work for the CIA was, according to the McClaughrys' deep research, "merely a continuance of what he was already doing in full concert with the coordinated efforts of British, American, and Canadian intelligence agencies—with funding through the respective Defense departments. The CIA money later on was just that, an additional source of funding." In 1948, Cameron wrote that

> extremely interesting and provocative things . . . are happening to our conception of science. It is the inmost germinal place of our future. I reiterate my belief that psychiatrists, with their unique position between the medical and social sciences, have a special responsibility to act as leaders and guides in entering and opening up this new territory.[8]

In a speech he gave in Ohio in 1952, Cameron stated the following: "We have a very considerable obligation to undertake social engineering. . . . We have before us an exciting chapter indeed—a new attack upon individual diseases by the release and direction of the forces of the group. In mental hospitals opportunities are unparalleled for progress in this field."[9] In "Brainwashing in Red China: The Calculated Destruction of Men's Minds," published in 1951, CIA propagandist Edward Hunter wrote:

> Brain-washing is indoctrination, a comparatively simple procedure, but brain-changing is immeasurably more sinister and complicated. Whereas you merely have to undergo a brain-cleansing to rid yourself of "imperialist poisons," in order to have a brain-changing you must empty your mind of old ideas and recollections. . . . Evidently, in a brainchanging, a person's specific recollections of some past period in his life are wiped away, as completely as if they never happened. Then, to fill these gaps in

memory, the ideas which the authorities want this person to "remember" are put into his brain. Hypnotism and drugs and cunning pressures that plague the body and do not necessarily require marked physical violence are required for a brainchanging (p. 11).

Another member of the MKULTRA team who worked at McGill with Ewen Cameron was Donald Hebb, the man whose experiments Diamond claims Cohen volunteered for. At a 1951 secret meeting at the Ritz Carlton Hotel in Montreal, Hebb proposed that by "cutting off all sensory stimulation . . . the individual could be led into a situation whereby ideas, etc. might be implanted."[10] This appears to be what is happening to the subject in the above photograph, who may or may not be Leonard Cohen.

In *Control of The Mind: Man And Civilization*, a symposium edited by Seymour M. Parher and Roger H. L. Wilson for the University of California, San Francisco Medical Center, there is a piece by Hebb titled "The Role of Experience." This is also the title of a radio presentation Hebb gave in late 1961 or early 1962, for a series called "Control of the Mind," also recorded at the San Francisco Medical Center, under sponsorship of the Center's Division of Continuing Education in Medicine. Hebb outlined the rationale for the McGill-MKULTRA program as follows:

What I am saying implies that civilization depends on an all-pervasive thought control established in infancy, which both maintains and is maintained by the social environment, consisting of the behavior of the members of society. The mind is not an absolute, with properties that are the same in radically different circumstances. What we are really talking about in this symposium is mind in an accustomed social environment, and more particularly a social environment that we consider to be the normal one. It is easy to forget this, and the means by which it is achieved. The thought control that we object to, the "tyranny over the mind of man" to which Jefferson swore "eternal hostility," is only the one that is imposed by some autocratic agency, and does not include the rigorous and doctrinaire control that society itself exercises, by common consent, in moral and political values. I do not suggest that this is undesirable. Quite the contrary, I argue that a sound society must have such a control, but let us at least see what we are doing. . . . The problem of thought control, or control of the mind, then, is not how to avoid it, considering it only as a malign influence exerted over the innocent by foreigners, communists, and other evil fellows. We all exert it; only, on the whole, we are more efficient at it.

7.4.   DEEP BACKGROUND

"I want to be the kind of hero/I wanted to be/When I was seven years old/A perfect man/Who kills"

—LEONARD COHEN, *"The Reason I Write"*

In April 1959, both Cohen and his mentor Irving Layton received Canadian Council grants. Cohen's "proposed project was to write a novel drawn from visits to the ancient capitals of Rome, Athens, and Jerusalem," which the Canadian Council agreed to fund. With $2000 in his pocket, Cohen left Canada. In late 1959 to early 1960 (apparently on his way to Jerusalem), Cohen sojourned in Hampstead,[11] London, along with several friends from Montreal such as Nancy Bacal. (Bacal went on to be one of the first people to interview Pink Floyd and became a teacher at Esalen, the California hub for the human potential movement; more on her below.) In London, Cohen met Jacob Rothschild, who suggested Cohen go to the Greek island of Hydra, with specific mention of Nikos Hadjikyriakos-Ghikas's mansion. Ghikas had just married Barbara Hutchinson, Jacob Rothschild's mother, after she divorced Victor Rothschild, Jacob's father.

Cohen quickly established a new social circle in London [meeting] Elizabeth Kenrick, part of a Cambridge set. She, in turn, introduced him to Jacob Rothschild, later Lord Rothschild, [who] encouraged Cohen to visit [Rothschild's] mother [in Hydra], promising to write her to say that Cohen was coming. Layton had predicted Cohen's departure. (Nadel, p. 73)

Cohen arrived in Hydra in 1960, after a visit to Jerusalem. Allegedly he took to it at first sight.

ADT: Diamond told me Cohen tried to visit the Ghikas mansion on his arrival but was refused entry (presumably by a servant); he cursed the house and the next day it burned down. This may be true, but if so it did not happen until 1965. Ghikas was in London at the time and blamed his servant. He never returned to Hydra again.[12]

In 1960, only weeks after arriving there, Henry Luce's *Life* magazine (a major asset in the CIA's Operation Mockingbird*) published a photospread of Bohemian life on Hydra, in which Cohen was prominently placed with his guitar.[13] In 1961 (still working on his Canadian Council-funded novel?), Cohen visited Cuba, shortly after the revolution and right before the Bay of Pigs US invasion occurred. He was arrested as a spy on the beach, but eventually released. The invasion began and he was again arrested at the airport while trying to leave, supposedly having been mistaken for a Cuban soldier trying to escape. He was "miraculously" able to escape from custody (See Nadel, p. 95–97).

In 1962, Cohen returned to London and hung out with Bacal and her boyfriend, the gangster-turned-black activist Michael X. X and Bacal formed the London Black Power Movement. Cohen later boasted about his friendship with Michael X on Canadian TV, joking (?) that X had promised him a country.

ADT: Diamond considers it likely X was an agent provocateur and/or patsy, and mentions that he shows up in a memoir by Kathy Etchingham, a girlfriend of Jimi Hendrix. Apparently, Michael X threatened Hendrix a few months before JH's death in 1970.

Having had his poetry picked up by the leading Canadian publisher McClelland and Stewart in 1961, Cohen's novels *The Favorite Game* and *Beautiful Losers* were published in 1963 and 1966. None of his work sold especially well, and by 1965, by all rights—the strange *Life* magazine photo-shoot and an unusual degree of prizes and government funding notwithstanding—Cohen was still a fairly little-known poet.

---

* Operation Mockingbird was a secret campaign by the CIA to influence media, initiated in the 1950s by Cord Meyer and Allen Dulles. Its origins date back to the OSS and the Second World War. Luce's *Time-Life* was a central weapon in this cultural war, and presumably still is.

Despite this, in 1964–5, the National Film Board of Canada (NFBC, founded to create propaganda during the Second World War) produced an hour-long documentary about Cohen called *Ladies & Gentlemen, Mr. Leonard Cohen*. The documentary begins with a humorous anecdote about Cohen's visit to an unnamed mental institution. Cohen also talks about why he went to Cuba, his "deep interest in violence," and how he "wanted to kill or be killed." He refers to his friendship with Michael X, without naming him. Towards the end, the documentary shows Cohen mingling with a young Bohemian crowd, with a voiceover about how Cohen is especially "interested in young people." He is seen playing guitar and singing at a party.

Soon after the film is released, Cohen professes to be disillusioned by his lack of success as a poet and novelist and opts to change horses midstream and become a folk singer. In 1967, he moves to New York and joins Andy Warhol's Factory crowd, hanging out with Lou Reed, Niko, and Bob Dylan. In no time at all (after playing a few folk festivals), he signs a contract with John Hammond Jr., one of the most famous talent scouts in music history, as well as a Vanderbilt. Cohen's song "Suzanne" becomes a hit for Judy Collins before Cohen has recorded a single song. In 1967, Cohen appears (as "Singer") in *The Ernie Game*, directed by *Ladies & Gentlemen* co-director Don Owen for the NFBC. The film is about a man released from an asylum, struggling to survive in society.

Also in 1967 (before his first album was even released, in December of that year), Cohen returned to London where he played live on the BBC's Julie Felix program. Julie Felix belonged to a countercultural circle along with Michael Hollingshead.[14] Purportedly a major player in the (MKULTRA-linked) CIA-LSD operation of the period, Hollingshead supplied LSD to the likes of Roman Polanski, Cohen's buddy Alex Trocchi, William Burroughs, Paul McCartney, Eric Clapton, Donovan, and the Rolling Stones.[15] Also during this period (according to *Acid Dreams*), Cohen was said to have visited the LSD guru John Starr Cooke, in Mexico (along with Andrija Puharich):

> Cooke was sequestered at a secluded outpost in Cuernavaca, Mexico . . .
> At Cooke's instructions a half-dozen [Psychedelic] Rangers were dispatched to various psychedelic hot spots in North America and Europe

[including] Millbrook* to try and influence the thinking of Leary's clan and lure some of them back to Mexico where Cooke was leading seances while high on acid. Among those who are said to have visited the crippled psychic were Ralph Metzner, songwriter Leonard Cohen, Andrija Puharich, who conducted parapsychology and drug experiments for the US military in the late 1950s (Lee & Shlain, p 158).

Cohen was in London in 1968, and recorded songs for John Peel. After releasing two more albums, Cohen began touring for the first time in 1970. He named his band The Army, and ended his concerts with a military salute.

ADT: When Diamond first saw Cohen perform, she and her friends, she told me, went into a trance state. She also claims that Cohen's hypnotic stage talents were able to calm down an unruly crowd at the Isle of Wight festival in 1970, after which Kris Kristofferson allegedly said, "Leonard's our boy." Diamond also believes Kristofferson was an undercover operative.

Kristoffer Kristofferson was born in Brownsville, Texas. His father, Lars Henry Kristofferson, was a US Army Air Corps officer (later a US Air Force major general). Kristofferson earned a Rhodes Scholarship to Oxford University and then joined the US Army and attained the rank of captain. He became a helicopter pilot after receiving flight training at Fort Rucker, Alabama and completed Ranger School. During the early 1960s, he was stationed in West Germany as a member of the 8th Infantry Division. During this time, he formed a band and began his music career. At the 1970 Isle of Wight festival, Cohen performed with The Army, right after Jimi Hendrix "had set the stage on fire. Someone had also set fire to the concession stands just before Cohen was to perform" (Nadel, p. 178). Cohen biographer Ira Nadel then quotes Kris Kristofferson: Cohen "did the damnedest thing you ever saw: he Charmed the Beast. A lone sorrowful voice did what some of the best rockers in the world had tried to do and failed" (p. 178).

By Cohen's own account, when Cohen first met Janis Joplin at the Chelsea Hotel, she was looking for Kris Kristofferson and he claimed (rather unconvincingly, one supposes) to be him.[16] There are a number of rumors

---

* Millbrook was the site at the Hitchcock Estate which became the nexus for Timothy Leary's psychedelic movement in the 1960s, and where Leary conducted the bulk of his research. It was owned by the CIA-affiliated Mellon Hitchcock family.

that the Chelsea Hotel was used as a CIA front. Certainly, it was a hot-bed of countercultural activity, of sex, drugs, and rock and roll celebrities (the Hotel's literary pedigree went back to Mark Twain, but figures known to reside there in the 1960s included William Burroughs, Arthur C. Clarke, Joan Baez, Bob Dylan, Jimi Hendrix, Allen Ginsberg, and Kristofferson). It seems likely it would have been on the US intelligence radar, and even of interest as a potentially invaluable venue, not only for observation and infiltration, but for active application (as a honey trap, for example).

To give some wider context for these speculations, a brief description of Operation Midnight Climax. Initially established in 1954 for the CIA as a sub-project of MKULTRA, by Sidney Gottlieb, MC consisted of a web of CIA-run "safehouses" in San Francisco, Marin, and New York City, "decorated like brothels." Prostitutes were recruited "to pick up johns at bars, bring them back to the safe house, give them LSD without their knowledge, and then have sex with them" while CIA officers watched through one-way glass. The project documents state that the purpose of the experiments was to test the effects of LSD on unwitting subjects under field conditions that mimicked an interrogation of a foreign operative. Several significant operational techniques were developed via Midnight Climax, involving sexual blackmail, surveillance technology, and the use of mind-altering drugs in field operations. The program was soon expanded, and CIA operatives began dosing people in restaurants, bars and beaches—and presumably hotels.

> In one of the memos contained in the MKULTRA files for these projects, however, another purpose of the safe house operation is revealed. The CIA was actually testing the performance of "Jekyll-Hyde" identities they had created in the prostitutes. They wanted to see if they could make female spies or female agents with alternate controllable personalities. Another purpose of these experiments was to test the CIA's Manchurian Candidate prostitutes under conditions that mimicked a field operation. The johns were given LSD as part of the cover for testing the CIA's female Manchurian Candidates prior to their use in actual operations (the mission being to have sex with and extract information from targets). The recruitment of street prostitutes provided an additional layer of cover for the testing of the Manchurian Candidates, plus it provided free live pornography for the CIA officers.[17]

Documents released under the Freedom of Information Act reveal a number of these operations in New York in the 1960s—the heyday of the Chelsea Hotel—though in all of them the location has been redacted. Ira Nadel describes the Chelsea Hotel during this period as being "notorious as the residence for the emerging underground music and writing scene, with its thick walls, high ceilings, and a management that had 'an iron regard for privacy.'" It also had "a flourishing drug culture." Nagel quotes Cohen saying that one "went on a lot of involuntary trips [there] just accepting the hospitality of others" (p. 143). If that doesn't sound like a CIA safe house, then I don't know what would.

Winding up our partial timeline: in 1973, a few days before the Yom Kippur war began, Cohen travelled to Israel. He joined the Israel Defense Forces (IDF) but did not fight, being considered more useful as a singer to boost soldier morale.[18] This clearly illustrates, in a less-controversial way, the overlap between army training and the development of performance skills for crowd control, and why a gifted folk singer might be considered an asset to military intelligence operations. Immediately after his stint in the IDF, Cohen flew from Israel to Asmara, Ethiopia, where he supposedly wrote "Chelsea Hotel" (about Janis Joplin). The Ethiopian revolution/civil war began soon after his visit, in early 1974. So far as I know, the only mention of Asmara in all the Cohen biographies refers to his writing a song there. Whatever his reasons were for being there, they appear to have been lost to history (i.e., deemed immaterial).

ADT: Diamond claims the hotel in Asmara appears to be another meeting place for intelligence operatives.

In "Field Commander Cohen," the song he released in 1974, Cohen refers to himself as "our most important spy . . . parachuting acid into diplomatic cocktail parties [and] urging Fidel Castro to abandon fields and castles." But that's OK, he's just being ironic. In 1974, apparently on a roll, Leonard Cohen was quoted as saying, "War is wonderful. They'll never stamp it out."

There were another forty years to Cohen's life, no doubt as rife with clues and anomalies as the preceding ones, but since space and time are limited, the only specific reference I will make to this period is Cohen's accountant, Kelley Lynch. Lynch was sentenced to eighteen months in jail in 2012 for embezzling over $5 million from Cohen's bank account. I have spoken to Lynch directly and, as might be expected, her version of events is radically different to Cohen's.[19] Lynch told me by email:

> Leonard Cohen spent millions upon millions of dollars developing his false narrative which was then propelled into the public realm through lawsuits, articles, interviews, press releases, biographies, and other PR techniques. There is an unfair advantage when a celebrity, with liability on the horizon, hires an army of lawyers, is assisted by LAPD's TMU (a celebrity unit) in manufacturing a false narrative, and highly unethical and nearly Satanic prosecutors take their so-called case before LA Superior Court. The Court literally resembles a fascist enterprise engaged in all sorts of racketeering. It serves no truth seeking function, suppresses the truth and actual facts every step of the way, perjury/fraud are "litigation protected" tactics, and the appellate division rubber stamps the trial court. This is a very perverted system of "justice."

Lynch added that Cohen's conduct with her "was unwholesome and thoroughly twisted" but that "as LC himself has stated: his public persona was a 'cover' operation." In a private correspondence similar in essence to public declarations she has made, while going significantly further out on a limb, Lynch wrote to me:

> I can confirm that LC personally advised me (my mother and others) that he was a participant in CIA's MK Ultra Program. He also informed me (and others) that he was a member of a CIA reconnaissance team during the Bay of Pigs, etc. "Our most important spy" who clearly, as Ann [Diamond] noticed, sent messages to his fans related to "alpha, omega, delta, and mockingbird." The manual of LAPD's celebrity unit shows how they employ similar tactics and use psychologists to intimidate, coerce, discredit, and torment individuals. Leonard Cohen and his "team" . . . have used malicious and unconscionable tactics against me and it is very clear (after reviewing this manual and the tactics used) that this is how their cases are manufactured. The use of fraud restraining orders is of the utmost importance. To quote Jeff Dunn of this unit: "Detectives should view restraining orders as tools rather than deterrents. We are seeking to place legal parameters around behavior that would

otherwise not be criminal. We expect the suspect to violate the order, with the knowledge that we can now justify an arrest where none was possible before."

7.5.   ZEN COHEN

"I'd say it's all from real situations. The experience is real but one tries to treat the experience imaginatively."

—LEONARD COHEN, *1973*

Leonard Cohen, in his own words:

"I saw powerful governing men in black suits
I saw them undressed
in the arms of young mistresses
the men more naked than the naked women
the men crying quietly
. . . .
It was tied up with the newspapers
I saw secret arrangements in high offices
I saw men who loved their worldliness"
("I Had It for a Moment")

"You had to open little boys
with a penknife.
I loved your statement to the press
'I didn't think he'd mind.'
Goodbye articulate monsters
Abbot and Costello have met Frankenstein.
I am sorry that the conspirators must go
the ones who scared me by showing me
a list of all the members of my family.
I loved the way they reserved judgment
about Genghis Khan."
("Disguises")

"Should I suffer
the smallest humiliation
at your hand
I will k--l you
and your entire family"
("Dear Mailer")

"You went to work at the U.N.
and you became a spy
for a South American government
because you cared for nothing"
("You Went to Work")

"Any system you contrive without us
will be brought down"
("Any System")

"You have many things on your mind
We think only of revenge"
("One of these days")

"This is war
You are here to be destroyed"
("This is War")

"What embrace
satisfies the child
who will not kill?"
("Stay")

"When they poured across the border
I was cautioned to surrender,
this I could not do;
I took my gun and vanished."
("The Partisan")

This last quote perhaps should come with a trigger warning. It is from *Beautiful Losers*:

> I want thirteen-year-olds in my life. Bible King David had one to warm his dying bed. Why shouldn't we associate with beautiful people? Tight, tight, tight, oh, I want to be trapped in a thirteen-year-old life. I know, I know about war and business. I am aware of shit. Thirteen-year-old electricity is very sweet to suck, and I am (or let me be) tender as a hummingbird. Don't I have some hummingbird in my soul? Isn't there something timeless and unutterably light in my lust hovering over a young wet crack in a blur of blond air? . . . . Bittersweet is the cunt sap of a thirteen year old (pg. 309).

Ann Diamond points out that there is another meaning of Hummingbird, mentioned by author Jerzy Kosiński, that of a high-level intelligence operative often occupying a cultural portfolio. She is referring to his novel Cockpit, in which a "hummingbird" is "an agent whose real identity is kept from other agents and is often disguised as a cultural official, a businessman, an artist, or writer."[20] In his last, posthumous album, *Thanks for the Dance*, the last track—Cohen's very last word to the world—is called "Listen to the Hummingbird."

7.6.   AN ALIBI FOR SOMETHING NOBODY'S EVER BEEN ABLE TO TALK ABOUT

"When I was a young man my friends and I thought we were famous and believed that every time we met for a beer it was a historical event. I grew up before television so it was easier to create one's own mythology, but we truly believed that Montreal was a holy city, all of us were sainted, gifted beings, our love affairs were important, our songs immortal, our poems deathless, and we would lead lives of delicious self-sacrifice to art or God."

—LEONARD COHEN, *1988*

There is a large collection of Cohen interviews called *Leonard Cohen on Leonard Cohen*—pop history is written by the winners—and reading it, I found myself wondering how it was possible that someone capable of such depth and insight could be involved in the sort of deep state/organized crime activity which Ann Diamond's testimony indicated. Of course, as Hayden stresses, the idea that depth and insight, even kindness and humility, cannot co-exist with (or be a front for) sociopathic behaviors is really no more solid than the belief that great art shows the soul of the artist, and is "all we need to know" about him or her.

The facts speak for themselves, however, and while the above facts do not make up a fully coherent counter-narrative to the official Cohen story, they do suggest that aspects of Cohen's life, personality, and actions have been strategically deemphasized. This implies that the accepted history of Leonard Cohen is unreliable, and that Cohen is an unreliable narrator.

While reading the interviews in the book, I found myself less and less impressed by Cohen's apparent wisdom and aplomb, and increasingly turned off by what I began to see as a subtle kind of condescension, self-importance, and messianic proselytizing *posing* as humility and self-effacement. The proof, for me, was in how adoring these pieces invariably were. Almost every one of them introduces the conversation with commentary about how gracious, kind, humble, and beguiling a man Cohen is and how excited and honored the interviewer is to be meeting him. Time after time, the pieces stress his legendary status and how, as an artist, he is just a feather or two away from a full set of wings.

It's interesting to note, in this regard, that not only many of the writers but Cohen himself all refer to his songs as "prayers" (including Bob Dylan). But prayers for what? Is the holy man praying for sufficient humility to inspire worship? Or is "the little Jew" patiently waiting for his people to have their revenge?

> *Who is it whom I address,*
> *who takes down what I confess?*

Another thing I noticed in the book was how frequently Cohen used the same terms, phrases, and descriptions, sometimes verbatim. This makes his sage-like persona look increasingly mask-like, a routine, a shtick. I found myself wondering if Cohen's master-shtick was appearing to be a man without a shtick.

> If you want a lover
> I'll do anything you ask me to
> And if you want another kind of love
> I'll wear a mask for you

There is one interview, towards the end of Part III, which is a marked exception. It's with Richard Guilliat for the *Sunday Times*, dated December 12, 1993. Cohen is obviously drunk, and talks more like a sexual predator than a holy man. As well as recording, without judgment, Cohen's drunken crassness, Guilliatt writes this:

> Unlike many Canadians, Cohen is a passionate defender of the American ideal, but the solutions he sees to the country's problems are surprisingly authoritarian—more police on the streets, the censoring of violent television, the application of force. "At certain times of crisis, like in every other society, extraordinary and emergency measures have to be invoked . . . The fact is that the predators—on all levels, whether it's Wall Street or the streets—are about to take over."

Was this a moment when the mask slipped, I wondered? *In vino, veritas*? Cohen's unaddressed alcoholism bleeds through the pages of this book, yet no one questions the holiness of that.

Of course this is observation, not evidence. If it were presented as an argument, it would more likely be interpreted as evidence of my own prejudice against Cohen, now that I have begun to adopt an alternate version of "the Man." But from my point of view, it is an essential part of the reassessment process. Evidence causes shifts in perception, and shifts in perception allow for previously unseen evidence to be seen. I have heard Ann Diamond's experiences of Cohen, and been privy to Kelley Lynch's damning testimony. And after placing Cohen's public persona in the new context provided by these testimonies, what I have started to see, or imagine I see, is less the charming raconteur and droll connoisseur of love and life, more the clever dissembler of information, the well-trained manager of perception.

He will speak these words of wisdom
Like a sage, a man of vision
Though he knows he's really nothing
But the brief elaboration of a tube

Another thing about those "prayers": so much of what Cohen says, particularly in the latter part of his career (the post-Prozac years, from 1990 to his death in 2016), is devoutly religious, both in tone and content, but without paying lip service to any specific religion or deity. Cohen is downright pious, and yet somehow he gets away with it. How often has religious rhetoric and sentiment been a cover for a legion of sins? Often enough for us to smell a rat when we hear its scratching? Don't we know the signs by now, that only the worst of sinners prays so much?

In an unrecorded conversation with Ann Diamond, we talked about how the desire to get to the truth of Cohen wasn't primarily a desire to expose him as a liar and a thief (or possibly worse), but stemmed from a need to identify a false representation of reality, as a way to move towards a truer one. The saintly sage Cohen, whom so many admire, revere, even worship, is, in my view, a counterfeit. Granted, he was a very *good* counterfeit. The MKULTRA team didn't mess around, and Cohen may have been among their proudest accomplishments, from that period at least, in terms of a successfully engineered "hummingbird" with an extremely high public profile. He was an almost flawless representation of the good (and successful!) poetic soul, the man of high art and sensual lusts who was both a worldly success *and* a spiritual servant. Holy mount Zion! In the halls of rock and roll, he is practically the Messiah.

You don't know me from the wind
You never will, you never did
I'm the little Jew
Who wrote the Bible

Yet all the while working for the Man? Perhaps this is the most important job a socially engineered cultural icon such as Cohen (if such he was)
can do for the System? By presenting a counterfeit spiritual and artistic currency, he helped ensure we wouldn't look for the real thing. And if we ever
happened to stumble on it, we would be unlikely to recognize it because it
wouldn't match the sort of style and grace—the superficial charm—we have
been conditioned, by straw sages like Cohen, to expect.

> *The war was lost, the treaty signed*
> *I was not caught, I crossed the line*
> *I was not caught, though many tried*
> *I live among you, well-disguised*
> *I had to leave, my life behind*
> *I dug some graves, you'll never find*
> *The story's told, with facts and lies*
> *I had a name, but never mind*

This is from page 93 of *Leonard Cohen on Leonard Cohen*, "The Romantic
in a Ragpicker's Trade," by Paul Williams:

"Forgive me for asking"—it may have seemed a significant question
made banal, but it needed an answer—"what are you trying to achieve in
your songs; what is your ambition?"

"To create a vapor and a mist," Cohen responded, "to make oneself
attractive, to master it . . . Really, it's all an alibi for something nobody's
ever been able to talk about."

And I said, 'This can't be me, must be my double.

8

CUL-DE-SAC

8.1. HOLLYWOOD DRUG DEAL
GOES HORRIBLY WRONG!

"[Y]ou never know the real truth about anyone. So who cares?"

—ROMAN POLANSKI, *Playboy 1971 interview*

Returning in now, circle-like, to the place we started, Cielo Drive, Los Angeles, August 1969. As we re-embark, it seems only fair to let the "victim" speak for himself at least one more time. The nature of my thesis means I have a vested interest in establishing Polanski, and by extension Hollywood, as complicit with, if not actual accomplices in, the Cielo Drive murders. This alone is reason to be cautious. Add to this, there is the fact of a whole cultural movement (#MeToo, etc.), currently tearing down statues of white men (literally) and redacting the names and reputations of former cultural icons, most especially when they are accused of crimes against women, as Polanski is. This movement strikes me as one more culturally engineered revenge fantasy and cynically exploited "outrage harvest," geared towards scapegoating white males (though also white women, who are currently undergoing their own "ritualistic humiliation"*). Since all

---

* "It's 2020 and one of the most popular trends on the internet is the ritualistic humiliation of women. Specifically of white, usually middle-aged women. They're called

187

this mimetic scapegoating is both a reaction against and a major contributing factor to the growing instability of the cultural institutions, I am wary of adding momentum to it *in any way* with this current text.

At a more personal level: even now, Polanski's version of events—a version he has never diverged from since the murder happened—causes a great deal of cognitive dissonance in me whenever I read or hear it. Despite all the evidence to the contrary, I find myself *believing* Polanski, and hence doubting my own arguments, wondering if this book is participating in an unfair condemnation ritual. The reader should also have the opportunity to doubt, and/or to share my cognitive dissonance, as two opposing versions of reality walk side by side, and yet never meet. Here is poor Roman's testimony, then, from his 1971 *Playboy* interview:

> It was sickening, the way the press sensationalized something that was already sensational. This was a subject I knew more about than anybody else, a subject very near to my heart. I had long known that it was impossible for a journalist to convey 100 percent of the truth, but I didn't realize to what extent the truth is distorted, both by the intentions of the journalist and by neglect. I don't mean just the interpretations of what happened; I also mean the facts. The reporting about Sharon and the murders was virtually criminal. Reading the papers, I could not believe my eyes. *I could not believe my eyes!* They blamed the victims for their own murders. . . . *Goddamn* them! The victims were assassinated two times: once by the murderers, the second time by the press. . . . And they all believed there had to be a logical motive, so they slandered us with articles about the "wild parties that led to the massacre"—which is an exact title of one newspaper story—and the connections to Jay Sebring and [Frykowski] with certain anonymous drug dealers. . . . But there is something magical about the printed word, so the average reader says, "Well,

---

'Karens'. And the hatred for them is off the scale. It has become a bloodsport. Mobs of the supposedly virtuous love nothing more than to hunt these women down, film them, post the content online, and then sit back and watch as the women's lives are destroyed by armies of Karen-haters." "The hatred for 'Karens' is out of control," by Brendan O'Neill, *Spiked*, June 25, 2020: https://www.spiked-online.com/2020/06/25/the-hatred-for-karens-is-out-of-control/

if they print it, it must be true" . . . . *Time* magazine said [Frykowski] had "sinister connections to which even the tolerant Polanski objected." Where do they get this stuff? I ask you. Where do they get it? (Randall, p. 307–8.)

As I will demonstrate, there was plenty of fire behind the smoke of these "rumors," so this part of Polanski's outraged testimony, at least, rings resoundingly false—fortunately for this book's thesis, since it introduces the possibility that *all of it* is likewise a kind of masterful performance to maintain a necessary fiction. On the other hand, much of Polanski's distress seems genuine to me, and so it may be wrongheaded to try and categorize his statements either as fiction or as nonfiction. This is something that's hard enough to do with books, and human beings are at least as complex as books. It's perhaps more likely that Polanski—like Whitley Strieber, whose "masterful performance to maintain a necessary fiction" I deconstructed in *Prisoner of Infinity*—is fragmented, and so both lying and telling the truth at the same time. (Rather like movies do.) Polanski asks the *Playboy* interviewer:

How could the press accept that as an explanation? These were all very good people, and this was a happy, blameless period of my life. . . . We all tried to help each other, we were happy at each other's success, and it was beautiful, and so new to me . . . . It seemed to be a kind of peculiar, happy dream. But there was nothing freaked out, sinister or immoral about it (Randall, p. 308–9).

Lastly, and most difficult of all to feel cynical about, there are Polanski's heartfelt(?) defenses of his murdered wife:

And Sharon—it was fantastic what they were attributing to her. In death, they made a monster out of her. A monster out of the sweetest, most lovable human being. She was kindness itself to everybody and everything around her—people, animals, everything. She just didn't have a bad bone in her body. She was a unique person. It's difficult to describe her character. She was just utterly good, the kindest human being I've ever met, with extreme patience. To live with me was proof of her patience, because to be near me must be an ordeal (Randall, p. 309–10).

That last is an interesting admission, one that's confirmed, as we will see, by the few Hollywood insiders who failed to keep to the script (some of whom Polanski rails against in the interview). At the end of the day, there is little one can do to determine the sincerity of Polanski's words; all we can do is examine them for accuracy. And if, as I think the material that both precedes and follows this section shows, the facts fail to support Roman's version of reality, then we must consider the possibility that he is, not only emotionally distraught, confused, and possibly deeply delusional, but also actively and consciously *lying*—as any successful aggrandizer must. If so, and if what Polanski is lying to protect is his very life, and/or his freedom and sanity, then we could expect someone in such a position to call on all their talents and give the most convincing performance possible. I don't offer this as a theory, or even an opinion; only as a question that should remain open as you read the following.

◆

"Now here I was in Hollywood, in the place that belonged more to my dreams than to my reality, at the threshold of where everything would be handed to me, and I felt absolutely no thrill."

—ROMAN POLANSKI, *Playboy 1971 interview*

The belief that "black hoods were found [at the Cielo Drive murder scene], and some sort of black aprons shaped like a downpointed ace of spades" (Sanders, p. 251)—elements Polanski singles out in his autobiography *Roman* as examples of sordid Hollywood gossip-mongering—persists to this day. And the occult aspects to the killings did seem to become especially central once the tabloid press got a hold of the story. If so, I suspect it is with a deeper purpose than merely selling papers (for one thing, they are fully compatible with the Manson-as-Satanic-Mastermind narrative). For years, I heard that Anton Szander LaVey was a "consultant" on *Rosemary's Baby* and that he played the barely glimpsed part of the devil in the film; I even repeated the claim in two of my books, presenting it as evidence of a genuine "satanic" element in Polanski's life, and hence in the Manson murders (one of the convicted killers, Susan Atkins, did know LaVey). Yet it probably wasn't true, being more likely fabricated by LaVey himself, whether for the

purposes of self-mythologizing or the more elaborate ones of mythic management (not that it's either/or).

As far back as I can remember, I have been familiar with the idea of
the tabloid press being salacious, irresponsible, sensationalistic, and lacking
journalistic and moral integrity. No doubt there is truth in this, and extreme
and shocking stories *are* sometimes invented whole-cloth by irresponsible
journalists hungry for a scoop, because people *do* seem to have a taste for
the salacious. But it's worth asking how exactly such an appetite became
so pervasive—and why. As is discussed in Outtake # 5 (page 471), the "free
press" is really nothing of the sort, and *Time* magazine is every bit as much a
propaganda wing of US intelligence as the *National Enquirer*. This suggests
it's not only "salacious" reporting that we should be on guard against, but
also the reassuring, middle-of-the-road, "nothing-to-see here" kind. And the
idea of a gutter-level press, muddying the waters by introducing "lurid" and
"sensationalist" elements relating to sexual depravity, drugs, mind control,
satanic rituals, organized crime, or government conspiracies, seems central
to the "spin doctoring" of the more reputable press. Yet it seems that often,
extremely sordid or disturbing stories that are derided as yellow journalism
have just as much basis in fact, or first-person testimonies, as more readily
accepted, less lurid accounts—and sometimes considerably more so.

On the other hand, it's not possible to rule out the possibility that
much of this stuff *is* confabulated, not by lazy and opportunistic journalists, however, but by Hollywood masters of persuasion like Robert Evans
or Roman Polanski. At this point a new question arises: how much of the
"devil-stuff" is manufactured, not *after* the fact, via false testimonials and
disinformation, but *before* the fact, in the propagation of movie myths, the
enactment of crimes, and the private kinks of the rich and famous? And how
much is done so deliberately, both to discredit the stories and, at the same
time, to make them more terrifying and titillating?

In subsequent chapters, I will outline how psyop exploits superstitious belief to manipulate and terrorize a target audience. Because of this,
I have become increasingly wary of including overtly satanic or occult
elements—or even the subject of CIA mind control, which is a secular
form of the occult—because there seems no way to know how much is
deliberate exaggeration, distortion, or outright invention, designed to
imbue shadowy organizations with an exaggerated degree of supernatural

power and knowledge. The possibility that there was a post-Cielo Drive murders psyop to create the *belief* it had all been carefully planned, and that Manson was a CIA MKULTRA puppet, can't be ruled out. Nor can we rule out the possibility that it *was* a preplanned military operation (as Mae Brussell believed), an act of domestic terrorism.[1]

Celebrity sex and drug orgies, and the corresponding opportunity—or necessity—of a criminal/political underworld involvement in the murders, on the other hand, doesn't seem to me to have any obvious advantages in terms of spreading shock-and-awe, and this element does seem to have been downplayed somewhat, even in alternate research circles. Perhaps the most central quote, floating around since 1969, is the one Ed Sanders sources in a friend of his, Allen Katzman, a poet and the editor of the underground newspaper, *The East Village Other*, who spoke to Dennis Hopper at the time. Hopper had been living with Michelle Phillips, having cast her in *The Last Movie* (this would have been before she hooked up with Jack Nicholson):

> He explained that the four murder victims had been involved in a sado-maso club run out of Mama Cass' house. A coke dealer had "burned" Sebring and Frykowski for a large amount of money, and as revenge he was kidnapped by them, taken to Mama Cass's where in front of twen-ty-five prominent rock and movie stars he was "stripped, whipped and buggered." Hopper implied his source was Michelle Phillips. After that, the tale went, vengeance occurred (Sanders, p. 251–52).

In some ways, Hopper's statement (if he truly said it, as far as I know he never confirmed it) is perhaps the central testimony around the Tate murder, at least in terms of pointing towards a concealed layer of intrigue and a possible motive for the murders that has nothing to do with race wars or cult brainwashing. As we'll see, however, there are many layers to an onion. A classic movie—*Chinatown*, say—has a surface story, under which there may be a more complex plot that few viewers ever fully bother to follow. Beneath *that*, there is a subtext which viewers don't ever need to become consciously aware of to appreciate the movie. And under *that* layer, there is, as *16 Maps of Hell* attempts to reveal, an almost entirely hidden, "occult," or encoded set of signifiers, meant exclusively for those "in the know." As with elaborately con-structed movies, so with real-world events such as the Cielo Drive murders.

8.2.   CHAOS!

"I separate love from sex. For many people, fornication is
immoral. Strangely enough, it seems supremely moral to me
to have sex with a girl I've met in a harbor at St. Tropez. Sex is
beautiful. No one gets hurt."

—ROMAN POLANSKI, *1971 Playboy interview*

Of all the books on Manson, O'Neill's *Chaos* probably goes the furthest
to uncovering this second layer of reality, and, as will come as no surprise
by now, the thread that weaves the two worlds together is that of organized
crime, with a particular emphasis—as we saw in the case of Evans—on the
Los Angeles drug trade. O'Neill recounts that, after Tate and Polanski left
for Europe in 1969, Wojtek Frykowski and Abigail Folger "threw parties all
the time. The door was open to anyone and everyone. The crowds got row-
dier, the drugs harder—not just pot and hash, but an abundance of cocaine,
mescaline, LSD, and MDA, which was then a new and fairly unheard-of
synthetic Frykowski was especially enamored of" (p. 58–9).

MDA is closely related to MDMA (both were first synthesized during
the same period, 1910–12, by German pharmaceutical companies). MDA
(street name Sally) can be used as an adulterant to illicitly produce MDMA
(street name Molly), but they are said to be "similar enough that MDA is
sometimes sold as MDMA."[2] A decade after Frykowski and friends were
partying with Sally, Molly—by then known as ecstasy—became the most
popular drug on the club scene, birthing a whole new subculture (rave). It
may also be significant that the first ever scientific paper on MDMA was
published in Poland (Frykowski and Polanski's homeland), in 1960.[3]

O'Neill, like Nicholas Schreck, believes that Frykowski wanted "in" on
the MDA market, and that he negotiated a deal with "his new friends" and
became "a middleman between them and Hollywood" (p. 59; this is an area
Sanders' *The Family* gives wide berth). According to O'Neill, these were the
same three dealers Frykowski threw out of Cielo Drive, as cited by Polanski
in *Roman* as the reason for the "rumors" about his friend's involvement in
the drug scene. Apparently Frykowski and co. kissed and made up, however, since the dealers became regulars at Cielo Drive parties, presumably

due more to their drug connections than their social graces. According to O'Neill, one of these men was Pic Dawson, who "had been the subject of Interpol surveillance for drug smuggling as early as 1965 [and had] gained entrée in the Polanski crowd through his friendship with Cass Elliot" (p. 67). Elliott, a.k.a. Mama Cass, also fraternized with Dawson's two associates, Billy Doyle and Tom Harrigan. According to Dave McGowan's *Weird Scenes Inside the Canyon*, Doyle was the victim of the whipping and rape, as witnessed by Michelle Phillips and recounted to Dennis Hopper (p. 208).[4] *Restless Souls* (the 2012 book written by Tate family and friends) also mentions a "third-hand rumor, a variation of Jim Mitchum's story on Billy Doyle," coming via Candice Bergen, that Frykowski and others were burned by Doyle and for revenge they "tied him to a tree and raped him in front of an audience of twelve" (p. 87).

So, with all of these smoking guns and flying bullets, how exactly did the Helter Skelter narrative manage to take such a total hold of public consciousness that the deep background of drug deals, sex orgies, and S & M Hollywood porn became irrelevant? Ignoring Sanders' account (he was after all a music industry insider), Mae Brussell, Schreck, and O'Neill all seem to agree that the original spinner of the tall tale that captured a nation was Susan Atkins (also known as "Sexy Sadie"). As Brussell explained in 1971:

> A man named Lawrence Schiller made a record with Jack Ruby on January the 2nd 1967 in which Ruby said there was no conspiracy to kill Oswald. . . . January the 4th, two days later, Ruby was dead. . . . Now this same Lawrence Schiller is the man who gave Sue Atkins $150,000 to turn the state's evidence to say that Manson masterminded the murders. She made $150,000. It was described as an unusual legal trick. Joseph Ball, who worked with the Warren Commission [JFK murder investigation], was with parties involved in the Sharon Tate massacre. George Shibley, who worked with Sirhan—and McKissick was in his office—they worked with the Sirhan [alleged RFK shooter] case. They were in on the Sharon Tate case. The lawyers overlap.[5]

There are far too many threads in this one paragraph to untangle all of them (the Sirhan Sirhan overlap would take us all the way into satanic mind control terrain), so I will focus just on the one: Lawrence Schiller, a man

I had never heard of before reading the Brussell transcript. Born in 1936, Schiller was a highly successful American film producer, director, and screenwriter who also worked for *Life* magazine, *Paris Match, The Sunday Times, Time* and *Newsweek* as a freelance photojournalist. His first book was called *LSD* and published in 1966. He worked on *Butch Cassidy and the Sundance Kid* in 1969, wrote *The Killing of Sharon Tate* in 1970 (a book Schreck recommends for including some of the mafia elements), and made a documentary about Dennis Hopper in 1971. He contributed photographs for two books on Marilyn Monroe (including one by Norman Mailer), and collaborated with Mailer on the script for *The Executioner's Song* (about murderer Gary Gilmore). He worked on a book with O.J. Simpson during the O.J. trial, and after Simpson's acquittal he co-wrote a book about the case. In 2014, his photographs were used for a book on Barbra Streisand.

Returning to Atkins, Schreck claims that, the moment she was arrested,

> mafia attorneys [Paul Caruso and Richard Cabellero] swooped in to protect her; she told a story to them that was sold to the media . . . and then distributed throughout the world that made it sound like the murders were an attack on random victims for some sort of vaguely defined revolutionary purpose. [Atkins] was guided to tell the cover story even before anyone knew what had happened.*

Schreck asks an important question that, in thirty years of reading about the case, I had never heard asked before: "how does a penniless hippie girl, 19 or 20, have two very expensive lawyers who have been well known to represent underworld and drug dealer figures come in to defend her?" If we

---

* Schreck's contention that the Cielo Drive murders were all just a drug deal gone wrong, and that Tate wasn't even meant to be there, seems to me a reach. The crime had so many essential elements of a psyop, including the uncanny way it completed the fictional narrative of *Rosemary's Baby*—by inverting it—that to put it all down to lucky coincidence (lucky for the psyop managers, I mean) seems as big a reach as claiming it was micromanaged from the start. Schreck's description of the drug and entertainment underworld that Manson moved within prior to the murders is suspiciously void of any mention of undercover police operatives or intelligence agents, as if there were no overlap between these worlds. But Schreck is an ex-Satanist with perhaps as much incentive to downplay the element of the occult in the murders as the "tabloid" press had to milk it.

believe "the mainstream mass media Manson myth," Schreck underscores, "it is one of the criminals who devised it."*

8.3.   A SHADOW OVER HOLLYWOOD

"The theater of cruelty is 'sorcery' in a very telling sense. As aesthetic terrorism, it amounts to a sacramental language for materializing the unwanted demons of experience."

—CARL RASCHKE, *Painted Black*

This is how I wrote about *Chinatown* in *The Secret Life of Movies* (2009):

Polanski takes the role of "the man with the knife," the snickering, white-clad "midget" who slices open Jack Nicholson's nose as a warning to mind his own business. What could be better evidence of Polanski's canniness in exploiting his own tragedy for sensationalist effect—playing up to the public's association of him with knives and bloodshed—and of his stubborn refusal to turn over a new leaf? Polanski—an avowed atheist with a fascination for occult themes—did not have it in him to learn from his mistakes. But as a filmmaker he was beginning to seem something of a one-trick pony. Without savagery to fall back on, his vision was growing

---

* O'Neill concurs in *Chaos* and calls Atkins' testimony "the blueprint for the official narrative of the murders" (p. 262). Also: "Charles Watson was basically an independent drug dealer on the fringes of the Manson group, sometimes deeply involved but more often off on his own, with his own criminal enterprises. . . . He was very good friends with Terry Melcher, who lived in the Polanski house before Sharon Tate and Roman Polanski. [He also] knew Dennis Wilson very well and he had been to parties with Manson at the Cielo Drive house. Dennis Wilson also introduced Sharon Tate to Manson and Watson at some of these parties. . . According to Manson, the first time he met Sharon Tate was at the home of Elvis Presley, when Elvis was in Las Vegas; some people who were a part of what was called the Memphis mafia, that Manson knew, Dennis Wilson knew them, and they would go to gambling parties held at Elvis's house and that's where he first met Sharon Tate." https://midnightwriternews.com/mwn-episode-026-charles-manson-and-the-myth-of-helter-skelter/

grim and empty and oppressive. . . . If the scenes in which he himself
appears, or in which (that fellow movie director with a sadistic streak of
humor) John Huston plays Noah Cross, the arch corrupter, are the only
scenes that have much life in them, it's because these are the only times
Polanski's wicked predilection for evil gets full play (p. 134).

In *The Matrix*, the currency that keeps the machinery of control going
is our own attention. Likewise, the Hollywood dream factory would seem
to be powered by our own somnambulism. "Hollywood has always been
a cage," John Huston said, "a cage to catch our dreams" (Dehgan, p. 91).
And in *Chinatown*, Huston tells Nicholson: "You see Mr. Gittes, most people never have to face the fact that, at the right time and the right place,
they're capable of—*anything*." Apparently, it is not enough for criminal
masterminds (of whom Manson is at worst a pale imitation) to constantly
retraumatize us; they are after our unbending loyalty and devotion too, our
never-ending, rapt attention. This is probably the most insidious aspect of all
to the Hollywood cage, because it both points to and conceals our consent
to, our complicity with, an ultimate form of evil.*

   In the first book I ever read about Polanski (*His Life and Films*), Barbra
Leaming recounts an incident that occurred during the filming of *Cul-de-
Sac*. *Cul-de-Sac* was written by Polanski and Gérard Brach and involves a
couple, living in a large island house in Scotland, whose lives are interrupted
by the arrival of mobsters seeking refuge. It ends in death and madness. The
shoot, as conceived by Polanski, required a very long continuous shot in
which the two male leads (Donald Pleasance and Lionel Stander) are arguing
on the beach, while the female, played by Françoise Dorleac, is swimming
naked in the ocean. Despite near-zero temperatures, Polanski required several takes for the shot. By the third take:

---

* In *Chaos* O'Neill mentions the persistent rumor that Manson visited Cielo Drive soon
after the murders, "arriving with some unknown companion to rearrange the scene"
(p. 263). Manson has hinted that he left the pair of eyeglasses found at the scene purposely
to confuse investigators. This is a particularly curious detail since the murder mystery in
Polanski's *Chinatown* revolves around a pair of eyeglasses found at the scene of the crime.

Dorleac had darkened from blue to purple . . . she was half frozen. The director seemed unconcerned. He was not certain he had what he needed. "We're going again!" he said. The shot was set up for a third time. Dorleac stripped off her robe, and plunged into the water and collapsed. Crew members rushed in to save her. She began to menstruate, and the company doctor feared that she might have suffered a minor heart attack. The set exploded into pandemonium. The usually aloof British crew had reached its limit. The shop steward announced that the crew would go on strike if Polanski continued in his mistreatment of the actress. At last he had to back down (p. 43).*

The *Cul-de-Sac* anecdote, which I quoted in a footnote in *The Blood Poets*, brought to mind, then and now, Hitchcock's remark, quoted by Donald Spoto in *The Dark Side of Genius*: "I always believe in following the advice of the playwright Sardou: 'Torture the women.'. . . The trouble today is that we don't torture the women enough" (p. 483). Hitchcock was known to torture his actresses off-screen as well as on.[6] In today's #MeToo climate, his reputation would never survive the fall-out of his borderline monstrous behaviors. And then we have John Huston's confession that "the secret to direction"—i.e. to his own success—is "sadism." Huston, lest we forget, best friend and party-goer with George Hodel.

In *The Power of Ritual in Prehistory*, Hayden uncovers what seems to be the *identical core pathologies* at the heart of these ancient sorcerous practices: "the main purpose of the secret society was to terrorize women," he writes; and: "the secret society's 'simple purpose is to conjure up infernal terrors and render each other assistance in keeping their women in subjection'" (p. 89–90). As Carl Raschke observes in *Painted Black*,

---

* Polanski underplays the incident, in considerably less detail, in *Roman*, and is unrepentant: "We watched as a small procession made its way up the beach, carrying an inanimate Françoise. Everyone was exaggeratedly solicitous about her. Already quick to complain whenever they got a chance, the whole crew seized upon this incident as if it were the last straw. Françoise had apparently fainted because of the cold, and they did their best to make me feel like a monster" (p. 240).

to the Dadaists, civilization and the idealized imagery of womanhood that held it together was a fraud perpetrated by the death instinct. . . . The 'secret language' to be spoken amid the crypts of dead, ancient religions was violence and desire—in other words, the compulsion to rape. . . Dadaism imagined a great liberation and a great terror as virtually one and the same climax (p. 182).

8.4.   WHAT IT TAKES TO MAKE IT IN HOLLYWOOD

"The real Humphrey Bogart and the real James Cagney are actors—I mean the ones you know. The real ones, they died in here. In other words, we die so you guys can play act us. We got to be the bad guys so you guys can be the good guys. But in reality we know that you're not the good guys, that you guys are worse than we are."

—CHARLES MANSON

A story disclosed in 2012 via the popular site, *Crazy Days and Nights*, is that legendary film actor Kirk Douglas violently and repeatedly raped actress Natalie Wood in a hotel room when she was only sixteen years of age.* Rumors about Wood's rape have been around at least since 2001, when Suzanne Finstad's biography *Natasha* alleged she was raped when 16 by an unnamed powerful actor.[7] Based on Finstad's timeline, this would have

---

* Hollywood rape stories go back all the way to Fatty Arbuckle (there has been some speculation that Arbuckle was framed, but this does not mean no rape occurred), and the number of movie stars who have been sexually abused as children or teenagers is impossible to gauge—especially when it comes to male movie stars, who are even less likely to talk about it. Marilyn Monroe was sexually abused during her childhood in foster care homes, and was also one of the first public figures to discuss it. Rita Hayworth was raped by her father as a young girl. Anne Heche likewise from the age of a toddler. Tim Roth, also a survivor of incest. Billie Holiday raped at twelve. Gabriel Byrne sexually abused as a child training to be a priest. Oprah Winfrey raped at nine. Ashley Judd as a child. See: https://www.ranker.com/list/celebrities-who-were-sexually-abused/celebrity-lists

occurred just before the *Rebel without a Cause* shoot began, and Dennis Hopper has said that she told him about it at the time (according to Finstad, Wood was having affairs with both Hopper and director Nicolas Ray at the time, see p. 167, 170). *Crazy Days and Nights* reported the event in graphic detail (*trigger warning*):

> One day [Wood] was invited to meet with this movie star about an upcoming major role. This man was a legend already, and was very powerful. . . . Without even discussing the film, this actor—drunk already—began making a pass at her. She politely declined, and excused herself. He wouldn't have it. He literally threw her down, slapped the hell out of her, and ripped her clothes off. He shouted obscenities at her, continually punched and held her arms so tight he left scars and bruises. He raped her repeatedly, spitting on her, and did permanent damage to her body. She was bleeding everywhere, with a battered face. She passed out. When she came to, the actor was still in the room gloating, and told her to come see him tomorrow night and he might give her the role. He laughed at her as she fell down, her legs so wobbly and weak. She gathered her torn clothes, and tried to walk out of the hotel and to her car—blood and semen running down her legs and bruises already forming on her face. She could barely make it back home in her car. She wanted to kill herself, so ashamed of what happened. The damage to her psyche was permanent, and haunted her forever.[8]

Crazy Days and Nights claimed that Wood's mother "said she must have made the actor mad and offended him," that Wood was taken to a hospital secretly, and that, although the studio knew about it, there were no repercussions for the powerful movie star, who is described as "a money machine." While Wood never named him publicly, her friends and family allegedly knew the truth. "Even after marriage and kids, if she saw this actor anywhere—she would almost convulse and cry." The "blind item" winds up by naming the two parties:

> So when the time comes, and the now 95-year-old Kirk Douglas, the superstar actor, finally dies, there will be tributes and honors about him.

Just remember that he is a monster who never repented, apologized, nor showed any sorrow for destroying the lives of others. Especially the life of that young beloved actress named Natalie Wood.[9]

In 2018, on a 12-part podcast about Wood's life, Wood's sister Lana revealed that the attack occurred inside the famed Chateau Marmont Hotel during an audition, and that it went on "for hours." According to professor Cynthia Lucia, Wood's rape was brutal and violent.[10] At the time of writing this, Kirk Douglas is 102 years old. He published his most recent book in 2017, at the age of 100. A *Guardian* piece, from that same year by Hadley Freeman (a woman in her late thirties at the time) eulogizes Douglas for all 2,600 words. There is one hint of darkness, however, when the piece mentions Douglas' self-confessed "mother complex":

"I constantly sought from the women around me a mother substitute." His search certainly was constant: from Rita Hayworth to Marlene Dietrich, it is hard to name a famous actress from the mid-20th century who wasn't seduced by Douglas. At one point he fretted to his analyst that he thought he might be impotent after a disappointing encounter the night before. "You tell me that you had sex 29 nights in a row with different girls. On the 30th, you say you're impotent," his doctor replied drily. "You know, even God rested after six days."

"'I was a bad boy,'" Douglas adds, "a little sorrowfully."[11]

◆

"You are asking me to psychoanalyze myself and that's not something that interests me at all."

—ROMAN POLANSKI, *Playboy interview, 1971*

Was Polanski's treatment of Dorleac an isolated incident? In *Repulsion*, Thomas Kiernan quotes Françoise Dorleac's sister Catherine Deneuve (the star of *Repulsion*) on Polanski, describing him as "a tender, humorous little boy off the set. . . . But on the set he was a brutal tyrant . . . an unforgiving, intolerable despot whose temper and impatience knew no bounds. He would scream the most outrageous, obscene things to me when we were shooting. Then, at night, the most endearing words came from his mouth" (p. 204).

According to Polanski's friend Kenneth Tynan, in his *Esquire* article, Polanski viewed a woman standing up unasked to be "tantamount to an act of insurrection."* Kiernan quotes a Hollywood actress (anonymously): "Revenge is a big thing with him, and he particularly enjoys humiliating women. . . . he goes out of his way to debase them" (p. 72). In *The Family*, Ed Sanders quotes Walter Chappell, a "long-time friend of Sharon Tate" who photographed her on a number of occasions: "during the first days on the set of the film *Dance of the Vampires*, Roman made Sharon walk around three days nude" (p. 460; Chappell also claimed that "Sharon Tate didn't dig the occult and was sucked into it by Mia Farrow").

In *Infamous Players*, Peter Bart quotes an assistant director on *Rosemary's Baby* describing Polanski's direction of Mia Farrow: "He's trying to break her down. . . . That's his idea of getting a performance. She's going to have a nervous breakdown if this continues" (p. 214). Earlier, Bart quotes a Polish producer: "Roman is a great guy but he's also a sociopath" (p. 205). Bart also told *Chaos* author O'Neill: "that crowd was a little scary. . . . There was an aura of danger around them . . . . an instinctive feeling that everyone was pushing it and things were getting out of control" (p. 50). O'Neill claims that "Polanski had established a pattern of abuse, emotional and physical" in his relationship with Tate. A friend of Sharon, anonymously, describes Polanski as "one of the most evil people I ever met . . . he had smashed Tate's face into a mirror, and, on another occasion, forced her to watch a recording of him having sex with another woman. He cheated on her constantly, and made sure she knew about it." According to actress Elke Sommer, Tate "wasn't herself when she was with him. She was in awe, or frightened, he had an awesome charisma." And there was "a horrendous sickness surrounding [Sharon's] relationship [with him]. She was quite lost."

---

* "The Polish Imposition," by Kenneth Tynan, *Esquire*, September 1971, p. 122: https://classic.esquire.com/article/1971/9/1/the-polish-imposition Polanski's rebuttal to *Playboy*: "Ken, who is a good friend, knows absolutely nothing about my emotional-sexual relationships with women. . . . so you shouldn't treat seriously what Ken says about my feelings toward women" (Randall, p. 324).

O'Neill even managed to get Bill Tennant, Polanski's manager at that time, to go on record. Bill Tennant is an interesting case study unto himself: he went from the slums of East LA to becoming the "superstar agent" and manager who got Peter Fonda *Easy Rider* and Polanski *Rosemary's Baby*. That job led to the thankless task of identifying the bodies at Cielo Drive. In the 1970s, he became a vice President at Columbia Pictures, in the period leading up to the David Begelman embezzlement scandal. After that, for reasons unknown, his career bottomed out so severely that he wound up homeless in Los Angeles. The closest he got to reestablishing himself in Hollywood was—according to Peter Bart in 1993—"selling sandwiches to movie crews off a catering truck."[12] There is surprisingly little information about him online, but according to IMDB, Tennant died in 2012. As far as I know, the first and only time he gave an interview about the Tate murder was with O'Neill, who tracked him down in London.

"Roman is a shit," Tennant told O'Neill. Echoing something O'Neill had heard from other friends of the couple, Tennant said there were two versions of the story: "So what story do you want to tell? The one about this little prick who left his wife alone [with Frykowski, Sebring, and Folger], these wankers, these four tragic losers, or do you want to talk about a poor kid, Roman Polanski? . . . There was nothing innocent about [the murders]. It was retribution." In Roman, Polanski admits he was having sex again within a month of Tate's death. According to Tennant, this was an understatement: within a week of the murders, Polanski and Warren Beatty were "partying it up . . . nobody cared or gave a shit about Sharon Tate. Not because they weren't nice but because she was expendable. As expendable as an actor whose option comes up and gets dropped" (O'Neill, p. 65–66).

According to Thomas Kiernan: "Since Tate's murder, Polanski had been indulging his predilection for having sex with children, thirteen- to fourteen-year-old girls preferably, as a way to assuage his grief." Kiernan quotes a cell-mate of Polanski from his period of incarceration in 1977: "He started having sex with young people because he couldn't bear to be with regular women . . . . So he went after these young girls" (p. 251). In relation to Polanski's drugging and raping a minor in 1977, Kiernan quotes LAPD detective Phil Vanatter, saying that Polanski "just couldn't unde
rstand why screwing a kid should be of concern to anyone. He'd screwed plenty of girls younger than this one, he said, and nobody gave a damn" (p.

82–83). Kiernan quotes "a woman who knew Polanski well in England" in the 1960s on how the

> British-American society and showbiz crowd he hangs out with in London has a big thing about young girls. I've actually heard some of those chaps compare notes on who has had the youngest. And when they find what they consider to be a really good one, it's a matter of honor that they pass her around themselves (p. 97).*

8.5.   IMPENETRABLE SCREENS & THE BID FOR INVULNERABILITY

> "Roman formed himself once he began to understand film. He made of his personality and character a screen—a hard, impenetrable screen—against which he projected the image of himself he wanted the world, the viewer, to accept. . . . Then he developed feelings with which he shaped the image."
>
> —JERZY KOSIŃSKI *(author of The Painted Bird, Being There), quoted in Repulsion*

The most contemporary example of an artist in the aggrandizer-imposer mold is probably Quentin Tarantino, whose *Once Upon a Time in Hollywood* is a *literal* Hollywood revenge fantasy and a bizarre attempt to reconsolidate the official history-myth of Manson, even while revising it and creating a parallel universe in which the murders never happened. Tarantino's depraved revenge fantasy came out the same year as Tom O'Neill's *Chaos*, as if in a conscious act of damage control. Its primary purpose is to *reassert* the childlike innocence of the victims (to the point of making Tate seem simple-minded), while serving up the "Manson" crew ("Tex" Watson, Susan Atkins, Patricia Krenwinkel) as blood-offerings to save the innocent Hollywood lambs.

---

* Polanski told *Playboy* in 1971: "I didn't make it with a chick until I was 17 and a half, which I think is very late" (Randall, p. 322).

The manner in which Tarantino has Brad Pitt and Leonardo DiCaprio dispense of the Manson clan—smashing the women's faces in repeatedly until they are bloody pulps—would have been unthinkable within any other context besides that of preemptively avenging—and thereby preventing— the murder of "poor Sharon, beautiful Sharon," her unborn baby, and the others. It is a theater of cruelty disguised as divine intervention. Kael's derogation of *The Exorcist* perfectly applies here: *Once Upon a Time in Hollywood* is "in the worst imaginable taste—that is, an utterly unfeeling movie about miracles" (1976, p. 249).

Tarantino was a close friend of Harvey Weinstein (who called Miramax "the house Quentin built"). He executive-produced the "torture porn" of Eli Roth's *Hostel* and *Hostel 2*. He is a known tormenter of actresses, in the Hitchcock-Polanski tradition (e.g. Uma Thurman on *Kill Bill*).[13] He is also a public defender of Polanski—insisting the 13-year-old girl plied with drugs and sodomized was "down with partying with Polanski." (He later retracted his statement,[14] and also apologized for not blowing the whistle on Weinstein.)[15] With *Once Upon a Time in Hollywood*, Tarantino stepped up, or came out, as an agent of mythic engineering in the Hollywood-Manson war. Is there a "tell" in the fact that the hero, played by Brad Pitt, murdered his wife and got away with it? (As depicted, he even seems justified in doing it.)

Besides the Barbara Leaming book, I also read Thomas Kiernan's biography of Polanski (*Repulsion*) in my early teens. Yet you would never guess it based on how deep my admiration for the director went, and how long it lasted. Somehow, the many damning passages in Kiernan's book seemed to have left no imprint on my consciousness. Passages that seem invaluable to me now, in breaking a lifelong spell, went in one eye and out the other back then. The above quote from Kosiński, for example, which continues:

> Since he could not use deep feelings, which are not easily controllable and imply the same vulnerability he had as a child, he substituted superficial feelings and, you might say, appetites. In fact I would describe Roman even today as a man of deep appetites rather than deep emotions. [H]e is dominated by appetites rather than emotions. Appetites cannot be hurt. They can only be satisfied or denied (Kiernan, p. 138–9).

Kosiński was a close associate, even friend, of Polanski, and the same is true of Kenneth Tynan, who echoed these impressions in his description of the director in 1971: "He armors himself against showing anything that might be construed as weakness. . . all weakness corrupts, and absolute weakness corrupts absolutely. . . . His aim is quite simply to be invulnerable, physically as well as psychologically."[16]

Most of these testimonies have been overlooked, however. Polanski has, until recently at least, been a master manipulator of the press in maintaining his image as a misunderstood and maligned genius. As Kiernan quotes an anonymous "friend" of Polanski:

> Roman has never shared his true thoughts with the press. That's because he has no "true" thoughts—that is, no philosophy, no worldview. What Roman says to the press is really no more than words, whatever he's thinking at the time. For the press to presume that they can get to the bottom of Roman from what he says is absurd. He's very good at putting up a smokescreen of statements and ideas. But in reality he is a man who operates not on ideas or principles, but on instincts. He seems and does the things that his instincts tell him are worth having and doing. And he avoids the things his instincts say are not worthwhile. He cares little about consequences, except when it comes to making movies (p. 266).

✦

> "You just try to keep alive with Roman, or you go under. Ask him why he's so obsessed by the bloody and gruesome, behaving like some kid in a candy store."
>
> —JOHN CASSAVETES[17]

Polanski was the mentor figure whom I admired from afar and whose fullest success came when I was only one year old. Tarantino, born four years before me, came to prominence in 1992, at a time when my own life had hit rock bottom. I disliked *Reservoir Dogs* for its sadism, and I resented Tarantino his success. Since he was my peer, he was not a mentor but *a rival*. Like me, Tarantino grew up on Marvel superheroes and was "a comic book geek."[18] He worked in video stores in the 1980s, just as I haunted them during the same period; like myself, he had a special penchant for B-horror movies. As a teenager (as documented in *Seen and Not Seen*), I even enjoyed "torture porn" back when it was known simply as "video nasties," before the erotic under layer was fully acknowledged in the general discussion.

There is a reason it wasn't acknowledged, and still isn't given the serious attention it deserves. The erotic under layer to the terrorization of women is something I have still not fully reconciled myself to, even after forty years of first uncovering it in my own psyche. I have no doubt it is why, in the last stages of rewriting this work, just weeks before printing, I have found myself reorganizing the first part around the theme of torturing women. This is the nature of the wound: that I have no choice but to keep returning to it until it is fully healed. My first admission to this dark detour of my adolescence was in (my first published work) *The Blood Poets*. It took fifteen years for me to go into gory detail with *Seen and Not Seen*. In both cases, I was ostensibly writing from, and about, my immersion in movie culture; yet, at the haunted heart of that obsession—the hub of an angry wheel—was an unnatural predilection for woman-torture.

Although I have no way of knowing the precise moment I became aware of being aroused by such imagery, as I wrote in *Seen and Not Seen* it was watching and masturbating to Sam Peckinpah's *Straw Dogs* (the first VHS video I ever rented) that was undoubtedly the watershed moment. That this "awakening" coincided with the brief spate of "video nasties" in the UK is something I can only regard now as a kind of satanic providence: not merely that these films were available, but that they were *advertised* to me—by the moral outrage around them—making it inevitable I would track them down and consume them. As bad as *I Spit on Your Grave* was, the one that disturbs me the most, looking back, is *The Last House on the Left* (1972). Wes Craven's first film, it was a Manson-family-inspired torture and revenge melodrama in which two attractive young women are raped, tortured, and murdered by a gang of wandering hippies (who are later murdered by one of the women's parents). In the most horrific scene, a young woman is held down by the gang while they cut into the flesh of her chest with a knife. At the age of thirteen or fourteen, I watched this scene and was powerfully aroused by it. I didn't understand why; and while it would be wrong to say I didn't care—I knew there was something wrong with me, and it bothered me— I didn't care *enough* to suppress my feeling of arousal but rather gave into it. I even hunted the film down again in my early twenties, for the same purpose.

The truth is, I still don't understand how I could allow myself to indulge such responses and not be stricken with remorse, or terror, or both. I understand the psychological reasoning (as discussed in *Seen and Not Seen*); but there remains a split in me: one part is excited by this material, another is horrified by it and disgusted by how it excites me. That split can't be healed, apparently, by any amount of psycho-logic or deductive reasoning; nor can guilt or shame do anything but exacerbate the lesion. I have written that *16 Maps of Hell* is an attempt to get to the bottom of my Hollywood obsession; I now believe it is also fueled by a need to understand how I could have such physiological responses to imagery that I consider now, as then, to be essentially appalling. I need to know how and why I have been complicit in the forging of dark entertainment out of the torture of women.

✦

> "The simplest Surrealist act consists of dashing down into the
> street, pistol in hand, and firing blindly, as fast as you can pull
> the trigger, into the crowd. Anyone who, at least once in his life,
> has not dreamed of thus putting an end to the petty system of
> debasement and cretinization in effect has a well-defined place in
> that crowd, with his belly at barrel level."
>
> —ANDRÉ BRETON, *Second Manifesto of Surrealism*[*]

Ironically, by the time Tarantino was helping to legitimize such imagery as "torture porn," it had been fully identified as a form of sadistic masturbatory fantasy. Yet, partially through Tarantino's stamp, it also gained avant-garde "cool," as part of the cinema of transgression, the theater of cruelty advocated by Artaud, George Bataille, Nitsch, Buñuel, Beckett, Polanski, and the Surrealists. For the release of *Django Unchained*, a UK *Channel 4* interviewer asked Tarantino why he was "so sure there's no link between enjoying movie

---

[*] I quoted this favorably in my own "Crow Manifesto" back in the late 1990s, for my first ever website, as part of an attempt to start a "New Surrealism" movement—mercifully failed.

violence and enjoying real violence?" Tarantino's reaction is telling—his indignation verges on apoplexy:

> Well I'm not going to tell you why I'm so sure. Do not ask me a question
> like that. I'm not biting. I refuse your question. . . . I'm not your slave
> and you're not my master. You can't make me dance to your tune. I'm not
> a monkey. I'm here to sell my movie. This is a commercial for the movie
> make no mistake. I don't want to talk about what you want to talk about.
> I don't want to talk about the implications of violence. . . . It's none of
> your damn business what I think about that. I don't have any responsi-
> bility to you to explain anything I don't want to.[19]

Presumably, Tarantino is fully aware of the implications of violence
in his films and is simply refusing to take responsibility for it, rather than
arguing against it. He is pleading the fifth and hiding behind the plausible deniability that is standard operating procedure in Hollywood (it's just
entertainment and only squares and prudes say otherwise). Yet Tarantino's
reaction is so virulent it suggests a deep insecurity. Perhaps he knows he has
no way to defend his love of violence that wouldn't reveal his true character
and motivations? In the interview, he appears to be attempting the art of
imposition, that "quality of temperament or personality . . . to impose one's
will on others [and] dictate the conditions—social, moral, sexual, political—
within which one can operate with maximum freedom." If so, he is doing
it very poorly. Caught in an annoying situation that threatens to expose his
true values, he doesn't charm his way through it but simply bludgeons his
opponent into submission.*

Compared to Polanski, Tarantino is a low-level operator (both in terms
of cinematic artistry and charismatic grace/imposition skills). But then, his
back is also a lot closer to the wall, and in 2020—all of Tarantino's efforts at
damage control notwithstanding—even Polanski's fifty year spell of invulnerability may finally be on the point of breaking. Since 2010, at least five women

---

* Judging by the comments on the video, Tarantino's audience doesn't much *care*. They
are more inclined to see it as the great genius giving the lowly yellow journalist what he
deserves. The press is considered the enemy in Hollywood, though indispensable to its
dispensations.

have accused him of severe sexual assault at varying ages: Charlotte Lewis, at age 16 (though her allegations were compromised by inconsistencies[20]); Robin (last name not given), also at 16; Renate Langer, at age 15; Valentine Monnier at age 18; and youngest of all was Marianne Barnard, who claims Polanski sexually assaulted her at the age of ten[21] (significantly, more recent articles do not refer to Barnard at all). Monnier claims her rape was "extremely violent" and that Polanski "pummeled me until I gave in and then raped me, making me do all sorts of things."[22] The first backlash against Polanski is strictly, and predictably, cultural: the French directors' guild has moved to suspend him from their ranks.[23] That'll learn 'im.

As a teenager, deeply conflicted about being aroused by woman-torture, I tried my hand at filmmaking, but was, mercifully, never able to take the torture from the imaginary into the actual. I failed to make the transition from sadism consumer to sadism producer, and so consigned myself to the "also-rans," the ones who fail to make the secret society grade. I lacked the predilection for evil required for success in Hollywood. As the successful heir to Polanski, a Hollywood *enfant terrible*—Tarantino not only represents the dream of super-status I was denied, he also points to *why* it was denied me—why, despite my openness to being possessed by the aesthetics of terror, and despite all my early efforts to prove it, the Hollywood fairy tale was never for me. I lacked the temperament of the imposer.

8.6.   NOT A LOVE STORY

> "Toward the end of the film, I have so many enemies that I consider whether I should flee the country. But this ballsiness that everybody is accusing me of is necessary to deflect all the vicious attacks that people will make on your film, from start to finish. . . If I've learned one thing about filmmaking, it's that it requires not only talent but the stamina to resist all these attackers."
>
> —ROMAN POLANSKI, *Playboy 1971 interview*

When I first began assembling *16 Maps of Hell*, I did not expect to be revisiting the Cielo Drive murders; and when I decided, or rather realized, I would be doing so, my aim became simply to review it through a lens which I hope this present book provides. That was of course naïve of me. One cannot pull on a worm without waking up the whole can; one lead, one quote, leads to another, expanding outward exponentially.

This present deep-dive by no means aspires to reaching any sort of conclusion regarding the Manson-Hollywood war, and I have left out much material for the sake of brevity. My intention here is not so much to understand what happened that night and why, but to what extent Polanski, and Hollywood, were involved in and complicit with the murders. Even here, my deeper goal is a smaller and more personal one: can my lifelong affection for Roman Polanski withstand a sustained exposure to the facts? This question is, however, a microcosm for the larger question posed by *16 Maps of Hell*, which is my latest attempt to extract the Hollywood implant from my soul.

In the first parts of *Chaos*, when the author Tom O'Neill was working on an article for *Premiere* magazine that eventually became the book (twenty years later), everyone he tries to talk to in Hollywood refuses to talk to him. Peter Bart considers this fact "fascinating" in and of itself (p. 51)—but really, is it any wonder?

> Picture a spiderweb so dense with connections and tendrils that it looks like a solid sheet of fabric. . . . The Hollywood cliques that had seemed, at the start, so discrete and isolated were all mixed up with one another, much more than Bugliosi had made it appear. Plus, then and now, people weren't always willing to be upfront about who they hung out with (O'Neill, p. 66–7).

Manson the artist who is also a drug criminal and pimp, who got screwed over by the music industry and cheated out of his piece of the Hollywood pie and who took revenge on the industry, is central to the accepted explanation of what occurred in 1969 at Cielo Drive. Yet I suspect that both Manson as the avatar of evil and Tate as the paragon of innocence are manufactured images, and for exactly the same purpose: to keep us lost in a movie plot of good and evil. They prevent us from recognizing that Manson moved freely within the Los Angeles music and movie world, and if he never made it within it, it was not due to lack of talent *or* connections, but something more obscure and "occulted" (he was from the wrong social and economic *class*).

In the preceding chapters, I explored the eerie parallels between filmed representations and reality as evidence of criminals' desire to flaunt their untouchability by crowing about their crimes. So what of the parallels between the storyline of *Rosemary's Baby* and the reality that both preceded and followed it? The film is about what Guy Woodhouse (John Cassavetes) has to do to gain access to the Hollywood inner circles, which is precisely what the film did for its director, Polanski. It may not be a leap from here to ask, what exactly did Polanski do to get his Paramount gig, and did it, in some roundabout and twisted way, lead to the sacrifice of his own wife's unborn child to another kind of "devil cult"?

In *Painted Black*, Carl Raschke describes Kenneth Anger's *Inauguration of the Pleasure Dome* as "crafted to celebrate the spring equinox of 1966, when Crowleyite prophecies of the 'new age' were supposed to be consummated and LaVey would proclaim the 'second coming' of Satan" (p. 109). Raschke then quotes Anger: "My reason for filming has nothing to do with 'cinema' at all. . . It's a transparent excuse for capturing people. . . I consider myself as working Evil in an evil medium." Raschke adds: "No more gripping confession about the broad-ranging strategy of aesthetic terrorism could have been uttered" (p. 111). 1966, of course, was the year Ira Levin set *Rosemary's Baby* and it was published right on time. Polanski went to great lengths to recreate the period exactly, albeit only two years later, for his film. As I wrote in *The Blood Poets*: "A serious artist and a respecter of the mysteries (though a self-professed atheist), Polanski made every effort towards authenticity" (p. 73; I was using "mysteries" to refer to arcane knowledge traditions). Is it a reach to ask if *Rosemary's Baby* was meant as a mainstream continuation of these same dark magical workings?

More mundanely, as already mentioned, there are some striking parallels between what appears to have been going on at Cielo Drive, during the period leading up to the murders, and the case of Jeffrey Epstein, some thirty or forty years later, with his party-mansions complete with hidden cameras and sex parties, all for the purpose of sex-trafficking, home-movies, orgies, blackmail, and high-level, intelligence-backed manipulations. Or, for that matter, George Hodel's mansion depravities two decades previously.

Polanski's manager Bill Tennant told O'Neill in *Chaos* that "there was a kind of FBI-slash-CIA aspect of the LAPD [that] knew everything there was to know" in Hollywood (p. 66). If so, this would have depended on insider sources, moles within the local communities.

In a 1991 interview with Ron Reagan Jr., Charles Manson gives a free-associative spiel of vivid imagery in which he lets slip that "Leno LaBianca was killed for a black phone book with all the numbers in it, the phone numbers that control the music market." As O'Neill writes in *Chaos*, "Atkins said that they killed the LaBianca couple because of something to do with 'blackmail,' although she couldn't elaborate" (p. 263). Jeffrey Epstein's notorious black book contained the numbers of many of his high-profile clients in the entertainment industry, and became a crucial piece of evidence after his arrest. In the interview, Manson barks theatrically: "What are you doing up on my stage? Who controls *what* on this set, and who is the *man* on this set? Clark Gable?"

> When you see Sharon Tate's body laying there all naked and murdered, dead—do you think I had something to do with that? That was the altar [or alter—as in sub-personality]. It had nothing to do with me. It was the turn-around of the whole world. It was the Aryan woman that was being brought up from the head for *Rosemary's Baby*. *They* was the cult. Did they tell you about all the films that they got with the dogs and chauffeurs, that came out of the black and white, when Yul Brynner and Peter Sellers paid $30,000 to get the videotapes back, that they had done with the pornography, where they was gobbling on each other's knobs in the closet, with Sharon, poor Sharon, beautiful Sharon? I'll give you something that may be beneficial to your awareness![24]

Since this was Manson talking, no one paid much attention. Yet the evidence indicates that Polanski's friend Frykowski *was* connected to the drug trade in LA, and that his connections may have gone all the way back to Poland, before he arrived in the US. (Even official Hollywood chronicler Peter Bart, in *Infamous Players*, p. 230, refers to Polanski's Polish friends as "shady characters from Eastern Europe.") Perhaps Polanski was also hooked into organized crime circles, and was only granted access to the Hollywood elite by agreeing to cooperate with the LAPD-FBI-CIA intel network (and operations like COINTELPRO and CHAOS), in some capacity. That would mean that the murder of his wife, as well as what occurred in 1977 (when he was arrested for drugging, photographing, and having various kinds of sex with a 13-year-old girl in Jack Nicholson's home), would have been a case of the chickens coming home to roost (i.e., Polanski being brought in line by the same apparatus he was part of). This seems especially likely considering that the judge who threw the book at Polanski in 1977 was Laurence J. Rittenbrand, "the great friend of Robert Evans's consigliere, Sidney Korshak" (Russo, p. 449).

Is it possible that the borders between avant-garde artists, organized criminals, psychological operatives, and state-created psychopaths could be so porous? Perhaps the better question is, how is it that, for my whole adult life, I have struggled to maintain the illusion of a clear-cut distinction—with the result that, by aspiring to be a filmmaker-artist, while being ignorant of the necessity of also aligning with the shadowy forces behind Hollywood, I was pursuing an impossible dream? When alienated teenagers identify with Manson (stick his poster on their walls or wear his image on their T-shirts), it's because they want to transgress, to feel dark, edgy, and powerful. Eventually, they get over it (most of them at least), because they figure out there's nothing cool about murdering pregnant women (something Manson never did anyway). But what of those, like me, who identify with avant-garde Hollywood filmmakers with "tragic" personal histories who get caught red-handed and are forgiven, and who continue to receive honors and awards? Is there a way out of a mistaken identification when there's no way to see the error of it, to see what's behind the mask?

The story told about Manson is as fantastic as any movie plot, though with all the necessary elements of truth to make it convincing; and like any good movie, it points to a wider, deeper truth. What if a deep criminal background, a utility to intelligence operations, and the demonically inspired torture of women (not to say the sacrifice of babies) is what it takes to *make it* in the entertainment industry? A reach, perhaps, though based on the example of George Hodel, perhaps not so much of one. If Polanski's—or Huston's, or Hitchcock's, or whoever's—works are fueled by a deep, possibly unconscious, desire to purge some terrible weight from their souls, is it possible to separate that torment from the demented need to torture women for the sake of "art"?

There may be a fine line between art that winks at an affinity for evil, and art that's fueled by a desperate need to receive absolution *for* it (Michael Powell's *Peeping Tom* comes to mind—the film that destroyed his career). If Polanski or Nicholson or Evans or Huston are admitting to their own evil in the coded or "twilight" language of movie art, and if, in place of judgment, they receive awards and accolades—what better way to appease their conscience could there be? To add one more twist to the plot, if the crimes they commit are central to how these men became established in the first place— the rites of passage of secret societies and organized crime—then perhaps publicizing them is also a way to show off their credentials? If you've got it, flaunt it: because there will always be others coming up behind you, trying to take it for themselves.

So much for the Hollywood love story that ended in tragedy. I have come away from this latest pass, which I pray will be my last, over the Manson-Hollywood war, inclined to believe that Polanski fits the bill of "charismatic monster and mind-controller" considerably better than does Charlie Manson. And Manson, in turn, begins to appear *relatively* innocent by comparison—a true scapegoat, selected (and yes, "trained," like any good actor) to bind the Hollywood community together. It was a sacrificial ritual to appease the dark gods and blood-cement the fairy tale. Once Upon a Time in Hollywood.*

---

* If there is a strange doubling between "Tex" Watson and Manson, the same might be said of Manson and Polanski: one year in age between them (Manson 1934, Polanski 1933), two inches difference in height (Manson 5'2", Polanski 5'4"), both thin with shaggy brown hair, round faces, and clefts in their chins.

Part Two

THE FORGETTING CHAMBER

"The audience is like a giant organ that you and I are playing. At one moment we play this note on them and get this reaction, and then we play that chord and they react that way. And someday we won't even have to make a movie—there'll be electrodes implanted in their brains, and we'll just press different buttons and they'll go 'ooooh' and 'aaaah' and we'll frighten them, and make them laugh. Won't that be wonderful?"

 —ALFRED HITCHCOCK, *quoted by Ernest Lehman*

"Those who are mind-controlled want to control others. . . . Hitchcock's mastery of the film medium was cruelly shadowed by his impotence (perhaps literally) as a husband and a father. [H]e tortured his actresses not only to create his 'art' but out of unconscious hostility towards his mother. The two drives, creative and destructive, were one obsession. To be a master of the world means, above all, never letting one's guard down. It means allowing the inner guardian to master you, because otherwise, the Master Plan will come all unraveled."

 —JASUN HORSLEY, *Seen and Not Seen*

9

THE PLAYER

9.1. DEPP BACKGROUND
(MY SECOND TRIP TO HOLLYWOOD)

"If California is a state of mind, Hollywood is where you take its temperature. . . . It's the place where our children learn how and what to dream and where everything happens just before, or just after, it happens to us."

—ROSS MACDONALD

In 1999, I published *The Blood Poets*, a two-volume set of film writings and cultural analysis. In early 2001, after the books came out, I traveled from Guatemala (via the UK and Canada) to Los Angeles to do some "networking." I had cards printed up with "Movie Shaman" on them. It was my first trip to Hollywood since I had fallen ill in 1987, and I was a very different person. On the first or second night, I went to a night club, something I rarely did in those days. I was less motivated by the desire to get laid by this point than by the hope of running into some "Hollywood people" and making vital connections. I had mostly given up drinking, smoked a little tobacco and the occasional joint, but I had just discovered a powerful hallucinogen called salvia divinorum, which I began using on a regular basis around this time (I believed shamanically).

I don't remember if I was high on weed when I went to the club; I would guess not, though what I am about to recount might sound like it. Within half an hour or so, I met two young guys in their twenties, friendly and good-looking. One of them resembled Sean Penn so much that (he said) he was able to get the best tables at local restaurants simply by going along with their assumptions. The other guy looked like Johnny Depp, and somehow I ended up dancing with both of them, in a mildly hallucinogenic state. I remember feeling like I had gone through the looking glass and, via this improbable encounter with movie-star *doppelgängers*, was being mysteriously initiated into the secret sorcery world of Hollywood.

In the few days I was there, surreal encounters notwithstanding, I didn't have any luck making real-world connections with Hollywood insiders. I called up Pauline Kael at one point (she had received and praised *The Blood Poets*), to see if she could hook me up with anyone; she assured me her Hollywood connections were less than zero, so we chatted about Brian De Palma instead. I did manage to get copies of the book to De Palma and David Lynch (I left it at Lynch's house), and I got a draft of my 200-page script, "Bring Me the Head of Sam Peckinpah," to Johnny Depp, whose home address I had managed to procure via a mutual acquaintance (artist Craig LaRotonda). Depp's house was rumored (falsely) to have been Bela Lugosi's old house, a castle-mansion with a curious history.* I was met at the

---

* "The mansion was built by George Campbell Carson, an itinerant miner who in 1906 invented the side-charge hopper (whatever that is) that revolutionized ore processing. [It] cost $500,000 and took six years to complete. It was finished in late 1933 but George died less than a year later in 1934. Carson's family tried to get his money but [his wife] won in court and kept the mansion. For a time in the late 1930's she stayed in the house and gave several well-publicized parties for children but by 1941 it was being rented by ex-Ziegfeld Follies dancer 'Queen' Patricia Noblesse Hogan and used as a combination guest-house/rooming house. . . . Howard Hughes' mysterious right-hand-man Noah Dietrich lived there in the 1950's and Motown legend Berry Gordy in the 1960's and 1970's. Gordy hosted parties for 300 to 400 people. Super-agent Marvin Mitchelson lived there in the 1980s and Johnny Depp bought the castle in 1995. In 2007 he was reportedly renting the house to Orlando Bloom. Because of its resemblance to a Bavarian castle, 1930's Hollywood tour guides told people Bela Lugosi lived there (they've been lying to people for almost 90 years; most of the tour guide info given today is pure fiction). But he never did." "1486 North Sweetzer—The Real Story of Mt. Kalmia, 'Dracula's Castle,'" *The Movie Land Directory*: https://movieland.wordpress.com/2007/09/14/1486-north-sweetzer-the-real-story-of-mt-kalmia-draculas-castle/

iron gates by "Pink," Depp's manservant, who took the script and promised me Depp would read it.

Later, I dreamt about that house. In the dream I was not quite "myself," more like Marilyn Manson or some other Gothic vampire-type. There was a lot of partying going on in the Mansion and I was smoking some super-strength salvia divinorum, a batch strong enough to kill. In the dream there was someone I wanted to dispose of, a voodoo-practicing black man. He was not a threat to me, but by killing him I stood to profit. I took him up to a private room, a den hidden behind a sliding wall. He took out some "coasters" that were like Tarot cards and that were also quite deadly (they were related to DMT in some way). I caused the man to die, using the DMT; I was quite clear in my mind what I was doing, and I felt (at the time) perfectly reconciled to my deed—without guilt or remorse. It seemed a small price to pay for what I stood to gain. But, as in an Edgar Allan Poe tale, the horror of consequences soon ensued. By that fateful act of murder, I had sealed a lifelong pact with the forces of darkness.

The dream was one of those epic all-nighters that covered a period of years. Over time, both the house and my life went to utter ruin. The body of the black man rotted for a time in the secret den, before being "buried" when the hidden wing was sealed off completely (Poe again). Meanwhile, I continued to sicken, sinking deeper and deeper into despair, while the house went steadily to Hell. By the time Depp returned, he could barely even recognize his property. I wrote the following day in my journal:

The ensuing events are unclear; all I know for certain is that I am suffering the hideous torments of the damned, and of my oppressively guilty conscience over such a selfish and despicable deed; but above all I am stricken with an awareness that I am given over to Evil Forces, that I have sold my soul. It is all terribly Faustian. At a later stage of the dream, I am back to "myself" again, but with a personal memory of these events. I am waiting at a customs check and they are looking through my green army bag, at the bottom of which is my German great coat, inside the pocket of which is a magik pouch with the salvia and pipe (all of this is true enough to reality). I am positive it will be found, and that the terrible consequences will come crashing down on me. (Salvia has become more than just a drug: it has become a murder weapon!) This, I know, is my Karmuppance. But they don't find it, and by some miracle I am saved. Apparently my sins are forgiven.

God knows what this dream implies. I felt for a while, during the night, as though I really WERE damned, given over to the Darkness, that I had fallen into a trap Aeons in the making, and become the slave and prey of primordial, malignant forces. But I "know" now, in the light of day, that this could never happen. I am not so foolish as that, am I? Surely not! But whatever this dream—past-life recall dressed up in modern pop garb (Depp and Manson), or an experience taken from the collective race memory banks, and contemporary to my own time—it has given me a most sobering taste of the stakes at which we are playing, in this life-and-death (and beyond death) Game.

Or an early map of Hell, rashly ignored?

9.2.   DON'T LET THE MATRIX TELL YOU WHO YOU ARE

"The result [of propaganda] need not be an improved memory, which in fact is not very important, but that what is transmitted goes, generally without any specific recall whatsoever, to build action, and that is the effect most desired."

—FREDERIC CHARLES BARTLETT, *Political Propaganda*

Undaunted by nightmare warnings from my unconscious, I pressed on. In late 2001, I moved back to London (from Guatemala) and began living in Hampstead on government support. Hampstead village is among the most expensive areas of London and definitely the nicest. My mother's neighbor was the famous broadcaster, author and parliamentarian, Melvin Bragg, and I had Jonathan Ross (England's answer to David Letterman) just down the street. Helena Bonham Carter and Tim Burton lived nearby in Belsize, and I would see them from time to time on the street. In October 2002, Bonham Carter was filming *The Heart of Me* on Hampstead Heath, and I had caught her eye. Emboldened by the curiosity in her glance, I went over to introduce myself. She was giving an interview on a park bench and her mother was with her. Later, I had a dream in which we were looking into each other's eyes, smiling beatifically. It was such an intense dream that I became convinced we were destined to be, or at least work, together. I decided to court her, sending flowers and messages via the film's publicity office.

I was aware it was a mad scheme but I was unable to stop myself. I became so immersed in my fantasy that Helena and I were meant to be together that I started channeling it into a script, a non-technology version of *The Matrix*, inspired by Carlos Castaneda and my own salvia-boosted experiences as a "sorcerer," with lucid dreaming in place of simulacra and cybernetics. It was called "Ariadne's Thread" and it was about a young sorcerer, part of a group of sorcerers, who meets a movie star—just as I had—and then finds her in his dreams—just as I had. He is told by his sorcerer teacher that she is "one of us," and given the task of recruiting her.

The script began with a recreation of what was actually occurring in my life, vis a vis Helena, after which it gradually morphed into my fantasy of what *should* happen. In the script, the young sorcerer gets past first-base with the movie star, and ends up writing a script about their encounters. She agrees to be in it, thereby exiting the world of Hollywood to make an indie movie, turning the sorcerers' gonzo project into a movie-star-endorsed enterprise. This enables the sorcerers' to get a coded message about their existence into the world, alerting other sleeper-agents to their calling.

I left red roses and a message for Helena. I wrote the script in a few weeks. I got the number of Helena's parents and spoke to her father about her. I sent a copy of the script to their address. I never heard back. A while later, I sent a second letter (stalker, *me?*), this time taking a more "sorcerous" approach, in which I warned Helena that Hollywood was a dark web of social control and that, as an unwitting agent of it, she should extricate herself before the end came. I signed the letter "Tyler." You get the picture. Hampstead was a rarefied neighborhood, and while the trees and high quality of oxygen might have helped me to keep my sanity, the celebrities on every corner helped keep my insane fantasy life going.

Fantasy spilled all the way into reality—aptly enough—when I embarked on a movie project called *The God Game: An Investigation into the Illusory Nature of Reality*. The idea for it came to me in a dream and involved spending a day with actors exploring their innermost psyches on film, culminating with an imaginative enactment of their deaths. Instantly galvanized by this dream-vision, I set about recruiting volunteers via the

London newsletter for actors, Shooting People. I received dozens of submissions and became gleefully immersed in auditioning charismatic men and beautiful women in my Hampstead apartment. Overnight, I had become a filmmaker!

Once I had secured my "cast," all I needed was a digital camera and someone to hold it. I called on Michael LaBurt. Fittingly enough, I first met Mike in Hollywood, in 2000, during my "movie shaman" jaunt (having befriended his sister Tara in Guatemala). Mike and I only hung out for one night, during which we went (fittingly enough) to Depp's Viper Room where I broke out solo on the dance floor, much to Mike's amusement. Mike was traveling around and agreed to join the project and bring his high-end Canon digital camera along with him. Soon after he arrived in London, after perhaps the third or fourth day's shooting, Mike's unique and forceful personality began to take over the *God Game* project. Little by little, he started to assume the role of the director of a whole new film, with myself as the star. The idea appealed to my vanity (doesn't every director secretly want to be a movie star?), so I went along with it.

Initially, Mike wanted to find some crack whores for me to interact with. Then he wanted to have me sit in a circle for a month without moving, speed up the footage and create one minute of screen time. I dragged my feet on both these ideas (for different reasons), and Mike grew impatient. He felt I was setting unnecessary limits on what we could or couldn't do as filmmakers. If reality was a second-hand illusion, he argued, a B-movie he didn't want to sit through, much less imitate, there were no limits outside of the ones we placed on ourselves. Pushing the boundaries of art meant pushing the boundaries of morality. Mike was so passionately persuasive that, if he'd suggested we kill someone for the movie, I might not have known he was kidding. And since I was versed in the same traditions as he was, I didn't disagree with the *theory*—only drew the line at certain kinds of practice.

Eventually, we settled on the idea of me playing "the One," a real-life Neo whose mission was to find his sorcerer tribe (just like my script for Helena) and awaken them from the matrix by whatever means necessary. Our film was to be an improvised blend of documentary with fiction (called Dogme Surrealism), in which I would don a costume (black suit and shades) and offer "the red pill" to the actor-volunteers I had already recruited. The red pill was salvia divinorum, which by then I had sworn off using, due to what I can only term a psychotic break in Guatemala, during the previous summer. As indicated in my Depp dream, I still kept some of the substance in my shaman's pouch, however, as a sorcerer's "ally." As risky as I knew Mike's proposition to be, I also found it irresistible as an exercise in "reality-manifesting." I drew up a treatment and explained to the remaining actors the nature of our new enterprise.

Several of the actors refused to participate. One of them even panicked and broke down in tears. I put an ad in Shooting People for more, mentioning the experimental nature of the project, but a complaint was filed that I was trying to lure people into a cult. In the end, only a couple of people agreed to smoke salvia on film. One of them had a powerful vision of entering another realm where she met a mysterious being with horns and a long black cape, and her experience ended up as part of the sixth and final episode of *The God Game*. As with all the *God Game* shoots, it included an imaginary enactment of her death; several years later, I discovered she actually had died, later that same year. She died of cancer, but whether she had been diagnosed when we filmed her, I don't know.

The new project, *Being the One*, collapsed a couple of weeks later. Both Mike and I reached the point where we could no longer say how much of what we were doing was a stunt, and how much was real. I didn't know to what extent Mike really *believed* I was the One or was only pretending to believe it. I didn't know how much *I* believed it. The reason I didn't know whether I believed it or not was that the idea of being the One did not begin with Mike's suggestion, nor even with seeing *The Matrix* and over-identifying with that story. It began many years before, probably in my mid-twenties, around the time I first read Aleister Crowley's *The Book of the Law* (c.f. *The Vice of Kings*). The idea that I was somehow chosen by God for a special mission grew during my late twenties and early thirties, peaking, aptly enough, around the age of 33 (in 2000, the year my brother was crucified, and the year after *The Matrix* was released). By that time, I was more or less fully persuaded that I was, or that it was my destiny to become, a living avatar of Lucifer. This idea was rooted in a decade or more's occult study, psychedelic-use, and shamanic self-initiations, and it fused seamlessly with the mythic auto-invention inspired by the movie, and then a couple of years later by our own movie project. Eventually this led to a crash and burn period in my late-thirties (I landed at 39, just in time for a new life to begin at forty, see 9.4). Before that, in 2005, I wrote a book about my Lucifer-obsession, called *Answer to Lucifer* (after C.G. Jung's *Answer to Job*); it included the following passage:

> *I am a living incarnation of the force or entity known, among countless other names, as Lucifer. I am that force or entity. I am that. I am.*
>
> There. Now I have said it, we can all breathe more easily. My cards are face up on the table. Everything else I write can now be judged in the light of this, the hand I have played, and through the lens of this "delusion," or this revelation, should any of you be wise to me.
>
> Please note at this juncture, however, as we embark upon my tale, that I am careful to identify myself as *a* human incarnation of Lucifer, and not as *the* human incarnation of Lucifer. I have no illusions about this, for I have no reason to imagine that the force or entity of which I speak is so limited or narrow (or conventional) as to require a single host for His manifestation. This would be an assumption founded in grossest vanity and not in knowledge, inspired by ego alone, and not by vision. Intuition tells me—well, why be modest, *Lucifer* tells me (for though He is I, I am not yet He)—that there are *many* of us currently manifesting His intelligence. How many I cannot say, only that it is not so many as to in any way diminish the exclusivity and the honor of being so chosen.
>
> Which brings me to my second observation. I may as well state, right off the bat, that I do not perceive this state of affairs to be *in any way a bad thing*. Being a living embodiment of Lucifer is not the same—nor is it even remotely equivalent to—what Christians talk of as satanic possession. It is true, I suppose, that Lucifer possesses this body, even as I possess the garments that clothe it, or a car that I may drive it. But the difference between devil possession and identification with Lucifer is the difference, roughly, between a car thief who hotwires any old piece of junk he can find and unceremoniously dumps it after a couple of joy rides, and a master mechanic and scientific genius who painstakingly designs and constructs his automobile from scratch, forging the parts with loving hands and assembling the perfect, personalized vehicle for a cross-country journey from one end of the Earth to the other (and possibly back again). This is the difference I speak of, and this is why, I repeat, I do not perceive this state of affairs in any way as a *negative*.

Be all that as it may, what transpired in 2002–3 was that the rubber of the "Lucifer-vehicle" hit the road of the world, and with hindsight it was probably somewhere bang in the middle of the spectrum between drug-addled joy ride and spiritual voyage to the ends of the Earth. The first clue, perhaps, or one of them, was when Mike and I watched our movie project fall apart. If blurring the line between reality and fantasy was what Dogme Surrealism was all about, *losing* that line meant being increasingly unable to manage the practical aspects of filming. As the One, I was too busy trying to save souls to think about making movies. I got lost in the Method, and quite literally lost the plot.

Mike carried on his travels, and a few weeks later, I wrote *Matrix Warrior* in a period of two weeks. It was accepted for publication by Orion Books within a week of finishing it. Orion timed it to come out with the release of *Matrix Reloaded*, in May 2003, and I traveled to Cannes with my partner at the time, Liz Wu, and Mark Lawn (the first volunteer for The God Game) to attend (or haunt) the festival, where Reloaded was scheduled to premiere, out of competition. From my journal at the time:

Cannes was interesting. Certain elements intervened to ensure I get copies of the book to Keanu and the Wachowskis, though now I have seen the sequel, I wonder if there's any sense in it. They all seem to be utterly plugged in. Hollywood is the enemy, may as well face it. But one of our gang (my friend, Mark) ran into Agent Smith (Hugo Weaving) at Soho House, and since he was carrying copies of the book, he approached him and handed one over. Hugo looked pleased and said, "Keanu would love a copy!" Mark produced another copy and handed it over. The following day I went into Cannes again with a friend and between us we deduced where the Matrix *crew were staying (huge* Reloaded *banners hanging outside the Carlton being our first clue). I bluffed the receptionist into giving me the room number for publicity, went up and inscribed a couple of copies for Keanu and the Wachowskis.*

I found out later that he and the rest of the cast left Cannes in disgust, if not shame, at the crack of dawn after the vitriolic response to Reloaded. *Apparently there was a backlash from French critics against the infiltration of the festival by Hollywood blockbusters, and* Reloaded *got the brunt of the attack. At least that's the story I heard, sometime later. Poor Keanu. One of the reasons I was so keen to hook up with him was because I had a dream with him some nights*

*before. He was depressed and discouraged (when I saw the sequel, I knew why).**
*I told him that, little by little, he would lose his sense of self and all fear would
go along with it. He had to do this a little at a time, so he could learn to disguise
his transformation, otherwise people would assume he had gone insane. It seemed
like sound advice.*

*I left our number on a separate note in the book, in case he wanted to meet
up. Of course I was unable to abolish entirely the hope that Keanu would call.
And of course he didn't. All this was just another detour from my true purpose,
which is not to make connections within the matrix, obviously. Equally plain,
Keanu and his $50 million might come in handy, but only if he's able to grok our
true purpose. This seems increasingly unlikely, dreams notwithstanding.*

Seeing Matrix Reloaded *has deflated my spirits considerably, however
indulgent that may be on my part. It's a necessary disillusionment, but the result
is that not only have I lost faith/interest in the Wachowskis and the* Matrix
*phenomenon, but also, to a lesser extent, in the book. My worst fear has been
realized. The book must stand alone, or fade away like a bad dream, along with
the rest of the* Matrix *hoopla.*

9.3.   IN THE DOGHOUSE: CASE STUDY # 9,
BILL MECHANIC

"Electric information environments, being utterly ethereal, foster
the illusion of the world as a spiritual substance. It is now a
reasonable facsimile of the mystical body, a blatant manifestation
of the Anti-Christ. After all, the Prince of this World is a very
great electric engineer."

—MARSHALL MCLUHAN, *letters, 1969*

In 2005, I published *Dogville Vs Hollywood* for Marion Boyars,
Pauline Kael's UK publisher, about the war between independent cinema

---

* Perhaps this was the source of what later became the "Sad Keanu" meme?

and Hollywood. The book began with the line: "Talking of creative integrity in Hollywood is akin to preaching chastity in a whorehouse." A few pages later, I wrote: "Since corruption comes not before but *after* death has occurred, a system that is corrupt is by definition already dead." I laid out my argument as follows (I've updated the text to bring it more in harmony with my present timbre):

> There is a saying in the legal world, much used, little publicized (for obvious reasons): "Any prosecutor can convict a guilty man; it takes a great prosecutor to convict an innocent man." If such "game rules" have now replaced more traditional moral principles in modern institutions such as Law, Politics, and Hollywood, then the same basic principle might afford us a better understanding of the world of mass media. For the thrill of the challenge, and a perverse satisfaction at the rank stupidity of the public, publishers may (for all we know) take special pride in turning the most execrable books into bestsellers.
>
> Naturally, this is a rationale/motivation that can only come about when a nihilistic contempt for readers has supplanted a love of literature, and the same applies in the legal world when it comes to justice. In Hollywood, this sinister game seemed to have reached its apotheosis, around the turn of the millennium, with works like *Phantom Menace* and the *Matrix* sequels; now in 2020, we have an endless stream of superhero summer blockbusters that—no matter how tawdry or inept—are guaranteed to recoup their costs and garner a tidy profit for the studios, for all concerned in fact, and even receive rave reviews from respected periodicals. Most diabolically of all, moviegoers seem to be fooling *themselves* into feeling satisfied by these bloated spectacles, probably due to their previous investment in the characters and storylines, a kind of nostalgic residual affection that is being exploited and steadily debased.
>
> In Robert Altman's *The Player*, the Faustian producer-executive played by Tim Robbins makes a quip, after having murdered a scriptwriter he believes was blackmailing him: "I was just thinking what an interesting concept it is to eliminate the writer from the artistic process. If we can just get rid of these actors and directors, maybe we've got something here." Hollywood has yet to succeed in this goal, but it is getting close. Many big Hollywood movies are worked on (even during shooting) by so

many different writers-for-hire that the end result is that the movies seem to have been written by no one, or not to have been written at all. With "deep fake" technology, actors will soon be expendable. A seemingly inexhaustible stream of basically worthless movies make money for studios to make more worthless movies with, keeping the public hungry for ever-more movies. The medicine that forever promises but never quite delivers a cure is a blueprint for never-ending addiction and everlasting dominance. Hollywood über alles, worlds without end.

Not surprisingly, the book did not find favor in Hollywood, or anywhere else for that matter (though the opening line was voted "best first line of the week" by *The Sunday Times*). It landed with an inaudible splash, causing almost no observable ripples. While working on the book, I started a correspondence with actor-turned-director Keith Gordon (*Back to School*— as Robert Downey's roommate—*Dressed to Kill, Mother Night, The Singing Detective*) which continued for several years. I had listed Gordon at my website as "the no. 1 most underrated film director" (Kubrick was the most overrated), and I managed to make contact with him by email. Compared to where I was situated in my endless struggle to get my emails answered, Keith Gordon had "made it." But compared to other Hollywood filmmakers, he was struggling just to be noticed and could barely get his movies financed (he now works in TV). It made perfect sense he was the only Hollywood player whose attention I was able to get. Keith was even good enough to read a few of my scripts and provide feedback.

In full Hollywood-storming mode during this period, I also somehow managed to catch the attention of a couple of big-leaguers: Lorenzo di Bonaventura, the producer of *The Matrix* (I sent him a copy of *Matrix Warrior*), and Bill Mechanic, who worked at Disney for nine years and then was CEO of Fox Filmed Entertainment from 1994–2000. At Fox, he was responsible for production, marketing, distribution, international theatrical activities, home video and pay TV, and it was under his guidance that Fox produced the worldwide top grossing films in 1995, 1996 and 1997, *Die Hard with a Vengeance, Independence Day*, and *Titanic*. That particular stint, as well as films like *X-Men, Ice Age, Minority Report, Moulin Rouge, There's Something About Mary, Braveheart, The X-Files,* and *True Lies,* made Twentieth Century Fox the number-one studio in worldwide box-office gross revenue in 1998, and made Mechanic a very rich and powerful man.

But there was more to Mechanic than titanic returns. While running Fox, he created three new film divisions: Fox 2000, Fox Searchlight Pictures, and Fox Animation, overseeing the production of *Girl 6, Looking for Richard, She's the One, Boys Don't Cry, The Full Monty, Sexy Beast, Bulworth, Office Space, Ice Storm*, and *Waking Life*. Mechanic also greenlit Fincher's *Fight Club*, released in 1999. Some rumors have suggested that Rupert Murdoch—the owner of Fox—hated *Fight Club* so much he had Mechanic fired the following year. Whatever the reason, his tenure as studio head came to an end, and by the time I was corresponding with him, he was attempting to make a new start as an independent producer and not having a great deal of success (*Coraline, Dark Water, The New World*). He eventually had a hit with Mel Gibson's *Hacksaw Ridge* (2015), but during the period we corresponded he was closer in stature to Keith Gordon than Steven Spielberg, industrially speaking, and involved in "the Sisyphus-like task of getting pictures made in any way possible" (Mechanic to author). This would have undoubtedly been why he had time to correspond with an unknown quantity like myself.

I'd got a hold of Mechanic's email via a site called *Everyone Who's Anyone—in the Monolithic, Misanthropic, Malevolent, Mashugana Media and Entertainment Monopoly that Rots Your Mind, Robs You Blind and Keeps You a Slave from Cradle to Grave: A Writer's Guide to The All-Pervasive Propaganda Cabal*. The site is run by an elderly frustrated writer called Gerald Jones who loves to bitch about how no one will read his book, *Ginny Good*. He claims to have sent out "at least 200,000 'query' letters over the past seventeen years" (in June 2019), and got all of nowhere. For his efforts, he has managed to amass a vast archive of industry people's email addresses, which he has generously made available to everyone. In those days the site had a search function, so I used it to try and find emails for all the Hollywood talent I was dying to make contact with. Predictably enough, I found that many of the emails (Mel Gibson's or Steven Spielberg's) didn't work (if they ever had, the A-listers would surely have closed their accounts after a few unwelcome emails); but that didn't stop me from trying dozens of them out. I think Mechanic was the only real Hollywood insider I got a response from.

In 2007, I sent him an early draft of a script I had written called *Grasshopper* (see 9.4.). His response was roughly what F. Murray Abraham says to Oscar Isaac in *Inside Llewyn Davis*: "I don't see any money here."

I don't think Lorenzo di Bonaventura ever read any of my scripts, but he did take my call once, also in 2007. To date, this was my one and only chance to do a bona fide Hollywood pitch. I had a bunch of ideas—too many—but the main one was *The Keepers*, an epic tale of the Nosferatu I had been working on that I believed was going to be "*The Godfather* of vampire movies." I thought I had prepared for the meeting but it turned out I hadn't. I flubbed it badly, so badly that I apologized halfway through for "doing the Hollywood pitch thing." Lorenzo assured me, "There's nothing wrong with a Hollywood pitch, Jake." (I went by Jake back then.) I was so out of the loop I was apologizing for trying to give Lorenzo what he had taken my call to get! Later, I realized that I had also unwittingly tipped my hand: not only was I not a Hollywood player, I had no intention of turning myself into one. My apology was a passive-aggressive act of self-effacement, after which Lorenzo stopped answering my emails.

A bit later, when I was writing for the *Film Festival Magazine*, I did an email interview with Mechanic that included this exchange:

You must have known Murdoch and half the studio brass at Fox was going to hate Fight Club, *and that you would be first in line to take the heat.*

I knew it would kick up a shit storm. I knew it would lead to a confrontation, most likely with Murdoch. In this case, I would have left my job
if I had been unable to perform the duties I was hired to perform, which
were to make films I absolutely believed in. . . . But ultimately and honestly, I caused the film to get made because I thought it had a chance to
be a great movie. That it would do for a generation what *Blow Up* did for
me; make artists want to become filmmakers, make audiences go home
and argue about a film instead of forgetting it before they reached the
front door. . . . My job running a studio was to make money. My goal
was to make good movies. When I did my job well, I made good movies
that made money.

You're quoted in Biskind's Down and Dirty Pictures *[talking about Bob
and Harvey Weinstein]: "Bad behavior doesn't get punished in this business."
Care to elaborate?*

What I think I meant was that success breeds contempt in many people. They forget all the people who participated in their success and feel bulletproof. It allows some of the worst human behavior to surface. This doesn't happen to everyone. As someone once said to me, assholes don't happen overnight. They are just waiting for their chance to come out.

How about good behavior? Does that get rewarded?

Good behavior on the other hand almost never gets rewarded. But then good behavior usually isn't searching for rewards.

In the case of Bill Mechanic, two things come to mind. He may well have been sincere when he spoke to me about his love of movies and his desire to make great ones that also made money for the studio. But he was also involved, wittingly or not, in globally distributing US imperialist propaganda like *Die Hard with a Vengeance* and *Independence Day*. The smaller, more personal and prestigious movies he did gave credibility to that propaganda machine. By garnering acclaim, they increased Fox's power and influence in the world, and, in theory, his own. It's possible that, with *Fight Club*, Mechanic went too far out on an already thin limb, and that the film really did ruffle some elite feathers, whereupon Mechanic had to be made an example of. Yes, "edgy," semi-subversive movies that pass for art do need to be included in our roster to maintain our credibility; but we wouldn't want it to become a habit! Firing Mechanic after *Fight Club*, while it wouldn't alert the general public to anything untoward, might have sent a message to other high-ups not to bite the hand that fed them.

9.4.   A GRAND DARK EMPTINESS

"Not half a dozen men have ever been able to keep the whole equation of pictures in their heads."

—F. SCOTT FITZGERALD, *The Last Tycoon*

After I first fell ill in Hollywood in 1987, over the ensuing twenty years, I suffered on an almost daily basis from intense body pains, headaches, sore throat, relentless stomach problems, night sweats, and frequent bouts of exhaustion. My condition was worst of all in the mornings: I would wake after a night's rest, drained of all energy, soaked in sweat, my body a seething mass of discomfort, racked by an indescribable feeling of contamination. Many days, I barely had the energy to get out of bed. Usually I did so by sheer will alone. I eventually gave the condition-that-began-in-Hollywood a nickname: "The Grinch." It was only in 2007, while seeking incapacity benefit, that I underwent a series of interviews and tests and my condition was diagnosed as Chronic Fatigue Syndrome (CFS).

This was after I had moved back to London from Guatemala, with my cat and little else. I had no money or means of income, but I knew I could collect Unemployment and Housing Benefits, at least for a year or two, just as I had back in 2002. There was no earthly reason, as far as the government was concerned, why a failed writer needed to live in the *chichi* neighborhood of Hampstead, but fortunately, I was able to give my aging mother as an excuse. Within a few months, I was secure and settled enough to gaze into the grand dark emptiness my life had become. Licking my wounds on government support, staring at the desert of the real, I found myself wondering—*How* did *I get here?*

I had nothing but time, and I sought ways to engage myself besides walking on the heath, watching movies, and (occasionally) surfing the net for porn. I'd discovered movie torrent sites, an endless resource of distraction. All of these movies *seemed* like treasures—the promise never seemed to fade—but they usually turned to shit within a few minutes of watching them. In the worst moments, I would find myself watching another crappy movie, stuffing my face with popcorn and Kettle crisps, when it would suddenly hit me that I wasn't even *enjoying* the experience. I was caught up in a vainglorious struggle to recapture a lost time, when this behavior *had* been fun. I would wake up the next day with my junk food hangover, sickness and despair hanging over me like a toxic cloud.

I was still working feverishly on my creative projects, a couple of blogs and a number of scripts, including *Grasshopper*. Inspired by the endless drudgery of my existence at the time, I posed a question: what if someone tried to make every day *exactly alike*? This gave me the idea of an extreme OCD sufferer who tries to turn himself into a robot so he doesn't have to make any decisions, ever again. He maps out his day precisely, to the minute, repeating each day without variation. Since he still has sexual urges, he abducts a young girl, imprisons her in his basement, and tries to turns *her* into a robot too, a sex slave, a flesh and blood suck doll.

The curious fact was that, no matter how many times my Hollywood dream failed, it seemed to rise up again, like a Phoenix (a dark one). After ten, twenty, thirty, years of seeking, aspiring, struggling, I was no closer to my goal, spiritually *or* materially, than when I'd started. They say failure is a great teacher; I had made significant progress in that department. I had been joking that life better damn well begin at forty, because mine had ended at thirty-nine. So why was I still holding on? Why couldn't I give it *all* up? One day I made a decision: if nothing came of my efforts by the time I turned forty, I would drive a stake through the Hollywood vampire's heart; I would shoot the beast with a silver bullet, cut off the zombie's head and burn the body; I would close the coffin on the dream forever. Goodbye, good riddance, *adieu!*

I announced my intention at my MySpace page, determined to keep to it. Time passed and I turned forty. A couple of days later, I found a private message from Michael Falvetta: a fan of *Matrix Warrior*. He had read my announcement and told me not to abandon hope. He worked at an independent film company in New York, he said, and he wanted to hear about any screenplays I had written. The message was sent on my fortieth birthday. The ego had landed.

9.5.   A DREAM WITHIN A DREAM

> "Being confident that there is ground beneath one's feet when one needs to plant them firmly is an enabling condition of making a sober judgment."
>
> —RAIMOND GAITA, *"Even Socrates drew the line at spin"*

Bubbling with excitement, I sent Michael my epic Sam Peckinpah biopic, and soon after that I sent him *Grasshopper*, still a work in progress. Months passed before I heard that Michael loved the Peckinpah script and had passed it on to his boss, Marissa Polvino (he had since moved to another NY production company, this one called Straight Up Films). Sometime after that, I heard that she loved it too. I was reeling. At that time, Straight Up was developing a David Mamet biopic, and Michael told me that Marissa thought that, in my sympathetic treatment of such an unsavory character as Peckinpah, I had done a better job than Mamet! In August 2007, Michael told me that Marissa wanted to put the Peckinpah project into development. At some point, he assured me, they would "make me an offer."

Michael also liked *Grasshopper* and passed it along to Marissa, who said she wanted to produce it too! My life was exploding into new possibilities, spinning off in every direction; I could no longer tell fantasy from reality. Michael and I began discussing directors and actors for the projects: Johnny Depp or Guy Pierce for the Peckinpah project, with Sean Penn or Alejandro G. Iñárritu directing; Kristen Stewart, David Morse, and David Thewlis for *Grasshopper*, with some crazy talk about Cronenberg and (more realistically) Chris Cunningham for director. I began spending long periods on my bed lost in elaborate fantasies of hanging out on the set with A-listers in Mexico and making Oscar speeches.

At that time, I was banned from entering the US for a marijuana infraction, going back to my early-twenties (I had come in through Canada in 2001). Since most of the Peckinpah script was set in Mexico, the chances were it would be filmed there, meaning I would be able to hang out on set! I wasn't fantasizing about drug parties or nubile groupies, just buddying up to Sean Penn and Johnny Depp, being the screenwriter, the man behind it all, giving advice and feedback and being treated as one of the "gang" (being ushered into the secret society—I was conveniently forgetting what I knew about how scriptwriters are generally treated in Hollywood). The fantasies weren't elaborate, but they were hooked into a much grander one, that of the unleashing of my own still-untapped shamanic potential, of getting to walk with the gods. The dream was coming true. My daily ritual of meditation became almost impossible—all I did was fantasize.

Oddly, the peak of the fantasy coincided—exactly six months after that first fateful message—with the launch of my brother Sebastian's memoir,

Dandy in the Underworld. Just a few days before the launch, we had got into an argument. Ostensibly, he was trying to "save" me from my despair. He was convinced that the gulf between my talent and my aspirations was the source of all my unhappiness. What this translated into, however, was him doing what he had always done: trying to keep me in "my place" and prevent me from stealing his thunder.

By the time the book launch came around, I was flying so high on my Hollywood horse that I didn't care. It was the perfect revenge after all his put-downs. Ironically, he was lost in similar fantasies, with pending film deals and US book tours. We were Cain and Abel, making our offerings to Mammon, in endless competition for the prize. His was accepted, mine was rejected. Just as my brother's dream was coming true, my own ended, as swiftly and mysteriously as it began. Michael got into an argument with Marissa and was fired. All the projects he'd brought to her were firebombed along with him.

There may be a lesson in this, an ultimate one: better your dream dies, than you do.

9.6.   STAR-STALKING

"There is nothing more terrifying or despair-inducing than loss of contact with reality; but what could be more unreal than the life of a movie star?"

—JAKE HORSLEY, *"Fame Kills:*
Heath Ledger & the Twilight of the Gods"

While I was "developing" *Grasshopper* with Michael and Marissa, I had decided, after much thought, that the ideal actor for the role of Jeffrey, the sympathetic maniac, was David Thewlis. Thewlis is perhaps best known (in England at least) for his role in Mike Leigh's apocalyptic *Naked*, and for playing one of the magicians in the *Harry Potter* series. So when I heard Thewlis was giving a reading from his new novel in the West End, I was determined to get the script into his hands, by whatever means necessary. I printed up a copy, put on my old "Neo" black suit, and headed to the reading, full of determination and excitement.

It was a medium turn-out of maybe thirty people, with a smattering of *Harry Potter* fangirls. I sat in the front row. Thewlis read from his novel and did it well (there was a lot of dialogue so he was acting a lot). Half the time I was looking at him, I was imagining him as Jeffrey. No doubt about it, I thought: he's my guy. At question time, no one wanted to start so I got the ball rolling. Since his novel was about a painter, I asked him if he was a painter. He said he wasn't but that his older brother was, then hinted that there was possibly some rivalry there: a familiar scenario. I asked him what had inspired the novel and he told a funny anecdote about working on *The Island of Dr. Moreau* with Marlon Brando. He'd chosen the art world for his novel, he said, because of how similar it is to the film world.*

The Q & A was mostly between the two of us, and towards the end, as I kept on asking questions (once everyone else had run out), he blurted out, "I like you!" which got a big laugh (including from me). I was still asking questions when they were trying to round things up. Thewlis was funny, affable, and relaxed, unlike any other celebrity I'd seen before, in the flesh or otherwise. My last question to him was whether he'd ever wanted to do stand-up. He said he never had and that he didn't think he could do it, but that he admired people who did. I told him he seemed like a natural, where-upon he got shy and thanked me. "I don't know what to say," he said.

---

* "Reluctant to write about his own profession, Thewlis—who collects early 20th-century portraits, paints a little himself, and spoke to the artists Damien Hirst, Gillian Wearing and Stuart Pearson Wright for research—was inevitably drawn to its similarities with the art world. 'I was interested in the idea of celebrity. . . some very untalented people getting very successful and making a lot of money for not a lot of work, sometimes. And I was interested in rivalry between friends.' Thewlis has lost friends to his celebrity. Judging by the uncomplicated way in which Billy Connolly, Paul Auster, Bill Nighy and Kathy Burke pop up in conversation, new alliances are easier to maintain than some ancient ones. He is quite sanguine about this. 'Yeah. Certain people became . . . ungracious. You couldn't go round and tell a story about Marlon Brando—obviously the biggest star I've ever worked with—because they'd roll their eyes and go [yawning], "Oh, Marlon Brando . . ." So you think, OK, should I not tell a story about playing chess with Marlon Brando? The friend-ship becomes pointless if I can't share my life with you, I can't tell you what's happening.'" "A funny thing happened . . .," by Harriet Lane, *The Telegraph*, 25 Aug, 2007: https://www.telegraph.co.uk/culture/3667486/A-funny-thing-happened....html

After it was over people lined up for signings. I went to the toilet, got some water, and hung out on the edge of things, waiting for my chance, thinking, "Don't fuck up!" Thewlis had what looked like his "people" with him: two blonde women, one of whom was at least eight months pregnant. I approached and told Thewlis that I didn't have a book to sign but that I wanted to introduce myself. At first his eyes looked wary, then warm as we shook hands. I told him I was a writer.

"I know you're busy," I said, "*I don't want to impose.*" He nodded appreciatively, as if agreeing. It was then that things started to get weird. Instead of just telling him I had a script I wanted to give him, I asked if he had a few minutes while I asked a couple of things.

"More questions?" he said. And just like that, the mood changed.

Both Thewlis and the pregnant woman started saying he was very busy and had to go. I could tell right away he was feeling cornered. His people were trying to extract him from the exchange before it turned into "a situation." Instantly, I started to feel like a pariah, but I pressed on.

"I love your work," I said, dully, feeling anything but love. "I've written a script that I hope is, um, 'in development'"—I probably even put the quotes around it—"and, uh, I think you'd be great for the part."

I could hear my voice and it intensified my distress. There was absolutely no conviction in it and I could see Thewlis' eyes glazing over. It was as if I'd turned into an automaton—or Jeffrey from *Grasshopper*! I was reading a script I didn't believe in, lines I knew that he, a movie star, had heard a thousand times before.

Inevitably, Thewlis mirrored my artificiality and, just as I had done, he became a different person. By this time, he was just being polite to avoid a scene. We were locked into roles neither of us wanted to play. His manager (the pregnant woman) stepped in and handed me her card. I took it automatically. Thewlis was making noises about sending the script to an agent, etc.

"I don't have an agent," I stammered.

"That's how it's done," he said, "even the big guys do it that way."

"Yeah, but I'm a small fry."

He wasn't having any of it. The manager was still trying to get me to talk to her, so Thewlis, who was standing up now, could make a clean getaway.

"I just wanted to finish telling David something," I said to her.

He said, "Sure, while I put my coat on." Fortunately he didn't sound unfriendly.

"I have the script here," I said. "It's in a stamped-addressed-envelope!"

Thewlis looked surprised. It took him a few seconds to register that I actually had the script right there with me. When the penny dropped, he said, "OK, let me have it."

I felt a rush of relief. I went and grabbed the script without saying anything else. I came back and handed it to him. I was back to myself again, the spell of miserable toad-pariah had broken as quickly as it had fallen over me and I was all smiles and confidence again. I told him I really appreciated it, and shook his hand.

"Great to meet you," I said. He smiled and the warmth between us returned.

"Thanks for asking all those questions," he said. His manager seconded it.

I told him he was welcome and got the hell out of there while everyone was still smiling.

Afterwards, I went over it my mind endlessly, squirming at every recall. Why had I tried to soften Thewlis up before giving him the script? If I'd only come right out and asked him, I could have avoided all that misery and embarrassment. Looking back, I realized he probably thought I was trying to get his home address or email and that I wasn't going to leave without it. The very qualities that had made me such a positive presence at the Q & A— enthusiasm, confidence, engagement—had suddenly started to seem like the qualities of a stalker. I had left the real world and entered into a negative parasocial relationship.

What had happened at my end was simple enough: I got all tangled up in the transition from a friendly and pleasant dialogue of equals to the world- lier, desire-based, ego-bound roles of "unknown scriptwriter approaches movie star." I lost the plot and found myself recast in a thankless bit part that gave me no room to improvise. Thewlis and his people—more accurately the whole cultural machinery of celebrity power games—took over the narrative. In that narrative, I was a loser to be dispatched with as quickly, politely, and painlessly as possible.

I emailed his publicity manager later for an interview but nothing came of it. I never heard back from any of them, and despite the stamped- addressed-envelope, Thewlis never returned my script.

While I was working on this segment, I looked into what Thewlis had been doing since then. In 2017, he was in *Wonder Woman* and *Justice League America*. He was even then working with James Cameron on not one but *two* *Avatar* sequels, due in 2021 and 2023.

Maybe in a parallel universe, he did *Grasshopper*, I thought, and avoided a terrible fate. Or maybe in that universe, *Grasshopper* got made and I got pulled into one and became a Hollywood "player". . . ?

10

THE SWEET SMELL
OF SUCCESS

10.1. THE GAY MAFIA

> "[I]t seems like some Hollywood bigwigs may be trying to turn
> women against men and men against women, may be trying to
> drive a wedge between the sexes. Ominously, Hollywood appears
> to be somewhat successful in fostering antagonism between the
> sexes. Witness the soaring divorce rate, number one. Then there
> is this remark by author Tama Janowitz: 'This will sound goofy,
> but I think they put something in the water in New York to make
> men not like women very much. . . . They don't seem to have
> much use for women.'"
>
> —MIMI READ, *"Literary Misfit," New York Times*

When Rock Hudson was asked how many top actors in Hollywood
were homosexual, Hudson replied: "If you mean gay, or 'bisex-
ual'. . . then maybe most. . . . Trust me. . . America does not
want to know."[1] As uncontroversial a critic as Roger Ebert has written that
"gays were everywhere in the movies, right from the beginning."[2] On the
other hand, the suggestion that there might be a homosexual clique wielding
a disproportionate amount of power and influence in Hollywood is one I
had not come across in four decades of reading about the film industry, or

even in my study of deep politics, social engineering, or "conspiracy culture." Yet among the gay community, it is apparently no secret, as Michelangelo Signorile makes explicit in *Queer in America: Sex, the Media, and the Closets of Power*:

> Many of the powerful gay men are known to each other, part of a *secret network*. . . Stars and starlets trying to make it up the Hollywood power chain have always slept with power brokers in order to move up; there has always been an ample supply of young men ready and willing to have sex with those at the top in gay Hollywood (p. 260, emphasis added).

In 1995, *Spy* magazine ran a piece called "The Gay Mafia."* The article stands almost alone within mainstream coverage, at least what's currently available online (and at that barely). This itself seems like a noteworthy fact, one I will come back to. The *Spy* article describes a homosexual Hollywood clique as "a power so far-reaching it's mind-boggling." (It qualifies this statement by adding: "Does being straight get in the way? Is there a heterosexual glass ceiling? Probably not.") The piece begins:

> Despite numerous denials, the Gay Mafia *does* exist, in hierarchical factions. "Like the Jews who came to Hollywood in the Twenties and Thirties," writes [gay psychotherapist] Doug Sadownick in *L.A. Weekly*, "gays have found the industry an extraordinary contradiction: an opportunity to reap extravagant rewards, while, at the same time, being forced to deny their cultural identities." How does one go about reaping rewards while denying who they are? By forming a powerful clique—an assemblage of like-minded industry people amongst whom they can feel "themselves" and with whom they can share their strongest desires: power and sex. A top talent manager says of the clan: "Do they protect and screw each other? The [Gay] Mafia? Completely" (p. 44).

---

* *Spy* was a satirical monthly magazine based in New York City that ran from 1986 to 1998 and specialized in lampooning US media and entertainment industries. It also looked into the (slightly) darker side of celebrity culture. The article quoted is a 100% non-satirical piece.

One of the main focuses of the *Spy* piece is David Geffen, the music and movie executive who built up a vast Hollywood-based empire in the 1970s and 1980s, including Geffen Records and DreamWorks, formed with Steven Spielberg and Jeffrey Katzenberg. Geffen was an early financial supporter of President Clinton and came out of the closet in 1992, soon after which, *Out* magazine placed him at the top of its list of the fifty "Most Powerful Gay Men and Women in America."*

The *Spy* article describes Geffen as being an exemplary of the upper echelons of this "family": a man "who can end a career with a phone call." An actor "with 20 pictures to his credit" says of Geffen: "I knew I was in the big leagues when I slept with [him]." Geffen dismisses the idea of a Gay Mafia as "just another homophobic, nasty kind of thing that jealous queens make up." But Geffen's influence extended well beyond the entertainment industry, as in the case of the arrest of a pimp, David Forrest, who ran a male prostitution ring whose services Geffen procured. The police told *Spy* that Geffen's name wouldn't be mentioned in the trial, because they considered him untouchable (p. 48).†

Another alleged member of the GM cited in the article is Barry Diller, creator of the Fox Broadcasting Company and one-time head of Paramount Pictures. Diller, the piece states, has been outed as homosexual by the press but has yet to formally come out of the closet. (His sexual orientation is not mentioned on Wikipedia at the time of writing.) Journalist Andrew Goldman Former claimed, in 2015, that he was fired from the *New York Times Magazine* for asking Diller's wife, fashion entrepreneur Diane von Furstenberg—whose company advertises in the paper—about her husband's homosexuality.[3]

---

* As an interesting detail, Geffen's voice can be heard on Barbra Streisand's 1985 *The Broadway Album*, in the song "Putting It Together," as the voice of a record company executive schmoozing with Streisand. Streisand has always been hugely popular with the gay community, and is considered a leading spokesperson for gay rights. This footnote was more relevant when there was a chapter about Barbra Streisand as a possible MKULTRA subject, see Brice Taylor's *Thanks for the Memories*. The chapter didn't make the Outtakes section, but will be available as a PDF for supporters of the *16 Maps of Hell* campaign.

† The article does stretch credibility when it refers to Neil Jordan as gay; if true, then Jordan's cover is unusually deep: he has five children from two marriages.

One film executive quoted in the *Spy* article describes Diller as "more *mean* than gay. The worst stories you hear [are] about him being nasty and horrible . . . he's made grown men cry, and he's enjoyed it. And he would fuck with people and play with their minds for the sheer pleasure of taking them apart" (p. 46). Another source suggests that Diller "has what he wants in his mind already. . . . He doesn't want [to be out the closet]. He wants it the way it is." Diller's ability to control the public perception, the piece argues, is "a cornerstone of his power."

The piece mentions how the Creative Artists Agency (CAA), one of the biggest talent agencies in Hollywood, obliged its executives (in 1995) to get married before being promoted. This suggests that plausible denial was at that time an essential factor to the functioning of the (alleged) Gay Mafia: "if you're gay and closeted in Hollywood, it might be best to stay that way. Most would agree that it wouldn't be beneficial even for the most powerful individuals, like Diller, to come out . . . an attitude fostered not only at the individual level, but at the institutional level, as well."

Diller's response to all this in *Out* magazine (quoted by *Spy*) was this: "I don't even know what [the Gay Mafia] means, so I don't know how to respond to stuff like that. It's all silly talk."

◆

> "[Y]ou can't live in Hollywood and get along in this business . . . and have issues with gay people. . . . If you can't work with gay people, you're gonna have a difficult time in Hollywood. There's plenty of gay people and they're in positions above you. You're not going to get your movie directed. I don't have a problem with it—they've just turned into a mafia and demanding everyone apologize for every joke and retract every statement. It's turned into something that's bigger than it is. I've lived in this town my whole life and never seen it like this."
>
> —ADAM CAROLLA, *quoted in "Adam Carolla: The gay mafia is real,"* *by Daniel D'addario, Salon, May 19, 2014*

The next example in the *Spy* article is producer Howard Rosenman (*Father of the Bride*). The piece claims Rosenman was blacklisted for many years for making a (very minor) public criticism of Geffen (essentially: "Don't piss him off"), but that he managed to get back into the game over time. It implies this was partially via his involvement with "the Circle of Fire" sex orgies. The Circle of Fire, says an anonymous insider, "has all the stars involved in it. . . . It's this group of young, really good-looking guys that travel around everywhere, from coast to coast, and cater to big orgy parties. They fly these guys out en masse, and they just party, party, party. Like at Stan Kamen's house out in Point Dume . . . that was so far out that no one would hear the screams" (p. 46).

Stanley Kamen was one of Hollywood's best-known and most successful talent agents and represented Barbra Streisand, Warren Beatty, Steven Spielberg, and Robert Redford. One of his former employees describes him as "the original gay power broker. . . . He had it all, and the [straight] guys who came off his desk idolized him." His sexual orientation was never mentioned, however, and he was treated with "reverence built out of fear." The fear was "based on what will happen to you" (p. 48). He died in 1986 of AIDS,[4] which was perhaps why it was safe to name him as one of the hosts of the Circle of Fire orgies.

Like Jeffrey Epstein, Howard Rosenman was born in Brooklyn. Despite his Palestinian ancestry, he served in the Israeli Defense Forces as an extern medic in his early twenties. He became a producer in 1976 and made Streisand's *The Main Event* as his second feature, in 1979. When quoted in the *Spy* article, Rosenman demonstrates a capacity he shares with Diller for shifting perspectives according to the occasion. He insists (in the *Spy* piece) "there's no homophobia in the industry. . . . It's a very liberal industry [and] people are much more tolerant than anywhere else." After that, he appears to contradict himself by calling Hollywood "a very conservative industry. It's sort of like Wall Street." The confusion is partially dispelled when he adds this proviso, "You have to establish yourself first. . . . If you set a good impression, then you can let people know you're gay."

Apparently, the rules in Hollywood around sexuality, as with other things, change according to who you know and, most of all, how much power you wield. At the same time, as the actor who slept with Geffen suggests, achieving power depends on getting into bed, sometimes literally, with the power-brokers for whom the rules do not apply. Power in Hollywood, as elsewhere, depends not just on compliance but on complicity.

The article ends with Disney, citing five top Disney creative executives, "not to mention a host of underlings," as being homosexual. Yet "despite all the gay power concentrated at the top, Disney still has its wholesome imagine [sic] to maintain. . . . There is a whole level of deception there, and I think they work very hard to maintain that level of deception" (p. 49).

10.2.   CASE STUDY # 10: THE FALL OF MIKE OVITZ

"The history of Hollywood is filled with stars who started out
at the bottom of the chain, essentially as prostitutes, became
networkers, and went on to become stars or power brokers, but
remained networkers, continuing to ingratiate the powerful. Still
others, actors mostly, will always be prostitutes, willing to put
out for whatever they can get in return. There has never been
a shortage of them, male or female. They will always flock to
Hollywood."

   —MICHELANGELO SIGNORILE, *Queer in America:*
   Sex, the Media, and the Closets of Power

As regards diligence in maintaining deception, Disney may not be alone. A search for "gay mafia" online brings up few results that aren't in the context of alleged homophobia or, in one striking case, a kind of public meltdown. In a 2008 interview with *Vanity Fair*, Michael Ovitz, who was for a time considered the "Most Powerful Man in Hollywood,"™ stated, on record, that a "gay mafia" was largely responsible for his company's failure.[5] The back-story: Ovitz co-created and managed the previously cited CAA for twenty years, after which he retired and opted for a stint as President of Disney from 1995–97, under CEO Michael Eisner. In the same interview, Ovitz complained that he was blocked every step of the way by Eisner (whom he fingers as a member of the GM).

Ovitz quit Disney and, in 1998, formed the Artist Management Group, the premise of which was to pair a "supergroup" of managers with a film-and-television-production company—pretty much equivalent to starting a new studio. For reasons political as much as economic, the AMG hemorrhaged money from its inception on; Ovitz was forced to cut his losses and sold the company in 2002 to Jeff Kwatinetz, for an undisclosed amount. Kwatinetz merged it into his management group, The Firm, and Ovitz was left with nothing to do but publicly lament the monumental collapse of his new project and his Icarus-like plummet from the Hollywood heights.

In his prime, Ovitz was as verified a Hollywood insider as it's possible to be, which means there can be little doubt that his epic crash-and-burn was the result of pissing off the wrong people. The *Vanity Fair* article supports this view, up to a point:

> CAA's zenith [was] during the 1980s, when Ovitz, emerging as an Armani-clad, Sun Tzu-quoting Zen warrior, packaged his clients into one blockbuster movie after another and was crowned the arrogant sovereign of a merciless city. These were the years when his rivals say power went to his head, when CAA's slash-and-burn tactics created enemies the way a hurricane produces raindrops.

The point at which the piece abandons him, inevitably, is more or less when Ovitz starts talking about a Gay Mafia. While not actually deriding the idea, the article is careful to couch it in language that insinuates paranoia and delusion, and then to counteract Ovitz's claim of a GM with non-denial denials from on high. The two most emphatic denials it relies on come, not surprisingly, from Geffen and Diller.

> "You're not serious," Diller says. "Wow. He said that on the record? Wow . . . Wow. Wow. I'm stunned. I'm stunned. I'm stunned. I think it's . . . uh . . . uh . . . it's worse than unfortunate, notwithstanding his completely understandable anguish. A statement like that is . . . uh . . . uh . . . is . . . is . . . is beyond unfortunate. It's fairly rotten."

It's hard to say why the article includes every stutter and pause Diller makes here. Perhaps it is to assist the reader in appreciating his performance of astonishment and concern? On the other hand, Diller's astonishment may well have been genuine, if not for the reason implied. The fact Ovitz was breaking the velvet omertà might, genuinely, have been a cause for both amazement and alarm. Geffen's response is an even ballsier piece of gaslighting:

"Oh, please," says Geffen. "A Gay Mafia? This is so crazy. This is insane.
I think he needs a psychiatrist. It's so paranoid, and so crazy, and so
irresponsible, and makes him look like such a nut. It's beyond crazy. On
a scale of 1 to 10 crazy, it's 11. . . . He's made a fool of himself, and he's
made a huge failure of his life. To say you've been brought down by the
Gay Mafia and its allies is as crazy as anything I've ever heard in my life."[6]

There are few methods more effective for undermining someone's credibility than to use words like "needs a psychiatrist," "paranoid," "crazy" (x 5),
"failure," and "made a fool of himself." The Ovitz interview came a full 13
years after the *Spy* article, which means Geffen could have been reasonably
sure that most readers—if they ever heard the term Gay Mafia before—
would have forgotten all about it and would be easily persuaded that it had
spilled wholly out of the lobster pot of Ovitz's addled brain.

But there's another reason for Geffen to play the indignant care troll:
Ovitz is, or was, an insider, and presumably a master of public relations. He
would have been fully aware of just how risky it was to speak of a "secret
clique of Hollywood homosexuals" conspiring to destroy him. If his career
weren't already in flames, it would have been career suicide. As he himself
put it in the interview:

> This is a big roll of the dice for me. . . . Up to the moment I stepped in
> here, I doubted whether to do it. Instinctively, I just don't know if it's
> the right thing. . . I'm just going to say what I'm going to say, and let the
> cards fall where they may. I think it's the low road out for me. But it's a
> lose-lose proposition. If I say nothing, I get killed. If I talk, it comes off
> as sour grapes.

Actually, it came off a fair bit worse than sour grapes, as Geffen, and
presumably Ovitz, well knew. Geffen *had* to call Ovitz crazy, because the only
other reason Ovitz would make such a claim publically is—if it were true.

There's a third element to Geffen's masterful rebuttal, and this one is
subtler still: Geffen's tone and choice of words—Diller's too—emphasizes,
not just the idea of Ovitz's insanity, but also, implicitly, his homophobia. It
suggests that his charges can only be driven by irrational fear, hatred, and

prejudice. This signals to others that Ovitz is not just crazy but malignant, "rotten," and that to take what he says seriously is to participate in that rot.

Of course, Ovitz made a public apology soon after; but even so, his career was over. Today he is an active Silicon Valley investor, with no apparent remaining ties to Hollywood. In *Who Is Michael Ovitz?: A Memoir* published in 2018, he refers to his comments to *Vanity Fair* about a "gay mafia" as "more absurd than poisonous" (p. 337).

10.3.   THE USUAL SUSPECTS: CASE STUDY # 11, BRYAN SINGER, GARY GODDARD, & DEN

> "He's just a poor boy from a poor family. Spare him his life from this monstrosity."
>
> —QUEEN, *"Bohemian Rhapsody"*

The testimonials about the use of sexual favors, and sexual leverage, in Hollywood are so many and so widespread as to brook no argument from even the most star-struck quarters. Marilyn Monroe is said to have spent the first part of her career in Hollywood on her knees. After signing a contract at Twentieth Century Fox in 1951, she gushed: "I have sucked my last cock!"[7]

Producer Julia Phillips quipped: "There is an old saying that Hollywood makes whores out of the women. That hasn't changed. These guys really do feel more comfortable in the company of hookers because that is how they see women."[8] Actor Woody Harrelson admitted: "Every [acting] business I ever entered into in New York seemed to have a casting couch. . . . I've seen so many people sleep with people they loathe in order to further their ambition."[9] Actress Jenny McCarthy went into more detail:

> LA is the worst place in the world to try to feel secure. The girls that moved out there at the same time as me, I watched them fizzle and turn into walking on the streets at night. You see that in the movies and hear about casting couches—which I thought were just big fluffy

couches—but you don't know till you experience it how corrupt it is. I
was the only girl in my clique who wasn't sleeping with someone to get
a job.[10]

Producer Chris Hanley (*American Psycho, The Virgin Suicides*) divulged
at his class reunion, at Amherst College in Massachusetts: "Almost every
leading actress in all of my 24 films has slept with a director or producer
or a leading actor to get the part that launched her career."[11] A 2018 *USA
Today* survey about the entertainment industry "found that almost every
one of hundreds of women questioned—a startling 94%—say they have
experienced some form of sexual harassment or assault in their careers in
Tinseltown."[12] And so on. Generally speaking, these disclosures tend to leave
out the homosexual angle (the casting couch is usually assumed to involve
women giving favors to men), not to mention (until Corey Feldman spoke
out) the pedophilia one. This would seem to be a combination of insider
"discretion" (i.e., secrecy) with media squeamishness (or ideological caution).

It's fair to wonder, for example, if Mike Ovitz mentioned (unquoted)
the Fire Circle during his interview with *Vanity Fair*, and if not, why not?
Possibly he knew *Vanity Fair* would never run it anyway, or perhaps even, in
his frustration, he knew to draw the line between career-suicide and actual
suicide? Clearly, there was an awful lot he could have spoken about, some
of which was even a matter of public record. And since that time, while the
term Gay Mafia has barely resurfaced, the evidence for its existence has,
verily, proliferated.

For readers not familiar with the Bryan Singer case, what follows is a
rough, sparse, timeline of the accusations leveled and the (so far minor) consequences he and his cohorts have suffered. The first intimations of power
abuse in Singer's history date as far back as 1994, though word did not come
out about this for over twenty years, once Kevin Spacey was already a dead
shark in the water. In December, 2017, Gabriel Byrne told *The Sunday Times*
how filming on Singer's *The Usual Suspects* was temporarily shut down due to
Kevin Spacey's "inappropriate sexual behavior."[13] Byrne and the other actors
claimed not to have learned the reason until years later, though they certainly
heard the rumors. And if the industry heard them too, it didn't care: Spacey
won his first Oscar for the film.

Singer's follow-up film was *Apt Pupil*, based on a Stephen King novella about a twisted relationship between a Nazi war criminal and a 16-year-old boy. (Hindsight is 20-20: no great mystery why Singer chose this subject matter for his next film since it provided him with easy access to a potentially endless stream of young boys.) While shooting in 1997, the parents of Devin St. Albin, age 14, filed suit against the film's producers, claiming Singer had filmed St. Albin naked for a shower scene without asking their permission. Several other young actors also sued for the same reason; the case was dismissed for "insufficient evidence."[14]

The same year, the Digital Entertainment Network (DEN) founded in 1996 by Marc Collins-Rector and Chad Shackley, added Brock Pierce to the team. Pierce was a 17-year-old former Disney child actor who (according to Amy Berg's 2015 documentary *An Open Secret*) was introduced to DEN by Singer. Singer later became a DEN investor. DEN aimed to create original episodic video content for the 14-24 audience, and by 1999 it had over 200 employees, a $58 million valuation, and had received investments from Microsoft, Dell, and Chase. (Making DEN an openly-gay-oriented, yet hardly a marginalized, group.) Shackley boasted at the time of their plans "to become the Time Warner of the Internet." Collins-Rector and Shackley also became known for "wild parties" at their Los Angeles estate that were often attended by Singer. The estate served as the setting for the early internet TV show, *Chad's World*, which was loosely based on Shackley's life. A November 2007 *Radar* article about DEN described the show as a "gay pedophile version of *Silver Spoons*."

In June 2000, DEN filed for bankruptcy. A month later, and a week after the *X-Men* premiere, *X-Men* actor Alexander Burton (Pyro), along with Mark Ryan and "Michael E," filed a lawsuit against DEN founders, alleging that they had offered them jobs, coerced them into taking both prescription drugs and controlled substances, and sexually and physically assaulted them. The case was settled confidentially; the three claimants were allegedly awarded several million dollars. The following month:

> a federal grand jury indicted Collins-Rector on criminal charges of trans-
> porting minors across state lines for the purpose of sex. The founding trio
> of DEN then fled the country, and were arrested in Spain by Interpol

in May 2002 where they also found guns, machetes, and "an enormous collection of child porn," according to Spanish police reports. Collins-Rector spent 18 months in [Spanish] prison and [when extradited back to the US] registered as a convicted sex offender.

Somehow, Bryan Singer avoided any blowback from these twin scandals (the second of which I never even heard about), and ten halcyon years went by without untoward event, during which time he helmed two more superhero movies (and produced a third), and made *Valkyrie*, with Tom Cruise as a good Nazi.

In October 2011, film director and actor Roland Emmerich went on record saying that Bryan Singer's parties traditionally hosted scores of "twinks" (gay slang for a young man in his late teens to early twenties) at a "Pride weekend party" each June. "When [Singer] makes a New Year's party, there's like 600, 700 twinks running around." Emmerich wasn't complaining, exactly, since he attended the parties himself. He just felt they were "getting out of hand."

Three years went by without much comment from the industry. Then, in April 2014, former child actor, Michael F. Egan III, filed a civil lawsuit against Singer. Egan alleged that, between August 1 and October 31, 1999, when he was 17, "Singer flew him to Kailua, Hawaii multiple times under the guise of discussing movie roles but fed him cocaine, alcohol, and other drugs and anally raped him." The claim document stated that Singer:

> manipulated his power, wealth, and position in the entertainment industry to sexually abuse and exploit underage Plaintiff through the use of drugs, threats, and inducements which resulted in Plaintiff suffering catastrophic psychological and emotional injuries. Defendant Singer did so as part of a group of adult males positioned in the entertainment industry that maintained and exploited boys in a sordid sex ring. [Page 2 of "Michael F. Egan v. Bryan Jay Singer"]

Egan then added three former DEN investors to his suit against Singer: former Fox and NBC executive Garth Ancier, onetime Walt Disney Television president David Neuman, and producer and theme park designer Gary

Goddard. Egan claimed that all three men drugged and sexually abused him at parties, both in California and Hawaii. Two months later, however, Egan's attorneys dropped him as a client, reportedly after Egan refused to agree to a settlement of $100,000 (which suggests that he was not lying). "This exact kind of take-it-and-shut-up deal is why I decided to stand up in the first place," Egan was quoted as saying. "Being silenced goes completely against what I believe in and offers no protection for other vulnerable children."[15]

10.4.   DEN OF INIQUITY

"Actors live dependent on being validated by other people's opinions. . . . The good actors are all screwed up. They're all in pain. It's a profession of bottom feeders and heartbroken people."

—SHIA LABEOUF[16]

Also in April 2014, Florida-based attorney Jeff Herman, who had filed lawsuits against Goddard and Singer, gave a news conference in which he vowed to "expose every Hollywood pedophile and predator [he] can identify."[17] Brian Claflin came forward to testify. Claflin was a 17-year-old from Utah who met a man from Santa Monica at a gay nightclub before his senior year. The stranger told him he "was the most beautiful boy he'd ever met" and that he, the stranger, knew "some very rich and powerful people that wanted to meet me and could possibly get me a job." The man flew him to L.A. on his 18th birthday and took him to an Encino mansion where he was "introduced to what I was told were the most powerful people in Hollywood."[18]

In May, shortly after agreeing to testify, Claflin talked to his parents on Skype while he "barricaded himself in his bathroom, afraid of men he said were stalking him from his roof. On June 2, 2014, Claflin texted his father to 'have a handgun nearby.'" Three days later, he was hit by a train in a tunnel of the Berlin subway. German authorities concluded Claflin's cause of death was "massive head trauma resulting from presumed suicide by train impact." Herman claimed that Claflin was one of many people he heard from "around the world who said that they were abused by people in Hollywood." He said that Claflin had been an errand boy at the DEN mansion in Encino and as such, had important information. Claflin was fearful, he said, that "somebody was going to try to kill him" because he knew too much about a "gay Mafia in Hollywood."[19]

In August 2014, Egan voluntarily dropped his claim against Singer, and in June 2015, his former attorneys made a formal apology to Ancier and Neuman (not Goddard), as well as a seven-figure settlement paid out to them for damages. In December 2015, Egan was sentenced to two years in prison on unrelated charges of conspiracy to commit securities and wire fraud. Egan's alleged abusers have used this as evidence of his shady character and proof that his claims were fabricated.

In the interim, however, in May 2014, another person came forward, this time anonymously, also alleging that Singer and Goddard sexually assaulted him as a minor. He was 14 in 2003, when he says Goddard (then 48) contacted him over social media, luring him with promises to meet Hollywood players like Bryan Singer, who could help him become an actor. At 15, the plaintiff ("John Doe") and Goddard began "an online sexual relationship," and Goddard introduced him to Singer over the phone. In 2006, according to the suit, Singer and Goddard lured the plaintiff to the premiere of *Superman Returns* and then invited him to Singer's suite to show him some Superman memorabilia. Both men "started grabbing John Doe in a sexual manner," and when he resisted, Goddard "brought in a man to beat him up." Singer then sexually assaulted him. John Doe also claimed that Goddard had sex with him when he was 16. But then in July 2014, Doe dropped Singer from the case, and in October 2014, his attorneys also dismissed the claim against Goddard. Is a pattern starting to emerge?

In June 2016, actor Noah Galvin, star of the canceled ABC sitcom *The Real O'Neals*, told *Vulture*: "Bryan Singer likes to invite little boys over to his pool and diddle them in the fucking dark of night." Soon after, he retracted his statement and then *Vulture* deleted it.[20] In October 2017, just after the Weinstein scandal broke, actress Evan Rachel Wood tweeted "Let's not forget Brian [sic] Singer either." The tweet was deleted sometime later.[21]

On November 10, 2017, actor Anthony Edwards (*Zodiac*) wrote a short piece on *Medium* describing his own experience of exploitation by Goddard:

When I was 14 years old, my mother opened the door for me to answer honestly about the rumors she had heard about Gary Goddard—who was my mentor, teacher and friend—being a pedophile. I denied it through tears of complete panic. To face that truth was not an option as my sense of self was completely enmeshed in my gang of five friends who were all led by this sick father figure. . . . My vulnerability was exploited. I was molested by Goddard, my best friend was raped by him—and this went on for years. The group of us, the gang, stayed quiet.[22]

Goddard's publicist denied the allegations. Goddard left his company later that month, and the Goddard Group was renamed Legacy Entertainment.

In other apparent unofficial consequences, in December 2017, Bryan Singer was fired as the director of *Bohemian Rhapsody*, and his Bad Hat Harry production company began vacating the Fox lot. Singer's former publicist, Simon Halls, stated that Singer was no longer a client. Unconvincingly, Singer claimed he had been fired for taking time off to be with a sick parent. But two days later, on December 7, 2017, Cesar Sanchez-Guzman filed a lawsuit against Singer. The same attorney who had represented—and abandoned—Egan and "John Doe" filed a case on behalf of Sanchez-Guzman. Sanchez-Guzman alleged that Singer both orally and anally raped him in 2003, while they were sailing on a yacht near Seattle. He was 17 at the time.

Singer denied the charges. Despite being fired as director, his name remained on the film. *Bohemian Rhapsody* became the highest-grossing musical biopic and the highest-grossing biographical film of all time, the highest-grossing drama film (without action or fantasy), and the highest-grossing LGBT film. It received multiple awards and nominations, won four awards at the Academy Awards, including Best Actor (Rami Malek), and was the film with the most wins at that ceremony. It was also nominated for Best Picture. Due to the renewed sexual abuse allegations against Singer, the British Academy of Film and Television Arts removed Singer's name from the film's nomination for the BAFTA Award for Best British Film.

Beelzebub, meanwhile, has a devil put aside for him. As with the case of Goddard, this name-redaction policy oughtn't to be viewed as punishment, or even as consequences *per se*, merely as the necessary survival strategy of an industry that can't *afford* truly diabolical press. If there's punishment inferred, it is not for any crimes committed, but for having the bad judgment to be caught, thereby drawing fire to the industry as a whole. Celebrities who become identified with vice, rather than with glamor, rapidly lose the name which the industry bestowed upon them, and their power goes along with it. To remain in power, the powerful must be quick to distance themselves from all rumors of abuse, that the name of Hollywood remain untarnished.

For the bohemian life to continue to be the stuff of rhapsody, poor boys must die.[*]

10.5.   PEDOPHILIA VS. HEBEPHILIA, HOMOPHOBIA VS. HETEROPHOBIA

"I know what you want. Oh sure, they may have tried to separate
us, but what we have is too strong, is too powerful. I mean, after
all we shared, everything you and I, I told you my deepest darkest
secrets, I showed you exactly what people are capable of, I shocked
you with my honesty, but mostly I challenged you and made you think
and you trusted me, even though you knew you shouldn't."

—KEVIN SPACEY, *"Let Me Be Frank"*

When Kevin Spacey was accused in 2016 of showing pornography to a 16-year old—while undoubtedly very sleazy and sad behavior—some of us might have been tempted to ask what made it *deviant*, precisely, in a climate of child beauty pageants, Miley Cyrus' twerking, and explicit sex education for grade school kids.[23] Compared to what almost *everyone* in Hollywood, and just about everywhere else these days, is doing, do 16-year-olds really *need* sad,

---

[*] The lyrics of "Bohemian Rhapsody" take on such a radically different and more sinister character within the context of this present chapter that it would seem almost to validate mind control survivors' claims that popular music may sometimes be encoded with trigger language, aimed at victims of sexual abuse. Even that, by extension, it can be used to "program" the larger audience-base with subtly-charged content—i.e., for mass mind control.

sleazy movie stars to lure them into porn and sexual irresponsibility when they are gorging on a culture designed to do just that? In some ways, exaggerating the gravity of these *peccadilloes*, and referring to Spacey (as Susan Sarandon and one of his victims did) as a pedophile, may present a bigger problem than Spacey ever could.

If wanting to have sex with a fourteen-year-old makes someone a pedophile, by this definition, there's probably not a sexually active man alive who, given the right circumstances at some point in his life, wouldn't fit the bill and find himself "beyond the pale." At the risk of appearing to be a pedo-apologist (I am not), we are biologically predisposed to want to have sex with pubescents, because pubescence is a biological signal of fertility. The moral code of society is as indifferent to biological imperatives as biology is to social codes (witness the growing insistence that biology no longer determines sex). This makes social codes for behavior dangerously out of touch with reality, which in turn creates the perfect breeding ground for actual deviants to flower in.

Technically, a desire for pubescents is known as *hebephilia*, and whether or not it's pathological, and whatever its moral implications may be, it is obviously not the same as the desire to have sex with prepubescent children. Since both are equally illegal, however (at least in some parts of the world), they tend to get lumped together as a single vice. The problem with this ought to be apparent to anyone thinking logically and not merely reacting emotionally. If a sexual abuser is condemned by society as a pedophile, when his or her sins correspond with a far less unusual—even a biologically standard—predilection, then a whole lot of people are going to feel sympathy for this "pedophile," even if they are too afraid to express it (unless they are Oscar-winning filmmakers). Pedophilia then becomes a much less clear-cut problem—it becomes something closer to what homosexuality once was: a socially condemned sexual preference that is *assumed* to be pathological and harmful, but that is so widely practiced that, eventually, we have to seriously rethink our ideas about the parameters of consensual sex, in order not to demonize a whole social subset of people.*

---

* Pedophiles are currently rebranding themselves as "maps," or minor-attracted people, including nomaps, the non-offending sort—an acronym that gives unexpected new meaning to the title of this book.

The same is true of Harvey Weinstein. When sexual harassment—or casting couch methods—become akin to rape, an awful lot of undisciplined men may start to feel like rapists—or at least in danger of being accused as such—if they express any sort of testosterone at all. After Weinstein was busted, several other people came forward making accusations about "sexual misconduct." A woman who was a 17-year-old production assistant on the 1985 film adaptation of *Death of a Salesman* claimed that Dustin Hoffman "was openly flirtatious, he grabbed my ass, he talked about sex to me and in front of me."[24] From this we can deduce that Hoffman is an asshole. But at what point does news become gossip?

The context here is organized, systematic sexual abuse in the entertainment industry. On the one hand, accounts like this are the tip of an iceberg that could sink Hollywood and even society as we know it. On the other hand, if they are not *seen* as such, if they are not *contextualized* within the necessary deep sociopolitical background, if the focus is on individual behaviors and not the system that creates and enables them, they are just flotsam, trivialities. I suspect that this is all part of the program: orchestrate an organized overreaction and you can create a corresponding upsurge of the opposite, namely, of unspoken (even unconscious) sympathy for the condemned. Over time, the Spaceys and Weinsteins—and even the Singers and the Goddards—become victims of unjust social condemnation—martyrs. This is exactly the way pedophiles once tried to represent themselves back in the 1970s.* The time wasn't ripe back then. At a surface glance, it would seem to be even less ripe now. But that might only be because we are still on the blind side of a tipping point. These monsters may really be ahead of the curve.

✦

> "That which cannot be wholly concealed should be deliberately displayed."
>
> —QUENTIN CRISP *(a line my brother later stole)*†

---

* E.g., the Pedophile Information Exchange, an offshoot of the National Council for Civil Liberties in the UK in 1974–1984. See *Vice of Kings* for the full story.

† Another Crispism that my brother stole, the description of movies as a "forgetting chamber," which in *Seen and Not Seen* I attributed to Horsley rather than Crisp. One more win for "the ecstasy of influence."

In 2018, while still in the news for his sexual infractions, Kevin Spacey came out as gay after many years of it being more or less public knowledge. His hope, presumably, was to obfuscate accusations of sexual abuse being made against him (by boys as young as fourteen at the time) with a show of "courage" in coming out of the Hollywood closet. It backfired, because no one was in the mood either to congratulate Spacey on his courage, or to assume a more sympathetic stance because of his homosexuality. Instead, he was accused of opportunistic timing and, worse, of tainting homosexuality by associating it with child abuse.

It's easy to see how Spacey might have misplayed his hand here. Accusations of homophobia, for example as leveled by David Geffen and Barry Diller against Mike Ovitz, can be, and presumably are, used as an instant "get-out-of-public-scrutiny-free-card" by anyone cunning and desperate enough to use it. Many people will not only back down at the first insinuation that they are acting out of prejudice, they may even suffer profound cognitive dissonance—the lurking fear that they are unconscious bigots—and the resulting loss of moral ground.

When I first stumbled upon the term "gay mafia," it was via an online piece called "The Homosexual Movement's Connection to Hollywood." An online search brought up a Wikipedia page that groups the phrase with "Velvet Mafia, gay lobby, Lavender Mafia, Homintern," referring to all these as "pejorative terms." The article links to another page, entitled "Homosexual agenda (or gay agenda)," a term it describes as introduced by "sectors of the Christian religious right" (primarily in the US) and as

> a disparaging way to describe the advocacy of cultural acceptance and normalization of non-heterosexual orientations and relationships. The term refers to efforts to change government policies and laws on LGBT rights-related issues. Additionally, it has been used by social conservatives and others to describe alleged goals of LGBT rights activists, such as recruiting heterosexuals into what conservatives term a "homosexual lifestyle."

While investigating the possibility of a homosexual power clique in Hollywood—something that runs on principles not wholly dissimilar to those of the mafia, say—it would be naïve to think that the subject can be approached independently of ideological concerns. Probably, this ideological embargo is the main reason why my search failed to turn up many articles on the subject—even of the online sort—that *didn't* stem from conservative Christian groups and writers who are already being labeled homophobes by many liberals, and therefore had little to lose by exploring the subject. (I did not find the Ebert piece quoted above anywhere online, I had to refer to an essay on the website of the conservative Christian group, Heterosexuals Organized for a Moral Environment, or HOME.)

In the Western world, homosexuality is not just socially condoned, it is actively celebrated. Gay pride has been fully legitimized via the legalization of gay marriage, which happened in the US in 2015. Denmark was the first country to legalize it in 1989, and since then (as of 2020), 27 other countries have followed suit: Argentina, Australia, Austria, Belgium, Brazil, Canada, Colombia, Ecuador, Finland, France, Germany, Iceland, Ireland, Luxembourg, Malta, Mexico, the Netherlands, New Zealand, Norway, Portugal, South Africa, Spain, Sweden, Taiwan, the UK, the US, and Uruguay. Further proof of the normalization of homosexuality is (something Barbra Streisand fought for) allowing gays and lesbians to openly serve in the military (the US was one of the last of the "developed" nations to overturn its ban on homosexuality in the military, in 2010).

For a great many people today, to be critical of homosexuality as a "lifestyle"—or even to describe it in such outmoded terms—is to betray one's bigotry. Ironically, to do so risks facing the sort of condemnation once reserved for homosexuals (what goes around, comes around). As mentioned earlier, the word homophobia appears to be a misnomer that has become normalized. As Vicki Klafter wrote in 2015:

> It was first used in the 1960s by a psychiatrist in a speech to describe a morbid fear of homosexuals. After that though, pop culture mangled the Latin roots of it and turned it into a relative umbrella to hold over anything that expresses any aversion or disagreement with LGBT people. In fact, the first place the word appeared in print was *Screw*, a pornographic magazine, that used it to describe a heterosexual male's fear that other men might think he's gay.[25]

Since heterophobia means a fear of difference, logically, via the same Latin roots, homophobia means a fear of sameness. This means that an automatic prejudice against homosexuals, because of their different sexual orientation, might technically be better known as *heterophobia*. And heterophobia is a condition shared by some homosexuals too—why exclude them?—perhaps particularly when it comes to male homosexuals regarding female heterosexuals, with whom they naturally compete. Even Geffen's dismissal of the idea of a gay mafia as the creation of "jealous queens" suggests that bitchiness knows no sexual borders.

This probably isn't the place for a deep discussion on the world of homosexuals or the social prejudices, both against it and within it. But what does seem relevant here—and why I have juxtaposed the mostly derided suggestions of a "gay mafia" with the legally documented charges of systematized homosexual abuse made against Bryan Singer and his cohorts—is the *overlap* between the homosexual "lifestyle" (and/or self-identification as gay) and the abuse and exploitation of young people, including children (though what constitutes a child, culturally speaking, is an ever-moving line).

Child sexual abuse—generally lumped under "pedophilia"—is as widely condemned as homosexuality is now embraced, so even to suggest an overlap—or rather, to point to the existence of one—is a risky endeavor that invites accusations, once again, of homophobia. Alternatively, it could imply an attempt to normalize pedophilia—it would depend on whether the context belonged to the "conservative" or "progressive" end of the spectrum.

As a practicing pederast—a man with a sexual preference for adolescent males—it may be that Spacey was himself unaware of the difference between his sexual orientation and "regular" homosexuality (it being only really clearly defined in a legal sense). In the same way, perhaps Roman Polanski—a European with a different cultural and moral attitude to the subject—was unaware of the (moral) distinction between seducing an adult and seducing (or drugging and raping) a thirteen-year-old girl? When it comes to masters (and mistresses) of the "art of imposition," the modus operandi is that of *circumnavigating the need for consent*, by manipulating others into giving you what you want, even when it goes against their own interests. The point I wish to make is a subtle one: when it comes to moral boundaries, cultural context is everything, and we do not actually *know* what sort of boundaries exist within the culture of imposer-celebrities and power politics. This makes it difficult to interpret the behaviors of members within it who appear to have committed social, legal, and moral infractions, but who may only have got caught doing something that's considered *quite normal within their own circles.*

The difference between the heterosexual abuse of a minor and the homosexual abuse of a minor is a social and cultural as well as a sexual difference. There is no taboo around heterosexuality in general, since the human race has literally been doing it since the race began. With homosexuality, on the other hand, most especially within Judeo-Christian societies, there is now a two-sided controversy. There is the culturally-sanctioned belief that the act itself is "unnatural" or immoral, which is the old Judeo-Christian taboo. Then, more recently (in the past fifty years or so), there has been the emergence of a *new* social taboo, the taboo of suggesting that homosexuality is unnatural. There can be little doubt which paradigm is the dominant one in Hollywood. As Nina Jacobson, a former Universal exec put it, "Now at [the Music Corporation of America], you would have a bigger problem if you were a homophobe than a homosexual."[26]

10.6.   THE BRO CODE

"Being initiated into a secret society—a 'band of warrior brothers' that exists apart from and is superior to civil society— can be intoxicating."

—DOUGLAS VALENTINE, *The CIA as Organized Crime: How Illegal Operations Corrupt America and the World*

In *The Power of Ritual in Prehistory*, Hayden makes starkly apparent the correlation between ascending the ranks of secret societies and personal or family wealth:

The initiation feasts in some groups constituted the greatest undertaking of a man's career. Initiation costs could be enormous and sometimes entailed many thousands of blankets, as well as bracelets, decorated boxes, food, kitchen ware, canoes, pelts, shells, masks, and other wealth items, in one case enough to fill a square that was 100 feet on a side. The higher one progressed in the ranked positions of the secret societies, the more costly and exclusive the initiations became (p. 38).

More significantly still for our present purposes, Hayden underscores the relationship between wealth, power and the breaking of taboos: "as wealth increases, the wealthy are more likely to feel entitled to good things, and that they see themselves as above normal laws and morals." This is, he claims, "an aspect of tribal and chiefly [sic] aggrandizers repeatedly observed by ethnographers" (p. 17).

In the Encyclopedia Britannica, taboo is defined as "the prohibition of an action based on the belief that such behavior is either too sacred or too dangerous and accursed for ordinary individuals to undertake." In the preface to *Totem and Taboo* (first published in 1918), Sigmund Freud wrote that, while "taboo still exists in our midst . . . totemism is a religio-social institution which is alien to our present feelings; it has long been abandoned and replaced by new forms" (p. ix). Freud defines totem as relating to "the tribal ancestor of the clan, as well as its tutelary spirit and protector [whose] character is inherent not only in a single animal or a single being but in all the members of the species." He describes festivals "at which the members of a totem represent or imitate, in ceremonial dances, the movements and characteristics of their totems" (p. 2). While ancient totems were usually animals or plants—or images thereof—it is not so great a stretch to propose modern-day celebrities, who are mostly encountered by us (in parasocial interactions) via images, as a new form of the ancient tradition of totemism.

In Freud's interpretation, "the two basic laws of totemism" are also the original taboo prohibitions: "namely not to kill the totem animal, and to avoid sexual intercourse with totem companions of the other sex." He defines the basis of taboo as "a very primitive prohibition imposed from without (by an authority) and directed against the strongest desires of man" (p 30); it is "a forbidden action for which there exists a strong inclination in the unconscious" (p 28). "An individual who has violated a taboo," Freud warns,

> becomes himself taboo because he has the dangerous property of tempting others to follow his example. He arouses envy; why should he be allowed to do what is prohibited to others? He is therefore really contagious, in so far as every example incites to imitation and therefore he

himself must be avoided. But a person may become permanently or temporarily taboo without having violated any taboos, for the simple reason
that he is in a condition which has the property of inciting the forbidden desires of others and of awakening the ambivalent conflict in them.
Most of the exceptional positions and conditions have this character and
possess this dangerous power. The king or chieftain rouses envy of his
prerogatives; everybody would perhaps like to be king (p. 28–29).

Or a movie star. From this, it can easily be seen that, whatever the
privileges of the exceptional (the celebrities or chieftains who preside over
a community), there is *a prerogative to keep these privileges occulted*, lest the
common man be infected by mimetic desire to emulate the breaking of
taboos as a means to attain special status.

> It is equally clear how the violation of certain taboo prohibitions becomes
> a social danger which must be punished or expiated by all the members
> of society lest it harm them all. This danger really exists if we substitute
> the known impulses for the unconscious desires. It consists in the possi-
> bility of imitation, as a result of which society would soon be dissolved.
> *If the others did not punish the violation they would perforce become aware*
> *that they want to imitate the evil doer* (p. 29, emphasis added).

Because the desire to violate taboo continues in the unconscious, while
being consciously forbidden and resisted, we "assume an ambivalent attitude" towards taboos: in our unconscious we "would like nothing better
than to transgress them but [we] are also afraid to do it . . . and the fear is
stronger than the pleasure" (p. 27). At the same time, because the breaking
of the taboo is associated with the special status and privilege of "kings,"
its forbidden or "criminal" nature is inseparable from its (partially hidden)
sacred dimension—making it all the more desirable (i.e., we desire to break
the taboo *because* it is forbidden). "The magic power attributed to taboo goes
back to its ability to lead man into temptation; *it behaves like a contagion,*
because the example is contagious" (p. 30, emphasis added).

The point about taboos—and why there is no way for me to avoid
the (taboo!) subject of a gay mafia, much as I might wish to—is firstly

that, because they pertain to boundaries, *they bind a society or a community together*. Secondly, breaking taboos is not merely charged for us because we risk being ostracized, but also because *it presents an opportunity for being initiated into a subset of society via the secrecy and risk that taboo-breaking engenders*. Historically, homosexuals have needed to stick together and form secret cliques, precisely because society has condemned them, and there is a certain kind of power that arises out of forming secret cliques. The history of homosexual cliques in the UK, for example, goes back at least as far as 1897, when The Order of Chaeronea was founded by George Cecil Ives (friend of Oscar Wilde), for the cultivation of a homosexual, ethical, cultural and spiritual ethos. Chaeronea was secret because homosexuality was illegal at that time, and homosexuals needed a means of underground communication, both to find one another and to pursue their shared interests together.

The idea of a "gay mafia" doesn't only imply that homosexuals gather together and support one another, however, but that they also wield a particular kind of power and influence within society at large. It's here that the controversy enters. One way to possibly neutralize that controversy is to perform a thought experiment: rather than thinking of a "gay mafia" being homosexuals conspiring to gain a disproportionate kind of power within Hollywood, what if a group of men are conspiring to extend their power and influence, and have discovered that homosexuality—either as a cloak or a practice, or both—is an invaluable means of doing so?

"Gay pride in the industry?" a Hollywood screenwriter is quoted in the *Spy* article: "Red ribbons? That's such crap. They only do things because it's a good career move." This presents a kind of Gordian knot hypothesis. Suggesting that some allegedly gay men might be using their identification as a cynical ruse to manipulate people may *seem* to be casting aspersions on homosexuality—but this is precisely what makes it effective *as* a ruse, because it makes it almost impossible to discuss it without appearing to malign a subset of individuals already historically victimized by society. If there is power in secret cliques, this is especially so in the case of a clique that identifies as a *victim class*.

✦

"Domination is the main form of deviance, and victimization
a way of attracting sympathy, so rather than emphasize either
their strength or inner worth, the aggrieved emphasize their
oppression and social marginalization."

—CONOR FRIEDERSDORF, *The Atlantic*

In *Queer in America: Sex, the Media, and the Closets of Power*, queer
activist Michelangelo Signorile writes,

An industry built predominantly by immigrant Jews at a time of rabid
and overt anti-Semitism in America and the rest of the world, Hollywood
has always been a place where the "other" is actually in power, while at
the same time it is a victim of society's prejudices and thus easily manipulated by the larger power structure of Washington.[27]

Few could deny that there is a form of power, of social clout, to be
gained by assuming the role of victim within certain circles in Western society. As the taboo has shifted from the condemnation of homosexuals to the
condemnation of "homophobes," this has afforded a degree of unprecedented power to anyone who self-identifies—even covertly—as homosexual.
It is surely not hard to imagine that some people might want to cynically
take advantage of such easily assumed power and status? Isn't it possible that
the combination of two factors—the solidarity of shared taboo-breaking,
combined with the special privileges of identifying as a victim of social prejudice—might account for why powerful men in Hollywood find advantage
in identifying as homosexuals—*whether or not they truly are*?

There's another factor to consider here. The use of taboo for social
control, which underlies the formation of communities, has a very specific,
microcosmic application. As has come out recently in the case of Jeffrey
Epstein, sexual honey-pots are extremely effective as means to compromise
individuals and blackmail them into compliance. For a honey-pot to work,
it has to be offering something that is socially forbidden. Simply put, if you
lure someone into committing something that can potentially ruin their
careers, their marriages, even land them in jail, you have them where you
want them.

Keeping homosexuality in the realm of an open secret that, while no longer deemed immoral *per se*, might still seriously hinder a person's career in Hollywood—even just maintaining the *belief* that this is the case—means it still has the special charge that makes it useful as an instrument of control. Those already inured to the practice, and immunized to fear of exposure, can then wield it as leverage over those *not yet aware of the actual social climate they have entered*. A gay mafia, therefore, might not simply be a matter of a sexual preference given free reign, but of *intentional seduction strategies* and rites of passage, ways to bring "newbs" in and submit them to a form of subtle control. After which, if they prove useful, compliant, and agreeable, they can be recruited into the order. How many victims of Bryan Singer, Goddard, and the DEN of iniquity have kept silent because their careers were furthered as a result of submitting to abuses? How much did Anthony Edwards' career as a movie star result from his unwanted initiation at the hands of Goddard?

The use of controlled taboo-breaking suggests that Hollywood is a kind of weird twilight zone, or parallel world, where the forbidden is juxtaposed with the compulsory, and what is proscribed is also prescribed. Perhaps entering it involves the gradual discovery that actions you feared might ostracize you are now the very things you are expected to commit in order to *avoid* ostracization? Such a "wonderland" dynamic (where up is down and black is white) is described by James Palmer in "The Bro Code: Booze, Sex, and the Dark Art of Dealmaking in China," which describes how, in the corporate world of China, committing criminal acts—especially of the sexual variety— is a means of binding men (and presumably women) together "through the power of taboo and mutual self-exposure, or at least the pretense of it."

The power of the experience, Palmer writes, "comes from the mutual pleasure of shared transgression, the feeling of a shared secret." The maxim of the Bro Code: "It's better to do one bad thing with your boss than a hundred good things for your boss."

> Over time, this can extend to an actual exchange of what criminologist Diego Gambetta [in *Codes of the Underworld*] calls "hostage-information," mutual knowledge of each party's sins that acts as a powerful guarantee neither will break their agreements. [V]ice serves as a kind of screen, weeding

out the rare few who might have moral qualms about future dealings. It tells both sides that they're playing by the same rules. . . . Refusing to play the game, on the other hand, comes at a sharp cost.[28]

In the case of Singer, Goddard, and Spacey, we have alleged sexual predators with an apparent bent towards homosexuality. But as has often been said, rape is not about sex but about power. Perhaps in Hollywood sex is not about sex, either, but about power? In her famous 1979 book *The White Album*, Joan Didion wrote:

> There is in Hollywood, as in all cultures in which gambling is the central activity, a lowered sexual energy, an inability to devote more than token attention to the preoccupations of the society outside. The action is everything, more consuming than sex, more immediate than politics; more important always than the acquisition of money, which is never, for the gambler, the true point of the exercise (p. 296).

There may have been a degree of dissembling going on here—Didion was also a Hollywood scriptwriter with Gregory Dunne (*The Panic in Needle Park, Play It as It Lays*, based on her novel, *A Star Is Born, True Confessions*, and *Up Close & Personal*)—but also, perhaps, a kernel of truth? Many people assume that everything comes down to sex, and that this is nowhere more true than in Hollywood, which has turned sexual charisma into an industry of mass seduction. But if the ultra-rich no longer see money as a means to buy things but as counters—chips—by which to measure and augment their power, perhaps in a society where sex is as freely available as bread and Netflix to the rest of us, something similar applies? Perhaps sex no longer becomes about pleasure, *per se*, but a means of establishing and extending power and control over others?

For Singer, Spacey, Geffen, Diller, and the "Gay Mafia," homosexuality may likewise be a means to a more "transcendental"—if truly deviant—end.

11

TOUCH OF EVIL

11.1. CASE STUDY # 12:
DAVID FINCHER & *MINDHUNTER*

"Among businesses in general, the CIA has long had a
special relationship with the entertainment industry, devoting
considerable attention to fostering relationships with Hollywood
movers and shakers—studio executives, producers, directors,
and big-name actors. . . . These are people who have made a lot
of money basically creating make-believe stuff. A lot of them, *at
least the smarter and more self-aware ones*, realize what they do
makes them ridiculously rich but also ephemeral and meaningless
in the larger scheme of things. So *they're receptive to helping the
CIA in any way they can*, probably in equal parts because they are
sincerely patriotic and because it gives them a taste of real-life
intrigue and excitement."

—JOHN RIZZO, *Company Man (emphasis added)*

In season two of David Fincher and Joe Penhall's *Mindhunter*, the FBI
crack team of Ford and Tench take a visit to both Charles Manson and
Charles "Tex" Watson. As we saw in Part One, there is every reason
to question the official "Helter Skelter" version of "The Manson murders."
Manson was not even at the scene of the Sharon Tate murder, while Watson

has been credibly established to have committed several of the killings that night with his own hands. As conspiracy researcher Mae Brussell expressed it all the way back in 1971:

> Nobody talks about it being Charles Watson's massacre. That's the boy who killed seven people. But the news media associates the name Charles Manson. He made the picture on the cover of *Life*. He is the man that you associate with killing Sharon Tate. Many people don't even know the name Charles Watson, because you're not supposed to know it. [Watson] did the murders. And Manson was never in the homes where seven people were killed. Now if that isn't a topsy-turvy, crazy world I don't know what it is. Now how did you—how does your mind get affected to only associate the murder with one man, and let the other man get off the hook like this?

In the same radio show, Mae Brussell called California "an important state in terms of conspiracies to kill candidates and presidents, and to effect national policy." She considered the murder of Tate and the others "a political massacre."

> In this strange world of covert overthrow of the governments and clandestine armies and secret operations, the problem we're facing is that you're working with two realities: you're working with what we assume is the real way to function and move. And then we're working with a system of what we call power: exchange of power, economic power, power over people; controlling their lives. And in order to do that *you disguise certain persons and send them into roles to influence; they become actors on a stage and they influence our minds in a way that is not real but affect a reality that will touch us later.*[1]

The eerie thing about this is that Hollywood actors also come in handy for cementing the characters of "lifetime actors," or undercover operatives, as in Mindhunter season two when an actor (Damon Herriman) is cast to play Charles Manson, and then cast again by Quentin Tarantino in his revisionist history, *Once Upon a Time in Hollywood*. The actor who plays Watson in Mindhunter gives his standard "Manson-made-me-do-it" line, and the FBI never questions his story. Why would they? They've probably already seen *Aquarius* and all the other movie and TV fictions keeping the myth alive.

For a full discussion of David Fincher's role as Hollywood disinformation agent—most overtly with *Zodiac*—see Outtake # 6 on page 475. I excised it when I realized that the thesis of *16 Maps of Hell* had become so thoroughly buried under layers of data that even I had trouble finding it. But what seems possibly indispensable, that I will attempt to boil down to its essential parts in the present chapter, is the intersection between the aesthetics of terror (the torture of women, children, and men), occult ritual, intelligence operations (psyop), and what has been popularized over the last sixty years or so—since Ed Gein formed the basis of Hitchcock's *Psycho*—as "the serial killer."

The first season of *Mindhunter* features Ed Kemper, as the principal serial killer being interviewed. The scenes were based on filmed and recorded interviews with Kemper, and many of the lines given to the fictional Kemper were recreations, sometimes word for word, of those dialogues. The impression, as with Fincher's *Zodiac*, is one of painstaking accuracy of detail, in these scenes at least (much of the show is obviously fictionalized). But a fictional representation of a historical case—just like a court testimony—is characterized not only by what it includes but what it leaves out. And one thing that *Mindhunter* leaves out—like almost all representations of serial killers—is deep (state) background.

For example, prior to Kemper's arrest, there was media speculation that the murders were connected to a devil-worshiping cult. On trial, Kemper "testified that the killings arose from fantasies that began to build in his head during his confinement at Atascadero." Attorney Jackson confirmed this when he testified that Kemper "had told California Youth Authority officials of 'evil forces within him which tried to control his behavior'" (McGowan, 2004, p. 156–7). All of this points to the kind of multilayered, high-level sociopolitical complexity which David Fincher's talents were recruited to help "simplify" and streamline into an official narrative, for both *Zodiac* and *Mindhunter* —the second season of which covered the Atlanta child murders (see Outtake # 7 on page 483).

None of the truly anomalous elements make the final cut of *Mindhunter*. As the show also makes subtly explicit (via the overlap of medium with message), the FBI's appliance of psychological studies has really worked together—in synthesis—with popular entertainment to create the "profile" of the "serial killer." This strange synthesis of truth and fiction is even apparent in the ways alleged serial killers supposedly seek emotional gratification via mass media exposure, and even how they sometimes base their crimes on *fictional narratives*—either that or come up with apparently fictionalized motivations, as David Berkowitz, "Son of Sam," is shown to have done in season two.

By merging pathological violence with quasi-supernatural or occultic qualities, these narratives turn the serial killer into the equivalent of the mythic vampire or werewolf. And as we'll see, more than one of the serial killers during that key period on the West Coast in the early 1970s was literally a blood drinker. In *Programmed to Kill: The Politics of Serial Murder*, Dave McGowan writes that "no fewer than six serial killers/mass murderers" (Charles Manson, Stanley Baker, Edmund Kemper, Herbert Mullin, John Findley Frazier, and the Zodiac) were operational within the Santa Cruz/San Francisco metropolitan area "in a span of just over four years." This was also the time the term "serial killer" entered the vernacular (probably in 1974, though its first use has been traced all the way back to 1930). What's more, the serial murders occurring during the period McGowan cites weren't even restricted to these six men's (alleged) crimes:

> the bodies of at least fourteen young women and girls were found, nude and with their belongings missing, in Northern California between December 1969 and December 1973. In the immediate vicinity of each of the bodies "was found an elaborate witchcraft symbol of twigs and rocks." Remarkably enough, the crimes collectively attributed to these men did not even account for all the ritualized homicides that occurred in the Bay area during that time (p. 136).

McGowan goes on to describe the brutal 1974 Santa Cruz murder (at Stanford University) of Arliss Perry, whose body was found in Stanford Memorial Church, arranged into the sort of grisly ritualistic "artwork" that has now become a trope of serial killer movies and TV shows—including Fincher's *Se7en* and the immensely popular first season of HBO's *True Detective*—all chillingly foreshadowed by the Black Dahlia murder in 1947 (the year the CIA was born). The prime suspect in the murder, Bill Mentzer (according to McGowan), was a known associate of Charles Manson, as well as of Abigail Folger, one of the victims of the "Manson killings." Later, Mentzer was connected to the alleged "Son of Sam" killer, David Berkowitz. As discussed in Chapter One, he was eventually convicted of the infamous *Cotton Club* murder of Roy Radin, who was in negotiations with producer Robert Evans at the time.

A circle that ever returneth in.

11.2. MAKING MOVIE MYTHS AROUND ORGANIZED CRIME

"Every executive learns eventually, of course, that power in Hollywood can be as ambiguous, elusive, and ephemeral as the acclaim that leads to it. The power can even be mystical, just like the institutions of Hollywood itself. Hollywood—its mores, its *modus operandi,* even its *raison d'être*—has been shrouded in myth since movies began and remains so today. And anyone who has held power for very long has found it necessary to fathom the truths behind the myths. *They have had to learn where real power resides and where it does not.* And they have had to accept and accommodate those aspects of the institution of Hollywood that are eternally mysterious and impenetrable by computer analysis."

—DAVID MCCLINTICK, *Indecent Exposure (emphasis added)*

The narrative around the infamous Zodiac killings was created by a combination of the killings themselves, letters and phone calls from the supposed killer, police investigations, newspaper articles, extensive TV coverage, Robert Graysmith's best-selling books (which Fincher's movie sticks closely to), and movies like *Dirty Harry*. With the codes, ciphers, and cat-and-mouse games, the weird overlaps with popular fiction, the occult references, murders timed with equinox dates, and the multimedia propagation of all these elements, the Zodiac killings had all the earmarks of sociological propaganda taken to the level of psychological warfare.

The Zodiac killer (or killers) was believed to have been inspired by the movie *The Most Dangerous Game*, a 1932 pre-Code adaptation of the 1924 short story by Richard Connell, also published as "The Hounds of Zaroff." The story and film is about a big-game hunter from New York stranded on an island in the Caribbean who is hunted by a Russian aristocrat.* The Zodiac killings (as reported by the mainstream media at least) "inspired" the 1971 Don Siegel movie *Dirty Harry*, with Clint Eastwood as a San Francisco cop who hunts and executes a serial killer, Scorpio (Andy Robinson). Pauline Kael called that movie *"an almost perfect piece of propaganda for para-legal police power"* (1975, p. 387, emphasis added). The movie is referenced in Fincher's *Zodiac*, when the police detective played by Mark Ruffalo—upon whom Harry Callaghan was supposedly based—attends a 1972 screening of the film and walks out in distaste. Art inspires life inspires art inspires life— isn't that the essence of sociological propaganda?

One thing *Zodiac* gets right is that the killings suggested military or ex-military involvement (the two main suspects in the film are ex-Navy men). One of (David Fincher's favorite leading man) Brad Pitt's earliest movies was *Spy Game*, with Robert Redford, for director Tony Scott (who gave Pitt one of his first roles in the Quentin Tarantino-scripted *True Romance*). The filmmaker Alex Cox named Scott as a CIA asset at his blog, which lists actors, directors, writers, producers and studio execs with links to the CIA, including Tony Scott.[2] Scott threw himself off the Vincent Thomas Bridge in San Pedro, California, in 2012, an act his brother Ridley described as "inexplicable."[3]

Like other Scott movies (most notably *Top Gun*), *Spy Game* is a fairly obvious piece of US military propaganda in which Pitt plays a sniper-assassin in Vietnam, trained as part of the Phoenix program. The Phoenix program was a US military operation which frequently recruited from Navy Seals and was designed to identify and destroy the Viet Cong via infiltration, capture, counter-terrorism, torture, and assassination. It was also designed to instill

---

* It has been adapted (more or less loosely) for the screen, roughly once a decade, as *Game of Death* (1945), *Run for the Sun* (1956), *Bloodlust* (1961), *The Woman Hunt* (1971), John Woo's *Hard Target* (1993), *Surviving the Game* (1994), *The Eliminator* (2004), and most recently the B-movie *The Most Dangerous Game* (2017).

terror into Vietnamese citizens resistant to US presence, by any and all means necessary, including the rape, torture, murder, mutilation, and dismemberment of men, women, and children, sometimes in unbelievably grisly ways. It was designed to send a message. As journalist Douglas Valentine writes in The Phoenix Program: America's Use of Terror in Vietnam, "Central to Phoenix is the fact that it targeted civilians, not soldiers." And, he adds in The CIA as Organized Crime, its terror campaign may have extended into domestic realms as well as foreign:

> The fascistic merging of government and corporate forces against the public interest is the most insidious facet of Phoenix in American society. And it is done with the full cooperation of the corporate media, which exploits each and every mass murder we endure, whether it is a terrorist attack or not—like the gay attacker's assault on the gay nightclub in Orlando—to terrorize the public into consenting to greater restrictions on civil liberties and more wars overseas (p. 65).

In *Programmed to Kill*, McGowan painstakingly presented the many links between the spate of "serial killers" beginning in the 1960s to US military involvement, and specifically the Phoenix program. Henry Lee Lucas, for example, claimed to be working for the "Hand of Death" CIA-linked Satanic cult as an assassin, and after his conviction for eleven murders, he confessed to hundreds more. Lucas' death sentence was mysteriously commuted by then-governor of Texas, George W. Bush, an especially anomalous act, as Texas is known for its lack of clemency around the death penalty.[4] A 2019 Netflix series seemed designed to try and bury the mysteries and anomalies of the Lucas case by reducing them to a combination of Lucas' fantasy life, police incompetence, and opportunism on both sides. Significantly, there is no mention in the show of the Hand of Death cult. Nor are any of these disturbing ties between seemingly solitary killers and larger networks referenced in *Spy Game* or *Zodiac*, or in *Mindhunter*.

McGowan reports another rash of "serial killings" that began in nearby Sacramento, California, in 1977, eventually attributed to Richard Chase, colloquially known as the "Vampire of Sacramento" and "The Dracula Killer." Oddly enough, the disgraced production head of Columbia pictures, David Begelman, was developing a film version around a similar case at the time his crimes came to light, that of Vaughn Greenwood, the "Skid Row Slasher" of Southern California, who cut his victim's throats from ear to ear and allegedly drank their blood (see *Indecent Exposure*, p. 16). McGowan writes:

> These killers—Chase, Manson, Kemper, Mullin, the Zodiac, Frazier and Baker—heralded the dawn of a new era that soon had established "serial killers" as an ever-present part of the American landscape. Before 1960, fewer than two serial killers a year were reported nationwide. By 1970, the number had climbed to six per year; by 1980, to nearly twenty per year. By 1990, nearly three-dozen serial killers a year were being reported across the country. The years covered by the occult bloodbath in Northern California, 1967 through 1973, correspond precisely to the years that the Phoenix Program in Vietnam was in full operation (although similar programs, under different names, existed prior to 1967). In September 1973, the head of the Phoenix operation, William Colby, was appointed as the new Director of the Central Intelligence Agency. Phoenix had officially come home (p. 137).

In August 1984, *Life* ran an article, "An American Tragedy," claiming that in 1983, 5000 people were killed by serial killers in the US.

Insofar as there are ties between the entertainment industry and organized crime, and between organized crime and intelligence agencies and covert military operations (including sex and drug trafficking), then the ways in which the entertainment industry depicts organized crime takes on entirely new ramifications. It becomes a key factor in our incapacity to understand—or even perceive—the interlinking of only *seemingly* disparate worlds. Every criminal conspiracy includes the means to cover its traces; in the case of organized crime and entertainment media, one obvious reason for criminals to want to take control of Hollywood might be just this: *to create myths that obscure the truth around their activities.* Think Jimmy Savile or Jeffrey Epstein, expanded outward to include an entire "pop" culture. . .

✦

"[O]ver the next quarter century the CIA, through its placement of its people throughout the media, including Hollywood and television, resurrected its mythic image—phoenix-like—from the fleeting and rarely examined ashes Valentine had reduced it to. Using what the CIA officer Frank Wisner called the agency's 'Mighty Wurlitzer'—its deep penetration of the news and cultural apparatus—it played the American people to a tune of CIA heroes defending the 'homeland' from mad Muslim terrorists and evil drug dealers besieging the U.S. citadel through deception and direct attack. Movies, television shows, cognitive infiltration of the mainstream media across platforms repeated the message over and over again: We are the good guys in this mythic battle of good against evil. We are defenders of the 'Homeland.'"

—EDWARD CURTIN, *2017 review of Douglas Valentine's*
The Phoenix Program

So if Fincher, with *Zodiac* and *Mindhunter*, is claiming one thing while doing something closer to the exact opposite—isn't that a kind of *under-cover work?* From an informed (some might say paranoid) perspective, it is perhaps not so simple. Insofar as Hollywood itself is an ongoing organized crime/intelligence psyop, then clearly David Fincher is part of it, as is any-one making films in Hollywood. But insofar as any hypothetical ongoing organized crime/intelligence psyop entails giving a degree of freedom for self-expression (creative autonomy) to its assets in order to reap the benefits of the acclaim they receive, then Fincher is also an autonomous artist work-ing within the Hollywood system. It's not a question of either/or, then, but both/and.

We can speculate that the US intelligence community wants its agents to maintain artistic credibility and lets them do some of their own proj-ects (even when seemingly subversive) to ensure their subsequent assigned projects have the respectability of their "brand." (Propaganda Films was the name of Fincher's first company. His work with corporate advertising, both

---

* Joe Penhall is the actual "creator" of *Mindhunter*, an English playwright who spent six years working on a film about Idi Amin, *The Last King of Scotland*. His research included flying to Uganda and meeting Idi Amin's henchmen. He had his name removed from the film, ostensibly after other writers worked on his script. "Joe Penhall, 10 Screenwriters to Watch," by Adam Dawtrey, *Variety*, June 18, 2008: https://variety.com/2008/film/markets-festivals/joe-penhall-1117987704/

pre- and post-*Fight Club*, is discussed in Outtake # 6.) Or we can speculate that these artists are "rewarded" for their government work with the freedom to initiate their own projects, even when superficially (or deeply) subversive, as in the case of a *Fight Club* or a *Counselor*. In either case, it's really six of one and half a dozen of the other.

In the fascinating book about David Begelman's long history of embezzlement at Columbia pictures, *Indecent Exposure*, David McClintick (an investigative reporter for the Wall Street Journal) breaks it down neatly:

> Acclaim is as important to executives as it is to stars, for it is through acclaim that most show-business executives obtain and consolidate their power. The acclaim of making a successful movie or TV show, whether the executive deserves it or not, usually is accompanied by the power to make more movies and TV shows. The acclaim for making *several* successful movies or TV shows, whether the executive deserves the acclaim or not, often leads to the opportunity to run an entire studio or network. [This in turn] usually opens larger vistas. . . *to play a major role in determining how the nation and indeed the world are entertained* (p. 39–40, emphasis added).

In this simple equation, acclaim equals power and influence, ergo *artistically prestigious projects are essential to the extension of State (and industry) propaganda's reach*. Just as much as terror is.

11.3. WHEN EMPIRE ACTS

> "We're an empire now, and when we act, we create our own reality. And while you're studying that reality—judiciously, as you will—we'll act again, creating other new realities, which you can study too, and that's how things will sort out. We're history's actors . . . and you, all of you, will be left to just study what we do."
>
> —KARL ROVE, *Deputy Chief of Staff during the George W. Bush administration (as quoted by Ron Suskind)*

The tendency of power—in the sociological sense of status, influence, authority and control—is to seek to extend itself over time, if possible indefinitely, by whatever means necessary. The question of benevolence and malevolence is secondary—even irrelevant—to this tendency, since everyone believes in the goodness of his or her motivations and whatever motivates us is ipso facto "good." What *is* relevant is the means power employs to extend itself, and the ways in which this may be observable in our culture, society, and, most importantly, our personal lives.

Advertising and economic expansion provide a fairly good template, I think, for mapping these means. In the case of advertising, perception management and behavior modification are primary both as ends *and* means, since to manage perception is to modify behavior, and vice versa. Advertising works by making us feel differently about a product so we will buy it. Whether the psyop "lite" of advertising or the psyop heavy of military takeovers, the goals may change according to the agencies creating them, but the methodologies remain the same.

We all know (or think we do) that corporations and their algorithms manipulate our perceptions in order to influence our decisions (what we buy, consume, watch, "like," or recommend to others). Through means subtle and coarse, fair and foul, corporations work day and night to exploit our values as a means to sell their products to us. The coarser means include sexual stimulation, on the one hand, and the shock tactics of fast-cutting, loud music, bright lights, and overtly violent imagery, on the other. The aim is to turn us into *latahs*, to induce a trance-like state of cultural-possession in which we will obey commands without ever realizing we are doing so. At the same time, in a circular fashion, the products themselves are designed to shape and mold our values, to make those values, and by extension us, more easily exploitable—and to keep us in a state of shock and suspended disbelief. The aim is always the same: to get or keep us "on-side."

As above so below: As corporations operate, so do governments, military, intelligence, educational, legal, medical, and all other institutions. The higher up the sociocultural strata we go, the less easily identifiable the products become: a candidate, an administration, a policy, an ideology, a culture, these can all be seen—to one degree or another—as products, manufactured carriers of values that are themselves carried by the values we already possess—or are possessed by. All these things act as *delivery devices*—like actors on a stage inducing mimetic contagion—to inject, and infect, both our inner and outer worlds with their contents. One way or another, they *in-form* us, dictating our behavior in such a way that we remain oblivious to being controlled. *Latahs.*

In order for a ruling class or body to maintain and increase its power and influence in the world, it has to persuade ever larger numbers of people to depend on it. Love and worship are optimal attitudes, but where these cannot be inspired, fear and subjugation will do, as demonstrated by the afore-cited anecdote about Stalin and the chicken. As anthropologist Hutton Webster notes (quoted by Brian Hayden):

> The members of the inner circle . . . come to realize what a means for personal advancement is to be found in the manipulation of the tribal ceremonies. The tendency will then be constantly to widen the gap between the initiated and the uninitiated, and to surround the organization so formed with every appliance for working on the fear and awe of the outsiders (p. 340).

Showing the people just enough to terrify and inspire awe in them with both your power and lack of moral limits—without giving away anything that can be used against you—is standard tactics in war, known as "shock-and-awe." Also known as rapid dominance, shock-and-awe is technically the use of overwhelming power and excessive displays of force to paralyze the enemy and destroy their will to fight. But this is an overly simplified understanding of the term that only applies to actual combat, and "shock-and-awe" takes on much more sinister and far-reaching implications when juxtaposed with what is known about *latah.*

Implicit in the infamous Karl Rove quote above (though Rove has denied saying it[5]) is the idea that what we take for history—or reality—is designed, like a horror movie, to distract us from what is *really* going on, behind the scenes and off-stage, where the real horror is. The game of history, like the magician's trick, somewhat paradoxically, is designed to keep us enthralled. The word enthralled comes from *thrall*, a Viking word for serf or slave: a person in bondage. Fitting then that we describe an especially effective movie or TV show as *enthralling*. Our masters *create* what we take for reality; and by the time we are starting to see through it, they have already prepared a new layer—a new series—to lure us into.

11.4. PSYCHOLOGICAL OPERATIONS
FIELD MANUALS

> "The psychological distress symptoms of traumatized people
> simultaneously call attention to the existence of an unspeakable
> secret and deflect attention from it. This is most apparent in
> the way traumatized people alternate between feeling numb
> and reliving the event. The dialectic of trauma gives rise to
> complicated, sometimes uncanny alterations of consciousness,
> which George Orwell . . . called 'doublethink,' and which mental
> health professionals, searching for calm, precise language, call
> 'dissociation.'"
>
> —JUDITH LEWIS HERMAN, *Trauma and Recovery**

In the past, the "psyop" was the stuff of "conspiracy theory"; in 2020, while the term psyop may still carry some disreputable baggage, the reality which it refers to—much-discussed in media studies—has become thoroughly integrated into our lives. As these paramilitary procedures have trickled down and multiplied via mimesis, both conscious and not, they have entered not only into corporate advertising and mass media, but into social networking as well. *Latahs*, after all, are not only the victims of shock-and-awe-induced cultural-bondage, but also the carriers and promulgators of it.

What follows are some passages taken from U.S. military Field Manual, FM 3-05.30 MCRP 3-40.6, dated April 2005, "Psychological Operations" (emphasis added).

---

* Herman is professor of clinical psychiatry at Harvard and director of Training at the Department of Psychiatry at Cambridge, Massachusetts

PSYOP are a vital part of the broad range of United States (U.S.) diplomatic, informational, military, and *economic* (DIME) activities. The
employment of any element of national power, particularly the military
element, has always had a psychological dimension. Foreign perceptions
of U.S. military capabilities are fundamental to strategic deterrence. *The
effectiveness of deterrence hinges on U.S. ability to influence the perceptions of
others.* The purpose of PSYOP is to induce or reinforce foreign attitudes
and behavior favorable to U.S. national objectives. PSYOP are characteristically delivered as information for effect, used during peacetime and
conflict, to inform and influence (p. 1-1).[6]

This passage underscores the essentiality of psyop to government and
military maintenance of economic power. And while the emphasis on *foreign* target audiences implies that psyop are not implemented domestically,
this is almost certainly a misrepresentation due to the classified nature of
domestic psyop.

The mission of PSYOP is to influence the behavior of foreign target audiences (TAs) to support U.S. national objectives. PSYOP accomplish this
by conveying selected information and/or advising on *actions that influence the emotions, motives, objective reasoning, and ultimately the behavior
of foreign audiences.* Behavioral change is at the root of the PSYOP mission. Although concerned with the mental processes of the TA, it is the
observable modification of TA behavior that determines the mission success of PSYOP. . . . *PSYOP help shape both the physical and informational
dimensions of the battlespace.* (p. 1-2, emphasis added)

Once again, to inflict shock is to induce trance, manage perception,
and modify behavior. In a certain sense, shocking a Target Audience is secondary to the inducing of a trance state (the shocks are means, the end is
awe); but in another sense the shocks are primary, since without them the
Target Audience will not be receptive to the commands. At the same time,
the only way to confirm that *latahs* have been created is by observing their
behaviors. Psychological operations proceed on the understanding that,
not just human society but awareness itself (informational dimensions) is
a *battlespace*.

Even as one plan is about to be executed, planners are turning their attention to the next anticipated operation. Flexibility, adaptability, and adjustment are critical to all planning. The importance of adjusting PSYOP plans and series in response to events in the battlespace cannot be overemphasized. PSYOP planners must be agile to be successful in an environment that has simultaneous and competing requirements to plan for an event that is in itself an ongoing process. At any given moment, PSYOP forces may be disseminating messages while military forces are executing a PSYACT in support of PSYOP objectives. (5-1)

This passage points to the necessity of constant improvisation within the field. It indicates how, as a Target Audience's perception of reality is altered via manufactured "messages," their behaviors will also change in ways that can't be predicted with 100% accuracy by the controlling forces. Since, presumably, there is no clear dividing line between passive media manipulation and that of *live-action theater* (in which psychological operatives interact more directly with Target Audiences), to some degree, the Target Audience is itself shaping the nature of the psyop by forcing it, the psyop, to adapt to the very changes it is bringing about. In marketing, this is similar to the old "supply and demand" question, a mutually reinforcing feedback loop in which the one is constantly creating and augmenting the other.

"Most PSYOP activities and accomplishments in Panama were hardly noticed by either the U.S. public or the general military community. But the special operations community did notice. The lessons learned in Panama were incorporated into standing [sic] operating procedures. . . . Operations DESERT SHIELD and DESERT STORM employed PSYOP of an order of magnitude and effectiveness which many credit to the lessons learned from Panama." USSOCOM Report, "Psychological Operations in Panama during Operations JUST CAUSE and PROMOTE LIBERTY," March 1994. (5-1)

This passage is self-explanatory and conveys how every psyop serves not only to manipulate a Target Audience but also as a form of field-testing for psychological operatives to learn from and pass information back and forth, thereby improving their skills and methods and becoming ever more "operational." Another way of stating this might be to say that, with each effective psyop, the battlespace of human society and human awareness is becoming ever more "secured."

> As one of the five core elements, PSYOP integrate their activities with those of electronic warfare (EW), military deception, OPSEC [operations security], and computer network operations to create a synergistic effect. PSYOP serve as a focal point for persuasion and influence strategy. PSYOP forces facilitate targeting by analyzing the various factors that affect and influence the behavior of an adversary, such as religion, ethnicity, economics, politics, culture, region, history, leadership, geography, demographics, and national interests. They use this analysis to nominate targets in order to change the behavior of TAs in order to deter conflict (whenever possible), facilitate military operations, and to support and communicate national objectives. (7-4)

This passage indicates the wide range both of technological means and of target audiences, and suggests that not merely populations but entire "disciplines" (i.e., fields of human interest and endeavor) have been "weaponized." One way to better understand this might again be to compare it to coarser forms of marketing, such as "product placement," when a movie or TV show is used to "sell" specific products to an audience *without it consciously noticing or remembering*. In this far subtler form, areas of human interest such as religion, economics, and the arts can be employed (reshaped) as *carriers for the desired messages or ideologies—or, more simply stated, commands.*

> Media analysis is the structured, deliberate tracking and analysis of opponent and neutral media (TV, radio, Internet, and print). Properly performed media analysis, although time-consuming and linguist-intensive, can identify trends and become predictive when the supported force considers a potentially unpopular activity. To be truly effective, media analysis must be conducted on a daily basis. PSYOP units usually do not have the organic personnel sufficient to accomplish this task. The TAAD [Target Audience Analysis Detachment] of the PDC [product development company] is best suited for conducting media analysis. (8-5)

This passage clearly indicates an alliance—even a continuum—between corporate marketing research and military strategy. Media analysis, like everything else when it comes to military application, has an active as well as passive aspect. Nothing the military incentive undertakes (and this would include not only the entire intelligence, legal, and police community but also to a degree the entire corporate world) is done without the aim of *aggressive application*. To analyze media is to understand how to manipulate media; ditto with human psychology, religion, science, and so forth.

11.5.   THE MONOPOLIZATION OF SUPERNATURAL POWER BY THE RULING CLASS

> "[T]he monopolization of supernatural power by the ruling class
> functioned to produce fear, awe, and acquiescence on the part of
> the uninitiated populace and supported an exploitative system.
> There was a wide range of tactics used to intimidate, persuade,
> or coerce people into compliance with the professed ideological
> claims, rules, and actions of secret societies, but foremost among
> the tactics used was terror. [T]he function of secret societies
> on the Northwest Coast was to dominate society by the use of
> violence or black magic. Accounts by some informants portrayed
> them as 'terroristic organizations.'"
>
> —BRIAN HAYDEN, *The Power of Ritual in Prehistory*

During the Vietnam War, the Joint United States Public Affairs Office (JUSPAO) regularly sent out PSYOP Policy to be used by the troops in the field. Policy Number 36, dated May 10, 1967, describes guidance to be followed by all U.S. elements in Vietnam, beginning with the title "THE USE OF SUPERSTITIONS IN PSYCHOLOGICAL OPERATIONS IN VIETNAM." It poses a two-part problem, "To devise guidelines for the exploitation of enemy vulnerabilities provided by superstitions and deep-ly-held traditional beliefs"; and "To be aware of and accommodate those superstitions of friendly forces and populations that may have a bearing on military operations."

"A strong superstition or a deeply-held belief shared by a substantial number of the enemy target audience," it continues (emphasis added), *"can be used as a psychological weapon* because it permits with some degree of probability the prediction of individual or group behavior under a given set of conditions."

The manual cautions that using enemy superstition as a starting point for psychological operations requires that "one must be sure of the conditions and control the stimuli that trigger the desired behavior. The first step in the manipulation of a superstition as an enemy vulnerability *is its exact identification and detailed definition of its spread and intensity among the target audience"* (emphasis added). This exploitation of enemy superstition requires ascertaining that "The superstition or belief is real and powerful" and that manipulating it is not only possible, but that it will "achieve results favorable to the friendly forces." These are modern applications of what is clearly an ancient set of principles, however. As Hayden writes in *The Power of Ritual in Prehistory*, "Secret society members did not shirk from using any tactics they could to impress and intimidate their fellow villagers, no matter how gruesome"; and they "often used terror indiscriminately to enforce their grip on power" (p. 2, 12).

> Members of secret societies had many rights and privileges, and thus formed "a rude but powerful aristocracy" . . . . Indeed, the pervasive use of terror is difficult to explain in any other terms than the imposition of control by those seeking power. It did not fundamentally result from any desire for conviviality, attraction of mystery, or curiosity. Nor was the use of terror compatible with any altruistic or communitarian assumptions about organizers' motives. Instead, the psychological picture of secret society leaders and organizers corresponds very closely, if not exactly, to the personality characteristics of typical aggrandizers who tended toward sociopathology (p. 340).

Entirely independent of Hayden's archeological research, in the 1990s the study of human sacrifice in early American cultures gave rise to the "Social Control Hypothesis": that *the previously undisclosed reason for human sacrifice was to raise some members of the community to the top of the social hierarchy, while keeping others at the bottom.* Building on this hypothesis, a paper was published in 2016 based on a series of new studies. It was called "Ritual human sacrifice promoted and sustained the evolution of stratified societies," by Watts, Sheehan, Atkinson, Bulbulia, and Gray:

> What the results show is that . . . the practice of human sacrifice may have helped to hasten the development and separation between various layers of social status. . . . human sacrifice instilled fear and at the same time demonstrated the power of the elite. . . . This system could have been an early means to build and maintain power, which was a step to the development of complex societies and more formal political systems. [M]any of the rituals surrounding sacrifices seemed to aim for the utmost gore—with some ceremonies delaying the moment of death for many hours. "*It's not just a matter of killing efficiently. There's more to it than that . . . The terror and spectacle . . . was maximized*" (emphasis added).[7]

According to retired "Superstition Psyop" Sergeant Major, Herbert A. Friedman, one of the prime American proponents of the use of superstition for terror tactics was General Edward Lansdale, for whom successful psychological warfare depended on "a firm understanding of the socio-cultural beliefs and myths of the target." Lansdale served as the CIA's chief operative in the Philippines during the early 1950s counterinsurgency campaign against the country's Huk rebels.*

> In the most famous operation, which may or may not be true, it is alleged that [Lansdale] was told of an area known to be harboring Hukbalahap guerrillas. A combat psychological warfare squad was brought in and, under Lansdale's direction, planted stories among town residents of an *asuang* or vampire living on the hill where the Huks were based. A famous local soothsayer, they said, had predicted that men with evil in their hearts would become its victim. After letting the story sink in, Lansdale's ambushers waited for a Huk patrol to pass along the trail,

---

* "The Hukbalahap Rebellion was a rebellion staged by former Hukbalahap or Hukbong Bayan Labansa Hapon (Anti-Japanese Army) soldiers against the Philippine government. It started during the Japanese occupation of the Philippines in 1942 and continued during the presidency of Manuel Roxas, and ended in 1954 under the presidency of Ramon Magsaysay." http://www.psywarrior.com/SuperstitionPSYOP.html

quietly snatched the last insurgent, punctured his neck with two holes, hung the body by the ankles to drain it of blood, then put the corpse back on the trail. When the guerrillas returned to look for their missing comrade they found the bloodless corpse, obviously killed by an *Asuang* (vampire). The entire Huk unit packed up and left the area in great haste.

As if to indicate the centrality of pop culture to psyop, at this point Friedman inserts the poster for the 1973 Philippine movie, *Son of the Vampire*:

Friedman provides a similar example in the exploiting of the North Vietnamese fear that, if they died far from home, and their bodies were denied a proper burial, they would become "wandering souls" after death.

The operation was code-named "Wandering Soul." Engineers spent weeks recording eerie sounds . . . similar to the sounds employed during a scary radio show or movie . . . designed to send shivers down the back. These cries and wails were intended to represent souls of the enemy dead who had failed to find the peace of a proper burial. . . . The purpose of these sounds was to panic and disrupt the enemy and cause him to flee his position. Helicopters were used to broadcast Vietnamese voices pretending to be from beyond the grave. They called on their descendants in the Vietcong to defect, to cease fighting.[8]

Consider the implications of a *domestic* appliance for exploiting popular superstitions to manipulate perceptions and behavior (e.g., *The Exorcist*). Consider movements such as Antonin Artaud's theater of cruelty and Nitsch's orgy mysteries, Dadaism and Surrealism, or the slasher movies of the 1980s (the bastard children of Hitchcock's *Psycho* and Powell's *Peeping Tom*), or the Zodiac killings and the whole real-time "genre" of serial killers, the modern secular equivalent of the *asuang* for Philippino soldiers (most especially when an occult or satanic element is added). All of these examples make it clear why, as the inheritor of the "advance-guard," pop culture, and Hollywood specifically, might be central to the art and science of psyop: namely, the inducement of culture-bondage, or *latah*.

11.6. PLANET ILLUMINATI

"The conflict between the will to deny horrible events and
the will to proclaim them aloud is the central dialectic of
psychological trauma. People who have survived atrocities
often tell their stories in a highly emotional, contradictory, and
fragmented manner that undermines their credibility and thereby
serves the twin imperatives of truth-telling and secrecy. When the
truth is finally recognized, survivors can begin their recovery.
But far too often secrecy prevails, and the story of the traumatic
event surfaces not as a verbal narrative but *as a symptom*"
(emphasis added).

—JUDITH LEWIS, *Herman Trauma and Recovery*

Organized murders, pedophilia, and other forms of "satanic" abuses seem designed to enflame the already combustive, superstitious, fear-based imagination of a community and to lure them into a new level of nightmare (so-called "mass hysteria," "psychic contagion," or "moral panic"). One potentially desirable effect of such psyop would be to manage the target audience's perceptions towards seeing the State as *both diabolic and Godlike*. It also seems to function as a highly effective tool of *schismogenesis*, as can be glimpsed, perhaps, by how opinion on these accounts is so strongly divided between those who accept the reality of them (sometimes unquestioningly) and those who dismiss them as the result of religious hysteria and/or the exploitation of hordes of unethical psychotherapists (for example). Yet on both ends of the spectrum, ironically, a massive conspiracy is imagined. Ditto with the way in which, COINTELPRO-aided or not, the Atlanta murders acted as a wedge of paranoia between black and white, and rich and poor, in the community (see Outtake # 7 on page 483).

In the case of Lansdale's soldier-vampires psyop, we might ask "Was that reality or make-believe?" The answer is not either-or but both-and. Real people *were* killed as part of a real military strategy, and a fake supernatural element was incorporated to spread shock, awe, and superstitious dread. The soldiers who committed the acts of violence were not required to believe they were vampires, however, or even to believe in vampires, any more than General Lansdale needed to believe in the supernatural to plan the psyop or Friedkin needed to believe in the devil to make *The Exorcist* (though it did help for him to claim to, just as it helped Polanski to deny it; see 16.6).

In many of the cases examined here, real abominations were certainly committed, even while more lurid, fantastic, overly "satanic" (even supernatural) aspects were simultaneously pushed forward and suppressed (as with the whole UFO tangle, see *Prisoner of Infinity*). Yet these elements may not even have been strictly essential or integral to the acts being committed, any more than an abduction experience depends on the existence of aliens. Or, if these elements *are* integral to a given experience, then they are like "special effects" that make a movie that much more persuasive, like the "mechanical and impersonal" use of state-of-the-art, nausea-inducing special effects, subliminal sound and imagery, and backmasking in *The Exorcist*.

We might ask the same question of the supposed serial killers or of Joker-copycat shooters: how much do they *believe* in their ostensible motivations, and how much are they merely assuming the appearance of belief as a terror tactic? And at what point does a conscious suspension of disbelief become involuntary possession by the narrative being enacted—cultural bondage to "the Method"? Lansdale's soldiers—like Polanski's and Friedkin's and Fincher's actors—*did* need to embody that superstitious belief and *make it real*. And since the killing was real, and the blood-draining was real, mightn't they find themselves, like actors trained in the Method, increasingly unsure at what point the movie ends and reality begins? As Hayden writes:

> Undoubtedly some people did believe various claims, but equally certain from the accounts of secret societies is the fact that many people did not believe the claims but simply viewed them as a means of manipulating people. Even if people exhibited public compliance to beliefs or norms, this would not necessarily have meant that they privately believed in them or even accepted them (p. 18).

Hayden adds, however, that any individuals who failed to accept secret society claims or dictates "were targeted and frequently eliminated one way or another." Spies were engaged "to identify such individuals," to prevent awareness that "the appearances of the spirits were really humans in masks." Those who did discover the truth were "either inducted into the society (if deemed desirable) or killed outright" (p. 39).

The "occultic" aspect of accounts of organized ritual abuse, and of the various "serial killings" depicted in *Mindhunter*, may of course be absolutely real. Forces of the occult—and the ancient sorcery rituals of secret societies—may also in some sense be real (Hayden avoids getting into this question, understandably). But whatever the case, and whatever those involved actually believe, they certainly appear to be essential to the managing of *perception*—first of the victims and then of the larger public that hears these accounts—as a means of adding an extra dimension of psychological dread to the physical shock and horror. The prowling predators at loose in our cities and in our backwaters and forests become harbingers of superstitious terror in exactly the same way Lansdale's vampires did: they are administrators of shock-and-awe whose purpose is to induce the trance-like terrorized state of culture-bound *latahs*.

Since there exists a spectrum of awareness in any given target audience, the exact same methods can't be applied to everyone. (You can't fool all the people, etc.) All possible responses in the target audience's perception, therefore, have to be covered. Supernatural elements not only play upon the superstitious fears of one target audience, they also serve to make the accounts seem ridiculous to another (people who are contemptuous and dismissive of religious and superstitious belief). For this demographic, the supernatural element, rather than making the accounts more terrifying, increases their apparent *absurdity*. But for both demographics, the result is the same: they are having their heads screwed on backwards. *Gradual schismogenesis* drives people towards whichever end of a spectrum they are closer to. To this end, I once wrote, "There is a worldwide conspiracy [i.e., agenda] to create the *illusion* of a worldwide conspiracy." Yet the opposite may also be true: there is a worldwide conspiracy, or agenda, to discredit the idea of a worldwide conspiracy. All the bases are covered.

This brings us full circle and back to Stalin's chicken. If a people are terrorized by a power they do not consciously see as their enemy but as their protector and caregiver, they will be forced to project benevolence onto the state precisely *because* of how fearsome it appears to be. This depends on the terror being measured in just the right proportions. The art of domestic psyop is to ensure that the terror not be so great as to shock the target audience into awakening, because awakening could lead to a revolt, uprising.

The point of a psyop is not to keep it secret, but to have control over the narrative that emerges around it. This requires people to be clued into, made to suspect, the truth, or several layers of it at least, but never be allowed to quite confirm it or understand how many layers and how they can be made to fit together. This sort of mix of awareness with ignorance is what allows the more *superstitious* aspect of belief to remain predominant. Since there's no official confirmation or explanation, there's no consensus, and no consensus means no way for people to really talk about it or to make sense of it. When rumor, fact, sensationalized reportage, disinformation, entertainment media, and plain lies are all inextricably tangled up, people's consciousness gets tangled up with them. We know at some level the true depths of the horror being revealed—and are terrorized by it—but we aren't able to fully re-cognize it, and so there's no way to act upon it—or even to talk coherently about it. People can't organize to *resist* an enemy that is never fully identified, one that remains, like occult forces, shrouded in a fog of manipulated information.

The main thing in such social and psychological *schismogenesis* is that people never make a conscious choice but only react to "the advertising." It doesn't matter if they buy Pepsi or Coke, as long as they keep imbibing the sugar; as long as the *latahs* tear off their clothes and submit, then the theater continues to unfold.* As long as the narratives we subscribe to—globalism, nationalism, Marxism, neoliberalism, alt-right-ism, racial realism, ethno-nationalism, postmodernism, nihilism, theism, occultism, conspiratorialism—are manufactured as vehicles to capture our attention, direct our choices, and modify our behaviors down pre-prepared State channels, we will continue to sink deeper into dependency and distrust, away from autonomy, self-awareness, or compassion.

This may be why those who gravitate towards a more conspiratorial perspective tend to wind up stranded on Planet Illuminati, where the movie playing depicts an all-powerful, all-controlling satanic elite of possibly superhuman dimensions. If people are going to start wising up, it's expedient (for the perception managers) that the "red pill" leads them deeper into fear and loathing, dissociation, narcissism and obsession and not towards embodiment, acceptance, wisdom, peace, understanding, or love. Like traumatized children, we are rendered powerless in the face of something so vast that it is seemingly incomprehensible to us. Our trauma becomes our God, and our traumatized state becomes our traumatizer-State.† Seeing, or remembering, the movements of a dark Empire, we both believe and disbelieve our perceptions. Not knowing which of our responses to believe, we are paralyzed to act.

---

* Following the mass shock event of 9/11, during the period of increased safety measures, people eventually agreed to take their shoes off at airport security, which in some cultures is as an act of submission.

† See Greg Mogenson, *A Most Accursed Religion: When A Trauma Becomes God.*

12

MASTERS OF THE UNIVERSE

12.1.   GENERATING AVATARS

> "In this world, the Marvel super-hero becomes emblematic
> of a new kind of individualism that stands in that indefinable
> space between the margin and mainstream society. The hero
> is essentially presented as a misfit, as a social and scientific
> aberration, who is accidentally given super-human powers that
> are in conflict with and even undermined by the convulsions of
> his/her human personality."
>
> —MARINO TUZI, *"Individualism and Marginality"*

Tarantino's *Once Upon a Time in Hollywood* presents the possibility
of using movies to create parallel universes in which things go
how we would like them to go. Tarantino is probably seen, at least
by his defenders, as daring and innovative for using mere cinema to revise
history. But of course, movies have always been about creating false realities
that entice us to blot out reality, and Tarantino is only making explicit what
was always implicit to the "service" Hollywood provides: high-level fairy
tales—a.k.a., psyop, or suspension of disbelief.

One way to better understand the century-long appeal of movies and
visual media—and the efficacy of psyop—is as *an externalization of a natural
process of consciousness.* Specifically, with reference to the prefrontal cortex

complex, which is where what we think of as voluntary thought occurs, *where we work things out*. One of the ways we work things out is by creating simulated versions of reality and "generating avatars" of ourselves to send into these "hypothetical worlds" and see how they survive.[1] This means that fantasy, of whatever sort, isn't only a way to escape reality or to relieve the stress of everyday existence, but also a way to learn to better navigate our lives.

The question that underlies every quest, once our basic survival needs have been addressed, is "Who am I?"[2] It's the job of movies, state propaganda, psyop, and genuine inspirational art, to provide an answer—though the answer of course varies greatly. What all of these various media share, when it comes to providing real or pseudo-transcendental answers, is a preoccupation with that which transcends nature, i.e., both destruction and death (often violent) and *the supernatural*. Or, from the more sophisticated or avant-garde perspective, the *surreal*: what is *above* reality. When we sit down in front of a movie (a good one), we get to forget our lives, even our very identities, for two or three hours. But this is only insofar as we are able to immerse ourselves inside *a fabricated life/world* and become voluntarily lost in it. Paradoxically, our desire to escape our lives is coupled with a search for *a new sense of identity* via the passive act of vicariously identifying with a fictional construct, a fake reality.

When we watch a movie, we're entering not only into a virtual world but also a virtual *self* custom-made *for* us (albeit on a mass-scale). This false self provides us with a way of moving around inside the virtual environment of the movie, thereby gaining *vicarious experience*. Besides the sheer entertainment value of such a process, when we watch a movie, TV show, or play a video game, we're also trying out new possibilities as individuals. This suggests there may be something innate about our enjoyment of movies that relates both to survival, at the primal level, and to self-awareness or self-discovery, at the more philosophical or spiritual level.

By the same token, there's something dangerous about such voluntary symbiosis. If movies are a form of involuntary creative thinking, dreaming awake, even possession, then whenever we enter into a film narrative, we may actually be taking on all of the elements of that narrative *as if it was our own creation*. If so, we would not only become inextricably bound up in these narratives while we are "innocently" enjoying them, we would also be allowing our consciousness—our very identities—to become permanently spliced *to* them.

One of the most striking changes in the movie industry in the past fifteen years or so (roughly since the first *Spiderman* trilogy, *X-Men* films, *The Dark Knight* series, and—the capstone—the massive success of 2008's *Iron Man*) is the rise of the superhero movie. If we include the *Star Wars* franchise and animated entries from DreamWorks and Pixar, the whole US film industry is currently supported by one superhero franchise or another. What was once the geeky margins of comic book and Sci-Fi conventions has now entered full-blown into the mainstream, to the extent that, if a movie star wants to be on the A-list at this point, the only surefire way is to star in a superhero franchise.[3]

There is a weird sort of mirroring here, or perhaps a glimpse into parallel universes, because an A-list Hollywood movie star is—short of Elon Musk, or, at the other end of the social scale, joining the military or police force—about as close to a real-world superhero as one can get. That said, our world, as one might expect with a parallel universe, is like the Bizarro world to the Marvel or DC universe, where superheroes are entirely unknown in their ordinary lives, and often feared and reviled by ordinary people. They are also supposed to have given up all worldly desires to serve a higher cause. In that sense, real-world cultural heroes like Musk or Robert Downey Jr.— not to mention the tech-ed out police and military personnel, including "supersoldiers"—are significantly closer to the supervillain type. Ironies— and inversions—abound.

*

"Give me the child for the first seven years and I will give you the man."

—JESUIT SAYING[4]

I was around seven or eight when I first discovered superhero comics. Coincidentally that's more or less where my chronological memory begins. (It's also when I began to experiment with my sexuality.) I was captivated by the Marvel characters the Fantastic Four, the X-Men and the Silver Surfer, but my main point of entry into the Marvel universe was Peter Parker: an awkward, socially inept teenager who creates a secret life for himself as the wise-cracking, web-swinging Spiderman. Before pubescence was more than a blip on the horizon for me, superhero comics hinted at the hidden potential of my body, at impossible possibilities and worlds of mystery and wonder.

It's easy enough to see how these tailor-made fantasies for alienated pre-adolescents to retreat into—struggling with the uneasy transformation of their sexuality—were also coded primers for the spiritual path (especially considering how sexless, even monkish, some of these heroes were). In the process of seeking an escape into "amazing fantasy," I was unwittingly feeding the fires of a lifetime of spiritual striving—the lonely heroic quest to separate from the milling crowds and ascend, on trails of glory, to Valhalla. Even if, like Siddhartha or Norrin Radd (the Silver Surfer), I would have to sacrifice everything to get there. My passion extended beyond just reading about superheroes; pretty soon I was creating my own. I wrote and drew Spiderman comics (one of the few things I remember doing with my brother, as kids) and then I dreamed up my own cast of superheroes, with Captain Solar as the center of my system (fittingly enough; his nemesis was Gasmaster—a very body-centric power). The same evolution, from receiving to transmitting, consuming to manufacturing, happened with movies, as already recounted. Another passion of this period, from pre- to post-adolescence, was David Bowie; before that it was Elvis, mostly because of my sister's devotion to him. (Later, I chose David Byrne, see 14.5.) Bowie was the protean rock idol whose specialty was self-transformation. Elvis self-transformed too, in a horribly non-volitional way: he bloated, sagged, and melted before our disbelieving eyes.

"I'm not a prophet or a stone age man, just a mortal with potential of a superman," sings Bowie in "Quicksand." The track ends side one of *Hunky Dory*, the first Bowie album I ever heard, on the rare occasions I got to hang out in my brother's room. I chose these same words to adorn a painting I did of Bowie, at around twelve or thirteen, of his *Aladdin Sane* incarnation. The first Bowie songs I remember liking were "Oh! You Pretty Things!" and "Life on Mars," also on *Hunky Dory*. Years later, I found out that Bowie had been heavily into the occult during this period, and probably the first time I ever heard the name Aleister Crowley was while listening to "Quicksand."*

---

* The song begins: "I'm closer to the golden dawn, immersed in Crowley's uniform, of imagery."

Without knowing it, I was being seduced onto the path of pursuing occult power.

I drew my own comics; I stitched together a Spiderman costume for my Lone Ranger action figure. Later, I spent hours and hours writing film reviews and screenplays: all ways to become actively involved in the self-invention process and allow my fantasy life to spill over into reality. It gave me the feeling of being more than just an idle dreamer (like so many teenagers), as the biological goal of maturation became the social goal of self-promotion and aggrandizement. By raising the ego up to a higher plateau, the goal became to create the "enlightened" or spiritualized superego of the artist-genius. Fantasies of being a mutant, a powerful loner, an otherworldly androgyne, or a successful Hollywood filmmaker like Polanski, were all ways to turn alienation from a curse into a birthright—into destiny. The splinter was real, but the only way to deal with it was to escape into fantasies of "being the one."

The fantasy of super-heroism is about, not service, but empowerment—which is precisely what it has in common with being a Hollywood movie star. As Jonathan Lethem writes in *Ecstasy of Influence*: "Spiderman was a wunderkind-outcast identification available to anyone who'd mixed teenage grandiosity with even the mildest persecution complex, let alone real persecution" (p. 153). An idea further accentuated by *Gizmodo* in 2016: "So baked into the superhero genre is an acknowledgement of deep-seated rage, against those who have made us feel powerless, and a craving to have the power to make everybody respect us."[5]

Not exactly the psychological recipe for a community benefactor, is it?

The correlation between superhero fantasy and Hollywood aspirations is made explicit in the case of former A-list actor Nick Cage (who played *Ghost Rider* in a 2007 turkey, before Marvel had become synonymous with Midas). Cage is the nephew of Francis Coppola, and early in his career he changed his name to avoid charges of nepotism. He took his new name from a Marvel super-hero, Luke Cage:

> As a child, these colorful superheroes that could fly, or were horrifying like Ghost Rider and the Hulk, with this tremendous rage or these supernatural powers, provided an escape for me from my mundane existence, from my lack of friends or my inability to communicate well with people.

They liberated me. . . . I would look at the cover of the *Ghost Rider* comic book in my little home in Long Beach, California, and I couldn't get my head around how something that scary could also be good. To me it was my first philosophical awakening—"How is this possible, this duality?"

"Who am I and how can I enter the world in a way that is safe?" are questions that every child and teenager wrestles with. Movies of all kinds—none more than the superhero kind—present the knotty paradox of mass-produced, personalized fantasies that appeal to the alienated outsider in all of us, to the spotty adolescent who never grew up. They are corporate mass media that glorify "individuation" (specialness) as a Homeric odyssey, a violent break from the herd, and they offer carbon-copy cues to follow, as a way to *simulate* the appearance and experience of individuality.

Hopefully, the contradiction in this is self-evident: millions of kids (many of whom have now grown up to be adults) found lonely solace, as I did, by escaping in their rooms into fantasies of being Superman, Hulk, Captain America, Spiderman, an X-Man, or the Batman (or the Joker), fantasies that were both shared *and* private. Many or all of these heroes were transformed, in a kind of science-fantasy glorification of MKULTRA, through applied violence. Whether it's Jason Bourne, Wolverine, the Hulk, Captain America, or the more emotional impacts suffered by the Batman (and even Superman), these characters have all undergone physical, emotional, and psychological transformation through extreme trauma. It's hardly any wonder, then, that they have gone onto discover, develop, and consolidate their new identities primarily through *the use of violence*.

12.2. PROPAGANDA MACHINE

"All forms of violence are quests for identity."

—MARSHALL MCLUHAN

According to a study presented at the American Academy of Pediatrics in 2018, "Superheroes in Hollywood blockbusters conduct more violent acts on screen than the villains they are battling." This would seem to confirm the rule of Empire, "might is right": ass-kicking = heroism. Films like *Captain America: Civil War, Batman Vs Superman, Suicide Squad, Avengers: Age of Ultron, Deadpool,* and *Ant Man,* the study claimed, showed more acts of violence by the films' protagonists than the antagonists.

> "Children and adolescents see the superheroes as 'good guys,' and may be influenced by their portrayal of risk-taking behaviors and acts of violence," said the study's lead author, Robert Olympia. . . . According to the abstract of the study, the most common violent act of superheroes was fighting, with 1,021 instances, followed by destruction of property, murder, bullying, intimidation and torture. For villains, use of a lethal weapon was most common, with 604 instances counted. The researchers who conducted the study pointed to previous studies that have shown an increase in aggressive behavior in children when parents signal approval of violence by passively watching superhero films with them.[6]

If superheroes are models of positive identification (self-imaging) for children and adolescents (and adults who grew up on comic books); and if central to that identification is the ability and willingness to commit violence; it should come as no surprise to learn that superhero movies are considered highly effective as military propaganda. The proof is everywhere, but to cite just one example: the makers of 2019's *Captain Marvel* relied heavily on US military officers as consultants and advisers, employed dozens of active-duty US soldiers as extras, and shot several scenes on a US military base. Proud of their contribution, the US Department of Defense promoted the film on its website and social media accounts after its release, boasting of its involvement in the film's production. The directors, Ryan Fleck and Anna Boden, returned the favor by doing a PR event for the Pentagon. Afterwards, the DoD screened the film with the directors present, "to highlight Air Force collaboration with Disney and the inspiration behind the main character's warrior ethos: 'higher, further, faster.'"

In a curious twist, *Captain Marvel* supplants the male comic book hero with a female version of himself, and so was marketed as a feminist (or should that be transgender?), hence progressive (i.e., left-leaning), superhero movie! *Elle* magazine celebrated it as, "the Highest Grossing Movie with a

Female Lead Ever." As is so often the case in Hollywood, however, ostensibly progressive breakthroughs in cultural representation were seamlessly blended with US militarist propaganda. Captain Marvel (played by Brie Larson) has two close allies: Nick Fury (Samuel L. Jackson), a former CIA agent who finds himself directionless in life after successfully defeating communism in the Cold War; and Maria Rambeau (Lashana Lynch), another fighter pilot in the US military. The three team up in a benevolent, US military-backed mission to try to save a race of misunderstood underdog refugee aliens known as the Skrulls from annihilation by the Kree, a belligerent galactic superpower.[7]

Another wolf-in-sheep-clothing was the 2018 *Black Panther*, also produced by Marvel Studios and distributed by Disney. With its mostly black cast, this was also sold as progressive filmmaking, yet it too featured a CIA agent who—in good US-interventionist fashion—helps save the hero's *absolute monarchy* from a revolution led by anti-imperialists. Just as *Captain Marvel* was supported by the DoD, *Black Panther* was "aggressively promoted by the CIA on social media."[8] *Cui bono*? As Mark Bowden wrote in "Why Are We Obsessed with Superhero Movies?" these movies

> depict a Manichaean world populated by gods, or superheroes and super-villains, in endless conflict. Christian imagery is freely evoked, but the faith itself is dramatically contradicted—forget about turning the other cheek; the ideal here is to kick evil's ass. There is little in them for the religious right; they are socially liberal, big on female empowerment, and so inclusive they embrace even a trash-talking alien raccoon. The extraordinary success of *Black Panther* rests in part on creating a counter-myth to centuries of racist depictions of Africa, where it sets a hidden kingdom wiser and more technologically advanced than the wildest visions of Afro-Centrism.[9]

The irony of the military-industrial complex using its entertainment arm to produce a Hollywood revenge fantasy designed to rouse black audiences into epiphanies of racial pride needs no further expostulation. Yet even Spike Lee apparently drinks at the Marvel cooler these days. He saw the film four times and claimed it "changed everything, especially for people of color."[10] Christopher Lebron (also black) must have seen a different movie, one he described, in "Black Panther Is Not the Movie We Deserve," as "a shocking devaluation of black American men."[11] But whether or not black people were fooled, white liberals lapped it up. *Black Panther* not only did massive worldwide business, it received almost unanimous accolades. The ultra-liberal *The Guardian* gave it four stars, calling it "a subversive and uproarious action-adventure, in which African stereotypes are upended and history is rewritten."

By the winners, of course. Mission accomplished.

12.3.   VOLUNTARY SYMBIOSIS

> "In both neoliberalism and superhero movies, politics and
> big political decisions happen because the elite (politicians or
> superpeople or supervillains) make them happen. Society is ruled
> over by benevolent philosopher-kings (plutocrats or superheroes
> or both) who watch over us and aid only when needed; much
> of the superhero-movie narrative is devoted to litigating the
> benevolent philosopher-king's specific ideals ("with great power
> comes great responsibility"), and how they might work out best
> for the people at large."
>
> —KEITH A. SPENCER, *"Peak Superhero"*

The popularity of superhero movies isn't really anything new, but it is a magnification, or *centralization*, of a previously more marginal pattern of fantasy-identification via the glorification of violence—raw power—that brings the revenge fantasy all the way to the front and center of our "supercul-ture." As such, it may be that it is also revealing something that was hitherto concealed: that gods watch over our world, and they aren't necessarily benign (though they know how to make us think they are).

The super-heroic journey is a gross, over-literalization of the indi-viduation process—the means by which we become whole, autonomous individuals, independent from social and familial conditioning. The way in which it literalizes this process is most obvious—and distorted—in how the transition from ordinary socialized human to superhero involves killing or dying, or both. The idea that violence is necessary to break free from the Borgian hold of the group-mind—to escape the matrix pod of cultural identity—is perhaps evidence of how much our culture *depends* on a form of emotional and psychological violence to socialize us and impose its spell upon us. We need a nail to drive out a nail, as most overtly dramatized with the first *Matrix* film. Neo and the others pursued their liberation through the wanton slaughter of human simulations, with no concern that these simulations were connected to living beings in pods who die for real when they die in the matrix (because "The body cannot live without the mind").

Another aspect of this "liberation through violence" myth is how much socialization, while making us compatible with culture and society at large, also alienates us as individuals from one another, because it cuts us off from our inner, felt sense of *who we are*. And alienated souls—mind-bodies alienated *from* their souls—cannot connect to one another at a soul level, only at a purely social, cultural one. (Hence audience cults such as sci-fi and comic book conventions have replaced communities.) We are forced to use the language of culture and socialization to even *recognize* one another, and this secondary language homogenizes us and makes us all essentially the same. This was even literalized by how audiences (once upon a time pre-covid-19) huddled together in the dark to watch movies. Now they are watching them alone on their iPhones. The global village has replaced the actual village, and in the process, it has become an electronic simulation.

It's worth pondering what it says about us that, as we proceed unchecked on our journey into simulated realms, we're watching movies and TV shows—and playing video games—that depict extreme forms of destruction and violence, all for *relaxation*! The question of whether the brain knows the difference between watching simulated images of violence and real violence is one that has not been satisfactorily answered. It seems as though it does but also doesn't—which is why movies and simulations work at all. Watching violent entertainment is only exciting because we are able to vicariously experience the action, to feel a terror or a rage that's safe *because* it's simulated. At the same time, with those mirror neurons firing and the frontal cortex involved in working out deep, survival-related issues, there's part of us that really *doesn't* know the difference, because *that's how it works*. This is most readily apparent in the (exponentially increasing) popularity of internet porn.

From depression to erectile dysfunction, porn appears to be hijacking our
neural wiring with dire consequences. . . . The properties of video porn
make it a particularly powerful trigger for plasticity, the brain's ability to
change and adapt as a result of experience. Combined with the accessibil-
ity and anonymity of online porn consumption, we are more vulnerable
than ever to its hyper-stimulating effects.[*]

In other words, we can't get no satisfaction, and the harder we try, the
worse it gets. Psychiatrist Norman Doidge: "When pornographers boast that
they are pushing the envelope by introducing new, harder themes, what they
don't say is that they must, because their customers are building up a tolerance to the content." [12] Pornhub analytics indicate "that conventional sex is
decreasingly interesting to users and is being replaced by themes like incest
and violence."[13] What's more: "The perpetuation of sexual violence online
may cause real-life incidences to escalate."

The regions of the brain that are active when someone is viewing porn
are the same regions of the brain that are active while the person is actually having sex. Marco Iacoboni, a professor of psychiatry at University
of California Los Angeles, speculates that these systems have the potential to spread violent behavior: "the mirror mechanism in the brain also
suggests that we are automatically influenced by what we perceive, thus
proposing a plausible neurobiological mechanism for contagion of violent behavior."[14]

"Porn use has been correlated with erosion of the prefrontal cortex—the region of the brain that houses executive functions like morality,
willpower and impulse control." Damage to the prefrontal cortex in adulthood is termed *hypofrontality*, and it "predisposes an individual to behave

---

* "Watching pornography rewires the brain to a more juvenile state," by Rachel Anne Barr,
The Conversation, November 27, 2019: https://theconversation.com/watching-pornogra-
phy-rewires-the-brain-to-a-more-juvenile-state-127306 The definition of "pornography"
(as compared to erotic art) is a cultural one that is forever mutating. It is used here in a
fairly wide sense of: media expressly and more or less exclusively created, and used, as an
aid to masturbation, mostly devoid of any artistic aspirations or qualities.

compulsively and make poor decisions." As Rachel Anne Barr writes, "It's somewhat paradoxical that adult entertainment may revert our brain wiring to a more juvenile state. The much greater irony is that while porn promises to satisfy and provide sexual gratification, it delivers the opposite."[15]

Somehow, two aspects of existence that, at a visceral level, are as far removed as is possible to imagine—sex and violence—are on the verge of becoming synonymous for us in the realm of media-generated simulations. And if movies of mass destruction have become forms of relaxation for us, it can only be because, like porn, such images temporarily relieve, while in the long run exacerbating, a feeling of internal tension that we have already pushed into our unconscious. Simmering just below the surface, this repressed rage and *potential* violence—traumatized libidinal forces—make our daily lives increasingly anxiety-filled; and since we experience ever-increasing stress levels that *don't* correspond with actual physical threats but only with emotional and psychological ones (such as being electronically dissed on social media), we feel like we increasingly *need* the relief of escaping into violent and/or sexual fantasy.*

To relax us, the fantasy needs to be intense enough to drown out these real-world anxieties with a simulated, massively exaggerated version *of* them. And so we have more and more electronically-generated anxiety, including the anxiety of feeling increasingly removed from our physical environment and having our nervous systems electronically stimulated! So we need, or think we need, electronically-simulated pseudo-experiences of physical (violent or sexual) engagement with reality to calm us down! The global village is becoming a Roman circus.

To be clear, westerners *are* under constant threat even of physical violence, of a sort, but in ways that are difficult for them, for us, to consciously acknowledge, much less counteract. This is from "Why America's a More Violent Society Than You Think":

---

* In the 2003 documentary based on *Easy Riders, Raging Bulls*, John Milius spoke briefly about how, when he knew him, George Lucas would talk about how pornography was "the answer," seeing as how all that was really needed was "a warm room" and "people really don't care what room. [I]f he hadn't done *Star Wars* or *American Graffiti*," Milius suggests, "he would probably own this huge porno network today, and would probably be even richer than he is."

Americans aren't just at the risk of being shot, or their kids shooting each other—they're forever at the brink of losing their livelihoods, homes, belongings, incomes, families, health, and even their lives. Bang! Gone. The specter of ruin, just one step away, is relentless, and it never ends, tires, or changes.* Hence, the average American lives his whole life under an ever-present billy-club of threat and intimidation—of genuine and very real violence befalling them, if they're not "productive" or "useful" or "employable" (or even "healthy" or "strong" or "young") enough. [16]

In contrast, the extraordinary American, who never has to worry about poverty or foreclosure, is part of an even more dangerous jungle. Working, for example, for an "organization where it has become normal to sacrifice one's personal life and one's ethical standards to career success . . . people with deep-seated psychological problems or serious addictions often rise to the top. [In such a milieu,] *pathology actually is a pre-condition* for making the extraordinary personal sacrifices and ethical compromises required for success."[17] Pathology has progressed from being a side-effect of our culture to a precondition.†

One inevitable side effect of the constant struggle to achieve or maintain affluence (security), whether social, economic, emotional or psychological—and the ever-present possibility of either committing or being a victim of violence, or both—is dissociation. Movies, TV shows, and video games are *technological dissociation aids:* central to their efficacy is the use of shock, of simulated violence—most especially unnatural and senseless violence—to *trigger* us into a *latah* trance state, disconnected from sensory reality.

Related to this is the fact that, when we become desensitized to the consequences of violence, we have a correspondingly greater capacity for committing gratuitous or "senseless" acts ourselves. If, when we encounter violence, we dissociate, like Paul Bateson or the subjects of Dr. West's

---

* To say the situation never changes is an error, as we are all now aware, in 2020's post-covid 19 world, and the relentless specter of ruin grows to apocalyptic dimensions.

† The idea that "Wealth can be bad for your soul" is "not just a hoary piece of folk wisdom" but "a conclusion from serious social science, confirmed by statistical analysis and experiment. The affluent are, on average, less likely to exhibit empathy, less likely to respect norms and even laws, more likely to cheat, than those occupying lower rungs on the economic ladder." "Privilege, Pathology and Power," *New York Times,* January 1, 2016.

experiments taken to "the limits of human experience"; and if, when we dissociate, we disconnect from our bodies; we also reduce our capacity for empathy for *other bodies*—just as William Friedkin described a rush of killer instinct when faced with the bully. Without that capacity, we become closer to a machine than an organism, able to commit violence without remorse and without experiencing the pain of our victims. Like Roman Polanski, in his bid for total invulnerability, we become a hard, shiny screen fueled by appetites. We have un-passed the Turing test and sacrificed our sensitivity—our humanness—in exchange for power. We have gone "super."

12.4.   DREAM CATCHERS & CHILD CATCHERS

> "The origins of their shared universe would lie in a combination
> of corporate imperatives to sell toys and a creative process
> borrowed from television that put writers and their ideas in
> charge. [T]he people who thrive in the movie business today and
> the near future will be those who can straddle the line between
> giving studios and global audiences the franchise they demand
> while cultivating the creativity that cinema needs, in the long run,
> to survive."
>
> —BEN FRITZ, *The Big Picture*

If our fight-flight responses are constantly being triggered by (and for) our entertainment, and if this is what we think of as relaxation, it becomes necessary to ask: where does that imagery go after we turn away from the screens? As Pauline Kael wrote, there may be no way to exorcise these movies: since they stay in our system as simulated memories, they continue to operate just below the threshold of our conscious minds. So what is that language of movie violence doing, down there in our unconscious minds, to and with our bodies? Is this a less-literalized version of mind-controlled sex slaves, Manchurian Candidate assassins, or the *latahs* of South-East Asia?

Now that *16 Maps of Hell* is in its final chapters, it's to my surprise that I find myself approaching the strange intersection, or *vesica piscis*, between superhero myths, violent revenge fantasies, the aesthetic terrorism of the avant-garde, and—inevitably, inescapably—child sexual abuse. The obvious correlation—the element that's undeniably common to both ends of this dark rainbow spectrum, from innocent to corrupt childhood "fantasy"—is that of *power abuse*. It's here that our loosely mapped triad of organized crime, intelligence skullduggery, and the sins of the Hollywood elite all signal loudly, not as merely complicit with, but as dependent, if not founded, upon elaborately malevolent forms of abuse.

With absolute power, comes absolute abuse; but also, far more grimly and less fully recognized (mostly because of how grim it is), it is only via absolute abuse that absolute power can be gained. In such far-reaching psychosocial, psychosexual mechanisms, as mapped in my last book *Vice of Kings*, it's not merely that the opportunity to sexually exploit the weak and the young is a perk of power; it is that power of this sort is both consolidated and increased via acts of ruthless exploitation. As I partially delved into already, the intersection of child sexual abuse and Hollywood is darkly visible in the ways in which the influence of "progressive" art movements like Dadaism, expressionism, Surrealism, and postmodernism (some of which were covertly supported by the CIA and other agencies) has bled through into pop culture via avant-garde artists, musicians (like David Bowie was for me), writers, and filmmakers.

The sacred cow of academia, Michel Foucault, advocated the same "theater of cruelty" of the Dadaists and—presumably—of George Hodel. Foucault "followed the lead of the Marquis de Sade . . . one of his prime intellectual and moral heroes [though] Foucault felt that Sade 'had not gone far enough.'"* In terms of the individual, interpersonal dynamics of sexual and other forms of abuse, it's well known that, the more a perpetrator abuses

---

* A recent biographer of Foucault, James Miller, believes "Foucault's penchant for sadomasochistic sex was itself an indication of admirable ethical adventurousness. . . In other words, Miller attempts to enroll in the ranks of virtue behavior and attitudes that until fifteen minutes ago were universally condemned as pathological. Many of his critics have cheerfully followed suit. [For example:] 'sadomasochism was a kind of blessing in Foucault's life. It provided the occasion to experience relations of power as a source of delight.' [And:] 'Foucault extended the limits of what could count as an admirable human life.' [Or:] Foucault 'expanded modern knowledge in profoundly important and original ways.'" Miller offers "clear and nonjudgmental (even supportive) analysis of the tools and techniques of what he considers a mutually consensual theater of cruelty." "The perversions of M. Foucault," by Roger Kimball, *The New Criterian*, March 1993.

his or her victims, the greater his or her power over them potentially grows (Stalin and the chicken). But it's not yet even dimly understood, in terms of collective, inter-social dynamics, how this might work within entire organizations and communities—even societies.

A starkly obvious, easily citable example of the intersection between superhero mythmaking and sexual abuse, including of minors, is the afore-described Bryan Singer and his longtime collaborator, Gary Goddard. Singer more or less made his career via the *X-Men* franchise, while Goddard demonstrated an even more prodigious aptitude, as well as a predilection, for "childish things," beginning his career at The Walt Disney Company in 1974 as an original cast member of, and later directing, the Hoop-Dee-Doo Musical Revue at Walt Disney World Resort's Fort Wilderness. Goddard went on to work at Walt Disney Imagineering, where he developed concepts for theme parks EPCOT, Tokyo Disneyland, and River Country, among others. His first company, Gary Goddard Productions, was formed in 1980, and in 2002 he started a new company, Gary Goddard Entertainment (later The Goddard Group), based in North Hollywood. The company, under Goddard, created several large-scale attractions for Universal Studios, including The Amazing Adventures of Spider-Man, Terminator 2/3D: Battle Across Time, Jurassic Park: The Ride, Conan: A Sword and Sorcery Spectacular, Star Trek: The Experience (in Las Vegas), and Kongfrontation. The Goddard Group is known as "a themed entertainment integrator" and includes theme parks, resorts, casinos, retail malls, Broadway shows, and films. Besides his work with Bryan Singer on many superhero movies, Goddard also created the TV shows *Captain Power*, *Mega Babies*, and *Skeleton Warriors*, and directed the 1987 movie *Masters of the Universe*.

Clearly, Goddard loves children, and clearly he knows how to create environments to attract them. One of his victims was Brian Caflin, who, as already described, died on Berlin train tacks weeks after agreeing to testify about a Hollywood "Gay mafia." "In his statement, Claflin said that, in 1999, he was brought to the Beverly Hills home of Goddard, who had directed one of his favorite childhood movies, *Masters of the Universe*."[18]

Another, possibly even starker, overlap is the little-known fact that Jeffrey Epstein, before his fall from grace, fraternized heavily with the scientific community.[19] The Jeffrey Epstein VI [Virgin Island] Foundation plays "an active role in supporting neuroscience research around the world," and is

"one of the largest funders of individual scientists . . . dedicated to investing in science research and education throughout the world."[20] Via these
and other channels, Epstein funneled large amounts of his fortune into the
tech industry, in the pursuit of technological "marvels"—including the bid
for superpowers. As mentioned, Epstein was a member of John Brockman's
Edge Foundation: Third Culture.

> Edge consists of individuals who create their own reality and do not
> accept an ersatz, appropriated reality. The Edge community consists of
> people who are out there doing it rather than talking about and analyzing
> the people who are doing it. [Yet Edge's] full range of exclusive events
> would not have been possible without Epstein's largesse. . . . While he
> was bankrolling Edge, Epstein attended its events. So, too, in the early
> 2000s did Sarah Kellen, who is alleged to have helped arrange Epstein's
> sexual abuse of underage girls. [21]

In a 2019 article, the writer and researcher Evgeny Morozov described
Edge as:

> a perfect shield for pursuing entrepreneurial activities under the banner
> of intellectualism. Infinite networking with billionaires but also mod-
> els and Hollywood stars; instant funding by philanthropists and venture
> capitalists moving in the same circles; bestselling books tied to soaring
> speaking fees used as promotional materials for the author's more sub-
> stantial commercial activities, often run out of academia.[22]

Morozov maps Brockman's role in shaping the digital and intellectual
world, citing his correspondences with Marshall McLuhan, Stewart Brand,
and Gregory Bateson. He describes Brockman as "a true 'organic intellectual' of the digital revolution, *shaping trends rather than responding to them*"
(emphasis added). The idea of shaping cultural trends rather than responding
to them brings to mind Rove's gnomic description of the imperative of empire
to create realities while the rest of us stand around analyzing its creations. It
also raises the question of how, exactly, culture makers like Brockman shape
cultural trends without responding to existing trends. It is because they exist
in their own separate culture, looking down on ours? A superculture?

One future billionaire (now alleged trillionaire) and early Edge member was Jeff Bezos, who attended a 1998 Edge dinner called "World Domination, Corporate Cubism and Alien Mind Control at Digerati."[23] In 2003, Martin A. Nowak, Director of the Program for Evolutionary Dynamics at Harvard University, described Epstein as "one of the most pleasant philanthropists. . . Unlike many people who support science, he supports science without any conditions. There are not any disadvantages to associating with him."[24] Famous last words.

One especially relevant name in Epstein's little black book is Eric Ellenbogen, President and Chief Executive Officer of Marvel Enterprises from 1998 to 1999, co-founder (with John Engelman) of Classic Media, and head of DreamWorks Animation's television division. Another worth mentioning is former Marvel Entertainment Group owner Ronald Perelman, who founded Marvel Studios shortly before Marvel filed for bankruptcy, in December 1996. Apparently what appear to be as two, or three, or four, separate worlds may actually be one, as the science industry, sex trafficking and women-branding cults such as NXIVM, deep state machinations, and superheroes all coexist harmoniously, side by side in the superculture.

12.5. THE NEW ONE PERCENT (THE SCIENCE AND ENTERTAINMENT EXCHANGE)

"All that is relevant is how interesting is the story that someone invents to explain the origin of the universe. . . There is a struggle between two or three or even ten different poets. Who can invent a funny, amusing, or interesting story so that everyone immediately thinks, 'That's what must have happened!'"

—HEINZ VON FOERSTER, *Guggenheim fellow, fellow of the American Association for the Advancement of Science*

The cinematic universe (whether Disney, *Star Wars*, Marvel, or DC) takes immersive entertainment to a new level. It's exciting to people because it creates the feeling that the story is spilling over the edges of the movie itself, into other movies and thereby, potentially, into life itself. And a strange symbiosis between medium and message seems to be occurring here. The more technologically-enhanced our visual media gets, the more it becomes about technological enhancement, *per se*. It was only with CGI, for example, that it became possible to recreate the sort of superhero-action previously restricted to comic books and cartoons. As if in unconscious concession to this technological "blessing," the superhero movies that have been emerging have placed special emphasis on the ways in which new forms of technology are inseparable from, and central to, the emergence of these superheroes.

To be fair, this was always an element, whether the advanced Krypton tech that got Kal-El to Earth, Bruce Wayne's wealth and engineering know-how, the cryogenics that teleported Captain America from 1945 to the 1960s, or the radiation that created the Hulk and Spiderman and the space flight that created the Fantastic Four. But even so, the fact that Iron Man has become the center of the Marvel Cinematic Universe, when he was never close to that in the pulp equivalent, probably can't be accounted for exclusively by the casting of Downey Jr. In 2017's *Homecoming*, even the most "down-home" hero, Spiderman, was "rebooted" via Tony Stark's intervention, as a tech-heavy hero with an "instant-kill" function on his suit.

Once again, there are visible agendas implementing this "photo-synthesis" of fantasy and reality. In 2008, the National Academy of Sciences began the Science & Entertainment Exchange, offering a link up with Hollywood. One science advisor involved in the exchange, Dr. Clifford V. Johnson, a professor of physics at the University of Southern California in Los Angeles, worked as a science consultant on the *Thor* and *Avengers* movies. His job was "to study how our existing universe works," to help the filmmakers "build a different universe with its own rules," and "help make it consistent." The physicist braved multiple security checkpoints to get into their writers' room ("It's really like entering the Avengers Tower"), where he "tossed ideas about the kinds of physics that could resonate with some of the things they wanted to do with the story." To his delight, he watched the show and found that the writers had dumped whole chunks of this wisdom into the dialogue. In many cases, the science drove the story. "I see physics as storytelling," Johnson says. "To some extent, all of science is."[25]

The Science and Entertainment Exchange is a branch of the US National Academy of Sciences (NAS) that launched in November 2008. Its avowed function, as the official partnership between NAS and Hollywood, is to connect "entertainment industry professionals with top scientists and engineers to create a synergy between accurate science and engaging storylines in both film and TV programming." Its overriding goal "is to use the vehicle of popular entertainment media to deliver sometimes subtle, but nevertheless powerful, messages about science." This also entails "re-cultivating how science and scientists truly are in order to rid the public of false perceptions on these topics." (Superhero movies allow the public to see what real scientists are like—got that?) At the same time, SEEX "helps the science community understand the needs and requirements of the entertainment industry, while making sure science is conveyed in a correct and positive manner to the target audience."

One of the first acts of business of SEEX (E-SEX?) was to connect Alex McDowell, the production designer for the 2009 *Watchmen* adaptation, with the physics professor James Kakalios, author of the book *The Physics of Superheroes*. Kakalios was selected as a science consultant in part because of his ongoing efforts to use popular media references to motivate the public to take an interest in science. In the run up to the theatrical release of *Watchmen*, Kakalios and the University of Minnesota produced a short video explaining the science—the "science"—behind Dr. Manhattan's super powers. Is it any wonder Alan Moore took his name off it?

Ann Merchant, the Science and Entertainment Exchange manager, offers a garbled summation of the project: "The scientists also they know how inspired they were by the movies and the television shows that they watched as kids. [W]e're trying to create the superheroes of tomorrow, that the next generation of scientists that will solve all the problems." Apparently, the SEEX agenda runs two ways: not only are they trying to imbue superhero fantasy with a dab of realism and use it as a Trojan Horse to incept future generations with some "scientific" know-how; at the same time, they want to use superhero fantasy—or more exactly, the attempt to make it real—as a way to juice up dry old science. "The next generation of scientists . . . will solve all the problems" by creating "the superheroes of tomorrow." How exactly the creation of superheroes is going to solve things like poverty, drug and alcohol addiction, or domestic abuse, is anyone's guess; but that's OK, none of these things gets much playtime in the Marvel Cinematic Universe either.

12.6.   A NEW ORDER OF ATTACHMENT

"The human delusion lies in the belief that the human being is
the basis of reality and the final goal of the evolution."

—JOHN BROCKMAN, *By the Late John Brockman*

Jeffrey Epstein apparently shared in this Hitlerian vision of science
as the means of genetic reengineering humans into superhumans. Alan
M. Dershowitz, a professor emeritus of law at Harvard, recalled a lunch
Epstein hosted in Cambridge, Mass., during which "he steered the conversation toward the question of how humans could be improved genetically."
At a 2006 island conference,* ostensibly on the subject of gravity, "Epstein
wanted to talk about perfecting the human genome. [He] was fascinated
with how certain traits were passed on, and how that could result in superior
humans."[26] John Brockman made his vision for humankind explicit in his
book (first published in 1969) *By the Late John Brockman*: "Man was nothing more than a model, a technique. It is now necessary to construct a new
model, a new system of abstraction, no more truthful than the old one. . ."[27]

While the fantastic solutions being imagineered into existence are
only for the chosen few, the promise, of course, is all-inclusive. An event in
downtown Los Angeles in late 2016 was called "The Science of the Marvel
Universe," co-produced by The Great Company and SEEX, funded by
Google, Huawei, a Chinese electronics company, and the Alfred P. Sloan
foundation, a nearly century-old organization founded by the chairman of
General Motors. It was an all-day event with speakers and panels and an exhibition of props and artefacts from "the Marvel Universe." (Thor's hammer
was kept behind vibranium shields.†) One of the speakers was Alicia Jackson,
a former DARPA employee and the current CTO (Chief technology officer) of Drawbridge Health. Drawbridge Health is a medical company that
allegedly "developed a device to draw blood without pain and chemically
stabilizes it for transport." A blood industry, get it? The company was created

---

* Stephen Hawking attended, and was photographed on the "Island of Sin."

† This is a joke.

by GE Ventures, the venture capital subsidiary of General Electric, and is headquartered in Menlo Park, California. Blood-extraction-and-trafficking are the foundation of the creation of tomorrow's superheroes? Is that because they are equivalent to yesterday's Vampires?

Whatever the correct mythological update, Jackson begins her speech at the event by sharing how, ever since she was little, she wanted to be Superwoman. "In fact I *am* Superwoman as far as I'm concerned!" she crows, then asks the audience which of them believe they, too, are superheroes. After an awkward pause, she drops the punchline: "At least one percent of you are, for real!" Apparently, the new one percent has been announced, after which comes the full body of Jackson's inspirational talk:

> When the human genome project started over a decade ago, we began sequencing millions of individuals looking for those genetic mutations that make us susceptible for disease. . . . As we learn more about what genetic code leads to what superpowers, you can imagine a world in which we actually get to pick and choose. [T]his is a near future, when you will have the choice that goes beyond just what disease do I want to prevent, to what traits do I want to enable? . . . What makes a hero? It's the transition from the normal to the super.*

The dream factory is dead. Long live the dream factory. The lure of the tech, the promise of superpowers and heroic status and endowment, and the "price" (or perk?) of ultra-violence, are all key elements in luring audiences ever further into a form of "ecstatic" disembodiment. As these fantasies inspire the tech, the tech not only reshapes the next generation of fantasies, it also seeds the real-world aspirations: the "is" of technology determines the "ought" of humanity, as what is merely possible becomes desirable, and

---

* "The Science of Super," *YouTube*: https://www.youtube.com/watch?v=S_8Bs5X78aw I am indebted to Tom Secker at *Spy Culture*, and his pithy response to the Jackson speech: "A drawbridge is something you pull up to prevent access to your town or castle—in short it's a way to keep out the plebs and the bandits. That's not a reassuring image for a company engaged in the transhumanist science of creating superpowers. Though I guess that depends which side of the drawbridge you're on." Or which side of the eye of the needle. "ClandesTime 131," *Spy Culture*, Jan 7, 2018: https://www.spyculture.com /clandestime-131-science-entertainment-exchange/

finally essential. The transhumanist drive towards downloading or upload-
ing our consciousness, videogames, Netflix binging, Smart phones, Google
glasses, and most recently, microchip implants, are all different ways of luring
us into alternate universes—Bizarro worlds—that are increasingly immersive
but also increasingly artificial, corporate-created, and profit-driven.

In the meantime, as above, so below: the old Hollywood studio system
has morphed into corporate internet giants like Amazon and Netflix, which
offer a totally different platform. To give a real-world example, in the peak
period of the DVD market, Walmart sold DVDs at $5 *less* than the wholesale
cost, simply to lure people into the store where they would buy other stuff
(this is known in the retail business as "loss leaders"). People in turn bought
movies they had never seen rather than rent them from Blockbuster, for the
convenience of not having to return them. Roughly 15% of DVDs sold in
the mid-2000s "were never removed from their shrink-wrap" (Fritz, p. 17).

I cite this as a microcosm for the entertainment industry itself, and
even of the whole of Western culture: seemingly "artful" products are merely
there to lure us into maintaining our dependency on a system that's designed
to sell us endless crap in order to keep on expanding. At the end of it, we
become "Walmart People," batteries to fuel the matrix, and half the time we
don't even bother to enjoy the "art" anyway, because *just owning it is enough*.
As Ben Fritz writes:

> Amazon didn't make movies primarily to make money from movies. It
> used movies to draw attention, to increase engagement, and to dominate
> people's time and digital behavior so they would ultimately buy more
> stuff from the company. The solution [indie producer] Ted Hope had
> long wanted, one that would keep feeding intelligent moviegoers and the
> culture at large with truly artful cinema, had finally revealed itself. All he
> needed was a company that, at its core, couldn't care less about movies
> (Fritz, p. 200).

Like Walmart with its loss leader DVDs, corporations like Amazon and
Netflix make movies and TV *as bait* to get people to come to their sites and
subscribe. The corporations that make this product don't give a damn about
the quality of the product, about movies or TV *as an art form*, or even as a
form of entertainment. All they care about is creating brand loyalty: reeling

people into the Avengers Tower of their multinational virtual realms and making sure they never leave.

Nowadays, people wear not just superhero-emblazoned clothing but corporate caps and T-shirts with pride. Like cattle, they volunteer to be branded as part of the herd. Another way of putting this is that people may be offering themselves up for adoption *by* the corporations, who then become like surrogate parents. And if corporations are legally identifiable as individuals, what's to prevent them from becoming our legal guardians? Workers will take—are *already* taking—the microchip in the same spirit, because it shows loyalty to their brand, and because it facilities their movements, vertically or horizontally, within it.[28]

Underneath the shiny, electronic surface, the world is becoming a more and more terrifying place, directly augmenting our imagined need, not just for escapist fantasies, but for real-life gods and heroes to save us. Total immersion of the orphans of Mother Earth inside an electronic simulation of her body offers a new order of attachment for the attachment disordered. Once upon a time in Hollywood, like all fairy tales, has only one ending. Torture the women; prolong the dream life; live perpetually ever after.

13

THEY LIVE

13.1.   THE OVERMEN

"Terrifying visions were manufactured of what could happen to
people or communities if supernatural forces were unleashed.
Among others, the cannibal spirits in the forests of the American
Northwest Coast waited to possess uninitiated people who
then attacked and ate people in their communities, all vividly
enacted in ritual displays not unlike Hollywood horror movies
of vampires or zombies that threatened communities or even all
of humanity. Only the secret societies claimed to be able to save
their world."

—BRIAN HAYDEN, *The Power of Ritual in Prehistory*

As the preceding summation of "superhero science" makes clear, there
is a strange equivalency between the superhero myths and those
that drive Silicon Valley. Figures such as "Elon Musk, Steve Jobs,
Mark Zuckerberg and other techies are depicted in mass media and pop culture in the same reverent tones normally reserved for superheroics, as though
they alone toiled to produce their companies' products."[1] Just as Downey Jr.
based his portrayal of Tony Stark on Elon Musk,[2] so, in a reciprocal feedback

loop of truth and fantasy, Mark Zuckerberg designed a digital personal assistant he claims was inspired by the AI assistant in *Iron Man*.*

And if scientists and technological officers want to be superhuman, then movie stars are unlikely to be satisfied for long with just *playing at* superheroes. Sooner or later, they will want to get their hands on the tech, and start saving the world in real-time. Robert Downey Jr., erstwhile-drug-fuck-up-extraordinaire but as-of-2020-highest-paid-movie-star-in-the-world, sensing that rust never sleeps and his stint as Iron Man cannot continue forever, went seeking, like the tech-wizards of SEEX, a way to weave reality from fantasy. He found himself at a similar event to "The Science of the Marvel Universe," this one literally from MARS: the geek-friendly acronym for Amazon's new, premier, open-to-the-public "Machine Learning, Automation, Robotics and Space." In June 2019, in Las Vegas, MARS hosted a conference from "AI legends, astronauts, and other dignitaries," and invited Tony Stark to be a keynote speaker. Downey Jr.

> delivered a witty speech that somehow weaved together the history of the Marvel Cinematic Universe, the evolution of Stark's Iron Man suits, allusions to his own troubled history with drug addiction, the actual history of AI and its pioneers, with a series of jokes using the Amazon Alexa voice and Matt Damon—including a videotaped guest appearance by Damon [the star of 2015's *The Martian*].[3]

At the end of his talk, RDJ announced the launch of a new initiative called "Footprint Coalition." Its goal? To employ robotics, AI, and technology "to clean up the Earth and reverse its carbon footprint." Downey's fame, he confided at the MARS conference, gives him access to all sorts of people (including Elon Musk, presumably). "I was at a table with super smart, impressive, expert folks about six months ago," Downey bragged,

---

* "These men imagine themselves in the mold of superheroes, and society at large imagines them just the same—the screenwriters insert their tropes into their films. Do an internet search for 'Elon Musk will save the world' if you want to rot your brain with thinkpiece after thinkpiece about his singular brilliance." "Peak superhero?" by Keith A. Spencer, *Salon*, April 28, 2018: https://www.salon.com/2018/04/28/how-superhero-films-became-the-guiding-myth-of-neoliberalism/

"and the following statement was made: 'between robotics and technology, we could probably clean up the planet significantly, if not entirely within a decade." This plan—which has been termed "the coalition"—was promised to officially launch by April 2020. (At the time of writing this, June 2020, there has been no word since that announcement, suggesting another slice of Muskian sky-pie.) Downey stated that he was willing to spend "the next 11 years" working on the project, perhaps meant to balance the 11 years he had just spent working on becoming the world's highest paid actor, and on helping to turn the Marvel Universe into the most lucrative movie franchise in history.[4] Also, considering that Tony Stark dies saving the universe at the end of *Avengers: End Game*, "I've got to do something," he joked (?); "I'm unemployed."[5]

The process by which humans invented gods to represent the mysterious forces of both nature (the body) and the unconscious (the soul) has been techno-boosted into the postmodern age, as warrior-kings and shaman-priests and other cultural leaders and demagogues give over to tech-celebrities, and, ultimately, tech-celebrities playing tech-gods or tech-superheroes, or in the case of *Thor*, both. If the postmodernist, post-industrial age "is defined by a lack of guiding social or biblical myths," what do we get? Superhero movies—"a full expression of the sociological myths of capitalist empires."[6] Stripped down to their essence, these myths revolve around the modern myth of progress—a word that only took on its present day meaning in the early 19th century. The Iron Man needs oil (as well as a heart), and oil is the life blood of the Western world.*

✦

"Historically, the racist caricature of the Jew is of someone who somehow is simultaneously weak and yet controls the world, or significant aspects of it. So one could say that the wimpy secret identity was the Jewish creators' way of saying

---

* The concept of progress as known today was apparently introduced via early 19th-century social theories, specifically those of social evolution as described by (for example) Auguste Comte and Herbert Spencer. The myth of progress established the marketplace for the currency of individual accomplishment, making competition and status central to our sense of identity and self-worth.

that we're powerful, in an individual sense, not wimps, and
guided, individually and as a group, by the selfless desire to do
good. . . . It's also a comment on the immigrant desire, Jewish and
otherwise, to both be part of the society—be Clark Kent—and
also be separate from it as a being of superhuman power."

—DANNY FINGEROTH, *Disguised as Clark Kent: Jews,
Comics and the Creation of the Superhero*

In superhero movies, even more than in comic books, the fundamental
paradox (and the lie of the neoliberal meritocracy) is that anyone can become
a god. The oxymoronic nature of this ideal is mostly avoided by excluding
ordinary community members from the narratives entirely, *save as potential
victims*. For example, even though many superheroes depend on high-tech
(considerably more so in the movies than in the original comic books), they
somehow manage to make their weaponry alone or with minimal help: "the
labor force is invisible":

Superman's ice castle, Iron Man's suit, Wakanda's intricate mining system, Batman's gear and vehicles—in the real world, these things might
take decades to construct, and would require the collective labor of
thousands if not millions of human beings. . . . Superhero movies are
obscurantist: in presenting the myth of the self-made (super)man, they
conceal the hard economic facts of the labor that, in reality, such supermen would require.[7]

In this and in other ways, superhero movies are "the sustaining creation
myths of neoliberalism [and] the political equivalent of an immune system
response to a growing populist tide":

They celebrate and rehash the underlying tenets that keep neoliberalism's
subjects from revolting. These include the idea that technology is inherently progressive; . . . that police are ultimately good; *that some people
are born or created superior and that we should trust in them; that there are
benevolent rich people who can undemocratically rule over us*, a situation
that is made OK because they donate to charity sometimes; and finally,

that democracy isn't always good, because some people are inherently criminal or evil, and thus the commoners need strong leaders to control and rule over us.[8]

Like a scientistic cult, the superhero team—Avengers or Justice League— helps to reconcile the tension between the desire to be part of the community and the drive to autonomy, individuation, and independence (specialness), by introducing a *second* collective made up of superior figures, technocrats, or gods. A cryptocratic group of secret identities. The superhero team is defined by its power, its use of force for overcoming evil; this presents a problem of its own. Since superheroes only arise as a necessary solution for insurmountable problems within the human community, they are defined in opposition to that threat, whether real or manufactured, whether stemming from super-villains or some other transcendental menace (e.g., climate change, or as of 2020, covid-19). Without this external threat, superheroes have no function, no *raison d' être*, within the community that gives them their specialness.

The oppositional function of the superhero—I punch, therefore I am—leads to a negative identity complex that can be easily redirected onto the community at large, and indeed *must* be, as soon as the external threat is vanquished or seen as the illusory ruse that it is. In Western stories, the gunslinger becomes a potential threat to the community he is protecting once the original threat is gone. In the same manner, the community member who aspires to become *superior* easily finds him- or herself in opposition to the community s/he wishes to rise above. Just so cults tend to become increasingly pitted against the world, both from the perspective of the cult and that of the world. What's more, the aspiring ascendant may wind up in mimetic rivalry with the gods—the cryptocratic elite—who do not allow anyone to enter their ranks without severe trials.*

✦

---

* Is this what we got to glimpse, from the outside, with a case such as Robert Downey Jr.? Was Downey forced to undergo a horrendous rite of passage and be reduced to a virtual nothing before being given access to "the A-List"? If so, then perhaps a case like Heath Ledger's shows what happens when the soul in question lacks the necessary resilience to endure the tribulations?

"The establishment has so protected itself, unless you submit to the saturation indoctrination and adopt all its values, you can't get in."

—DOUGLAS VALENTINE

I don't think it's coincidental that, whether it's X-Men, Avengers, or the Justice League of America, the current successful superhero movies are more and more about teams. As an adolescent, I was particularly taken with the Marvel teams, and with hindsight, what I was really seeking, in my fantasy identification with costumed heroes, wasn't adventure, excitement, status, or power; it wasn't even freedom, though that comes closest. I was seeking a sense of belonging, for the family I never felt I had.

In *The X-Men*, to a lesser extent *The Fantastic Four*, and even *The Avengers*, it's not their powers that unite these heroes so much as their sense of alienation and estrangement in a world that sees them as a threat (similar to the Roy family in *Succession**). This is what first brings them together, and it's the affinity that grows between them that keeps them together. That's what I was responding to when I read those comics, and it's probably the deeper appeal of superhero movies today. As children struggling to make it through adolescence and into adulthood, with only corrupt or damaged living role models to imitate, our sense of alienation begins with our family but may eventually include—for a time at least—the whole world.

Our desire to be "super"—to identify with the fantasy role models of comic book superheroes and movie stars—is inseparable from feelings of anger, resentment, revulsion, and the desire to rebel.† Since the heroes

---

* It can be no coincidence that far and away the best TV show or movie I saw in 2019, the one that brought me closest to total immersion, was Jesse Armstrong's *Succession*, about the fucked up family of an entertainment magnate. One reason why *Succession* is so outstanding may be that it's a case of the cultural elite making a show about *themselves*, one that isn't quite so dressed up in the bells and whistles of custom-made self-idealizations meant to appeal "democratically" to the masses. (It's also written by a Brit.)

† An obvious "secular"—non-superheroic—version of a compensatory tribal fantasy for alienated teenagers is John Hughes' hugely popular 1985 movie *The Breakfast Club*, in which a bunch of misfits go from surly hostility to group-bonding during a shared detention, with the common adversary of the adult teacher, and by extension the school system, to bind them together. The superhero team makes teenage revolt the whole *raison d'être*, and so it becomes never-ending as a form of negative identity-maintenance.

in these movies are individually defined by their capacity for violence—by their uncontainable power—they can only be at peace together, can only work as a functioning family, so long as their force and aggression is directed *outside* the group, towards a common enemy. Even then, they still bicker and tussle. Stan Lee brought soap operatic angst and human frailty to the superhero comic, giving the characters "contradictory but essentially human qualities. [And in recent years], it appears that it is the Marvel postmodernist sensibility that has become pervasive in the comic book super-hero genre."[9]

> At times, destructive, evil super-mutants are rehabilitated and join the forces of good. On other occasions, well-meaning super-heroes are misunderstood or feared by the general population. Sometimes, these super-heroes unwittingly make terrible situations worse because they are unable to deal with their own personal insecurities. The archetypal Marvel Comics super-heroes, such as Spider-Man and the X-Men, have to cope not only with their social isolation as individuals and with *the constant repression of their desires.* They also must also [sic] deal with the fact that their super-hero *activities are met with mixed responses from the people whom they are trying to protect from harm.*[10]

Note the parallels between the italicized passages above and what may be the experience of the ruling elite in relation to us, the ruled. As already indicated, the superhero myth is like a childish representation of a dark sociopolitical reality that is, diabolically, both a collective ("bottom-up") attempt to see and assimilate that reality, and an elitist (top-down) effort to keep us slavishly enthralled *to* it. In a similar way to that of elite transgression described previously, "post-modern super-heroes are unable to fully detach themselves from the world that has rejected them." They are "unable to be part of the world that has instilled in them the emotions and desires that govern their existence"; but nor can they exist wholly independently *of* that world.[11] This means they have to find—or create—a new community to belong to, a *secret* one. Whether it is forming a transegalitarian secret society, entering a cult, or assembling a super-group, the common element is *initiation into a secret clique by undergoing whatever psychosomatic (often sexual), and (one way or another) criminal rituals of symbolic (or literal) transformation it requires.*

Central to the occupying mind armies of the superculture is just how far our corporate-created fantasies have removed us from a direct, lived experience of simple, mundane reality. One reason for this, besides the obvious (that fantasies are meant to provide escape), is that the people who create these fantasies, by and large, are living in a world so far removed from ours that it's the sociocultural equivalent of a parallel universe, a veritable "secret society"—or virgin island. In the past decade, we have seen "superhero culture's evolution from nerd culture to monoculture"[12]— all by apparent design. By forging a new social reality out of our dreams, our overmen may begin to walk freely amongst us.

13.2.   BRAINS IN A MOVIE VAT

"Only when conditioned reflexes have been created in a man and he lives in a collective myth can he be readily mobilized."

—JACQUES ELLUL, *Propaganda*

As an adolescent, the most exciting adventures I had were taking the early train to London (the sparrow's fart, as my stepfather called it) to visit the (aptly named) Forbidden Planet—the giant comic book store on Denmark Street, also known as Tin Pan Alley.* I would arrive soon after opening time and enter into that magical realm to gaze upon rows and rows of comic books and breathe in the exquisite odor of pulped paper. I would spend the entire day there, slowly and carefully selecting the few comics which my money could buy. I would travel back on the early evening train, looking them over lovingly but not yet reading them. Finally, I would carry my prizes

---

* It gained this nickname for being a location for metalwork and then housing numerous music publishers' offices, music shops and independent recording studios. The Rolling Stones recorded there, David Bowie hung out at the Gioconda café, Elton John wrote songs at offices on the street in the 1960s, and the Sex Pistols lived above No. 6 and recorded their first demos there. The Helter Skelter music bookshop was also based on the street.

up to my bedroom, climb into bed or curl up on the carpet with a packet of crisps and covertly secured lumps of cheddar cheese, to settle blissfully into the world of amazing fantasy. It was the one space I could fully disappear.

Now four decades later, the superhero industry depends on offering a similar kind of total immersion to children and adults. This requires characters we can relate to and sympathize with, become one with, so the movie becomes correspondingly meaningful to us. As already described, using media to try out different experiences comes naturally because this kind of imaginative speculation is how we learned to survive. Despite the committee-driven nature of these superhero fantasies, they do need to be sufficiently well-rendered for audiences to suspend their disbelief and forget the kind of nonsense they are consenting to. This requires that the people involved in making the movies *take it seriously enough themselves* to do justice to the subject matter.

Simply put: for audiences to fully disappear into a fictional world, the creators of that world must achieve—or at least simulate—an equal degree of immersion themselves. Only then can they infect audiences with it (mirror neurons). This is why even summer blockbusters, which are easy to dismiss as crass corporate products, generally don't succeed if that's *all* they are. They have to be infused with love, passion, dedication, and devotion—or at the very least, a cynically manufactured simulation of them (plus the right ideological message). This means finding and recruiting personnel who genuinely *believe* in these things, or at least know how to fake it. And the line between fakery and belief—as discussed with Lansdale's Philippines vampire psyop, and as we may be seeing with many of these high-tech "solutions"—is not always a clear one. I found this out for myself, when I graduated from drawing my own comic books and writing movie scripts as a child and adolescent to a multimedia attempt at "being the One" in my early thirties. That endeavor included a film (unfinished until five years later, *Being the One*), a book (*Matrix Warrior*), and a number of interviews and articles (including one for *Fortean Times*) in which I played the role of "the One." I was one of the many who were called, and for a time I felt chosen. Fortunately, I failed to make the grade and squeeze through the eye of the Hollywood needle (I dodged that bullet).

An example of a dedicated "geek talent" who did make it through the needle is Simon Kinberg, born 1973, the writer or co-writer of *X-Men: The*

Last Stand, Sherlock Holmes, X-Men: First Class, X-Men: Days of Future Past, Fantastic Four, The Martian, Deadpool, X-Men: Apocalypse, Logan, Deadpool 2, Dark Phoenix, and *The New Mutants*.

> Understand him, in fact, and you can understand some of the most important themes of the recent *X-Men* movies, hidden beneath the sound and fury of superpowered mutants battling over the fate of the world. You might even see these adaptations of Marvel's most famous superhero team as personal stories of his. . . . "The truth is that I find myself in these movies. I'm not writing them on an assembly line," he said. "My brain is always living in these stories, even when I think I may die from the flu" (Fritz, p. 174, 181).

When the writer's "brain is always living in these stories," there's a good chance the movies that result from such a fevered *symbiosis* will be, likewise, easily habitable and welcoming vats for audience brains to stew inside. This has been termed "narrative transportation," a phenomenon that manifests itself in the affective and cognitive responses, beliefs, attitudes, and intentions of audiences swept away by a story and "transported" into a narrative world that *modifies their perception of their world of origin*.[13] The theory of narrative transportation (a variation on suspension of disbelief) proposes simply that, when we lose ourselves in a story, our attitudes and desires adapt to better reflect that story—*just as if we are adapting to a surrogate reality situation*. During the process of identification-immersion into story,

> the reader [or viewer] loses access to some real-world facts in favor of accepting the narrative world that the author has created. This loss of access may occur on a physical level—a transported reader may not notice others entering the room, for example—or, more importantly, on a psychological level, a subjective distancing from reality. While the person is immersed in the story, he or she may be less aware of real-world facts that contradict assertions made in the narrative.[14]

TL;DR: When in Rome, we naturally start to do as the Romans do. The narrative transportation thesis is that: 1) "transportation may make narrative experience seem more like real experience." 2) "Direct experience can be a powerful means of forming attitudes." And 3) "to the extent that narratives enable mimicry of experience, they may have greater impact than nonnarrative modes."[15] Narrative transportation is dependent above all on our empathy for the characters within the story and the imagination with which the storyline is imbued and made real to us. Of essence to this process of "transportation" (suspending disbelief) is how our "world of origin" (i.e., the real world) becomes partially inaccessible to us, marking a clear spacial divide between "here" (the surrogate reality) and "there" (original reality), as well as one in time, between the present and the past.

The literature on the subject indicates that narrative transportation is *more unintentionally affective than intentionally cognitive in nature*—in other words, we respond to it unconsciously *at a bodily level*, more than consciously at an intellectual one. This brings us back, via a different route, to Socrates' "phantoms of reality" and theatrical mimesis, and to the cultural bondage of *latah*. As with these methods, the effects of affective narrative transportation increase over time (they are accumulative) and endure for longer and longer periods. It follows also that, the more we succumb to narrative transportation in our formative years, a) the more susceptible we become to it; and b) the more intense or immersive we require the experience to become.

The authors Appel and Richter coined the term "Sleeper effect" to describe how, over time, *the influence of narrative transportation deepens and leads to increasingly pronounced transformation of our attitudes, intentions, and desires, our perceptions and behaviors.*[16] And as transportation into a fictional narrative causes us to internalize the elements, perversely, *the greater our certainty becomes that our perceptions are correct.* The more we suspend our disbelief, in other words, the more strenuously we come to *believe*. Believing is seeing, and seeing is, to an unknown degree, *creating*. A 2014 essay on narrative transportation claims that the formation of immersive narratives not only allows for the mirroring of our reality but also *co-constructs* it:

> As such, stories could cause profound and durable persuasion of the transported story receiver as a result of his or her progressive internalization. . . When stories transport story receivers, not only do they present a narrative world but, by reframing the story receiver's language, they also durably change the world to which the story receiver returns after the transportation experience.[17]

We can check out of the Superhero Cinematic Universe—but can we ever leave? It's an invisible work force: the consumer consumed.

13.3.   AMERICA'S INNER EMPIRE

> "I hate superheroes. I think they're abominations.
> They don't mean what they used to mean."[18]
>
> —ALAN MOORE

Every star creates a shadow, and the brighter the star burns, the darker the shadow. The ironic counterpart to the dream of techno-salvation via the reification of adolescent fantasies is—a frequent trope of the movies and comic books—that absolute power corrupts absolutely. This truism is the very inverse of the neoliberal assertion that those who are bestowed with power will wield it responsibly.* This split between the hopeful fantasy and the historically grim reality is evidenced by how *The Guardian*, when not praising superhero movies for their progressive positivity, is warning us that they're spawning demagogic monsters. A March 2016 article, "America's need for superheroes has led to the rise of Donald Trump," argued that, in the wake of 9/11, while Americans were attempting to process the collective trauma, "superheroes [began] to rise to a reconfigured position in popular culture. Suddenly they represented the more complex and terrifying evil that America was facing."[19] And that evil was—the dark side of democracy—populism!

The *Guardian* piece refers to an increasing polarization "under the pressure of the dichotomous political party machines" that is culminating with a presidential candidate who is "more Lex Luthor than Superman . . . whose stock philosophy tends towards vigilantism, laying the groundwork for the

---

* This scenario is dramatized quite effectively in the first couple of episodes of the 2019 TV show, *The Boys*, based on a comic by Garth Ennis. Perhaps the first superhero fiction I have seen that briefly picks up the gauntlet thrown down by *Watchmen* and runs with it. After a couple of episodes, however, it settles back into the same old shit.

superhero movie to turn away from external enemies and instead focus inwards."[20] "Inwards" does not refer to introspection, however, but civil war. The article cites two movies from 2016, *Captain America: Civil War* from Marvel, and *Batman Vs Superman* from DC, both of which focus on "the clash between trusting the mechanisms of democracy and fighting against it to preserve a different—anti-establishment—version of freedom." Both these films "are steeped in the uniquely American pop-culture belief that vigilantism is sometimes better than the law." *The Guardian* illustrates its point in lurid terms: "Each time Trump urges supporters to 'knock the crap' out of a protester, he is triggering an urge to resort to violence, the urge that is so satisfyingly played out in every superhero movie."

What the article fails to address is how, exactly, this is anything new as regards American policy. And in case you think this is simply a standard liberal position against violence, think again, for the times they are a-changing. To paraphrase "Dirty" Harry Callaghan in *Magnum Force*—a movie that posited the same (false) dichotomy between vigilante violence and the state-sanctioned kind—there's nothing wrong with punching, so long as the right people get punched. Never mind that *The Guardian* would glowingly endorse *Black Panther* in 2019 because of its themes of "anti-racism." In February 2017, ten days after Lex Luthor had been officially inaugurated as POTUS, *The Guardian* was offering up its own brand of anti-vigilante vigilantism. After white nationalist Richard Spencer was punched in the face during a speech, *Guardian* journalist Nesrine Malik made a video that begins: "In principle it's never OK to hit anyone, Nazi or otherwise, *but . . .*"

Jon Snow's paternally bestowed wisdom in *Game of Thrones* is "Everything before the word 'but' is horseshit," and where Malik's "but" leads to is, of course, the whole *raison d'être* of her video. Her position is: "Some positions simply cannot be entertained, let alone argued about." In other words, "knock the crap out of protestors" you don't agree with. "Why should we be better?" she asks. "This philosophical Achilles heel is paralyzing liberal democracy." "Going high is not a suitable response." Ergo, low blows are what *some* opponents require.[21] But if the liberal progressives are agreed to behave no better than Nazis, why should we care which side wins? As of 2020, black-masked Antifa activists (in Portland Oregon, for example) are freely using violence in the name of combating fascism—not only against anyone who disagrees with them but against anyone who tries to report factually what they are doing![22] Donald Trump has become the monster that everyone on the correct side of the ideological divide is willing to become monsters to battle against. The divide has become a yawning abyss.*

◆

"I don't know, but I wonder if the root of the emergence of the superhero in American culture might have something to do with a kind of an ingrained American reluctance to engage in confrontation without massive tactical superiority."

—ALAN MOORE[23]

For the scientistic dream of superpowers to have any traction at all in the collective psyche—and to be a working business and social control model— it has to ensure that, as with any good movie, we suspend our disbelief. This

---

* At the time of writing (July 2020), following the murder of George Floyd in Minneapolis in May 2020 at the hands of a white police officer, there has been an outbreak of civil conflict across the US apparently resulting in a drastic reduction of police power, causing mass resignations by police (for example, "almost three-quarters of Washington, D.C. cops are ready to quit the force." "Nearly 75 percent of disgruntled DC cops," etc., by Andrew Court & Rachel Sharp, *The Daily Mail*, June 20, 2020: https://www.dailymail.co.uk/news/article-8442531/Nearly-75-percent-DC-cops-want-quit-NYC-murders-increased-70-percent.html). The situation has been building for some time. In Seattle, two years ago, cops "were called racist murderers by Socialist Seattle Councilmember Kshama Sawant . . . There was a 'mass exodus' of cops at the time. . . . Councilmember Debora Juarez says it's not just 'a few bad apples' in the police department. She said the whole tree is rotten. Fearing she'll be impeached, Mayor Jenny Durkan pushed cops under the bus and sacrificed them—and their East Precinct—to placate a group of protesters that will never vote for her and a council she will never control. . . This news will, of course, be celebrated by the very Antifa groups the city and activists pretend don't exist . . . . This is their literal plan: to wear officer's [sic] down until they quit." ("Rantz: 'Ashamed' of department, Seattle cop explains why it's time to quit," by Jason Rantz, *770KTTH*, June 10, 2020: https://mynorthwest.com/1932903/rantz-seattle-cop-quitting-ashamed-protests/) Antifa, meanwhile, is denounced by Donald Trump as a terrorist organization while leftist pundits deny it even exists. A vigilante proxy army of murky political and corporate interests, it is both easier to control and significantly less unaccountable even than State police are. And meanwhile there are the police robots, lined up in who knows what numbers inside military factories and corporate warehouses, some of which have already been deployed. ("Are Police Robots The Future Of Law Enforcement?," by Mike Thomas, *Built In*, May 30, 2019: https://builtin.com/robotics/police-robot-law-enforcement)

requires that it address problems that are either wholly imaginary or so large (*super*-problems, such as climate change or covid-19) that most of us cannot get to grips with *as* problems and so cannot gauge the validity of the proposed solutions. To illustrate this point better, for the remainder of this chapter, I want to explore some growing problems that the emerging new superhero "ethic" either ignores or is actually helping to augment. Together, these problems suggest a human situation of truly apocalyptic dimensions; and yet, as I hope to show, the Superhero, as such, is much closer to a world-ending plague*—or to the dragon of Revelation—than the Second Coming.

In a 2017 article in the *Nation*, Danny Sjursen asked: "Who hasn't noticed in recent years that, thanks in part to a Pentagon program selling weaponry and equipment right off America's battlefields, the police on our streets look ever less like kindly beat cops and ever more like Robocop or the heavily armed and protected troops of our distant wars?"[24] In the US, over the last 40 years or so, "as Washington struggled to maintain its global military influence," urban police "have progressively shifted to military-style patrol, search, and surveillance tactics, while measuring success through statistical models familiar to any Pentagon staff officer." This "new look" for an increasingly militarized police force is oddly congruent with how Batman, via the Nolan movie franchise, and in the interests of realism, has come to increasingly resemble a SWAT team member. Parapolitical urban reality and comic book fantasy have converged, giving birth to a dark dystopian vision of state-sanctioned vigilantism and domestic occupational forces, a vision of American society "embracing its inner empire."[25]

The *Nation* article points out that the individuals who join the military and the police are often "the very same people, since veterans from our wars are now making their way into police forces across the country." This is directly observable with "the highly militarized SWAT teams proliferating nationwide that use the sorts of smash-and-search tactics perfected abroad in recent years." In Springfield, Massachusetts, for example, "police anti-gang units learned and applied literal military counterinsurgency doctrine." The article makes some sobering comparisons of "police violence at home to our imperial pursuits abroad or the militarization of the policing of

---

* Written before the alleged "pandemic" broke in March 2020.

urban America to our wars across the Greater Middle East and Africa." It lists degradations, racial and ethnic stereotyping, illegal searches, equipment and trade tools, and torture. It describes the militarized police forces acting like an occupying army, as "St. Louis cops taunted protestors by chanting 'whose streets? Our streets,' at a gathering crowd."

If military police act like they are occupying an enemy territory when they police their own country—and still get to feel like superheroes while doing it—it can only be because their allegiance is no longer, if it ever was, with "the people," but with the overlords who provide their tech and give them their orders. They are choosing to be on the winning side, even as the gulf between the haves and the have-nots widens into a bottomless chasm.

13.4.   THE EXPENDABLES

> "Marvel declared bankruptcy in 1996 and spent the early 2000s
> loaning out properties like Spider-Man and the X-Men to movie
> studios for chump change. It had come up with the table stakes
> for what became the MCU [Marvel Cinematic Universe] by
> essentially betting the House of Ideas, putting up 10 of its most
> potentially-valuable properties—including Captain America,
> Dr. Strange, Black Panther, and the Avengers—as collateral in
> exchange for a $525 million loan from Merrill Lynch in 2005."
>
> —ALEX PAPPADEMAS, *"The Decade Comic Book Nerds*
> *Became Our Cultural Overlords"*

According to *The Guardian* in 2018, by 2030, "the richest 1% will own two-thirds of global wealth."[26] This rapid process of transegalitarianism, roughly between 2008 and 2015, has seen "the greatest transfer of wealth in the history of the world . . . Some $4.5 trillion was given to Wall Street banks with the American people picking up the IOU and getting little more than working ATMs for the misery."[27] Research from Oxfam claims that "the richest *85 individuals* have as much as half the global population—around 3.5 billion people";[28] we have entered, without ever consciously consenting to it, "a new Gilded Age, where an ever greater share of the national pie is held by the same families, and passed down from generation to generation."[29]

The remaining 99% of Americans, meanwhile, are dying "deaths of despair": their life expectancies "stagnating or declining [as] their dwindling economic opportunities spur them toward drugs, alcohol, and suicide." The casualties of the failure of the American Dream—or more accurately, the collateral damage of its success for a tiny few—now tallies at "more than 700,000 Americans—about the population of Boston."[30] Not insignificantly, perhaps, "nearly 90 percent of people who try heroin for the first time these days [in 2015] are white," and most of them "found heroin through prescription painkillers."[31] This is apparently all in keeping with the applied principles of neoliberalism, which "sees competition as the defining characteristic of human relations [and] redefines citizens as consumers, whose democratic choices are best exercised by buying and selling, a process that rewards merit and punishes inefficiency."[32] The proof? Amazon owner Jeff Bezos is now "a good candidate for first trillionaire"[33]—that's a million *million* dollars, enough to give everyone on the planet $100 and *still* be a multi-billionaire.

"Deaths of despair" would seem on the cards, then, not only for the old and/or the economically obsolete. A 2019 research paper, cited by *Time* magazine,[34] claimed that, between 2009 and 2017, rates of depression among kids ages 14 to 17 increased by over 60%. For ages 12 to 13, it was 47%, and 18 to 21 46%. Rates roughly doubled among 20 to 21-year-olds.

> The same trends held when the researchers analyzed the data on suicides, attempted suicides and "serious psychological distress"—a term applied to people who score high on a test that measures feelings of sadness, nervousness and hopelessness. Among young people, rates of suicidal thoughts, plans and attempts all increased significantly, and in some cases *more than doubled*, between 2008 and 2017 [emphasis added].

That's twice as many suicides among young people as less than a decade before. "[O]ne change that impacted the lives of young people more than older people," according to Jean Twenge (professor of psychology at San Diego State University), "was the growth of smartphones and digital media like social media, texting and gaming."[35]

Technology is designed to utilise the basic human need to feel a sense of belonging and connection with others. So, a fear of missing out [FoMO] is at the heart of many features of social media design. . . . People using digital media do exhibit symptoms of behavioural addiction. These include salience, conflict, and mood modification when they check their online profiles regularly. Often people feel the need to engage with digital devices even if it is inappropriate or dangerous for them to do so.[36]

Back-alley drug deals between corporate IT and deep state superheroes, marketing shiny pseudo solutions that make a few individuals unbelievably rich while consolidating a living hell for the rest of us? Dr. Nicholas Kardaras coined the term "digital heroin" in 2016, and while some critics considered the term, and Kardaras' arguments, alarmist, by 2018, "the Department of Defense had created a new designation for the death certificates: death due to 'electronic distractions,' where the fathers had been up for days gaming as their babies died of neglect."[37] Babies are being sacrificed so infantilized adults can live.

Erik Peper, Professor of Health Education, and Richard Harvey, Associate Professor of Health Education (both at San Francisco University), argue that "excessive use of smart phones bears striking similarities to those diagnosed with substance abuse" and that "the heaviest smartphone users exhibited the greatest degree of depression, anxiety and loneliness, and isolation." Smartphone use "begins forming neurological connections in the brain in ways similar to how opioid addiction is experienced by people taking Oxycontin for pain relief—gradually." The net result, as with substance addiction, is that "social media technology may actually have an adverse effect on nurturing and developing new social connections," causing loneliness due to "the absence of body language and other social cues normally associated with face-to-face communication." Not that we aren't receiving stimulation, but that all of it is coming from the tech:

The bells and whistles of the smartphone—pings, chimes, vibrations, push notifications—lure us in to peek at them by activating the same neural circuits in our brains that activate the flight or fight response— such as incoming danger from a predator. "But now we are hijacked by those same mechanisms that once protected us and allowed us to survive—for the most trivial pieces of information," added Peper.[38]

A term like digital addiction does have its drawback. As Dr. Jenny Radesky, an assistant professor of developmental behavioral pediatrics at the University of Michigan, cautions, "calling problematic technology use a clinical 'addiction' . . . locates the illness or problem within the individual, rather than the digital environment that is shaping the individual's behavior, often through methods that are intentionally exploitative or subconscious."[39] And if we are becoming addicted to life-sapping IT, it is wholly by design:

> The tech companies do know that the sooner you get kids, adolescents, or teenagers used to your platform, the easier it is to become a lifelong habit. . . . It's no coincidence . . . that Google has made a push into schools with Google Docs, Google Sheets, and the learning management suite Google Classroom. Turning kids into loyal customers of unhealthy products isn't exactly a new strategy. Some estimates find that major tobacco companies spend nearly $9 billion a year, or $24 million a day, marketing their products in the hopes kids will use them for life. The same principle helps explain why fast-food chains offer kids' meals: Brand loyalty is lucrative.[40]

Tellingly, the higher up the Silicon Valley social scale we go, the more concern about this there is, albeit only for themselves and their kids. Bill Gates, former CEO of Microsoft, "implemented a cap on screen time when his daughter started developing an unhealthy attachment to a video game"; it was Gates family policy "not to allow kids to have their own phones until they turned 14." Steve Jobs, former CEO of Apple, likewise "prohibited his kids from using the newly-released iPad." Tim Cook, current Apple CEO, admitted in January 2018 that "he doesn't allow his nephew to join online social networks." His admission came on the heels of "other tech luminaries, who have condemned social media as detrimental to society." Needless to say, this doesn't stop them designing it or making gargantuan profits off it. If children are being turned into living batteries, all the better to power the IT industry.

13.5.   THE HOSTILE TAKEOVER OF CHILDHOOD

> "The biggest reason for Hollywood's booming Comic Book Age,
> of course, is technology. Computer imagery can now bring even
> the most outlandish images of comic book fantasy to life. They
> are exactly what I dreamed about as a boy."
>
> —MARK BOWDEN, *"Why Are We Obsessed With Superhero Movies?"*

In one of his last interviews, Alan Moore (who announced his retire-
ment from the public sphere in 2014, though he did speak at Northampton
University in 2017) gave a more nuanced reading of his earlier comments to
The Guardian about superheroes. The "embracing of . . . children's characters," he said, "seems to indicate a retreat from the admittedly overwhelming
complexities of modern existence. [H]aving given up on attempting to
understand the reality [we] are actually living in," we have opted to escape
into "the sprawling, meaningless, but at-least-still-finite 'universes' presented
by DC or Marvel Comics."[41]

Such a retreat from the overwhelming complexity of existence may
extend all the way into an attempt, not merely to manufacture and gaze
upon but *to escape all the way into* a fake universe: a perfect copy of (the
most glamorous parts of) childhood, waiting to welcome us back. This
diabolic intersection between our tendency to dissociate from reality and
regress, and corporate and political psychological warfare, has been termed,
within the social sciences, "the hostile takeover of childhood."[42] And there's
no getting around the fact that (not counting 2009's *Watchmen*) Marvel and
DC superhero movies—*Guardian* raves notwithstanding—are seriously
under-developed and/or emotionally-arrested works. As Mark Bowden put
it: "Plot lines are an afterthought, and dialogue is often breezily incoherent. . . . They are formulaic, completely driven by commercial calculation,
largely written by committees under strict studio supervision . . . . full of
sound and fury—imaginatively costumed, star-studded, often well-acted,
stunningly crafted—signifying nothing, at least on purpose."[43]

With *Watchmen* in the 1980s, comic books were rebranded as graphic
novels, which, as Moore also pointed out, made them more *respectable* as
adult-fare. The superhero movie adaptations, with their high-production

values, A-list casting, and *relatively* smart scriptwriting, and with their post-modernist irony and self-satirical elements—most overt with *Deadpool*—are now allowing adults to groove to characters originally created for their amusement as children and adolescents. Many of these same adults *grew up* on comic books, as I did, and so they already have a strong affection for the characters and plotlines (or at least for the genre). The excitement of seeing them rendered in *real-time*, as moving images, incarnated by talented actors and *realized* via CGI and costumes, magnifies the nostalgic allure of bygone times. It allows these future-shocked, failed-jock adults to *re-experience* the joy of being a child again, to gaze upon marvels with new-old eyes.

This may also be by design. In a 2006 lecture by Benjamin R. Barber, author of *Consumed—How Markets Corrupt Children, Infantilize Adults & Swallow Citizens Whole*, Barber argues that global consumerism

> *seeks to encourage adult regression*, hoping to rekindle in grown ups the tastes and habits of children so that they can sell globally the relatively useless cornucopia of games, gadgets and myriad consumer goods for which there is no discernible "need market" other than the one created by capitalism's own frantic imperative to sell. [C]orporations are vying "more and more aggressively for young consumers" while popular culture "is being smothered by commercial culture relentlessly sold to children who [are valued] for their consumption."

Barber coined the term "infantilist ethos" to describe a psychosocial trend extending beyond corporate culture, and into politics and religion, where "dogmatic judgments of black and white . . . displace the nuanced complexities of adult morality." In their place, we get "sex without reproduction, work without discipline, play without spontaneity, acquisition without purpose, certainty without doubt, life without responsibility and narcissism into old age and unto death without a hint of wisdom or humility."[44] All this heralds what Jacob Bernardini, in a 2014 paper, called "The Birth of a New Social Figure: the Kidult:

> infantile adults, unable to take responsibilities . . . husbands in their forties who spend hours playing the same video games that obsess adolescents, fathers verbally and physically involved in fist fights at their

children's game, politicians and managers who behave like impulsive teenagers, young adults who live with their parents, watch cartoons and see in marriage and in parenting an obstacle to their independence.*

The "postmodern adult" Bernardini argues, "is by now characterized by an unprecedented infantilist nature" that is "constantly promoted by the media and tolerated by institutions":

Television schedules, for example, have gradually lost their original ped-agogic and cultural depth in favor of fun and entertainment; the movie industry is increasingly focused on kidult movies, sequels, remakes, com-ics and cartoon superheroes at the expense of the complexity of plot and dialog; in publishing one sees motivational books and novels apparently addressed to children or adolescents (think of the Harry Potter phenom-enon); Internet use, by adults, seems to be increasingly linked to ludic motivations, especially through social networks, while that of video games has assumed a nostalgic-escapist function that promotes the regression of the adult male to a utopian world of fantasy and virility, and to the consequent escape from family obligations and social responsibilities.[45]

Like Michael Jackson in his Neverland, Bernardini's kidult "lives an artificial youthfulness as infinite potentiality, he lives in a universe in which any valence to diversity between young and adult has been subtracted and [where] the lack of distinction between the two became a character-izing element." (The possible connection between collective infantilization and widespread pedophilia becomes starkly apparent via this diagnosis of "lack of distinction.") Barber and Bernadini's prognosis is echoed by Simon Gottschalk in "The Infantilization of Western Culture." Citing Frankfurt School scholars, Herbert Marcuse, Erich Fromm and other critical theo-rists, Barber suggests that the whole of Western society may be suffering from arrested development. What's more, our "failure to reach emotional,

---

* Jacopo Bernardini holds a PhD in Social and Political Theory and Research. He is an Assistant Professor of Sociology and Methodology of Social Research at the Department of Institutions and Society of the Faculty of Political Sciences, University of Perugia (Italy).

social or cognitive maturity," he argues, "is not due to individual shortcomings. Rather, it is *socially engineered*" (emphasis added). The "infantilist ethos becomes especially seductive in times of social crises and fear . . . its favoring of simple, easy and fast betrays natural affinities for certain political solutions over others. And typically not intelligent ones."[46]

✦

> "You know, I used to think it was awful that life was so unfair.
> Then I thought, wouldn't it be much worse if life were fair, and
> all the terrible things that happen to us come because we actually
> deserve them? So, now I take great comfort in the general
> hostility and unfairness of the universe."
>
> —J. MICHAEL STRACZYNSKI

Now that everyone wants to be a superhero, a surgically enhanced, socially uplifted justice warrior, the tech is offering a solution that's ever-more state dependent and corporate-based, and sourced ever more in fantasy than science. The message is this: technological transformation is to be desired, and it has little or nothing to do with tuning to our interior spaces, to the subtle life of the soul, or with connecting to the community around us. Since the universe is unfair (aging, disease, death), we are morally obliged to impose our own laws upon it, starting with our own bodies. The solution is to be found outside of us, in the tech and on the world stage, where the gods parade their latest fashion-apps, a place where shame is outlawed and pride is the cardinal virtue. "In an era defined by individualism and our individual identities, there is no 'we,' only 'I,' to paraphrase Ayn Rand or Margaret Thatcher. We have to do things alone, just as we are the superheroes of our own imagined story arcs."[47]

This creates an impossible, intolerable paradox for human beings. In a culture in which celebrity is the highest goal and everyone wants to be famous, whether or not we ever recognize the irreconcilable contradiction in this, sooner or later we must face the fact that, while many are called (if they respond to the advertising), few are chosen. All this leaves is to increase the fervor of one's identification with, and allegiance to, the chosen few, the self-made übermenschen whose station is, like the stars, one of high visibility.

In such an arrangement, to see is not only to worship, but to practice the sincerest form of flattery there is.

But by imitating a cartoon-sourced, computer-generated form of humanness, the ordinary celebrity seeker and aspirant to superhero status is essentially putting all his chips on a single unicorn, that of state science's promise to deliver a technology indistinguishable from magic (about as likely as finding Thor's hammer). To further cement this allegiance requires grand acts of *hubris*, extravagant gestures, impossible claims, endless demands for unearned praise and instant entitlements, and increasingly wild claims of imaginary (or delusional) accomplishments. Whatever, in short, it takes to *reify the grand illusion of our specialness*. The superego made flesh, a sovereign selfness, a solar hero star-eater who is I-sol-ate but at the same time surrounded by lesser planets whose only duty is to bow down and worship us, and thereby affirm our specialness.

This violent quest for a supreme-status sovereign identity transcends all questioning or criticism or consequence. It is accountable to no one. In faithful imitation of our benefactors, it is the aspiration of the tyrant, and it becomes of necessity more and more oppositional, not only to society but to nature and biology, to our ancestry, which is to say to our fathers, to God, and to reality itself (against our own bodies). All of this is presumably why the dark side of the superhero mythos is manifested via ever more contradictory and narcissistic rationalizations for *excess force*.

Perversely, we the dreamers dreaming the brave new world into being are also the batteries that power it: perpetual infants who must be endlessly policed and surveilled, both coerced and forced into compliance and servility, *for our own good*. As both evidence and instrumentalities of this regressive tendency within us, the massively popular superhero movies indicate a collective *will* to offer ourselves up for re-possession by the superculture. In return for our voluntary self-sacrifice, we get to return to a prepubescent (though highly sexualized) state, and become bricks in an invisible, all-pervading architecture of collective regression.

AI = the State of Assisted Infantilization?

13.6. CRYPTOCRACY'S COMING OUT PARTY

"Shane represents the radical individualism of the American
West, the ultimate self-made man. . . . What the narrative tells
the American reader or filmgoer is that this is what a true hero
consists of. The boy is starstruck by Shane; he wants to grow
up to be just like him. I imagine films with John Wayne or Clint
Eastwood have had a similar impact on the American psyche.
But exactly what is it that is being idealized? Shane might as well
have landed from the moon. He is a one-dimensional character,
bereft of all human ties. His horse and his gun are apparently the
only serious attachments in his life. He's a kind of atom, floating
in interstellar space—an ideal millions of Americans aspire
to. From inside the narrative, Shaneworld is dignified, heroic
(and very masculine). Looking at it from the outside, however,
it comes off as a species of insanity—alienation taken to its
logical conclusion. . . . 'Don't go, Shane, don't go!' the boy cries
at the end of the film. But Shane goes. He has, in effect, been
apotheosized as a god. To stay, after all, would have been human."

—MORRIS BERMAN, *"Shane," 2019*

One of the recipients of Jeffrey Epstein's financial favor was Ben
Goertzel, vice chairman of Humanity Plus, a transhumanist organization
whose goal is "to deeply influence a new generation of thinkers who dare to
envision humanity's next steps." Goertzel is also chief scientist at Hanson
Robotics, the company that created the "AI robot Sophia," as well as the
founder and current CEO of SingularityNET, a company that "focuses on
bringing AI and blockchain together to create a decentralized open market
for AI."[48]

Epstein also helped fund Goertzel's Hong Kong open source AI
programming group, OpenCog, one of whose goals is "to take the basic
intelligence of virtual avatars programmed for the screen, and transfer that
to a robotic structure." "The challenge in all of this," Jeffrey Epstein said in
2013, "is to create a robotic nervous system that can perceive concepts in its
environment." Other dystopian fantasies that Epstein was funding included

"Growing a 'brain in a dish,' the prospect of creating designer babies, and the possibility of detecting the first signs of extra-terrestrial intelligence."[49] Though Epstein was previously paying his salary, Goertzel told *The New York Times* a month before Epstein was reported dead, in July 2019, "I have no desire to talk about Epstein right now. . . The stuff I'm reading about him in the papers is pretty disturbing and goes way beyond what I thought his misdoings and kinks were. Yecch."[50] Yet despite his non-denial denials, Goertzel continues to work on the various projects Epstein helped to bankroll, and he is far from alone.

It should come as little surprise that this wonder tech has a habit of failing. This is assuming that our overlords are genuinely attempting to achieve their stated goals, and not merely inventing stories to get us to suspend our disbelief, invest our hopes, and carry on buying stuff to keep the wheels of neoliberal capitalism turning (in which case, they are succeeding admirably). Elizabeth Holmes' promise of "on the spot blood testing technology" via Theranos, for example, a "company valued at $9 billion from some of the most prominent investors out there," turned out to be "a complete sham."[51] Similarly Watson—"the IBM project that was supposed to turn IBM's computing prowess into a scalable program that could deliver state-of-the-art personalized cancer treatment protocols to millions of patients around the world"—got all of nowhere.[52]

Even more techno-utopian face-egg resulted from the Mars One Mars colony and reality TV show that is now known as "The Fake Mission To Mars That Fooled The World." "Four years ago [in 2015], you couldn't go a day without hearing about Mars One" and its plan "to launch their first robotic mission in 2020." Despite thousands of volunteers and a final list of the chosen hundred Martian immigrants, the company was "declared bankrupt as of January 15, 2019, with less than $25,000 in its accounts." It's since been dissolved.[53] Back on Earth things haven't gone much better: Mars-cheerleader Elon Musk promised to build "a prototype tunnel system under Los Angeles since 2016 in a bid to relieve traffic congestion." The project was "linked to the billionaire's futuristic 'hyperloop' concept of pods suspended on magnets travelling hundreds of kilometres an hour through vacuum tubes," and promised to create "a new kind of private, public and commercial transport system using special vehicles propelled on electric skates." In Spring 2019,

Musk's tech-vision was downsized, "in favour of a more conventional solution—a car in a tunnel."[54]

And so it goes. When the invisible empire acts, it creates its own reality, leaving us enthralled by the echoes of former fictions, even while it spins the latest episode around us. Silicon Valley, like Washington and Hollywood, is a town of confabulators. We, the people, meanwhile, are forever condemned to map the effects of causal agencies which remain invisible to us. That the roots of the modern techno-savior and tech-enhanced superhero reach all the way back to ancient religious myths is no secret. That they are also inextricably entangled with shamanic secret society rituals, as a mode of deceptive sociopolitical manipulation via elaborate threat-promises of supernatural, or super-scientist, forces, including terrorism, is less understood. In *The Power of Ritual in Prehistory*, Brian Hayden writes that

> supernatural power could also be transferred from one individual to another by means of "shooting" a crystal into the person who fainted or was "killed" by the shock of the power, but then was revived and eventually returned to a normal state by removing the crystal from his body. Supernatural power was portrayed as dangerous (rather like electricity or nuclear power), although secret society members knew how to get it and use it without harming themselves. . . . Demonstrations of this raw power involved the possessed person destroying property, tearing off people's clothes, biting people, and cannibalism (p. 46–7).

If a sufficiently advanced technology is indistinguishable to us primitives from magic, what of übermenschen—or ruling elite—so far beyond (or beneath) us we can't even comprehend how they operate? Are they indistinguishable to us from monsters? Is it here that aliens, gods, and superheroes meet and merge with zombies, vampires, werewolves, and other protean nightmare figures of folklore? Now, allied with technology, the State is assuming a similar kind of promethean grandeur, and a looming, draconian stature. The Vampire State is both the natural ally and inevitable nemesis (because rival) of the Superhero. Whether it's Superman or Thor, Wonder Woman or Black Panther, many superheroes spring from aristocracy (even Batman and Mr. Fantastic are fabulously wealthy): "super-ness and individualistic societies are interlinked; there will never be a superhero who originates from a robust democracy or an anarchist commune, because *those societies don't create individual hero myths*."[55]

While superheroes "are, by definition, more powerful and more import-ant than the state" (Spencer), paradoxically, they also *stand in* for the State: they represent the basic benevolence of *the super-power*, rendered as literal and tangible (and semi-human) reality. Their power is their benevolence, their might makes them right. At the same time, also somewhat paradoxi-cally—though this is consistent with the various law enforcement, military, and intelligence arms of the US state—they are non- or even *anti*-democratic agencies that use the ideology of democracy to keep the masses in their place, and do so without ever having to reveal their *essential allegiance to tyranny*. A benevolent dictatorship is one in which the tactical superiority of our rulers is so obvious and paralyzing that we have no choice but to *assume* benevolence, because anything else would be intolerable to us. Our rapt obedience then makes it possible for our dictators to maintain the guise of benevolence. All of this sets the stage for the coming out party of cryptocracy. "Indeed, most pop culture nowadays posits that there is no alternative future: either we will meet our untimely end soon (something foreshadowed by the current glut of dystopian art), or we let a few benevolent 'supermen'—be it Bill Gates or Donald Trump—lead us unilaterally to a world they control and manage."[56]

Force, violence, flamboyance, uniqueness, extreme (and absurd) assertions of identity, are all being enacted in ever-multiplying, ever more outrageous forms, via identity politics, political correctness, the assertion of feeling and desire over biological reality, body modifications, Antifa move-ments and extinction rebellions, and, the inevitable shadow, mass addiction, poverty, violence, suicide, and despair. The enemy of "democracy," mean-while, without irony, is populism: the people are not only unfit to rule, they are unfit to choose their rulers anymore. Trump is the joker card that trumps we the people, ushering us into a new age of post-populist techno-autocracy. When we can no longer trust human beings—either to vote or to lead—the stage is now set for the post-human techno-god to enter. And whatever occurs on the world stage, we will all be watching it on our smart phones anyway.*

---

* Possibly in lockdown, earning carbon credits for doing nothing but consume mass media and shop online.

14

THIS MUST BE THE PLACE?

14.1. DIGITAL APOCALYPSE

"As things fell apart, nobody paid much attention."

—TALKING HEADS, *"Nothing But Flowers"*

Where is it all leading? To an epoch of mass infantilization in which "civilization is not an ideal or an aspiration, it is a video game"?[1] According to a 2014 TED talk by Ray Kurtzweil, director of engineering at Google, we are currently undergoing the birth pangs of a brave new world of digitized post-humans:

> Twenty years from now, we'll have nanobots, because another exponential trend is the shrinking of technology. They'll go into our brain through the capillaries and basically connect our neocortex to a synthetic neocortex in the cloud providing an extension of our neocortex. Now today, I mean, you have a computer in your phone, but if you need 10,000 computers for a few seconds to do a complex search, you can access that for a second or two in the cloud. In the 2030s, if you need some extra neocortex, you'll be able to connect to that in the cloud directly from your brain.[2]

Kurtzweil believes—or claims to—that he can resurrect his dead father via nanotechnology, old DNA, and computer-harvested memories. He believes—or claims to—that we can convert our memories and consciousness—our "minds"—into digital quanta and upload them to the cloud, and/or that our brains will be linked via microchip implants to artificial intelligence by the 2030s. Elon Musk, for his part, believes—or claims to—that we are *already* living inside a simulation, and presumably that there is no longer *any* actual biological basis to our existence (if there ever was). These men are not warning us; they are promising us a brave new world of post-humans. The assumption is that we will all coexist blissfully once we are electronically linked up, and that having the power to create our own virtual realities will lead to the creation of a perfect world, even though the one we are living in (simulated or not) is about as far from utopia as is possible to imagine. (And they have imagined further.)

Yet so far, early attempts to create interactive virtual online worlds have mostly ended up being a kind of X-rated *Roger Rabbit* world of dark-web sexual possibilities, a meat market for humans to pursue their paraphilias and fetish-objects to their heart's content, anonymously and free (relatively) from consequences (the universe is unfair, remember, so consequences are to be avoided). Over 90% of Second Life "residents" engage in virtual sexual relations and "approximately 10% of their time spent in the online environment is devoted to cybersex." According to Second Life Wikipedia: "A big part of all Inhabited Land is used for sexual activities. This includes from small parcels to entire sims." PSE (Porn Star Experience) is a Second Life sexual encounter that needs no explanation. Common Second Life constructions are orgy rooms which "usually have far more male avatars looking for quick no commitment low detail sex. Some orgy rooms are seeded with sex-bots or with avatars to give out slsex." There is also a "family orientated beach infamous for being a meet and mingle place for those looking for *very young flesh*." And so on. Is this Ray Kurtzweil's and Elon Musk's idea of utopia? Or Jeffrey Epstein's? Is there a difference?

This fake world where everything is permitted (because nothing is real) has of course spilled over into the real world (AFK, away from keyboard life), for example via a rising demand for body modifications in which the physical body is treated more and more like an avatar to be customized to every last whim of the end-user. There may be a fetishistic logic to this: the more homogenized our internal, corporate-colonized, monocultural identity becomes, the more twists and turns we need to do to the external body self, just in order *to experience, and assert, our individuality.*

To give the most visible example, transgenderism,* along with some of the social trends mapped in the last two chapters, has seen an increase of over 4,000 percent in the UK between 2009 and 2018.† This involves injecting children with puberty-blocking drugs, some as young as 10 years old. Likewise in the US, there is "a growing push to inject children with drugs to stall the onset of puberty."[3] Many of the major corporations, meanwhile (especially the IT Silicon Valley kind, such as Google, Apple, Facebook, and Twitter), are fully on board with sexual transitioning, making it both a powerful ideological engine of cultural identification and a multi-billion-dollar industry. Perhaps related, in many states in the US, it is now a "hate crime" to explore gender dysphoria from a psychotherapeutic perspective, to the extent that a professional may lose his or her license for attempting to do so. This despite the fact that transgender identification (suffering from what was previously known as gender identity disorder) can lead to voluntary sterilization and double-mastectomies for children as young as 13 years-old.[4]

The desire to surgically "enhance" (slice bits off) one's body is a tech-given right, one firmly in synchronization with the transhumanist drive to

---

* Gender dysphoria or "transgenderism," the feeling of being in the wrong-sex body, is often (though not always) accompanied by the desire to surgically and/or chemically "convert" from one sex to the other (or somewhere between the two). This condition spills over into less common forms of body dysphoria (unhappiness), including racial and species dysphoria, which can also lead to surgical and chemical body modifications (Michael Jackson being the most famous example). Then there's "body integrity dysphoria," or "transablism," a desire to have body parts removed, the logical endpoint of which is the desire to get rid of the body, i.e., die.

† Stories about the massive rise of "transgender hate crimes" are also doing the rounds, though these statistics are somewhat more ephemeral for a number of reasons. Firstly, since transgender ideology and identification itself is enormously on the increase, so-called hate crimes may only be increasing in tandem with that. Secondly, stories about "transphobia" are often used politically as a means to stress the necessity of affirming gender-transitioning as healthy and normal (even for children). Thirdly, "hate crime" now legally includes things such refusing to use the "correct" pronoun or denying that men identifying as women are *actually biological women* even before undergoing any kind of surgery. This makes it difficult to determine the accuracy of these reports.

slough off the body entirely, and migrate to a solipsistic simulacra of existence. This tech-identity politics continuum is insinuated by how, in 2020, the American Dialect Society chose "they" as their Word of the Decade, referring to people who identify their gender as neither entirely male nor entirely female. The society, founded in 1889, has picked only two other "Words of the Decade": "web" for the 1990s, and "Google" as a verb, for the 2000s.[5] Biased, who?

Since the dawn of the internet, that's to say, since IT became fully embedded in our lives (or our lives in it), the language has been rapidly mutating and boundaries have been dissolving. To return to the most easy and pervasive example: pornography has now moved beyond an industry into something we may not yet have words for, a multidimensional space for instant sexual gratification in which the retailer and the consumer have become largely indistinguishable, where self-exploitation has become an assertion of freedom from exploitation, and any suggestion of consequences is deemed akin to Puritanism. At the same time, the line between sex and violence—as already described in the long-term effects of porn—has become blurred out via forms of pornography that not only realistically simulate torture, rape, and murder but are actual, real-world footage of it. Snuff movies have gone from being an urban myth to a largely unacknowledged but all-pervasive *fact of life*, without anyone really noticing—with the curious result that, even while they are now accessible to anyone of any age with internet access, snuff films are still being referred to in some circles as myths!

For example, Luka Magnotta, a male escort who apparently would do anything for notoriety, created a grisly real-life LARP-ing project that included YouTube videos of his "kills," and the mailing of human body parts to prominent Canadian politicians. Whether or not he had help (he claimed he was being forced to commit his acts), the videos started with suffocating and drowning kittens (as well as feeding one to a python) before graduating to the murder of an Asian gay man, in a recreation of a scene out of *Basic Instinct*. By the end of his online killing spree, Magnotta seemed to be committing his crimes at least partially as a way to bait the amateur social network sleuths who were trying to track him down via their Facebook group. In the process, he helped pioneer a new form of grisly participatory entertainment media—at least that is how it was presented in the (highly entertaining) 2019 Netflix documentary, *Don't F*** with Cats*.

The confusion between reality, fantasy, and staged acts in which the two coexist inextricably—including acts of torture, rape, and murder—is both symptomatic and causative of an erosion of our *desire* to distinguish between these things. In the age of the deep fake, it not only seems futile to question what's real, it becomes irrelevant. By the same token, when everything is permitted (when a loss of reality leads to a deficit in empathy and increase in cruelty), it is more and more tempting to believe that nothing is true. And through this swirling chaos glides the idealized selfie of the superhero, his-her hard body glistening with the fluids of former conquests. The ascension of the infantilized superego, whose shadow is the fully empowered, sexually insatiable, and infinitely engorging id-monster, gives a whole new meaning to "baby-boomer."

Perhaps the perfect image for this techno-dystopia is the afore-mentioned children of military men, for whom the Department of Defense had to create a new category for their death certificates: "due to electronic distractions." These electronically distracted parents "don't take care of the house, themselves, the kids or even the pets when they are gaming. They don't even stop to go to the bathroom, they drink power drinks then they urinate in the bottles and they are lined up under the TV they are gaming on."[6]

The logical next step is for the parents to start wearing the diapers.

14.2.   THE DEATH OF PARTICIPATORY DEMOCRACY

"An individual can be influenced by forces such as propaganda only when he is cut off from membership in local groups. . . . An individual thus uprooted can only be part of a mass. He is on his own, and individualist thinking asks of him something he has never been required to do before: that he, the individual, become the measure of all things. . . . Thus, here is one of the first conditions for the growth and development of modern propaganda: It emerged in western Europe in the nineteenth century and the first half of the twentieth precisely because that was when society was becoming increasingly individualistic and its organic structures were breaking down."

—JACQUES ELLUL, *Propaganda*

In *Revolt of the Elites: The Betrayal of Democracy*, Christopher Lasch makes a similar point to Ellul's above, albeit from a different angle of approach: "Having been effectively excluded from public debate on the grounds of their incompetence," he writes, "most people no longer have any use for the information inflicted on them in such large amounts." According to Lasch, it is community debate alone that "gives rise to the desire for usable information. In the absence of democratic exchange, most people have no incentive to master the knowledge that would make them capable citizens" (p. 11–12). Information overload, then, as the flip side of ignorance, breeds passivity, cynicism, and despair.

As Lasch points out, "democracy" means not so much "rule of the people" as *strength* of the people. He also emphasizes the need for people to be strong in something besides numbers: *to be competent to organize themselves.* Participatory democracy "works best when men and women do things for themselves, with the help of their friends and neighbors, instead of depending on the state" (p. 7–8). For people to run a community, they have to be self-reliant. Symmetrically, to develop the self-reliance and competence to run a community, we need the opportunity—the freedom—to get it wrong. I have experienced this first-hand in the last few years and I can state with confidence that *there is no substitute* for the development of individual autonomy and competence via sustained, positive interactions with a local community. And if there is, it is certainly not the substitute of "electronic community."

For Lasch, the decline of communities was inseparable from the failure of participatory democracy. People who live together in a community share experience, ideas, and knowledge on a day-to-day basis, thereby developing collective competence, even wisdom. This used to be how we learned about life as children: less in schools—never mind via comic books, TV shows, or Smart Phones—than in the street, watching adults on the sly, interacting directly with them, and improvising at being grown-ups without adult supervision. Observation, interaction, experimentation.

> Democracy requires a vigorous exchange of ideas and opinions. Ideas, like property, need to be distributed as widely as possible. . . . It is the act of articulating or defending our views that lifts them out of the category of "opinions," gives them shape and definition, and makes it possible for others to recognize them as a description of their own experience as well.

In short, we come to know our own minds only by explaining ourselves to others (p. 10, 170, emphasis added).

A few centuries back, Shakespeare was considered popular entertainment for the masses. Now it's *The Walking Dead* and *The Avengers*. In ancient Rome, the rulers gave people bread and circuses. Alone in my room as a lost adolescent, I had Marvel comics and lumps of cheddar cheese. How many people today seek a sense of well-being—fake community—watching Netflix and eating TV dinners? If the cryptocratic elite—and all of modern science and medicine—have done an amazing job at keeping we, the people, comfortable, it's safe to say it has nothing to do with benevolence or compassion. And if we, the people, are more comfortable than at any other time in history, does gaining the world really benefit us, if we have to lose our (communal) soul to do so?

The equation is simple, and deadly: to participate in the superculture, we are required above all never to grow up or connect to reality. In exchange, we have the "nanny state," a government that "babies" the populace by taking charge of all of its needs, even if it kills them. A grisly example of this: in the London Grenfell fire of 2017, 72 people died. The first report of the Grenfell Inquiry indicated that "the London Fire Brigade's 'stay put' policy prevented some families from escaping [and] fewer people would have died if the LFB had changed its strategy and adopted different methods earlier on during the fire." Tory MP Jacob Rees-Mogg concluded from the report that "'the chances of people surviving' the fire in Grenfell would have increased if they had ignored the fire service's advice to 'stay put' [and] that if he had been in that burning building, he would have left [because] 'It just seems the common-sense thing to do.'"[7]

Rees-Mogg received a lot of blowback for his remark and was accused of blaming the victims for being stupid. Infantile would have been a more accurate description, but the point remains the same: adults, with children in their care, opted to remain inside a burning building because authorities told them to. Being cut off from the challenges, responsibilities, and rewards of community life doesn't only prevent personal growth, it can be deadly—for both actual and adult babies. By the same token, when people in what's left of a community are too busy amusing themselves to death to grow up, community crumbles from the inside. People who never get fresh air or exercise grow flabby, stiff, hollow-eyed, ornery and insatiable. They become zombies, dreaming of being superheroes.

✦

"The individual super-heroes are presented as orphans, as having no real family support system. This lack of family contributes to an overriding sense of isolation and simmering, personal desperation. Their super-human abilities have compounded their marginalization . . . . As a group, who are under the guidance and tutelage of Prof. Xavier, the X-men and women have constituted a new sense of family among themselves."

—MARINO TUZI, *"Individualism and Marginality"*

As mentioned, I first began devouring Marvel comics at around age seven. When I was an adolescent, around eleven or twelve, I became especially enraptured by the original *X-Men* comics. The idea of a group of outsiders, united by their shared alienation, perfectly satisfied both my desire to be different—or more precisely, since I *was* different, to have my uniqueness appreciated by others—with an acute loneliness, the desperate, aching *need* for meaningful human relationships. It's really not so different now. The seeking of my "tribe" was something I over-literalized and over-dramatized in my twenties and thirties, as a result of which I unconsciously reenacted my formative, fractious family experiences (as one does). It was only in my forties, when I met a spiritual teacher called Dave Oshana, got married, and, a few years later, started running a small town thrift store with my wife, that I began following something other than my own personal preferences for "assembling" a team, and entered into something like a true soul-tribal experience. There isn't much that can be said about this, besides that it defies any kind of expectations or intentions about what "community" is.

In those early formative years, the comic book stories I immersed myself in may have helped me to plug into a profound longing, to stay connected to an intuitive sense of where I was trying to get to in my life, and in myself. But by the same token, by providing such spectacularly exaggerated, garish, and childish distortions of an almost infinitely subtler truth, they also led me, over time, as adulthood arrived, to seek satisfaction in all the wrong places, via epic accomplishments, heroic feats, superiority over others, occult elitist philosophies, shamanic stunts, magical doctrines, psychedelic drugs, even at times forms of violence, self-traumatization, and self-victimization.

The familiarity, even, paradoxically, the *humanness* of these comic book *übermenschen* was really what made them attractive to me, not their powers or their violence. This was demonstrated whenever a supervillain "crossed over" to the other side (as when the Sub Mariner fell in love with Ben Grimm's girlfriend, Alicia): it was always through an awakening of his heart. My guess is that it's central to the pleasure provided to today's viewers—especially younger ones—that these stories allow them to project their own dysfunctional family lives—their frustrated relationships, or lack of them—onto the screen or page. They need to be able to imagine, for an hour or two, how much more bearable it would be, if only they could be united with other, kindred souls, bound together in a common cause. Maybe then all our incomprehensible soul power could at last find a healthy, healing outlet?

14.3.   VEHICLES OF LONGING

> "If you are too much of a purist you might miss that the rose grows in the shit-field sometimes."
>
> —JONATHAN LETHEM, on *The Liminalist*

As I recounted in *Vice of Kings*, I was raised in an elitist British family environment, inculcated with the belief that "the people" were unfit to organize their sock drawers, much less society. On the other hand, since I rejected my own family programming, I didn't believe in the elite's ability to do so either. I saw democracy as a sneaky ruse to trick "the people" into consenting to slavery. I still see it that way. But in 2016, when my wife and I took over a thrift store in our little town, for the first time ever I found myself obliged to participate with my community on a regular basis. This meant serving the poor and disenfranchised especially, who, though they may not be the most damaged of people, are certainly the most visibly so. It became a daily opportunity to connect to other humans—to literally *serve* them—in the most mundane and ordinary context possible. If only in order to do my job well, I had no choice but to downsize my expectations and learn to see, and nurture, whatever was good in people, no matter how hard it might be. It was, you might say, a crash training course in humility and compassion, and in the essentiality of community connections. (Our entire livelihood now depends on the good will of our community, just as members of that community depend on us.)

To give a less mundane example: In January of 2019, I participated in a trauma-healing workshop for men. The workshop was by donation and involved a variation of Systemic Family Constellations, an alternative therapeutic method which draws on elements of family systems therapy, existential phenomenology, and, of all things, Zulu tradition.* Systemic Family Constellations aim to reveal, in a single session, unrecognized family dynamics that span multiple generations, to *dissolve negative ancestral patterns* by interacting with representatives of the past, and facilitate an acceptance of the tangible reality of our circumstances. The workshop took place in the garage of a house belonging to one of the participants, a father of four, of First Nation (Native American) and Irish-Scottish ancestry. Even here, the walls of his garage were covered with posters of superheroes—mostly Marvel, with a few Superman and Batman. (The supercultural virus extends its reach into every last garage?)

What I noticed very quickly in that garage space was how comfortable I felt surrounded by total strangers; not because of mutual nostalgia for superheroes, but from a shared acknowledgment of the impact of trauma on all our lives. Trauma victims (which includes all of us) are less like superheroes than spies who never come in from the cold. Sitting there in that garage, very much out of my element and outside my comfort zone, I found another, quite unexpected form of comfort. Partaking in a mutual need to acknowledge, express, and heal our traumas, I entered into a *human love field*. This might seem like a wild digression from everything that's come before. But the question is, how *do* we make the transition together from enthrallment

---

* *Zulu*—Michael Caine's break-out movie—was a recurring viewing experience in our household when I was a child. Of course, it is about Brits slaughtering Zulus, not Zulus performing ancestral healing ceremonies.

to a propaganda-fueled will to power of a cunningly created superculture to love and community? How do we follow the map to the exit without making improbable leaps of continuity or suspending disbelief? Is it even possible?

Perhaps the answer is that what we are seeking—the exit—was always right here, and all that needs to happen is an unsuspension of disbelief and a suspension of distraction? Maybe what we are seeking is not in technological simulations of transformation and empowerment but in the midst of the mundane: not because we decorate our garage walls with superheroes, but because a garage is not only a garage?*

◆

"The real evocation and mystery inherent in the comic form
is found in the white lines of border between panels, where the
imagination of the reader is energized and engaged."

—JONATHAN LETHEM, *The Ecstasy of Influence*

In a conversation I had with the author Jonathan Lethem for *The Liminalist* in 2016, Lethem made this observation: "as a practical matter, when you go back to the Marvel Comics, or any comics that entranced you . . . those comics can seem weirdly crapulous and thin; when you go back and try to revisit the exact episodes or sequences that meant so much to

---

* To give a more topical example of community in action: the *16 Maps of Hell* fundraiser was 100% independent of "Hollywood," the corporate system (not counting PayPal), publishers, editors, agents, and myriad gatekeepers. It was the result of a more or less direct (though mediated) interface with the future readers of the book. The shift of emphasis from the world out there, as a monolithic system of values whose favor I spent the previous forty years courting, to a small, organically emerging community of 200 or so likeminded people, was obvious and startling to me. The process essentially stripped the culturally-incepted goal of "fame" (worldly status via success) down to its most basic (I hope non-neurotic) components: a direct exchange between author and readers, with book and money as the objective, visible currencies, inside of which, perhaps, is an infinitely more valuable currency. The fundraiser afforded me an unprecedented experience of validation as an author, as well as suggesting a whole new criteria for "success."

you. And yet, they also remain charged as a kind of vehicle for your search."[8] I experienced this viscerally a few years ago. While writing *Seen and Not Seen*, I went looking for images online of the covers of UK versions of the Marvel comics I grew up on. I became so transfixed by what I found that I printed them up, in full color on cardboard, and assembled an album so I could gaze reverentially at the images. It was similar to what it's like to *almost* remember a dream: the pull of another world, another life, an intense *block of memory* that I could only glimpse peripherally, but that seemed to promise the dissolution of my present existence and the re-immersion into another, lost, vastly more enticing reality.

In Richard Schickel's *Conversations with Scorsese*, the director describes an almost identical experience when, in the early seventies, he "started to become obsessive about collecting" movie posters:

> It was part of this urge or impulse to possess the cinema experience. The posters promise something. They really do. A special dream. . . . it's absurd, in a way—you can't possess the film because you didn't make the film, and you can't possess the moment that the film was projected. It's like chasing a phantom. The only way you can try to possess films is to make your own films (p. 358–59).

Of course, what those comic books signified to me, like the movie posters for Scorsese, was *childhood*. The cover or poster image wasn't where the action was: that was on the inside. The cover was the door I had opened, all those years ago, over and over, to enter into that world. As my adult self, I knew that to try and re-read those comic books invariably—and almost instantly—led to disappointment, disinterest, even distaste. The *promise* of those covers was the closest I could get to recreating the feeling and the sensations from that time. To gaze upon them was like approaching a vortex that, if I gazed long enough, might pull me all the way *in* there and *back*— back to where I belonged, back to innocence. The vehicles of my longing might be crapulous and thin, but the longing was soul-deep and, most essentially of all, that which I was longing for was within reach.

14.4. THE SPACE BETWEEN

"The meaning and the power in so many of those comics, and in
comics *per se*, has to do with the vacuum, the space, the gutters
between, where your mind has to make this extraordinary leap
to connect: first within one panel, to connect the verbal stuff,
the balloons and the captions, with the drawing . . . there's a
leap being made, an interpretive fusion is required in the mind
of the . . . reader, to put those elements together. And an even
greater leap is required immediately thereafter, to jump from that
panel across the gutter—this apparently inconsequential gap of
nothingness [that's] actually a terrifying . . . abysmal space that
we just learn to ignore—to the next panel."

—JONATHAN LETHEM, on *The Liminalist*

Many of us have movies we loved as children that we re-watch as adults
and still enjoy. Because love is blind, the spell of nostalgia is strong enough
to blur out those movies' many limitations; in such cases, intense familiarity
breeds not contempt but loyalty and devotion. We say these films "stand
up," and in some cases this may be true (*Jaws* is a movie I loved as a child
that still seems flawless today). But, in many more cases, what we mistake for
"stand-up-ness" is more likely an overwhelming desire to *relive* the original
experience; it's as if our refusal to put away childish things trumps the sadly
impoverished reality. We suspend our disbelief. We recalibrate our interior
spaces so as to reconstruct our outer reality and (re-)experience transportation into the narratives. If ghosts need the living to animate them, the
experience of re-immersion in old movie love only works because we *regress
to a childlike state* and allow ourselves to be *re-possessed*.

Curiously enough, when Lethem waxed lyrically about this hidden power of our shared comic book love as a vehicle for a deeper search,
we hadn't been speaking about superheroes at all, or about the difference
between movie and comic book representations. We'd been talking about
the perils of cultural enthrallment, coexisting impossibly, maddeningly, with
the sheer inescapability of it. I had raised Lethem's own example of the New

York Mets, his favorite baseball team of "lovable underdogs," the backstory to which was *the threat of community-owned baseball teams*. The Mets were created as a way of countering this threat by awarding New York City a glamorous new, privately-owned team instead. Despite his awareness of this history, Lethem remained a loyal Mets fan. He had suspended his disbelief.

Lethem's response to my probes was that even cynical corporate sub-terfuges can—through the miracle of participation—transcend their origins and become authentic vehicles for "quasi-community," existing for other souls to have an experience of, as he put it, "commingling in an egoless bath of human affection for tribalism"! It was, he argued, a question of "people feeling connected just to feel connected." He wasn't arguing that the means were justified by the end, but that they were in some sense incidental to it.

It was at this point that I came back with the example of our shared affinity for Marvel comics, something we both knew were really kids' stuff, with the bloated military-industrial movies (which we both disliked) to prove it. Lethem pointed out how the parts within us that *connect* to those cultural commodities remain real, even if what they are connecting to, or through, isn't. In Lethem's unexpected response, he used the example of *the space between* the panels in comic books, as a metaphor for the space between human souls. The act of weaving together flat and disparate images and text with the force of our own imaginal desire, he felt, bound us together in *our shared search for meaning*. It was a vehicle that only our common longing fueled, and therefore it was our longing that determined the ultimate destination.

> [A]nd this action is such a form of human liveliness and projection and creativity that what matters in the comics, perhaps, is the action of the reader in enlivening all of this stuff. [W]hat makes us *one* at that moment is that we both committed ungodly resources of our own creative spirit to collaborating with those drawings, to make them into something large, and to uncover their implications, some of them of course accidental, half-assed, barely intended, or cynically intended, by the creators. And it's in that, in what you might call the formalistic urgency of our work to make those comics live, that we are *as one* through them. It's about complicity and the interpretive energies which become so potent that they become creative: they make a world.[9]

Startling and innovative—and mysterious—as Lethem's reading of the situation is, I think it can be applied, and confirmed, on many different levels, from the mundane (or immanent) to the transcendental. The original appeal and fascination of superhero comics, for me, was strictly metaphorical. Though I dreamed of meeting my Marvel Girl and joining a super-group, I also knew that these dreams were unrealizable in any kind of literalized—infantilized—form. Secret identities and superpowers were a gaudy dramatization of a *felt sense* about the *possibility* of a hidden dimension to my existence. They were pointing towards the secret life of the soul. I am convinced I was not wrong about this, even if I made the mistake of over-literalizing that sense due to my supercultural entrainment, and so succumbed to the counterfeit. We *are* vastly greater, more mysterious and magical, than we imagine—or even *can* imagine (hence the limitations of these fantasies, however creative). I am *still* seeking this lost aspect of reality. I think we all are. I think it is our one true love.

The greatness, the vastness, of the overlooked world of the soul is internal and eternal, not external or worldly/temporal. This is why superheroes *are* strictly for kids, or should be. Because in life, there are (or at least *were*) no serious aspirations to give those fantasies a foothold in our lived reality. Yet the line between imaginary-metaphoric and actual and attainable is not so clear to children today. Just as those backwards-straining, arrested-developed, nostalgia-soaked adults have clung to childish fantasies of empowerment, and even as the CGI movie upgrades have rendered them more and more realistic *as* fantasies, so technological advances (real or confabulated) in the world have rendered these fantasies more and more seemingly feasible *as* reality. What was once obvious, and relatively benign, metaphor, even to a child, is now a kind of deranged, doomed aspiration for adults, collectively dreaming—seriously—of being upgraded to an epic life of superheroic existence. And all the while, our mundane reality goes rapidly to hell.

As my brother used to remind me, unhappiness is the gulf between our aspirations and our ability to realize them. And the more epic the aspirations, the more epic the fail.

14.5.   IT'S (NOT) LOVE:
CASE STUDY # 13, DAVID BYRNE

"Niels Bohr distinguished two kinds of truths. An ordinary truth
is a statement whose opposite is a falsehood. A profound truth is
a statement whose opposite is also a profound truth."

—FRANK WILCZEK, *The Lightness of Being*

Poetically speaking, there's only one reason this book exists: ever since
I gave my soul to Hollywood, I have been trying to get it back. If I hadn't
found something of irresistible value and meaning in movies as a child,
adolescent, and adult, I would never have been compelled, later in life, to
identify all the ways in which the superculture is not what it seems, is somehow inherently corrupt, *bad for my soul.*

Obviously (I hope it's obvious), there's a contradiction in this, if only
for the overly literal-minded who see everything in square screen black and
white, never in technicolor widescreen. Even if all of my writing on the subject has been precisely aimed at separating them out, the evil of Hollywood
culture is, in a certain sense, inseparable from the good. And now, as we
near the end(?) of this many-book process, I feel ready to reclaim what is
good, having identified all the ways in which it became—and always was—
inextricably tangled up in what is not-good.

As mentioned, one of my deepest and most lasting cultural influences
was Talking Heads. When I first write this, it is August 1, 2019, about six
weeks after attending a Dave Oshana spiritual retreat in Finland. Once
again, I confirmed there a strong desire to shift my orientation *away* from
darkness, into the light, away from fear, dread, and suspicion, towards love,
joy, and radical acceptance. And the question again arose: after decades of
work in the deconstruction business, where the focus has *always* been on the
dark side of the psyche and society, as what is most in need of exposing and
dissolving—*Neti Neti*, here we go again˙—can I somehow bring this new
orientation to the worksite without upsetting the crew overmuch?

---

* "Not this, not that," the basis of the spiritual path to reject everything that is not truth
until only truth remains. Roughly.

Shortly after returning from the retreat, I wrote a blogpost about my experiences. It was about connecting to other souls as a means to discover the truth of who we are. It was about finding love via acts of self-expression, and deepening self-expression through receiving and feeling love. I referred in the post to this "new feeling," which was what the blogpost was about, and right away I realized it was the title of an early Talking Heads song—introduced on *The Name of This Band is Talking Heads* with, "The name of this song is 'New Feeling,' and that's what it's about." In the same moment, it occurred to me how apt the lyrics of the song were. They go like this:

> *It's not . . . yesterday . . . anymore*
> *I go visiting. I talk loud*
> *I try to make myself clear*
> *In front . . . of a face . . . that's nearer*
> *Than it's ever been before*
> *Not this close before*
> *Nearer than before*
> *Not this close before*
> *It is . . . is a million . . . years ago*
> *I hear music, and it . . . sounds like bells*
> *I feel like my head is high*
> *I wish . . . I could meet . . . everyone*
> *Meet them all over again*
> *Bring them up to my room*
> *Meet them all over again*
> *Everyone's up in my room*

One of the tasks Dave (Oshana, not Byrne) gave me after the retreat was to look back over my life and, rather than seeking evidence of crime, conspiracy, and abuse, identify interventions of the angelic kind. I knew what he meant: I have always felt blessed, watched over, supported, by something unseen, perhaps in exact proportion to how I have also felt cursed, persecuted, oppressed by the visible world. In a certain sense, the acute awareness of the latter has allowed me to also acknowledge the former. Because without it, faced with such odds, I might have truly been lost.

I wondered if something was coming more fully into awareness that had first been seeded decades before, clearly represented by this song (a song I first heard around the age of 16), and by others like it. I told my wife about it, since she also has a lifelong affection and affinity for Talking Heads (and, along with Lethem, we both especially treasured *Fear of Music*). It wasn't something we had bonded over, so much as one stitch of a golden thread of confirmations that we *were* kindred spirits. As far back as our teenage years, we had been tuning to the same station; we were souls seeking one another without even knowing, except remotely, what we were seeking.

We talked about how David Byrne, during those early years, was, like we had been, lonely, geeky, socially awkward, painfully shy, maybe even cold and detached—yet artistically gifted. In order to develop his potential for creative self-expression, he formed a band in 1975, joining forces with Tina Weymouth and Chris Frantz, then later Jerry Harrison. Like the X-Men, he found a surrogate family of outsiders (they were first called The Artistics, and were quickly nicknamed The Autistics). From interacting with the other musicians, Byrne began to open up and slowly emerge from his autistic shell. It was a slow process of moving from not-seen to seen. "It might take ten years or so"—and it did: his coming out party was *Stop Making Sense*, in 1984.

✦

"When my love
Stands next to your love,
I can't define love
When it's not love.
It's not love.
It's not love.
Which is my face
Which is a building
Which is on fire"

—TALKING HEADS, *"Love --> Building on Fire"*

As mentioned, before Bowie, before Byrne, my first musical identification figure was, the reincarnated Egyptian pharaoh himself, Elvis. I inherited a love of Elvis from my sister, but you would never know it by how wildly my passion burned. I remember saying, to whoever would listen, probably my sister and mother but not my brother, that, if I ever got a chance to see Elvis (he died when I was ten), I would dress up as a girl and push to the front of the stage so he would kiss me. Talk about identity confusion.

When I was eight or nine and Elvis had not yet left the building, I would dance to his songs and sing the words. The two songs I particularly burned to were "Burning Love" and a lesser known song called "I'll Take love" (it first appears in the movie *Easy Come, Easy Go*, released the year I was born). I can recall the intensity with which I sang the words, dancing wildly in front of the stereo. The words I put the most energy into were these: "So let them *have* their wealth and fame! Eat caviar and drink champagne!"* I remember that I sang these lines with venom and scorn, but also joy. I was the child of enormous wealth, and I never received much love from my father—or even from my mother that wasn't toxic—so it's no wonder I expressed angry satisfaction and defiance singing these lines. Elvis understood, at least. And did he ever! (Talk about toxic mother-love.)

Elvis' brand of song was *all* about love, but he himself drifted further and further from it, to die alone—legend has it—on his toilet eating a peanut butter and ice cream sandwich (or whatever it was). If Elvis represents the dark side of culture, that pretends to be something majestic and romantic and glorious even as it's spiraling down the toilet into darkness, despair, and isolation—the hell of an inability to love—then Talking Heads represented the other end of the spectrum. It was a place where the irony was so thick there was no chance of ever mistaking anything for sentimentality. When they sang about Heaven, it was lovely and haunting but laced with *ennui*. When they sang about love, they called it "not-love" (the love that can be spoken is not true love). Byrne was like Elvis turned inside out, the alienation was on the outside, the romance and the passion safely protected within. But for those who were able to tune in, the message, however distant and strange, was clear.

---

* "Some people think that their success/Is all they need for happiness/But there's a pleasure, I think more of/Measure for measure, I'll take love/Pound for pound, oh yeah, and ounce for ounce /Love is all that really counts!/So let them have their wealth and fame!/ Eat caviar and drink champagne!/You're all the treasure I'm dreaming of/Measure for measure, I'll take love!" (Elvis, "I'll Take Love")

A crucial element of this transmission is in how Byrne learned to express himself *in new ways* through the lyrics of the songs he wrote. He wrote intellectually stimulating (autistic) songs about how he was *feeling*, as a way to explore those feelings and express them in a manner that felt safe to him: first of all to the other band members, and then later to audiences. It's unlikely Byrne would have been comfortable expressing his new feelings directly, so instead he put them into the lyrics of the songs. But of course, the other band members would have known, or at least intuited, that he was singing about them and that, therefore, he was also singing *to* them. This fact need never be openly acknowledged for the love to be communicated, and delivered.

> *But now I'm speaking out*
> *Speaking about my friends*
> *Now I'm speaking out*
> *Thinking about my friends*

One of the ways Byrne disguised the love he was daring to express in these words was, with the collaboration of the band, by nesting them in quirky, jerky melodies that were the very inverse of emotional or sentimental. Because of this, when Talking Heads wrote and performed "Naïve Melody" in 1983, for the album *Speaking in Tongues* and the subsequent *Stop Making Sense* tour, it was referred to as Byrne's first love song. Yet all the time he had been wearing his heart on his album sleeve. Seen and not seen.

Nonetheless, for me, it was the words—of *Fear of Music*—that first got under my skin and led to my decades-long, one-sided para-romance with Byrne. I even recall where I was when the penny first dropped: I was by the side of a lake (Ullswater) outside our tent while camping in the Lake District with my best friend at that time, Justin. We were around 15 years old. He had heard the album too, independently of me, and somehow we wound up repeating the words of "Cities":

> *Think of London. A small city.*
> *Dark. Dark in the daytime.*
> *People sleep. Sleep in the daytime.*
> *If they want to. If they want to.*

We both laughed in a mixture of delight and bemusement at the strangeness of the words; after that, as if a shared passion had been sealed, a mutual vehicle of longing discovered, we listened to all the Talking Heads songs both together and apart. (I even bought all the bootlegs I could find when I went to London.) Byrne's lyrics became a constant opportunity and challenge for quoting, whenever circumstances allowed. This was often, because Byrne's lyrics (especially from the first four great albums) are like clippings of mundane conversation that he plucked from everyday life, then inserted into the band's jagged, edgy musical arrangements. The uniquely mundane flavor of the lyrics made the songs stranger and more otherworldly, and the music made the words seem almost surreally mundane. It was an irresistible challenge to find opportunities to return the words to their natural habitat, that of mundane conversation. "You look exhausted: I'll do some driving; you ought to get you some sleep."

What moves me still about Talking Heads' and David Byrne's early output is, once again, how it switches or reverses the focus, and the allegiance, away from the grandiose, the epic, the extravagant, and back to where we actually *are*—where the body *is*—to the mundane, ordinary, everyday banality of existence—but in such a way as to demolish, gently and humorously, the illusion of banality. Rather than trying to manufacture or consume visions of epic splendor that allow us to disappear into a dissociative fantasy, the artistry is in perceiving the ordinary in extraordinary ways and so moving the emphasis from what's being perceived—the everyday, always with us—to that which is doing the perceiving. If beauty is in the eye of the beholder, then what makes art "art," is not the artist but ourselves.

At the same time as those early Talking Heads songs seemed to collide with the most staggeringly profane aspects of existence—not to flinch from the worldliness of the world—they also shimmered with Byrne's strange autistic intelligence. It was the language of alienation, celebrated (they were songs, after all). Byrne wrote lyrics like you would imagine an alien observing human customs would speak—or an angel. It was love, in a non-ordinary way.

14.6. BAND ON FIRE

"And now I'm busy . . . busy again."

—TALKING HEADS, *"New Feeling"*

The act of jamming together, of working on the songs, of creating *via the development and observation of human relationships*, was Byrne's way of discovering and then acknowledging this new feeling—perhaps even of discovering it *by* acknowledging it. The love, affection, and affinity growing between himself and the other band members became the substance of the songs. In a certain sense, then, all the songs were about this *experience—the new feeling—of making songs together*. Kindred souls had found each other in a world of darkness and alienation. Now they were finding new ways to experience, and *express*, aspects of themselves previously unknown to them. By *being together* creatively, the band members were reflecting one another across a social, cultural *abysm*, drawing out new forms of being from one another, new refractions of light, in the call and response process of "jamming."

This—a band jamming together until they are able to "stop making sense" (and start making love)—is both a metaphor *for* and a literalization *of* the poet Dante's description of God's love: the way isolate souls discover connections and correspondences between them, the way they become aware of existing as part of *a network of souls*. This shared discovery is like the Christian idea of "Heaven," where bands of angels sing the only song there is, forever.

The journey of one lonely soul connecting up with kindred spirits and so discovering his "soul team"—which I sensed when I first heard *Fear of Music*—was even visually enacted in *Stop Making Sense*, the 1984 Talking Heads concert movie directed by Jonathan Demme, which I first saw in London, at age 17. The film begins with Byrne, alone on the stage, playing "Psycho Killer" with a boom box, the solitary adolescent alone in his room. He is joined for the next set by Tina Weymouth, to sing "Heaven," after which they are joined by Weymouth's partner, Chris Frantz, for "Thank You For Sending Me an Angel." Finally Jerry Harrison joins them and they play "Found a Job." The psycho killer had a taste of heaven through his music, was sent an angel, or three, to love and support him, then found a job: a

mission in life to create his own TV shows instead of imbibing the crap provided by the culture. Think of Bob and Judy: they're happy as can be.

After that, the core-four are joined by the five unofficial African members, who came aboard as the band's musical style evolved, making up nine in
all. Even the crew is made visible towards the end of the film; and then, last of
all, the audience is seen for the final encore ("Cross-eyed and Painless"). With
the release of the film, this audience expanded to include the whole world.
The individual discovering himself via the gradual, "tentative decisions" it
requires to move slowly away from isolation towards connection, eventually
connects to the whole world. And by connecting to the world he discovers
himself, because he discovers that the world is in him, as much as he is in
the world. "The one you are looking for is the one who is looking," wrote St.
Francis of Assisi. A straight line exists between him and the good thing, wrote
Byrne. It's a hard logic to follow, but somehow, he doesn't get lost.

This is just an example, but it is meant to offer a blueprint. It's certainly
not meant to present David Byrne as the author's personal idea of "a true
artist," since I am well aware that the same deconstructive lens applied so
ruthlessly to other individuals in this book might also be applied to him,
possibly at the cost of my enduring fondness. The opening track on *Fear of
Music*, "I Zimbra," for example, uses Dadaist Hugo Ball's poem for its lyrics,
indicating an affinity with the Surrealists. Tina Weymouth told *Rolling Stone*
in 1983 that members of the band were using cocaine during the *Stop Making
Sense* period. David Byrne's 1986 movie *True Stories* is an unabashed celebration of Americanism with barely a whiff of Byrne's previous aesthetic edge
of alienation. The director of *Stop Making Sense*, Jonathan Demme, went on
to direct the execrable bit of agitprop and serial killer chic, *The Silence of the
Lambs*. On that film, *Mindhunter* author John E. Douglas was a leading consultant and the Scott Glenn character was loosely based on him (see Outtake
7). Demme even gave a blurb for the reissue of *Mindhunter*.

Right at the time of finalizing this book for printing, Chris Frantz's
memoir *Remain in Love* was released, along with some accompanying articles and interviews. Many of them focused on Frantz's descriptions of David
Byrne as avaricious for limelight, selfishly stealing credit wherever he could
get it, and pushing himself forward in the tell-tale manner of the aggrandizer-imposer. Frantz even refers to "David's need to aggrandize himself at the
expense of others"![10] He also told *The Guardian*: "If you knew David Byrne,

you would not be jealous of him,"[11] though this is possibly a bit of self-talk on the part of the most marginalized member of Talking Heads.*

What I wish to illustrate with the Talking Heads example is that "art" and propaganda is less a polarity than a spectrum. First of all, I think it illustrates a mysterious process that's central to the cultural convention known as art: that creative self-expression works, in its pure form, as a means to discover one's essence, one's soul nature, and that this only happens by connecting to other souls. Secondly, I want to point out how, whatever is happening socio-politically, culturally, and criminally, within and through the entertainment industry as a whole, *souls are involved.* What they are involved in, consciously or not, is not exploitation, manipulation, or deception (that's just the surface), but *a necessary collective attempt to uncover our true natures.* (Even the attempt to conceal, reveals.)

Never for money: always for love. If Byrne had been making art purely, or even primarily, to try and make a name for himself, to try and make it *in* the world by becoming *of* the world, to try and garner approval and validation from it, and alleviate his alienation that way, the songs would have been meaningless to me. Instead, he developed and applied his songwriting abilities to *articulate his alienation* and to, not assert but simply *air* ("Hit me in the face, I run faster!") his experience of *being* an anomaly, a misfit. This primary orientation allowed him to uncover connections—genuine, non-parasocial ones—to those in his environment who were similarly alienated (if to a lesser degree) fellow anomalies. His string of tentative decisions, his finding a line and knowing its direction, led to elective affinities. His heart *did* have a will of its own; he *was* born with the things that he knew. It was a happy day for all involved (at least while it lasted).

---

* On a more personal note, I tried to get an early copy of *16 Maps of Hell* to Byrne for his 68th birthday via a couple of *seemingly* open channels, and received no response. If we have heard of someone, they have probably been coopted. But the transmission may still reach us. The closest to a true creative genius I would feel comfortable citing at this stage in my disillusionment process would be—another David—Dave Oshana. Unsurprisingly, Oshana doesn't create artistic products at all, making it unlikely he will ever leave any lasting mark upon culture. If the thesis of this book is even halfway correct, it stands to reason that a true genius would be antithetical to both the ends and the means of "superculture," as currently configured. In this regard, my being forced to self-publish this work also speaks in its favor!

Something deeper is occurring here, always. Even the most compromised or corrupt of individuals is driven by their unconscious—and unconscious is another word for soul. There is only one agenda at work where the psyche is concerned, finally, and that is the quest for wholeness. As a prepubescent lonely boy, dancing to Elvis, and later as a solitary adolescent, writing scripts and comic books in his room, diligently transcribing the lyrics of Talking Heads songs (when they didn't come with the album), getting them wrong but making them my own, I was tuning into the "noise between stations." It was the frequency of angels. My mistake was the one we all make, that of confusing the messenger (the medium) for the message, and so falling into the trap of culture. Even angels are only emanations from the source.

There was really no way for me to avoid doing this, however. I was a boy in need of parenting. The transference that happened between me and Elvis, and Bowie, Eastwood, Polanski, Byrne, and all the rest—my culture-provided parasocial family network—meant that, in the act of receiving the nourishment I needed, like the gosling that mistakes a football for its mother, I was imprinted. The signal I was receiving so hungrily, though it came to me *through* these agents of culture, didn't come *from* them. It came from elsewhere.

✦

"Transmit the message, to the receiver
Hope for an answer someday"

—TALKING HEADS, *"Life During Wartime"*

On July 5th 2002, I went to see David Byrne perform at the Ocean, in Islington, for the "Look into the Eyeball" tour. I was near the front and was dancing as much as space allowed. At one point during the show, after "Naïve Melody," the crowd spontaneously began chanting the singer's name, in a simple musical refrain: "David Byrne, David Byrne, David Byrne; David Byrne, David Byrne, David Byrne." I was caught up by the moment too and found myself singing along. The band accompanied our song—it was our song now—and Byrne could only stand there, at the front of the stage, and look out at us, blushing slightly, beaming with joy. We had turned the tables: now he was *our* audience, and what we had to share was our simple love and appreciation for what he had given us. It was payback. On the other hand, we were singing *his* name, making us essentially a congregation of Byrne worshippers. He had harvested our attention, and now we were feeding it back to him and making him fat.

After the show, I went to the stage door and at that precise moment, Byrne came out to smoke a cigarette. I shook his hand and introduced myself. It had been such a beautiful show that I felt all my teenage love and admiration rekindled. I mentioned how remarkable the audience show of appreciation had been. He said something about how it was especially unusual for London. "Yes, I said, "we are normally so reserved!" He laughed. I told him he was greatly loved, then I asked him if he had heard of *The Blood Poets*. He said he hadn't, so I told him briefly about how, whether he remembered or not, he had given his permission for me to quote his lyrics in the book, without asking for any recompense (he was the only musical artist who had done that; The Rolling Stones had asked for several thousand dollars to use a single line from "Sympathy for the Devil"!)

I said that I had asked the publishers to send him a copy and he replied that they might have done (if so he didn't recall). I pulled out a copy I had brought with me. He took it and said "Wow." I offered to sign it, he agreed and handed it back to me. "Quite a turn around," I said, "Me giving you my autograph." I pulled out my pen and as I did so, a second pen next to it fell to the ground. As I was writing in the book, I noticed my hand was trembling. Byrne meanwhile picked up the fallen pen and placed it back in my upper jacket pocket. I handed him the book, he thanked me, and, finishing his cigarette, went back inside.

The receiver evokes the transmission, giving rise to the performance as a means by which the awakened soul can be articulated. *It can happen.* But it is like lightning in a bottle: so rare and fleeting that it is only likely to occur once in a lifetime. And the lighting is already in us: why would we ever want to bottle it? If I gave my soul to movies, pop songs, comic books, and novels, if I gave it to culture at large, then my soul is *in* those things, and they are in it and *of* it. It is a collective soul, a world of light waiting to open our eyes up, split into a billion fragments. There is nothing, finally, that is not this soul. Just as there is nothing, finally, that is not-love. Which is a building. Which is on fire (time for Elvis to leave the building?).

15

MAPS TO THE STARS

15.1. POPCORN & CIRCUSES

> "Literary criticism teaches the power of symbolic
> transformation, or processing experience into ideas, into
> meaning. . . . one must, above all, understand the archetypal
> power of the myth of the hero. That way you can transform,
> through words, Joe the Plumber or even a mass murderer,
> into a national hero. [The CIA] create the myths we believe."
>
> —DOUGLAS VALENTINE, *The CIA as Organized Crime*

If you ever had a problem with rats in your house, you may have discovered that smart rats learn to avoid traps. There are ways of getting around this: putting tastier, more delicate food in the traps, making sure there are no other sources of food in the house, placing scraps of food *around* the trap, so the rats come close enough to smell the luxury food. The CIA-corporate-military-entertainment-myth-making-mind-control complex mapped in *16 Maps of Hell* employs similar methods, and we are the rats. To continue to lure us in to its traps, it's obliged to find ever more rarified products (art and artists). This includes scattering scraps of true creativity that really *are* free and pure, to give us a false sense of security and draw us closer in.* The primary aim is to strip us, over time, of our innate faculty, and of all opportunity, to find nourishment through our own resources. Cutting us off from both nature and human community, and even the finer aspects of culture, means we become less and less discerning and more and more desperate for anything that will satisfy our longing. Until one day, *SNAP!*

What makes us easy prey is the same thing that gave the Rolling Stones' their biggest hit: chronic dissatisfaction. The point is, if we are going to resist the deceptive spell and the insidious allure of cultural propaganda, we need to get filled up with—fully satisfied by—more rarefied kinds of cultural sustenance, including what transcends culture entirely, such as, in the words of David Byrne, "rocks and trees and physical culture."[1]

In *Beginning to See the Light*, feminist author Ellen Willis (the first pop music critic for *The New Yorker*) presents her vision of art, specifically rock music of the 1960s and 1970s, as an inextricable mix of top-down propaganda with bottom up subversive-rebellion. Art, she writes in her first introduction, "has always been in some sense propaganda for ruling classes and at the same time a form of struggle against them. . . . on the deepest level it is the enemy of authority." Even popular art

> is never simply imposed from above, but reflects a complicated interplay of corporate interests, the conscious or intuitive intentions of the artists and technicians who create the product, and the demands of the audience. . . . But the forms invented . . . have an autonomous aesthetic existence. They convey their own message, which, like the content of advertising (or the content of pop lyrics) is *essentially hedonistic*. Implicit in the formal language of mass art is the possibility that given the right sort of social conditions, it can act as a catalyst that transforms its mass audience into an oppositional community (p. xvi-xvii, emphasis added).

History, I think, has given the lie to this naïvely optimistic perception (also shared by Camille Paglia). In her second introduction to the book, written in 1992, Willis mentions having seen *Thelma and Louise* and how much she loved it, especially its "give me liberty or give me death" ending,

---

* To give just one example, the much-loved cult film *Harold and Maude* came out of the crime and depravity nexus that got Robert Evans and Peter Bart their gigs at Paramount.

in which the anti-heroine uber-chicks drive their convertible off a cliff rather than face the consequences of their crimes and submit to The Patriarchy. Shortly after, Willis describes the world she wants to help bring about as "a polyglot, cosmopolitan culture in which boundaries break down and individuals are free to reinvent themselves, not just affirm what they've inherited" (p. xxxii). I found myself wondering, somewhat idly, how Willis (who died in 2006) might have felt if she had lived long enough to see the realization of her dream in which, by 2020, the increased freedom to reinvent ourselves has translated, quite literally, into a whole new vocabulary of dysphoria.

While it was difficult for me to take Willis seriously after reading about her blind embracing of a tawdry little revenge fantasy like *Thelma and Louise*, it did help me see something more clearly: the power of Hollywood product is in how it appeals to us at a subrational, visceral level of awareness, and no amount of critical or sociopolitical acumen makes us immune. If the medium is the message, then what we "love" about movies is precisely this: that they bypass, and neutralize, our rational faculties and reduce us to little children again (albeit to be diddled by unsavory caregivers). Movies and TV shows rely primarily on visual communication, after all (as well as adverts, pop videos, and comic books), and they function—as in Hitchcock's vision of total brain enrapture—like an orchestrated symphony of emotional triggers, a kind of sign language that employs all the body and impacts all of our senses. Movies tap into our cultural unconscious and push buttons that have been installed there long ago, for precisely this function and purpose. Like rats in a maze, we keep receiving the dopamine hit we have grown addicted to.

To coopt and assimilate—*in-corporate*—the "Dionysian" eruptions of the id into the super-egoic structures of power may be a way both to neutralize the former and transform the latter; or it may be that (to whatever degree) these very "urges" were already incepted and/or simulated within the masses by *agent provocateurs* assigned to create a controlled counterculture. The question of whether the top infiltrates the bottom in order to harness and direct its uprising, or the bottom "sells out" on its way to the top is surely not one of either-or but both-and. And the essential realization that this present work has attempted to facilitate is that of the fundamental futility of any kind of rebellion that is coupled to the idea of social liberation *as an end rather than a means*. Freedom means freedom *from* the matrix, not freedom within it. Liberation means getting free from society's internal conditions, not changing the external ones.

Insofar as social liberation has been an end and not a means, and has always ended up being about freeing the self within society rather than getting society's hooks out of the "self," it has invariably come down to the hedonistic pursuit of pleasure as a rejection of social restraints. This, in itself, amounts to little more than adopting a set of values in direct opposition to the (perceived) oppressive social climate, as a way to assert one's liberation from it ("an oppositional community"). As if society's *de*-liberation only reaches to the surface of our bodies, rather than extending all the way to our insides. As if we can become free merely by acting *as if we are free*, rather than by identifying and dissolving everything that has been installed in us that prevents us from acting freely. So the dichotomy of state oppression and control (top-down propaganda) vs. popular rebellion and hedonism (bottom-up art) is a false one, a bad cop-good cop routine of both the State *and* the People. Circuses need audiences as much as audiences need circuses.

This age-old control system of combining oppressive political structures with rock and roll "rebellions" is the same as it ever was, with popcorn and movies replacing bread and circuses. And the circus, to keep us enthralled, must provide not just the relief of entertainment, but a compensatory fantasy of freedom, rebellion, and revenge. (Above all, it's the freedom to indulge our fantasies without consequences that we are seeking.) This ensures the collective id energy—that Dionysian uprising Willis and Paglia invested all their ideological dreams into—goes nowhere but back into the system that unleashed it, to be stimulated and harnessed and exploited for the system's sustenance and maintenance. Fantasies of liberation that center around the indulgence of the id (hedonism and the freedom to pursue pleasure) are always ripe for exploitation; and judging by the long-term evidence, they rarely if ever lead to autonomy or true community (which is a necessary context for autonomy, as well as the natural result of it). The reason for this may be simple: the urges of the id are less our liberators than the original slave-masters of the human spirit.

15.2. QUEEN OF DRAMA:
CASE STUDY # 14, BILLIE WHITELAW

"Now the whole world will know we have done crimes."

—MAP TO THE STARS

In 2007, during the period I was working on *Grasshopper, The Keepers*, and *Shooting the Ghost* (my Peckinpah script), dreaming of my up-and-coming Hollywood success, I met Billie Whitelaw. Whitelaw was famous in two separate but interconnected worlds, theater and movies. She'd had a close working relationship with the playwright Samuel Beckett for two and a half decades, until Beckett's death in 1989. According to Whitelaw's obituary, she was Beckett's "muse. He would write parts in experimental plays for her which she would often perform to the point of exhaustion," making her "one of the foremost interpreters of [his] works."[2]

In her final years, Billie lived a few doors down from George Orwell's old house in Hampstead, just off the heath. By the time I moved back there, my mother and Billie had become close acquaintances, if not quite friends. There was just two years in age between them and they shared a number of interests (my mother was a Samuel Beckett fan and also volunteered at the John Keats society). Between spring and autumn of 2007, when Billie was in her mid-seventies, I visited her perhaps four or five times. Usually this would entail me dropping something off for her and her inviting me in. She was a hard woman to say no to, especially since I was also ever-so-slightly starstruck, if only because she played the evil nanny in *The Omen*, my no. 1 movie for all of a month when I was fourteen. (David Thewlis was in the 2006 remake.) She was also in Hitchcock's *Frenzy*, though I never had the good sense to ask her about Hitch.*

Though I never stayed for more than an hour, I found Billie easy enough to talk to, if eccentric, scatty, and erratic. Her cat liked me and this

---

* Other films she did: *Mr. Arkadin*, with Orson Welles, *Charlie Bubbles*, with Albert Finney and Liza Minelli, *Start the Revolution without Me*, with Donald Sutherland, Stephen Frears' *Gumshoe*, John Boorman's *Leo the Last*, *The Krays*, and *Quills*, about the Marquis de Sade. Her last film role was in 2007's *Hot Fuzz*.

seemed to impress her. Over time, however, I discovered that Whitelaw was a raging egomaniac, and worse, didn't even know it. She was also desperately lonely because, as impossible as she was, most of her friends had abandoned her. On my visits, she always asked a lot of questions, and like most people I enjoyed talking about myself. With hindsight, however, it was more like she was gathering intel than being friendly. I began to realize that Billie's "gifts"—even her offers of gifts—not only had strings attached but hidden bombs inside them. They were like Trojan Horses. I realized it was a mistake to talk to her as one would to a normal person. She was a one-woman Chinese whispers factory, latching onto a couple of things without registering the rest, then twisting them into her own fantasy narratives. All her stories seemed to involve her selfless efforts to help others, and how she was met with ingratitude and indifference.*

To give one example: she suggested I contact a friend of hers, John Calder. The John Calder publishing company had published Beckett's works in his day, but by then it was a very small publisher that had little in common with my writing. I didn't follow up on her suggestion, after which Billie got it into her head that my mother had *asked* her to help me find a publisher. She became indignant, both with my mother for asking her for help and with me, for my ingratitude and lack of commitment. She repeatedly quoted her "friend" Alec Guinness at me (they were in *Hotel Paradiso* together in 1966), "Success depends on concentration!" She also repeated her erroneous version of the John Calder non-incident, incessantly telling both me and my mother that I wasn't focused enough to succeed.

The most dramatic example of her malignant meddling began benignly enough. Billie mentioned, either to me or my mother, that she was friends with Desmond Davies, the director of *The Girl with Green Eyes*, a 1964 British film starring Peter Finch (Howard Beale in *Network*) about a young girl just out of convent school who enters into a romantic relationship with an older man (Finch). It was Davies' only film of note besides *Clash of the*

---

* Editor's note: The context is there, but could be made explicit: Whitelaw as unconsciously displaying and (also unconsciously) seeking to instill in others imposer techniques: playing loose with the facts, reframing everything sympathetically to herself, providing unwelcome pressure based on a subjective set of standards, etc.

Titans. Sometime in late spring of 2007, Billie offered to get me a copy of Davies' film on VHS and to send *Shooting the Ghost* to him. Of course I agreed. I watched Davies' film with my mother and enjoyed it, and Davies read my script and wrote me a thoughtful letter. He thought the script was very good and offered some rudimentary suggestions. I wrote a letter back thanking him, and that was that. Or so I thought.

A couple of months later, in late July, as my fantasy wave to Hollywood glory was starting to build, I found out from my mother that Billie had got it into her head that I had decided to quit writing. After the John Calder incident, I had told her—as a way to get her off my back—that I wasn't really interested in getting published right now, as it never seemed to make any difference anyway. The fact I was still working on several scripts, including the Peckinpah one—that I was probably working more ferociously on scriptwriting than at any other time in my life and had even *told* her about it—made no difference to her. She told Davies I had quit writing, and Davies—*or so she claimed*—was furious that I had wasted his time.

My mother meanwhile complained to me that Billie wouldn't stop calling her—as many as eight times in a single morning!—and decided to get caller ID to screen her calls. Feeling as if Whitelaw was stalking her, she actually referred to her as "evil"—a word I had never heard her use for anyone, not even Hitler. Having worked herself up into a frenzy of indignation over my imaginary decision to quit writing, Billie was now telling my mother how irresponsible I was and that she (my mother) needed to "take me in hand"! My mother told her it was nothing to do with either of them and that she didn't want to hear about it, at which point, Billie hung up on her.

The more I heard from my mother about what Billie was saying about me, the angrier I got. "I don't want to hear anything more about Billie!" I snapped. "It's only making me hate her!" We were playing right into Billie's witchy hands, dancing to her dark Gothic tune. Eventually, I got so disgusted by it all that I decided to have nothing to do with Whitelaw anymore. My mother felt the same way, and left a message for Billie, telling her not to call anymore.

I called up Davies meanwhile and left a message on his answering machine. I said I had heard from Billie that he was angry with me because of what she'd said about my quitting writing. I assured him I was still working

on the script. "Billie creates her own reality," I said, "then inflicts it on others.'"
An hour or two later, Davies called my mother: he had no idea what Billie was
talking about! He had received a nice letter from me and would have replied if
I'd put a return address on it (I only put an email address on). Apparently we
had all been strung along by the nanny of Antichrist.

I don't recount this here to tarnish Billie Whitelaw's reputation or
to spice up this work with inside gossip. Only because, with all of the
"Hollywood connections" I was making, or breaking, during this period,
Billie was possibly the most up-close-and-personal, and hence the most
significant. In retrospect (though I *was* probably aware at the time), Billie
Whitelaw's behavior, as well as being perhaps typical of a particular kind of
lonely, half-psychotic old lady, might also indicate what sort of aggrandizer-
imposer personality it takes to succeed in the entertainment industry—and
how they do it. Knowing Billie Whitelaw, I gradually came to understand,
meant being cast in an ongoing psychodrama created for her amusement. It
was a kind of Beckett-like sense (and reality) deprivation chamber, designed
to pass on the charge of her trauma (see 16.5).

As a seasoned actress, however, Billie knew how to turn on the charm,
and even *after* I knew how toxic she was I still fell for it. She *appeared* warm,
polite, concerned, bright, and involved; but behind the friendly façade lurked
a black agenda. No wonder she was cast in *The Omen*, I thought: her dark art
was to create conflict and turn people against one another. She sowed discord
between my mother and me, for example, by telling my mother things I
never actually said, putting extra strain on our already highly strained relationship. It was as if, unable to live without drama, Whitelaw compulsively
staged her own absurdist theater, then cast anyone foolish enough to get
close to her. Above all, the melodramas woven out of her interactions with
myself and my mother seemed fueled by her ongoing obsession with having
made it in the world of the arts. They centered on her power to assist or

---

* Editor's note # 2: But how intentionally deliberate is she rather than unconsciously
rearticulating and repeating behaviors done to her? She comes across *as not very good at
it,* and maybe also *not entirely aware of what she's doing*—both of which would contribute
towards her never rising above the bit-roles she was tossed: that is to say, she tried out for
the imposer, mostly failed, was relegated to something like an automaton—a victimizing
victim rather than a true imposer.

block others from doing the same. Yet her "favors" were rigged to detonate a Molotov cocktail of fury and indignation the moment I failed to cooperate or to show the requisite degree of appreciation, compliance, and respect.

"She uses her fame to draw people in, and then abuse them," I said at the time. Nearing the end of this exploration, it sounds like a Hollywood microcosm.*

15.3.   THE THING THAT DIDN'T HAPPEN: CASE STUDY # 15, THE AUTHOR

> "I believe nothing of my own that I have ever written. I cannot accept that the products of minds are subject-matter for beliefs."
>
> —CHARLES FORT

Bringing together all of my impressions and ruminations on the nature of Hollywood/pop culture into one place has required some awkward juxtapositioning of perspectives and a lot of hopscotching around in time. This is presumably because one of the main, probably the primary, driving forces behind my writing was always to make something conscious that was mostly unconscious, namely, my pact with "Hollywood" and with the dark—but also light-bearing—forces which the word encompasses for me, and, with any luck, now also for the reader.

Mind control/sociocultural conditioning is something that, by its nature, leaves no traces we can identify—until we begin to shake its spell and see ourselves more clearly. Like scars from wounds inflicted before we were born, that we are assured are merely natural features of our being, like trying to see the mote in one's eye, the nature of coerced consent to unwholesome values and practices is that it neutralizes our capacity to perceive the nature of the covenant we have cut—and been cut for.

---

* Following this melodrama, in August 2007, Whitelaw called my mother and apologized, and I did speak to her again. I never ascertained how conscious she was of her behavior.

This is a possibly long-winded explanation for why, in the final pages, I want to hop back to a piece I wrote in 2017, as what I thought at the time would be the ending to *another* book, *The Kubrickon*. The reason is two-fold: firstly, because I have not been able to complete these final chapters (including a promised "rough draft of the exit") to my own satisfaction (or, for that matter, the satisfaction of a couple of early readers). Secondly, because this unused piece addresses the core nature of my own Hollywood obsession, and so seems more likely to bring us closer to a genuine "way out" than the previously included study of David Lynch (see Outtake # 8 on page 495) and more philosophical material about the nature of "the culture trap."

When I first quoted the Fort line above, in *The Lucid View*, I was aware of consciously pretending not to believe many of the theories and interpretations I was presenting in that work. This was a conscious strategy to avoid discrediting myself—or more accurately, the ideas being presented, which were already pretty disreputable—with more skeptical readers. By the time I wrote *The Kubrickon*, things seemed to have reversed themselves, and I found myself in the odd position of not quite believing the things I was arguing for (including my own critical judgments about Kubrick). It was not that I disbelieved them or held contrary views, only that I could no longer get fully *behind* them. Like Fort, I can't accept that the products of my mind are subject matter for belief. I recognize and respect the power of belief, and because of that, I can't fully believe in anything I believe in.

It ain't over till it's over. While I was finishing up *The Kubrickon*—so I thought, back in 2017—I spontaneously remembered a line from a (highly critical) review of *The Blood Poets* and realized at once that it belonged in that work (and now in this current one, twenty years later). The review was from Oliver Harris, of the University of Keele in the UK—a countryman—and came out in 2001. I don't think I saw it until at least ten years later, as a result of—that most illicit of authorial pastimes—typing my name into Google. Happily, I managed to find it again by doing the same, in a PDF online, and I reproduce the quote that seems so significant to me now. The author of *Blood Poets*, Harris wrote, "hates Kubrick for gate-crashing the Hall of Fame, which always remains his abiding obsession."

It's not clear whether Harris meant my abiding obsession was for the Hall of Fame or for gate-crashing it; but either way, he not only scored a bullseye, he split his first arrow with his second.* Peer reviews are a time-honored tradition of academia, one that serves to hold researchers to an impersonal standard and let them know when they are in danger of "thesis creep" (or creepy theses). Harris upheld that tradition honorably, even if it took me almost twenty years to appreciate it.

Thesis, antithesis, synthesis.

✦

Remember when your identity was still forming? How could you? More precisely, with what would you remember it? The lens the spectacle-maker uses to build a better lens, at a given point is tossed aside, or built into the new lens. And so on. All our discernment and taste about movies is created by watching movies—what else can it come out of? The first ones that get to us, lay the foundations thereafter. There is nothing less objective than movie taste, and there is nothing objective about taste. Or, for that matter, about perception.

The author Joseph Chilton Pearce made a career out of writing books about the war between nature and culture. He described a classic battle between good and evil, complete with its own death-star and (life) force (guess which was which). The central premise to his thesis—which focused on brain development and biology—was something I call The Thing That Didn't Happen. According to Pearce, the human brain is designed to develop in such a way that, during or just after adolescence (i.e., with the awakening of our libido), the frontal lobe of the brain becomes fully active and we enter into whole-brain functioning awareness. Spiritual-traditionally, this is called "enlightenment," the arrival, emergence, or return to no-self selfness, to non-survival-oriented, non-mind-based, holistic consciousness that experiences itself as fully connected to and in harmony with its environment.

---

* Harris' review was almost wholly excoriating and only half-insightful, the other half being more of an ideocratic attack than an analysis, as when he took me to task for (of all things) lack of tokenism: "It almost goes without saying that Horsley's gallery of 'blood poets' is . . . exclusively white and male." (Talk about shooting the messenger!) But the insights Harris did provide were dandies—even if I was less than receptive to them when I first read it. The truth, like medicine, often tastes bad.

Due to the deleterious effects of an overly complex cultural environment, however, the Event never happens and we remain locked inside the self-protective, highly reactive, egocentric identity construction which characterizes the first stage of self-awareness. This constructed identity is what comes into being (it would be temporarily if all went well) between an identity-free child state and a fully adapted and autonomous, identity-free adulthood. In Pearce's model (due to birth trauma and other early interference), we wind up stuck in pre-adolescence. Pearce attributes the feeling of immense letdown which so many of us experience as we enter into adulthood—if not kicking and screaming then with massive reluctance—to this deep, biologically instilled sense that something epic and life-changing has failed to occur.

Naturally, we continue to seek this thing that didn't happen, even long after the window of opportunity has closed (the brain has stopped developing). And naturally, we transpose our sense of that inner lack, that disappointment or need, outside ourselves, onto the things of the world. It's usually at middle-age that the penny fully drops and we become conscious of the immense disappointment we are carrying around with us. As our options start to run out one by one, the likelihood of A Big Event That Will Transform Our Lives is slowly whittled away to nothing. Think of all those characters in novels, movies, and TV shows (and our lives—and *us*), lamenting (to their children, their partners, or whoever): "This isn't how I thought it was going to be." How could it be, when our life force got diverted from the get-go?

I tried to write about this in *Seen and Not Seen* (cf. "Peddlers of Astonishment"), referring to how I grew up (from age seven or so) with a profound attachment to Marvel super-heroes. A bit later (though I continued to read comic books into adulthood), it was Hammer horror movies, and then, finally, as I entered adolescence, Clint Eastwood and David Bowie stepped in, or up, to provide me with an adult-ified projection of self-liberation and empowerment. Culture had hijacked my development and coopted it for its own dark ends (building the Death Star[*]); and then,

---

[*] Editor's note # 3: metaphor could be teased out—a monolithic source of world-destroying, with all participants militaristically uniformed and arranged in power hierarchies, etc.

over time, it became my friend, ally, and caretaker. Culture offered ever-new promises to fill the aching void left by biology's failed ones. And so it went, or so I did, digging the hole of my premature burial, deeper and deeper with each wishful wave of my lightsaber (or fake .44 Magnum). Each artifact of fantasy I could amass helped buffer me from the formless phantom menace of an increasingly dark reality.

15.4. IDENTITIES IN MOTION

"Loving Hollywood cinema by loving Pauline Kael, what Horsley really loves is, of course, Art with an old-fashioned capital A. Accordingly, *The Blood Poets* is a remarkably unapologetic work of evaluation and canonisation, committed to sacramental archetypes and individualist expression, while seemingly unaware of a mass of underpinning essentialist assumptions. . . . For Horsley, the film critic not only has to 'assign credit and blame' but, more profoundly, aspires to be 'an artist whose work depends wholly upon the art of others' (I: ix), which is to say, aspires to the same heroic individualism of his individual heroes—the pantheon of great directors. In this light, the foregrounded idiosyncratic agenda of *The Blood Poets*—quirky detours into pop-occult theory, asides on gnostic tradition, pearls of wisdom from Carlos Castaneda, Charles Fort, and sundry others—has to be read as Horsley's own bid for that all-important capital A."

—OLIVER HARRIS

Of course (once again), Harris was 100% right in the above passage: *The Blood Poets* was not an academic thesis about movie violence. It was many things (a love letter to Kael, a delivery device for paranoid awareness, a sustained rant against my father's dislike of violent movies, and a hopeless bid to gain the attention of Hollywood); but, while it was published by an academic press, it was not an academic work, not really. Above all, it was a sustained, wildly undisciplined, stream-of-consciousness exploration of a personal obsession; in other words, something that probably never should have been submitted for academic peer review. But *c'est la guerre.* If Icarus wants to fly that high, Icarus can expect to land with a thud. I didn't gate-crash Hollywood, but I did gate-crash the halls of academia, and apparently Harris didn't like it.

So why is it that I enjoy writing about movies so damn much? This is the question that pursued me in the last stages of writing *The Kubrickon,* in 2017–18, and that has pursued me all the way to the (shaky) end of *16 Maps of Hell.* The answer is that it takes me back. It takes me back to a time when I was first imprinted by these cultural artifacts—when they meant so much to me that it was as if my life depended on them. Movies (and comic books, and albums and songs, and yes, books about movies) were objects of power animated by adolescent desire. By re-handling them, by turning them over and over in my writer-mind's eye and hand, I am, I think, hoping to reclaim that power I lost to them. Or at least, to regain the experience of losing it, which is just close enough to having had it that it will have to do (you can't lose what you never had).

I loved comic books and movies before I cared about art, with or without a capital "A." It wasn't that any dream would do; but as long as the dream was technicolor enough to coat my monochrome reality, then it would do—exactly what I needed it to do. And what I needed to do was escape. Naturally, with time and maturation, learning to discern between dreamscapes (becoming a film critic) became part of the ritual of submitting to them. I wanted—needed—to be seduced, persuaded, even deceived, to succumb, to surrender my sense of reality to another. Like any game, to be meaningful it couldn't be too easy. The measure of the seduction was art: how artfully could I be lured into an imitation of a no-self (childhood) existence, one that simultaneously offered the empowerment fantasy of a fully-functioning identity that matched how I wanted to be as an adult self? The more compelling it was to me, the more seductive, the more I could identify with it and use it to build my moving fortress in which to enter the world, without ever having to be really exposed to it.

Lethem again (one last time, this from *Ecstasy of Influence*):

It may be latent in human psychology to model the world on a fall from innocence, since we each go through one. [A]s a culture we're disastrously addicted to easy fantasies of a halcyon past, one always just fading from view, a land where things were more orderly and simple. . . . For that reason, so many really smashing cultural investigations open up a window onto the truly disordered and frequently degenerate origins of things we've sentimentalized as pure and whole and pat. [It is] a revelatory nightmare of evidence that the place we came from is as deep and strange as any place we might have been ourselves, or might imagine we are on the way to going (p. 142).

We all dream of being little children again, even the worst of us (*The Wild Bunch*). Is that because we are still children, dreaming of being adults (often the worst kind)? To refer back to Kael again—one last time?—this is from her closing statement from her career-making attack on Andrew Sarris and the auteur theory, "Circles and Squares":

Can we conclude that, in England and the United States, the auteur theory is an attempt by adult males to justify staying inside the small range of experience of their boyhood and adolescence—that period when masculinity looked so great and important but art was something talked about by poseurs and phonies and sensitive feminine types? And is it perhaps also their way of making a comment on our civilization by their suggestion that trash is the true film art? I ask: I do not know (1965, p. 319).

It's curious to note that, elsewhere, I have argued for pulp as the true film art as well as for the great importance of masculinity. Perhaps I have gone some ways to proving Harris wrong by turning out to be a poor sort of "Paulette," after all?* Yet Kael's most interesting point in the above is the one that dovetails with my past/present argument, that all my own film theorizing—and now

---

* "Paulette" was the term coined for a bevy of male critics both influenced and endorsed by Pauline Kael, their den (or hen) mother. See *Seen and Not Seen*, "The Movie Nomad."

Hollywood conspiracy theorizing?—has been revealed to me as an attempt to justify staying inside that small range of experience of my boyhood and adolescence—yet also, finally, a valid attempt to get free of it. (Can there be one without the other?)

Peckinpah's assumption in *The Wild Bunch* is that, as adult males, we all want to return to (relative) innocence; but why would we want that when we know, from a mix of experience (dim memories) and observation that, with innocence came unbearable exposure, vulnerability, and pain? The answer I think is that we are trying to get back to a place and time *before* the thing that was supposed to happen didn't happen, in the hope that, somehow, this time, it will. The tragedy of this unconscious reenactment compulsion is that, what most effectively transport us back to childhood are the very same artifacts and associations—those cultural power objects—that trapped our attention in the first place by providing a surrogate experience of The Thing we were waiting for, and so helped prevent it from happening (because our attention was elsewhere). In other words, by trying to follow my attachments to cultural objects and personalities (Art) back to the beginning, so I can dis-identify with them and extricate myself from their illusory magic—drown out the serpent's whisper—I may only be holding more tightly to them, like a drowning man clinging to a sinking ship.

Or like Pike and his wild bunch, cradling their rifles like babies, as they march inexorably towards the closest they can ever get to a true expression of adult masculinity.

◆

"The things you own, end up owning you."

—TYLER DURDEN

The above is never truer than of what we believe. Opinions are not just like assholes: they make assholes of us all. Being right is only a state of mind.

I was always one to hold fast to my convictions, especially when it came to movies. Don't even try to tell me *K-Pax* is a good movie, or *Field of Dreams* or *Gravity* or *Silence* or *12 Years a Slave* or (now) *Once Upon a Time in Hollywood*. It won't wash with me. I will end you. (Actually, it's more likely I will avoid your eyes and change the subject. There are few experiences more uncomfortable than listening to people talk about bad movies they love.) As much as my "aesthetic responses" feel like unquestionable facts of life, I know that, really, they can't be much more than tricks of light. Why believe in my own judgments about movies when I doubt my ability to even know what's real? The answer may be: because it's all I've got? So what happens if I let go of that "all," and see that it's really nothing much of anything? What then?

I am the unreliable narrator who can't be trusted to represent the facts of the matter (facts all come with points of view), whose perspective just twists the truth around. But, my judgment about movies is impeccable, i.e., when it comes to discerning good illusion from bad illusion, I am a master of taste. Do these two facts go together? I am the unreliable narrator who reassures you, "You can trust me, I'm a critic" (parasocial deconstructionist). Because, if we aren't able to tell what's real, the need to choose a really good illusion becomes paramount.

The movies I love lie beautifully when they tell me who I am. I wrote *The Blood Poets* based on simple logic: I wanted to write a book about movies and focus on the movies I loved the most. Most of the movies I loved were violent, so I wrote a book about movie violence. The one question I never addressed was why? Why the love of violence? I skipped it by focusing on the world and not the self. I took it as *a priori* given that the best art (or Art) is imbued with violence of one sort or another because that is the world we live in. Yet, so far as I knew back then, my world was not an especially violent one, so why the fascination for violent art? That is the secret I kept from myself: that my own identity, long before I first laid eyes on John Wayne or Kirk Douglas or Clint Eastwood, was forged through violence. And the hidden aspect of my movie love was not that I loved violent movies but that I loved movies violently. My identity depended on an ability to say "This is good and this is bad." To judge, even as I was judged. And in every violent judgment, there is condemnation.

The part that seems most vital to my sense of who I am is the part that condemns anything and everything that questions its control: it is a system of defense. Taste is a terrible mistress, a narcissistic mother and a moveable fortress. It is a prison made of promised but forbidden pleasures. A tree of knowledge.

15.5.   THE WRONG PILL

> "If the Wachowsky [sic] brothers are Horsley's best hope of
> realizing this vision of poetic brotherly radicalism, then I can only
> think that Morpheus must have given him the wrong pill."*
>
> —OLIVER HARRIS, *review of The Blood Poets*

So where does Stanley Kubrick come into this exactly, when none of his artifacts made it into my adolescent mojo pouch? The answer, I think, has to do with what Kubrick represented, even then. This was the thing I most wanted to happen, the identity I was desperately aspiring to become: the legendary filmmaker. What better way to hold onto my fantasy that the objects of my dream life were real than to learn how to make these objects myself? My .44 Magnum replica was a faintly embarrassing continuation of my stuffed animals, *Star Wars* action figures, and James Bond Moon buggy. It worked for a while but then had to be put away with the other child-ish things. Ditto my "idea" of becoming a cop in San Francisco (live the dream—enter the nightmare), which was about as likely as my becoming an astronaut. To be a filmmaker was a logical, practical next step for my fantasy life to live on. Most excitingly of all, I could start immediately, writing scripts and (rather more childishly) drawing mini-posters and writing imaginary reviews of the movies I would someday make. (The only one I remember was called *Houses in Motion*, after the Talking Heads song. It starred Robert De Niro and Jessica Lange and was about domestic strife. Ha. De Niro and Lange did go onto star together—ten years later, which might have been

---

* Harris called this, and *then some*; there currently *are* no Wachowski brothers, since both have since joined the open secret society of "men who turned themselves into women" (see next chapter). On August 4, 2020, *Vanity Fair* published "*The Matrix* Was a Trans Allegory, Confirms Lilly Wachowski," by Yohana Desta. Quoting Larry-turned-Lana: "I'm glad that it has gotten out that that was the original intention. . . The corporate world wasn't ready for it." But now it is, since the matrix-world built by Lana and Lilly has apparently caught up with the corporations' best-laid blueprints. Cultural revision-ism is written by the winners. See: https://www.vanityfair.com/hollywood/2020/08/the-matrix-trans-allegory-lilly-wachowski

roughly the release date of *Houses in Motion*—in Martin Scorsese's worst movie at the time—*Cape Fear*. It was about domestic strife, B-movie style.)

As Oliver Harris rightly calls it, from this time on (with the help of my own dysfunctional family conditioning, which included reverence for artists), I was indeed angling for induction into the Hall of Fame, for greatness, cultural permanence, for an identity to last the ages, in short, the closest equivalent I could manufacture for the missed boat of "enlightenment." For the goal to fill the hole where my soul had failed to show, or at least for it to promise to, for the dream to *do* (seem real), it depended on the culture in question—Hollywood—being itself real, trustworthy and true. That world I courted had to be able to recognize, affirm, accept, and reward my offering—my holographic dream-self—and all its works. There would be no satisfaction in entering Valhalla if I wound up surrounded by clowns and fakers. Nothing less than the gods would do for company.

Along with Hitchcock and a tiny handful of others, Kubrick was probably the closest to being recognized as a cinematic deity and—here was the rub that created the splinter—I didn't like his movies! What was wrong with this vision? If Kubrick had gatecrashed the party, what was the point in my trying to get in? (The party was in my mind and it never stopped—but I didn't know that yet.) More cryptically—even further below the threshold of my awareness back then—what did Kubrick have to do to attain his place in Valhalla? *What was the price of admission to the ranks of culture makers*—i.e., those who forge the artifacts from which lesser mortals such as myself assemble our own desperate, second-hand, identity matrices, all the while harboring the childish illusion that the dream is real? *What was the price and was I willing to pay it?*

Like the Wizard giving fake diplomas to Dorothy's gang of losers, the need to believe in the Wizard's sorcery is almost insurmountable. Is it enough for us to still believe that the one who creates the illusion of a Wizard is himself a wizard for doing so? To believe that his openly bogus artifacts—his placebo blessings—will bestow upon us our missing parts? Apparently so. But what about the Wizard—how can he believe? All that's left for the culture maker is to believe in his own power to create illusions, and in the power—the reality—of the culture that bestowed the power on him, in exchange for eternal servitude, like Jack in the Overlook. Then the price paid becomes not merely a way *into* the fake kingdom, but a way to re-animate the corpse-like illusion that a false kingdom is worth entering.

Is there any prison more confining than the prison created by legend? It's here that the deepest corner of the Culture Trap (what I called the Kubrickon, i.e., Kubrick-con) is found, and *this* is the corner I have to gain access to. (In this present enterprise, that is: not the Hall of Fame but the dungeon of endless aspiring.) I would do so not by aligning with power, but by identifying my own inner compulsion to achieve it, and by confronting my hapless, hopeless aspirations for all the spectral rewards I began chasing after, all those years ago.

✦

Everyone has heard of Mother Nature, but what about Mother Culture? The Matrix has you: just don't let it tell you who you are.

We are hard-wired to imbibe. If we don't get the breast when we need it, we just keep on reaching, our lips twisted into a permanent pucker of expectation. Just like a duckling that "imprints" onto a football when no mother duck is around, those of us whose parents were absent on arrival (or, for later generations, were floating about in helicopters with bullhorns tracking our every move, which is hardly preferable), we took our reassurance wherever we could. We wound up tattooed with cultural imagery. Like *A Scanner Darkly*'s Bob Arctor inside his scramble suit, we had an identity for every occasion.

And here also is exactly the complex from which this book emerged: the reason why a lack of agreement over movies has been such a seemingly disproportionate and exaggerated source of frustration and anxiety for me. Kubrick's films (*Eyes Wide Shut* above all, a film I was resolute in not citing in *16 Maps of Hell*) are only the most concentrated example of that dissonance between me and the culture I am beholden to and was weaned on. Evaluating what is good and bad in a movie, and which movies are good or bad (or ugly), and why, became, quite early in my development, a substitute for (or at least equivalent to) determining the difference between true and false perceptions of reality, between delusion and reality. And that ability is 100% essential to a feeling of being safe in our environment. I was propagandized.

The objects we are biologically hardwired to "fixate" on, to associate with strong feelings of pleasure, comfort, love, joy, or the opposite feelings, are natural objects found in our natural environment, there to imprint us and develop our capacities for survival and well-being. They are items of our training: water, air, fire, earth, fruit and other plants, wild life, other humans, "rocks and trees and physical culture." Knowing the difference between an animal we can eat and one that might eat us (or kill us), or between a plant that can save our lives and one that can end it prematurely, this ability is really, truly, something to get attached to and "build an identity" around. It is hardly equaled by learning to discern the difference between a Talking Heads song (good) and an Eagles one (bad), or between *Taxi Driver* and *Death Wish* (you decide: I trust you). Or *Alien* and *2001* (Oops, I think I just lost you—maybe forever).

"Can I trust you and will I be safe in your company?" is pretty much the most fundamental question for one human being to ask of another. But we can't find out by asking, so how do we gauge the answer? Isn't it by ascertaining the extent to which you and I share the same values (good and bad), the degree to which we can see eye to eye? And until we can do that, how do we know what the other might be capable of when our back is turned? You might start comparing *They Live* to *The Wild Bunch*, or something, and then where would we be?*

The answer, alas, is more or less exactly where we always were, ever since the Thing That Didn't Happen, didn't happen. Arrested and detained, without knowing the charges, a post-truth Joseph K., wandering endlessly through the virtual corridors of movie development hell.

15.6.   HOMELAND SECURITY

"We'll know our disinformation program is complete when everything the American public believes is false."

—WILLIAM CASEY, *CIA Director, 1981 to 1987*

---

* In-joke, almost private, for those who have close-read *Seen and Not Seen* and/or Lethem's *They Live*.

So let's go back to the beginning one last time. My attic room went across the whole length of the house and included a storage area, a bedroom, and a living room; it had its own staircase with a latched door at the foot of it. There was an intercom system linking the living room to the kitchen, so I could be alerted when meal times came around. This was my space—my boy cave—and I rarely emerged from it except to come and go to school. I have hardly any memories of my mother coming up there. It was my mad scientist's laboratory, and there was delicate work afoot. Naturally, it was off-limits to anyone not included—and that meant especially my mother. This was my fortress against that, against them, most especially against her.

The slanting walls consisted of cardboard panels between naked wooden beams, with a window in both of the main sections. The cardboard made it easy to staple pictures and posters up, mostly of movies, of Clint or Debbie Harry. On the wall over my bed was a poster of *Where Eagles Dare*, the first Eastwood movie I ever saw, the one that sealed the deal. The only other movie poster I can recall (besides an anomalous *Quest for Fire*, a movie I never bothered to see) was a small print of an ad for Russ Meyer's *Super Vixens*. The breasts I never got fed by.

There were two single beds running along each bedroom wall, no more than three feet between them, with matching duvets. The spare bed was for my two or three friends when they stayed over. My comic book collection and stuffed toy menagerie (they also had super-powers) was stored in the unfurnished area past the bedroom, on the other side of a door. There was a small bookshelf at the head of my bed, with *Edge* Western novels (and I presume my Pan Horror stories and James Herbert collection), as well as a DC pocketbook series of Superman stories and Marvel collections of early Spiderman stories. A low white table was on the right side of the bed, for water, books, and assorted items. A small TV and VHS video recorder was past the table on the right of the bed, a growing pile of VHS movies stacked somewhere nearby. This was the scene of my crimes which now the whole world knows I have done.

Some of the first movies I ever owned were *High Plains Drifter*—lifted from the local Video 2000 rental store—*Raiders of the Lost Ark*—one of the first mass-marketed video releases, I bought it for £19.99—*Taxi Driver, Easy Rider, Midnight Express, American Werewolf in London, Local Hero, Rosemary's Baby*, and *Harold and Maude*. Most of these were pirated from rented copies (by hooking up two video recorders with cables) and whenever possible I would steal the empty cases from video stores to make my acquisition complete. I even went to great pains to make the sticker on the cassettes as authentic as possible. Ownership of these cherished movies was paramount to my project: to literalize my adoption of them as objects of my interior space. I probably didn't appreciate it then, but my adolescence placed me on the very cusp of opportunity, when movies were becoming something that could be owned. I was also on the cutting edge of the revolution: by 1982 only 10% of houses in the UK owned video recorders, never mind a kid in his room!

By the time I was nineteen and had a home of my own (with my sister), an entire wall of my bedroom was covered with movies, stacked side by side like books. Having these movies meant my identity was fully on display: one glance from a visitor (of which there were scant few) and they could see what I was made of. They were my entrails, the values I defined myself by, values that, paradoxically, I was able to hide behind. They were a substitution of my interiority, proudly displayed on the outside, the movies that made the man. By allowing myself to be culturally colonized, I turned my soul into a stronghold. I created homeland security from an ongoing state of emergency.

It was here that I enacted, on an almost nightly basis, the ritualistic slaying of my mother via countless replays of video nasty-collected rapes and murders. Torturing the women—little did I know I was unconsciously training myself for induction to the Hall of Fame of Hollywood secret society life. At the same time, my daily invocations of San Clinton, the animus with no name, continued unabated, even as they expanded to include new icons: Woody, Marty, Bobby, Al, Elvis, Bowie, David Byrne. In *A Fistful of Dollars*, the Man with No Name is asked why he is risking his life to save an endangered family he barely knows. He answers, "Because I knew someone like you once, and there was no one there to help." Of course he was talking about himself—who else could it be? Film legend has it that this was the line Eastwood came up with to replace several pages of dialogue, stuff he knew instinctively would only diminish his character. And of course—along with the Peckinpah wisdom about bad men dreaming of being children again—this had to turn out to be the key to the whole damn thing. The philosopher's stone, buried in the dirt.

✦

I do not believe that the products of my mind are subject matter for belief—but what are beliefs if not products of my mind? So then, again, if I do not believe in my own beliefs, where does that leave me?

When I write about the greatness of *The Good, the Bad, and the Ugly* (showing in my local theater on the night I first wrote that), the badness of *Eyes Wide Shut*, or the ugliness of *A Clockwork Orange*—when I discuss the dark forces behind Roman Polanski or Leonard Cohen, *The Exorcist* and *Black Panther*—I am arranging a collection of beliefs and data-points into a coherent, many-paged essay-argument, in such a way as to persuade the reader that I am right, that I am reporting a factual observation and not just an article of faith. Who am I hoping to persuade? Is it the joy of cultural propaganda I want to communicate or the agony of it? Clearly it's both. If I want to demonstrate the Hollywood mind control conspiracy to those who love and revere Hollywood, it can only be the thin end of a psychic wedge that must end for me, at its thickest point, the point where *everything I love* must face this Holy Inquisition I have unleashed, like a forest fire. I must kill all my darlings to be free of their endless demands.

An infant only recognizes how much it loved the womb as it is dragged unceremoniously from it. There is barely time for goodbye in such an apocalypse, and no time at all for looking back. Say goodbye to the last frontier: as the door closes, you are going to wind up on one side or the other: either in the homestead (the security of the homeland, d'oh!) or the endless desert where the search goes on, forever. What has John Wayne to gain out there but more pain? It's what defines the hero, after all, the gain of pain, the endless self-stimming of the Westerner pitted against, not just the wilderness, but the inevitability of progress that will strip even that wilderness (wildness?) from him. Reality is a big emptiness that illusion fills up, like Cable Hogue's water hole on a wagon trail to nowhere.

If all forms of violence are quests for identity, I have found the Hollywood conspiracy and it is us. When the thing doesn't happen, the negative identity which the (for our purposes male) child assembles—lacking a father to emulate—as a defense against the annihilating narcissism of the mother (and all parents are narcissists, because the violent quest doesn't end with having children, it just becomes truly catastrophic), the very anti-narcissistic narcissistic identity takes hold, like a hole that can never be filled. And it is filled with rage against women.

The State can't tell us who we are and nor can culture; only mother and father know best. Top-down and bottom up, it's all the same construction. No matter how "pop" our fortress of identity is, or how much we think we are choosing it as a customized vehicle to enter "the world," we are still tied by the psychic umbilical cord to our original culture, the one that spawned us. The primal waters of Big Mother, who watches over us no matter how far we wander from home. It is this that drives the Westerner to wander, as if distance could ever make such a bond anything but stronger.

When I first wrote this section I was writing on an old pier on a lake, in the sun, in British Columbia, around noon on a July Thursday afternoon in 2017. The natural peacefulness of the place was, as usual, broken up and polluted by motor boats ridden by bored rich people burning endless gasoline like there's no tomorrow in their frenetic quests for identity. Earlier, a man went by in his canoe and interrupted my writing stream by shouting out, "It must be a really good book!" Apparently the insinuation was "to have my nose in it while surrounded by all this beauty." Did the man mistake what I was doing for reading, or did he recognize the signs of a frenetic and fevered *auteur* at work? Or—even longer odds—did he even recognize me from town as the "local author" (and thrift store owner)? Beggars of celebrity cannot be choosers.

Since my pen was clearly in view, moving rapidly, I chose to go with the latter. Why not? I get to choose what I believe, and so do you.* (You can believe that or not.) I chose to believe that—for all its naked contortionism and desperate grabs for attention, however much it may have Hollywood icons muttering in their premature graves, and despite the obvious futility of another cultural artifact denouncing the artificiality of culture—this must be *a really good book.*

If not, I still have the lake.

---

* Editor's note # 4: This could be more explicitly linked to the matrix pills image— when you finish the next chapter, outtakes, etc., and put the book down, you'll have to face your life, and believe . . . whatever you want to believe (or not; for those familiar with the pills suprametaphor, it jumps off the page).

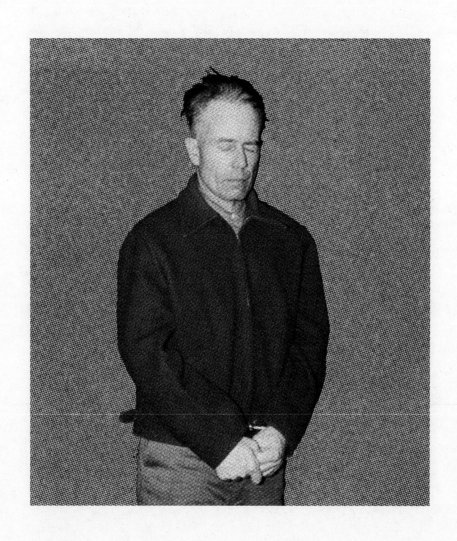

16

I CONFESS

16.1. NO MORE MAPS OF HELL

"The artist seeks to improve upon Nature, which is basically
hubris, the promethean urge, and perhaps only the sublimation,
after all, of his urge to destroy it. . . . Every artist is a 'reformed'
psychopath; every psychopath a frustrated artist."

—JAKE HORSLEY, *The Blood Poets*

The night after first completing this chapter, on July 15, 2020, I
listened to a tape I had made thirteen years previously, on July 15,
2007. On the tape, I recounted a dream in which I was fighting
with my ex-partner, Liz.

*I told Liz that I almost felt like a different person. She accused me of being
negative so I stormed off and climbed some stairs to get away from her. I was
going to sit on the stairs and turn out all the lights so she wouldn't be able to find
me. I wanted to disappear.*

*I began watching an interview with Roman Polanski. He was lit by red
light, looking very satanic. He was very aware of satanic stuff. He didn't seem evil
but he was acknowledging these forces. He was talking hypothetically, without
giving away that he believed in this stuff, talking "as if" (as regards* Rosemary's
Baby, *for example). But I knew that he actually was acknowledging his involvement with those forces. He talked about people who, if they believed enough in*

something, they could create it. They created the devil with enough components, like a carpenter building a table: they just got together the components and they created a devil.

It was through listening to him that I received information about Egyptian royalty—a man and a woman who had come to despise each other—and I realized that Liz and I were being possessed by past selves. It wasn't me who felt anger and hatred for her, it was another being that took me over, and I couldn't actually resist it. I managed to force myself to say "This is not me!" It was like being a puppet and wresting control for a moment: I had to force the words out and overlay them on top of what the being wanted me to say.

This being hated Liz, or the being in Liz that was also fighting, and they were both using us to get at each other, like dead spirits. The giveaway was that I actually enjoyed hurting Liz, and I didn't understand it. It made me feel terrible, as if there was something deeply wrong with me, and that compounded the problem because I then drew further away from Liz out of a feeling of guilt. But it was all because of these beings.

I took Liz upstairs to watch Polanski, so she would understand.

◆

> "Working on your book would be an act of biting the hand that feeds me at the moment [and] I think that one would be asking a publisher to bite the hand that feeds them by publishing a book that takes on a system they are invested in. Or if your theory is true—they would give you an advance then bury your book to protect their fellow media mafia."
>
> —LITERARY AGENT, *to author, on* 16 Maps of Hell

The last few books I have written were all difficult to finish.* With *16 Maps of Hell*, I deliberately set myself a hurdle at the start by intending to

---

* *Seen and Not Seen* veered into dark and difficult waters in its final chapters, as it shifted unexpectedly from a movie autobiography to the attempt to understand my brother's death and the family skeletons that predestined it. *Prisoner of Infinity* required a hiatus of three years before it finally came to term. *Dark Oasis* took almost ten years to complete and release—mostly because of the open-ended subject matter and my uncertainty about publishing. With *Vice of Kings*, I went as far into the wound as I could without losing the plot entirely, but the work still feels incomplete to me.

make a 180° turn in the final chapters, from darkness to light. My first mistake. When traveling through Hell, turning back is not an option. Actually, the way the book evolved, it had already begun to spiral out of my control with what was originally the fourth and final part (then called "Eyes without a Face"), as superheroes and scientism made a non-sequitur-entrance and the narrative dragged its author into the apocalyptic present. On top of that, I was trying to propose a solution, a way out, a cure, where until then I had always contented myself with diagnostics. I wanted to give myself a no-get-out-clause—ironically, a *huis clos* or no exit—to knocking my predilection for darkness on its head. "No more maps of Hell!" The result is the book you have, with any luck, just read.

The first two readers to give feedback—on an earlier and very different draft of this book—were young, intellectual, university-trained males. When both expressed disappointment, even frustration, with the ending, it occurred to me that a prison break from Hell might not involve a tidy resolution or a satisfyingly cathartic, Hollywood-style ending but something closer to the opposite (as in the much-reviled, vastly underrated *The Counselor*): a rude awakening that breaks the contract of narrative transportation and leaves the reader stranded and parched in the desert of the real. Perhaps, I thought, I have to abandon hope to leave Hell, as well as enter?

The pathology that has been under examination over the past few hundred pages—that is at the core of this world, with Hollywood as the most virulently enflamed example—is that of the *desire for specialness*. To elevate our constructed identity to the "A-list" of existence and enter the Hall of Fame is the Luciferian bid to perfect a false identity and reign in Hell. Fame is the starkest, most grotesque, absurd, and widespread manifestation of the desire for specialness in all its hollowness. What compromises this present work (no cultural artifact is without compromise) is the degree to which it was written as the final fling of a lifetime's effort to storm heaven by asserting its author's specialness. These attempts, in their very voraciousness, continue to feed the Hollywood machine, as what we resist, grows stronger. Even as I am attempting to uncover some great secret here (the exit to Hell), I am also, with another part of me, *doing all I can to conceal it.* This presents a seemingly impossible dilemma. Can I reveal my effort to conceal?

With *16 Maps of Hell*, I have once again thrown my psychological complex on the operating table, and on the mercy of the reader. Merely by witnessing this, you also participate in the dissection. I am hoping it will prove the *post-mortem* of that complex and not its preservation, that the corpse I leave behind is my own inner Dorian Gray in all its putrefaction. I am hoping that the Hollywood-as-Hell-complex mapped here is the shell I leave behind, and that what you have read is not only a thorough diagnosis of the disease but an early application of a cure that maps the first indications of recovery. I hope, but I must abandon hope in order to simply *see*.

If this isn't "meta" enough, there's still one more layer of the onion to peel. Having raised the funds to release this work, I began proof-reading the MS before sending it to my index-builder. What was my shock when I discovered that, apparently, I had changed so dramatically since completing it that large passages, whole chapters even, left me cold. The meticulous assemblage of biographical detail about movies and their makers felt tedious and lifeless, even dispiriting. The problem wasn't the subject matter; it wasn't even that anything was necessarily missing. It was that the themes of the book, the deeper meanings, were invisible. If they were there at all, they were buried under all the data, much of which *was* sort of numbing because, let's face it, Hollywood personalities are not the most vital or inspiring of human beings.

Perhaps the fault was not in the stars but in myself, I thought, hopefully? Maybe I was simply jaded from over-exposure to the material? It wasn't until I reached what was then Chapters Eleven and Twelve, on the New Hollywood nexus of Hodel, Huston, Evans, and Polanski, that I saw a way out and through this unexpected cave-in. I realized that, with a few short, sharp strokes, those chapters all but made my case for Hollywood as a cavern of dark sorcery. I then made an impulsive decision, half rational, half intuitive, to place them at the start, and immediately, I began to glimpse a whole new structure and impetus for the work—a narrative *drive*. It was then that I realized that this book couldn't *really* be about Hollywood corruption, at all, since that was so easy to establish with the first couple of chapters. The theme of the book was something subtler, darker, and more artfully concealed; so artfully, in fact, that I had failed to discover it.[*]

---

[*] The irony of having to totally restructure this book at the eleventh hour was that I had taken an enormous amount of care in structuring it, mathematically, as never before, to make it almost perfectly symmetrical and evenly distributed. There was no ostensible reason for this, I just noticed at some point how obsessive I was about getting the chapters

✦

"As has been documented, the use of terror and violence was especially directed against women and children."

—BRIAN HAYDEN, *The Power of Ritual in Prehistory*

16 Maps of Hell describes an internal war between mind and body that leads to a split—a wound—between body and soul. This wound is both enacted and perpetuated via the systematized torture of women (and children), on the one hand, and the creation of dissociated realms of empowerment—hierarchies of abuse—on the other. Now, not merely in the final stages but past the presumed finish line—in the book's afterlife, so to speak—I am obliged (or compelled) to attempt, before the reader's unbelieving eyes (unsuspend disbelief if you please), to bring those hidden themes to the light *of my own awareness*, knowing that the only way I will succeed is if my pen is sufficiently in communication with—or in service to—my unconscious, and if my unconscious is sufficiently coherent to provide the insight I am seeking.

Good thing I am self-publishing, I thought, otherwise these massive last-minute revisions and significant additions would not be possible. Even so, it is *highly* risky to try and incorporate fresh insights at the last moment because, without the luxury of time to let them ferment and sprout, they may fail to mesh with the rest of the book. To Hell with it! I choose to trust that my readers prefer a diamond in the rough to a polished lump of coal. This last addition is therefore considerably more speculative and further out on a limb than I wanted—or dared—to go with the rest of the book. It is a provisional hypothesis offered as we reach the end of the (newly organized)

---

roughly the same length, and decided to go *with* that rather than against it. It turned out that my over-determined structure was just scaffolding that had to come down. Possibly, it was a way for me to keep from being overwhelmed by the material and feel like I was in control of it. If so, I think the cost was that there was no space for *the inner life of the text* to emerge and express itself. This was probably also the *point*: to prevent myself from *seeing* what I was trying to see by writing the book.

work and head hopefully—but I hope not blindly—towards what may or may not be the exit.

I'd assumed the exit from Hell would be where the light was (see 14.5–14.6). It has turned out that, even if this is so, the darkest part of the terrain also has to be pushed into, through, and past, to get to the light behind it. Where the darkest portion of the map is, there seek the light. Because it is what we are most firmly committed to keeping hidden that holds the key to enlightenment.

✦

"All the darkness in the world cannot extinguish the light of a single candle."

—ST. FRANCIS OF ASSISI, *The Little Flowers of St. Francis of Assisi*

The discovery I made with *Seen and Not Seen* was that, if the real reason I write is to unravel my own crucial fictions, to identify the secret I am keeping from myself, then all of my previous writings are coded messages, left behind by my unconscious for my conscious mind to someday unravel. They are hinting at things I was unable to see directly, or to admit to, transmitting the truth *despite myself*, a truth concealed in the text itself, like dream-movies that play beneath my waking awareness.

No amount of confession can cleanse the soul if we don't fully know what it is we have done. What is not owned cannot be absolved. This is why my books have become increasingly self-referential, and more and more evidently the same work, circling back and back to an original wound that first leaked them. And this is why the most meaningful clues I find are not in the movies or the culture, but in *what I have already written about these things*. It's not Peckinpah or Polanski, Hitchcock or Kubrick, Strieber or Castaneda, de Ruiter, Crowley, or Savile—or even my brother—that hold the secrets to my enthrallment; it's the *intersection* between those things and me, the psychic *vesica piscis* in which this dream-story is unfolding. No doubt this is due to an original enmeshment or introjection, a Christ-like wound that never healed. If this work only finally found its narrative thrust when I identified a protagonist to mirror myself in Roman Polanski, it is because it is only by making visible the fusion that occurred in my adolescence between

Polanski's psyche and my own—an unholy parasocial alliance, as indicated by my dream—that I am able to undo the *latah* of cultural bondage, and dismantle the devil inside.

In this regard, it can surely be no coincidence that the very first pages of my first published work, *The Blood Poets*, are about two films, *Psycho* and *Peeping Tom*, that I find now resurfacing—independently of my conscious will or design—in the final pages of this culminating work. It is because the themes I found in those films are central to the mystery that my adult life has been consumed by the need to solve. Little did I know. Once upon a time in Hollywood? I truly *believed* this was all just entertainment.

16.2.   THE HITCHCOCK JOKE: CASE STUDY # 16, ALFRED HITCHCOCK/ED GEIN

"That's why I take pride in the fact that *Psycho*, more than any of my other pictures, is a film that belongs to filmmakers, to you and me."

—HITCHCOCK, *to Truffaut, 1962*

One of the very first Pauline Kael essays I ever read was a long 1975 piece called "Fear of Movies," defending violence in movies. Kael singled out *Psycho* in the article as one of the few violent movies she objected to. Referring to it as "a borderline case of immorality," she objected above all to "the director's cheerful complicity with the killer" and his "sadistic glee." "It was hard to laugh at the joke," she wrote, "after having been put in the position of being stabbed to death in the motel shower." Despite her reservations, Kael described *Psycho* as "a good dirty joke, even if we in the audience were its butt" (all quotes 1980, p. 436). *The Blood Poets*, as Kael herself wrote to me after reading it, was like a book-length letter to Kael, in which I riffed off her own writings throughout. The riff began in the book's introduction, when I commented on Kael's reading of *Psycho*:

> In *Psycho* we have perhaps the first intimations of a trend still several years to come: the hero as psychopath (perhaps complemented by what Kael observes as the director as murderer?) . . . The audience's *unconscious* feeling that the director somehow identified with the killer, that he was indeed playing out the whole horrible scenario as a kind of grand guignol jest, would serve, above all, to further consolidate their sense of dis-ease, of menace, and of being somehow caught, beyond their power to escape, *in anything but good hands* (Horsley, 1999, p. xxiv, xxi, emphasis added).

It is strange to consider now what I intuited back then: that the film geniuses I admired were not to be trusted; stranger still that it didn't stop me from aspiring to become one of them.

Psycho was based on a novel by Robert Bloch, supposedly inspired by Ed Gein, the convicted murderer and body snatcher from Wisconsin, active in the 1950s (he died in a mental home in 1984). In fact, Bloch later clarified that he based his novel

> on the situation rather than on any person, living or dead, involved in the Gein affair. . . . I knew very little of the details concerning that case and virtually nothing about Gein himself at the time. It was only some years later, when doing my essay on Gein for "The Quality of Murder," that I

discovered how closely the imaginary character I'd created resembled the real Ed Gein both in overt act and apparent motivation.[1]

Such intuited similarities included how Gein was said to have been greatly impacted by his mother's death and kept her bedroom in pristine condition for years after—something both Bates and Gein had in common with Jimmy Savile (who was also a necrophiliac[2]). Though Gein was only charged with the murder of two women, both of whom he said resembled his mother, he disinterred many others with the same likeness. But it was the grisly use to which Gein put the female body parts that cemented his horror legend. After his arrest, police searched Gein's house and found:

> two shin bones, four human noses, a quart can converted into a tom-tom by skin stretched over both top and bottom, a bowl made from the inverted half of a human skull, nine "death masks" (from the well preserved skin from the faces of women), ten female heads with the tops sawn off above the eyebrows, bracelets of human skin, a purse made with a handle of human skin, sheath for a knife made in human skin, a pair of leggings made from human skin, four chairs with the seats being replaced by strips of human skin, a shoe box containing nine salted vulvas of which his mother's was painted silver, a hanging human head, a lampshade covered with human skin, a shirt made of human skin, a number of shrunken heads (*Ed always joked that he had a collection of shrunken heads*), two skulls for Gein's bedposts, a pair of human lips hanging from string, *Ed's full woman body suit constructed with human skin and complete with mask and breasts*, Bernice Worden's heart in a pan on the stove, and the refrigerator which was stacked with human organs. The bodies of 15 different women had been mutilated to provide Gein's trophies (emphasis added).[3]

The first body Gein dug up (in 1947) was that of his mother, who died in 1945. "Twisting her head off with his bare hands, Ed took the head and shrunk it."[4] (Some joke. Ed Kemper had similar issues: he murdered his mother and then raped her severed head.) Gein acted; Bloch imagined;

Hitchcock, Anthony Perkins, and Janet Leigh *re*enacted. So who "created" Norman Bates? Did Gein ever see *Psycho* and if so, what did he think of the fictionalized recreation of his life?* We could say that Hitchcock was an artist and that he victimized no one; or we could say that, as an artist, he took Gein's "work" and adapted it in such a way as to turn an entire nation, for generations to come, into the paying victims of his terror campaign. Both are true, but neither is quite accurate.

Ed Gein, the 20th century prototype of the serial killer, dug up his mother and other corpses, murdered her symbolically by killing women in her likeness, and made clothing out of women's skin and body parts. Gein was the inspiration, if that's the word, not only for *Psycho* but for two other celebrated horror movies, *The Texas Chain Saw Massacre*, and *The Silence of the Lambs*. *The Silence of the Lambs* was the most critically acclaimed horror movie since *The Exorcist* and won the five principal Academy Awards in 1991. As crude and manipulative a movie "psyop" as *The Exorcist* in its day, the film juxtaposed its mythical *übermensch*-as-psychopath, Hannibal Lecter (a "secular" vampire), with Buffalo Bill, a serial killer who murders women and removes their skins in order to build himself a woman-suit, à la Gein, literally *putting himself inside the body of a woman.*

"For Ed Gein," his biographer wrote, "cutting up women who reminded him of his mother and preserving parts of them served two contradictory urges: to bring her back to life and to destroy her as the source of his frustration" (Schechter, p. 180). It seems apparent—if controversial to state these days—that *turning oneself into a woman* by surgically "robbing" the necessary body parts could satisfy both these urges, by essentially *replacing the mother's body with one's own* (or vice versa).[†] In *The Blood Poets*,

---

* One pathologist on the Ed Gein case, Dr F. Eigenberger (a woman), speculated that the seed of Gein's murderous impulses might have been planted by comic books and movies, "a speculation prompted partly no doubt by the discovery of Eddie's massive collection of quasipornographic crime publications and partly by contemporary concerns over excessive comic book violence, a controversial issue in 1950s America" (Schechter, p. 91). This was written in 2010, and the insinuation is that such concerns were unfounded and seem merely "quaint" to us today. This may be a faulty assumption, as we'll see.

† When an insatiable hunger for the mother's body is combined with the fear of being annihilated by/within it, there is a terrible push-pull, fight or flight, fuck or freeze struggle, in both the psyche and the body, that goes on indefinitely, offering no relief. This is

I described the artist as "reformed" psychopath who seeks to create a perfect copy of Nature (Art, capital "A"), as the sublimation of his (or her) urge to destroy it. Is this the culturally endorsed expression of Gein's (and Norman Bates') need to re-possess the mother's body and transform himself into a copy of her—*via the destruction of women's bodies*? If so, then Hitchcock and Gein may have been closer—in both temperament and technique—than has been formerly supposed.

◆

> "You know that poor, tortured soul Jimmy Stewart played in *Vertigo*? Well, that's Hitch."
>
> —VERA MILES *(Jessica Biel)*, *Hitchcock*

In the quote that opens Part One of this book, Carol J. Clover writes, "as the audiences of horror film in general are to the directors of those films, female is to male. Hitchcock's 'torture the women' then means, simply, torture the audience" (p. 52–3). Hitchcock, as the pioneer of the modern horror film, perceived the movie-going audience as essentially *passive*, receptive, and treated them accordingly. The audience, obligingly, was waiting to be "penetrated" by Hitch's violating camera/gaze, a gaze Clover equates with Norman Bates' knife, a correlation literalized that same year by Michael Powell's *Peeping Tom*, which in Clover's words maps "the symbiotic interplay of the sadistic work of the filmmaker and the masochistic stake of the spectator, an arrangement *on which horror cinema insists*" (Clover, p. 199, emphasis added).

Hitchcock's cinematic sadism would seem consistent with his sexual impotence in his married life, at least after the birth of his daughter Alma (the name means "soul"). By all accounts, Hitch's sex life outside of his movies *was* painfully dysfunctional, a case of "chronic abstinence . . . complicated by his obesity and . . . chronic impotence. Yet *his interest never waned*" (Whittey,

---

something I have, over the course of my writing "career," been mapping within my own divided consciousness, not only by telling but by *showing* that schism: hence writing has been for me a way *in* to the superculture, on the one hand, and a way to break *out* of it, on the other. Let not the left side of thy brain know what the right side is up to, for you cannot serve two masters except by splitting yourself in two.

p. 394). So what, pray, did he *do* with that interest? In the chapter on *Vertigo* in *The Secret Life of Movies*, I wrote:

> Sex repressed must come out willy-nilly, and since it is such a powerful (creative) force, it almost invariably comes out as violence: wanton, irrational violence, as often as not aimed at the object of sexual desire that awoke the forbidden impulse in the first place. All this is basic, textbook stuff, and *Psycho* diagnosed the American nation (on the very brink of the assassinations and the Vietnam war) as suffering from *a chronic and crippling mother complex*, a case of terminal repression that could only lead to explosive results (emphasis added).

Hitchcock told Truffaut in 1962, "it's generally the woman who has the final say on which picture a couple is going to see. In fact, it's generally the woman who will decide, later on, whether it was a good or a bad picture." This may be a key observation for understanding both Hitchcock and the art and grammar of suspense cinema that he helped to develop. Though Hitchcock's remark is much more specific and literal than the archetypal principle indicated by Clover's text, it is, I think, equally suggestive. Hitchcock's inference is that the "male gaze" (a phrase coined by feminist film theorist, Laura Mulvey) is *subject to the female one*: that men follow *the woman's lead*, not only about which movie to see, but how to evaluate what they are looking at.* The idea that the male gaze is submissive to the female gaze is consistent with the idea of a maternally-enmeshed psyche and a mother-enthralled culture, making it fitting that *Psycho*—the über-text of mother-bondage whose central murder act is preceded by an act of male gazing—is the movie text *par excellence* that diagnoses this condition. It is also the prototype for the modern horror movie, specifically the slasher film that brought woman-torture all the way from the *avant-garde* into the mainstream.

One of the many disturbing implications of all this is that it is not only *men* who wish to see women in peril, and who experience an erotic charge from images of females being tortured. It may also, even primarily,

---

* As a way of seeing women and the world, the psychology of the male gaze is comparable to the psychology of scopophilia, referring to both the aesthetic and the sexual pleasures derived from looking at someone or something.

be *women*. If so, this would presumably be from an altogether different perspective, one more fully identified with the victim than the persecutor. Nonetheless, our assumptions are seriously challenged once we allow the primacy of the female gaze over the male. And almost certainly, all this relates to an unconscious desire to reenact an early trauma, i.e., women who have been traumatized in early life may find relief in reliving the trauma via horror movie enactments, just as men may desire to unconsciously enact their revenge, as I was doing as an adolescent, while watching *Straw Dogs, Last House on the Left,* and *I Spit on Your Grave*. In both cases (male and female), however, the sadomasochistic element seems likely to neutralize any actual therapeutic potential of such reenactments.

16.3. SORCERERS OLD & NEW

> "[T]hough he denies it, I suspect Roman believes in the existence of evil as an active force in the world."
>
> —KENNETH TYNAN, *"The Polish Imposition"*

While I was contemplating the task of radically reorganizing *16 Maps of Hell,* just weeks before sending it to the printers, certain parallels between Polanski and the works of Carlos Castaneda occurred to me.* Specifically,

---

* I have deconstructed the Castaneda mythos thoroughly elsewhere, but nonetheless a brief proviso may be in order: while Don Juan Matus (Castaneda's sorcerer teacher) may be a semi-fictional composite, and while many of the incidents Castaneda recounts (in his twelve books) may be heavily embellished, I am proceeding on the belief that the information/knowledge in the books—specifically around the sorcery practices of the old and new seers—is at least somewhat accurate, i.e., that there exist groups of "sorcerers" who adhere to these beliefs and put them into practice. It follows that these sorcerers must have been *somewhat* effective in doing so, since beliefs can only survive their application if they work at least *some* of the time. For more on CC, see *Prisoner of Infinity,* part two and "A Sorcerer's Corner: Carlos Castaneda's Doomed Romance with Knowledge," by Aeolus Kephas, *Auticulture,* 2011: https://boxes.nyc3.digitaloceanspaces.com/wp-content/uploads/Castaneda.pdf

I wish to cite what Castaneda described as the "old seers," in *The Fire from Within*: "terrifying men [whose] bid is to dominate, to master everybody and everything" (1984, p. 103). In *The Art of Dreaming*, two books later, Castaneda reveals that some of these old seers devoted much of their efforts—like Ed Gein—to *turning themselves into women*. In the case of the old seers, it was a bid to escape the predations of "inorganic beings," and/or to cheat death and attain virtual immortality. In Castaneda's fantastic narrative, this entailed a full, physical transformation.

> "Don Juan explained to me that sorceresses, in theory, come and go as they please in that world because of their enhanced awareness and their femaleness. . . . "The first part of the dreaming lesson in question is that maleness and femaleness are not final states but are the result of a spe-cific act of positioning the assemblage point," he said. "And this act is, naturally, a matter of volition and training. Since it was a subject close to the old sorcerers' hearts, they are the only ones who can shed light on it" (1993, p. 188, 210).

Castaneda's Don Juan goes further still, in claiming something trans-gender activists could wholeheartedly get behind: that sorcery is powerful not only to change one's sex but retroactively "correct" what sex one was born as:

> "I have already said to you that to be a natural man or a natural woman is a matter of positioning the assemblage point. . . . By natural I mean someone who was born either male or female. To a seer, the shiniest part of the assemblage point faces outward, in the case of females, and inward, in the case of males. The tenant's assemblage point was originally facing inward, but he changed it by twisting it around and making his egglike energy shape look like a shell that has curled up on itself" (1993, p. 219).

Before explaining why this may be significant at this 11th hour, I wish to introduce a second component, namely, the old seers' *bid for immortal-ity* (retaining their individual sense of identity beyond death) via the art of *dreaming*. Specifically, this requires *the use of consciously directed dreaming attention to create perfect replicas of this world and move into them.* The art of the old seers, Castaneda claimed, was so prodigious that many of them exist to this day in these otherworldly realms, within a bandwidth of the human consciousness—similar to Bardo realms in Eastern tradition. Castaneda describes meeting one of the old seers, a being capable of transforming into a man *or* a woman, and names him/her in the narrative: "the tenant."

The tenant, Castaneda writes, "came from a line of sorcerers who knew how to move about in the second attention by projecting their intent." An ancient "art of projecting their thoughts in *dreaming*" led to "the truthful reproduction of any object or structure or landmark or scenery of their choice." Castaneda claims that the tenant and the sorcerers of her line started by "gazing at a simple object and memorizing every detail of it."

> They would then close their eyes and visualize the object and correct their visualization against the true object until they could see it, in its completeness, with their eyes shut. The next thing in their developing scheme was to dream with the object and create in the dream, from the point of view of their own perception, a total materialization of the object. . . . From a simple object, those sorcerers went on to take more and more complex items. Their final aim was for all of them together to visualize a total world, then dream that world and thus re-create *a totally veritable realm where they could exist* (1993, p. 231–2, emphasis added).

The tenant's "art was to make that dream an all-inclusive reality," Castaneda writes: "the art of the old sorcerers, the most frightening thing there is" (1993, p. 259).*

A week before first writing this chapter, I received a review copy of a 2020 book called *The Big Goodbye: Chinatown and the Last Years of Hollywood.* Predictably enough, most of the book is a celebration of Hollywood's golden age and a reification of the myth around the dark nexus of power and influence that begins *16 Maps of Hell. The Big Goodbye* follows the making of

---

* If that last reads like the tag-line for a Hollywood horror movie, this may be very much the point. Castaneda, an LA-based fantasist who managed to create his own cult via his hugely successful esoteric mythic-fiction series, was known to fraternize in Hollywood circles. He has also been linked—including by his own admission—to intelligence agencies (*Prisoner of Infinity*, p. 123).

Chinatown through each and every stage of development. At one point, the book quotes an intern on set, who describes Polanski as

> using everything available to him to express his vision . . . filmmaking is about the details. This is the most all-encompassing art form in the world—musicians, painters, costumers, cinematographers, actors, every kind of talent—and Roman was the master of all of them. He was on top of *every single detail in the frame of every single shot* (p. 211, emphasis added).

The context here is "how a masterpiece was created," but I want to put it in a very different context, that of Castaneda's old seers—real or imaginary—with their obsessive, painstaking creation of surrogate realities through *dreaming*. Just as Polanski obsessively recreated the Los Angeles of 1937 for *Chinatown* and the New York of 1965–66 for *Rosemary's Baby*—as a surrogate reality to escape into—so audiences followed after him in droves, like the proverbial lemmings, into that "Paramount" forgetting chamber (a fantasy to trump reality). As *The Big Goodbye* testifies (the cover copy begins 'CHINATOWN IS THE HOLY GRAIL OF 1970S CINEMA"), the film became a "limited hang out" for thousands of film buffs to visit and revisit, over and over again, including, no doubt, in their dreams: a home away from home. The film consolidated Polanski's status in Hollywood as reigning film genius. Yet strangely, the film he made after *Chinatown* was an odd little Gothic horror-comedy shot in Paris. It was called *The Tenant*.

16.4.   THE FALSE EXIT

"[With *The Tenant*] Polanski never allows us to forget that we are watching a movie. He characteristically makes us question the motives that underlie our interest in *the false self of the filmic body he has created.* . . The analogy to Polanski's own audience is clear; for *we too may be looking for an alternate, false self upon which to project unacceptable impulses toward sexuality and aggression that we consciously deny to our 'real' selves.* . . . Polanski, with his usual contrariety, has forced the audience to face up to the squalid nature of our pleasure in the genre even as he has satisfied it. In *The Tenant*, Polanski pushes the psychology of the horror story to its limit."

—VIRGINIA WRIGHT WEXMAN, *"The Body as Theater"*
(emphasis added)

"A film sums up the experiences of my life," Polanski says in *The Big Goodbye.* "You absorb the experience, you assimilate it and you make a decision. A film sums up everything—whom I see, what I drink, the amount of ice cream I eat. It is everything. Do you understand? Everything" (p. 236). As all of this bubbled up in my consciousness, a line from *The Blood Poets*, quoted earlier, began to take on increased significance: "A serious artist and *a respecter of the mysteries* (though *a self-professed atheist*), Polanski *made every effort towards authenticity"* (p. 73, emphasis added). In fact, Polanski never expressed respect for "the mysteries" (on the contrary, as we'll see), even if his work seems to clearly convey it. But then, the best occultists keep their affiliations *hidden.*

The same might be said of Hitchcock. In the chapter on Brian De Palma in *The Blood Poets,* I described Hitchcock's oeuvre as "the first surrealist body of work in American cinema":

[His] films seem to take place within a specifically cinematic realm: the Hitchcock Universe. . . . Hitchcock's films are not realistic, but they're not fantastic either; they are a form of heightened realism, created by Hitchcock's subtle but precise control of the medium, which he directed towards an intensification of our reactions—our emotions—*in order to lead us into his dream world* [emphasis added]. This is roughly the definition of *surreal* (and of cinema also), as what is "above reality," and Hitchcock's preoccupation with violence, with murder, crime, intrigue, madness, obsession, and, of course, suspense, was due to his fascination not for the subjects themselves but for their *effects* upon the audience (p. 201–2).

Polanski has made similar statements about his approach to filmmaking. "I'm not preoccupied with the macabre," he said in 1971, "I'm rather more interested in the behavior of people under stress, when they are no longer in comfortable, everyday situations where they can afford to respect the conventional rules and morals of society" (Randall, p. 302). Clover posits the director/artist as psychopath-murderer-rapist, and the audience (member) as his victim. In 1999, as quoted at the start of this chapter, I described the artist as hell-bent on destroying nature, in order to replace it with *an image*.

We are back to the technology of dissociation: trauma inflicted on the audience-body that leads them into a state of disembodiment, a willing escape into the "second attention" of the movie-dream-world. The best way "to provide the public with beneficial shocks," Hitchcock said in 1962, "is through a movie" (Truffaut, p. 201). This "art" (or dark science) is *essential* to filmmakers, above all to those with a Surrealist bent. It is the art of inducing trance states, the art of *dreaming*. As I wrote in *The Blood Poets* of Polanski's *Repulsion*:

> Polanski has a natural instinct for what is cinematic, an instinct that can never be learned and which amounts to *a kind of wizardry* (Lynch had it too, for a time). He can make the most *ordinary acts or objects seem somehow extraordinary*, and for whole sequences at a time, the film achieves an almost mesmeric hold over us. The trancelike motions of Carol lead us slowly and inexorably into her own world, a world where nothing is familiar and *the smallest detail becomes charged with a hallucinatory power* (p. 59–60, emphasis added).

The theme emerging here may be so obvious that I have overlooked it for over twenty years. Filmmaking *is* sorcery, the modern technological development of an ancient art. This one clear insight renders any number of previously gnomic, incidental details suddenly compelling in their stark implications. For example, in the 1934 version of Hitchcock's *The Man Who Knew Too Much*, a married couple discovers evidence of a plot to assassinate a European head of state. To keep them quiet, the clique of spies abducts their *adolescent daughter*. The father hunts them down to a church where they are posing as a "mystery cult" called the Tabernacle of the Sun. He witnesses a ceremony that begins with an admonition that "those who have not yet become initiated into the mysteries of the first circle of the seven-fold ray" must have their minds & souls "purged and made clean [by submitting] to *a very simple process of control.*" The symbolism is straight out of Blavatsky's Theosophy; the scene is highly anomalous to the rest of the film, and even the rest of Hitchcock's oeuvre. The film itself combines murder plots (to be carried out at the Albert Hall, under cover of a *performance*), intelligence operatives, occult secret societies, rituals, hypnotic suggestion and mind control, and the abduction of a teenage girl, all in one "satirical" package!

In the 1980s, British director John Boorman told critic Michel Ciment:

> Hypnosis interests me a great deal, as does extra-sensory perception; and it's a field I've studied quite thoroughly. What's more, I believe that *the occult and the cinema are natural companions.* What we experience while watching a film is comparable to the occult in its atmosphere and in the illusion that is created (Ciment, p. 157–164, emphasis added).

At the very least, Hitchcock, Polanski, Friedkin, Boorman, and countless others were unconsciously continuing the legacy of Castaneda's old seers and Hayden's secret society sorcerers. But were they *consciously doing so?* Maybe *all* the major Hollywood filmmakers are? (Why did Friedkin, at the very peak of his career, give his remake of *The Wages of Fear* the title of *Sorcerer?*) To imagine that Hollywood filmmakers are part of a secret society of sorcerers practicing a dark art through movies may seem improbable. But to posit that such secret sorcery societies exist—as apparently they have throughout human history and pre-history—and that its members might *choose to use filmmaking* (and filmmakers) as a means to extend their domination over "everyone and everything," this is perhaps considerably less far-fetched. Yet oddly, the two claims are both the same. Maybe sometimes we have to turn a McGuffin inside out to see what's inside it?[*]

✦

> "For Trelkovsky [in *The Tenant*] death is given sovereignty over life, and his mind becomes a dis-ease of the body. His dissociated psyche then sets about slowly, inexorably, to destroy his body, to lead it (like the serpent with its wiles) to ruin with false promises and chimera. When finally the split-off is complete, Trelkovsky has 'become' his head—namely his fantasy projection of Simone. He has effectively denied his body completely (signified by his becoming a woman); at this point he is ready to 'translate' to the next dimension, and hurls himself from the balcony. This is also the point at which Trelkovsky enters the imaginal realm fully (not just mentally but physically) and his perceptions become unhinged. His world has become an organic, self-sustaining nightmare, a living hell.
>
> —JASON HORSLEY, *The Secret Life of Movies*

The possibility of some sort of "sorcerous" secret societal correspondences between Castaneda and Polanski—both Los Angeles-based (in the 1960s and 1970s), short, soft-voiced, exotic-accented, womanizing masters of trance fiction—is not unthinkable. A possibly more plausible explanation is that Castaneda drew on Polanski's film and Roland Topor's 1962 novel for the creation of his metafictional opus.[†] Whatever the case, after delivering

---

[*] Now men turning themselves into women has spilled over from the realms of "occult conspiracy to attain immortality" into a growing cultural trend or *zeitgeist* that is the capstone of an identity politics intersectionality endeavor: to assume the highest victim status, and hence the greatest power of retribution.

[†] Roland Topor was a French Jew of Polish parents who spent his early years in hiding from the Nazis and later became known as an illustrator, comics artist, painter, novelist, playwright, actor and filmmaker with a Surrealist bent. (Topor's *The Tenant* was re-released in October 2006 with an introduction by Thomas Ligotti.)

"the holy grail of 1970s cinema"—and before his fall from grace and flight from the US in 1977—Polanski made *The Tenant*, a film which, though far messier and less disciplined a work than *Chinatown*, is considerably more interesting and revealing.

Polanski plays the protagonist, Trelkovsky, who rents an apartment in Paris when the former tenant, Simone, throws herself out of the window. As if to make sure he will get to keep his new apartment, Trelkovsky visits her in hospital before she dies. Over time, with the mysterious conspiring of the neighbors (the film is like a male version of *Rosemary's Baby*, and/or *Repulsion*), he becomes increasingly identified with Simone, and as his mental degeneration proceeds, he gradually *turns himself into her*. *The Tenant* is about *a man pressured by those around him to turn himself into a woman*. The key monologue in the film, delivered by Polanski himself, is about loss of identity: "By what right," Trelkovsky asks, "does the head claim the title of myself?" In *The Secret Life of Movies*, first written in 2000 but not published until 2009, I discussed the film in a chapter called "The Man Behind the Mask":

> Along with *Don't Look Now* and very few other films, *The Tenant* is a rare case of a horror movie that communicates a genuine sense of the *occult*. It presents consensus reality as a club from which it is possible, at any time, to be ostracized, whereupon the *true* nature of reality can no longer be avoided. This "club" provides shelter and refuge from the forces of our own unconscious, and as such, most of us (like Trelkovsky) would do just about anything to stay within it. It may be hell, but at least we belong there (p. 139–40).

The exit from Hell is also the entrance, but apparently it is also a *false* exit—and vice versa. (Do not let the head tell you who you are.)

After throwing himself out of the apartment window, Trelkovsky ends up trapped inside Simone's body, being visited by his former (male) self. She/he is bandaged from head to foot, the only visible part a disembodied mouth, emitting an eternally recurring scream of despair. The image, I realized while revisiting this material, is similar, if not identical, to a Samuel

Beckett stage production I discovered while looking more into its star, my former neighbor, Billie Whitelaw. The play was called *Not I.*

> During rehearsals for the 1973 British premiere of Samuel Beckett's *Not I* (1972), actor Billie Whitelaw collapsed. Whitelaw's experience of sensory deprivation rehearsing a play written with her in mind is an evental intervention into the voice's capacity—or incapacity, as you will see—to embody the disembodied, or text. Such is the province and paradox of theatre: to be resonating chamber, or translator, of voice and text into sensate, corporeal space. The floating monologist of *Not I* is a mouth, a disembodied and isolated entity of voice severed from body. *Whitelaw's collapse from sensory deprivation while rehearsing this part*—an event of affect—indicates that Beckett's late plays, written after the 1960s, *develop a dramaturgy of disembodiment* that is procedural and sensory, rather than symbolist or cognitive.[5]

In Whitelaw's own words: "If you are blindfolded and have a hood over your face, you hyperventilate, you suffer from sensory deprivation. . . . And I hung on and hung on until I couldn't any longer. I just went to pieces because I was convinced I was like an astronaut tumbling out into space."[6] All in a day's work for the genius and his muse? To torture the women and get them to "sing," to express terror and pain that is music to the psychopath's ears, is the dark side of Eros, when the impotent lover becomes the aggrandizer torturer.

To play the woman like an "instrument" is to turn her body into an "organ," as Hitchcock did with his actresses, in order to do so with his audiences. It is to fully possess the female body and turn it into an extension of

---

* Samuel Beckett's influence on Polanski was considerable. Besides trying to make a film version of *Waiting for Godot* in the 1960s, Polanski played Lucky in a 1989 French film version. "Beckett himself supervised the piece, his last public act before his death four months later. Polanski had owed the playwright a professional debt that went back to [Polanski's 1958 short] *Two Men and a Wardrobe*, and few of his major films were free of at least one character, scene, or individual speech that could have graced the pages of [Beckett]" (Sandford, p. 374).

one's own agony. "Not-I!" is the disembodied cry of the body to the soul: "Why hast thou forsaken me?"[*]

16.5. THE GOD OF CARNAGE

"Fantasies of unhealthy minds are now treated as proven facts."
—ROMAN POLANSKI, *2020*[7]

There are a few more pieces to toss into the puzzle before closing the box. David Bowie, at the tail end of his decade-long immersion in occultism in the 1970s, recorded *Lodger*, in 1979, his 13th album.[†] The cover art shows Bowie with his nose broken, one hand bandaged (like Simone in *The Tenant*), his limbs splayed out at unnatural angles, as if from a high fall— much as Trelkovsky is seen at the end of *The Tenant*. In the video for one of the singles taken from the album, "Boys (Keep Swinging)," Bowie dresses as a woman. The title, *Lodger*, besides being an obvious variation of *The Tenant*, also echoes another film that slides neatly into this closing occult nexus: Alfred Hitchcock's *The Lodger: A Story of the London Fog* (1927), a silent movie which the director considered to be the first true Hitchcock film. The film is about the hunt for a Jack the Ripper-like serial killer in London, called "The Avenger," who targets young blonde women on Tuesday evenings. Based on a novel of the same name by Marie Belloc Lowndes about

---

[*] As an adolescent, it was less the images of atrocities committed against women's bodies that aroused me than the *sounds* the actresses made—the cries, gasps, and moans of pain and terror that issued from them—and the sounds of a woman in agony are not always easy to distinguish from cries of sexual ecstasy.

[†] "There was a theory that one creates a *doppelgänger* and then imbues that with all your faults and guilts and fears and then eventually you destroy him, hopefully destroying all your guilt, fear and paranoia. And I often feel that I was doing that unwittingly, creating an alternative ego that would take on everything that I was insecure about." Bowie quoted in "The Laughing Gnostic," by Peter-R. Koenig, 1996, 2017: https://parareligion.ch/bowie.htm:

the Jack the Ripper murders, Hitch's biographer described it as "the first time Hitchcock has revealed his psychological attraction to the association between sex and murder, between ecstasy and death" (Spoto, p. 91).

Perhaps also significantly, the film is about the persecution of an *innocent*, wrongly accused of the murders, who narrowly escapes the ire of a lynch mob. The theme of the persecution of "the wrong man" recurred throughout Hitchcock's film career. It is less characteristic of Polanski's oeuvre, though in 2019 he made *An Officer and a Spy*, based on the Dreyfus affair, which involved the false accusation of a French officer for espionage, and which is now seen as a case of anti-Semitic persecution, a "witch-hunt." In 2020, Polanski's film was nominated for a number of awards at the "French Oscars." Polanski chose not to attend out of concern the ceremony would turn into "a public lynching" due to the many protests against him for the many allegations of sexual abuse.*

---

* "Fearing 'public lynching', Polanski pulls out of France's César awards," *France 24*, Feb 27, 2020:   https://www.france24.com/en/20200227-fearing-public-lynching-polanski-skips -french-oscars-night *An Officer and a Spy* is based on the novel by Robert Harris, who wrote the book with Polanski in mind. A quick glance at Harris' history reveals the usual "tells" of an undercover intelligence "asset." Harris went to King Edward VII School, Melton Mowbray, where he edited the school magazine (a hall has now been named after him). He read English literature at Selwyn College, Cambridge, where he was elected president of the Cambridge Union and became the editor of the oldest student newspaper at the university, *Varsity*. After Cambridge, he joined the BBC (employees at the BBC are regularly MI5-vetted, see *Vice of Kings* p. 260), and worked on the massively successful news and current affairs programs, *Panorama* and *Newsnight*. At the age of thirty, he got a job as political editor of *The Observer*, a paper with well-known ties to British intelligence (via David Astor, see *Vice of Kings*). If all of this isn't enough to place the letters M-I-5/6 after Harris' name, consider also: his first book was on biochemical warfare, followed by more nonfiction works on Hitler, the Hitler letters, and a number of leading UK politicians. His second work of fiction, *Enigma*, was about code-breaking during the Second World War at Cambridge. In the 2000s, he became close friends with Prime Minister Tony Blair, as well as Polanski, and he based his novel *The Ghost Writer* on his association with Blair; he then wrote the screenplay for Polanski, giving Polanski his biggest critical and commercial hit since *The Pianist*. *An Officer and a Spy*, the 2013 Harris novel that Polanski filmed in 2019, was inspired by Polanski's longstanding interest in the Dreyfus affair. Since Polanski was facing his own "lynch mob" in 2018–19, something he could well have foreseen, five or even ten years earlier, the subject matter may have been strategically chosen.

In *The Tenant*, Polanski also plays a "wrong man" who, like many of Hitchcock's protagonists, ends up in the wrong place at the wrong time and is misidentified by everyone around him—not as a criminal but as the former tenant, Simone. He becomes possessed by her *image* and, via a kind of schizophrenic persecution complex, scapegoats *himself*. At the end, he offers himself up for ritual sacrifice to the community, as his suicide is enacted *before an ecstatic theater audience*. This only occurs once he has fully turned himself into a woman. As it was for Gein, and Bates, the possession is both ancient and infant—a matriarchal legacy forged in Hell.

✦

"I believe in the god of carnage. The god whose rule has been unchallenged since time immemorial."

—*CARNAGE (script by Yasmina Reza and Roman Polanski)*

Every book I have written on film has included pieces about Polanski. It is even possible to trace an evolving narrative through those works, a weird, divided consciousness from which, on the one hand, I am seeking evidence for Polanski's complicity with the darkness, and on the other—rather harder to find—for the possibility of his redemption. As I wrote at the start of this chapter, no confession can be complete if our worst sins remain unconscious, overlooked, disowned. When the psyche is fractured, as is the case with every trauma-driven "imposer," there is no possibility of a full reckoning. The closest Polanski seems to have come to such a soul-unburdening was in 1976 with *The Tenant*, which is why it remains his most heartfelt movie. As I wrote in *Secret Life of Movies*:

> And for once the cruel, cool malevolence of the director is equaled and balanced by the almost painful vulnerability of the actor. Polanski becomes his own victim here; not only is his suffering made real this way, but the director's torture is rendered more heartfelt and exquisite also. It is the perfect schizophrenic juxtapositioning of director-victimizer with actor-victim, the very essence of the divided consciousness. Polanski the director conceives, creates, and controls his nightmare vision with all the ruthlessness at his disposal; overseeing his own private circus of delirium, he pulls out all the stops and makes a carnival of despair. Meanwhile, down below, forever trapped inside the circle, Polanski the actor twists and writhes and squirms, a puppet on evil strings, lost in this abominable world of his own fantasy creation (p. 142).

This reading—while also being a universal metaphor that relates to all of us—might be specifically consistent with the dereliction of Polanski's talent after *The Tenant* (with very few exceptions, and as was most painfully apparent with the asinine occult whimsy, *The Ninth Gate*). Perhaps *The Tenant* was Polanski's attempt to get free of a band of "old seers" whom he had allowed to possess him, in exchange for his much-coveted success as a filmmaker? (A daring hypothesis, I admit.) This would make the film both the fullest expression of his talent and its swan song. The themes of the film amply support this reading, which should also include the possibility that the film *was* a kind of confession and penance combined. As with Michael Powell's *Peeping Tom* (though not quite to the same degree), the film was savaged by critics on its release. *The Tenant* as Polanski's "coming clean" or expiation ritual would seem to be supported by his subsequent banishing from the Hollywood mafia in 1977: the moment the initiate starts to show pangs of conscience is the moment he is deemed a security risk and must be ex-communicated poste-haste.*

All of these recent insights, and the accompanying data points, suggest to me that I am once again circling a very personal zone of trauma, an original wound, and that only by diving all the way back into it can I complete this current work(ing). So here goes: watching fictional footage of women being raped, tortured, killed and dismembered as an adolescent and young adult may not have simply been an unconscious way for me to channel (or sublimate) my rage against my mother but also a means to traumatize *myself*. The conditions of a male psyche that remains trapped by the mother's gaze (due to unhealthy bonding starting in the womb) includes a cell-deep, pre-verbal, precognitive *identification with the mother's body* (out of which we are all formed), as poor Ed Gein so gruesomely enacted. And if torturing women is an "occult" strategy to tear free of that psychic womb-space, it never actually *works*, because it only perpetuates the wound and keeps it festering and toxic. Whatever is done to the woman's body—actually or in imagination—is felt also in the child-man's body, *just as if being done to himself*.

This may be how ancient pacts are sealed. The following is from a never-published memoir I wrote in 2011, *Hang-Dog with a Hard-On*:

> My sadistic relish in dark imagery [was] *a safe outlet for my hostility*, the means not only to have revenge on my mother but, at a deeper level still, to disconnect from the feminine side of myself—to torture and abuse it into withdrawing entirely. This would have been a way to have power over it—or at the very least, *not to be controlled by it*. Having cut off from my own soul, the *anima*, in adolescence via my dark predilection . . . it was then inevitable that, in adulthood, I would be unconsciously drawn into occultism, and eventually into a bizarre and obsessive courtship with Lucifer—*as the only way to approach my disowned feminine side*. . . . The missing element in my understanding was the original cause for my

---

* Not that Polanski's repentance continued—he remained in the game and managed to fight his way back into the Hollywood canon (if not the US) in 2002 with a film about "the Holocaust"—always the safest and surest route to respectability in the arts.

sexual distortion, and the unconscious motivation behind it. As a result, instead of going directly to the wounded part of my psyche and inviting the disowned feminine back into awareness, I took the long way around and *embarked upon the occult path of knowledge.*

If anyone discussed in this work ever had a maternal attachment disorder, and the resultant combination of desperate longing for the woman's body with deep resentment against it (besides Gein, our canary in the matrix), it would be Polanski, whose mother was cruelly taken from him at the age of six by the Nazis and died in a concentration camp soon after. Polanski's childhood, as well as his later life, is, like Charles Manson's, practically a blueprint for "trauma-based mind control." This may be why Polanski has consistently insisted on his complete lack of interest in the occult, whether in 1971—"I am down to earth in my philosophy of life, very rationally and materialistically oriented, with no interest in the occult" (Randall, p. 303)— or in 2000—"I don't believe in the occult. I don't believe. Period."[8]

Does the sorcerer protest too much? My brother Sebastian—whose mother-bondage became apparent to me in the months leading up to his death (c.f. *Paper Tiger*)—also scorned the occult, even while everything about his life, public and private, screamed out an allegiance, if not an enslavement, to its principles and aesthetics. In both cases, Polanski and Horsley, the disdain for occultism was nested in, fueled by, a philosophy of nihilism that's perfectly consistent with occultist ethics: "Unfortunately there is no lesson to be taken," Polanski said in 1971 of the murder of his wife. "There is just nothing. It's absolutely senseless, stupid, cruel and insane. I'm not sure it's even worth talking about" (Randall, p. 319). Isn't this the same philosophy (or lack of one) that led both Macbeth and Guy Woodhouse in *Rosemary's Baby* to *their* acts of *hubris*? In both cases, their nihilism and materialism—their lack of belief or respect for occult forces—made them the perfect tools for those forces to wield. They were ripe for possession.

16.6.   MY BROTHER'S ROOM (VAULT OF HORROR)

"That's the nature of the beast. Trauma infects the psyche and
tries to pass itself on, down the generations. Making movies about
trauma and dissociation as Polanski did (as all of my favorite
filmmakers did, pretty much) is a way to exorcise those demons
without becoming a psychopath or a pariah. The trouble is that,
if demons animate the art, eventually the artist will become both
dependent on and vulnerable to those demons."

—JASUN HORSLEY, *Seen and Not Seen*

While working on this last rewrite and chapter, I asked myself a question: where was I first exposed to sexualized imagery of tortured women? The
question arose simultaneously with the apparent answer.

Like many younger siblings, I looked up to my brother and imi-
tated his tastes as a child. When I was an adolescent, he literally passed
his clothes down to me, most memorably in the form of an authentic Nazi
leather great coat, as well as his cast-off punk trousers. With 2020 hindsight (a penny that only fully dropped while writing this chapter), it seems
inescapable to me now that *my ferocious drive to become a successful filmmaker* was at least partially in imitation of my brother's driving ambition
to become a pop star, which was on full display when he was a teenager.
He played in a number of bands, and was especially enamored with the
blood-spewing, fire-breathing glam metal band, Kiss (the name allegedly
stands for "Knights in Satan's Service"). Whenever he played his favorite
album of theirs, *Destroyer*, I would sit secretly outside his bedroom door to
listen longingly to the one slow track, "Great Expectations." I certainly had
them, and those expectations were somehow bound up in loving, fearful
emulation of my brother.

This was the same period I was discovering comic books and movies as a tool of dissociation and self-immersion, as well as terrorizing gerbils.* As previously discussed, at the age of seven or eight I entered into the immersive fantasy world of Marvel superheroes. While my brother and I shared an enjoyment of those comics, he was more into Tintin; but also, for a time, EC horror comics. I have the vaguest of recollections of reading one of those EC comics, lying on his bed in his room while he was away. This is strange for me to consider, because entering my brother's bedroom was not something I undertook casually. The walls were covered top to bottom with magazine stills from his beloved Hammer horror movies, making it a fortress of horror, a shell of outer darkness that was a terrifying rite of passage for me to enter.† My friend Adam and I had to pass through that room to get to the trainset on the other side, and we would run through it with our eyes closed to avoid having to see the horrifying imagery (one image especially: a still from the 1966 Hammer movie *The Reptile*, of a predatory *female*).

EC horror and crime comics imported into Britain in the 1950s were *a forerunner of the video nasty*, and they incurred a similar kind of reaction, seen by many then, and even more so now, as a "moral panic." The partially successful attempt to ban certain horror films as "video nasties," in other words, had a *direct precedent* with the 1955 Children and Young Persons (Harmful Publications) Act:

> In the early 1950s lurid American "crime" and "horror comics" reached Britain as ballast in ships crossing the Atlantic: unsold copies were also imported from Canada and Australia. Few penetrated much further than the environs of the great ports of Liverpool, Manchester, Belfast and London. . . . Using blocks made from imported American matrices, ensuing British versions of *Tales from the Crypt* and *The Vault of Horror*

---

* Admittedly a one-off: "As a young boy (about eight), I was allowed to take two gerbils home from school for the weekend. At one point, I took them out of their cage, wrapped them up in a sweater, and threw them across the room. The creatures were terrified, though not physically hurt. I was sexually aroused by the act. I had no idea at the time why, or why I was doing it." *Seen and Not Seen*, p. 85.

† In a similar way, perhaps, the dandy outfits my brother wore in his final years, red velvet and top hats, a camp/occult version of Jack the Ripper—the "clothes that made the Horsley," as he put it—were also a kind of shell of outer darkness for him to hide inside.

were printed in London and Leicester to be sold in small back-street
newsagents. [P]arliamentary deputations of teachers and churchmen
feared American mass culture invading Britain. All gave voice to an
orchestrated groundswell of opinion demanding urgent government
action. "The problem which now faces society in the trade that has
sprung up of presenting sadism, crime, lust, physical monstrosity, and
horror to the young is an urgent and a grave one," thundered *The Times*
on November 12, 1954. "There has been no more encouraging sign of the
moral health of the country than the way in which public opinion has
been roused in condemnation of the evil of 'horror comics' and in determination to combat them."[9]

The Act prohibited imagery that portrayed "acts of violence or cruelty"
and "incidents of a repulsive or horrible nature" that might "corrupt a child
or young person into whose hands it might fall."

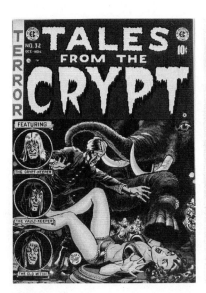 

In 5.6, I described how Clotaire Rapaille's long-term program of introducing Japanese children to coffee-flavored candy created a new generation
of adults susceptible to Nescafe's advertising campaign. Compare this now
to the roughly four-generation process—from 1950 to 2020—in which a
minority position (enjoying, or at least tolerating, graphic and horrifying

imagery of women being tortured) has now become a majority position, even as a former-majority, and its insistence that such imagery leads to serious psychological degeneration, has become a denigrated "moral minority."

How to import violent graphic imagery and ideation from the *avant-garde* of the 1920s into the mainstream, during a time when the cinema code would not allow such extreme content? Comic books formed a natural "bridge" between two worlds; most insidiously of all, they appealed to *children*. We now "know" the concerns of the Harmful Publications Act were silly and unfounded. How do we know? Because such imagery has now become normalized, just like the taste of coffee has to new generations of Japanese. The proof of the campaign's success—like all good takeovers—is in its invisibility.

✦

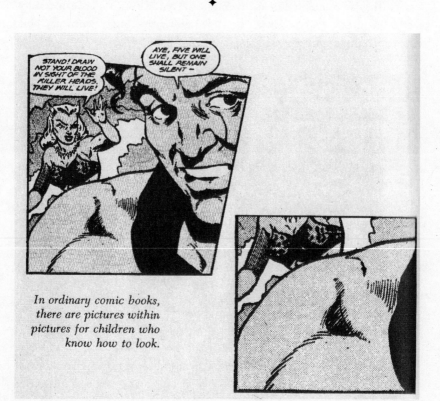

In ordinary comic books, there are pictures within pictures for children who know how to look.

"All that philosophy can do is to destroy idols. And that means not making any new ones—say out of 'the absence of idols.'"

— LUDWIG WITTGENSTEIN

Guy Woodhouse's initiation into the Halls of Fame in *Rosemary's Baby* requires sacrifice: Rosemary must be handed over to the devil and submitted to acts of torture, for the supplicant to show his willingness to *kill his soul,* to violate his own body, to be uncoupled from ordinary reality and translated to the "superculture," surreality. This is the process of aspiration, imagination, emulation, imitation, and initiation that I underwent with my brother. I saw his desire and I matched it; I sought to undergo the same ordeals, with my unmarked VHS tape of tortured women, mirroring the horror comics and grisly wall montage in my brother's room, to turn my trauma into my god and make the only offering that such a carnage lord would accept.

It now seems to me that I unwittingly adopted a form of simulated woman-torture as the means, not merely to enact revenge, but to *self-*trau-matize and trigger the dissociative mechanism within my psyche. When the nervous system is overwhelmed by violence, awareness retreats, flees, dis-incarnates into a psychic dream space, a "second attention," a forgetting chamber that violent comic books and movies helped to provide me with. Was this a form of unconscious self-initiation and self-training by which I was hoping to "ascend" to the disembodied state of the old seers, and so enter the new Hollywood—to join the artist-dreamers, both ancient and modern? Is *this* the secret of initiation rituals that slaughter the child and sacrifice the virgin, even to the point of dismembering and devouring the victim?

The dream which I recounted at the start of this last chapter underscores many of the primary themes of this book: Polanski's secret complicity with the satanic/occult; the idea of constructing a diabolic identity (or id-entity) by assembling the necessary components, as a carpenter builds a table (or a filmmaker makes a film); the possibility of being possessed by ancient (pos-sibly ancestral) spirits that drive people to commit sadistic violence against one another other; even the Egyptian iconography overlaps with *The Tenant* (Simone was an Egyptologist).

If I'd had that dream *after* finishing this chapter, it would have been remarkable enough, indicating that my unconscious was fully engaged in the process of working out this final "map" by providing clues at the last possible opportunity. The fact I had the dream *thirteen years previously, to that very day*, and that I happened to listen to a recording of it the night of completing this 16th chapter, is nothing short of uncanny. In a final twist that is truly *meta*, it confirms Castaneda's description of *dreaming* as a sorcerer's tool for shaping waking reality. Whatever I am working out here, with this final chapter, I was working on *unconsciously* thirteen years previously.

The parallels in all this are striking; the implications, while elusive, seem profound. Both Hitchcock's and Polanski's careers adhere closely to the ancient tradition of the old seers of Castaneda and, less fantastically confabulated, the secret society sorcerers Hayden tracks archeologically through pre-history. 1) to spread terror through the populace; 2) to torture the women and steal their creative power. 3) to use that power to create surrogate realities, dream matrices, artificial wombs, and attain virtual immortality. A central feature of these dream-worlds seems to be a dependence on luring souls to enter into them (attention harvesting), making of them a power source to keep the dream-world operational. What is Walmart without shoppers, a galley ship without slaves, the matrix without coppertops, or the Nosferatu without the blood of virgins to keep them youthful and strong?

The aim of this ancient sorcery is to recreate the original womb from the inside out: to colonize the mother's gaze (and body) and so have complete control over it. This is evident in the precise overlap between two seemingly disparate goals: turning oneself into a woman, on the one hand, and creating a surrogate, imagistic reality with which to replace physical reality, on the other. It seems fitting that the men behind *The Matrix*—the defining movie myth of surrogate reality creation and enslavement—have, since 1999, turned themselves into women.[*]

---

[*] Or at least would have us believe so. In fact, many men who self-identify as transwomen do not undergo the full surgery—i.e., have their penis and testicles removed and an artificial vagina constructed out of the skin tissue—but retain their male genitalia. Both Lilly and Lana Wachowski—as far as I can determine—have undergone full surgical intervention. (It is not easy to know, since in 2020 even to *differentiate* between a constructed vagina and a "woman-penis" is considered transphobic). One of the many ironies of transgenderism is how it reinforces the notion of gender identity, both socially and as determined by biology, through the insistence on surgical and chemical measures to "correct" one's sex. The irony becomes even starker in the context of the *Matrix* mythology,

In *Wandering God*, Morris Berman's attempt to get to the bottom of aggrandizer "vertical politics," Berman (after Marvin Harras) succinctly diagnoses the aggrandizer desire for power and prestige as "the search for a love substitute" (p. 75). Since the original source of love for every human being is the mother, the "will to power"—the art of imposition—is inseparable from the attempt to recreate one's mother and/or the womb. Since it is through the mother's gaze that our sense of subjectivity as infants develops, the attempt to recreate that gaze—as something *wholly validating*—is congruent with the desire to assemble *an artificially generated womb-space* and thereby invoke the original "love field" of the mother's body. Central to this sorcerous endeavor is the removal of any element of unpredictability or chaos that originally made that space unsafe or hostile to us. This infant urge to regress to an idealized experience of the womb involves *fusing the male gaze* (that of director-imposer-sorcerer) *with the female gaze* (the audience-victim in its various guises), so that *the mother is now subject to the son*. Symmetrically, ironically, and tragically, it also entails becoming possessed by the mother's unconscious and so becoming an instrument of her will, even beyond death.

Berman's summation of the cult of Isis (the ancient one, not the Islamic State in Iraq and Syria) in *Wandering God* is shockingly on point:

> In the *Phaedrus*, Plato uses details from the Eleusinian mysteries to create a picture of the soul ascending to heaven and undergoing a purification that allows new powers to enter it. The theme of death and rebirth is a constant one. . . Edith Weigert-Vorwinkel, in her essay on the Great Mother, points out that the word "fanatic" is derived from the mysteries, inasmuch as the Latin word *fanum* means "sanctuary," the place where the initiation was carried out. Hence, the followers of the Phrygian goddess Cybele (Magna Mater in Rome) were called *fanatici* (p. 146–7)

---

for it is the "false" (biological) avatar self, the one confined to the Matrix, being corrected, thereby reifying the idea that the Matrix can indeed tell us who we are, and has to be "reprogrammed" to tell us we are someone else. But then, transgenderism is a movement fueled by corporate opportunism as much as by ideological zeal.

A sanctum into which aspirants seeking a transcendentally empowering experience enter, and come out as "fans"? The parallels get even eerier: the fans who wished to level up and become acting priests in the Goddess cult

> used dance and music to enter ecstatic states. [T]his was accompanied by self-flagellation. At the peak of their frenzy, the initiated castrated themselves. Their genitals and clothing were then carried into the *fanum* or inner shrine (also called "the bridal chamber of Cybele"). After that, the [priests] wore women's clothing, wandering the countryside, performing ecstatic dances and breaking into prophecy. "*To be filled with the Great Mother, to be possessed by her, was the only form of life they desired*" (p. 147, emphasis added).

Ed Gein would surely have concurred. No wonder he was Hitchcock's ideal protagonist! A boy's best friend is his mother.

◆

> "Man is certainly stark mad; he cannot make a worm, and yet he will be making gods by dozens."
>
> —MONTAIGNE, *The Complete Essays*

I so much *wanted* to end this book on David Byrne and Dave Oshana. Instead I have wound up with Ed Gein dressed in women's skins. So be it. It ain't over till it's over. The only way to bid farewell to the darkness is to incorporate the darkest part of it. To put it even more explicitly: the only way to exit Hell is to integrate Hell. Whether or not they finally fit, the pieces of an overwhelmingly dark puzzle have come together in the last moments of writing this current work, as if waiting on the edges of my consciousness for the opportune moment to reveal themselves. Necessity is the mother of integration? Or necessity is the integration of mother? I was out of time for this realization and so, when needs must, the devil drives all of us into awareness. My cultural enmeshment with Hollywood, my unconscious complicity with the dark spellcraft it propagates, and my predilection for imagery of sexual violence against women, both of which began in my adolescence, are not two but one "complex." The desire to return to the womb, to get back to and inside the mother's body, is the desire to be submerged in an auto-erotic, polymorphously perverse, sensorial dream-world that is both intensely materialistic—visceral—and *disembodied.*

Now I have isolated and identified it, this theme to end all themes—the original myth of the aggrandizer-imposer—seems to me in evidence through these sixteen infernal maps. George Hodel's incest parties and macabre female mutilations as artworks; Jack Nicholson with his sister-mother complex; John Huston-as-Noah-Cross raping the land and his own daughter; John and Mackenzie Phillips; Jeffrey Epstein and Ghislaine Maxwell with their sex slaves; my own *Grasshopper*; Stalin with his chicken; Michael Jackson as the ultimate *puer aeternus*; young Billy Friedkin cinematically traumatized by his mother; Leonard Cohen with his oblique and dark-tinged worship of the female form; Kirk Douglas' Oedipal philandering; the Gay Mafia's mother-bonded men gathering into cliques to exclude women while reviling and abusing them (as well as young boys turned into receptacles and thereby also into women, "gay" men, transgender); the Phoenix program enacting secret society terror rituals of ancient times, and for the same purpose (shock-and-awe); the immersive superhero universes combined with scientism, social media, virtual porn worlds, and techno-boosted escapism, all more or less indistinguishable from the fictionalized horror narratives of Hollywood, comic books, and pulp fiction that have made (even before Ed Gein arose) the serial killer a secular monster for the postmodern age, and the techno-superhero our pseudo-savior. The pathogen is as plain as it is prolific: *the men who would be kings are men who turn themselves into women.* The creation of a surrogate reality to escape into and rule over, a matrix-womb that is a simulation of the lost maternal body, is achieved through the meticulous and painstaking assemblage of a mosaic of eidetic memory images, a celluloid (and cellular?) panopticon made up of copies of reality. A matrix.

However literalized it has been throughout history, it would seem that the sacrificial victim is, finally, *one's own body*, and the desired prize, immortality, is achieved through the translation or transference of our consciousness to *a disembodied phantom self*, a residual body image, a holographic replica captured, in the ether or in celluloid, or both, forever. Or rather "forever," since a counterfeit of the soul must remain forever time-bound, and so has no access to eternity—thank God.

Since there is nothing, finally, that is not nature, there is nothing that can replace (or distort, or corrupt) Nature. There are only endless strategies of distraction, a marketplace of attention, and elaborately built "devils" to prolong our agony and delay our inevitable awakening. The forgetting chamber of Hell plays endless reruns to keep us enthralled. But there are no movies in heaven.

OUTTAKES

Outtake # 1

HEATH LEDGER

THE CURSE OF THE JOKER (& THE DANDY)

"The aesthetics of terror has always been an ideological conspiracy to remake the world. And the power of media messages and symbols to activate the psyches of significant segments of the population brooks no dispute."

—CARL RASCHKE, *Painted Black*

When I first heard about Heath Ledger's death in January 2008, I found myself strangely and unexpectedly affected. Though I wasn't a fan of Ledger, for whatever reason, his death had an impact on me and I became aware of feeling an affinity for him previously unsuspected. Apparently, I was in a parasocial interaction with Ledger.

I put it down to unconscious or esoteric factors, such as his being a fellow Aries (he also shares a birthday with Robert Downey Jr., though I didn't know that at the time). Because of the sadness his death caused me, I wrote a piece about it for an independent journal called *Film Festival Magazine*. The magazine had just started up (in autumn 2007) and I'd been invited to write a monthly column, unpaid. I agreed because it gave me an excuse to keep knocking at the dream factory gates, trying to get interviews from "indie" movie stars like Ethan Hawke or up-and-comers like Kristen Stewart. The piece was called "Fame Kills: Heath Ledger and the Twilight of the Idols"

and it was about our (or my) "blind admiration and envy of movies stars"
and the corresponding fascination for the power and pleasures of fame.

> By worshipping material success in the guise of celebrities [I wrote], as if
> they were a higher life form, the public is drastically reduced in status and
> self-respect. And given a power and status previously only granted the
> forces of nature, is it any wonder if our human "gods" suffer from almost
> pathological ego inflation? The inevitable result of such inflation is a cor-
> responding enlargement of fears and doubts: since they can't possibly live
> up to the process of deification, they are oppressed and tormented *by* it.

I was attempting to make sense of Ledger's death, not so much by analyzing its circumstances as by exploring the context in which it occurred—as
made explicit with the piece's title. During this same period, I had just
undergone the bursting of my own Hollywood dream bubble, even as my
brother was on the verge of what looked like real success, including the sort
of Hollywood movie deal I had so long coveted. In the article, I describe a
"split between a star's public persona and their innermost, private self" as
creating "a shadowy realm [or] twilight world in which movie stars spend
most of their lives." This was something I could imagine, and to some degree
observe in my brother's behaviors, as his celebrity increased.

> In order to be successful, stars must balance these two extremes: the shim-
> mering public image to be worshipped—the magisterial play of light—and
> the shadow side which must be hidden from view at all costs. . . . The
> pressures of a life of high fame must be unimaginable, yet most of us are
> too busy envying the "perks" to consider the price paid to attain them. We
> are in awe of the Wizard; draw back the curtain and we will find a shabby
> old man, frantically pulling levers.

I found a surprisingly clear echo of these sentiments only *after* completing *16 Maps of Hell*, in a mostly forgotten French classic, *The Stars*, by
Edgar Morin:

> The festival quality of the stars' private-public life, the great love affairs,
> are obviously collective myths simultaneously secreted by the public and

fabricated by the star system. But this mythical life, we repeat, is in part actually lived by the star herself. The star is in effect subjectively determined by her double on the screen. She is nothing since her image is everything. She is everything since she is her image too. The psychology of the stars requires a brief incursion into the psychology of the dual personality (p. 65–66).

If attention is a kind of currency—even *food*—the more popular a character becomes, and the more narratives are successfully spun around it, the "stronger" that thought-form presumably grows. In the case of Father Christmas or Jesus Christ, whatever strange mix of myth, legend, and historical fact lies behind these characters, they are profoundly real in their effects, not just in our psyches but in our actions. Parents even pretend to *be* Santa to maintain the illusion, while priests claim to be representing the Pope, who is representing Peter, who is representing Christ. Through imitation we become image.

After Ledger's death, Jack Nicholson made a cryptic off-the-cuff remark to the reporter who informed him of it. Three enigmatic words, "I warned him," followed by a chuckle. No context was ever given for the remark, and as far as I know it's never been verified if Nicholson actually warned Ledger, and if so, about what. It's been assumed—given that he also played the Joker (not especially well) in Tim Burton's 1989 *Batman*, which was also presumably why the reporter mentioned Ledger's death—that Nicholson was referring to the potentially deranging effects of playing a psychotic super-villain.* Ledger, unlike Nicholson, was a Method actor. The Method directs the actor's thinking and will to activate unconscious content and processes,

---

* Nicholson went from intense, brooding, method actor in the Brando mode to an almost burlesque, buffoonish performer. Perhaps it was a conscious choice on Nicholson's part to keep his sanity intact while staying on top of the Hollywood game? Marlon Brando, close friends and neighbors with Nicholson, took a similar turn during the second decade of his career, in the 1960s, when he did so many bad movies, with openly clownish performances, that, by the time of *The Godfather*, he was considered washed up. Three generations of method actors, from Brando to Nicholson to Ledger, presents a loose lineage of legendary jokers. Perhaps Brando and Nicholson were, at some level, keeping at bay the demons of the unconscious—collective or personal—and/or the hidden forces of Hollywood, to avoid being turned into an unwilling sacrifice, à la Heath Ledger?

emotional memory and subconscious behaviors, and it does so "sympathetically" and indirectly. The actor's task is to locate internal motivations to justify his actions, most specifically to understand what his character wants to achieve in a given scene—hence the running joke of the amateur method actor, "What's my motivation?"*

Ledger's progress from little-known Australian TV personality to world-famous sex symbol, screen idol, and sacred cash cow for the Hollywood industry, is, to some extent at least, within the public domain of biographical fact. Based on this narrative, Ledger's personal struggle for success, and for excellence as an actor, led him to choose the role of the Joker, a role which offered him a new level of fame and fortune but which was also, possibly, a key factor in his drug meltdown and premature death. The latter, ironically, ensured him the fullest possible recognition from the industry, in the form of a gold-plated statuette.

---

* Part of "the Method" is to allow oneself to be *possessed* by the character one is playing, i.e., to fully internalize its qualities. Method acting has its origins in a systematic approach to training actors developed by Konstantin Stanislavski, the Russian theatre practitioner, in the first half of the 20th century. The Stanislavski system is based on the "art of experiencing," as compared to the "art of representation." Stanislavski further developed his system with more physically grounded rehearsals that came to be known as the "Method of Physical Action." For reasons too numerous to go into, Stanislavski's system was heavily promoted and advanced by other acting teachers (including former students), and his theoretical writings were widely translated. As a result, the system transcended cultural boundaries and became the predominant acting discipline in the West. The American Method focuses almost exclusively on psychological techniques, where Stanislavski's system included a more holistic, psychophysical approach. Via the tutelage of one of Stanislavski's students, Richard Boleslawski, the Method was developed in America by Lee Strasberg, Stella Adler, and Sanford Meisner and taught at the Actors Studio with a special emphasis on "emotional memory." Adler worked directly with Stanislavski, and was surprised to find that Stanislavski considered the emotion memory technique, which Strasberg made primary, as, at best, a last resort. Strasberg rejected this view and refused to modify his approach. Adler's most famous student was Marlon Brando and countless other American and British actors adopted the Westernized versions of the Stanislavski system, including James Dean, Julie Harris, Al Pacino, Robert De Niro, Dustin Hoffman, and Marilyn Monroe. Stanislavski's ideas—at least as recalibrated for Western appliance via Strasberg, Adler, and others—are now so commonly practiced that modern actors may apply them without even knowing they are doing so.

This is the first layer of the narrative. Although there may be evidence, as Nicholson's comment implies, that Ledger's career choices—specifically his engagement in the Joker role—led to his death, the case remains inconclusive at best. The rumor of a correlation between the Joker role and Ledger's death was mostly fueled by an interview Ledger gave in late 2007, while filming *The Imaginarium of Dr. Parnassus* in London. "It is a physically and mentally draining role" says the article; it quotes Ledger describing the Joker as a "psychopathic, mass-murdering, schizophrenic clown with zero empathy," before adding that, "as often happens when he throws himself into a part, he is not sleeping much."[1] After Ledger's death, his *Dark Knight* co-star, Christian Bale, refuted these speculations. He "recalled Heath saying: '[The Joker was] the most fun I've ever had, or probably ever will have, playing a character.'"[2] In 2017, Ledger's sister, Kate Ledger, insisted that playing the Joker had nothing to do with her brother's death, pointing out that he was already suffering from insomnia before taking on the role.[3]

Ledger's father Kim Ledger, on the other hand, in a documentary aired as part of the Netflix series *Too Young to Die*, claimed Heath "pretty well locked himself up in a hotel room for weeks [for the role]. He galvanized the upcoming character. That was typical of Heath. He would do that. He liked to dive into his characters, but this time he really took it up a notch." The documentary shows Kim flipping through Ledger's diary from the *Dark Knight* shoot, and we glimpse clipped images of the Joker and Malcolm McDowell's Alex, from *A Clockwork Orange* (a film and book with its own dark history). On one page of the diary, the words, "BYE BYE" are written in large letters.

Officially, Ledger's death was ruled an accident. He died from the combined effects of medications used to treat anxiety disorders and panic attacks by decreasing abnormal excitement in the brain (Valium, Xanax, and Restoril, a sleep aid). The toxicology analysis stated definitively: "the manner of death is accident, resulting from the abuse of prescribed medications." Ledger's body was found by Diana Wolozin, described as his masseuse. Wolozin arrived at Ledger's SoHo apartment in New York about 2:45 pm to give him a massage and found his bedroom door closed. At 3 pm, she called his cellphone, received no answer, entered the bedroom, and saw him in bed. She assumed he was sleeping and set up her massage table. When she found him cold to the touch, rather than call 911, she made three phone calls to actress Mary-Kate Olsen, a "friend" of Ledger's. Olsen didn't call 911 either, but instead called her "security guard" and sent him over to the apartment. Sometime later, Wolozin called 911.

According to the *New York Times*, police found no Diana Wolozin listed in the state database of licensed massage therapists, and made the point that "it is a felony to practice massage without a license in New York."[4] *People* magazine reported that Olsen and Ledger "were hooking up, but neither were particularly interested in making it exclusive. . . . They had a bond that was based on partying, and they had the same tastes in partying."[5] Due to Olsen's strange behavior, she was called for questioning and eventually agreed to speak, but only on condition of "immunity." Probably she was concerned about being charged for drug possession, or possibly dealing.

My brother struggled with addiction for many years, but as far as I knew at the time, he had been clean during the period leading up to the West-End premiere of *Dandy in the Underworld*, based on his memoir, on June 7, 2010. He thoroughly disliked the play, and no doubt this contributed to his relapse. As with Ledger, there is some suggestion that his life might have been saved if there had been a timelier intervention. His body was found by his long-term girlfriend, Rachel Garley, who claimed she last saw him at 8:30 in the morning of June 16, when he was going to bed after partying. She claimed she didn't come back until the next day, that his door was unlocked, and that this indicated "a dealer had been in and out."[6]

I knew from someone close to him that (whether or not it was a relapse) his agent, Ivan Mulcahy, had provided him with heroin in the days leading up to his death. Garley may well have also provided him with drugs on occasion, despite knowing of his struggle to get clean. (Is this why she made a point of mentioning his "dealer"?) The fact she left him on the morning of the 16th, in whatever state, and chose not to check in on him for over 24 hours, is at the very least neglectful behavior. Add to this the fact that Garley inherited my brother's estate and married Mulcahy soon after, and we have all the essential ingredients of a sordid murder-mystery tale.

In Ledger's case, the drugs involved were less obviously fatal, and the circumstances surrounding his death perhaps less obviously neglectful. But there is still room to wonder: at what point does a death wish become fully operational? The media painted a picture of a young, beautiful, and talented movie star with everything going for him who flirted with the dark side—both as an actor (admirable) and as a drug-user (foolish). Ledger's death was sufficiently shrouded in mystery to create ambiguity and doubt, as regards whether it had been accidental, intentional (suicide), or foul play. Officially, the police ruled out foul play almost immediately (as they did with my brother); and since no suicide note was found, there was little speculation that it was intentional. But when it comes to fatal drug abuse resulting from a self-destructive lifestyle and a toxic social set, the lines between accident and suicide, and even between suicide and murder, become blurry.

With friends like these, who needs murder plots?

TOM WAITS FOR NO MAN

"I truly wish I could've met Heath, I feel I could have helped him prepare before he took that role on. Jack Nicholson warned him. . . . Have a look in the history of the character of The Joker—because it results in delusion, insanity, believe you me I know [*laughs*]. Unless you understand beforehand just what it is, treat this force with the utmost respect and observance."

—JAZ COLEMAN, *lead singer of the band Killing Joke*

In 2012, *The Hollywood Reporter* ran a brief article titled "The Joker: Did Heath Ledger Take His Inspiration From . . . Tom Waits?" The piece singles out Ledger-Joker's "playful, dragged-down-a-country-road drawl" as seeming "like a unique invention. At least, until you listen to Tom Waits in this 1979 interview on Australia's *The Don Lane Show*."[7] I watched the video[8] and, the similarities are striking. I mentioned it in an email to Phil Snyder. I first met Phil online in 1998, while working on *The Blood Poets*. Snyder had written an article online about the mysterious, prankish secret society "the Sons of Lee Marvin" (SOLM), which Jim Jarmusch started with Tom Waits and John Lurie in the 1980s. Talking about it in 1992, Jarmusch told *Film Comment*: "Just the idea of Marvin's characters being outsiders and very violent appeals to me. Some seem to have a very strong code—*even if it's a psychotic one*—that he follows rigidly."[9]

Phil Snyder had also written about the "Great American Psychopath" (GAP) at his site, and we collaborated on a GAP chapter for *The Secret Life of Movies* a few years later that included a discussion of the Joker. Naturally, I assumed he would be interested in this collision between the GAP and the SOLM in popular culture. For years, Phil was "an obsessive watcher and listener to everything Tom Waits did" and had seen him live, twice, in his *Frank's Wild Years* play in Chicago. Phil responded:

> Not sure if anyone would believe me on this but it's true that, when I first saw the *Dark Knight* movie, and when Heath Ledger first appeared on screen shown only from the back, my immediate response was, "That's Tom Waits. He's doing Tom Waits." Something about his slouching stance, his posture, and later his voice. I think he might be holding a mask when he first appears and then he puts it on.

As for the SOLM connection, since "the bulk of Marvin's early career was dominated by psychopath characters," Phil wrote me, anyone who followed "the way of Lee Marvin" would be "naturally attuned to GAP themes."

> When I first formulated the GAP, I was also obsessively listening to *Frank's Wild Years* and what really cemented it for me was that the character I was drawn to in movies was similar to the character Waits was singing about. [Waits even] described the Frank character as "a dreamer and a psychopath." It seems pretty clear to me that Ledger studied Waits' concert film *Big Time*. . . There are a couple performances in particular that he seemed to copy: the posture here, a stance there, a vocal inflection, and so on [Email correspondence with author].

Apparently, Phil's "obsession" with Lee Marvin and Tom Waits was the thin end of a cultural wedge that had made its way all the way into Ledger's skull. And if Ledger was imitating Waits, who—or what—was inspiring Waits' own performance—itself highly mannered and "clownish"? Both Snyder's GAP thesis and his speculations about the SOLM circle around the question of how unconscious, or archetypal, energies can obsess us to the point of possession. In this regard, there is another alleged influence on Ledger's Joker that's even more suggestive of "occult forces"—and secret rituals—namely, Jaz Coleman of the popular metal band, Killing Joke. In 2008, shortly after Ledger's death, researcher Christopher Loring Knowles (author of *The Gods Wore Spandex* and *The Secret History of Rock 'n Roll: The Mysterious Roots of Modern Music*) wrote:

> Apparently, Ledger was directly involved in developing the Joker's look for the film. The original designs for the character . . . were nothing like what we saw on the screen. And given the fact that Ledger was handed Alan Moore's *Batman: The Killing Joke* as a starting point, we're just a Google search or two from Killing Joke singer Jaz Coleman, who is the Heath Ledger Joker's most compelling precedent. Particularly in the "Hosannas from the Basements of Hell" video, with the smeared clown makeup and long, greasy hair (that a lot of Batman fans didn't care much for). It's important to note here that both Alan Moore and Coleman are deeply involved in occult magic, particularly that of the Crowleyean variety.[10]

According to Knowles, the *Hosannas from the Basements of Hell* album was "how Jaz Coleman uses Killing Joke to channel his aggressions," and "filled with very heavy occult themes—songs dealing with Babalon ('Invocation') and Lucifer ('The Lightbringer') [and] titles like 'Walking with Gods' and 'The Judas Goat.'" Knowles suggested that, with Ledger's "modeling the new Joker off of Jaz Coleman's stage makeup . . . some sort of transference [was] at work."[11]

The occult origins of Killing Joke are far from hidden: "By [Coleman's] own admission, [he and] drummer Paul Ferguson . . . performed a ceremonial ritual to conjure the band into being, focusing their minds on finding people who 'shared our strong sense of mysticism and our studies.'"[12] When asked in 2015 about Ledger's death, Coleman said this:

> While he was shooting *The Dark Knight*, [Ledger] was listening to *Hosannas* and had my picture plastered everywhere in his caravan. He watched the *Hosannas* video, took my mannerisms, gait, and modelled his Joker on the rum-sodden Coleman of that period. Now this is a dangerous energy to work with unless you know what you're doing. I've been invoking the 11th path of the harlequin, madman or fool for three

decades, and *I use a mask system to protect myself.** This archetype of the
fool or Joker, with his Tourette's-like approach of saying things that other
people would naturally hide, is a zero—a void waiting to be filled with
knowledge.[13]

In 2010, Coleman was even more explicit:

> John Hicklenton [and] Brian Bolland, the artist who drew *Batman: The
> Killing Joke* . . . were both advisors on *The Dark Knight*, and played a
> part in getting old footage [of me] to Heath Ledger [in his preparations
> for the role of the Joker]—footage of me when I'm drunk or [acting] in
> *Year of the Devil*, all sorts of bits and pieces. . . . To be quite precise, we
> in Killing Joke refer to this energy of the harlequin, madman or fool as
> "the Eleventh Path of Divine Madness." It's an energy that constantly
> surrounds Killing Joke and what we've noticed about this energy is that it
> has its own consciousness, and its own agenda. . . . It doesn't like money;
> it doesn't like anything that goes against its agenda.[14]

From what I have seen of Coleman's stage performance (and besides the
white face paint), it has less obvious similarities to Ledger's Joker than Tom
Waits' persona of the late 1970s and 1980s (*Frank's Wild Years*) does, and it's
possible Coleman is playing up this angle for his own mythical engineering.
(For his part in the Imaginarium, Coleman was made Chevalier des Arts
et des Lettres by the French Minister of Culture in 2010.) On the other
hand, maybe there *is* a hidden tradition at work here, an invisible blueprint or psychic template that, as Coleman implies, all of these performances
were plugging into, consciously or not? (As far as I know, no one has asked
Coleman about Tom Waits, or Waits about Ledger.)

Coleman's assertion implies that, in order to act as a channel for
"Joker energies" and become a successful conduit for them (a SOLM or a
Jack Nicholson), it's essential to observe the protocol, i.e., the right magical

---

* This would seem to be a similar form of involuntary possession as Morin observed in
The Stars, when: "the archetypal beauty of the star acquires the hieratic quality of the
mask; but this mask has become perfectly adherent, identified with the face and dissolved
within it" (Morin, p. 44).

procedure. There is a rigid code, even if it's a psychotic one. Break it and, rather than being the magician conducting the ritual, you risk becoming a sacrifice to it. This would make Ledger like the dumb movie-hick crossing over Indian burial ground, inadvertently incurring the wrath of ancestral spirits. He broke the code and the code broke him. Maybe *that's* why Nicholson warned him?

In passing, *Dr. Parnassus*, which Ledger was working on when he died, featured Tom Waits playing Mr. Nick, a.k.a., the Devil. *The Guardian* called it "the role he was born to play."*

---

* "Tom Waits gives the devil his due," by Xan Brooks, *The Guardian*, Oct 8, 2009: https://www.theguardian.com/film/2009/oct/08/tom-waits-gives-devil-due In the script, Mr. Nick and Tony (Ledger's character) never meet. The closest they get is when Mr. Nick watches Tony from a clifftop and ruminates to Dr. Parnassus: "I hope they get that bastard. Tear him limb from limb. But they won't. He leads a charmed life, that one. I've been trying to nail him for years. I thought I had him this time. But, there's always some prat comes to his rescue. Talk about the luck of the Devil. Those weird markings you found on him, on his forehead. Those satanic-symbol, so-called things. What's all that about? Maybe they protect him in some way. I've never been into that black-magic stuff myself. Can't seem to get the hang of it. I know, pathetic isn't it?"

Outtake # 2

JAMES HOLMES
(DARK AURORA RISING)

Another, somewhat more complicated example of how the devil's imaginarium has a way of spilling out into ordinary society, with terminal results, might be the mass shooting in Aurora, Colorado, on July 20, 2012, during a midnight showing of *The Dark Knight Rises*. The official account of the event is as follows:

A gunman wearing a gas mask opened fire inside the multiplex theater, killing 12 people and injuring 58 more. The alleged gunman reportedly bought a ticket to the film, left before it started, went to his car, parked near the exit door, changed into protective clothing, and retrieved several guns. About 30 minutes into the movie, he reentered the theater through the exit door, dressed in black and wearing a gas mask, a load-bearing vest, a ballistic helmet, bullet-resistant leggings, a bullet-resistant throat protector, a groin protector, and tactical gloves. He was also (allegedly) listening to techno music through a set of headphones during the attack. Perhaps because other audience members had supposedly dressed up for the screening, many of them didn't react right away; some believed he was part of a special effects installation setup for the film's premiere, or a publicity stunt.

The attacker allegedly threw two canisters emitting gas or smoke, obscuring the audience members' vision, causing their throats and skin to itch, and eye irritation. He fired a 12-gauge Remington 870 Express Tactical shotgun at the ceiling and then at the audience, followed by a Smith & Wesson M&P15 semi-automatic rifle with a 100-round drum magazine,

457

which eventually malfunctioned. Finally, he fired a .40-caliber Glock 22 Gen4 handgun. He fired first towards the back of the room, then at people in the aisles. One bullet passed through the wall and hit three people in the adjacent theater, screening the same film. Witnesses said the multiplex's fire alarm system went off soon after the attack began. One witness said she was hesitant to leave because someone yelled that there was also shooting in the lobby (a significant detail).

Shortly after arriving on the scene, police apprehended a suspect whom they later identified as 24-year-old James Eagan Holmes. Initial reports stated that Holmes identified himself as "the Joker" at the time of his arrest (he had shocking red dyed hair). Holmes was a neuroscience doctoral student at the University of Colorado. In a subsequent news article for the *Los Angeles Times*, one of Holmes' college classmates described him as being "really into" superheroes; the article also reported that Holmes' apartment in Aurora was "decorated with Batman paraphernalia."[1] As a result of the incident, Warner Bros. cancelled the Paris, Mexico, and Japan premieres of the film and suspended its marketing campaign in Finland. Several broadcast networks also suspended television ads for the film in the US. The trailer for *Gangster Squad*, another Warner Bros. movie included in the screening of *The Dark Knight Rises*, was removed because it contains a scene in which gangsters shoot submachine guns at moviegoers "through" the screen. The film's director, Christopher Nolan, released a public statement after the event, as did other stars of the film. Christian Bale (Batman) paid a personal visit to the survivors and to the memorial in Aurora.

There is reason to question the official version of the event, of course, albeit at the risk of falling down the internet rabbit hole of "crazed conspiracy theories." A far-from-fringe source, *Business Insider*, reported that one witness told a reporter: "From what we saw [the shooter] wasn't alone . . . the second can of tear gas didn't come from his side." The article shares transcripts of a number of police radio communications that seem to confirm there was more than one attacker. For example, some three minutes after Holmes was detained, either in or next to his car, an officer says, "One of the shooters might be wearing a white and blue plaid shirt," to which the dispatcher responds, "Copy, outstanding shooter possibly wearing a white and blue plaid shirt." Two minutes later, an officer says, "The suspect is saying that he's the only one but I'm getting conflicting suspect descriptions from the witnesses out here." A full three-quarters of an hour later (over an hour after Holmes was detained), officers still mention other potential shooters: "Talking to people making statements, sounds like we have possibly two shooters, one that was in Theater 8 seated, another one that came in from the outside into Theater 9. Sounds like it was a coordinated attack."[2]

From such anomalies are conspiracy theories born, above all when left unexplained, or even unaddressed, by mainstream media and authorities. This naturally leads to increased online furor, investigations and speculation. One thing that was later doing the rounds was the discovery of seemingly random references in the movie, *The Dark Knight Rises*, to shootings that were still to come when the film was released. The word "Aurora" appears in red neon letters on top of a large skyscraper, as seen briefly during a scene in the film. Then there is a scene in which Commissioner Gordon (Gary Oldman) points to a map showing a targeted area identified as Sandy Hook, the only clearly visible words on the map. The Sandy Hook shootings occurred on December 14, 2012, five months after the Aurora shootings (which occurred on the film's release date). KDVR (a Denver-based subsidiary of Fox News) reported on January 2, 2013 (two weeks after Sandy Hook), that, since "the word 'Narrows' also appears on the map . . . the Narrows School District in Giles County closed all of its schools Wednesday. 'We have to take this as serious information,' Giles County Sheriff Morgan Millirons said."[3]

Anomalies of this sort present a double-bind: to dismiss them as pure coincidence is not only lazy and unimaginative but potentially irresponsible. Yet to a degree, it seems almost necessary, because the *apparent* alternative is to posit some kind of conscious conspiracy so complex and elaborate that it borders not just on paranoia but schizophrenia. It's more convenient to believe that Holmes—like John Hinckley Jr.—was a deranged fan who took fantasy to such an illogical and violent extreme that he *is* diagnosable as paranoid schizophrenic (at his trial, a court-appointed psychiatrist diagnosed Holmes as having schizotypal personality disorder, calling him mentally ill but legally sane!). This places the fault, not in the movies, the culture, or society (or parapolitical intrigue), but squarely in Holmes himself.

To suggest that the Aurora mass-shooting event was itself directed, like a kind of real-time movie with real-life casualties, is to risk being dismissed, in similar terms, as a paranoid nut-job. There is a third possibility, however, one that partakes of both, which is that movies (some of them at least) are designed precisely to generate such obsessive interest and disproportionate or unrealistic emotional involvement (parasocial fixations), and cause a corresponding loss of reality. This would certainly make them potential weapons of mass psychological warfare and *could*, in theory, lead to events like the Aurora shootings. From here, it's not such a reach to suggest that parasocial engineering might possibly *include* them too—i.e., that the shootings themselves were a form of domestic terrorism. In this regard, it may be helpful to cite Slavoj Žižek, the Lacanian psychologist and philosopher and movie commentator, on *Dark Knight*, in *A Pervert's Guide to Ideology*:

> The truly disturbing thing about *The Dark Knight* is that it elevates lie into a general social principle, into the principle of organization of our social political life. As if our societies can remain stable, can function, only if based on a lie; as if telling the truth—and this telling the truth is embodied in Joker—means destruction, disintegration of the social order. . . . The idea is, if the ordinary public were to learn how corrupt . . . the very core of our legal system [is], then everything would have collapsed, so we need a lie to maintain order. The truth is too strong [so] a politician should be a cynicist [sic] who, although he knows what is true, tells to ordinary people what Plato called "a noble fable," a lie.[4]

Admittedly, all this blurs the lines not only between truth, lie, and noble fable (or necessary psyop), but between paranoid schizophrenia and informed awareness. It might even do it to the degree we may wish to turn away from the whole godawful mess in despair and take refuge in the noble fable of official explanation, however many bullet holes there are in it. Added to this is the grim possibility that "conspiracy theorizing" has *itself* become a kind of parasocial networking, audience participation LARP-ing (live action roleplay), by which passive audience members get to experience a more direct and urgent involvement in the plots they imagine to be unfolding, transforming their lives more and more into something resembling a Hollywood movie (leveling up). It's not so hard to imagine, even, that such beliefs might be deliberately engendered—or at least cynically manipulated—either by movie manufacturers or intelligence operatives, or both. This would certainly be a means to increase the social impact of a given cultural product—even when it's negative impact—and thereby raise "mere movies" to the level of historical events.

Maybe the "naïve" audience members were right, and the Aurora shootings *were* a publicity stunt—a deadly one? In 2019, the movie *The Joker* was accompanied by predictions it would provoke similar sorts of public shootings, to the extent that some theaters had armed police on duty at screenings. Death, as the ultimate attention-grabber, is a great way to increase the harvest.

Outtake # 3

HARVEY WEINSTEIN &
GEORGE CLOONEY

"Bad behavior doesn't get punished in this business, and [the Weinsteins'] certainly doesn't. People just ignore it and say, 'They're good at what they do,' which they are."

—BILL MECHANIC, *quoted by Peter Biskind,*
Down and Dirty Pictures

Harvey Weinstein's sexual predations came to light in October 2017, more or less igniting the #MeToo movement. It all began when a *New York Times* article was followed by Ronan Farrow's *New Yorker* piece, reporting more than a dozen accusations against Weinstein of sexual harassment, assault, or rape. As happened after Jimmy Savile's death in the UK, this led to a snowball effect in which more and more women, most of them in the film industry, reported similar experiences (to date about eighty women have come forward).

While Weinstein continued to deny any nonconsensual sex, he was promptly fired from his production company Miramax, suspended from the British Academy of Film and Television Arts, expelled from the Academy of Motion Picture Arts and Sciences, resigned from the Directors Guild of America, left by his wife Georgina Chapman, and denounced by several leading figures in politics whom he had previously supported. The Los Angeles Police Department opened a criminal investigation against him for alleged rape, and New York and London police began investigating other sexual assault allegations. On May 25, 2018, Weinstein was arrested by New York police and charged with "rape, criminal sex acts, sex abuse and sexual misconduct for incidents involving two separate women." As of October 2019, Weinstein has settled all the charges with a $44 million payout.

Ronan Farrow's *Catch and Kill: Lies, Spies, and a Conspiracy to Protect Predators* recounts in minute detail the difficult process of making Weinstein's predations public. Central to the Weinstein affair is the fact that, whatever else Weinstein was, and is, exceptional he ain't. For example, Farrow quotes the producer of *Shakespeare in Love*, Donna Gigliotti, commenting that Weinstein "isn't guilty of anything worse than what a million other men in this business do" (p. 41). He quotes Elizabeth Perkins, one of Weinstein's countless victim of sexual assault: "Money and power enabled, and the legal system has enabled . . . Ultimately, the reason Harvey Weinstein followed the route he did is because he was allowed to, and that's our fault. As a culture that's our fault" (p. 130). Rosanna Arquette, meanwhile, went on record warning about "a cabal that was wider and deeper than Weinstein. 'This is the big boys' club, the Hollywood mafia,' she said. 'They protect each other'" (p. 242). Another object of Weinstein's predations, Emma de Caunes, told Farrow: "I know that everybody—I mean everybody—in Hollywood knows that it's happening. . . He's not even really hiding" (p. 251).

Beyond all doubt (and whatever Meryl Streep might claim*), this can only have been an "open secret" in Hollywood, and the same must be said for Jeffrey Epstein with his Lolita Island and sex parties. In 2002, for example, Donald Trump dropped blatant hints about the perks of being Epstein's travel buddy: "I've known Jeff for fifteen years. Terrific guy," Trump said. "He's a lot of fun to be with. It is even said that he likes beautiful women as much as I do, and many of them are on the younger side. No doubt about it—Jeffrey enjoys his social life."[1] Regarding Weinstein, Peter Biskind's *Down and Dirty Pictures* came out in 2004, and it paints a picture of Weinstein that, though it excludes any sexual abuses, is unequivocally monstrous. As far as I know, the book resulted in no repercussions for Weinstein.

---

* "One thing can be clarified. Not everybody knew. . . . And it's a shock . . . in terms of Harvey, I really didn't know. I did think he was having girlfriends." "Meryl Streep talks Harvey Weinstein, own harassment experiences," by Michael Rothman, *ABC News*, Jan 3, 2018: https://abcnews.go.com/Entertainment/meryl-streep-talks-harvey-weinstein-harassment-experiences/story?id=52115019

"Open secret"—as well as being the title of a 2014 documentary about child sexual abuse in Hollywood—is a popular oxymoron referring to something insiders are aware of but do not talk to outsiders about. By 2017, Weinstein had worked and/or partied with just about every major Hollywood player alive, and A-listers Matt Damon and Russell Crowe were even named as among his "enablers," having allegedly helped kill an earlier exposé on Weinstein.[2] Damon, along with other Weinstein bedfellows George Clooney and Ben Affleck, denied all knowledge and put their acting skills to maximum use in expressing shock and outrage at every press opportunity. Clooney was quoted by *The Daily Beast* on October 10, 2017:

> "It's indefensible. That's the only word you can start with. . . . I've known Harvey for 20 years. He gave me my first big break as an actor in films on *From Dusk Till Dawn*, he gave me my first big break as a director with *Confessions of a Dangerous Mind*. We've had dinners, we've been on location together, we've had arguments. But I can tell you that I've never seen any of this behavior—ever."[3]

Shortly after the interview, however, *ER* actress Vanessa Marquez tweeted that Clooney "helped blacklist me when I spoke up [about] harassment on ER," and that "women who dont [sic] play the game lose [their] career [as] I did." Earlier, in January 2017, Marquez posted on Facebook: "I was blacklisted and my career was over at 26. . . . Why are women afraid to speak up 'at the time?' Because everything they've ever worked for is RIPPED away from them. For being a goddamn victim and expecting protection."[4] Clooney issued a statement denying he had anything to do with casting on the show, and there the matter ended until August 2018, when "officers were conducting a welfare check at Marquez's home and she allegedly pulled out a 'BB-type' replica gun, causing an officer to open fire in response."[5] Marquez was killed.

This wasn't the first time Clooney—a friend of the Clintons, member of the Council on Foreign Relations, and actively involved in the Clinton-Bush Haiti Fund[6]—had come dangerously close to sexual scandal. In 2010, he was called as a witness in Italian Prime Minister Silvio Berlusconi's rape trial in Milan, for paying an underage prostitute for sex. The rape had allegedly occurred at one of Berlusconi's "elite orgies where male guests dressed as nuns and performed stripteases."[7] Clooney had attended some of these parties, and was called as a witness.[*]

All of this raises the question, once again: on which side of the screen is the more fantastic fiction unfolding? Movie fans and celebrity worshipers have always been fascinated by the lives of the rich and famous, even when they were being artfully airbrushed to appear squeaky clean or endearingly hell-raising. How much more so, now the cracks are starting to show?

---

[*] Clooney's father, Nick Clooney, was a former Corporal in the US Army who, after a start in radio, went on to become a journalist, anchorman, and television host; in 2004, he ran unsuccessfully for Congress. He has named Senator Robert Byrd, a member of the Ku Klux Klan in the 1940s, as a friend and mentor. George studied acting with leading Scientologist Milton Katselas, at his Beverly Hills Playhouse for 5 years, from 1982–1987, before his acting break in *ER*, which also starred the sexual abuse victim, Anthony Edwards. In 2013, WikiLeaks released 276 Global Intelligence emails that mentioned George Clooney by name. Global Intelligence fronts as an intelligence publisher while providing confidential intelligence services to large corporations, such as Bhopal's Dow Chemical Co., Lockheed Martin, Northrop Grumman, Raytheon and government agencies, including the US Department of Homeland Security, the US Marines and the US Defense Intelligence Agency.

Outtake # 4

KEVIN SPACEY
(A MIRRORED FUN HOUSE)

> "Our responsibility, as directors or producers, is to keep the
> heavy combat secret from the talent. So when I involved one of
> their angels [Robert De Niro], and made him aware of what goes
> on behind the scenes [at Miramax], I broke the code."
>
> —JAMES MANGOLD, *director of Logan, quoted by Peter Biskind,*
> *Down and Dirty Pictures*

In curious tandem with the Weinstein scandal, the Kevin Spacey affair
also kicked off in October 2017, when fifteen people leveled charges
against Keyser Söze for sexual assault, including journalist Heather
Unruh, filmmaker Tony Montana, actor Roberto Cavazos, Richard Dreyfuss'
son Harry, and eight people who worked on *House of Cards*. Spacey was
summarily fired from *House of Cards* and a Gore Vidal biopic he had done
(playing Vidal) for Netflix was shelved.* Spacey was also due to appear
in Ridley Scott's biographical film *All the Money in the World*, as industrial-
ist J. Paul Getty, but weeks before the release date his scenes were reshot with
Christopher Plummer. Spacey underwent the process of being redacted, or
"spaced out," as his mere existence became a blight upon the entertainment
industry.

Spacey's childhood backstory was filled in, however, somewhat sensa-
tionally, by the *Daily Mail:* Spacey's older brother claimed their father was a

---

* Vidal is (somewhat) known as a child sexual predator himself, as discussed in *Vice of
Kings.*

467

Nazi and that he, the elder brother, was raped by the father as a child.[1] A few years previously, the *Mail* also reported that Spacey

> attends political conferences—New Labour's, naturally, where he once turned up as a friend of Bill Clinton when the former president made a keynote address. But it is his relationship with another political figure that has raised eyebrows among the chattering classes. Sources say Peter Mandelson and Spacey have been friends for five years. Indeed, Mandelson—who was famously "outed" by former MP Matthew Parris on *Newsnight* in 1998—enjoys regular dinners with the star whenever they are both in London.[2]

Mandelson is linked to my own family, and his name comes up quite a bit in connection to organized child sexual abuse in the UK, as recounted in *Vice of Kings*.[3] And then there's the Epstein Connection: in 2002, Epstein "flew President Clinton, Kevin Spacey and Chris Tucker to Africa to explore the problems of AIDS and economic development facing the region."[4] According to his lawyers, Epstein was "part of the original group that conceived the Clinton Global Initiative."[5] At the 2010 Clinton Global Citizen Award ceremony, Spacey presented an award to Dr. Jean W. Pape for her work with AIDS treatment. The event marked "the culmination of the Clinton Global Initiative in New York."[6]

At the time of writing (2020), the criminal charges against Kevin Spacey have been dropped, primarily due to the death of one of his primary accusers, "John Doe"—with some irony, I note, the "name" of Spacey's satanically inspired serial killer in *Se7en*:

> The Los Angeles County District Attorney's office . . . said it would be declining the case filed against the Oscar winner. Prosecutors cited the death of the accuser during the course of their investigation. The man was an anonymous masseur who claimed the actor forced him to touch his genitals during a treatment at Spacey's Malibu home in October 2016. "The sexual assault allegations cannot be proved without participation of the victim. Thus, the case was declined," said charging documents provided to *The Times* by a D.A. spokesman.[7]

The death was reported first in September 2019, including the perfunctory statement: "There are no details yet on the circumstances of death."[8] No further details have been forthcoming since then, nor do any of the articles express the slightest curiosity.

◆

Some people naturally began to ask whether removing all traces of Kevin Spacey from the celebrity roster was a valid way to address the problem of predatory behaviors, much less their implications. But then, this was the same culture that wanted to change the title of the second *Lord of the Rings* movie (*The Two Towers*) after the World Trade Center collapsed in 2001, to protect its citizens from painful memories—or more accurately, to remove all negative associations with the product being sold. (Or the current trend for tearing down statues of politically incorrect historical figures.) This sort of redactive reaction is very much business as usual within the entertainment industry, as much as within the field of criminal conspiracies and espionage.

Inevitably, a roster of movie personalities began piping up with their two cents on Weinstein and Spacey. Woody Allen denied all knowledge of Weinstein's behavior and warned about a Hollywood witch-hunt. (As far as I know, no one asked him about partying with Jeffrey Epstein.) After Allen was trashed on social media, he rapidly backpedaled by calling Weinstein "a sad sick man." Tom Hanks said in *The Independent*: "Sure there were people who knew exactly what was going on." But: "[Weinstein's] name will become a noun and a verb. It will become an identifying moniker for a state of being for which there was a before and an after." Jeff Bridges commented to *Variety*: "Talk about facing your fear, he's gotta face his demons now. I wish him the best of luck with that, he needs to lean in and really face those things."

Meryl Streep: "The behavior is inexcusable, but the abuse of power familiar. Each brave voice that is raised, heard and credited by our watchdog media will ultimately change the game." This same watchdog media were quick to point out how, at the 2003 Academy Awards, Streep had joined in a standing ovation for convicted child-rapist Roman Polanski. How quickly we forget—and forgive. Bryan Cranston went on record calling Spacey "not a very good person" and opined that his "career now I think is over." A few days later, he was asked if there is a way back for Hollywood players accused of sexual harassment or assault. "Maybe so," he said: with time, society's forgiveness, and a "tremendous contrition on their part." Susan Sarandon commented on Spacey by stressing "the unfortunate thing is that he some-how tried to mix the idea of pedophilia and homosexuality, as if they had anything to do with each other."

Having emphasized this point (factually inaccurate, since pedo-philia and homosexuality have significant areas of overlap*) over all others, Sarandon added optimistically, "People have a short memory." By this she meant that Spacey might be able to salvage his career in time. But then she added: "[the abuse] couldn't happen if it weren't protected. . . . hopefully those days are over because everyone's discussing it." So much for Sarandon's point about short memories. Perhaps she forgot it already.

---

* To name just one: "Epidemiological studies find a positive association between child-hood maltreatment and same-sex sexuality in adulthood, with lesbians and gay men reporting 1.6 to 4 times greater prevalence of sexual and physical abuse than hetero-sexuals." "Does Maltreatment in Childhood Affect Sexual Orientation in Adulthood?," by Andrea L. Roberts, M. Maria Glymour, and Karestan C. Koenen, *Arch Sex Behav.* 2013 Feb; 42(2), p. 161–171: https://www.ncbi.nlm.nih.gov/pmc/articles/PMC3535560/ There is some uncertainty, in today's ideologically challenged climate, over whether some children are "naturally" homosexual and so attract male pedophiles, as compared to the more common-sense, if less politically correct, deduction, that sexual interference as a child compromises the development of adult sexuality. For more overlaps see *The Vice of Kings*, chapter 16, p. 117–125.

NATIONAL ENQUIRER & THE CIA

"They say you can fool some of the people all of the time.
Accordingly, I think we should concentrate on this group initially.
We can move on to the people you can only fool some of the time
at a later date if we deem it necessary."

—STEPHEN MITCHELL, *Ray D. Shosay's Journal*

One thing perhaps everyone can agree about, when it comes to Hollywood as much as politics, is that managing perception is central to how the world functions. We know there are vested interests in directing the flow of information, and that this relates to the drive for a more tightly controlled media and internet. Since Donald Trump became POTUS, Facebook, Twitter, YouTube, Apple, and Patreon have become increasingly proactive in helping to create a politically correct cyber-sphere.* And since there are, equally certainly, vested interests in discrediting or censoring stories of systematized, high-level sexual abuses—specifically the more fact-based accounts—it's fair to point out that inundating the web with fake news stories on the subject might be an effective means of doing so. Such stories serve to muddy the waters of a swamp of organized crime and its ties to the entertainment industry, in such a way as to intensify a growing divide in public perception that is becoming increasingly associated with *ideological affiliations*.

---

* Trump had a soft alliance with arch-conspiracy theorist Alex Jones, who in September of 2018 was roundly banned from his primary social media platforms.

The blurry zone between intelligence maneuvers, celebrity secrets, yellow journalism, and manipulation of public perception regarding what's true or false obviously predates the internet and the current furor over "Fake News" by several decades. The publisher of the notorious but still massively popular *National Enquirer,* Gene Pope Jr., for example, "worked briefly on the CIA's Italy desk in the early 1950s and maintained close ties with the Agency thereafter."[1] In *The Deeds of My Fathers: How My Grandfather and Father Built New York and Created the Tabloid World of Today,* Paul David Pope describes how the *Enquirer* refrained from publishing dozens of stories with "details of CIA kidnappings and murders, enough stuff for a year's worth of headlines" in order to "collect chits, IOUs [that] would come in handy when he got to 20 million circulation. When that happened, he'd have the voice to be almost his own branch of government and would need the cover." Other potential stories drew on documents proving the CIA financed Howard Hughes "to secretly fund, with campaign donations, twenty—seven congressmen and senators who sat on sub-committees critical to the agency [and] fifty-three international companies named and sourced as CIA fronts"—as well as "a list of reporters for mainstream media organizations who were playing ball with the agency."[2]

Regarding the CIA and *National Enquirer's* relationship to Hollywood, in "The Secret History of the National Enquirer," *DuJour* reported that

> Over the years, scores of celebrities and politicians were rumored to be making deals with the *National Enquirer* to conceal all manner of indiscretions, be it a DWI or other arrest on a minor charge, an intimate photo or video, an affair (particularly worrisome if it involved the spouse of another star), a gay or lesbian encounter or an out-of-wedlock child. In exchange for information on someone else or agreeing to an exclusive interview, stars were able to keep their secrets out of the spotlight. Confidential sources confirmed to *DuJour* that celebrities were essentially blackmailed to work with the *Enquirer* or else risk their improprieties appearing on the front page. It is alleged that Sylvester Stallone was told to cooperate or have a nasty exposé published. As agreed, such a story was not written, but a *National Enquirer* reporter gave the incriminating details to Hollywood private investigator Anthony Pellicano for one of his clients to use as leverage against Stallone. (Pellicano is currently

serving 15 years in federal prison for numerous RICO violations, including illegally wiretapping his clients.) Other prominent figures who reportedly cooperated under duress were Arnold Schwarzenegger, Burt Reynolds and Bill Cosby.[3]

Ronan Farrow's 2019 Catch and Kill provides confirmation of this discreet function of the tabloid press, via Farrow's discoveries regarding American Media, Inc. (AMI), the owner of *National Enquirer* until 2019 (when it was forced to sell the magazine to the Hudson Group). Farrow writes:

> Over the years, the company has reached deals to shelve reporting around Arnold Schwarzenegger, Sylvester Stallone, Tiger Woods, Mark Wahlberg, and too many others to count. "We had stories and we bought them knowing full well they were never going to run," [Farrow's source] said. One after another, the AMI employees used the same phrase to describe this practice of purchasing a story in order to bury it. It was an old term in the tabloid industry: "catch and kill" (p. 346–47).

From all this, it's pretty clear that mainstream media coverage of celebrity lives—at least some of it—is used as a means to influence and control celebrities, a machinery of blackmail and manipulation, before, above, and beyond being any kind of instrument of journalism. In a case such as Robert Downey Jr., for example, it appears the only reason we ever heard any of those stories—the only reason they got such wide play—is because they were not suppressed or "contained," i.e., *Downey was not protected*. This implies that the stories were being actively used as a means to punish him, get him back in line, or both, as well as to send a message to other celebrities.

National Enquirer articles and other lurid tales of Hollywood Babylon seem to have more than one target audience. There is an apparently primary, overt target audience of gullible, scandal-hungry masses who lap the stories up with nary a thought for veracity or confirmability. Then there is a more "discerning" intelligentsia who consider it beneath their interest, while at the same time regarding it as further proof of the common folk's salacious lack of discernment and of the yellowness of journalism. Neither demographic, one supposes, is aware of being hoodwinked. Then there would be the third and most important audience, that of Hollywood insiders, who would be aware that what they are seeing is not mere yellow journalism or malicious gossip, but the conscious appliance of power, blackmail, and control.

In the same way, while the mainstream reaction to much of the material cited in the present work is one of derision, still many people unquestioningly believe in the reality of claims around organized, ritualized child abuse and mind control within the entertainment industry, while others (presumably) *know* the truth of it. The first class of people—the believers—may not *care* if the accounts are made up or not, since they believe them to be true in "essence." In such people's minds, "Fake News" articles could even be a way for movie stars to go on record without having to suffer the consequences, since afterwards they can deny having ever said it! This could even be true— how would we know it if it were?

In a similar way, some stars now seem to be playing into the growing belief that they are mind-controlled mouth-pieces for the Illuminati. Or, like Kevin Spacey, they are happy to blur the line, in the public mind, between the corrupt characters they play in TV melodramas and the corrupt behaviors being attributed to them in the news. This might even be a way to apply their own pressure and manipulations, and potentially increase their immunity to blackmail—by showing that they have a strong fanbase of support, regardless of what is revealed about them.

One thing is clear: fact or fiction, dark legends sell. At a certain point, people may become effectively oblivious—or incapable of discerning— whether it's fact or legend, truth or rumor, most especially when real-life moral outrage is becoming a form of entertainment that's complementary with—even compensation *for*—the ironic detachment of dark make-believe fantasy.

Outtake # 6

DAVID FINCHER & *ZODIAC* (THE THIN END OF HOLLYWOOD HYPOCRISY)

"It takes all of those pieces of technology to deliver the thing and you want it all in service of that moment. Cinema is when you put an idea in somebody else's head, where you put an idea into seven hundred people's head, *at the same time*."

—DAVID FINCHER, *"A Life in Pictures"*

On the commentary track to *Se7en*, David Fincher comments that all filmmakers should make their thesis clear and that his thesis statement with *Se7en* (and in general) was to never use violence in a purely exploitative fashion, as an easy substitute for dramatic action (i.e., to titillate or excite). Fincher is an intelligent, articulate, and thoughtful guy, and listening to him, I *almost* believed him—about *Se7en* and *Fight Club* at least. But the same Fincher went on to make *Panic Room*, a violent piece of pulp; *Girl with the Dragon Tattoo*, a vacuous and repellent piece of S & M misandrist agitprop; and *Gone Girl*, a massively entertaining but extremely violent melodrama. Fincher was even planning to reunite with Brad Pitt for the sequel to the zombie apocalypse thriller, *World War Z, though that project has mercifully been cancelled*. All of this makes his anti-exploitation thesis *resoundingly hollow*, and I found myself wondering if it indicated the sort of high-level denial that's both *de rigueur* and almost entirely

unconscious—and invisible to insiders—in Hollywood. On the other hand, maybe it's not unconscious at all?*

If we look at Fincher's career more closely, we may discover that his father, Howard Kelly Fincher, worked as a bureau chief (also referred to as chief editor) for *Life* magazine, under the name Jack Fincher. (*Life* magazine—along with *Time*—was one of the major organs of the CIA's "Operation Mockingbird," as exposed by Carl Bernstein in 1977.[1]) On top of this, Fincher Sr. was a screenwriter who wrote a biopic on Howard Hughes, an alleged CIA affiliate. Unto this manor born, all doors flew open wide for young David: when he was two, his family moved to San Anselmo, California, where he had George Lucas for a neighbor. Inspired by the countercultural kitsch Western, *Butch Cassidy and the Sundance Kid*, Fincher began making movies at the age of eight.

At twenty-one, he got a job at George Lucas's Industrial Light and Magic and worked on *Return of the Jedi* and *Indiana Jones and the Temple of Doom* as assistant cameraman. His breakthrough came via "Smoking Fetus," a commercial for the American Cancer Society that stirred up controversy and got him his first music video gig, for Rick Springfield. Shortly after (reports vary), Fincher co-founded a video-production company called *Propaganda Films* (get it?) with future mass-destruction maestro, Michael Bay. Fincher made TV commercials for Levis, Converse, Nike, Pepsi, Revlon, Sony, Coca-Cola, and Chanel, and music videos for (among others) Madonna and Michael Jackson. His primary influences in this period were Tony and Ridley Scott. He also made a commercial with then-undiscovered model and future Mrs. Brad Pitt, Angelina Jolie, daughter of Jon Voight.

---

* Fincher's *The Curious Case of Benjamin Button*, also with Brad Pitt, stands out in the Fincher canon like a sore thumb. Based on a short story by F. Scott Fitzgerald, its title character is born an old man and ages backwards. One consequence of this is that, when he is physically eighty, he falls in love with a seven-year-old. On the commentary track, Fincher remarks: "Some people take umbrage with the notion that an 80-year-old man should be underneath sheets with a 7-year-old girl, and my response is, that's the fucking point of the scene!" (The sheets he refers to are of a makeshift children's "castle.")

Perhaps the most surprising thing about Fincher's career arc is that he went *back* to directing commercials, not only after his fiasco with *Alien 3* (1992, for which the studios gave him little creative control and which he abandoned in post-production), but also after *Panic Room*, in 2002. The man who made *Fight Club* in 1999 spent *half the following decade* making commercials for Coca-Cola, Nike, Motorola, and Heineken (with Brad Pitt!)! What's wrong with this picture?

"Advertising is the greatest art form of the 20th century," Marshall McLuhan said back in 1976. Out of vanity alone, Edward Bernays would probably have agreed.

✦

> "[Movie celebrities'] power and international celebrity can be
> valuable—it gives them entrée to people and places abroad.
> Heads of state want to meet and get cozy with them. Their film
> crews are given free reign everywhere, even in places where
> the US government doesn't normally have it. And they can be
> the voice of a US message that will have impact with foreign
> audiences so long as the audience doesn't know it is coming from
> the US government."
>
> —JOHN RIZZO, *Company Man*

A closer look at his career suggests there is barely a subversive bone in Fincher's body and that he is little more than a gifted errand boy for grocery clerks, all the way down to his Coke-soaked internal organs. Seen in this context, *Fight Club*—that searing denunciation of consumer culture— would seem to be likewise possessed of a split-personality. It implies there is nary a subversive frame in the whole film—not even subliminally—only a simulation of subversion, a controlled media opposition. While posing as edgy art, it doubles as an invitation to counterfeit consumer revolt and pseudo-awakening, offering, in the words of Guy Debord, "false models of revolution to local revolutionaries" (p. 28).*

---

* It may be worth mentioning that "anon" administrator(s) of the popular alternate news site *ZeroHedge* early-adopted Tyler D. as their avatar.

As a spectacle constructed with many layers of sophistication, beneath them all, perhaps, lurks an advertisement for itself, for the people who made it and the system that produced it. Like a calling card to get past the defenses of the cynical, alienated youth audience, *Fight Club* serves to thereby place its products—those hooks and levers that manage our perception—on our *insides*. Is there anything more pernicious than a phony rebellion, I find myself wondering, while still loving the film as it plays in my memory? Talk about split personality! Movies make Tylers of us all?

Arguably, there was even more perniciousness to come. In 2007, after five years pimping for Coke and Nike, Fincher made *Zodiac*, about the San Francisco serial killings of the late 1960s. *Zodiac* is based on two books by Robert Graysmith that purport to solve the Zodiac killings. (Graysmith is played in the movie by Jake Gyllenhaal, another movie star whose charms I am helpless to resist.) Fincher said this to the New York Times about the project: "I won't use anything in [Graysmith's] book that we don't have a police report for." He then added: "*It was an extremely difficult thing to make a movie that posthumously convicts somebody.*"[2]

The somebody in question was Arthur Leigh Allen (played in the film by John Carroll Lynch), and Fincher and his cast and crew certainly did a stand-up job of convicting him. I left the film (all four times I saw it) with my own conviction of his guilt. I should have known better, but I was somehow persuaded the film was a *reasonably* faithful historical recreation of events. It turns out that Fincher's two statements to the *New York Times* were *inversely* related: It was extremely difficult for him to make a movie that posthumously convicted Allen, *while still being able to claim* that he stuck strictly to police reports. The truth is, what he stuck to was Robert Graysmith's pet theory that implicates Allen, records be damned. Dig a little deeper (as only one in a thousand viewers ever will) and it turns out that

> many experts on the case have thoroughly dismantled Graysmith's book, exposing it as a mixture of myths, half-truths, and inventions concocted to present a non-existent case against an innocent man. [Nonetheless] many of his basic assumptions about the case are still widely accepted as correct by most theorists and investigators.[3]

The case against Graysmith's case against Allen is laid out in a painstaking online analysis of the film vs. the facts by long-time researcher Michael
Butterfield, who argues, convincingly, that "the foundation of distortions
and falsehood" in *Zodiac* was designed "to manipulate the audience opinion
regarding [Allen's] possible guilt."[4] Fincher and co. "made every effort to
ignore and gloss over the evidence" that undermined Graysmith's pet theory.*
Fincher claimed *Zodiac* drew exclusively on police reports, and today the
film is regarded as a classic police procedural movie. If Butterfield is to be
believed, it is closer to a tissue of lies. Butterfield even listened to the same
DVD commentary I did, albeit with a far more trained ear:

> Nowhere during his commentary does Fincher make any effort to cor-
> rect the historical record on any matters of real importance, and he
> only vaguely refers to problems with Graysmith's revisionist account
> of the case. At one point, Fincher refers to the Belli Birthday Call as
> Graysmith's "December 18 obsession," but the director does not inform
> his viewers that he and the filmmakers knew that the obsession had no
> basis in fact.[5]

Suspension of disbelief is the business Hollywood is in, and *Zodiac* proceeds as an artful deception that creates the atmosphere of a serious,
conscientious work that would never deliberately distort facts for dramatic
purposes, much less dishonorable ones. The same might be said of Fincher
himself. Yet if *Zodiac* is a tissue of lies, then Fincher is at the heart and center
of it. You would never know it from how the film was received. In a 2012
article called "*Zodiac* shows all the vital signs of historical accuracy," *The*

---

* For example, the evidence that key witness Don Cheney invented his stories to implicate Allen in the crimes; that the "thirteen points" cited by Graysmith in *Zodiac* did not
implicate Allen; and that the "lynchpins" of Graysmith's theory—the phone calls on the
night Darlene was killed, the terrifying "Lee," and the "birthday" call to Melvin Belli on
Allen's date of birth—"were easily refuted by the known facts."

Guardian described Fincher's movie as "a perfect example of how a historical film can be accurate, balanced in opinion, and a gripping thriller—all at the same time."[6]

Somebody sure wanted us to think so.[*]

---

[*] The operation was only somewhat successful, however: while the movie has no doubt closed the book on the Zodiac killings for many people, there are over a dozen books on the subject currently available, many of which came out after the movie, and few if any point at Fincher's and Graysmith's chosen "patsy," Arthur Leigh Allen. There is even a recent (mock?) conspiracy theory that 2016 presidential candidate Ted Cruz was the real killer. More pertinent to this current work, George Hodel's son, LA police officer Steve Hodel, has presented evidence that his father was involved in the killings.

Outtake # 7

THE ATLANTA MURDERS

SERIAL KILLINGS AS PSYOP

Season Two of David Fincher and Joe Penhall's *Mindhunter* focuses primarily on the Atlanta child murders. Naturally, I watched it wondering how, or if, it would square with my previous thesis of Fincher (witting or not) as a disinformation agent working within an entertainment industry that has ties to covert intelligence agendas, or psyop. Somewhat surprisingly, perhaps, the last episode of the second season does go a certain distance to acknowledging some of the deeper, darker implications of the Atlanta case. It mentions the pedophile connection, and acknowledges that the convicted killer, Wayne Williams, was never charged with any of the child murders (only with two adult slayings). It ends by showing that there was, and is, plenty of skepticism among Atlanta citizens that Williams was even the guilty party.

In the podcast series *Atlanta Monster*, several journalists collectively state that—despite the conviction of Wayne Williams—"this wasn't the work of one monster" but "a larger pyramid of players," a pyramid connected to a pedophile ring that operated out of several houses which many of the victims (both child and adult) frequented. They cite police inspector Vincent Hill, who went on record about "a real connection" between these houses and the murders. (There was also an occult ritual element to some of the crimes.) In the book *Mindhunter* is based on, author and FBI profiler

John E. Douglas (Holden Ford in the TV show) states his belief that the murders were never fully solved and that they were not committed by a single perpetrator.[1] Even so, it was his profile of Williams that helped get him convicted—just as *Zodiac* set out to posthumously convict Allen.

In the book, Douglas describes a conversation with a bank robber that, "like a bolt from the blue," gives him a lasting insight into criminal psychology: "there was something inherently deep within the criminal mind and psyche, that compelled him to do things in a certain way." As in a good movie script, he even puts it in the mouth of the criminal: "*It's what we are*" (p. 62). A bit later (p. 110), Douglas makes the dubious claim that, while many criminals (especially serial killers) aspire and fail to become lawmen, "few police officers go bad and commit violent crimes." I guess he never saw *Serpico*.

Douglas' summary of both the Charles Manson and the "Son of Sam" case histories (he spoke to both men, as dramatized in season two of *Mindhunter*), within the deeper context of what is known about these cases (as provided by books such as Maury Terry's *Ultimate Evil*, Dave McGowan's *Programmed to Kill*, or Tom O'Neill's *Chaos*), are almost indistinguishable from pulp fiction. Even if most of what Douglas includes in the book is true, or a close approximation of it, what he leaves out ensures the work acts as a transportation narrative in which Douglas is the white-knight-as-FBI-profiler battling the forces of chaos, making him every bit as heroic as a character played by Robert Redford or Jake Gyllenhaal (or Jodie Foster). Needless to say, there is no mention in here of pedophile rings, military psyop, the FBI's COINTELPRO, the CIA's MKULTRA programmed killers (at one point, Douglas dismisses dissociative identity disorder as a criminal defense in a couple of sentences), and only one fleeting and incidental reference to satanic cults.

Where Douglas allows the possibility of multiple culprits, he either downplays or rejects the idea of them working together. He has nothing at all to say about organized murder operations or snuff movies (Henry Lee Lucas is conspicuously absent from the book). In place of such complex and disturbing realities, *Mindhunter* relentlessly promotes the narrative of lone, disturbed, and socially "inadequate" white male psychopath (age 20–40), and pits a growing epidemic of these crazies against the brave new world of behavioral science (BS for short). In other words, Douglas' version of crime history is pretty much indistinguishable from Hollywood movies and TV shows from the past sixty years. Douglas even winds up his book by "solving" the Jack the Ripper murders, once again choosing the miserable social outcast over the politically connected, high-status suspects, all based on the circular logic that these are the sorts of people that commit these murders.

But if Douglas is really what he claims to be: a sincere law officer combatting a plague of lone psychopaths driven by dysfunctionality and wretchedness, one would think he'd strongly object to *The Silence of the Lambs*, with its portrait of Hannibal Lector as an übermensch with preterhuman intelligence and almost supernatural sensory capacities. The movie, directed by Jonathan Demme, and its many spinoffs are all based on books by Thomas Harris, whom Douglas claims consulted with him frequently. Demme's film not only glorifies Lector, it celebrates his "talents" and ends on a blackly humorous note by unleashing him on society to continue stalking "the lambs" (with a last line designed for laughs). If I had spent my life hunting depraved killers and commiserating with their victims' families, I would find this sort of nihilistic vision utterly reprehensible and deeply irresponsible (I haven't, and I do anyway). Yet Douglas cites it several times as a fair representation of his work, and even mentions how the Scott Glenn character may have been based on him. He offers no qualifications and never addresses the lack of even a rudimentary resemblance between Lector and the serial killer profile he has perfected and popularized. All he really says is how "daunting" it is

> for the new people coming into the unit, trying to blend in with all these "stars," especially after the film *The Silence of the Lambs* came out and such intense national interest was focused on what we do. . . . In fact, ever since Thomas Harris . . . writers and newspeople and filmmakers have been coming to us for "the real story" (p. 406, 409).

The reason for his diplomatic silence and tacit approval may be that *Silence of the Lambs* (like Fincher's *Zodiac* and *Mindhunter* in their way) conforms to a cultural program of sociological propaganda. Establishing the "profile" of the criminal and setting it in stone (in print and celluloid) is essential to creating and "enforcing" the reverse image of the lawman protecting society from agents of chaos. Without this boogeyman, it would not be possible to sustain a convincing narrative around the positive function of police, military, and intelligence agencies in society. But Douglas manages just that: reading the book, I found the idea that law enforcement officers and FBI agents are the good guys—despite everything I know to the contrary—halfway believable. I was effectively transported by the cunningly constructed narrative. Fittingly, the book has an endorsement from Jonathan Demme on the back cover: "John Douglas knows more about serial killers than anybody in the world." Intelligence and entertainment industry mutual back-scratching?

Unlike the thoroughly emasculated third season of *True Detective*, *Mindhunter* Season Two certainly doesn't attempt to tie everything up in a reassuring red ribbon, but instead leaves viewers with more questions than answers. So far, so good. So it's fair to ask, in the context of my thesis, what was the angle with *Mindhunter* Season Two? Why treat the subject matter at all when it only raises the lid on such a can of worms, and when it inevitably shines light on —and arouses curiosity about—a case in which the ties between "serial killers" and deep state intelligence operations were unusually visible?

One answer may be that this case was already in the process of being reopened, perhaps partially due to the afore-cited popular podcast *Atlanta Monster*. And the case actually *has* been reopened: *Rolling Stone* reported four days after *Mindhunter* Season Two aired, "A decades-old investigation into the gruesome murders of black children in Atlanta has been officially reopened, coincidentally converging with renewed interest in the case thanks to the second season of the Netflix series *Mindhunter*."[2] The article does not mention *Atlanta Monster*, and in fact it reads more like a plug for the show than a piece of reportage.

Here are some other things that so far aren't being focused on, or mentioned at all, in the renewed interest (many of them aren't mentioned in *Atlanta Monster* either): A significant number of the adult murder victims were in the business of procuring children for sexual use for clientele. Many of the murdered children, as mentioned in *Mindhunter*, were known to have had sexual encounters with adults and in some cases were last seen with known pedophiles. Yet, as also somewhat disclosed in the Netflix show, none of the identified sex offenders were seriously considered as suspects in the murders. Some were reportedly interviewed (as *not* seen in the show) and admitted to having sex with children; yet none were ever charged.[3]

As Dave McGowan writes in *Programmed to Kill*, Chet Dettlinger, a former Public Safety Commissioner and assistant to the chief of the Atlanta Police Department, "maintains that sixty-three 'pattern' victims were arbitrarily left off the official tally" and that "twenty-five of those victims were killed after the arrest of Wayne Williams." A number of adult victims were arbitrarily omitted, as well as many female victims (two of the earliest list victims were young girls). "A number of young boys were excluded as well, for reasons that appear to have been entirely arbitrary. . . . As Public Safety Commissioner Dick Hand has acknowledged, 'The list that was created by the Task Force, in my own personal opinion, was an artificial list'" (p. 330). This leads to the inescapable conclusion that John E. Douglas' profiling of the Atlanta murderer, since it was based on the list, would be equally inaccurate.

While *Mindhunter* doesn't fudge facts the way Fincher's *Zodiac* does— and refrains from attempting to convict a man (Williams) who has already been convicted—it does do its share of glossing over extremely relevant details. For example, author Dave McGowan points out that "Some investigators do not believe . . . Williams ever stopped his car on that bridge or that there was a splash that night"; that "the officer filing the report did not immediately report the splash, nor attempt to verify the source . . . nor request equipment to drag the river and recover the alleged object." He suggests that "it is certainly possible that the entire incident was fabricated to tenuously link Wayne Williams to the murders" (p. 335). There is nothing whatsoever to suggest this in *Mindhunter*, though it does refrain from making the splash audible in the "recreation."

Mindhunter makes a big show of the discovery of the incriminating green carpet fiber evidence upon which the state's case against Williams was almost entirely built. Yet McGowan's account argues that this evidence "had seemingly been planted to provide the state with some semblance of a case. It was claimed, for example, that fibers from Williams' car were found on one victim who had disappeared before Williams had even purchased the car" (p. 336). Also, Jimmy Ray Payne, one of the two adults Williams was charged with killing, "was not even initially considered a murder victim"— the original death certificate has his death as "undetermined." "Recognizing, however, that a homicide prosecution requires an actual homicide victim, the state later had the death certificate altered" (p. 336). McGowan also suggests that Williams "would have been acquitted if his defense team had not made another crucial 'error' by sending Wayne to the stand in his own defense" (p. 337).

In *Mindhunter*, John E. Douglas writes that he believes "the forensic evidence and the behavioral evidence points conclusively to Wayne Williams as the killer of eleven young men in Atlanta." He also states that "there is no strong evidence linking him to all or even most of the deaths and disappearances." He then adds, both ominously and obliquely: "young black and white children continue to die mysteriously in Atlanta and other cities. *We have an idea who did some of the others. It isn't a single offender and the truth isn't pleasant.* So far, though, there's been neither the evidence nor the public will to seek indictments" (emphasis added; all quotes, p. 238). This conveniently sidesteps the question of why Douglas chooses not to give more information about it in his book, but only to make gnomic hints of insider knowledge.

As mentioned, *Mindhunter* does hint, *very* obliquely, that the Atlanta political establishment may have been ignoring leads into an underground pedophile ring. What isn't hinted at, at all, is the possibility that political and business elites may have actually belonged to this underworld and were complicit with the killings. It's also possible that some of the murders, especially the adult ones (of which Williams was convicted of two) were part of a "cleanup" to prevent the network being exposed. Curiously, considering how much *Mindhunter* in general focuses on sexual sadism, it not only omits any reference to the sexual aspect of the Atlanta murders, but repeatedly stresses its absence. And yet "sexual abuse of the child victims was indeed of considerable significance." Also omitted in the murder descriptions is the fact that "at least some of the victims were not killed immediately, but were kept alive for an indeterminate period of time following their abductions" (McGowan 2004, p. 331). This is hardly a minor detail.

Another curious fact that *Mindhunter*, both the fictional TV show and the "non-fiction" book, leave out—its omission more easily justified since it didn't come fully to light until 2010—is that, in a CNN interview Williams gave at that time, he was questioned by Soledad O'Brien about an autobiographical story titled "Finding Myself." The story, O'Brien states, "reads like an autobiography" and recounts how Wayne was "recruited for espionage training as a teenager" at a "secret government camp hidden in the woods near this north Georgia lake." O'Brien describes it as "an account of your CIA training," to which Williams responds only, "We're not going to get into that"—four times in steady succession. When asked if the story is fake, he says simply "No." When asked again if he worked for the CIA, Williams reverts to his standard response, "We're not going to get into it." He eventually adds, "I'll let the document speak for itself. I'm not going to comment on that."[4]

TROJAN TV SHOWS, COINTELPRO, & SATANISM

"I happen to believe that the numbers [of child prostitutes] are far greater than we can imagine. . . I don't have a doubt in my mind that were we to adequately police this problem that we would find that it is far more pervasive than any of us ever have imagined."

—ATLANTA MAYOR BILL CAMPBELL, *NPR News, May 9, 2001*

In the context of the use of shock and superstitious dread to induce a trance state in a target audience—to turn them into *latah*-zombies obedient to commands, of whatever sort (see 3.5)—it's important to remember that the whole of Atlanta was reduced to a state of terror during the period depicted in *Mindhunter*. "Terror that rises from the threat of a faceless, relentless killer and grows to nearly paralyze an entire community builds slowly," wrote Atlanta citizen Vern Smith in *Newsweek* in 2019:

As a reporter covering the story for *Newsweek*, and as a parent, I was enveloped in the sense of foreboding that overshadowed everything. Normal routine was governed by the wait for the next bulletin that another child had gone missing. I spent weekends linking arms with strangers wearing red armbands, searching woods and behind old buildings, half-filled with dread at what we might find. The body of 7-year-old LaTonya Wilson, one of only two black girls on the list, had turned up on the very first volunteer search, on a Saturday in 1980. In an environment where everyone was a suspect, no one felt safe. One black father told me he'd advised his 10-year-old son: "Don't even trust your uncles."[5]

Rumors circulated through the black population that the FBI and CIA were involved in the killings. Yet these rumors are not included in *Mindhunter,* any more than the occult or sexual elements to the killings are. And barring the occasional hint of a pedophile ring, the only reference to any sort of criminal organization at work is when the Ku Klux Klan is raised, repeatedly, as a possible suspect in the killings. This idea is dismissed by the FBI protagonist Holden Ford, and it is presented in the show as a red herring—as a combination of black hysteria with lazy thinking.

Yet a 2019 article, "Secret investigation into KKK during Atlanta child murders uncovers fear of race riots" disclosed that:

> The investigation into a possible Klan connection to the Atlanta child murders lasted two months and ended one month before Williams was considered a suspect. The operation, conducted in secrecy by informants and top law enforcement officials, included weeks of physical surveillance, phone wiretaps and polygraph tests. The investigation focused closely on the death of Lubie Geter, outlining information that a Klan member could be responsible for the 14-year-old's murder. . . . According to documents, former FBI director Phil Peters asked for "it to be kept a separate investigation," stating that if the investigation "leaked out, it would possibly cause a race riot." . . . One of the informants testified that a Klansman tried to recruit him "to help on the child murders" and was advised that the KKK was, "creating an uprising among the blacks. That they were killing the children. That they are going to do one each month until things blow up."[6]

The Klan is a longstanding secret organization with occult trappings, and was so heavy infiltrated in the 1960s and 1970s by FBI agents as to be pretty much continuous with it. As Brian Glick writes in *War at Home: Covert Action Against U.S. Activists and What We Can Do About It*: "By 1965, some 20 percent of Klan members were on the FBI payroll. Many occupied positions of power: 'FBI agents reached leadership positions in seven of the fourteen Klan groups across the country, headed one state Klan organization and even created a splinter Klan group which grew to nearly two hundred members'" (p. 60). This "infiltration" was part of the FBI's COINTELPRO, and, as Glick also notes, "The most intense COINTELPRO operations were directed against the Black movement, particularly the Black Panther Party" (p. 11). To assume, therefore, that the FBI's interests were incompatible with those of the KKK would be premature.

No wonder then that Ford/Douglas has no interest in pursuing the possibility of KKK involvement, any more than in looking further into the pedophile houses. He has his "profile" based on an arbitrary list—a single black male in his late-twenties, etc., etc. Ford, of course, as played by Jonathan Groff, is firmly in the infallibly intuitive unorthodox detective mold. Even though we are shown that he is emotionally unstable, and in need of constant reigning in due to his lack of social skills, we are never made to doubt his almost mystical deductive powers. Whatever he believes, we can be reasonably sure it will turn out to be true, and when he expresses an opinion, or a hunch, we are signaled to trust in it. He is our reliable guide through the underworld of serial murders, and we are lost without him.

✦

Another reason the second season of *Mindhunter* focuses on Atlanta so much could have to do with the subject matter being ideologically sympathetic with the "Black Lives Matter" movement started in 2013. This helps to uphold the impression of Fincher, Hollywood, and Netflix, as a liberal, progressive, benevolent and socially responsible—and *relevant*—cultural hub of conscientious creativity. It follows that Trojan Horses—engines of military propaganda or psyop—need to be ever more artfully constructed, even as awareness of their existence increases.

The question of *relevance* is especially central here, because the Atlanta child murders were already attracting a lot of renewed attention and interest via the afore-mentioned podcast, *Atlanta Monster*. *Atlanta Monster* painstakingly chronicles the case history and sifts through the evidence, essentially concluding with a question mark regarding Williams' guilt: if not a patsy, the evidence presented indicates indubitably that he was part of a larger organization—and operation—and that he possessed few, if any, of the standard features of the "serial killer profile." This latter, of course, is what *Mindhunter*, the book *and* TV show, are busy validating. In fact, within the fictionalized narrative of Season Two, the Atlanta child murders are presented as the means by which FBI profiling receives its official validation and becomes fully operational.

The most essential thing about *Mindhunter*—if it's serving as a disinformation Trojan Horse—is to establish and maintain its credibility. This is, after all, the highest level of Hollywood propaganda we're talking about, aimed at fooling, if possible, that segment of the people most difficult to fool *any* of the time. This would include the growing demographic of conspiracy-culture aficionados, WikiLeaks followers, "Alt-Right" researchers, as well as, specifically, the followers of *Atlanta Monster*. Satisfying these viewers means not ringing any overly jarring bells that might shake them out of their Netflix trance, or engender any feelings of resentment, suspicion, or incredulity (to suspend disbelief is the prime directive, remember). *Mindhunter* does a commendable job here, as I said, of keeping the worm-can open, as regards the many intelligence community entanglements squirming therein—without, it should be said, pulling on any of them overmuch.

The primary narrative within *Mindhunter*'s depiction of the Atlanta child murders (as in the show overall) is of dedicated FBI agents hunting down the minds and motives of serial killers, creating effective profiling tools as the means—if not to fully solve a case—to protect American society from a new kind of predator. Yet in reality, there is no way an agent as diligent, intelligent, and intimate with the case as Holden Ford/John E. Douglas would not have known significantly more about the actual nature of the Atlanta child murders, and how they had little or nothing to do with "profiling serial killers"—unless this latter was a means to maintain a cover-up by redirecting the public's attention into a manufactured narrative. This makes Ford-as-Douglas, to whatever degree, complicit with the crimes he is supposedly trying to solve.

✦

"It is not inconceivable that the killings were performed as
human sacrifices. Some reports hold that several of the parents
reported to independent investigators that the bodies of their
children had crosses carved into their foreheads and chests. It
is also not inconceivable that the ritual killings were recorded as
snuff films."

—DAVE MCGOWAN, *Programmed to Kill*

One thing about the Atlanta murders that is somewhat implied in *Mindhunter* is that, once the FBI were sent down there—initially because of a bogus kidnapping call that made the case federal—the story went nationwide. At a certain point, "before the investigation was wrapped up, no less an authority than Vice-President [and former director of the CIA] George Bush [Sr.] even came to town, ostensibly to coordinate federal and local efforts and to make sure the investigation stayed on track" (McGowan 2004, p. 333). And now, in 2020, the Atlanta murders are all over both the real news and the entertainment news, and the case is officially reopened. All this is supposedly about the pursuit of truth and justice. But one thing about a psyop—*it only works if your target audience is made aware of it.*

Which brings us to the last, and critical, element of the Atlanta killings conspicuously absent from *Mindhunter*—despite again being fully in keeping with "serial killer profiles"—the occult (hidden) element. Admittedly, this does seem to revolve around a single witness and a couple of crime scenes; but even so, some of the details are striking. The witness in question was Shirley McGill, a Miami cocktail waitress whose story was made public by Roy Innis, head of the Congress of Racial Equality (CORE; an organization not mentioned in *Mindhunter*). In April 1981, McGill claimed that the Atlanta murders were committed by a satanic cult run by her ex-boyfriend, Parnell Traham. Traham was a (black) Vietnam veteran involved in a trafficking operation that brought drugs from Miami to Atlanta, Houston, and other cities. The operation, according to McGill, extended into ritual sacrifices and child abuse, as well as "business murders" for profit.

McGill claimed she worked as a bookkeeper for the drug operations, "purchasing used cars in Miami, packing them with drugs, and then delivering them to Atlanta and Houston. She also said that the ring had police protection and that at least one funeral home was complicit in disposing of bodies" (McGowan 2004, p. 338). McGill identified Wayne Williams (a photographer), as being involved in making snuff films of the rituals. She also stated that he did not take direct part in the rituals. She claimed that Traham delivered some of the murdered children to white men. When Innis delivered this story to the press in April 1981, it was received with skepticism.

With its witness under attack, CORE commissioned a battery of tests to gauge her veracity. McGill passed two polygraph examinations, repeated

her story under hypnosis, and was declared sane by examining psychiatrists. She was also able to lead investigators to remote sites that had
clearly been used for the performance of rituals (McGowan 2004, p. 338).

Also, a couple months before McGill came forward (on January 3, 1981),
an abandoned church and residency in southwest Atlanta was discovered via
an anonymous tip. Allegedly, parts of the house smelled like decaying flesh;
children's shoes and clothing were found, as well as axes and shovels, and two
Bibles nailed to the wall, both open to passages on murder and children. In
Painted Black, Carl Raschke wrote that, in the Atlanta neighborhoods where
the killings occurred, "a number of children have told police about satanic
sex abuse in which, they insist, they were compelled to drink both animal
and human blood." Some months after McGill came forward, searchers
stumbled upon a ritual site littered with the carcasses of slaughtered animals.
Prominent features of the site included a stone altar stained with blood and
a twelve-foot-high charred cross (McGowan 2004, p. 338).

Outtake # 8

DAVID LYNCH
(TOILET TO ETERNITY)

"I still get a little star-struck around David because he's so
unique. He's like another world you want to be a part of, and
you just want to please him in everything you do. (*Laughs.*) That
sounds weird. . . . He creates such an incredibly imaginative
world and it's so original and you just want to join that world at
whatever cost."

—NAOMI WATTS[1]

O ne of the central recurring problems that *16 Maps of Hell*
addresses—really *all* of my books, and maybe all *books*—is the
question of truth and how to identify it. Put more specifically,
which version of the narrative do we believe? This extends—or *in*-tends—to
our own internally generated narratives, which also conflict. Like the devil
and the angel on our shoulders, there is the part that tells us what we want to
believe, versus the part that lets us know what's actually happening.

In the summer of 2019, around about the time I first began working
on this book, I read David Lynch's auto-hagiography (it's a mix of biography, memoir, and canonization), *Room to Dream*. I found it a hard slog,
and the conclusion it left me with was that, either Lynch is a living saint, or
Lynch and his co-author (Kristine McKenna) were careful to omit anything
remotely negative that anyone had to say about him. Since I do not believe
that David Lynch is a living saint, I began to wonder if maybe everyone who
contributed to the book was subtly prompted, without actually being told,

or perhaps just intuitively sensed, that, if they wanted to be in this book, they would need to amp up their adoration to "11."

At one point, someone comments that Lynch's hair is a way of connecting to God. The statement seems slightly ironic but also slightly serious. (Lynch does have very cool hair, so much so that it's hard to imagine him without it. He is the movie director as rock star.) Countless people testify in the book about his amazingly positive energy, the joy he brings to the set, and how he makes everyone feel special, all of the time, and never does or says anything bad to anyone, ever. Though the book repeatedly emphasizes what a happy person Lynch is, one of the *only* non-glowing comments in the whole thing refers, casually, to his inability to function without very strict routines, coffee and cigarettes and donuts, and suchlike. I found myself thinking that this is hardly the mark of a healthy or "positive-energy" person.

The unceasing gush of testimonials became so oppressive to me in the end that I found myself wanting to believe that Lynch—like Leonard Cohen, an unabashed admirer of Ronald Reagan in the 1980s—is a closet psychopath who, like Leland Palmer (and as *Twin Peaks* actor Michael Anderson claimed), did terrible things to his daughter, Jennifer.* Or, less extreme but still light years from the book's Dorian-like portrait, something *Repo Man* director Alex Cox told me in 2015. Cox was at the house of some high school kids who attended a lecture by Lynch on Transcendental Meditation™. They made fun of Lynch's squeaky voice, and Cox mimicked them mimicking Lynch, saying, "I used to beat my wife, *every* day. TM: it works!"[2]

That Lynch used to beat his wife remains anecdotal, but it may be supported by something Lynch said to Lizzie Borden at the *Village Voice*, around

---

* "In an astonishing online attack, *Twin Peaks* cult actor Michael J. Anderson has unleashed a disturbing barrage of hate-filled vitriol on esteemed filmmaker David Lynch's reputation. The 'revelations' were posted up by 'Little Mike' on his Facebook profile photo. It reads: 'He totally did NOT rape his own under-age daughter and then write a television series about it. She totally has NOT lived under a DEATH THREAT from her own father, all her life if she ever told. He NEVER had his "best friend" murdered. And he DEFINITELY NEVER suggested to me that I should kill myself! There's a whole bunch of other stuff he never did either.'" "Michael J. Anderson Accuses Twin Peaks Filmmaker David Lynch of Being a Pedophile Rapist Murderer," *Data Lounge*, Aug 10, 2016: https://www.datalounge.com/thread/17409057-michael-j.-anderson-accuses-twin-peaks-filmmaker-david-lynch-of-being-a-pedophile-rapist-murderer

the time of *Blue Velvet*: "There are some women that you want to hit because you're getting a feeling from them that they want it, or maybe they upset you in a certain way. I see this happening. But I don't really understand it."[3] It has taken some major spin to prevent these aspects of Lynch's character from ending up all over the internet, and it's not hard to imagine how important that spin would be to securing his canonization. In the #MeToo climate that came fully into public awareness via the Weinstein scandal, Lynch's sainthood would be swiftly and permanently revoked in light of such allegations; even his own statement above, requoted in the present climate, could get him into hot water. This begs the question of how it is that *some* claims remain unsubstantiated rumors, quickly to disappear from public awareness, while others become international scandals. Presumably, it all depends whom the gods of spin wish to destroy, and why.

Room to Dream* also includes quite a few comments about how strange it is that such a happy, loving person as Lynch would have such fascination for dark, twisted imagery. Lynch, I believe, has eschewed psychotherapy as potentially interfering with his creativity, though his practice and promotion of TM is by now almost as central to his public persona as his dark movies. That said, no one in the foreseeable future is likely to refer to inner peace, collective positivity, or spiritual discipline as "Lynchian." What does seem to be in evidence is an ability to compartmentalize, a psyche that's split within itself and can alternate between poles of light and darkness which, like Sandy and Frank Booth, never get to meet. Perhaps that's why the robin at the end of *Blue Velvet* is artificial (and built by Lynch)?

*

> "It's very annoying, the notion that possessing genius is
> irrelevant to how people should behave, and that involvement in a
> masterwork, versus in a work that's forgettable, promises no extra
> benefit. Genius is no alibi, but neither is it a myth; it is a spirit
> that comes into the room. Later, you can say only that you had to
> be there."
>
> —SARAH NICOLE PRICKETT, *"Point of No Return"*

While *Room to Dream* deftly circumnavigates the conundrum of a happy camper with a festering unconscious, it gets busy combining the endless eulogizing with an appraisal and reappraisal of all Lynch's films and TV shows as masterpieces (except *Dune*, since the producer and studio can take the blame for that one). Apparently it's not enough to allow Lynch an ordinary career of hit and misses: in order to establish him as the saint of surrealist cinema and TV, *everything* he does must be proven equally great, even when it was painfully obviously *not* great at the time.

Tawdry works like *Wild at Heart* or *Fire Walk with Me*, or the second, longer portion of *Lost Highway*, are misunderstood works of genius being "restored" to greatness by the passage of time. Even *The Straight Story*—a forgettable whimsy—is referred to as a masterpiece. *Twin Peaks: The Return* doesn't need subjecting to aesthetic revisionism because, by the time it aired, Lynch's canonization was sufficiently complete for people to gush all over it immediately, despite its incoherence and self-indulgence (I gave up after four episodes). "Sometimes the network can give too much respect to an artist," said producer Tony Krantz of Lynch in 1999. Make that cubed for 2017.

Towards the end of *Room to Dream*, actor Robert Forster claims that, "Whatever David is doing, it is of a high order, and he may be a portal to the eternal, because he asks us to find that connection to the eternal in ourselves. . . . He is leading his audience toward the good." It is no longer enough to call someone a great artist, or even a genius; now he must be anointed as a human god. This is quite a bitter irony to me: after I first saw *Blue Velvet*, in 1987 at the age of twenty, I sent a postcard to a friend on which I wrote: "David Lynch is God!" It's as if, the more I have matured and extricated myself from slavish devotion to cultural creatives and their products, the more the world has sunk into that same swamp, until such misplaced religiosity has become the norm.

This culture-/self-worshiping madness reached its apotheosis for me with *Twin Peaks: the Return*, which alternated between really good, maybe great Lynch, and the worst, most self-indulgent Lynch, not just incoherent and boring but tasteless, inept, asinine, and almost unbearable to sit through. Now I am being assured that the 18-hour series is not only great TV but a means to lead humanity towards God™. What to make of this?

I see three possibilities: 1) people have been conned by a mixture of cultural hoodwinking and their own internal emptiness (the most appealing interpretation, since it allows me to feel superior); 2) I failed to recognize corporate-sponsored eternal goodness when I saw it (the least appealing option, since it makes me a failure, and possibly damned); 3) finally, neither, and a bit of both. Maybe each of us has our *own* way back to God, the eternal, and to goodness, and, while I ended up feeling like *Twin Peaks: The Return* was

Lynch's "punking" of the audience—similar to the way modern artists sell a piece of dried feces for a million dollars, the art being in the "stunt"—for others, it allowed a glimpse into the eternal (though I can barely read that back without flinching).

Still and good, the notion that a TV show can be a portal to eternity opens up an abyss of infinite possibilities in which *even a dried piece of feces* must also, surely, be granted said potential. It's as if Lynch and his backers and promoters want to push people deeper into a split within themselves: if audiences want to hold onto the idea, the experience, of being in the presence of greatness, they have to keep pushing away their felt sense that they are in the presence of shit. They have to keep coming up with ever more elaborate ways to persuade themselves that *this is art*—firstly, because of their belief in Lynch as a great artist; secondly, beneath that and less consciously, because of their need to believe in culture as a benevolent force in their lives.

This need to see everything Lynch (or Kubrick, or whoever) does as great requires an abandoning of critical faculties in lieu of blind worship. It stems from the need to see the artist himself as great, infallible, and perfect, rather than as an ordinary human being through whom lightning struck, once or twice. This in turn stems, as far as I can see, from the need to believe in great individuals, in people to admire and worship. Beneath that, I think, is really a narcissistic desire to *be* great oneself, to become a star. It's that infantile desire that fuels the delusion about great individuals out there to be worshipped: the desire to gain specialness by worshiping them—to join a cult and so gain access to "the goodness." Believe in Lynch (and Showtime TV) and you too will be saved.

There is a possibly even more pernicious aspect to this. Believing in Lynch also entails believing in the machinery of celebrity and the entertainment complex that recognized and supported Lynch's ascent from the very start, when he received an AFI grant to make *Eraserhead*. A system that, despite all the ways Lynch may have been blocked from doing some of the work he wanted to, has supported and elevated him ever since, and without which we would never have heard of him at all. The message of *Room to Dream*—it's there in the title—is that goodness, in the sense both of talent and virtue, is rewarded by success. It's the Protestant ethic: the system not only works; it provides a link to the eternal. All it requires is our undying allegiance.

Afterword

(ABOUT THE AUTHOR)

U sually this page is in the third person, but why pretend? It seems a bit dissociated to write about this guy "Jasun Horsley" when I have spent the last fifty years firmly locked inside that identity matrix.

In September 2020, I, the author, am on the verge of a massive change in perspective, readying to pull up stakes and move continents, even as the "world"—the socioeconomic and parapolitical superstructure that sustains the superculture mapped in this book—moves into increasingly Draconian "lockdown."

This book, *16 Maps of Hell*, may not be my last. It may not even be my last on these sorts of subjects to be published (I have at least two unreleased works written before it, *The Kubrickon* and *Neuro-Deviance*, possibly one book in two parts). But it is definitely an ending of some sort, and a new departure—judging at least by my rapidly morphing outer circumstances.

A few weeks ago, I had a dream of sorts, a vision. As I awoke from it, or before I did (time is meaningless here, as you will see), I saw that the nature of my true existence encompassed many existences, lives, timelines, and identity-selves. The dream-vision I was waking from was every bit as real as the dream-vision I was waking into, and yet the latter was one I considered my life. I knew now that it was nothing of the sort, or if it was, it was one of possibly countless existences occurring simultaneously.

I suspected that this experience was closely related to enlightenment, to where Dave Oshana was. I also suspected I wasn't ready for it, or even sure I especially wanted it. It seemed terrifyingly overwhelming. On the other hand, the person I took to be "me" was unquestionably and now palpably and experientially revealed as *not real*, as a kind of movie copy of a real life that was elsewhere unfolding. So where did that leave "me"?

When I placed my attention on my "life"—on the details that had been pushing on my attention the day before—it appeared as it was, unimportant, illusory. When I shifted my attention to my body, it felt solid and substantial, deeply at peace in a way that was new to me. I became aware of breathing, and of an impetus to breathe more deeply. Doing so was effortless ease, and far more engaging than my thoughts. I stayed with the feeling of breathing, immersed in the act of it. I began to realize then that nothing my body experienced "out there" was real—because it was being filtered through the mind-identity—but the experience *of* the body—of my awareness *in* my body—was where reality was located.

Then, last night, I had another dream-intimation of the edge of enlightenment. In contrast to the previous experience, this one was eminently desirable. I was on the streets of the town where I live, a block or so from home, thinking of my cat, Tuco. I closed my eyes and became immersed in the experience of an inner world, a world of boundless energetic being, drawing me towards it. I was aware of the possibility, the invitation, of turning fully "inside-out" so that the exterior world I perceived would be gone for good and the inner kingdom of the body would open to receive "me"— my awareness. It seemed infinitely inviting.

There was part of me that still saw the outer world of physicality, of objects and linear spacetime, as a necessary respite from this seemingly confined inner space, an escape. But that part was receding, no longer credible. I was ready to "flip"—to disappear into the infinity within.

If this final flip-over ever happens, there's obviously no way to say what my outer life will look like after that. It may become the proverbial "carry water, chop wood" life—or more likely the "saw wood, hammer nails" life of never-ending renovations—in which the life of the mind, of books and blogposts and podcasts and tweets, no longer has much attraction or relevance. But in the meantime, you can find the author at https://auticulture.com, where I have a weekly podcast *The Liminalist* and a regularly maintained blog, and where I invite readers and listeners to join online meetings and/or record conversations with myself to explore the ongoing mystery of existence.

If at some point none of this is happening anymore, then I invite you to follow what breadcrumbs I have left, and find me where I am.

I can also be reached (for now at least) at jasun@protonmail.com

BIBLIOGRAPHY

Adler, Tim. *Hollywood and the Mob*. London: Bloomsbury, 2007.

Andersen, Christopher, *Barbra: The Way It Is*. London: Aurum Press, 2007.

BACM Research, *Atlanta Child Murders—Wayne Williams FBI Files*. Paperless Archives, 2008.

Ballard. J.G. *Millennium People*. London: Harper Perennial, 2004.

Bart, Peter. *Infamous Players: A Tale of Movies, the Mob (and Sex)*. New York: Weinstein Books, 2011.

Bartlett, Frederic Charles. *Political Propaganda*. New York: MacMillan, 1940.

Bateson, Gregory. *Steps towards an Ecology of Mind*. University of Chicago Press, 2000.

Berman, Morris. *Wandering God: A Study in Nomadic Spirituality*. Albany: State University of New York press, 2000.

Bernays, Edward. *Propaganda*. New York: Ig Publishing, 2005.

Biskind, Peter. *Easy Riders, Raging Bulls*. New York: Simon & Schuster, 1999.

Biskind, Peter. *Down and Dirty Pictures*. New York: Simon & Schuster, 2005.

Breton, André. *Manifestoes of Surrealism*. University of Michigan Press, 1969.

Brockman, John. *By the Late John Brockman*. New York: HarperCollins, 2014.

Burger, Jeff. *Leonard Cohen on Leonard Cohen: Interviews and Encounters*. Chicago Review Press, 2014.

Burroughs, William. *Nova Express*. New York: Grove/Atlantic, Inc., 2011.

Castaneda, Carlos. *The Art of Dreaming*. New York: HarperCollins, 1993.

Castaneda, Carlos. *The Fire from Within*. New York: Washington Square Press, 1984.

Ciment, Michel. *John Boorman*. London: Faber & Faber, 1986.

Clover, Carol J. *Men, Women, and Chain Saws: Gender in the Modern Horror Film*. Princeton University Press, 1993.

Cronin, Paul (ed.). *Roman Polanski: Interviews*. Univ. Press of Mississippi, 2005.

Danny Fingeroth. *Disguised as Clark Kent: Jews, Comics and the Creation of the Superhero.* London: Bloomsbury Academic, 2007.

Debord, Guy. *Society of the Spectacle.* London: Rebel Press, 2002.

DeHaven Smith, Lance: *Conspiracy Theory in America.* University of Texas Press, 2013.

Dehgan, Bahman (ed.). *America in Quotations.* Jefferson: McFarland, 2015.

Douglas, John E. & Olshaker, Mark. *Mindhunter: Inside the FBI's Elite Serial Crime Unit.* New York: Simon and Schuster, 2017.

Edwards, Anne. *Streisand: A Biography.* New York: Little, Brown & Company, 2016.

Ellis, Bret Easton. *White.* New York: Alfred A. Knopf, 2019.

Ellul, Jacques. *Propaganda: The Formation of Men's Attitudes.* New York: Vintage Books, 1973.

Eszterhas, Joe. *Hollywood Animal.* New York: Knopf Doubleday, 2010.

Evans, Robert. *The Kid Stays in the Picture.* Los Angeles: Phoenix Books, 2002.

Falk, Ben. *Robert Downey, Jr: The Rise and Fall of the Comeback Kid.* London: Pavilion Books, 2014.

Farrow, Ronan. *Catch and Kill: Lies, Spies, and a Conspiracy to Protect Predators.* New York: Little, Brown, and Company, 2019.

Finstad, Suzanne. *Natasha: The Biography of Natalie Wood.* New York: Three Rivers Press, 2001.

Freud, Sigmund. *Totem and Taboo.* Mineola: Dover Thrift, 1998.

Friedkin, William. *The Friedkin Connection.* New York: HarperCollins, 2013.

Fritz, Ben. *The Big Picture: The Fight for the Future of Movies.* New York: Houghton Mifflin Harcourt, 2018.

Giles, David. *Illusions of Immortality: A Psychology of Fame and Celebrity.* Houndmills: Macmillan, 2000.

Gladstone, B. James. *The Man Who Seduced Hollywood: The Life and Loves of Greg Bautzer, Tinseltown's Most Powerful Lawyer.* Chicago Review Press, 2013.

Glick, Brian. *War at Home: Covert Action Against U.S. Activists and What We Can Do About It.* Cambridge: South End Press, 1989.

Goertzel, Victor and Mildred. *Cradles of Eminence: A Provocative Study of the Childhoods of Over 400 Famous Twentieth-Century Men and Women.* Boston: Little, Brown, and Co., 1962.

Hayden, Brian. *The Power of Ritual in Prehistory: Secret Societies and Origins of Social Complexity.* Cambridge University Press, 2018.

Herman, Judith Lewis. *Trauma and Recovery: The Aftermath of Violence--From Domestic Abuse to Political Terror.* New York: Basic Books, 2015.

Hiaasen, Carl. *Team Rodent: How Disney Devours the World.* New York: Random House, 2010.

Hoberman, J. *The Dream Life: Movies, Media, and the Mythology of the Sixties.* New York: New Press, 2003.

Hodel, Steve. *Black Dahlia Avenger: A Genius for Murder*. New York: Arcade Publishing, 2003.

Hofstadter, Richard. *The Paranoid Style in American Politics*. New York: Knopf Doubleday, 2012.

Horsley, Jake. *Dogville vs Hollywood: The War Between Independent Film and Mainstream Movies*. London: Marion Boyars, 2005.

Horsley, Jake. *The Blood Poets: A Cinema of Savagery*, volume 1, "American Chaos." Lanham: Scarecrow Press, 1999.

Horsley, Jason. *The Secret Life of Movies: Schizophrenic and Shamanic Journeys in American Cinema*. Jefferson: McFarland Press, 2009.

Horsley, Jasun. *Prisoner of Infinity: Social Engineering, UFOs, and the Psychology of Fragmentation*. London, Aeon Books, 2018.

Horsley, Jasun. *Seen and Not Seen: Confessions of a Movie Autist*. Winchester: Zero Books, 2014.

Horsley, Jasun. *The Vice of Kings: How Socialism, Occultism, and the Sexual Revolution Engineered a Culture of Abuse*. London, Aeon Books, 2019.

Hotchner, A. E. *Doris Day: Her Own Story*. William Morrow, 1975.

Huxley, Aldous. *Brave New World Revisited*. New York: Harper Perennial, 2006.

Joan Didion. *The White Album*. New York: Open Road Media, 2017

Kael, Pauline. *Deeper into Movies*. London: Marion Boyars, 1975, reprinted 2005.

Kael, Pauline. *I Lost it at the Movies*. London, Marion Boyars, 1965, reprinted 2002.

Kael, Pauline. *Reeling*. London: Marion Boyars, 1976, reprinted 1992.

Kael, Pauline. *When the Lights Go Down*. London: Marion Boyars, 1980.

Kiernan, Thomas. *Repulsion: The Life and Times of Roman Polanski*. London: New English Library, 1980.

King, Greg. *Sharon Tate and the Manson Murders*. New York: Open Road Media, 2016.

Kirk, Marshall, and Madsen, Hunter. *After the Ball*. New York: Doubleday, 1989.

Knight, Peter. *Conspiracy Theories in American History*. ABC-CLIO, 2003.

Lasch, Christopher. *Revolt of the Elites: The Betrayal of Democracy*. New York: W. W. Norton, 1995.

Leaming, Barbra. *Polanski: His Life and Films*. London: Hamilton, 1982.

Lee, Martin A. & Shlain, Bruce. *Acid Dreams: The Complete Social History of LSD: the CIA, the Sixties, and Beyond*. New York: Grove Press, 1992.

Lerner, Max. *America as a Civilization*. New York: Simon and Schuster, 1963.

Lethem, Jonathan. *Ecstasy of Influence*. New York: Vintage Books, 2012.

Lewis, C.S. *Screwtape Letters*. New York: Harper Collins, 2009.

Lynch, David and McKenna, Kristine. *Room to Dream*. New York: Random House, 2018.

Malloy, Oliver Markus. *Why Creeps Don't Know They're Creeps*. Bookmaester, 2017.

McClintick, David. *Indecent Exposure*. New York: HarperCollins, 2002.

McGilligan, Patrick. *Jack's Life: A Biography of Jack Nicholson*. London: HarperCollins, 1995.

McGowan, Dave. *Programmed to Kill: The Politics of Serial Murder*. Lincoln: IUniverse, 2004.

McGowan, Dave. *Weird Scenes Inside the Canyon*. SCB Distributors, 2014.

Meyers, Jeffrey. *John Huston and Art*. New York: Crown Archetype, 2011.

Moldea, Dan E. *Dark Victory: Ronald Reagan, MCA and the Mob*. New York: Viking Penguin. 1986.

Morin, Edgar. *The Stars*. New York: Grove Press. 1960.

Nadel, Ira B. *Various Positions*. Random House of Canada, 2010.

O'Neill, Tom. *Chaos: Charles Manson, the CIA, and the Secret History of the Sixties*. New York: Little, Brown, 2019.

Parfrey, Adam (ed.). *Apocalypse Culture*. Port Townsend: Feral House, 1990.

Parker, Sachi. *Lucky Me: My Life With—and Without—My Mom, Shirley MacLaine*. New York: Penguin, 2013.

Peary, Gerald (ed.). *Quentin Tarantino: Interviews*. Univ. Press of Mississippi, 1998.

Philby, Kim. *My Silent War: The Autobiography of a Spy*. New York: Modern Library, 2002.

Phillips, John. *Papa John*. New York: Doubleday & Company, 1986.

Phillips, Mackenzie. *High on Arrival*. New York: Simon and Schuster, 2011.

Polanski, Roman. *Roman*. New York: William Morrow & Co., 1984.

Pope, Paul David. *The Deeds of My Fathers: How My Grandfather and Father Built New York and Created the Tabloid World of Today*. Lanham: Rowman & Littlefield, 2010.

Plutarch. *On Sparta*. Penguin UK, 1988, 2005.

Randall, Stephen (editor). *The* Playboy *Interviews: The Directors*. Milwaukee Press, 2006.

Rapkin, Mickey. *Theater Geek: The Real Life Drama of a Summer at Stagedoor Manor, the Famous Performing Arts Camp*. New York: Simon & Schuster, 2010.

Raschke, Carl. *Painted Black: From Drug Killings to Heavy Metal: The Alarming True Story of How Satanism Is Terrorizing Our Communities*. New York: HarperCollins, 1990.

Rizzo, John. *Company Man*. New York: Simon & Schuster, 2014.

Ross, Colin A. *The C.I.A. Doctors: Human Rights Violations by American Psychiatrists*. Greenleaf Book Group, 2006.

Russell, Bertrand. *The Impact of Science on Society*. London: Routledge, 2016.

Russo, Gus. *Supermob*. New York: Bloomsbury, 2006.

Sanders, Ed. *The Family*. New York: Thunder's Mouth Press, 2002.

Sandford, Christopher. *Polanski*. New York, Random House, 2012.

Saunders, Frances Stonor. *Who Paid the Piper? The CIA and the Cultural Cold War*. London: Granta Books, 2000.

Schechter, Harold. *Deviant*. New York: Simon & Schuster, 2010.

Schickel, Richard. *Conversations with Scorsese*. New York: Alfred A. Knopf, 2013.

Schmidt, Jeff. *Disciplined Minds*. Lanham: Rowman & Littlefield, 2001.

Signorile, Michelangelo. *Queer in America: Sex, the Media, and the Closets of Power.* Univ of Wisconsin Press, 2003.

Smith, Adam. *The Theory Of Moral Sentiments.* Hard Press, 2020.

Spoto, Donald. *The Dark Side of Genius: The Life of Alfred Hitchcock.* Da Capo, 1999.

Statman, Alisa, and Tate, Brie. *Restless Souls: The Sharon Tate Family's Account of Stardom, the Manson Murders, and a Crusade for Justice.* New York: Harper Collins, 2012.

Straczynski, J. Michael. *Becoming Superman: My Journey from Poverty to Hollywood, with Stops Along the Way at Murder, Madness, Mayhem, Movie Stars, Cults, Slums, Sociopaths, and War Crimes.* New York: HarperCollins, 2019.

Terry, Maury. *Ultimate Evil.* Grafton, 1988.

Thomassen, Bjørn. *Liminality and the Modern: Living Through the In-Between.* London: Routledge, 2016.

Truffaut, Francois. *Hitchcock.* New York: Simon and Schuster, 1984.

Upton, Charles. *System of the Antichrist.* Ghent: Sophia Perennis, 2001.

Valentine, Douglas. *The CIA as Organized Crime: How Illegal Operations Corrupt America and the World.* Atlanta: Clarity Press, 2016.

Valentine, Douglas. *The Phoenix Program: America's Use of Terror in Vietnam.* New York: Open Road Media, 2014.

Wasson, Sam. *The Big Goodbye: Chinatown and the Last Years of Hollywood.* New York: Flatiron Books, 2020.

Whitty, Stephen. *The Alfred Hitchcock Encyclopedia.* Lanham: Rowman & Littlefield, 2016.

Willis, Ellen. *Beginning to See the Light.* Wesleyan University Press, 1992.

Wu, Tim. *The Attention Merchants.* New York: Vintage Books, 2016.

Zacharias, Ravi. *Can Man Live Without God.* Nashville: Thomas Nelson, 1994.

Zinoman, Jason. *Shock Value: How a Few Eccentric Outsiders Gave Us Nightmares, Conquered Hollywood, and Invented Modern Horror.* New York: Penguin, 2011.

NOTES

(All links last checked August 24, 2020. These end notes, inc. hyperlinks, can be found online at https://auticulture.com/end-notes-for-16-maps-of-hell/)

Introduction

1. Bart, Peter. *Infamous Players: A Tale of Movies, the Mob (and Sex),* Weinstein Books, 2011, p. 113.

2. "Making an exhibition of himself," by David Jenkins, *The Telegraph,* Jan 29, 2001: https://www.telegraph.co.uk/culture/4721300/Making-an-exhibition-of-himself.html

3. Richard Dreyfuss, *Easy Riders Raging Bulls,* 2003 BBC documentary directed by Kenneth Bowser.

Chapter 1

1. "The Polish Imposition," by Kenneth Tynan, *Esquire,* September 1971, p. 122: https://classic.esquire.com/article/1971/9/1/the-polish-imposition

2. "The Phoenix: The Manual of Sigma Alpha Epsilon," 2012 by Sigma Alpha Epsilon, Twelfth Edition, p. 36: http://data.sae.net/docs/Phoenix2012.pdf

3. "Deadliest Frat's Icy 'Torture' of Pledges Evokes Tarantino Films," by John Hechinger and David Glovin

December 29, 2013: https://www.bloomberg.com/news/articles/2013-12-30/deadliest -frat-s-icy-torture-of-pledges-evokes-tarantino-films

4. "Phi Beta Kappa Key Being Turned Down By Many Honorees," by Emily Bernstein, *New York Times,* May 26, 1996: https://www.nytimes.com/1996/05/26/nyregion/phi-beta -kappa-key-being-turned-down-by-many-honorees.html

5. "Behavior differences seven months later: Effects of a rape prevention program on first-year men who join fraternities," by John Foubert, Johnathan Newberry, Jerry Tatum, *NASPA* Journal. 2007, p. 728–749.

6. Richard Dreyfuss, *Easy Riders Raging Bulls,* 2003 BBC documentary directed by Kenneth Bowser.

7. "The Sins of the Father," by Sheila Weller, *DuJour*, May 25, 2015, p. 161-165: http://www.onedayshelldarken.com/wp-content/uploads/2015/06/DUJOUR-ARTICLE.pdf

8. Published by Steve Hodel as *Hodel-Black Dahlia Case File No. 30-1268: Official 1950 Law Enforcement Transcripts of Stake-Out and Electronic Recordings of Black Dahlia Murder Confession made by Dr. George Hill Hodel.*

9. "L.A. Confidential," by David Thomson, *New York Times*, May 18, 2003: https://www.nytimes.com/2003/05/18/books/la-confidential.html

10. "'The Black Dahlia' haunts American movies still," by Jeff Simon, *Buffalo News*, February 1, 2019: https://buffalonews.com/2019/02/01/jeff-simon-the-black-dahlia-haunts-american-movies-still/

11. "Film Studies: Who killed the Black Dahlia?" by David Thomson, *The Independent*, September, 10 2006: https://www.independent.co.uk/arts-entertainment/films/features/film-studies-who-killed-the-black-dahlia-415428.html

12. "Lost To America—The Unknown Brazilians: Raul Roulien," *Reviews By Josmar Lopes*, July 22, 2019: https://josmarlopes.wordpress.com/2019/07/22/lost-to-america-the-unknown-brazilians-raul-roulien/

13. "The Real-Life Hollywood Scandals Covered Up By Eddie Mannix, Leading Figure Of *Hail Caesar!*" by Caroline Frost, *Huffington Post*, August 7. 2016: https://www.huffingtonpost.co.uk/entry/hollywood-scandals-eddie-mannix_uk_577fa12ae4b0935d4b4aaf73?guccounter=1

14. "Where Is Tamar Hodel, Fauna's Mother In *I Am The Night*, Now?," by Elena Nicolaou, *Refinery 29*, Feby 11, 2019: https://www.refinery29.com/en-us/2019/02/224121/who-is-tamar-hodel-alive-fauna-mother-i-am-the-night

15. "The True Story of Tamar Hodel from *I Am the Night* Is Absolutely Harrowing," by Mehera Bonner, *Cosmopolitan*, Jan 28, 2019: https://www.cosmopolitan.com/entertainment/a26063508/tamar-hodel-true-story-i-am-the-night/

16. "Mackenzie Phillips Confesses to 10-Year Consensual Sexual Relationship With Father," by Russell Goldman, Eileen Murphy and Lindsay Goldwert, *ABC News*, Sept 23, 2009: https://abcnews.go.com/Entertainment/mackenzie-phillips-sexual-affair-dad/story?id=8647172

17. "Mackenzie Phillips, daughter of Mamas and Papas star, reveals their incestuous affair," by Veronica Schmidt, *The Times*, Sept 24, 2009: https://www.thetimes.co.uk/article/mackenzie-phillips-daughter-of-mamas-and-papas-star-reveals-their-incestuous-affair-wd8s2loqcsr

18. "Mackenzie Phillips Confesses to 10-Year Consensual Sexual Relationship With Father," by Russell Goldman, Eileen Murphy and Lindsay Goldwert, *ABC News*, Sept 23, 2009: https://abcnews.go.com/Entertainment/mackenzie-phillips-sexual-affair-dad/story?id=8647172

19. "Michelle Phillips and Friends Speak Out about Mackenzie's Incest Allegations." by Sheila Weller, *Vanity Fair*, September 25, 2009: https://stevehodel.com/wp-content/uploads/2019/05/Michelle-Phillips-and-Friends-Speak-Out-about-Mackenzie.pdf

20. "The Sins of the Father," by Sheila Weller, *DuJour*, May 25, 2015, p. 161-165: http://www.onedayshelldarken.com/wp-content/uploads/2015/06/DUJOUR-ARTICLE.pdf

21. "The sordid and possibly murderous secrets of Los Angeles's Sowden House," by Hadley Meares, *LA Curbed*, Oct 28, 2015: https://la.curbed.com/2015/10/28/9906764/sowden-house-george-hodel-black-dahlia

22. "The Sins of the Father," by Sheila Weller, *DuJour*, May 25, 2015, p. 161-165: http://www.onedayshelldarken.com/wp-content/uploads/2015/06/DUJOUR-ARTICLE.pdf

23. "Was Man Ray the Inspiration Behind the Black Dahlia Murder?" by Zachary Small, *Hyper Allergic*, March 28, 2019: https://hyperallergic.com/492217/was-man-ray-the-inspiration-behind-the-black-dahlia-murder/

24. "John Huston," *Interview* magazine # 25, Sept 1972, p. 45.

25. Bob Benson, *A Late-Inning Trilogy*, Page Publishing Inc, 2014, chapter 11.

26. "The Man Who Kept The Secrets," by Nick Tosches, *Vanity Fair*, April 6, 1997: https://www.vanityfair.com/news/1997/04/The-Man-Who-Kept-The-Secrets

27. "How Robert Evans Really Got His Paramount Job," *Hollywood Reporter*, May 24, 2013: https://www.hollywoodreporter.com/news/how-robert-evans-got-his-527416

28. "Robert Evans's Story Cover-Up for Satanism," by Michelle Steinberg, *Executive Intelligence Review*, vol 21, # 46, p. 77: https://larouchepub.com/eiw/public/1994/eirv21n46-19941118/eirv21n46-19941118_076-robert_evanss_story_coverup_for.pdf

29. "Millionaire movie producer Robert Evans, who pleaded guilty to," by John Pryor, *UPI*, Oct 7, 1980: https://www.upi.com/Archives/1980/10/07/Millionaire-movie-producer-Robert-Evans-who-pleaded-guilty-to/8789339739200/

30. "*Get High On Yourself*: Robert Evans' Coke-Bust Community Service Mega-Turd TV Special," Dangerous Minds, June 10, 2016: https://dangerousminds.net/comments/get_high_on_yourself_robert_evans_coke_bust_community_service_mega_turd_tv

31. "The Man Who Kept The Secrets," by Nick Tosches, *Vanity Fair*, April 6, 1997: https://www.vanityfair.com/news/1997/04/The-Man-Who-Kept-The-Secrets "There were rumors he'd been murdered, but they were never investigated." Peter Bart, *Infamous Players: A Tale of Movies, the Mob (and Sex)*, Weinstein Books, 2011, p. 256.

32. These passages are slightly reworked sections from *Dogville vs Hollywood*.

33. "The *Cotton Club* Killing," by David Treadwell, *LA Times*, Oct 9, 1988: https://www.latimes.com/archives/la-xpm-1988-10-09-me-5435-story.html

34. "Producer Robert Evans Invokes 5th at Hearing in Murder Case," by Dennis McDougal, *LA Times*, May 13, 1989: https://www.latimes.com/archives/la-xpm-1989-05-13-me-2729-story.html

Chapter 2

1. *The Kid Stays in the Picture*, last page of chapter one (no page number).

2. "How Robert Evans changed movies for ever—and for the better," by Ryan Gilbey: 24 Feb, 2017: https://www.theguardian.com/stage/2017/feb/24/hollywood-robert-evans-the-kid-stays-in-the-picture-simon-mcburney-royal-court

3. Ibid.

4. "The Roman Polanski Presence Still Looms Large In Hollywood Despite Academy Censure & Distributor Resistance," by Peter Bart, *Deadline*, June 12, 2019:

https://deadline.com/2019/06/roman-polanski-still-looms-large-in-hollywood-peter
-bart-column-1202631485/

5. "How 10050 Cielo Drive Went From Peaceful Dream Home To Manson Family
Murder Scene," by Erin Kelly, *All That's Interesting*, June 28, 2019: https://allthatsinterest-
ing.com/10050-cielo-drive

6. See for example, "What Started as a Book Review…" by Allan Weisbecker, Dec 17,
2019: https://blog.banditobooks.com/this-started-as-a-book-review/

7. "38 women have come forward to accuse director James Toback of sexual harassment," Glenn Whipp, *Los Angeles Times*, Oct 22, 2017: https://www.latimes.com/
entertainment/la-et-mn-james-toback-sexual-harassment-allegations-20171018-story.html

8. "Victor Lownes: An American Playboy In London," *The Eastern Terraces*, Jan 20, 2014:
https://theeasternterraces.wordpress.com/2014/01/20/victor-lownes-an-american-playboy
-in-london/

9. "Nikolas Schreck speaks about EVIL HOLLYWOOD," spahn ranch worker,
YouTube, Aug 15, 2019: https://www.youtube.com/watch?v=9QNkCqdpryI

10. "How the Epstein Case Explains the Rise of Conspiracy Theorists," by Mckay
Coppins, *The Atlantic*, July 12, 2019: https://www.theatlantic.com/politics/archive
/2019/07/epstein-conspiracy-theories/593605/

11. "Prince Andrew Might Have Been Caught On Tape With 'Sex Slave'", by Pooja
Bhagat, *International Business Times*, Jan 7, 2015: https://www.ibtimes.com.au/prince
-andrew-might-have-been-caught-tape-sex-slave-1407641

12. Ibid.

13. "Judge unseals more details in Jeffrey Epstein underage sex lawsuit," by Josh
Gerstein, *Politico*, July 7, 2015: https://www.politico.com/blogs/under-the-radar/2015/07/
judge-unseals-more-details-in-jeffrey-epstein-underage-sex-lawsuit-210065

14. "How a future Trump Cabinet member gave a serial sex abuser the deal of a lifetime," by Julie Brown, *Miami Herald*, Nov 28, 2018: https://www.miamiherald.com/
news/local/article220097825.html

15. Ibid.

16. Ibid.

17. Emphasis added. "It Sure Looks Like Jeffrey Epstein Was a Spy—But Whose?,"
by John R. Schindler, *The Observer*, July 10, 2019: https://observer.com/2019/07/
jeffrey-epstein-spy-intelligence-work/

18. "Jeffrey Epstein Moved Freely in Hollywood Circles Even After 2008
Conviction," by Tatiana Siegel & Marisa Guthrie, *Hollywood Reporter*, July 10, 2019:
https://www.hollywoodreporter.com/news/jeffrey-epstein-moved-freely-hollywood
-circles-2008-conviction-1223336

19. Ibid.

20. Ibid.

21. Ibid.

22. Ibid.

23. "Jeffrey Epstein: Financier and Science Philanthropist," *The Edge*: https://web.
archive.org/web/20120214162529/https://www.edge.org/memberbio/jeffrey_epstein

24. "Jeffrey Epstein's Intellectual Enabler," by Evgeny Morozov, *The New Republic*, Aug 22, 2019: https://newrepublic.com/article/154826/jeffrey-epsteins-intellectual-enabler

25. "'It's Going To Be Staggering, The Amount Of Names': As The Jeffrey Epstein Case Grows More Grotesque, Manhattan And Dc Brace For Impact," by Gabriel Sherman, *Vanity Fair*, July 17, 2019: https://www.vanityfair.com/news/2019/07/jeffrey-epstein-case-grows-more-grotesque

26. "Epstein Lawyers say evidence 'far more consistent' with murder than suicide," by Asher Stockler, *Newsweek*, Aug 27, 2019: https://www.newsweek.com/epstein-death-murder-suicide-victims-hearing-1456397

27. "Strange Things Are Happening on Epstein Island: Drone Footage," *Vigilant Citizen*, Sept 4, 2019: https://vigilantcitizen.com/latestnews/strange-things-are-happening-on-epstein-island-drone-footage/

Chapter 3

1. "Parasocial Relationships: The Nature of Celebrity Fascinations," Find a Psychologist, March 23, 2017: https://www.findapsychologist.org/parasocial-relationships-the-nature-of-celebrity-fascinations/

2. "Art, dandyism and the accidental death of a hedonist," by Cahal Milmo, *The Independent*, June 18, 2010: https://www.independent.co.uk/news/people/news/art-dandyism-and-the-accidental-death-of-a-hedonist-2003606.html

3. Ibid.

4. "Crazy in Love with a Smooth Criminal: An In-Depth Look at Parasocial Relationships and How Celebrities Affect the Relationship," Johnson & Wales University Scholars Archive, Winter 2016, p. 10: https://scholarsarchive.jwu.edu/cgi/viewcontent.cgi?article=1025&context=student_scholarship

5. Emphasis added. "Celebrity versus non-celebrity: parasocial relationships with characters in reality-based television programs," by Nicole Webb Henry, LSU Master's Theses. 3440, 2011, p. 13: https://pdfs.semanticscholar.org/b620/a749468e6caec799cc4f-d70095ce142fb9dd.pdf

6. *Illusions of Immortality: A Psychology of Fame and Celebrity*, David Giles, Macmillan International Higher Education, 2000, p. 271.

7. "Crazy in Love with a Smooth Criminal: An In-Depth Look at Parasocial Relationships and How Celebrities Affect the Relationship," Johnson & Wales University Scholars Archive, Winter 2016, p. 6: https://scholarsarchive.jwu.edu/cgi/viewcontent.cgi?article=1025&context=student_scholarship

8. Ibid., p. 6, 11.

9. "A farewell to my friend Sebastian, a true Soho eccentric," by Hermione Eyre, *The Independent*, June 20, 2010: https://www.independent.co.uk/news/people/news/a-farewell-to-my-friend-sebastian-a-true-soho-eccentric-2005614.html

10. "The Birth and Death of the Superhero Film," by Sander L. Koole, Daniel A Fockenberg, Mattie Tops, Iris K. Schneider, Jan 2014: https://www.researchgate.net/publication/257030125_The_Birth_and_Death_of_the_Superhero_Film

11. "Slave Revolt!" *US in Chains*, Aug 27, 2018: https://usinchains.wordpress.com/2018/08/27/slave-revolt/

12. Nidesh Lawtoo is a practicing psychiatrist, and the assistant professor of Philosophy at KU Leuven, in Belgium, who looks at Rene Girard's theory of mimesis through the lens of psychopathology and applies it to the study of hysteria and possession. Lawtoo has done extensive research that combines contemporary continental philosophy with literary theory with special focus on the role mimesis plays in genealogies of the modern subject (Nietzsche), phenomenology (Bataille), psychoanalysis (Freud), feminism (Irigaray), critical race theory (Achebe), deconstruction (Lacoue-Labarthe), and mimetic theory (Girard).

13. Emphasis added. "The Matric E-Motion: Simulation, Mimesis, Hypermimesis," by Nidesh Lawtoo, in *Mimesis, Movies, and Media: Violence, Desire, and the Sacred*, Volume 3, edited by Scott Cowdell, Chris Fleming, Joel Hodge; Bloomsbury Publishing USA, 2015.

14. Ibid.

15. "Aurora Copycat Effect: The Complete List," by Loren Coleman, *Twilight Language*, July 29, 2012: https://copycateffect.blogspot.com/2012/07/aurora-copycat-effect.html

16. "Regional Disturbances," by Lawrence Osborne, *New York Times*, May 6, 2001: https://www.nytimes.com/2001/05/06/magazine/regional-disturbances.html

17. Ibid.

Chapter 4

1. "Robert Downey Jr.'s 1st film EVER, just a kid," appreciez, *YouTube*, June 5, 2009: https://www.youtube.com/watch?v=_Jij2oLmOkc

2. Emphasis added. "Setting The Stage How A N.Y. Summer Camp Spawned A H'Wood Mafia," by Leslie Gornstein, *New York Post*, June 15, 2007: https://web.archive.org/web/20070618163938/https://nypost.com/seven/06152007/entertainment/setting_the_stage_entertainment_leslie_gornstein.htm

3. "Big Man, Big Heart? The Political Role of Aggrandizers in Egalitarian and Transegalitarian Societies," by Brian Hayden, in *For the Greater Good of All: Perspectives on Individualism, Society, and Leadership*, edited by Forsyth, Donelson R. and Hoyt, Crystal L., Springer, 2011, p. 101.

4. "Foot in the Door," by Michael Schulman, *The New Yorker*, July 19, 2010: https://www.newyorker.com/magazine/2010/07/26/foot-in-the-door-2

5. "Teenage flicks," by William Shaw, *The Observer*, March 3, 2002: https://www.theguardian.com/film/2002/mar/03/features.magazine

6. "Mind Your Manor," by Brian Scott Lipton, *V-Life*, June/July 2005, p. 28.

7. "I Want To Stand For Something," by Dotson Rader, *Parade*, Oct 5, 2008, p. 5.

8. "Childhood and Adult Sexual Victimization: Living in the Aftermath of Transgression and Quest for Restoration of the Self," Erwin R. Parson, Dawn M. Brett, and Alan S. Brett, p. 1-2.

9. *Cradles of Eminence: A Provocative Study of the Childhoods of Over 400 Famous Twentieth-Century Men and Women*, by Victor and Mildred Goertzel.

10. "The Secrets of Resilience: What does it take to conquer life's adversities? Lessons from successful adults who overcame difficult childhoods," by Meg Jay, *Wall Street Journal*, Nov 10, 2017: https://www.wsj.com/articles/the-secrets-of-resilience-1510329202

11. "Traumatic Bonding," *Encylopedia.com*: https://www.encyclopedia.com/social-sciences/applied-and-social-sciences-magazines/traumatic-bonding

12. "Michael Jackson's life showed us the journey from abused to abuser," by Hadley Freeman, *The Guardian*, March 26, 2019: https://www.theguardian.com/commentisfree/2019/mar/26/michael-jackson-abuse-abuser-sexual

13. "Is it still OK to listen to Michael Jackson? Fans give their verdict," by Nosheen Iqbal, *The Guardian*, March 9, 2019: https://www.theguardian.com/music/2019/mar/09/michael-jackson-fans-verdict-leaving-neverland

14. "*Succession's* Kieran Culkin on villainy, *Home Alone*—and Michael Jackson," by Benjamin Lee, *The Guardian*, Aug 21, 2019: https://www.theguardian.com/tv-and-radio/2019/aug/21/kieran-culkin-roman-roy-hbo-succession-home-alone-child-star-michael-jackson

15. "Macaulay Culkin Denies Jackson Molested Him" by Stephen M. Silverman and Johnny Dodd, *People*, May 11, 2005: https://people.com/celebrity/macaulay-culkin-denies-jackson-molested-him/

16. "Corey Feldman clarifies statements that seemed to defend Michael Jackson," by Lisa Respers France, *CNN*, March 5, 2019: https://www.cnn.com/2019/03/05/entertainment/corey-feldman-michael-jackson/index.html

17. "Barbra Streisand and Diana Ross are defending Michael Jackson," *Vox*, March 23, 2019: https://www.vox.com/2019/3/23/18278530/barbra-streisand-diana-ross-michael-jackson-didnt-kill-them-leaving-neverland-sexual-abuse-twitter

18. Ibid.

19. Clarke, Patrick, "Madonna on Michael Jackson: 'I don't have a lynch mob mentality,'" *NME*, May 7, 2019: https://www.nme.com/news/music/madonna-michael-jackson-interview-dont-have-a-lynch-mob-mentality-2485080

20. Wong, Curtis M. "Madonna Says Michael Jackson Is 'Innocent Until Proven Guilty'" HuffPost, May 7, 2019: https://www.huffingtonpost.ca/entry/madonna-michael-jackson-sexual-abuse-claims_n_5cd1adb7e4b04e275d50cdb4

21. "Michael Jackson albums climb the charts following Leaving Neverland broadcast," *The Independent*, March 9, 2019: https://www.independent.co.uk/arts-entertainment/music/news/michael-jackson-album-charts-leaving-neverland-child-sex-allegations-a8815081.html

22. "Michael Jackson's life showed us the journey from abused to abuser," by Hadley Freeman, *The Guardian*, March 26, 2019: https://www.theguardian.com/commentisfree/2019/mar/26/michael-jackson-abuse-abuser-sexual

23. "Michael Jackson fans sue singer's alleged abuse victims for 'damaging memory of the dead,'" by Sam Bradpiece, *CNN*, July 14, 2019: https://www.cnn.com/2019/07/14/europe/france-michael-jackson-case-intl/index.html

24. "Is it still OK to listen to Michael Jackson? Fans give their verdict," by Nosheen Iqbal, *The Guardian*, March 9, 2019: https://www.theguardian.com/music/2019/mar/09/michael-jackson-fans-verdict-leaving-neverland

25. "Michael Jackson's life showed us the journey from abused to abuser," by Hadley Freeman, *The Guardian*, March 26, 2019: https://www.theguardian.com/commentisfree/2019/mar/26/michael-jackson-abuse-abuser-sexual

26. "'I'm a martyr': Disgraced Harvey Weinstein believes he is a savior who was born to 'change the world' by taking the fall for sexual assaults." *Daily Mail*, Oct 31, 2017, by Chris Pleasance: https://www.dailymail.co.uk/news/article-5034597/Harvey-Weinstein-thinks-born-change-world.html

27. "Harvey Weinstein, Sabbatai Zevi and Tikun Olam," Nov 1, 2017: https://gilad.online/writings/2017/11/1/harvey-weinsteinsabbatai-zeviandtikun-olam

28. "Let Me Be Frank," Kevin Spacey, *YouTube*, Dec 24, 2018: https://www.youtube.com/watch?v=JZveA-NAIDI

Chapter 5

1. "Conspiracy Theory as Naive Deconstructive History," by Floyd Rudmin, *The President and the Provocateur*, Oct 10, 2015: https://presidentandprovocateur.wordpress.com/2013/10/05/conspiracy-theory-as-naive-deconstructive-history/

2. Ibid.

3. "Neurosis is the inability to tolerate ambiguity."

4. Quoted in *Streisand: A Biography*, Anne Edwards, p. 335.

5. Saarinen, E., & Hämäläinen, R. P. 2007. *Systems Intelligence: Connecting Engineering Thinking with Human Sensitivity*. In R. P. Hämäläinen & E. Saarinen (Eds.), Systems Intelligence in Leadership and Everyday Life: 39-50, Espoo: Helsinki University of Technology, Systems Analysis Laboratory.

6. "Walt Disney Goes to War," by Lisa Briner, Army Heritage and Education Center, April 7, 2009: https://www.army.mil/article/19340/walt_disney_goes_to_war

7. "The CIA Spies Behind Disney World's Secretive, Fake Cities," *Knowledge Nuts*, July 8, 2015: https://knowledgenuts.com/2015/07/08/the-cia-spies-behind-disney-worlds-secretive-fake-cities/

8. *Team Rodent: How Disney Devours the World*, by Carl Hiaasen, Random House Publishing Group, 2010.

9. Emphasis added. "Field Manual 33-1-1 - Psychological Operations Techniques and Procedures," US Army: http://www.enlistment.us/field-manuals/fm-33-1-1-psychological-operations-techniques-and-procedures.shtml

10. "The Spy Who Came Into the Fold," by Fred Kaplan, *New York Times*, Jan 3, 2014: https://www.nytimes.com/2014/01/05/books/review/john-rizzos-company-man.html

11. "Q&A: Roseanne Barr, on marijuana, the CIA, and how she is, in fact, the president," by Eric Spitznagel, *Esquire*, April 25, 2013: https://www.esquire.com/entertainment/interviews/a22334/roseanne-barr-interview/

12. "Forget Scientology, celebs are now falling for an even more sinister 'religion'" by Richard Price, *The Daily Mail*, April 21, 2013: https://www.dailymail.co.uk/femail/article-2312632/Introducing-Satanic-sex-cult-thats-snaring-stars-Peaches-Geldof.html

13. "What's with Hollywood's connection to Big Crime?" *National Post*, Jan 13, 2016: https://nationalpost.com/entertainment/movies/whats-with-hollywoods-connection-to-big-crime

14. "1,400 child abuse suspects identified," *BBC News*, May 20, 2015: https://www.bbc.com/news/uk-32812449

15. "Why Didn't Anyone Listen to Corey Feldman's Warnings About Pedophilia in Hollywood?" by Amy Zimmerman, *Daily Beast*, Oct 27, 2017: https://www.thedailybeast.com/why-didnt-anyone-listen-to-corey-feldmans-warnings-about-pedophilia-in-hollywood

16. See "The Age of Advanced Incoherence: Identity Politics & Identity Crisis,"by Jasun Horsley, 2018: https://boxes.nyc3.digitaloceanspaces.com/wp-content/uploads/Age-of-Advanced-Incoherence.pdf

Chapter 6

1. "The Multibillion-Dollar U.S. Spy Agency You Haven't Heard of," *Foreign Policy* March 20, 2017. https://foreignpolicy.com/2017/03/20/the-multibillion-dollar-u-s-spy-agency-you-havent-heard-of-trump/

2. "Louis Jolyon 'Jolly' West MKULTRA Subproject 43," *Mcclaughry's Blog*, Jan 23, 2016: https://web.archive.org/web/20170717065010/https://mikemcclaughry.wordpress.com/2016/01/23/louis-jolyon-jolly-west-mkultra-subproject-43/

3. *The C.I.A. Doctors: Human Rights Violations by American Psychiatrists*, by Colin A. Ross, Greenleaf Book Group, 2006.

4. Louis Jolyon West, "Psychiatric aspects on training for honorable survival as a prisoner of war," American Journal of Psychiatry, vol. 115 (October 1958), p. 329-336.

5. "Interview: William Friedkin On *The People Vs. Paul Crump*," by Donald Liebenson, *RogerEbert.com*, June 2, 2014: https://www.rogerebert.com/interviews/interview-william-friedkin-on-the-people-vs-paul-crump

6. "Phil Ochs and the Crucifixion of President John F. Kennedy," by Edward Curtin, *Dissident Voice*, Nov 16, 2018: https://dissidentvoice.org/2018/11/phil-ochs-and-the-crucifixion-of-president-john-f-kennedy/

7. "Think The Exorcist Was Just a Horror Movie? The Author Says You're Wrong," by Eddie Dean, the *Washingtonian*, Oct 19, 2015: https://www.washingtonian.com/2015/10/19/think-the-exorcist-was-just-a-horror-movie-author-william-peter-blatty-says-youre-wrong/

8. "*The Exorcist* Controversy: Film Used Tactics Previously Tested by US Government to Scare Audiences," by Nick Younker, *Latin Post*, May 30, 2015: https://www.latinpost.com/articles/56565/20150530/the-exorcist-controversy-film-used-c-i-a-tested-tactics-to-scare-audiences.htm

9. "Uncle Sam's Secret Sorcerers V," by Chris Knowles, *Secret Sun*, Sept 18, 2016: https://secretsun.blogspot.com/2016/09/uncle-sams-secret-sorcerers-v.html

10. Ibid.

11. Ibid.

12. B. James Gladstone, *The Man Who Seduced Hollywood: The Life and Loves of Greg Bautzer, Tinseltown's Most Powerful Lawyer*, Chicago Review Press, May 1, 2013, p. 237.

13. "Sidney Korshak, 88, Dies; Fabled Fixer for the Chicago Mob," by Robert Mcg. Thomas Jr., Jan 22, 1996: https://www.nytimes.com/1996/01/22/us/sidney-korshak-88-dies-fabled-fixer-for-the-chicago-mob.html

14. Ibid.

15. "The Man Who Wrote Secrets: James Ellroy to script lawyer biopic," by Stax, June 19, 2012: https://ca.ign.com/articles/2004/02/02/the-man-who-wrote-secrets

16. Roger Ebert, "Inside *Deep Throat*," *Chicago Sun-Times.* Feb 11, 2005.

17. "How Jimmy Savile revealed all in the psychiatrist's chair," *Channel 4 News*, Nov 2, 2012: https://www.channel4.com/news/how-jimmy-savile-revealed-all-in-the-psychiatrists-chair

18. "The Crooked Timber: A Conversation with William Friedkin," by Michael Guillen, *The Notebook*, Aug 13, 2012: https://mubi.com/notebook/posts/the-crooked-timber-a-conversation-with-william-friedkin

19. "William Friedkin: The Hollywood Flashback Interviews": https://thehollywood-interview.blogspot.com/2008/01/cruising-with-billy.html

20. "The True Story of Paul Bateson Is Much More Fascinating Than We See in *Mindhunter* Season Two," by Matt Miller, *Esquire*, Aug 19, 2019: https://www.esquire.com/entertainment/tv/a28746016/paul-bateson-bag-murders-mindhunter-season-2-episode-6-true-story/

21. This and following quotes in subsequent paragraph: "Why Cults Terrorize and Kill Children," by Lloyd deMause, *The Journal of Psychohistory* 21 (4) 1994: https://ritualabuse.us/ritualabuse/articles/why-cults-terrorize-and-kill-children-lloyd-demause-the-journal-of-psychohistory/

22. "A Street-Gang Movie Called *The Warriors* Triggers a Puzzling, Tragic Wave of Audience Violence and Death," *People*, March 12, 1979: https://people.com/archive/a-street-gang-movie-called-the-warriors-triggers-a-puzzling-tragic-wave-of-audience-violence-and-death-vol-11-no-10/

23. "William Friedkin on Witnessing a Real Exorcism 45 Years Later, and What *The Exorcist* Got Right," by Jamie Righetti, *IndieWire*, April 19, 2018: https://www.indiewire.com/2018/04/william-friedkin-real-exorcism-the-exorcist-accurate-1201954647/

Chapter 7

1. "Famous Alumni: Leonard Cohen, Musician," by Matt Ralph, *Summer Camp Culture*, Jan 12, 2013: http://www.summercampculture.com/famous-alumni-leonard-cohen-musician/

2. "Ewen Cameron: further reading," by Naomi Klein, *The Guardian*, Sept 8, 2007: http://www.theguardian.com/books/2007/sep/08/naomiklein1

3. "1951: CIA's psychological torture is rooted in experiments at Dachau, Project ARTICHOKE & MK-ULTRA," *Alliance For Human Research Protection*, Jan 18, 2015:

http://ahrp.org/1951-cias-psychological-torture-is-rooted-in-experiments-at-dachau-project-artichoke-mk-ultra/

4. "What Extreme Isolation Does to Your Mind," by Mike Mechanic, *Mother Jones*, Oct 18, 2012: http://www.motherjones.com/politics/2012/10/donald-o-hebb-effects-extreme-isolation

5. "The toxic legacy of Canada's CIA brainwashing experiments: 'They strip you of your soul,'" by Ashifa Kassam, *The Guardian*, May 3, 2018: https://www.theguardian.com/world/2018/may/03/montreal-brainwashing-allan-memorial-institute

6. "Donald Ewen Cameron," *The McClaughry's Blog*: https://mikemcclaughry.wordpress.com/the-reading-library/specific-persons/donald-ewen-cameron/

7. Ibid.

8. D. Ewen Cameron, "The Current Transition in the Conception in Science," *Science* #107 (1948): p. 558.

9. "Institute Shows Main Hospital Needs," *Journal of American Psychiatric Association*, Volume 3, Issue 9, Nov 1952, pp. 5-5: https://mikemcclaughry.files.wordpress.com/2016/06/ewen-cameron-speech-oct-20-1952-social-engineering.pdf

10. "Science in Dachau's Shadow: Hebb, Beecher, and The Development of CIA Psychological Torture and Modern Medical Ethics," by Alfred W. McCoy, published in the *Journal of the History of the Behavioral Sciences*, Vol. 43(4), Fall 2007, p. 401-417. Published online in Wiley Interscience (www.interscience.wiley.com).

11. "Leonard Cohen in London," *History is Made at Night*, Jan 6, 2014:
http://history-is-made-at-night.blogspot.ca/2014/01/leonard-cohen-in-london.html

12. "Interview: Nikos Hadjikyriakos-Ghikas," *dreamidamachine Art View*: http://www.dreamideamachine.com/en/?p=53

13. "They are still singing down at Dusko's, Hydra 1960," *Leonard Cohen Forum*, Feb 19, 2011: http://www.leonardcohenforum.com/viewtopic.php?t=25289

14. "Michael Hollingshead," *Source Watch*: http://www.sourcewatch.org/index.php/Michael_Hollingshead

15. "Secret London: LSD experiments at the World Psychedelic Centre," Peter Watts, *The Great Wen*, Nov 30, 2011: http://greatwen.com/2011/11/30/secret-london-lsd-experiments-at-the-world-psychedelic-centre/

16. "How Leonard Cohen Met Janis Joplin: Inside Legendary Chelsea Hotel Encounter," by Jordan Runtagh, *Rolling Stone*, Nov 14, 2016: https://www.rollingstone.com/music/music-features/how-leonard-cohen-met-janis-joplin-inside-legendary-chelsea-hotel-encounter-121067/

17. "Dr. Colin Ross on CIA Mind Control Doctors from Harvard to Guantanamo," *Constantine Report*, May 17, 2013: http://constantinereport.com/dr-colin-ross-on-cia-mind-control-doctors-from-harvard-to-guantanamo/

18. http://www.israelhayom.com/site/newsletter_article.php?id=11943

19. "Declaration of Kelley Lynch," *Ann Diamond's Weblog*, Nov 16, 2016: https://ann-diamond.wordpress.com/2016/11/16/declaration-of-kelley-lynch/

20. "Becoming Tarden (Installation view)," *New Digital Archive Museum*: http://ca.newmuseum.org/index.php/Detail/Object/Show/object_id/7592

Chapter 8

1. Emphasis added. "Transcription of Dialogue: Assassination. Broadcast of October 13, 1971," *The Mae Brussel website*: http://www.maebrussell.com/Transcriptions/16.html

2. "What Is MDA, or Sally, One of the Drugs Scott Weiland Overdosed On?" by Tessa Stuart, *Rolling Stone*, Dec 18, 2015: https://www.rollingstone.com/culture/culture-news/what-is-mda-or-sally-one-of-the-drugs-scott-weiland-overdosed-on-41307/

3. Bernschneider-Reif S, Oxler F, Freudenmann RW (November 2006). "The origin of MDMA ('ecstasy')—separating the facts from the myth," *Die Pharmazie*. 61 (11): 966–72.

4. "Inside The LC: The Strange But Mostly True Story Of Laurel Canyon And The Birth Of The Hippie Generation: Part XIX," by Dave McGowan, *The Center For An Informed America*, Aug 14, 2011: https://centerforaninformedamerica.com/inside-the-lc-the-strange-but-mostly-true-story-of-laurel-canyon-and-the-birth-of-the-hippie-generation-part-xix/

5. Emphasis added. "Transcription of Dialogue: Assassination. Broadcast of October 13, 1971," *The Mae Brussel website*: http://www.maebrussell.com/Transcriptions/16.html

6. "'Torture the women!' Hitchcock said—and he wasn't really joking," *Mail & Guardian*, April 5, 2013: https://mg.co.za/article/2013-04-05-torture-the-women-hitchcock-said-and-he-wasnt-really-joking/

7. "Natalie Wood 'raped as a teenager,'" *BBC News*, Aug 2, 2001: http://news.bbc.co.uk/2/hi/entertainment/1470142.stm

8. "Did Robert Downey Jr. Really Just Accuse Kirk Douglas of a Brutal Rape?" by Ryan Tate, *Gawker*, March 15, 2012: https://gawker.com/5893793/did-robert-downey-jr-really-just-accuse-kirk-douglas-of-a-brutal-rape

9. Ibid.

10. "Natalie Wood's Tragic Childhood Secret: Actress Was Raped 'For Hours' By Hollywood Star, Sister Claims," *Closer Weekly*, July 26, 2018: https://www.closerweekly.com/posts/natalie-wood-sister-lana-claims-star-raped-hours-teen-163518/

11. "Kirk Douglas: 'I never thought I'd live to 100. That's shocked me,'" by Hadley Freeman, *The Guardian*, Feb 12, 2017: https://www.theguardian.com/film/2017/feb/12/kirk-douglas-i-never-thought-id-live-to-100-thats-shocked-me

12. "Exec comes full circle after descent into despair," by Peter Bart, *Variety*, Feb 7, 1993: https://variety.com/1993/voices/columns/exec-comes-full-circle-after-descent-into-despair-1117859405/

13. "Quentin Tarantino's History of Disturbing Behavior Toward His Actresses," by Amy Zimmerman, *Daily Beast*, June 2, 2018: https://www.thedailybeast.com/quentin-tarantinos-history-of-disturbing-behavior-toward-his-actresses

14. "Quentin Tarantino apologizes for Polanski defense: 'I was ignorant,'" *The Guardian*, Feb 8, 2018: https://www.theguardian.com/film/2018/feb/08/quentin-tarantino-apologizes-for-polanski-defense-i-was-ignorant

15. "Tarantino on Weinstein: 'I Knew Enough to Do More Than I Did,'" by Jodi Kantor, New York Times, Oct 19, 2017: https://www.nytimes.com/2017/10/19/movies/tarantino-weinstein.html

16. "The Polish Imposition," by Kenneth Tynan, *Esquire*, Sept 1971, p. 122: https://classic.esquire.com/article/1971/9/1/the-polish-imposition

17. *Sharon Tate and the Manson Murders*, by Greg King, Open Road Media, 2016, chapter 10.

18. *Quentin Tarantino: Interviews*, Univ. Press of Mississippi, 1998: p. 20.

19. Quentin Tarantino interview: 'I'm shutting your butt down!'" *Channel 4 News*, 10 Jan, 2013: https://www.youtube.com/watch?v=GrsJDy8VjZk

20. "Roman Polanski Accuser, Charlotte Lewis, Lying?" by Eric Pape, *Daily Beast*, Jul. 14, 2017: https://www.thedailybeast.com/roman-polanski-accuser-charlotte-lewis-lying

21. "Roman Polanski accused of sexually assaulting 10-year-old girl in 1975," by Gwilym Mumford, *The Guardian*, Oct 23, 2017: https://www.theguardian.com/film/2017/oct/23/roman-polanski-marianne-barnard-allegations

22. "Woman accuses Roman Polanski of raping her in 1975 when she was 18," *The Guardian*, Nov 8, 2019: https://www.theguardian.com/film/2019/nov/08/woman-accuses-roman-polanski-of-raping-her-in-1975-when-she-was-18

23. "French directors' guild begins moves to suspend Roman Polanski," *The Guardian*, Nov 19, 2019: https://www.theguardian.com/film/2019/nov/19/french-directors-guild-arp-begins-moves-suspend-roman-polanski

24. "Charles Manson, 1991 Interview," True Crime Vids, *YouTube*, July 8, 2018: https://www.youtube.com/watch?v=yx732w-y99Y

Chapter 9

[Chapter 9 contains no end notes—*ed.*]

Chapter 10

1. Marshall Kirk and Hunter Madsen, *After the Ball* (NY: Doubleday, 1989), pp. 11-12. Cited in "The Homosexual Movement's Connection To Hollywood," by Wayne Lela, *H.O.M.E*: http://www.home60515.com/22.html

2. Roger Ebert, "Second Take: 'Closet' Looks Back at Movies' Gay Subtext," *Chicago Sun-Times*, April 26, 1996, "Weekend Plus" section, p. 20. Cited in "The Homosexual Movement's Connection To Hollywood," by Wayne Lela, *H.O.M.E*: http://www.home60515.com/22.html

3. "NYT Writer Says He Was Fired for Observing That Barry Diller Is Gay," by J.K. Trotter, *Gawker*, April 20, 2015: http://tktk.gawker.com/nyt-writer-says-he-was-fired-for-observing-that-barry-d-1696552554

4. "Hollywood's Newest Players," *Entertainment Weekly*, Sept 8, 1995: https://ew.com/article/1995/09/08/hollywoods-newest-players/

5. "Ovitz Agonistes" by Bryan Burrough, *Vanity Fair*, Sept 9, 2008: https://www.vanityfair.com/news/2002/08/ovitz200208

6. Ibid.

7. *The Genius and the Goddess: Arthur Miller and Marilyn Monroe*, by Jeffrey Meyers, University of Illinois Press, 2012, p. 29.

8. Dean E. Murphy and Terry Pristin, "'Hollywood Madam' Is the Talk of Tinseltown," *Chicago Sun-Times*, Aug. 9, 1993, p. 24.

9. Stephanie Mansfield, "Wild & Woody," *USA Weekend*, July 5-7, 1996, p. 5.

10. Cheryl Lavin, "Dumb like a fox," *Chicago Tribune*, Aug. 24, 1997, section 10, p. 16.

11. "News from the casting couch," *Chicago Sun-Times*, June 10, 2005, p. 52.

12. Maria Puente and Cara Kelly, "How bad is Hollywood's 'Me Too' problem?," *USA Today*, Feb 21, 2018, p. 1A.

13. "Usual suspect was Spacey for misbehaviour, claims Byrne," by Eithne Shortall, *The Sunday Times*, Dec 3, 2017: https://www.thetimes.co.uk/article/usual-suspect-was-spacey-for-misbehaviour-claims-byrne-m2q829vjv

14. For the source on this and all subsequent unreferenced data-points on the Singer abuse story, see "The Bryan Singer Timeline: a History of Allegations and Defenses, from Troubled Films to Sexual Assault Claims," by Jenna Marotta and Dana Harris, *IndieWire*, Dec 8, 2017: https://www.indiewire.com/2017/12/bryan-singer-sexual-assault-rape-allegations-timeline-1201903868/2/

15. "Lawyer Drops Accuser in Bryan Singer Sex Abuse Lawsuit," by Jessica Fecteau, *People*, July 30, 2014: https://people.com/crime/bryan-singer-sex-abuse-lawsuit-lawyer-drops-accuser-michael-egan-as-client/

16. "The Mixed-Up Life of Shia LaBeouf," by Dotson Rader, *Parade*, June 14, 2009, pp. 4-5.

17. "Must Reads: A notorious mansion. An alleged assault by a Hollywood producer. A suicide. What happened to Brian Claflin?" by Gus Garcia-Roberts, *Los Angeles Times*, May 11, 2018: https://www.latimes.com/business/hollywood/la-fi-ct-claflin-goddard-singer-20180511-story.html

18. Ibid.

19. Ibid.

20. "The Bryan Singer Timeline: a History of Allegations and Defenses, from Troubled Films to Sexual Assault Claims," by Jenna Marotta and Dana Harris, *IndieWire*, Dec 8, 2017: https://www.indiewire.com/2017/12/bryan-singer-sexual-assault-rape-allegations-timeline-1201903868/2/

21. Ibid.

22. "Yes Mom, There is Something Wrong: From victim to survivor" by Anthony Edwards, *Medium*, Nov 10, 2017: https://medium.com/@anthonyedwards/yes-mom-there-is-something-wrong-f2bcf56434b9

23. "Controversial sex education framework for California approved despite protest," by Colleen Shalby, *LA Times*, May 10, 2019: https://www.latimes.com/local/lanow/la-me-sex-education-california-20190510-story.html

24. "Brett Ratner, Dustin Hoffman the latest to be accused of sexual harassment, misconduct," *CBC*, Nov 1, 2017: http://www.cbc.ca/news/entertainment/brett-ratner-harassment-1.4381788

25. "Think twice before you use the word 'homophobia,'" by Vicki Klafter, Jan 22, 2015: http://www.dailynebraskan.com/opinion/klafter-think-twice-before-you-use-the-word-homophobia/article_ef960d84-a1e2-11e4-a266-f714fe6282e5.html

26. "Hollywood's Newest Players," *Entertainment Weekly*, Sept 8, 1995: https://ew.com/article/1995/09/08/hollywoods-newest-players/

27. Signorile, Michelangelo, *Queer in America: Sex, the Media, and the Closets of Power*, Univ of Wisconsin Press, 2003, p. 234.

28. "The Bro Code: Booze, Sex, and the Dark Art of Dealmaking in China," by James Palmer, *China File*, Feb 4, 2015: http://www.chinafile.com/reporting-opinion/postcard/bro-code

Chapter 11

1. Emphasis added. "Transcription of Dialogue: Assassination. Broadcast of October 13, 1971," *The Mae Brussel website*: http://www.maebrussell.com/Transcriptions/16.html

2. "Tony Scott's Suicide Note," by Alex Cox, The Blog of Alex Cox, Oct 7, 2012: https://web.archive.org/web/20121113115612/http:/www.alexcox.com/blog.htm

3. "Exodus: *Gods and Kings'* Director Ridley Scott on Creating His Vision of Moses," by Scott Foundas, *Variety*, Nov 25, 2014: https://variety.com/2014/film/news/ridley-scott-exodus-gods-and-kings-christian-bale-1201363668/

4. "Citing Facts, Bush Spares Texas Inmate On Death Row," by Allen R. Myerson, *New York Times*, June 27, 1998: https://www.nytimes.com/1998/06/27/us/citing-facts-bush-spares-texas-inmate-on-death-row.html

5. "Faith, Certainty and the Presidency of George W. Bush," by Ron Suskind, *The New York Times Magazine*, Oct 17, 2004: https://www.nytimes.com/2004/10/17/magazine/faith-certainty-and-the-presidency-of-george-w-bush.html

6. "Psychological Operations, Field Manual Headquarters No. 3-05.30," Department of the Army, Washington, DC, April 15, 2005: https://fas.org/irp/doddir/army/fm3-05-30.pdf

7. "Human Sacrifices May Lie Behind the Rise of Ancient Social Status," by Maya Wei-Haas, Smithsonianmag.com, April 4, 2016: https://www.smithsonianmag.com/science-nature/human-sacrifices-may-lie-behind-rise-ancient-social-status-180958646/

8. "Superstition Psyop," by SGM Herbert A. Friedman (Ret.), *Psiwarrior*: http://www.psywarrior.com/SuperstitionPSYOP.html

Chapter 12

1. Jordan Peterson "Maps of Meaning" lectures, # 5: https://www.youtube.com/watch?v=RudKmwzDpNY&list=PL26JJsMKQxwiACxEL9shrRcFHcORxshQq

2. Psychology educator and neuroscience researcher Roger Allan Drake has conducted research that suggests that selective activation of left prefrontal cortex might increase the likelihood that an attitude would predict a relevant behavior. Simply stated, people whose brain was more active in the left prefrontal areas seemed to pay more attention to statements with which they agreed while those with a more active right prefrontal area said that they paid attention to statements that disagreed. This is an example of defensive repression, the avoidance or forgetting of unpleasant information, which research has shown is related to left prefrontal activation. One way to increase persuasion would seem to be to selectively activate the right prefrontal cortex. This is easily done by monaural stimulation

to the contralateral ear. See Drake, Roger A; Bingham, Brad R (1985), "Induced lateral orientation and persuasibility," Brain and Cognition, 4 (2): 156–64.

3. "Six actors who play characters in the Marvel Cinematic Universe are among the highest-paid celebrities in the world, according to Forbes' 2019 Celebrity 100 list published on Wednesday." "6 Marvel Cinematic Universe actors who are among the highest-paid celebrities in the world," by Travis Clark, *Business Insider*, July 10, 2019: https://www.businessinsider.com/marvel-actors-who-are-highest-paid-celebrities-hemsworth-downey-2019-7#chris-hemsworth-thor-764-million-6

4. Sometimes attributed to Ignatius Loyola; according to *Three Myths*, by A. Beichman et al. (1981), p. 48, this saying was "attributed to him (perhaps mischievously) by Voltaire."

5. "This Year's Biggest Superhero Movies Are All About America's Descent into Fascism," by Charlie Jane Anders, *Gizmodo*, March 16, 2016: https://i09.gizmodo.com/this-year-s-biggest-superhero-movies-are-all-about-amer-1765086280

6. "'Good Guys' in Superhero Films Are More Violent Than Villains, Study Says," by Kevin Kelleher, *Fortune*, Nov 2, 2018: http://fortune.com/2018/11/02/good-guys-superhero-films-more-violent-villains-study/

7. "Hollywood's 'Captain Marvel' Blockbuster Is Blatant US Military Propaganda," by Ben Norton, Mint Press, March 13, 2019: https://www.mintpressnews.com/hollywoods-captain-marvel-blockbuster-is-blatant-us-military-propaganda/256196/

8. Ibid.

9. "Why Are We Obsessed With Superhero Movies?" by Mark Bowden, *New York Times*, July 6, 2018: https://www.nytimes.com/2018/07/06/opinion/sunday/ant-man-wasp-movies-superheroes.html

10. "Spike Lee Looks at the World Differently After *Black Panther*," by Jackie Strause, *Hollywood Reporter*, April 25, 2018: https://www.hollywoodreporter.com/heat-vision/spike-lee-black-panther-new-movie-blackkklansman-tribeca-talk-alec-baldwin-1105698

11. "*Black Panther* Is Not the Movie We Deserve," by Christopher Lebron, *Boston Review*, Feb 17, 2018: https://bostonreview.net/race/christopher-lebron-black-panther

12. "Watching pornography rewires the brain to a more juvenile state," by Rachel Anne Barr, *The Conversation*, Nov 27, 2019: https://theconversation.com/watching-pornography-rewires-the-brain-to-a-more-juvenile-state-127306

13. Ibid.

14. Ibid.

15. Ibid.

16. Umair Haque. https://eand.co/why-americas-a-more-violent-society-than-you-think-cf1c535e841e

17. Jacqueline Fitzgerald, "Merlin, we beg thee, thy magic, we need some here at the office," quoting Carol S. Pearson and Sharon Sievert, *Chicago Tribune*, Aug. 28, 1995, section 4, p. 3, emphasis added.

18. "Must Reads: A notorious mansion. An alleged assault by a Hollywood producer. A suicide. What happened to Brian Claflin?" by Gus Garcia-Roberts, *Los Angeles Times*, May 11, 2018: https://www.latimes.com/business/hollywood/la-fi-ct-claflin-goddard-singer-20180511-story.html

19. "Jeffrey Epstein Liked Palling Around With Scientists—What Do They Think Now?" by Neel V. Patel, *The Verge*, July 13, 2019: https://www.theverge.com/2019/7/13/20692415/jeffrey-epstein-scientists-sexual-harassment

20. "Jeffrey Epstein backs OpenCog Artificial Intelligence Research," by Peter Rothman, *h+ magazine*, Nov 14, 2013: https://hplusmagazine.com/2013/11/14/jeffrey-epstein-backs-opencog-artificial-intelligence-research/

21. "How Jeffrey Epstein Bought His Way Into An Exclusive Intellectual Boys Club," by Peter Aldhouse, *Buzzfeed*, Sept 26, 2019: https://www.buzzfeednews.com/article/peteraldhous/jeffrey-epstein-john-brockman-edge-foundation

22. "The Epstein scandal at MIT shows the moral bankruptcy of techno-elites," by Evgeny Morozov, *The Guardian*, Sep 7, 2019: https://www.theguardian.com/commentisfree/2019/sep/07/jeffrey-epstein-mit-funding-tech-intellectuals

23. "Jeff Bezos: Founder & CEO, Amazon, Owner, Washington Post, Founder, Blue Origin," *Edge*: https://www.edge.org/memberbio/jeff_bezos

24. "People in the News: Jeffrey E. Epstein," by Jaquelyn M. Scharnick, *Crimson*, June 5, 2003: https://www.thecrimson.com/article/2003/6/5/people-in-the-news-jeffrey-e/

25. "Marvel Science: Meet The Physicist Called In To Consult On Superhero Movies," by April Wolfe, *Village Voice*, May 18, 2017: https://www.villagevoice.com/2017/05/18/marvel-science-meet-the-physicist-called-in-to-consult-on-superhero-movies/

26. "Jeffrey Epstein Hoped to Seed Human Race With His DNA," by James B. Stewart, Matthew Goldstein and Jessica Silver-Greenberg, New York Times, July 31, 2019: https://www.nytimes.com/2019/07/31/business/jeffrey-epstein-eugenics.html

27. "The Éminence Grise," by Georg Diez, *Der Spiegel*, Nov 17, 2014: https://www.edge.org/conversation/eminence_grise

28. "Alarm over talks to implant UK employees with microchips," by Julia Kollewe, *The Guardian*, Nov 11, 2018: https://www.theguardian.com/technology/2018/nov/11/alarm-over-talks-to-implant-uk-employees-with-microchips

Chapter 13

1. "Peak superhero?" by Keith A. Spencer, *Salon*, April 28, 2018: https://www.salon.com/2018/04/28/how-superhero-films-became-the-guiding-myth-of-neoliberalism/

2. "Elon Musk: the real-life Iron Man," by Alex Hern, *The Guardian*, Feb 14, 2018: https://www.theguardian.com/technology/2018/feb/09/elon-musk-the-real-life-iron-man

3. "Actor Robert Downey Jr vows to save the world—with AI and robotics," *Business Insider*, June 5, 2019: https://www.scmp.com/magazines/style/people-events/article/3013241/actor-robert-downey-jr-vows-save-world-ai-and

4. "10 Highest-Grossing Movie Franchises of All Time," by Jennifer M. Wood, *Mental Floss*, March 18, 2019: https://mentalfloss.com/article/70920/10-highest-grossing-movie-franchises-all-time

5. "Actor Robert Downey Jr vows to save the world—with AI and robotics," *Business Insider*, June 5, 2019: https://www.scmp.com/magazines/style/people-events/article/3013241/actor-robert-downey-jr-vows-save-world-ai-and

6. "Peak superhero?" by Keith A. Spencer, *Salon*, April 28, 2018: https://www.salon.com/2018/04/28/how-superhero-films-became-the-guiding-myth-of-neoliberalism/

7. Ibid.

8. Ibid, emphasis added.

9. "Individualism and Marginality: From Comic Book to Film: Marvel Comics Superheroes," by Marino Tuzi, College Quarterly, Spring 2005, vol 8, # 2: http://collegequarterly.ca/2005-vol08-num02-spring/tuzi.html

10. Ibid, emphasis added.

11. Ibid.

12. "The Decade Comic Book Nerds Became Our Cultural Overlords," by Alex Pappademas, Medium, Dec 9, 2019: https://gen.medium.com/the-decade-comic-book-nerds-became-our-cultural-overlords-f219b732a660

13. M. C. Green, J. J. Strange & T. C. Brock (Eds.), *Narrative Impact: Social and Cognitive Foundations*, p. 315-341. Mahwah, NJ: Lawrence Erlbaum.

14. *Journal of Personality and Social Psychology* 2000, Vol. 79, No. 5, p. 701-721: http://www.communicationcache.com/uploads/1/0/8/8/10887248/the_role_of_transportation_in_the_persuasiveness_of_public_narratives.pdf

15. Ibid.

16. "Persuasive effects of fictional narratives increase over time," by Appel, M., & Richter, T., *Media Psychology*, 10(1), 2007, p. 113-134.

17. "The Extended Transportation-Imagery Model: A Meta-Analysis of the Antecedents and Consequences of Consumers' Narrative Transportation," by Tom Van Laer, Ko De Ruyter, Luca M. Visconti, and Martin Wetzels.

18. "Alan Moore: 'Why shouldn't you have a bit of fun while dealing with the deepest issues of the mind?'" by Stuart Kelly, *The Guardian*, Nov 22, 2013: https://www.theguardian.com/books/2013/nov/22/alan-moore-comic-books-interview

19. "America's need for superheroes has led to the rise of Donald Trump," by Annika Hagley, *The Guardian*, March 28, 2016: https://www.theguardian.com/commentisfree/2016/mar/28/america-superheroes-donald-trump-brutal-comic-book-ideal

20. Ibid.

21. "When they go low, going high is not enough—video," Nesrine Malik, Leah Green and Bruno Rinvolucri, *The Guardian*, Feb 1, 2017: https://www.theguardian.com/commentisfree/video/2017/feb/01/when-they-go-low-going-high-is-not-enough-video

22. "Antifa attack conservative blogger Andy Ngo," by Lizzie Dearden, *The Independent*, June 30, 2019: https://www.independent.co.uk/news/world/americas/antifa-attack-portland-andy-ngo-portland-proud-boys-alt-right-a8981331.html

23. "Legendary Comics Writer Alan Moore On Superheroes, The League, And Making Magic," *Wired*, Feb 23, 2009: https://www.wired.com/2009/02/ff-moore-qa/

24. "The Disturbing Parallels Between US Policing at Home and Military Tactics Abroad," by Danny Sjursen, *The Nation*, Oct 12, 2017: https://www.thenation.com/article/the-disturbing-parallels-between-us-policing-at-home-and-military-tactics-abroad/

25. Ibid.

26. "Wealth inequality is soaring—here are the 10 reasons why it's happening," by Dominic Frisby, *The Guardian*, Apr 12, 2018: https://www.theguardian.com/commentisfree/2018/apr/12/wealth-inequality-reasons-richest-global-gap

27. "The greatest transfer of wealth in history," by Michael Gray, *Gray's Economy*, Jan 11, 2016: https://mgray12.wordpress.com/2016/01/11/the-greatest-transfer-of-wealth-in-history/

28. Emphasis added. "World's First Trillionaire Is Alive Today," by James Vincent, *The Independent*, May 6, 2014: https://www.independent.co.uk/news/world/worlds-first-trillionaire-is-alive-today-9326532.html

29. "Thomas Piketty: The French economist forcing America to wake up to the end of The Dream" by Rupert Cornwell, *The Independent*, April 27, 2014: https://www.independent.co.uk/voices/comment/the-french-economist-forcing-america-to-wake-up-to-the-end-of-the-dream-9292308.html

30. "The True Cause of the Opioid Epidemic," by Olga Khazan, *The Atlantic*, Jan 2, 2020: https://www.theatlantic.com/health/archive/2020/01/what-caused-opioid-epidemic/604330

31. "Middle-Aged White Americans Are Dying of Despair," by Olga Khazan, *The Atlantic*, Nov 4, 2015: https://www.theatlantic.com/health/archive/2015/11/boomers-deaths-pnas/413971/

32. "Neoliberalism—the ideology at the root of all our problems" by George Monbiot, *The Guardian*, April 15, 2016: https://www.theguardian.com/books/2016/apr/15/neoliberalism-ideology-problem-george-monbiot

33. "How Many Trillionaires Are In The World?" by Joseph Gibson, *Celebrity Net Worth*, Dec 6, 2019: https://www.celebritynetworth.com/articles/billionaire-news/how-many-trillionaires-are-in-the-world/

34. "Age, Period, and Cohort Trends in Mood Disorder Indicators and Suicide Related Outcomes in a Nationally Representative Dataset, 2005–2017," by Jean M. Twenge, A. Bell Cooper, Thomas E. Joiner and Mary E. Duffy, and Sarah G. Binau, Journal of Abnormal Psychology, 2019, Vol. 128, No. 3, p. 185-199: https://www.apa.org/pubs/journals/releases/abn-abn0000410.pdf

35. "Depression and Suicide Rates Are Rising Sharply in Young Americans, New Report Says. This May Be One Reason Why," by Markham Heid, Time, March 14, 2019: https://time.com/5550803/depression-suicide-rates-youth/

36. "Digital addiction: how technology keeps us hooked," by Raian Ali, Emily Arden-Close, and John McAlaney, *The Conversation*, June 12, 2018: https://theconversation.com/digital-addiction-how-technology-keeps-us-hooked-97499

37. "Our digital addictions are killing our kids," by Dr. Nicholas Kardaras, *New York Post*, May 19, 2018: https://nypost.com/2018/05/19/our-digital-addictions-are-killing-our-kids/

38. "Digital Addiction: A Recipe For Isolation, Depression And Anxiety," by Robert Glatter, MD, *Forbes*, Apr 13, 2018: https://www.forbes.com/sites/robertglatter/2018/04/13/digital-addiction-a-recipe-for-isolation-depression-and-anxiety/

39. "Is 'Digital Addiction' a Real Threat to Kids?" by Perri Klass, M.D., *New York Times*, May 20, 2019: https://www.nytimes.com/2019/05/20/well/family/is-digital-addiction-a-real-threat-to-kids.html

40. "Silicon Valley parents are raising their kids tech-free—and it should be a red flag," by Chris Weller, *Business Insider*, Feb 18, 2018: https://www.businessinsider.com/silicon-valley-parents-raising-their-kids-tech-free-red-flag-2018-2/

41. "Last Alan Moore Interview?" *Pádraig Ó Méalóid AKA Slovobooks*, Jan 9, 2014: https://slovobooks.wordpress.com/2014/01/09/last-alan-moore-interview/

42. "Consuming Kids: The Hostile Takeover of Childhood," by Susan Linn, Jan 2004: https://www.researchgate.net/publication/245781723_Consuming_Kids_The_Hostile_Takeover_of_Childhood

43. "Why Are We Obsessed With Superhero Movies?" by Mark Bowden, New York Times, July 6, 2018: https://www.nytimes.com/2018/07/06/opinion/sunday/ant-man-wasp-movies-superheroes.html

44. "Consumed: The Fate Of Citizens Under Capitalism Triumphant: Three Lectures For The Shih Ming Teh Lectureship," Taipei: December, 2006, by Benjamin R. Barber: https://ce399fascism.files.wordpress.com/2011/05/barbers-3-lectures.pdf

45. "The Infantilization of the Postmodern Adult and the Figure of Kiduld," by Jacopo Bernardini, *Postmodern Openings*, 2014, Volume 5, Issue 2, June, p. 39-55: http://www.postmodernopenings.com/wp-content/uploads/2014/07/PO_June2014_1_39to55.pdf

46. "The Infantilization of Western Culture," by Simon Gottschalk, *The Conversation*, August 1, 2018: https://theconversation.com/the-infantilization-of-western-culture-99556

47. "Peak superhero? Not even close: How one movie genre became the guiding myth of neoliberalism," by Keith A. Spencer, *Salon*, April 28, 2018: https://www.salon.com/2018/04/28/how-superhero-films-became-the-guiding-myth-of-neoliberalism/

48. "Interview with Ben Goertzel, Chief Scientist at Hanson Robotics," by Lisa Chai, *Equities*, August 15, 2019: https://www.equities.com/news/interview-with-ben-goertzel-chief-scientist-at-hanson-robotics

49. "Scientific breakthroughs in 2015 that could change the world" by Steve Connor, Independent.co.uk [12.31.15] [From The Edge contributors]: https://www.edge.org/edgenews/2015

50. "Jeffrey Epstein Hoped to Seed Human Race With His DNA," by James B. Stewart, Matthew Goldstein and Jessica Silver-Greenberg, *New York Times*, July 31, 2019: https://www.nytimes.com/2019/07/31/business/jeffrey-epstein-eugenics.html

51. "Theranos: When a Culture of Growth Becomes a Culture of Scam," by Nicole Alvino, *Entrepreneur*, May 22, 2019: https://www.entrepreneur.com/article/332986

52. "What Went Wrong With IBM's Watson," by Felix Salmon, Aug 18, 2018: https://slate.com/business/2018/08/ibms-watson-how-the-ai-project-to-improve-cancer-treatment-went-wrong.html

53. "Goodbye Mars One: The Fake Mission To Mars That Fooled The World" by Jonathan O'Callaghan, *Forbes*, Feb 11, 2019: https://www.forbes.com/sites/jonathanocallaghan/2019/02/11/goodbye-mars-one-the-fake-mission-to-mars-that-fooled-the-world/#113970512af5

54. "'Scam': Elon Musk's 'hyperloop' project revealed as a car in a tunnel," *New Zealand Herald*, May 28, 2019: https://www.nzherald.co.nz/business/news/article.cfm?c_id=3&objectid=12234921

55. Emphasis added. "Peak superhero? Not even close: How one movie genre became the guiding myth of neoliberalism," by Keith A. Spencer, *Salon*, April 28, 2018: https://www.salon.com/2018/04/28/how-superhero-films-became-the-guiding-myth-of-neoliberalism/

56. Ibid.

Chapter 14

1. "Consumed: The Fate Of Citizens Under Capitalism Triumphant: Three Lectures For The Shih Ming Teh Lectureship," Taipei: December, 2006, by Benjamin R. Barber: https://ce399fascism.files.wordpress.com/2011/05/barbers-3-lectures.pdf

2. "Ray Kurzweil: Get ready for hybrid thinking," TED, YouTube, June 2, 2014: https://www.youtube.com/watch?v=PVXQUItNEDQ

3. "4,000% Explosion in Kids Identifying as Transgender, Docs Perform Double Mastectomies on Healthy Teen Girls," by Charlene Aaron, *CBN News*, Sept 19, 2018: https://www1.cbn.com/cbnnews/us/2018/september/4-000-explosion-in-kids-identifying-as-transgender-docs-perform-double-mastectomies-on-healthy-teen-girls

4. "U.S. Doctors Are Performing Double Mastectomies On Healthy 13-Year-Old Girls," by Jane Robbins, *New Federalist*, Sept 12, 2018: https://thefederalist.com/2018/09/12/u-s-doctors-performing-double-mastectomies-healthy-13-year-old-girls/

5. "Singular 'they' is voted Word of the Decade by US linguists," by Barbara Goldberg, *Reuters*, Jan 3, 2020: https://www.reuters.com/article/us-usa-word/singular-they-is-voted-word-of-the-decade-by-u-s-linguists-idUSKBN1Z21KF

6. "Our digital addictions are killing our kids," by Dr. Nicholas Kardaras, *New York Post*, May 19, 2018: https://nypost.com/2018/05/19/our-digital-addictions-are-killing-our-kids/

7. "Jacob Rees-Mogg is right about Grenfell" by Brendan O'Neill, *Spiked*, 5 November 2019: https://www.spiked-online.com/2019/11/05/jacob-rees-mogg-is-right-about-grenfell/

8. "Liminalist # 28: A Conspiracy of Secret Voices (with Jonathan Lethem)," by Jasun Horsley, *Auticulture*, Aug 22, 2015: https://auticulture.com/liminalist-28-a-conspiracy-of-secret-voices-with-jonathan-lethem/

9. Ibid.

10. "The Best and Worst of Talking Heads, According to Chris Frantz," by Devon Ivie, *Vulture*, July 21, 2020: https://www.vulture.com/2020/07/chris-frantz-best-of-talking-heads-worst-of-david-byrne.html

11. "Chris Frantz: 'If you knew David Byrne, you would not be jealous of him,'" by Jim Farber, *The Guardian*, July 21, 2020: https://www.theguardian.com/music/2020/jul/21/chris-frantz-talking-heads-david-byrne

Chapter 15

1. "Totally Nude," from *Naked*.

2. "Obituary: Billie Whitelaw," *BBC News*, 21 December 2014: https://www.bbc.com/news/entertainment-arts-29445982

Chapter 16

1. "60 years ago Norman Bates and *Psycho* were born in small-town Wisconsin," by Shane Nyman, *Appleton Post-Crescent*, March 5, 2019: https://www.postcrescent.com/story/entertainment/2019/03/05/robert-bloch-wrote-psycho-weyauwega-wisconsin-60-years-ago/2380385002/

2. "Savile told hospital staff he performed sex acts on corpses in Leeds mortuary," by Josh Halliday, *The Guardian*, June 26, 2014: https://www.theguardian.com/media/2014/jun/26/savile-bodies-sex-acts-corpses-glass-eyes-mortuary

3. "Case File—Ed Gein, the Butcher of Plainfield," by hiperaktiv, archived: https://web.archive.org/web/20111016184447/http://www.fortunecity.com/roswell/streiber/273/gein_cf.htm Note the url has "Strieber" in it, i.e., Whitley Strieber.

4. "Edward Theodore Gein, 'American Psycho,'" by Radford University students, Department of Psychology, Radford University: http://maamodt.asp.radford.edu/Psyc%20405/serial%20killers/Gein,%20Ed.pdf

5. Emphasis added. "'Only Her Mouth Could Move': Sensory Deprivation and the Billie Whitelaw Plays," by Corey Wakeling, *The Drama Review*, Volume 59, Number 3, Fall 2015, p. 91-107.

6. Ibid.

7. "Fearing 'public lynching,' Polanski pulls out of France's César awards," *France 24*, Feb 27, 2020: https://www.france24.com/en/20200227-fearing-public-lynching-polanski-skips-french-oscars-night

8. "Polanski's Demons," by Peter Howell, *Toronto Star*, March 3, 2000.

9. "Horror Comics: The Nasties of the 1950s," by John Sringhall, *History Today*, Vol. 44, No. 7, July 1994: https://www.questia.com/magazine/1G1-15654302/horror-comics-the-nasties-of-the-1950s

Outtake # 1

1. "In Stetson or Wig, He's Hard to Pin Down," by Sarah Lyall, *New York Times*, Nov 4, 2007: https://www.nytimes.com/2007/11/04/movies/moviesspecial/04lyal.html

2. "Heath Ledger's Joker Diary Is A Haunting Reminder Of His Commitment To The Role," by Stewart Perrie, *LAD Bible*, January 22, 2018: http://www.ladbible.com/entertainment/celebrity-film-and-tv-interesting-heath-ledgers-joker-diary-is-a-haunting-reminder-of-his-commitment-20180122

3. "Heath Ledger's fatal overdose wasn't a result of Joker role, claims sister," by Adam White, *The Telegraph*, 24 April, 2017: https://www.telegraph.co.uk/films/0/heath-ledgers-fatal-overdose-wasnt-result-joker-role-claims/

4. "Autopsy on Actor Is Inconclusive as Calls for Help Are Revealed," by Andy Newman and Al Baker, *New York Times*, Jan 24, 2008: https://www.nytimes.com/2008/01/24/nyregion/24celeb.html

5. "Inside Mary-Kate & Heath's Relationship," *People*, Jan 24, 2008: https://people.com/celebrity/inside-mary-kate-heaths-relationship/

6. "Sebastian Horsley died from cocktail of drugs, coroner rules," by Anita Singh, *The Telegraph*, 17 Aug, 2010: https://www.telegraph.co.uk/culture/art/art-news/7950312/ Sebastian-Horsley-died-from-cocktail-of-drugs-coroner-rules.html

7. "The Joker: Did Heath Ledger Take His Inspiration From . . . Tom Waits?" by Marc Bernardin, *Hollywood Reporter*, July 30, 2012: https://www.hollywoodreporter.com/ heat-vision/joker-did-heath-ledger-take-355883

8. "Tom Waits australia interview 1979 part 1," by JensdePens, *YouTube*, June 25, 2008: https://youtu.be/gCSc6E4yG9s

9. Emphasis added. "How to Join the Sons of Lee Marvin in Five Easy Steps," *Dangerous Minds*, August 27, 2013: https://dangerousminds.net/comments/how_to_join_the_sons _of_lee_marvin_in_five_easy_steps

10. "2008 in Review: The Killing Joke of the Dark Knight," by Chris Knowles, *The Secret Sun*, Jan 3, 2009: https://web.archive.org/web/20111104010145/http://secretsun. blogspot.com/2008/12/i-love-internet.html

11. "Killing Joker, part 2," by Chris Knowles, *The Secret Sun*, January 28, 2008: https:// web.archive.org/web/20111104161813/http://secretsun.blogspot.com/2008/01/killing -joker-part-2.html

12. "Killing Joke's Fearless Leader," by Ian Fortnam, *Metal Hammer*, September 15, 2015: https://www.loudersound.com/features/killing-joke-s-fearless-leader

13. Ibid.

14. "In Conversation with Killing Joke's Jaz Coleman," by Kyle Harcott, *Hellbound*, November 15, 2010: https://hellbound.ca/2010/11/jaz-coleman-interview/

Outtake # 2

1. "Aurora suspect's profile grows murkier," by Sam Quinones, Kim Murphy and Joe Mozingo, *Los Angeles Times*, July 23, 2012: https://www.latimes.com/archives/la-xpm-2012-jul-22-la-na-colorado-shooting-sider-20120723-story.html

2. "Police Audio Suggests There Were Multiple Shooters In The *Dark Knight* Massacre," by Michael B Kelley, *Business Insider*, August 7, 2012: https://www.businessinsider.com/ james-holmes-conspiracy-theories-2012-8

3. "Schools close after *Batman* theory connects Newtown, Aurora shootings; predicts future target," by Will C. Holden, *KDVR*, January 2, 2013: https://kdvr.com/2013/01/02/ batman-theory-connects-newtown-aurora-shootings-closes-school-district/

4. "Slavoj Zizek analyses Batman The Dark Knight," Frank Taylor, *YouTube*: https:// www.youtube.com/watch?v=XTFR4W8qLlQ

Outtake # 3

1. "Jeffrey Epstein: International Moneyman of Mystery," by Landon Thomas Jr., *New York* magazine, Oct 28, 2002: https://nymag.com/nymetro/news/people/n_7912/

2. "Matt Damon and Russell Crowe helped kill earlier *New York Times* expose about Harvey Weinstein, writer says," by Martha Ross, *Mercury News*, Oct 9, 2017: http://www.

mercurynews.com/2017/10/09/matt-damon-and-russell-crowe-helped-kill-earlier-new-york-times-expose-about-harvey-weinstein/

3. "George Clooney Speaks Out on Harvey Weinstein: 'It's Disturbing on a Whole Lot of Levels'" by Marlow Stern, *Daily Beast*, Oct 10, 2017: https://www.thedailybeast.com/george-clooney-speaks-out-on-harvey-weinstein-its-disturbing-on-a-whole-lot-of-levels

4. "Former 'ER' Actress Vanessa Marquez Shot and Killed by Police," by Gene Maddaus, *Variety*, Aug 31, 2018: https://variety.com/2018/tv/news/vanessa-marquez-er-shot-killed-police-1202923337/

5. "Shooting Of Ex-'ER' Actress Vanessa Marquez Prompts Wrongful Death Claim," by Anita Bennett, *Deadline*, Feb 20, 2019: https://deadline.com/2019/02/vanessa-marquez-wrongful-death-claim-shooting-police-south-pasadena-1202561511/

6. "'Hope for Haiti Now' telethon raises $57 million," *Reuters*, Jan 23, 2010: https://www.reuters.com/article/us-quake-haiti-celebrities/hope-for-haiti-now-telethon-raises-57-million-idUSTRE60M0E120100124

7. "George Clooney called as witness in Silvio Berlusconi trial," by Tom Kington, *The Guardian*, Oct 19, 2012: https://www.theguardian.com/film/2012/oct/19/george-clooney-witness-silvio-berlusconi-trial

Outtake # 4

1. "Kevin Spacey's father was 'Nazi child rapist,'" by Laura Collins, *Daily Mail*, Oct 30, 2017: https://www.dailymail.co.uk/news/article-5032809/Kevin-Spacey-s-father-Nazi-child-rapist-brother-says.html

2. "Why is Spacey so secretive?" by Paul Bracchi, *Daily Mail*, April 20, 2004: https://web.archive.org/web/20171030133448/https://www.dailymail.co.uk/tvshowbiz/article-300674/Why-Spacey-secretive.html

3. See "Blair Paedophile Minister? Ask Peter Mandelson," by Gojam, *The Needle*, April 28, 2014: https://theneedleblog.wordpress.com/2014/04/28/blair-paedophile-minister-ask-peter-mandelson/

4. "Financier Jeffrey Epstein once flew Bill Clinton and Kevin Spacey to Africa," by Ellen Cranley, *Business Insider*, July 7, 2019: https://www.businessinsider.com/jeffrey-epstein-traveled-with-bill-clinton-kevin-spacey-2019-7

5. "The one weird court case linking Trump, Clinton, and a billionaire pedophile," by Josh Gerstein, *Politico*, May 4, 2017: https://www.politico.com/story/2017/05/04/jeffrey-epstein-trump-lawsuit-sex-trafficking-237983

6. "Bill Clinton attracts Hollywood stars and business leaders to his annual Clinton Global Initiative," Nov 2010: https://www.telegraph.co.uk/news/picturegalleries/worldnews/8022788/Bill-Clinton-attracts-Hollywood-stars-and-business-leaders-to-his-annual-Clinton-Global-Initiative.html?image=14

7. "Kevin Spacey won't face criminal charges in groping case after accuser's death," by Nardine Saad, *LA Times*, Oct 29, 2019: https://www.latimes.com/entertainment-arts/story/2019-10-29/kevin-spacey-massage-therapist-criminal-case

8. "Kevin Spacey Accuser Dies in Midst of Sexual Assault Lawsuit," by Eriq Gardner, *Hollywood Reporter*, Sept 18, 2019: https://www.hollywoodreporter.com/thr-esq/kevin -spacey-accuser-dies-midst-sexual-assault-lawsuit-1240716

Outtake # 5

1. "The CIA and the Media: 50 Historical Facts the World Needs to Know," by James Tracy, *Information Clearing House*: http://www.informationclearinghouse.info/article42 768.htm

2. Ibid.

3. "The Secret History of the *National Enquirer*," by John Connolly, *Du Jour*: http:// dujour.com/news/national-enquirer-history-scandal/

Outtake # 6

1. "The CIA And The Media," Carl Bernstein, *Rolling Stone*, Oct 20, 1977: http:// www.carlbernstein.com/magazine_cia_and_media.php

2. Emphasis added. "Lights, Bogeyman, Action," By David M. Halbfinger, *New York Times*, Feb 18, 2007: https://www.nytimes.com/2007/02/18/movies/18halb.html

3. "The Phantom Killer," *The Unredacted*, 21 Feb, 2018: https://theunredacted.com/ zodiac-serial-murders-the-phantom-killer/

4. "Allen : The Movie," by Michael Butterfield, *Zodiac Killer Facts*: https://zodi- ackillerfacts.com/zodiac-theories/the-accused-the-accusers/allen-primed-suspect/ allen-the-movie/

5. "9–Fact Vs. Fincher–Conclusion," by Michael Butterfield, *Zodiac Killer Facts*: https://zodiackillerfacts.com/myths-legends/zodiac-the-movie-fact-vs-fincher/9-fact-vs -fincher-scene-by-scene-conclusion/

6. "Zodiac shows all the vital signs of historical accuracy" by Alex von Tunzelmann, *The Guardian*, Feb 23, 2012: https://www.theguardian.com/film/2012/feb/23/zodiac-signs -historical-accuracy

Outtake # 7

1. "What Are The Atlanta Child Murders? *Mindhunter* Season 2 Will Tackle These IRL Crimes," by Dylan Kickham, *Elite Daily*, Dec 5, 2017: https://www.elitedaily.com/p/what- are-the-atlanta-child-murders-mindhunter-season-2-will-tackle-these-irl-crimes-6783078

2. "Atlanta Child Murders Case Has Been Reopened," by Ej Dickson, *Rolling Stone*, Aug 20, 2019: https://www.rollingstone.com/culture/culture-news/atlanta-child-murders -case-reopened-mindhunter-874051/

3. See *Atlanta Child Murders—Wayne Williams FBI Files*, BACM Research, no year given.

4. CNN LIVE EVENT/SPECIAL, Atlanta Child Murders, *CNN*, 9-11p ET, July 18, 2015: http://transcripts.cnn.com/TRANSCRIPTS/1507/18/se.01.html

5. 40 Years After I Covered The Atlanta Child Murders, Trauma And Doubt Remain," by Vern Smith, *Newsweek*, Aug 27, 2019: https://www.newsweek.com/40-years-after-i -covered-atlanta-child-murders-trauma-doubt-remain-opinion-1456236

6. "Secret investigation into KKK during Atlanta child murders uncovers fear of race riots," by Neima Abdulahi, *Alive*, May 16, 2019: https://www.11alive.com/article/news/ investigations/secret-investigation-into-kkk-during-atlanta-child-murders-uncovers-fear -of-race-riots/85-7c06564c-baee-4b9f-a4d8-3b348bee41cf

Outtake # 8

1. "Point Of No Return," by Sarah Nicole Prickett, *Art Forum*, Jan 5, 2018: https://www .artforum.com/film/sarah-nicole-prickett-on-the-finale-of-twin-peaks-the-return-73381

2. "The Liminalist # 42: Hollywood Transgressor (with Alex Cox)," *Auticulture*, Nov 28, 2015: https://auticulture.com/liminalist-42/

3. "Is David Lynch Creepier Than His Movies," by Laurie Ouellette, *Utne Reader*, Jan/Feb. 1991, p. 15. See also: "Point Of No Return," by Sarah Nicole Prickett, *Art Forum*, January 5, 2018: https://www.artforum.com/film/sarah-nicole-prickett-on-the-finale-of-twin-peaks -the-return-73381

INDEX

*with a rough sketch of the exit